Tales of SUPERNATURAL LAW

D1500786

Batton Lash

EXHIBIT A PRESS

SAN DIEGO, CALIFORNIA

EVANSTON PUBLIC LIBRARY
1703 ORRINGTON AVENUE
EVANSTON, ILLINOIS 60201

Acknowledgments

"Herbert Has Risen from the Grave" originally appeared in *Wolff & Byrd, Counselors of the Macabre* issue 1; "Curse of the Werehouse" originally appeared in *Wolff & Byrd, Counselors of the Macabre* issue 2; the stories included in "Long Night's Journey into Day" originally appeared in *Wolff & Byrd, Counselors of the Macabre* issue 3; "A Host of Horrors" originally appeared in *Wolff & Byrd, Counselors of the Macabre* issue 4; "That Model Client" originally appeared in *Wolff & Byrd, Counselors of the Macabre* issue 5; "It Stalks the Public Domain" originally appeared in *Wolff & Byrd, Counselors of the Macabre* issue 6; the stories included in "Fungi and Dolls" originally appeared in *Wolff & Byrd, Counselors of the Macabre* issue 7; "Bar•Con" originally appeared in *Wolff & Byrd, Counselors of the Macabre* issue 8. All stories have been "remastered" for this collection: They have been completely relettered and retoned, and in some cases art has been redrawn.

Dedicated to Lovely Wife Jackie

Writer/artist: Batton Lash
Editor/letterer: Jackie Estrada
Technical consultant: Mitch Berger, Esq.
Art assists: Derek Ozawa, Nghia Lam, Melissa Uran, Dennis Caco
Production assistance: Melissa Uran, Trevor Nielson
Staff 'n stuff: S. Derma

10 9 8 7 6 5 4 3 2 1

Printed in the United States of America

ISBN: 0-9633954-9-1
ISBN 13: 978-0-9633954-9-8

Contents

Opening Statement

Oyez, oyez . . . welcome to the first volume in the *Tales of Supernatural Law* series. In this collection you will meet attorneys Alanna Wolff and Jeff Byrd (that's them in the accompanying illustration). They specialize in a very particular field of law: the supernatural and the supernaturally afflicted! Aided by their intrepid office manager, Mavis, the law firm of Wolff & Byrd, Counselors of the Macabre vigorously represents things that go bump in the night so they might have their day in court.

I originally created *Wolff & Byrd* over 25 years ago as a comic strip that ran in *The Brooklyn Paper,* a local weekly. The strip was picked up by *The National Law Journal,* where it ran for 14 years. I enjoyed doing the strip version, but over the years I yearned for a roomier format, where I could expand on the main characters' personal lives, introduce a more substantial supporting cast, and make use of a variety of storytelling techniques. My desire led to the formation of Exhibit A Press with my wife, Jackie Estrada, in 1994, and the publication of the first issue of the *Wolff & Byrd* comic book series. (I phased out the comic strip in the late 1990s to devote more time to the comic book series, which continues to this day under the title *Supernatural Law.*)

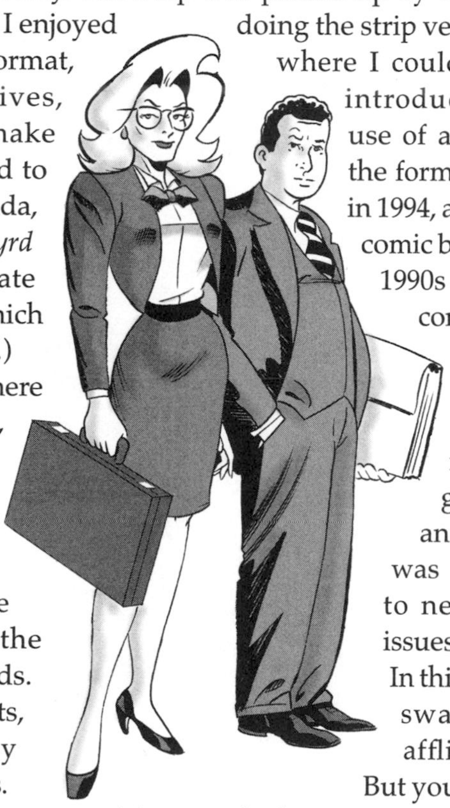

The stories collected here appeared in the first eight issues of the comic, and in them many of the longstanding "cast members" are introduced, including wild guy Toby Bascoe, supermodel Dawn DeVine, and the incorrigible Chase Hawkins, Esq. My goal was for each issue to stand alone and be accessible to new readers. However, ongoing subplots link the issues, so reading them in sequence offers extra rewards. In this book, you'll encounter vampires, zombies, ghosts, swamp monsters and all sorts of supernaturally afflicted folks who are in need of the firm's services. But you'll also learn a lot about Alanna, Jeff, and Mavis's personal lives—which can present challenges more unexpected and intimidating than anything the supernatural has to offer!

But judge for yourself. I submit to you now, volume one of *Tales of Supernatural Law, Featuring Wolff & Byrd, Counselors of the Macabre.*

Batton Lash

Herbert Has Risen from the Grave!

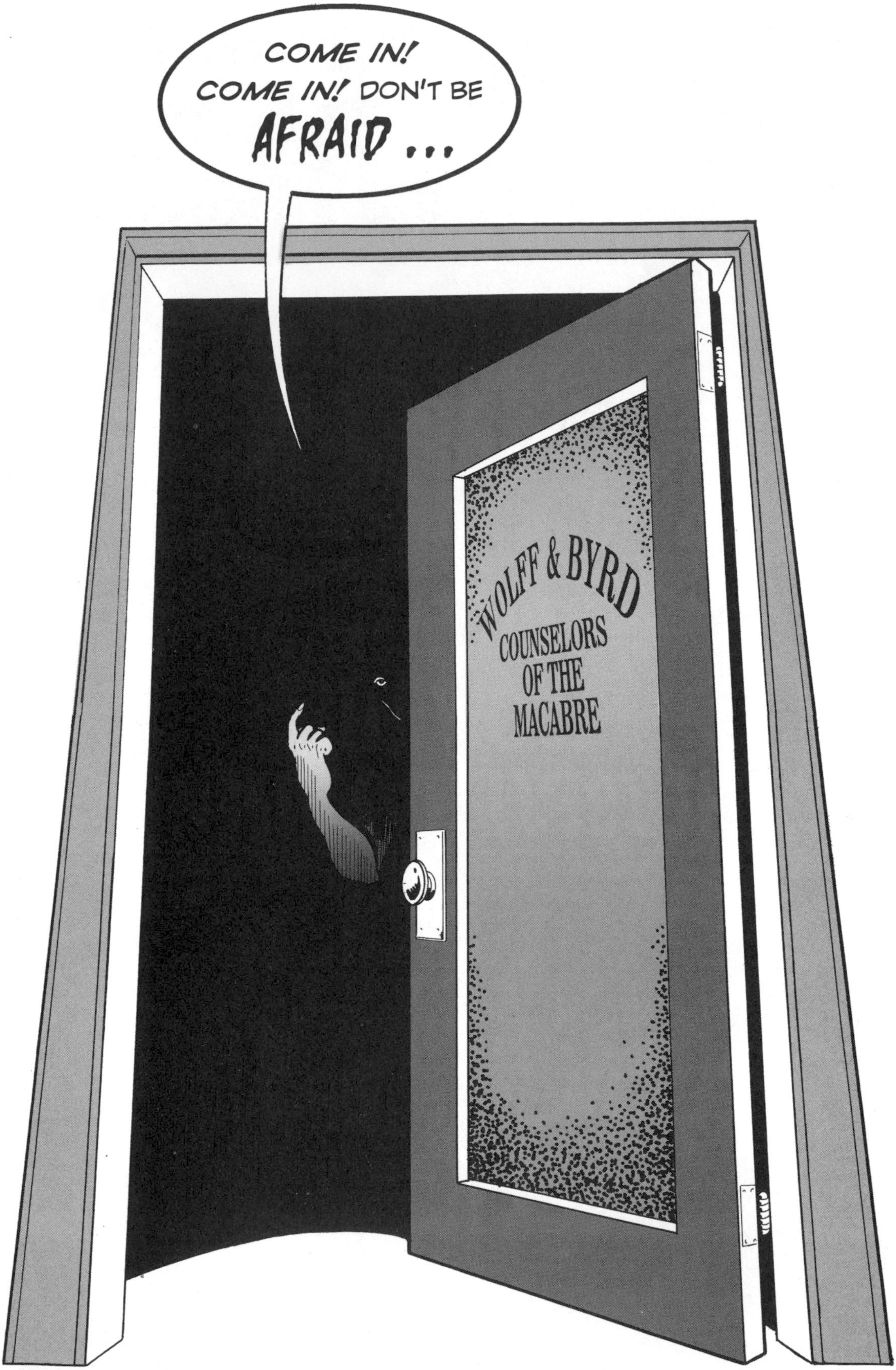
COME IN!
COME IN! DON'T BE
AFRAID ...
WOLFF & BYRD
COUNSELORS
OF THE
MACABRE

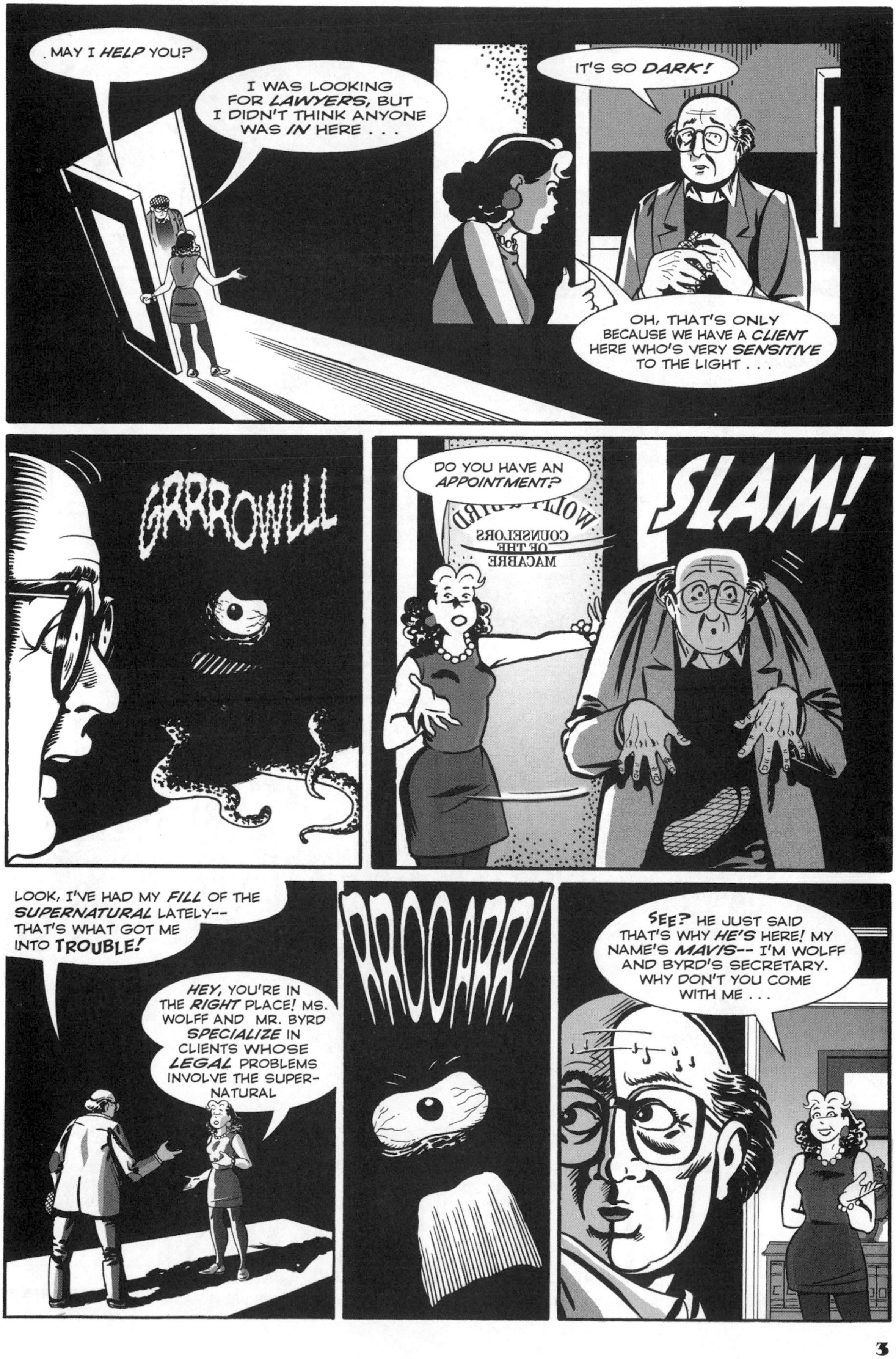

. MAY I HELP YOU?
I WAS LOOKING FOR LAWYERS, BUT I DIDN'T THINK ANYONE WAS IN HERE . . .
IT'S SO DARK!
OH, THAT'S ONLY BECAUSE WE HAVE A CLIENT HERE WHO'S VERY SENSITIVE TO THE LIGHT . . .
GRRROWLLL
DO YOU HAVE AN APPOINTMENT?
WOLFF & BYRD COUNSELORS OF THE MACABRE
SLAM!
LOOK, I'VE HAD MY FILL OF THE SUPERNATURAL LATELY-- THAT'S WHAT GOT ME INTO TROUBLE!
HEY, YOU'RE IN THE RIGHT PLACE! MS. WOLFF AND MR. BYRD SPECIALIZE IN CLIENTS WHOSE LEGAL PROBLEMS INVOLVE THE SUPER-NATURAL
RROOARR!
SEE? HE JUST SAID THAT'S WHY HE'S HERE! MY NAME'S MAVIS-- I'M WOLFF AND BYRD'S SECRETARY. WHY DON'T YOU COME WITH ME . . .

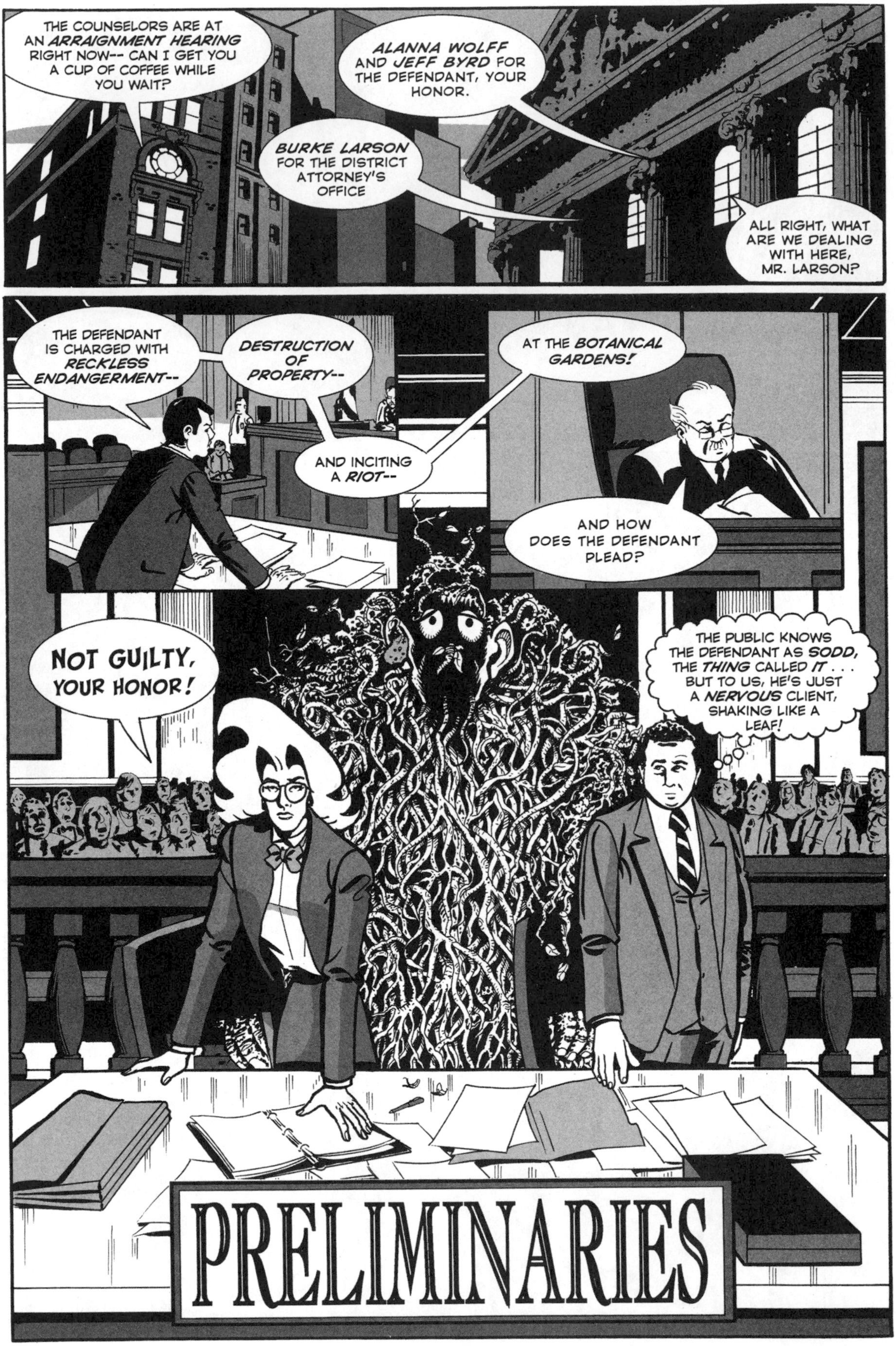
THE COUNSELORS ARE AT AN ARRAIGNMENT HEARING RIGHT NOW-- CAN I GET YOU A CUP OF COFFEE WHILE YOU WAIT?
BURKE LARSON FOR THE DISTRICT ATTORNEY'S OFFICE
ALANNA WOLFF AND JEFF BYRD FOR THE DEFENDANT, YOUR HONOR.
ALL RIGHT, WHAT ARE WE DEALING WITH HERE, MR. LARSON?
THE DEFENDANT IS CHARGED WITH RECKLESS ENDANGERMENT--
DESTRUCTION OF PROPERTY--
AND INCITING A RIOT--
AT THE BOTANICAL GARDENS!
AND HOW DOES THE DEFENDANT PLEAD?
NOT GUILTY, YOUR HONOR!
THE PUBLIC KNOWS THE DEFENDANT AS SODD, THE THING CALLED IT . . . BUT TO US, HE'S JUST A NERVOUS CLIENT, SHAKING LIKE A LEAF!
PRELIMINARIES

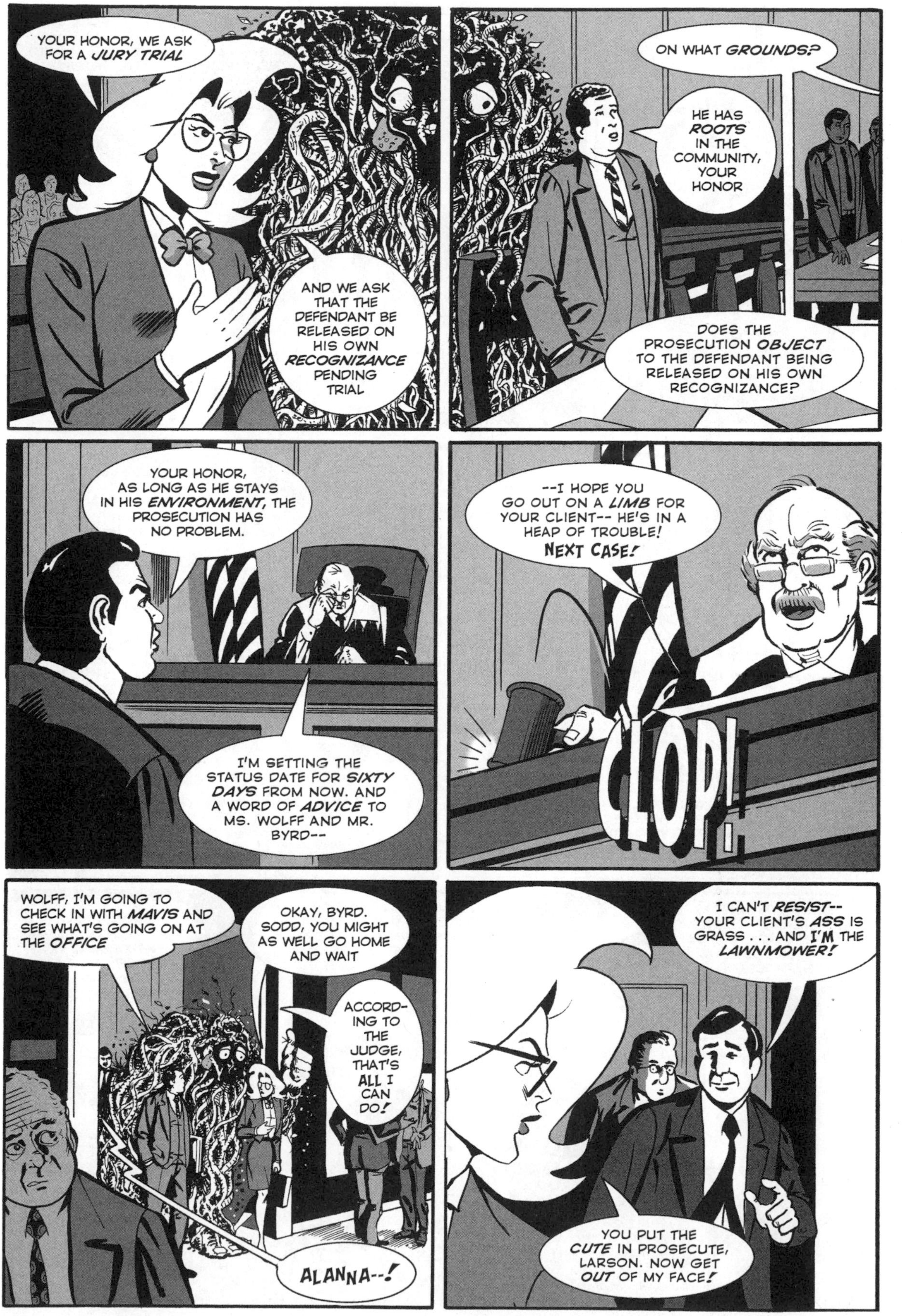
YOUR HONOR, WE ASK FOR A *JURY TRIAL*
AND WE ASK THAT THE DEFENDANT BE RELEASED ON HIS OWN *RECOGNIZANCE* PENDING TRIAL
ON WHAT *GROUNDS?*
HE HAS *ROOTS* IN THE COMMUNITY, YOUR HONOR
DOES THE PROSECUTION *OBJECT* TO THE DEFENDANT BEING RELEASED ON HIS OWN RECOGNIZANCE?
YOUR HONOR, AS LONG AS HE STAYS IN HIS *ENVIRONMENT,* THE PROSECUTION HAS NO PROBLEM.
I'M SETTING THE STATUS DATE FOR *SIXTY DAYS* FROM NOW. AND A WORD OF *ADVICE* TO MS. WOLFF AND MR. BYRD--
--I HOPE YOU GO OUT ON A *LIMB* FOR YOUR CLIENT-- HE'S IN A HEAP OF TROUBLE! **NEXT CASE!**
CLOP!
WOLFF, I'M GOING TO CHECK IN WITH *MAVIS* AND SEE WHAT'S GOING ON AT THE *OFFICE*
OKAY, BYRD. SODD, YOU MIGHT AS WELL GO HOME AND WAIT
ACCORDING TO THE JUDGE, THAT'S **ALL** I CAN DO!
ALANNA--!
I CAN'T *RESIST*-- YOUR CLIENT'S *ASS* IS GRASS . . . AND **I'M** THE *LAWNMOWER!*
YOU PUT THE *CUTE* IN PROSECUTE, LARSON. NOW GET *OUT* OF MY FACE!

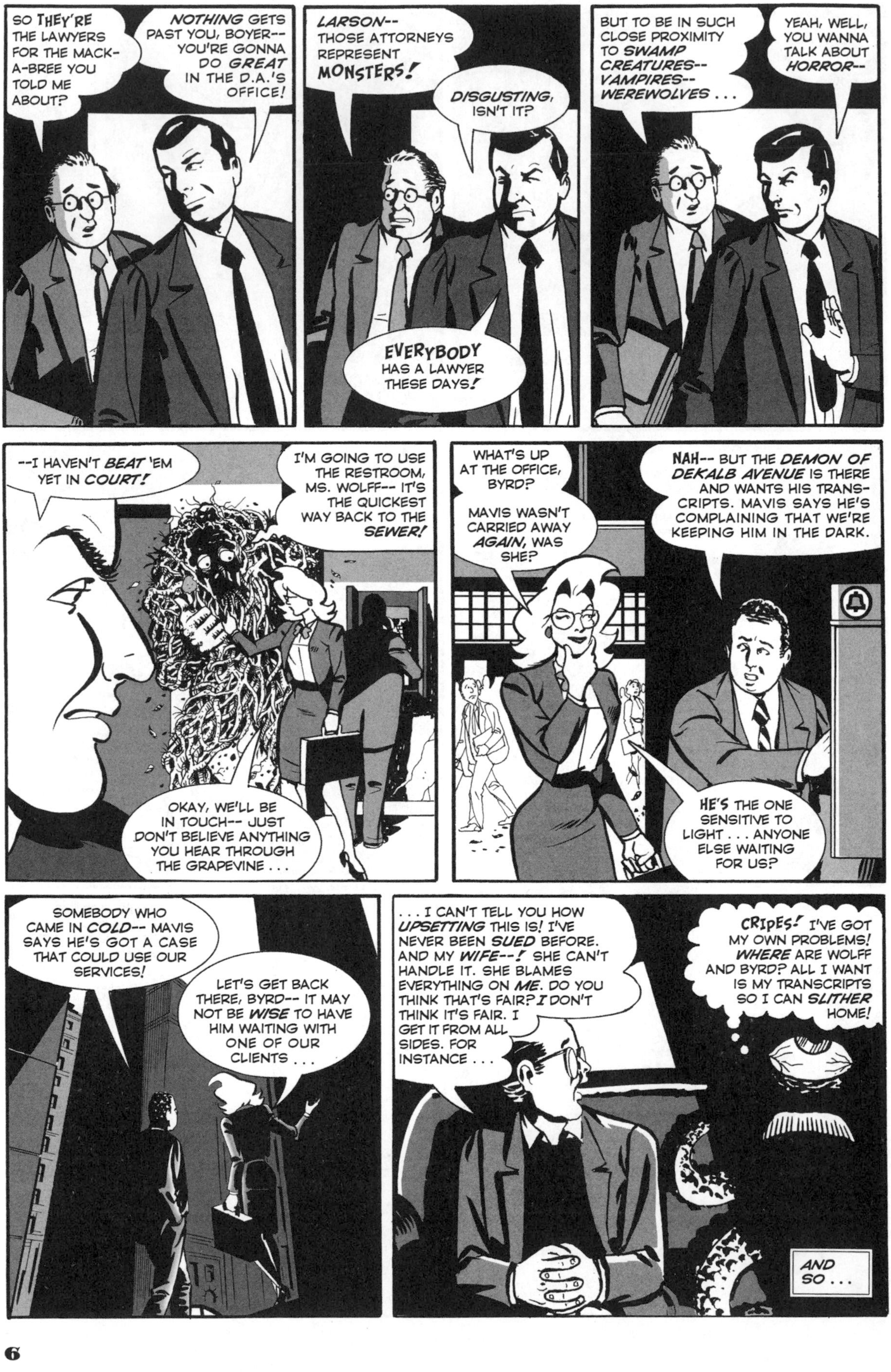
SO THEY'RE THE LAWYERS FOR THE MACK-A-BREE YOU TOLD ME ABOUT?
NOTHING GETS PAST YOU, BOYER-- YOU'RE GONNA DO GREAT IN THE D.A.'S OFFICE!
LARSON-- THOSE ATTORNEYS REPRESENT MONSTERS!
DISGUSTING, ISN'T IT?
EVERYBODY HAS A LAWYER THESE DAYS!
BUT TO BE IN SUCH CLOSE PROXIMITY TO SWAMP CREATURES-- VAMPIRES-- WEREWOLVES . . .
YEAH, WELL, YOU WANNA TALK ABOUT HORROR--
--I HAVEN'T BEAT 'EM YET IN COURT!
I'M GOING TO USE THE RESTROOM, MS. WOLFF-- IT'S THE QUICKEST WAY BACK TO THE SEWER!
OKAY, WE'LL BE IN TOUCH-- JUST DON'T BELIEVE ANYTHING YOU HEAR THROUGH THE GRAPEVINE . . .
WHAT'S UP AT THE OFFICE, BYRD?
MAVIS WASN'T CARRIED AWAY AGAIN, WAS SHE?
NAH-- BUT THE DEMON OF DEKALB AVENUE IS THERE AND WANTS HIS TRANSCRIPTS. MAVIS SAYS HE'S COMPLAINING THAT WE'RE KEEPING HIM IN THE DARK.
HE'S THE ONE SENSITIVE TO LIGHT . . . ANYONE ELSE WAITING FOR US?
SOMEBODY WHO CAME IN COLD-- MAVIS SAYS HE'S GOT A CASE THAT COULD USE OUR SERVICES!
LET'S GET BACK THERE, BYRD-- IT MAY NOT BE WISE TO HAVE HIM WAITING WITH ONE OF OUR CLIENTS . . .
. . . I CAN'T TELL YOU HOW UPSETTING THIS IS! I'VE NEVER BEEN SUED BEFORE. AND MY WIFE--! SHE CAN'T HANDLE IT. SHE BLAMES EVERYTHING ON ME. DO YOU THINK THAT'S FAIR? I DON'T THINK IT'S FAIR. I GET IT FROM ALL SIDES. FOR INSTANCE . . .
CRIPES! I'VE GOT MY OWN PROBLEMS! WHERE ARE WOLFF AND BYRD? ALL I WANT IS MY TRANSCRIPTS SO I CAN SLITHER HOME!
AND SO . . .

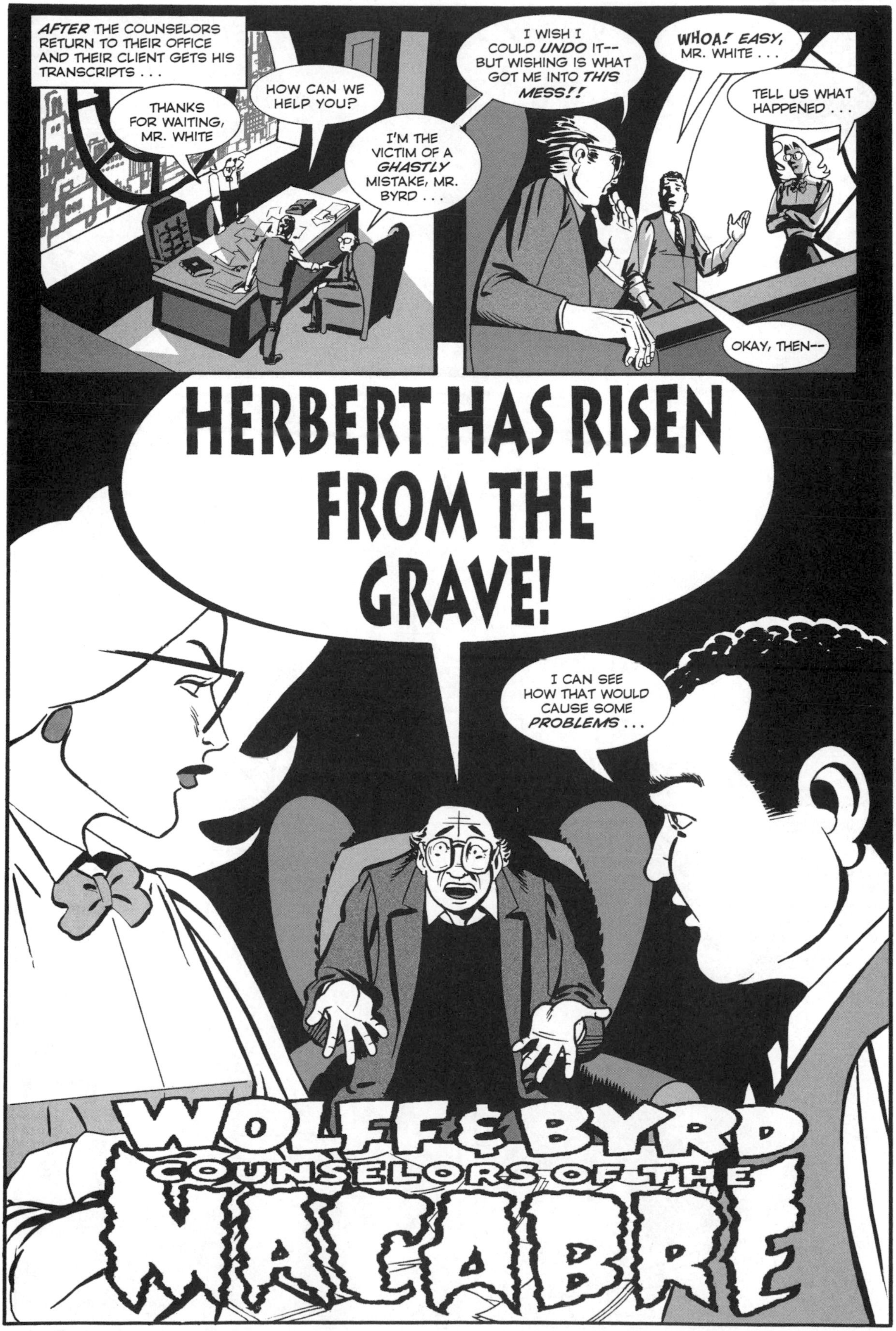
AFTER THE COUNSELORS RETURN TO THEIR OFFICE AND THEIR CLIENT GETS HIS TRANSCRIPTS . . .
THANKS FOR WAITING, MR. WHITE
HOW CAN WE HELP YOU?
I'M THE VICTIM OF A GHASTLY MISTAKE, MR. BYRD . . .
I WISH I COULD UNDO IT-- BUT WISHING IS WHAT GOT ME INTO THIS MESS!!
WHOA! EASY, MR. WHITE . . .
TELL US WHAT HAPPENED . . .
OKAY, THEN--
HERBERT HAS RISEN FROM THE GRAVE!
I CAN SEE HOW THAT WOULD CAUSE SOME PROBLEMS . . .
WOLFF & BYRD
COUNSELORS OF THE
MACABRE

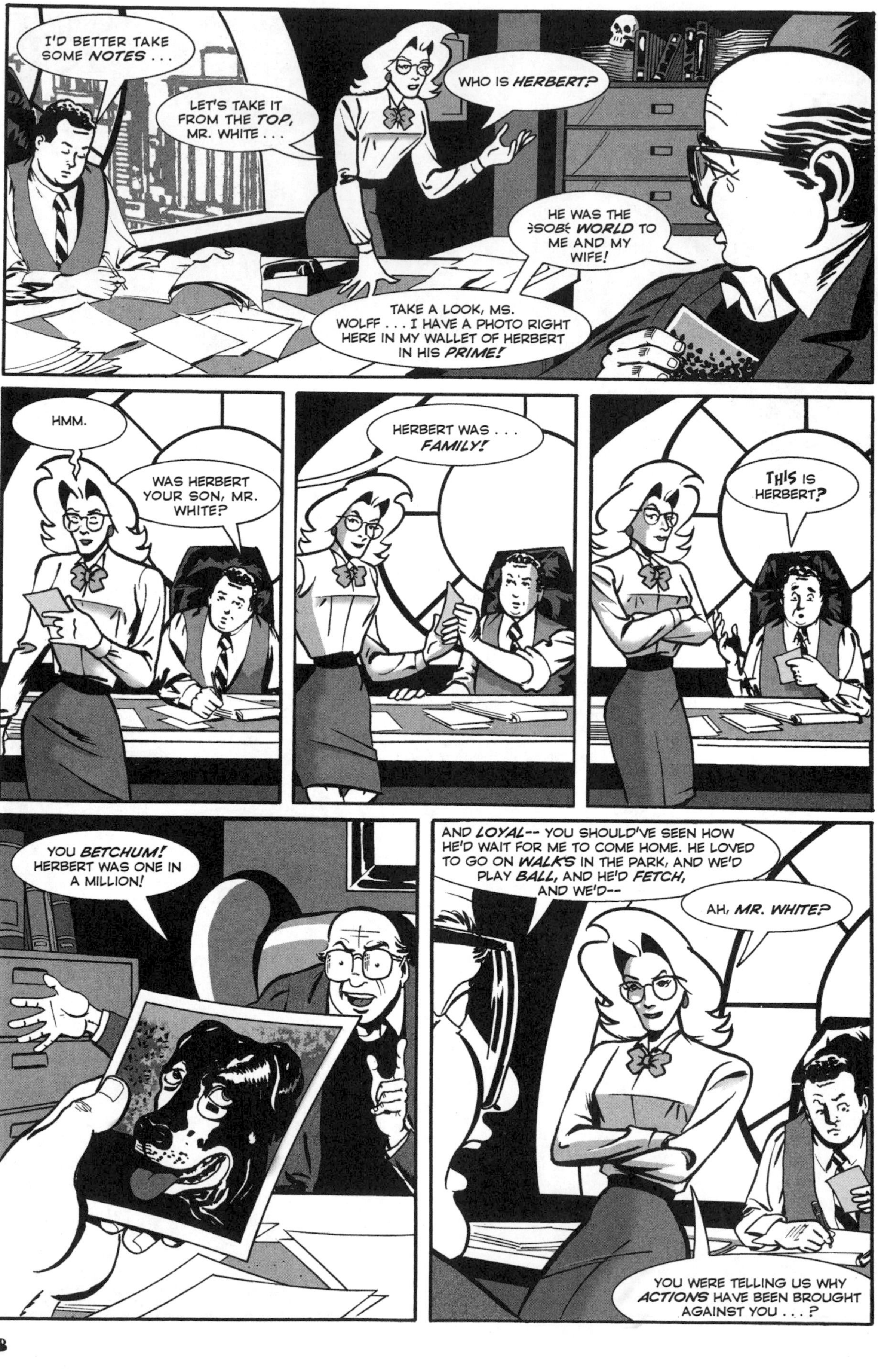
I'D BETTER TAKE SOME NOTES . . .
LET'S TAKE IT FROM THE TOP, MR. WHITE . . .
WHO IS HERBERT?
HE WAS THE *SOB* WORLD TO ME AND MY WIFE!
TAKE A LOOK, MS. WOLFF . . . I HAVE A PHOTO RIGHT HERE IN MY WALLET OF HERBERT IN HIS PRIME!
HMM.
WAS HERBERT YOUR SON, MR. WHITE?
HERBERT WAS . . . FAMILY!
THIS IS HERBERT?
YOU BETCHUM! HERBERT WAS ONE IN A MILLION!
AND LOYAL-- YOU SHOULD'VE SEEN HOW HE'D WAIT FOR ME TO COME HOME. HE LOVED TO GO ON WALKS IN THE PARK, AND WE'D PLAY BALL, AND HE'D FETCH, AND WE'D--
AH, MR. WHITE?
YOU WERE TELLING US WHY ACTIONS HAVE BEEN BROUGHT AGAINST YOU . . . ?

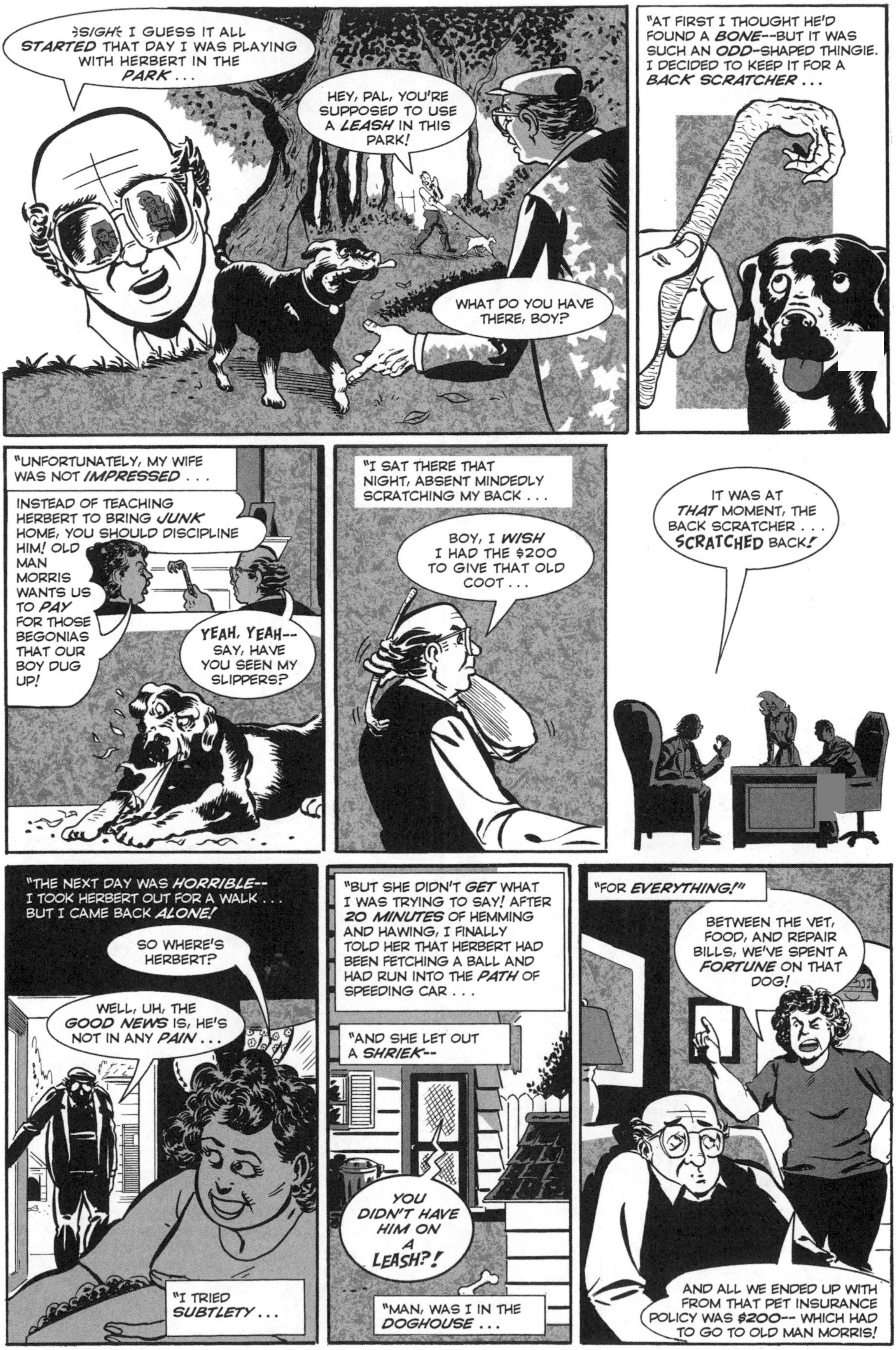

SIGH I GUESS IT ALL STARTED THAT DAY I WAS PLAYING WITH HERBERT IN THE PARK . . .
HEY, PAL, YOU'RE SUPPOSED TO USE A LEASH IN THIS PARK!
WHAT DO YOU HAVE THERE, BOY?
"AT FIRST I THOUGHT HE'D FOUND A BONE--BUT IT WAS SUCH AN ODD-SHAPED THINGIE. I DECIDED TO KEEP IT FOR A BACK SCRATCHER . . .
"UNFORTUNATELY, MY WIFE WAS NOT IMPRESSED . . .
INSTEAD OF TEACHING HERBERT TO BRING JUNK HOME, YOU SHOULD DISCIPLINE HIM! OLD MAN MORRIS WANTS US TO PAY FOR THOSE BEGONIAS THAT OUR BOY DUG UP!
YEAH, YEAH-- SAY, HAVE YOU SEEN MY SLIPPERS?
"I SAT THERE THAT NIGHT, ABSENT MINDEDLY SCRATCHING MY BACK . . .
BOY, I WISH I HAD THE $200 TO GIVE THAT OLD COOT . . .
IT WAS AT THAT MOMENT, THE BACK SCRATCHER . . . SCRATCHED BACK!
"THE NEXT DAY WAS HORRIBLE-- I TOOK HERBERT OUT FOR A WALK . . . BUT I CAME BACK ALONE!
SO WHERE'S HERBERT?
WELL, UH, THE GOOD NEWS IS, HE'S NOT IN ANY PAIN . . .
"I TRIED SUBTLETY . . .
"BUT SHE DIDN'T GET WHAT I WAS TRYING TO SAY! AFTER 20 MINUTES OF HEMMING AND HAWING, I FINALLY TOLD HER THAT HERBERT HAD BEEN FETCHING A BALL AND HAD RUN INTO THE PATH OF SPEEDING CAR . . .
"AND SHE LET OUT A SHRIEK--
YOU DIDN'T HAVE HIM ON A LEASH?!
"MAN, WAS I IN THE DOGHOUSE . . .
"FOR EVERYTHING!"
BETWEEN THE VET, FOOD, AND REPAIR BILLS, WE'VE SPENT A FORTUNE ON THAT DOG!
AND ALL WE ENDED UP WITH FROM THAT PET INSURANCE POLICY WAS $200-- WHICH HAD TO GO TO OLD MAN MORRIS!

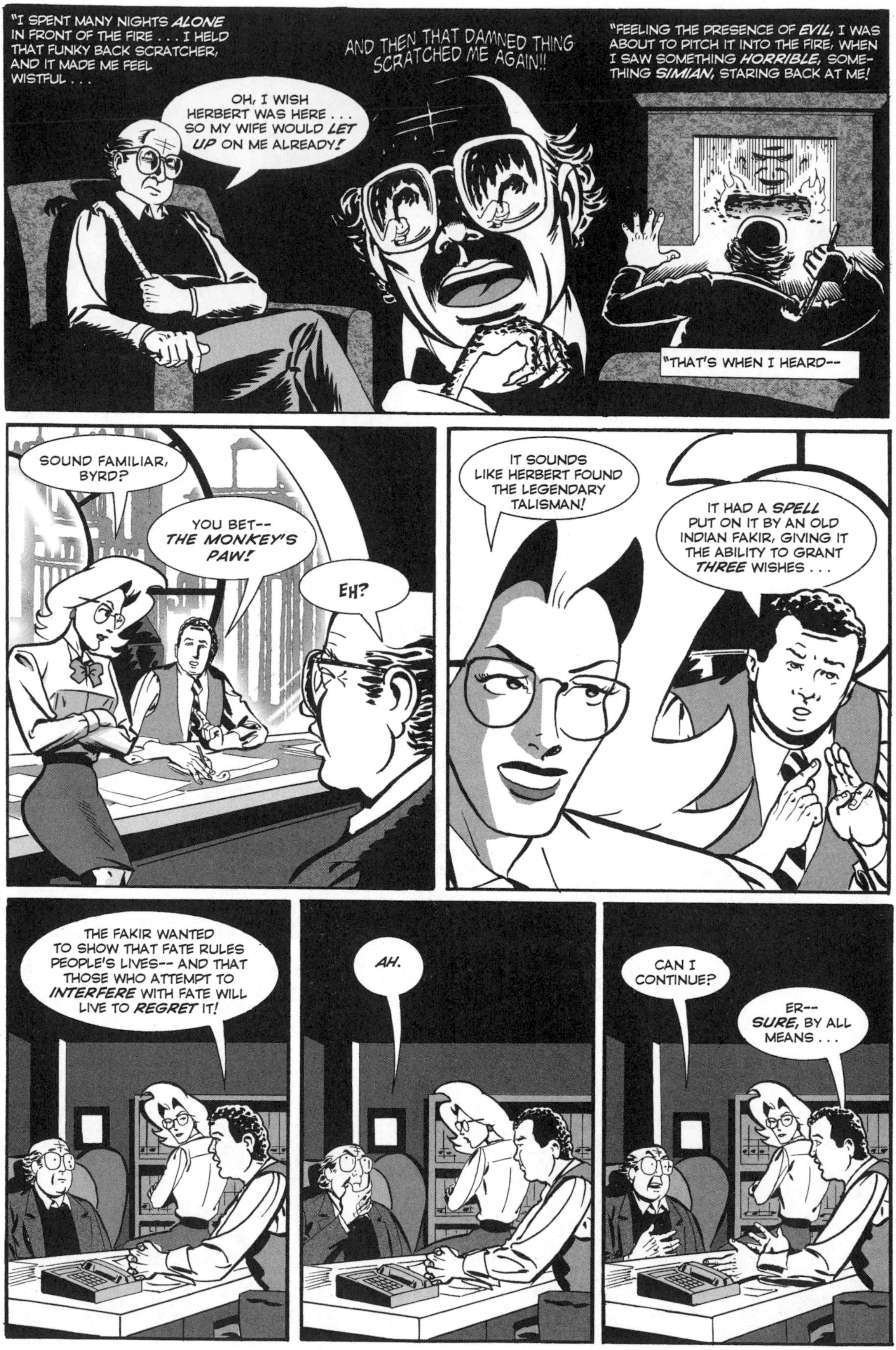
"I SPENT MANY NIGHTS ALONE IN FRONT OF THE FIRE . . . I HELD THAT FUNKY BACK SCRATCHER, AND IT MADE ME FEEL WISTFUL . . .
OH, I WISH HERBERT WAS HERE . . . SO MY WIFE WOULD LET UP ON ME ALREADY!
AND THEN THAT DAMNED THING SCRATCHED ME AGAIN!!
"FEELING THE PRESENCE OF EVIL, I WAS ABOUT TO PITCH IT INTO THE FIRE, WHEN I SAW SOMETHING HORRIBLE, SOMETHING SIMIAN, STARING BACK AT ME!
"THAT'S WHEN I HEARD--
SOUND FAMILIAR, BYRD?
YOU BET-- THE MONKEY'S PAW!
EH?
IT SOUNDS LIKE HERBERT FOUND THE LEGENDARY TALISMAN!
IT HAD A SPELL PUT ON IT BY AN OLD INDIAN FAKIR, GIVING IT THE ABILITY TO GRANT THREE WISHES . . .
THE FAKIR WANTED TO SHOW THAT FATE RULES PEOPLE'S LIVES-- AND THAT THOSE WHO ATTEMPT TO INTERFERE WITH FATE WILL LIVE TO REGRET IT!
AH.
CAN I CONTINUE?
ER-- SURE, BY ALL MEANS . . .

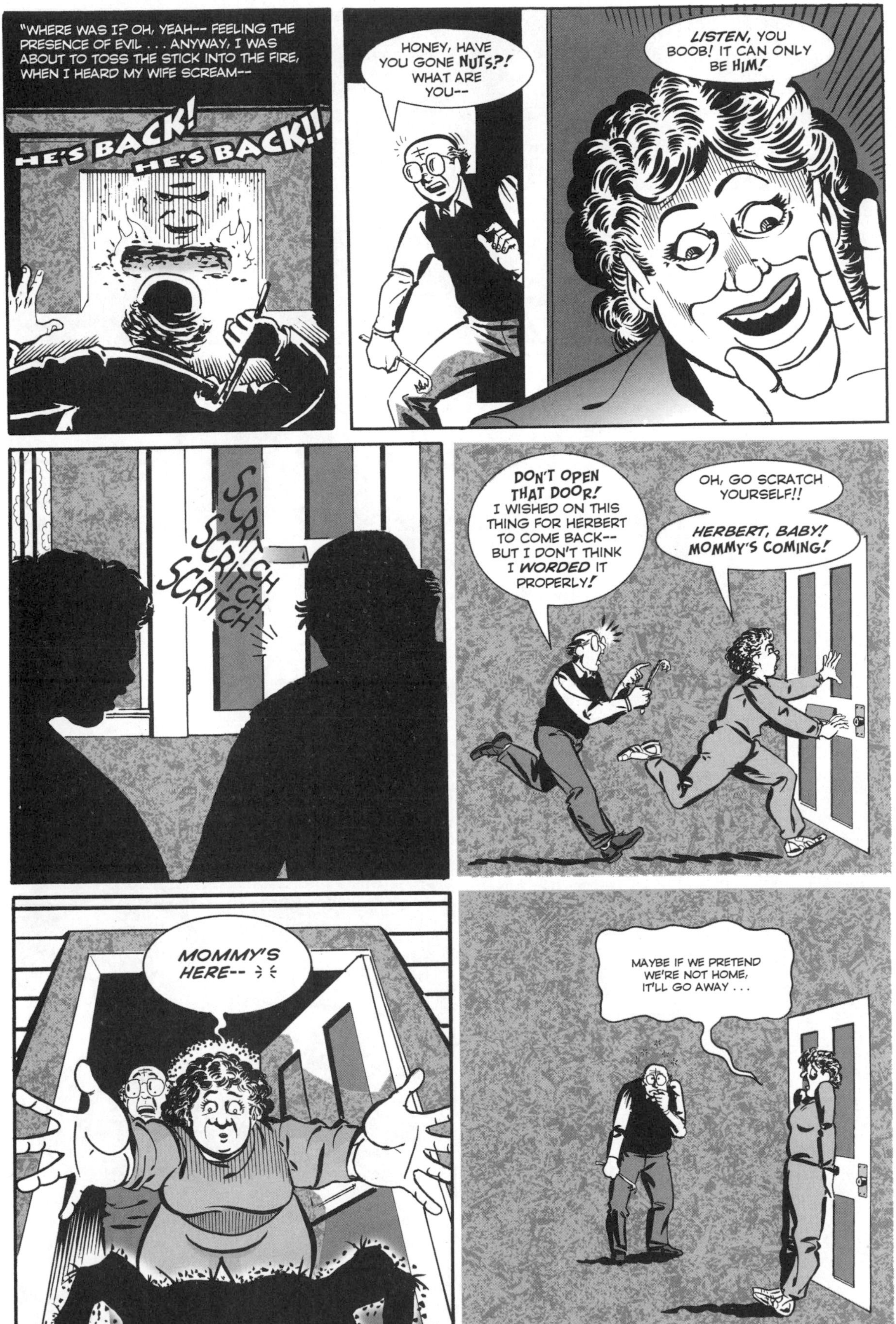
"WHERE WAS I? OH, YEAH-- FEELING THE PRESENCE OF EVIL . . . ANYWAY, I WAS ABOUT TO TOSS THE STICK INTO THE FIRE, WHEN I HEARD MY WIFE SCREAM--
HE'S BACK! HE'S BACK!!
HONEY, HAVE YOU GONE NUTS?! WHAT ARE YOU--
LISTEN, YOU BOOB! IT CAN ONLY BE HIM!
SCRITCH SCRITCH SCRITCH
DON'T OPEN THAT DOOR! I WISHED ON THIS THING FOR HERBERT TO COME BACK-- BUT I DON'T THINK I WORDED IT PROPERLY!
OH, GO SCRATCH YOURSELF!!
HERBERT, BABY! MOMMY'S COMING!
MOMMY'S HERE--
MAYBE IF WE PRETEND WE'RE NOT HOME, IT'LL GO AWAY . . .

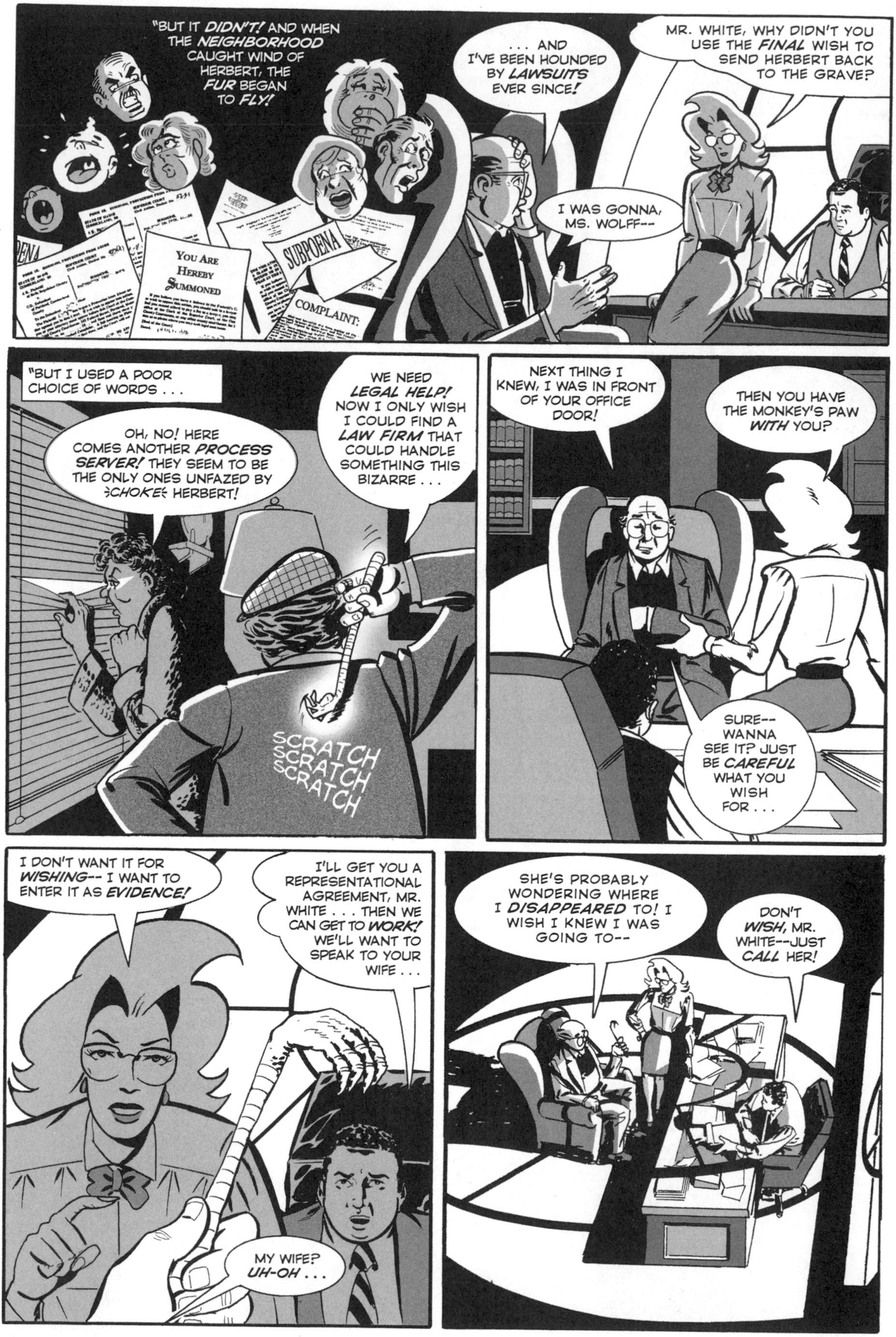
"BUT IT DIDN'T! AND WHEN THE NEIGHBORHOOD CAUGHT WIND OF HERBERT, THE FUR BEGAN TO FLY!
YOU ARE HEREBY SUMMONED
SUBPOENA
COMPLAINT:
. . . AND I'VE BEEN HOUNDED BY LAWSUITS EVER SINCE!
MR. WHITE, WHY DIDN'T YOU USE THE FINAL WISH TO SEND HERBERT BACK TO THE GRAVE?
I WAS GONNA, MS. WOLFF--
"BUT I USED A POOR CHOICE OF WORDS . . .
OH, NO! HERE COMES ANOTHER PROCESS SERVER! THEY SEEM TO BE THE ONLY ONES UNFAZED BY *CHOKE* HERBERT!
WE NEED LEGAL HELP! NOW I ONLY WISH I COULD FIND A LAW FIRM THAT COULD HANDLE SOMETHING THIS BIZARRE . . .
SCRATCH SCRATCH SCRATCH
NEXT THING I KNEW, I WAS IN FRONT OF YOUR OFFICE DOOR!
THEN YOU HAVE THE MONKEY'S PAW WITH YOU?
SURE-- WANNA SEE IT? JUST BE CAREFUL WHAT YOU WISH FOR . . .
I DON'T WANT IT FOR WISHING-- I WANT TO ENTER IT AS EVIDENCE!
I'LL GET YOU A REPRESENTATIONAL AGREEMENT, MR. WHITE . . . THEN WE CAN GET TO WORK! WE'LL WANT TO SPEAK TO YOUR WIFE . . .
MY WIFE? UH-OH . . .
SHE'S PROBABLY WONDERING WHERE I DISAPPEARED TO! I WISH I KNEW I WAS GOING TO--
DON'T WISH, MR. WHITE--JUST CALL HER!

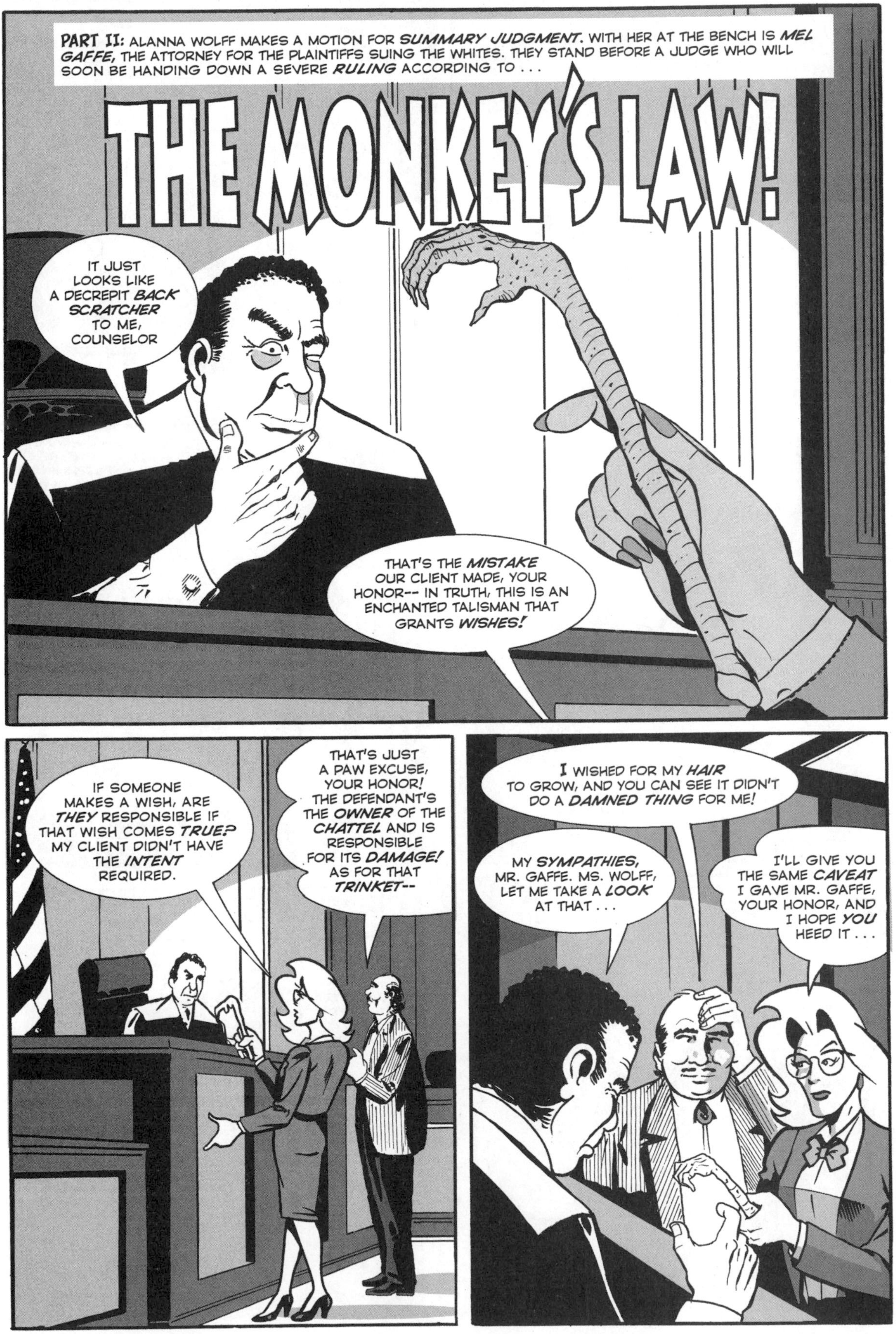
PART II: ALANNA WOLFF MAKES A MOTION FOR SUMMARY JUDGMENT. WITH HER AT THE BENCH IS MEL GAFFE, THE ATTORNEY FOR THE PLAINTIFFS SUING THE WHITES. THEY STAND BEFORE A JUDGE WHO WILL SOON BE HANDING DOWN A SEVERE RULING ACCORDING TO . . .
THE MONKEY'S LAW!
IT JUST LOOKS LIKE A DECREPIT BACK SCRATCHER TO ME, COUNSELOR
THAT'S THE MISTAKE OUR CLIENT MADE, YOUR HONOR-- IN TRUTH, THIS IS AN ENCHANTED TALISMAN THAT GRANTS WISHES!
IF SOMEONE MAKES A WISH, ARE THEY RESPONSIBLE IF THAT WISH COMES TRUE? MY CLIENT DIDN'T HAVE THE INTENT REQUIRED.
THAT'S JUST A PAW EXCUSE, YOUR HONOR! THE DEFENDANT'S THE OWNER OF THE CHATTEL AND IS RESPONSIBLE FOR ITS DAMAGE! AS FOR THAT TRINKET--
I WISHED FOR MY HAIR TO GROW, AND YOU CAN SEE IT DIDN'T DO A DAMNED THING FOR ME!
MY SYMPATHIES, MR. GAFFE. MS. WOLFF, LET ME TAKE A LOOK AT THAT . . .
I'LL GIVE YOU THE SAME CAVEAT I GAVE MR. GAFFE, YOUR HONOR, AND I HOPE YOU HEED IT . . .

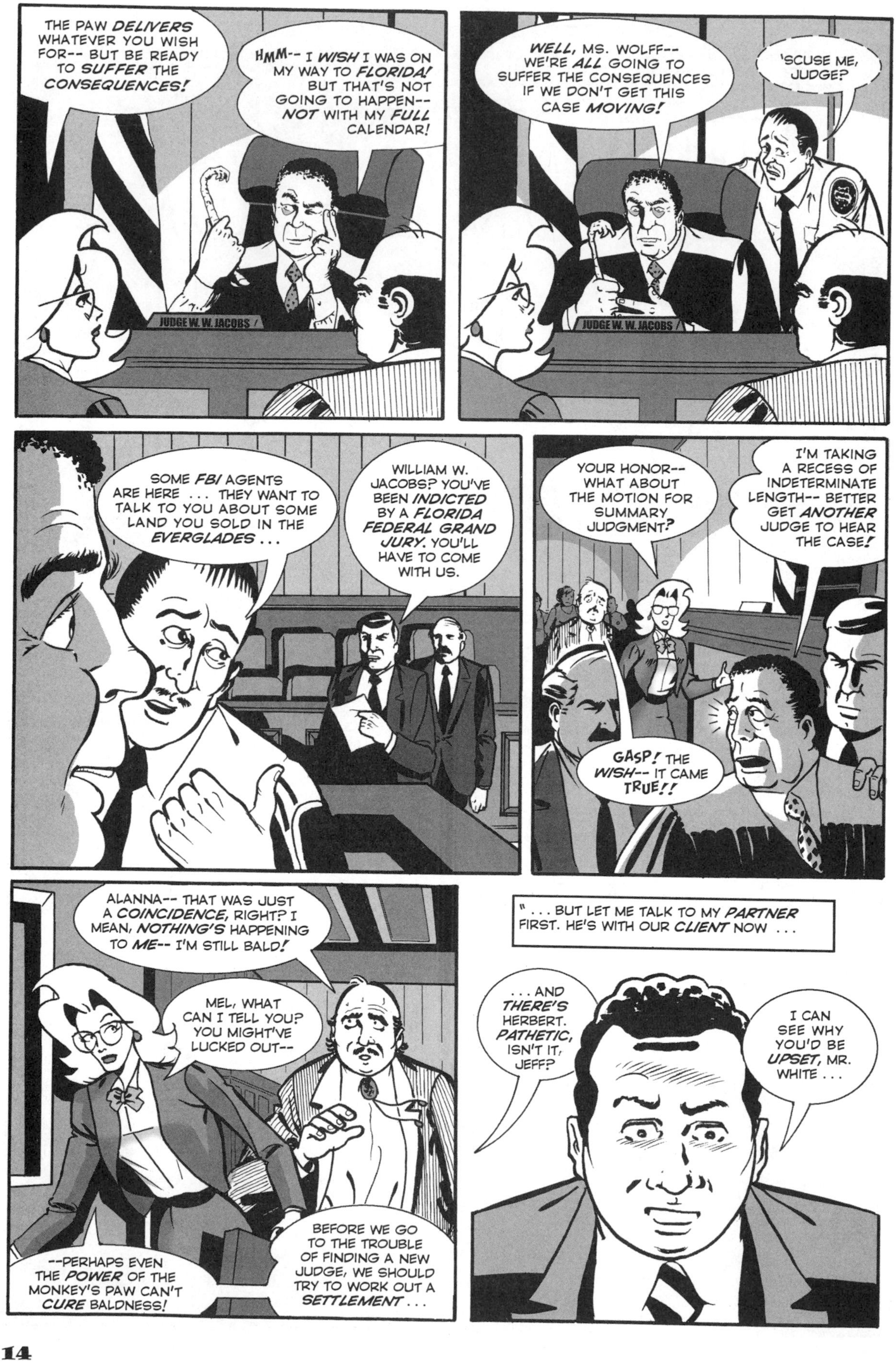
THE PAW DELIVERS WHATEVER YOU WISH FOR-- BUT BE READY TO SUFFER THE CONSEQUENCES!
HMM-- I WISH I WAS ON MY WAY TO FLORIDA! BUT THAT'S NOT GOING TO HAPPEN-- NOT WITH MY FULL CALENDAR!
JUDGE W. W. JACOBS
WELL, MS. WOLFF-- WE'RE ALL GOING TO SUFFER THE CONSEQUENCES IF WE DON'T GET THIS CASE MOVING!
'SCUSE ME, JUDGE?
JUDGE W. W. JACOBS
SOME FBI AGENTS ARE HERE ... THEY WANT TO TALK TO YOU ABOUT SOME LAND YOU SOLD IN THE EVERGLADES ...
WILLIAM W. JACOBS? YOU'VE BEEN INDICTED BY A FLORIDA FEDERAL GRAND JURY. YOU'LL HAVE TO COME WITH US.
YOUR HONOR-- WHAT ABOUT THE MOTION FOR SUMMARY JUDGMENT?
I'M TAKING A RECESS OF INDETERMINATE LENGTH-- BETTER GET ANOTHER JUDGE TO HEAR THE CASE!
GASP! THE WISH-- IT CAME TRUE!!
ALANNA-- THAT WAS JUST A COINCIDENCE, RIGHT? I MEAN, NOTHING'S HAPPENING TO ME-- I'M STILL BALD!
MEL, WHAT CAN I TELL YOU? YOU MIGHT'VE LUCKED OUT--
--PERHAPS EVEN THE POWER OF THE MONKEY'S PAW CAN'T CURE BALDNESS!
BEFORE WE GO TO THE TROUBLE OF FINDING A NEW JUDGE, WE SHOULD TRY TO WORK OUT A SETTLEMENT ...
" ... BUT LET ME TALK TO MY PARTNER FIRST. HE'S WITH OUR CLIENT NOW ...
... AND THERE'S HERBERT. PATHETIC, ISN'T IT, JEFF?
I CAN SEE WHY YOU'D BE UPSET, MR. WHITE ...

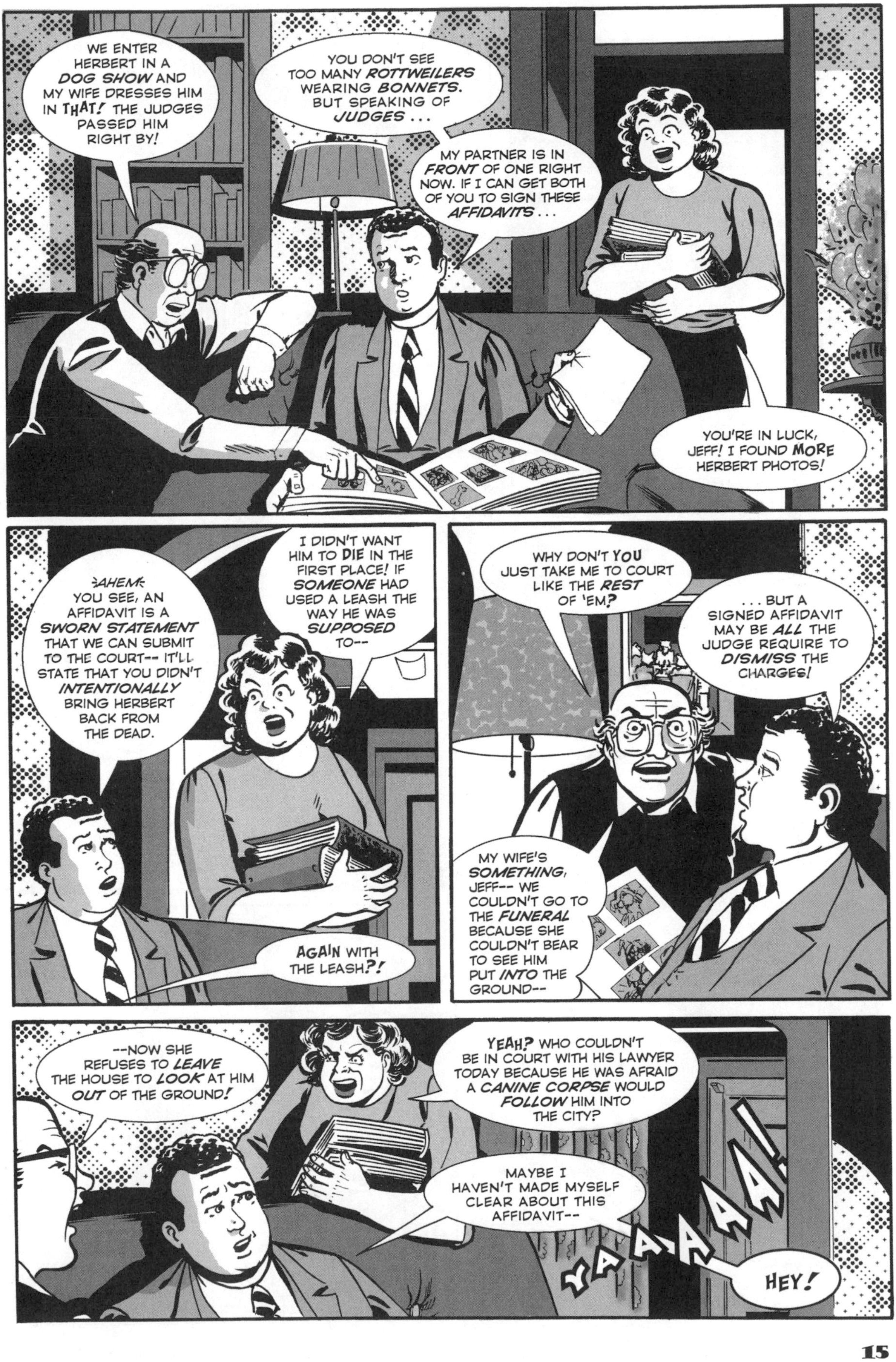
WE ENTER HERBERT IN A DOG SHOW AND MY WIFE DRESSES HIM IN THAT! THE JUDGES PASSED HIM RIGHT BY!
YOU DON'T SEE TOO MANY ROTTWEILERS WEARING BONNETS. BUT SPEAKING OF JUDGES . . .
MY PARTNER IS IN FRONT OF ONE RIGHT NOW. IF I CAN GET BOTH OF YOU TO SIGN THESE AFFIDAVITS . . .
YOU'RE IN LUCK, JEFF! I FOUND MORE HERBERT PHOTOS!
AHEM
YOU SEE, AN AFFIDAVIT IS A SWORN STATEMENT THAT WE CAN SUBMIT TO THE COURT-- IT'LL STATE THAT YOU DIDN'T INTENTIONALLY BRING HERBERT BACK FROM THE DEAD.
I DIDN'T WANT HIM TO DIE IN THE FIRST PLACE! IF SOMEONE HAD USED A LEASH THE WAY HE WAS SUPPOSED TO--
AGAIN WITH THE LEASH?!
WHY DON'T YOU JUST TAKE ME TO COURT LIKE THE REST OF 'EM?
. . . BUT A SIGNED AFFIDAVIT MAY BE ALL THE JUDGE REQUIRE TO DISMISS THE CHARGES!
MY WIFE'S SOMETHING, JEFF-- WE COULDN'T GO TO THE FUNERAL BECAUSE SHE COULDN'T BEAR TO SEE HIM PUT INTO THE GROUND--
--NOW SHE REFUSES TO LEAVE THE HOUSE TO LOOK AT HIM OUT OF THE GROUND!
YEAH? WHO COULDN'T BE IN COURT WITH HIS LAWYER TODAY BECAUSE HE WAS AFRAID A CANINE CORPSE WOULD FOLLOW HIM INTO THE CITY?
MAYBE I HAVEN'T MADE MYSELF CLEAR ABOUT THIS AFFIDAVIT--
YAAAAA!
HEY!

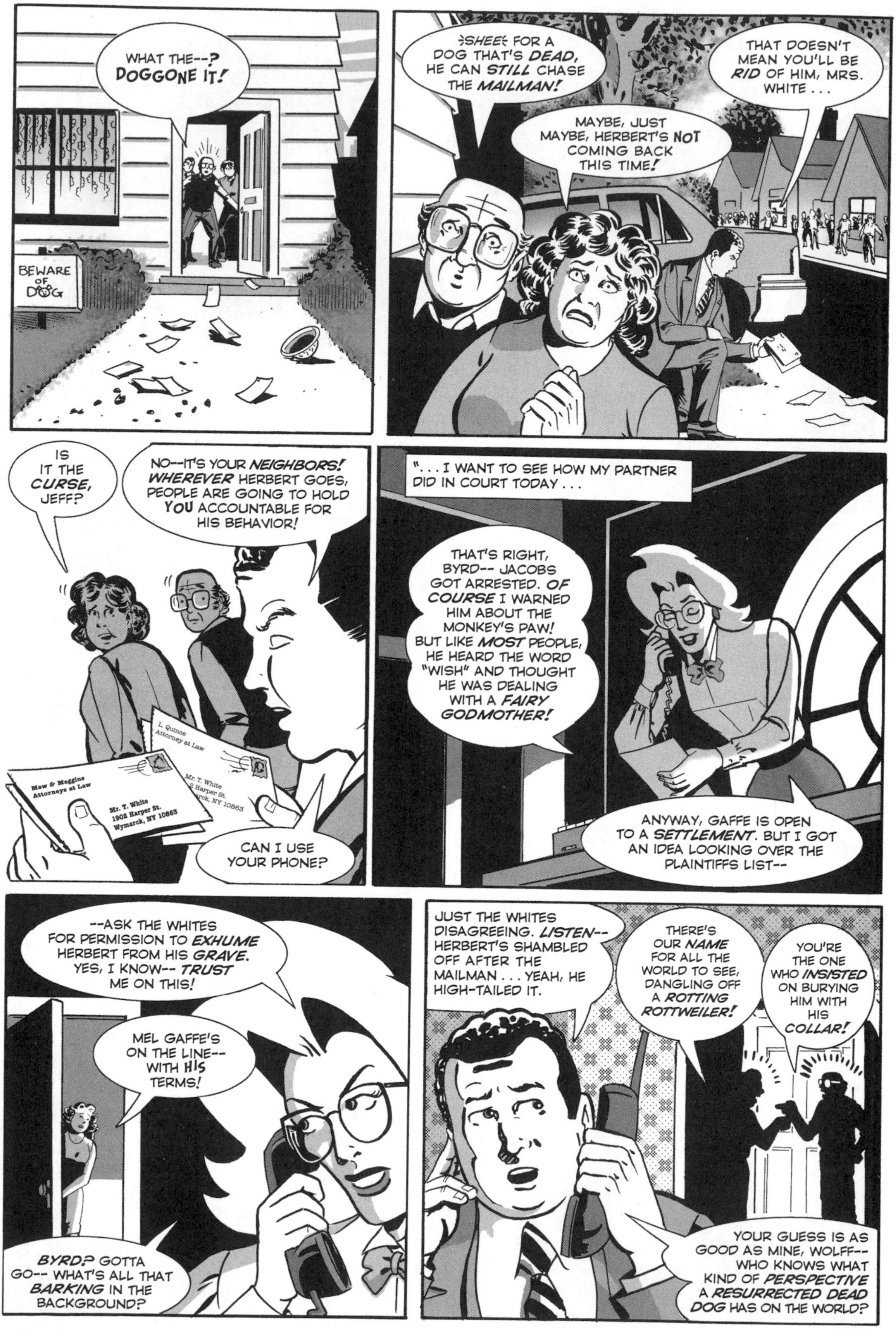
WHAT THE--? DOGGONE IT!
BEWARE OF DOG
>SHEE< FOR A DOG THAT'S DEAD, HE CAN STILL CHASE THE MAILMAN!
THAT DOESN'T MEAN YOU'LL BE RID OF HIM, MRS. WHITE . . .
MAYBE, JUST MAYBE, HERBERT'S NOT COMING BACK THIS TIME!
IS IT THE CURSE, JEFF?
NO--IT'S YOUR NEIGHBORS! WHEREVER HERBERT GOES, PEOPLE ARE GOING TO HOLD YOU ACCOUNTABLE FOR HIS BEHAVIOR!
L. Quince
Attorney at Law
Maw & Meggins
Attorneys at Law
Mr. T. White
1902 Harper St.
Wymarck, NY 10863
CAN I USE YOUR PHONE?
". . . I WANT TO SEE HOW MY PARTNER DID IN COURT TODAY . . .
THAT'S RIGHT, BYRD-- JACOBS GOT ARRESTED. OF COURSE I WARNED HIM ABOUT THE MONKEY'S PAW! BUT LIKE MOST PEOPLE, HE HEARD THE WORD "WISH" AND THOUGHT HE WAS DEALING WITH A FAIRY GODMOTHER!
ANYWAY, GAFFE IS OPEN TO A SETTLEMENT. BUT I GOT AN IDEA LOOKING OVER THE PLAINTIFFS LIST--
--ASK THE WHITES FOR PERMISSION TO EXHUME HERBERT FROM HIS GRAVE. YES, I KNOW-- TRUST ME ON THIS!
MEL GAFFE'S ON THE LINE-- WITH HIS TERMS!
BYRD? GOTTA GO-- WHAT'S ALL THAT BARKING IN THE BACKGROUND?
JUST THE WHITES DISAGREEING. LISTEN-- HERBERT'S SHAMBLED OFF AFTER THE MAILMAN . . . YEAH, HE HIGH-TAILED IT.
THERE'S OUR NAME FOR ALL THE WORLD TO SEE, DANGLING OFF A ROTTING ROTTWEILER!
YOU'RE THE ONE WHO INSISTED ON BURYING HIM WITH HIS COLLAR!
YOUR GUESS IS AS GOOD AS MINE, WOLFF-- WHO KNOWS WHAT KIND OF PERSPECTIVE A RESURRECTED DEAD DOG HAS ON THE WORLD?

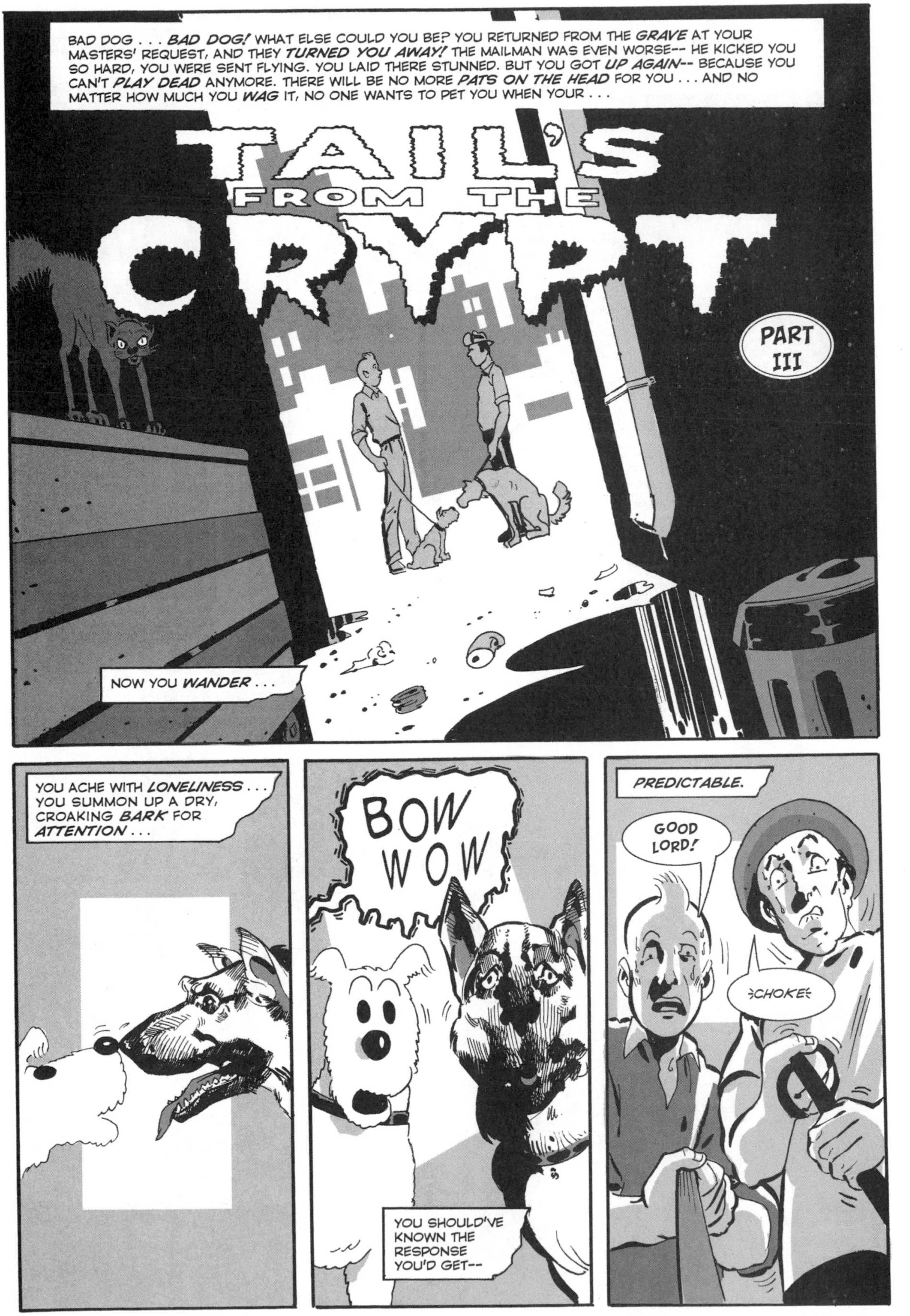

BAD DOG . . . BAD DOG! WHAT ELSE COULD YOU BE? YOU RETURNED FROM THE GRAVE AT YOUR MASTERS' REQUEST, AND THEY TURNED YOU AWAY! THE MAILMAN WAS EVEN WORSE-- HE KICKED YOU SO HARD, YOU WERE SENT FLYING. YOU LAID THERE STUNNED. BUT YOU GOT UP AGAIN-- BECAUSE YOU CAN'T PLAY DEAD ANYMORE. THERE WILL BE NO MORE PATS ON THE HEAD FOR YOU . . . AND NO MATTER HOW MUCH YOU WAG IT, NO ONE WANTS TO PET YOU WHEN YOUR . . .
TAIL'S FROM THE CRYPT
PART III
NOW YOU WANDER . . .
YOU ACHE WITH LONELINESS . . . YOU SUMMON UP A DRY, CROAKING BARK FOR ATTENTION . . .
BOW WOW
YOU SHOULD'VE KNOWN THE RESPONSE YOU'D GET--
PREDICTABLE.
GOOD LORD!
CHOKE

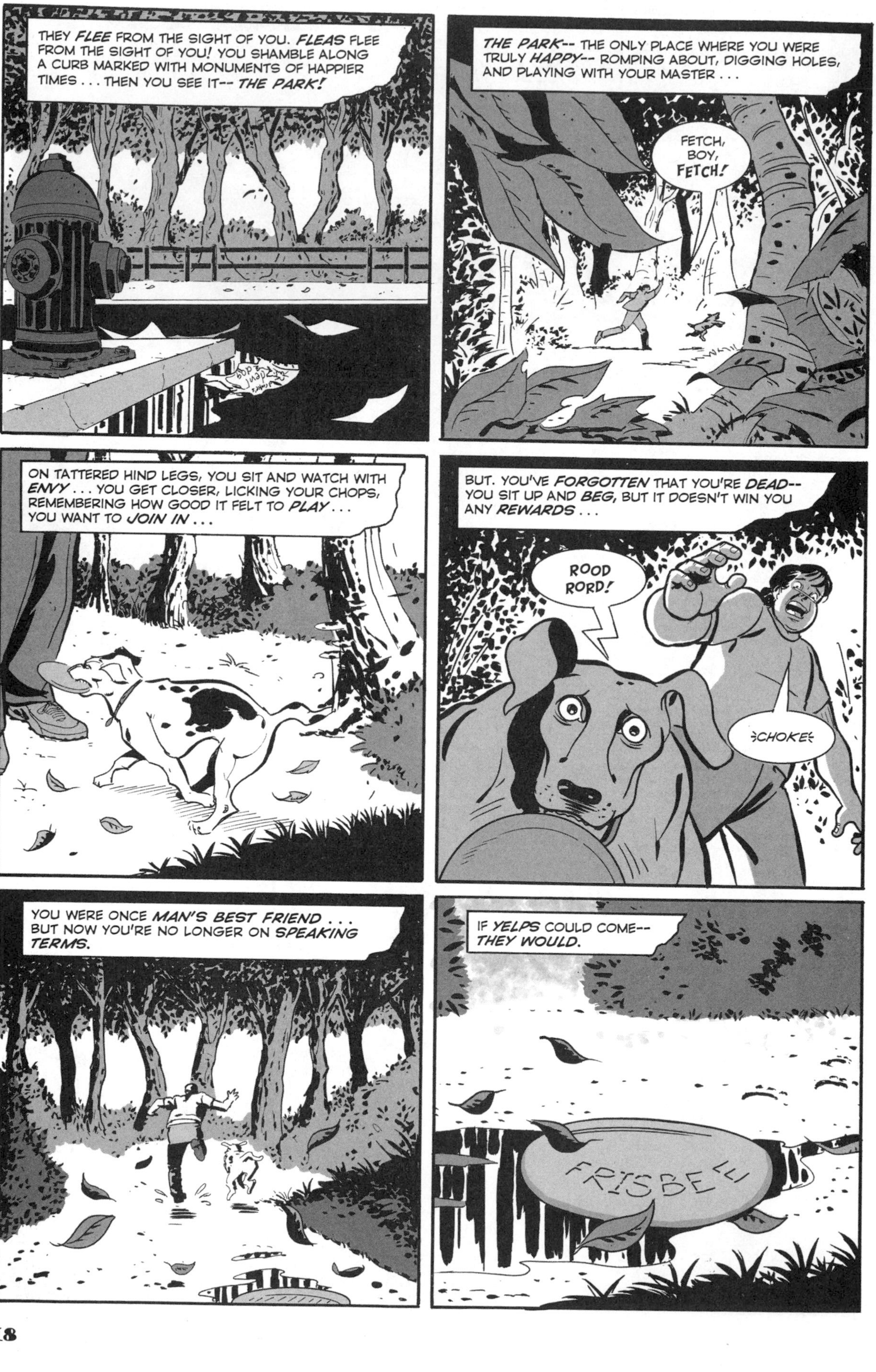
THEY FLEE FROM THE SIGHT OF YOU. FLEAS FLEE FROM THE SIGHT OF YOU! YOU SHAMBLE ALONG A CURB MARKED WITH MONUMENTS OF HAPPIER TIMES . . . THEN YOU SEE IT-- THE PARK!
THE PARK-- THE ONLY PLACE WHERE YOU WERE TRULY HAPPY-- ROMPING ABOUT, DIGGING HOLES, AND PLAYING WITH YOUR MASTER . . .
FETCH, BOY, FETCH!
ON TATTERED HIND LEGS, YOU SIT AND WATCH WITH ENVY . . . YOU GET CLOSER, LICKING YOUR CHOPS, REMEMBERING HOW GOOD IT FELT TO PLAY . . . YOU WANT TO JOIN IN . . .
BUT. YOU'VE FORGOTTEN THAT YOU'RE DEAD-- YOU SIT UP AND BEG, BUT IT DOESN'T WIN YOU ANY REWARDS . . .
ROOD RORD!
CHOKE
YOU WERE ONCE MAN'S BEST FRIEND . . . BUT NOW YOU'RE NO LONGER ON SPEAKING TERMS.
IF YELPS COULD COME-- THEY WOULD.
FRISBEE

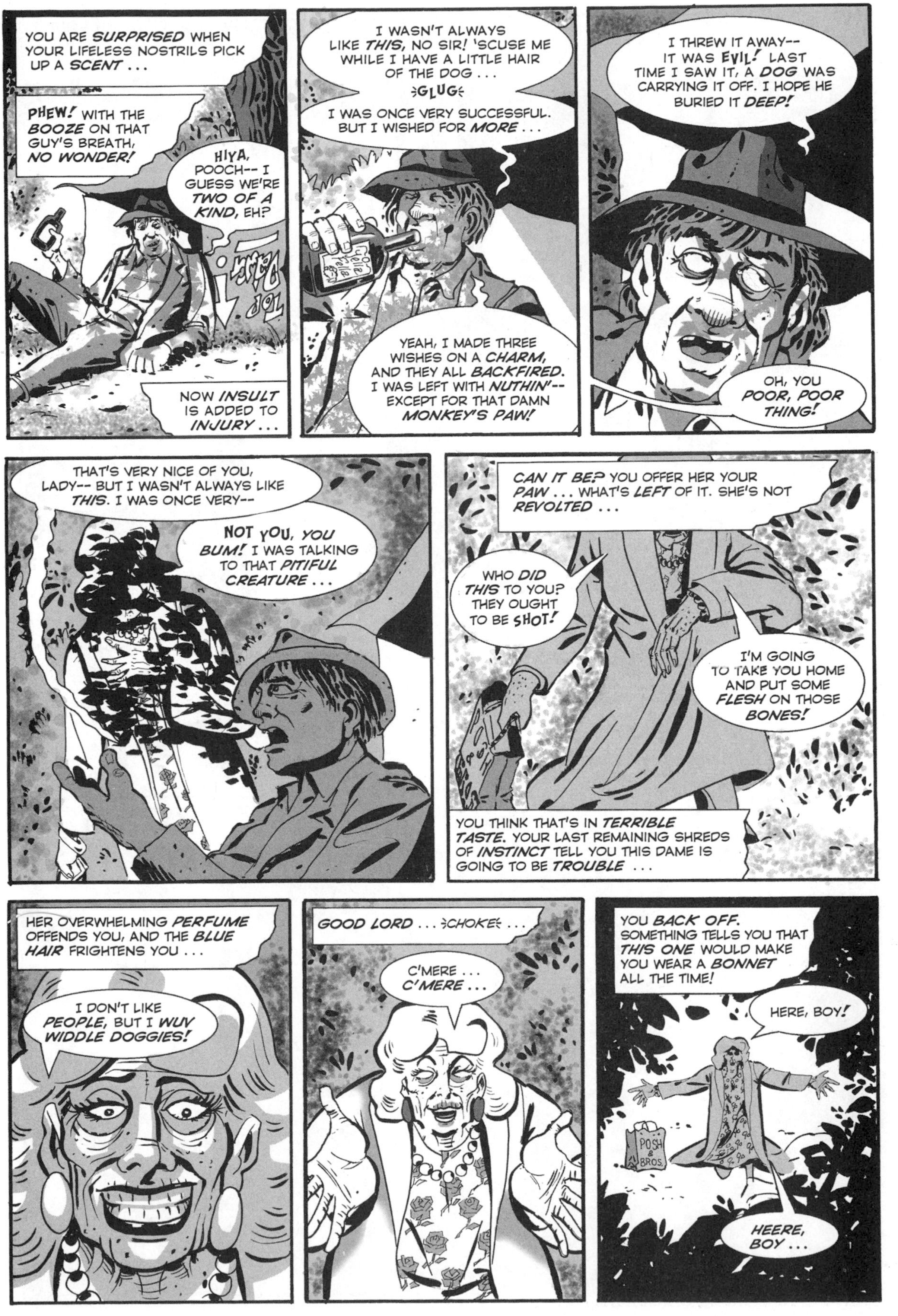
YOU ARE SURPRISED WHEN YOUR LIFELESS NOSTRILS PICK UP A SCENT . . .
PHEW! WITH THE BOOZE ON THAT GUY'S BREATH, NO WONDER!
HIYA, POOCH-- I GUESS WE'RE TWO OF A KIND, EH?
NOW INSULT IS ADDED TO INJURY . . .
I WASN'T ALWAYS LIKE THIS, NO SIR! 'SCUSE ME WHILE I HAVE A LITTLE HAIR OF THE DOG . . .
GLUG
I WAS ONCE VERY SUCCESSFUL. BUT I WISHED FOR MORE . . .
YEAH, I MADE THREE WISHES ON A CHARM, AND THEY ALL BACKFIRED. I WAS LEFT WITH NUTHIN'-- EXCEPT FOR THAT DAMN MONKEY'S PAW!
I THREW IT AWAY-- IT WAS EVIL! LAST TIME I SAW IT, A DOG WAS CARRYING IT OFF. I HOPE HE BURIED IT DEEP!
OH, YOU POOR, POOR THING!
THAT'S VERY NICE OF YOU, LADY-- BUT I WASN'T ALWAYS LIKE THIS. I WAS ONCE VERY--
NOT YOU, YOU BUM! I WAS TALKING TO THAT PITIFUL CREATURE . . .
CAN IT BE? YOU OFFER HER YOUR PAW . . . WHAT'S LEFT OF IT. SHE'S NOT REVOLTED . . .
WHO DID THIS TO YOU? THEY OUGHT TO BE SHOT!
I'M GOING TO TAKE YOU HOME AND PUT SOME FLESH ON THOSE BONES!
YOU THINK THAT'S IN TERRIBLE TASTE. YOUR LAST REMAINING SHREDS OF INSTINCT TELL YOU THIS DAME IS GOING TO BE TROUBLE . . .
HER OVERWHELMING PERFUME OFFENDS YOU, AND THE BLUE HAIR FRIGHTENS YOU . . .
I DON'T LIKE PEOPLE, BUT I WUV WIDDLE DOGGIES!
GOOD LORD . . . CHOKE . . .
C'MERE . . . C'MERE . . .
YOU BACK OFF. SOMETHING TELLS YOU THAT THIS ONE WOULD MAKE YOU WEAR A BONNET ALL THE TIME!
HERE, BOY!
POSH & BROS.
HEERE, BOY . . .

PART IV: *HERBERT HAS RISEN FROM THE GRAVE--* OR HAS HE JUST RETURNED FROM THE DEAD? THAT'S THE QUESTION *WOLFF AND BYRD* ASK. WITH THEIR CLIENTS' PERMISSION, THE COUNSELORS OBTAIN A COURT ORDER TO OPEN HERBERT'S GRAVE, SO THEY CAN COME TO . . .

TERMS OF INTERMENT

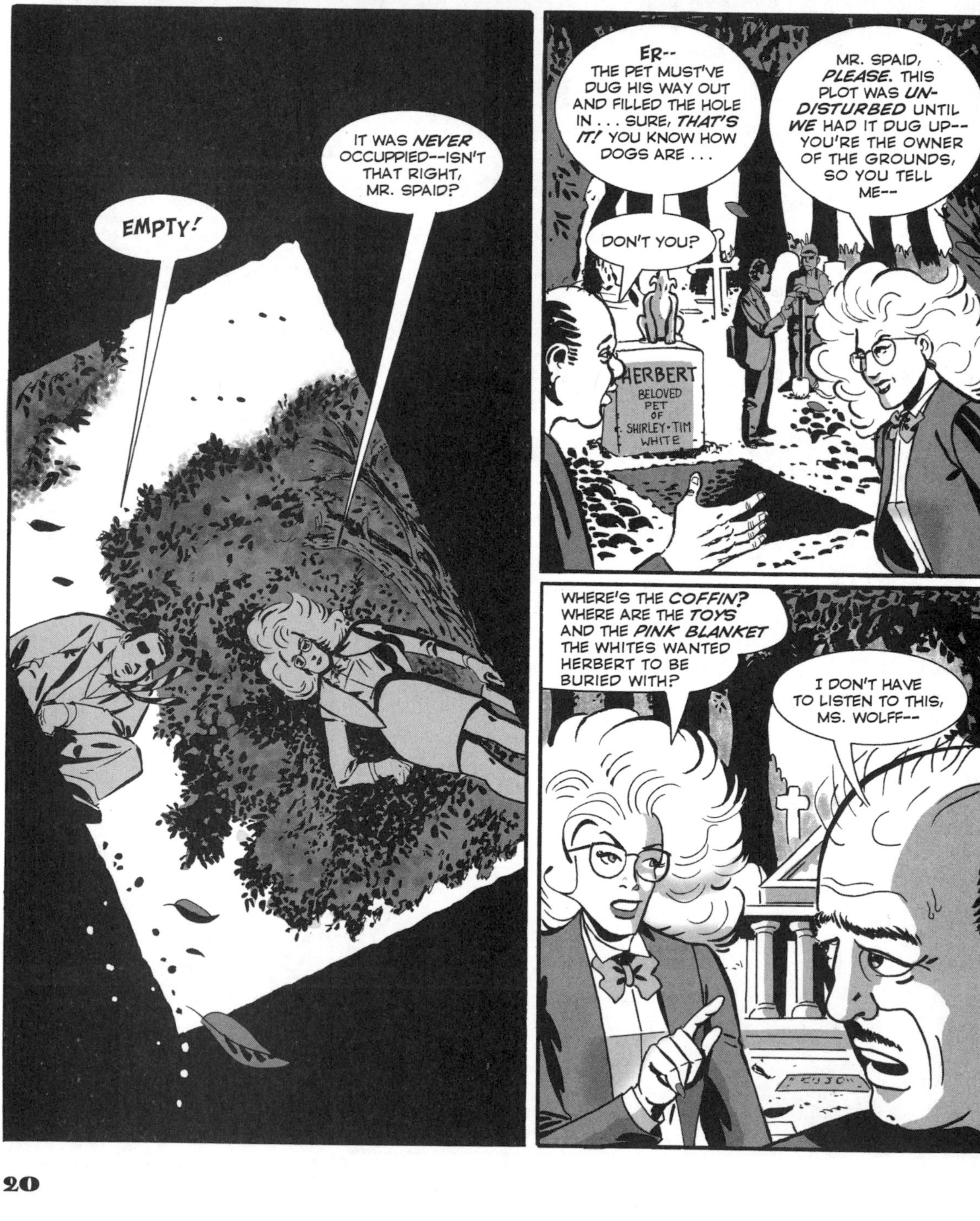
EMPTY!
IT WAS NEVER OCCUPPIED--ISN'T THAT RIGHT, MR. SPAID?
ER-- THE PET MUST'VE DUG HIS WAY OUT AND FILLED THE HOLE IN . . . SURE, THAT'S IT! YOU KNOW HOW DOGS ARE . . .
MR. SPAID, PLEASE. THIS PLOT WAS UN-DISTURBED UNTIL WE HAD IT DUG UP-- YOU'RE THE OWNER OF THE GROUNDS, SO YOU TELL ME--
DON'T YOU?
HERBERT
BELOVED PET OF SHIRLEY • TIM WHITE
WHERE'S THE COFFIN? WHERE ARE THE TOYS AND THE PINK BLANKET THE WHITES WANTED HERBERT TO BE BURIED WITH?
I DON'T HAVE TO LISTEN TO THIS, MS. WOLFF--

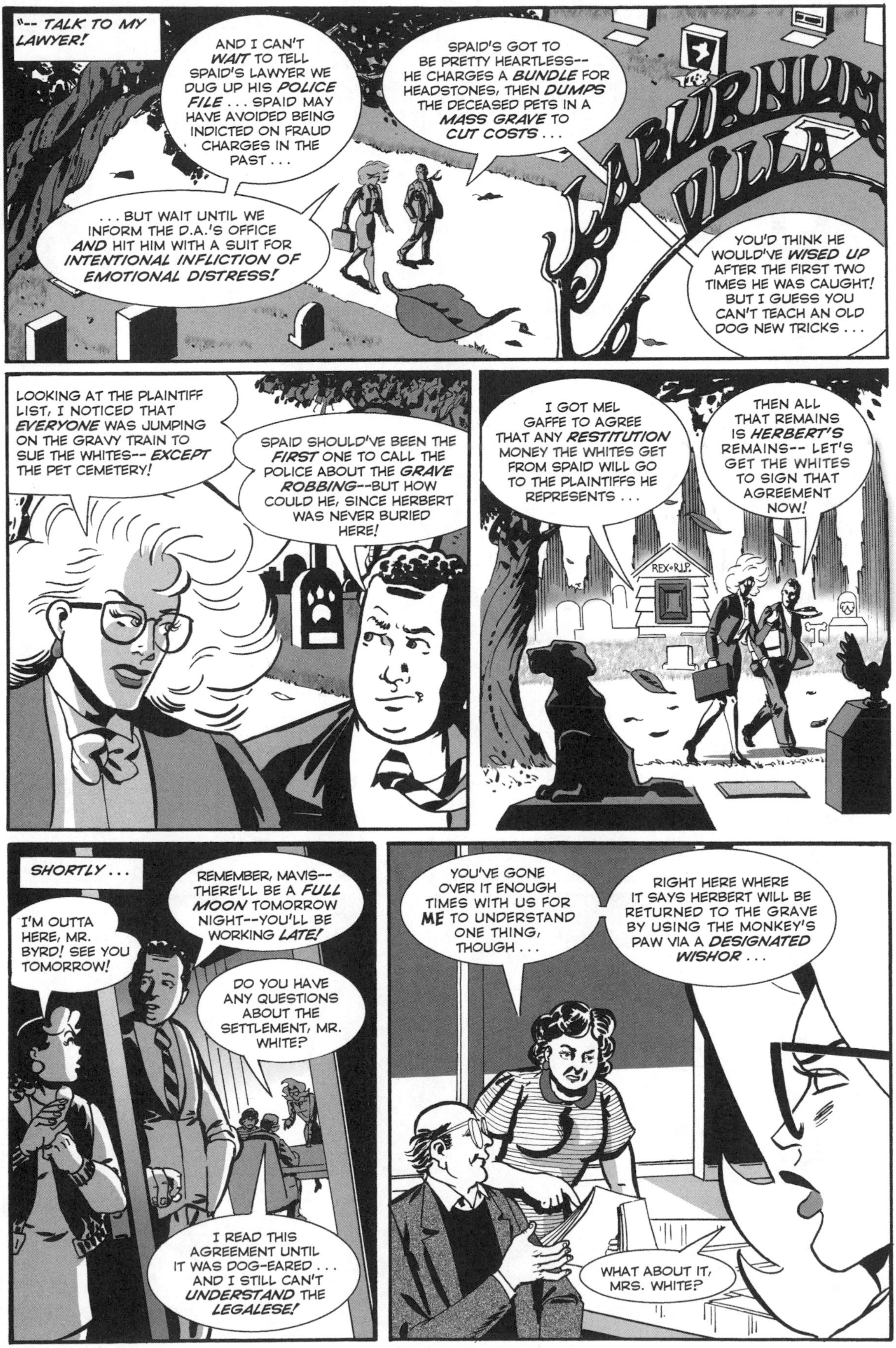
"-- TALK TO MY LAWYER!
AND I CAN'T WAIT TO TELL SPAID'S LAWYER WE DUG UP HIS POLICE FILE . . . SPAID MAY HAVE AVOIDED BEING INDICTED ON FRAUD CHARGES IN THE PAST . . .
. . . BUT WAIT UNTIL WE INFORM THE D.A.'S OFFICE AND HIT HIM WITH A SUIT FOR INTENTIONAL INFLICTION OF EMOTIONAL DISTRESS!
SPAID'S GOT TO BE PRETTY HEARTLESS-- HE CHARGES A BUNDLE FOR HEADSTONES, THEN DUMPS THE DECEASED PETS IN A MASS GRAVE TO CUT COSTS . . .
LABURNUM VILLA
YOU'D THINK HE WOULD'VE WISED UP AFTER THE FIRST TWO TIMES HE WAS CAUGHT! BUT I GUESS YOU CAN'T TEACH AN OLD DOG NEW TRICKS . . .
LOOKING AT THE PLAINTIFF LIST, I NOTICED THAT EVERYONE WAS JUMPING ON THE GRAVY TRAIN TO SUE THE WHITES-- EXCEPT THE PET CEMETERY!
SPAID SHOULD'VE BEEN THE FIRST ONE TO CALL THE POLICE ABOUT THE GRAVE ROBBING--BUT HOW COULD HE, SINCE HERBERT WAS NEVER BURIED HERE!
I GOT MEL GAFFE TO AGREE THAT ANY RESTITUTION MONEY THE WHITES GET FROM SPAID WILL GO TO THE PLAINTIFFS HE REPRESENTS . . .
THEN ALL THAT REMAINS IS HERBERT'S REMAINS-- LET'S GET THE WHITES TO SIGN THAT AGREEMENT NOW!
REX • R.I.P.
SHORTLY . . .
I'M OUTTA HERE, MR. BYRD! SEE YOU TOMORROW!
REMEMBER, MAVIS-- THERE'LL BE A FULL MOON TOMORROW NIGHT--YOU'LL BE WORKING LATE!
DO YOU HAVE ANY QUESTIONS ABOUT THE SETTLEMENT, MR. WHITE?
I READ THIS AGREEMENT UNTIL IT WAS DOG-EARED . . . AND I STILL CAN'T UNDERSTAND THE LEGALESE!
YOU'VE GONE OVER IT ENOUGH TIMES WITH US FOR ME TO UNDERSTAND ONE THING, THOUGH . . .
RIGHT HERE WHERE IT SAYS HERBERT WILL BE RETURNED TO THE GRAVE BY USING THE MONKEY'S PAW VIA A DESIGNATED WISHOR . . .
WHAT ABOUT IT, MRS. WHITE?

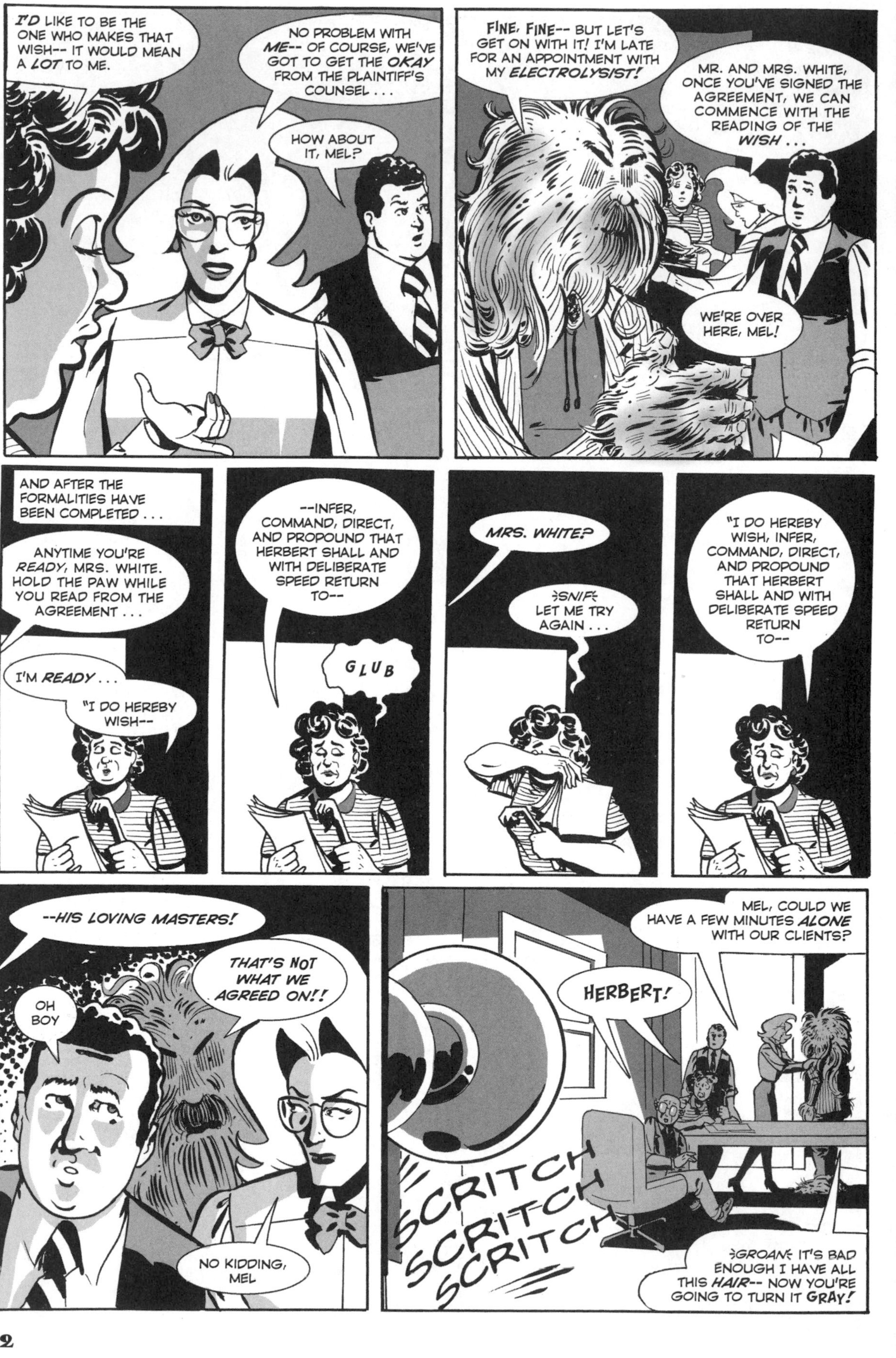
I'D LIKE TO BE THE ONE WHO MAKES THAT WISH-- IT WOULD MEAN A LOT TO ME.
NO PROBLEM WITH ME-- OF COURSE, WE'VE GOT TO GET THE OKAY FROM THE PLAINTIFF'S COUNSEL . . .
HOW ABOUT IT, MEL?
FINE, FINE-- BUT LET'S GET ON WITH IT! I'M LATE FOR AN APPOINTMENT WITH MY ELECTROLYSIST!
MR. AND MRS. WHITE, ONCE YOU'VE SIGNED THE AGREEMENT, WE CAN COMMENCE WITH THE READING OF THE WISH . . .
WE'RE OVER HERE, MEL!
AND AFTER THE FORMALITIES HAVE BEEN COMPLETED . . .
ANYTIME YOU'RE READY, MRS. WHITE. HOLD THE PAW WHILE YOU READ FROM THE AGREEMENT . . .
I'M READY . . .
"I DO HEREBY WISH--
--INFER, COMMAND, DIRECT, AND PROPOUND THAT HERBERT SHALL AND WITH DELIBERATE SPEED RETURN TO--
GLUB
MRS. WHITE?
SNIF LET ME TRY AGAIN . . .
"I DO HEREBY WISH, INFER, COMMAND, DIRECT, AND PROPOUND THAT HERBERT SHALL AND WITH DELIBERATE SPEED RETURN TO--
--HIS LOVING MASTERS!
OH BOY
THAT'S NOT WHAT WE AGREED ON!!
NO KIDDING, MEL
MEL, COULD WE HAVE A FEW MINUTES ALONE WITH OUR CLIENTS?
HERBERT!
SCRITCH SCRITCH SCRITCH
GROAN IT'S BAD ENOUGH I HAVE ALL THIS HAIR-- NOW YOU'RE GOING TO TURN IT GRAY!

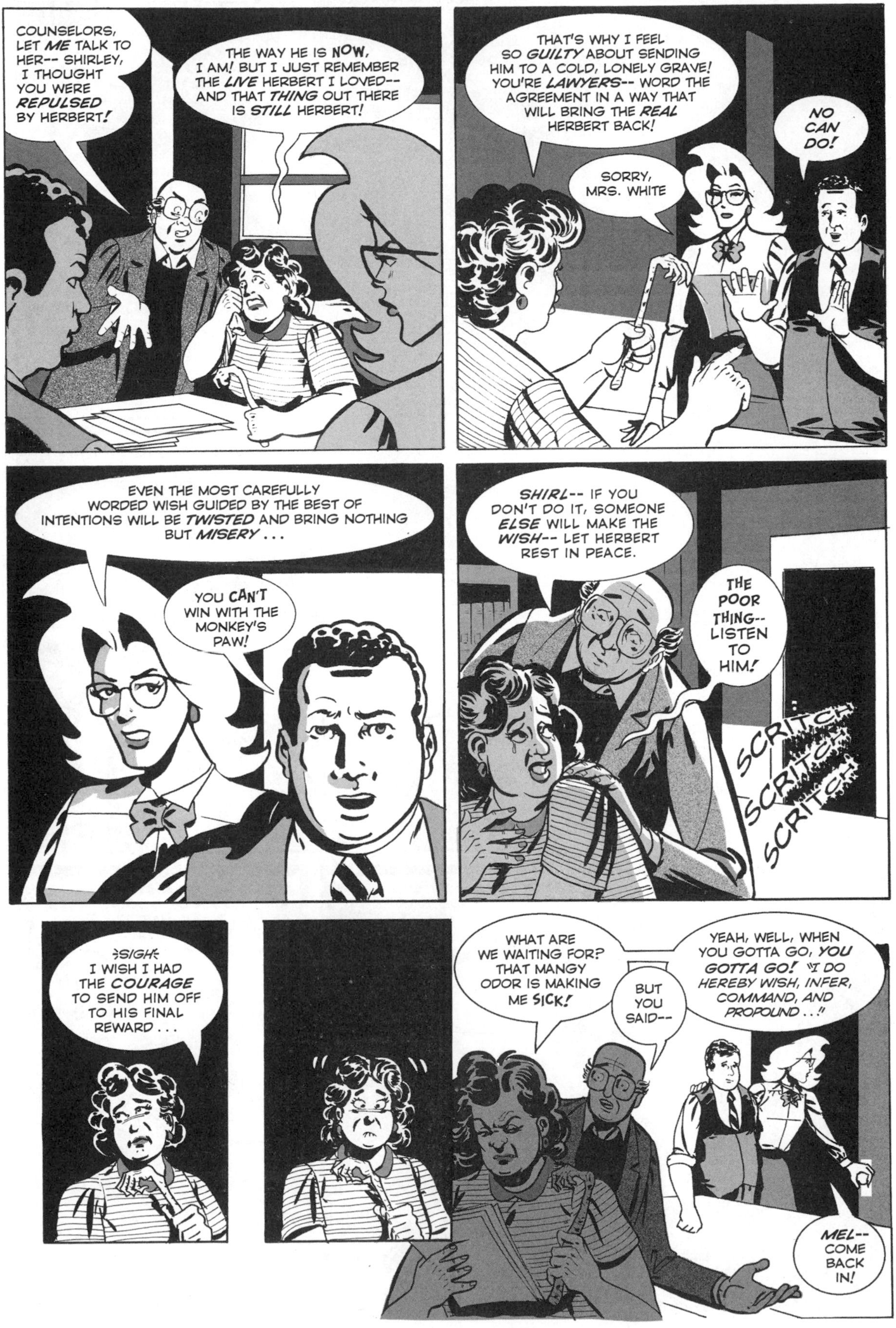
COUNSELORS, LET *ME* TALK TO HER-- SHIRLEY, I THOUGHT YOU WERE *REPULSED* BY HERBERT!
THE WAY HE IS **NOW**, I AM! BUT I JUST REMEMBER THE *LIVE* HERBERT I LOVED-- AND THAT *THING* OUT THERE IS *STILL* HERBERT!
THAT'S WHY I FEEL SO *GUILTY* ABOUT SENDING HIM TO A COLD, LONELY GRAVE! YOU'RE *LAWYERS*-- WORD THE AGREEMENT IN A WAY THAT WILL BRING THE *REAL* HERBERT BACK!
SORRY, MRS. WHITE
NO CAN DO!
EVEN THE MOST CAREFULLY WORDED WISH GUIDED BY THE BEST OF INTENTIONS WILL BE *TWISTED* AND BRING NOTHING BUT *MISERY* . . .
YOU **CAN'T** WIN WITH THE MONKEY'S PAW!
SHIRL-- IF YOU DON'T DO IT, SOMEONE *ELSE* WILL MAKE THE *WISH*-- LET HERBERT REST IN PEACE.
THE POOR THING-- LISTEN TO HIM!
SCRITCH SCRITCH SCRITCH
SIGH
I WISH I HAD THE *COURAGE* TO SEND HIM OFF TO HIS FINAL REWARD . . .
WHAT ARE WE WAITING FOR? THAT MANGY ODOR IS MAKING ME **SICK!**
BUT YOU SAID--
YEAH, WELL, WHEN YOU GOTTA GO, *YOU GOTTA GO!* "*I DO HEREBY WISH, INFER, COMMAND, AND PROPOUND . .!*"
MEL-- COME BACK IN!

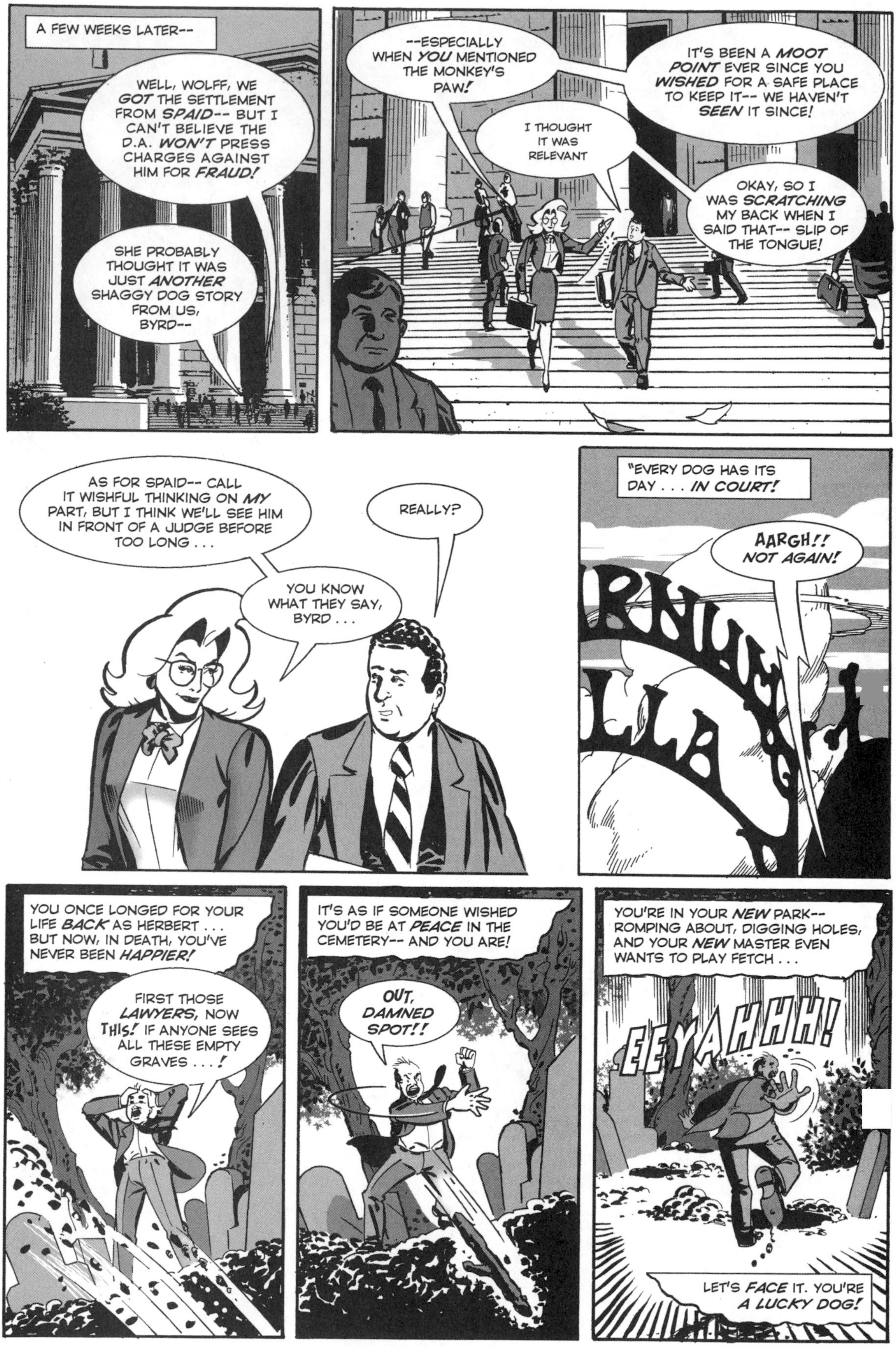
A FEW WEEKS LATER--
WELL, WOLFF, WE GOT THE SETTLEMENT FROM SPAID-- BUT I CAN'T BELIEVE THE D.A. WON'T PRESS CHARGES AGAINST HIM FOR FRAUD!
SHE PROBABLY THOUGHT IT WAS JUST ANOTHER SHAGGY DOG STORY FROM US, BYRD--
--ESPECIALLY WHEN YOU MENTIONED THE MONKEY'S PAW!
I THOUGHT IT WAS RELEVANT
IT'S BEEN A MOOT POINT EVER SINCE YOU WISHED FOR A SAFE PLACE TO KEEP IT-- WE HAVEN'T SEEN IT SINCE!
OKAY, SO I WAS SCRATCHING MY BACK WHEN I SAID THAT-- SLIP OF THE TONGUE!
AS FOR SPAID-- CALL IT WISHFUL THINKING ON MY PART, BUT I THINK WE'LL SEE HIM IN FRONT OF A JUDGE BEFORE TOO LONG . . .
REALLY?
YOU KNOW WHAT THEY SAY, BYRD . . .
"EVERY DOG HAS ITS DAY . . . IN COURT!
AARGH!! NOT AGAIN!
YOU ONCE LONGED FOR YOUR LIFE BACK AS HERBERT . . . BUT NOW, IN DEATH, YOU'VE NEVER BEEN HAPPIER!
FIRST THOSE LAWYERS, NOW THIS! IF ANYONE SEES ALL THESE EMPTY GRAVES . . . !
IT'S AS IF SOMEONE WISHED YOU'D BE AT PEACE IN THE CEMETERY-- AND YOU ARE!
OUT, DAMNED SPOT!!
YOU'RE IN YOUR NEW PARK-- ROMPING ABOUT, DIGGING HOLES, AND YOUR NEW MASTER EVEN WANTS TO PLAY FETCH . . .
EEYAHHH!
LET'S FACE IT. YOU'RE A LUCKY DOG!

Curse of the Werehouse

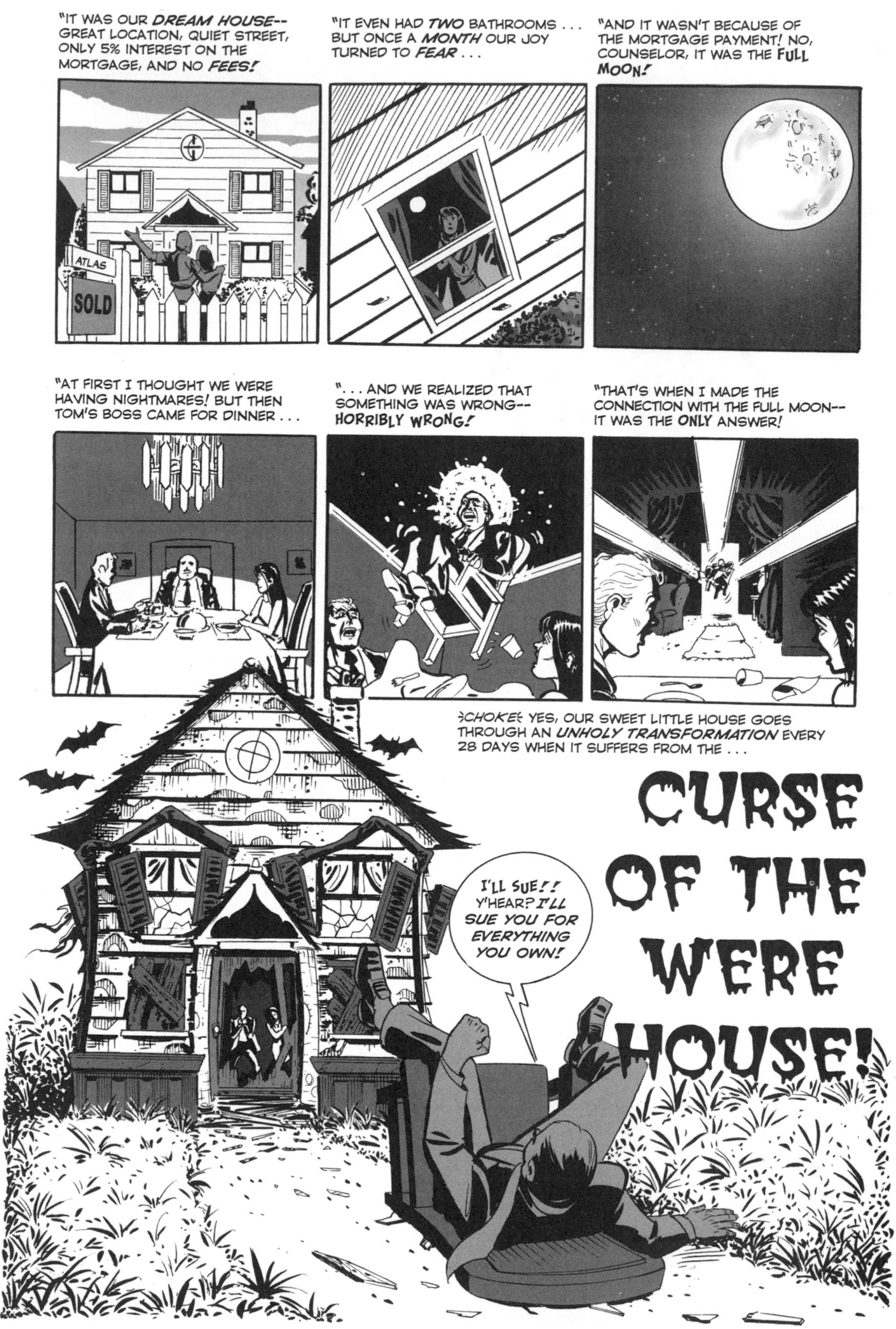
"IT WAS OUR DREAM HOUSE-- GREAT LOCATION, QUIET STREET, ONLY 5% INTEREST ON THE MORTGAGE, AND NO FEES!
ATLAS
SOLD
"IT EVEN HAD TWO BATHROOMS . . . BUT ONCE A MONTH OUR JOY TURNED TO FEAR . . .
"AND IT WASN'T BECAUSE OF THE MORTGAGE PAYMENT! NO, COUNSELOR, IT WAS THE FULL MOON!
"AT FIRST I THOUGHT WE WERE HAVING NIGHTMARES! BUT THEN TOM'S BOSS CAME FOR DINNER . . .
". . . AND WE REALIZED THAT SOMETHING WAS WRONG-- HORRIBLY WRONG!
"THAT'S WHEN I MADE THE CONNECTION WITH THE FULL MOON-- IT WAS THE ONLY ANSWER!
CHOKE YES, OUR SWEET LITTLE HOUSE GOES THROUGH AN UNHOLY TRANSFORMATION EVERY 28 DAYS WHEN IT SUFFERS FROM THE . . .
CURSE OF THE WERE HOUSE!
I'LL SUE!! Y'HEAR? I'LL SUE YOU FOR EVERYTHING YOU OWN!

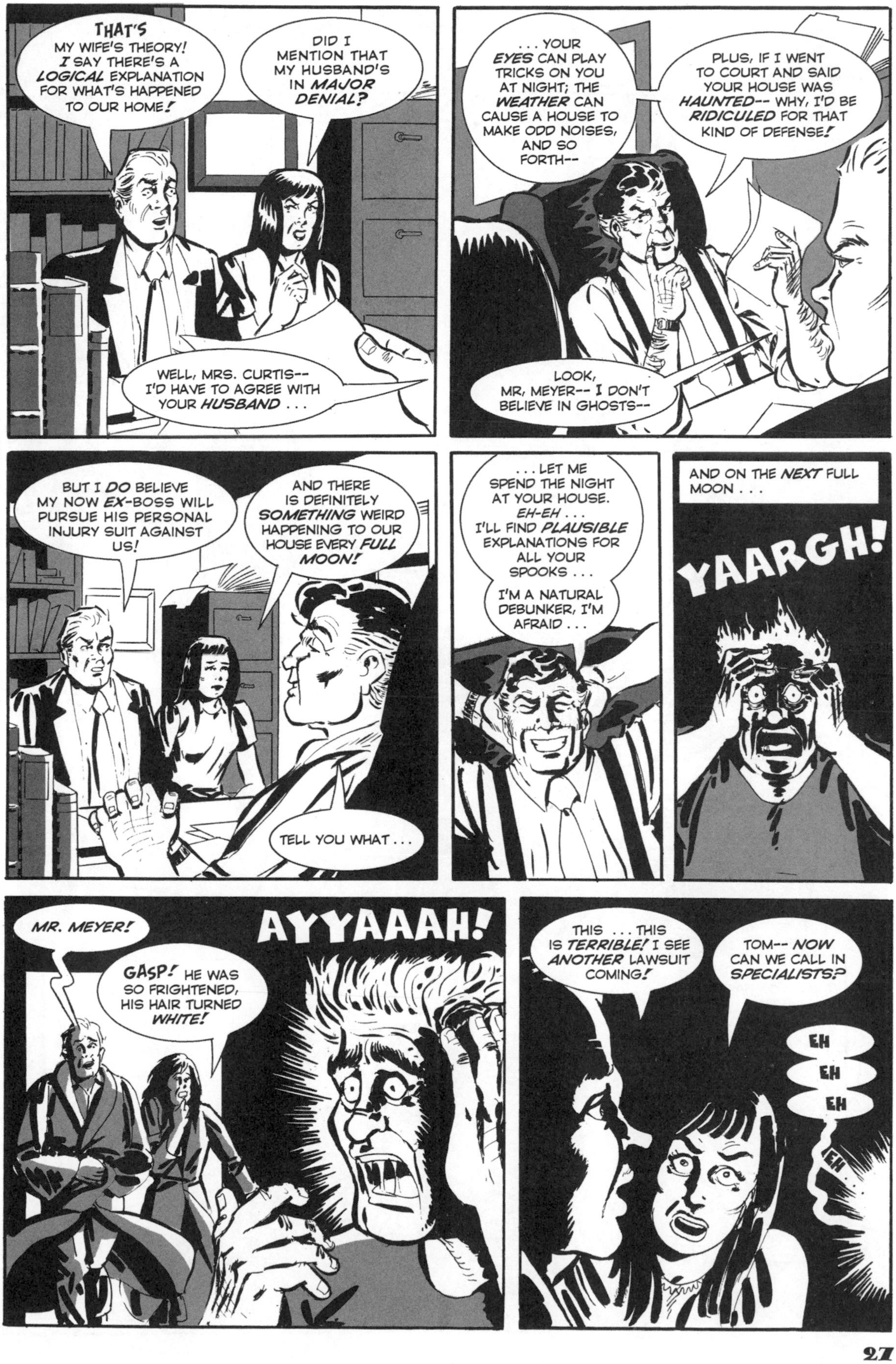
THAT'S MY WIFE'S THEORY! I SAY THERE'S A LOGICAL EXPLANATION FOR WHAT'S HAPPENED TO OUR HOME!
DID I MENTION THAT MY HUSBAND'S IN MAJOR DENIAL?
WELL, MRS. CURTIS-- I'D HAVE TO AGREE WITH YOUR HUSBAND . . .
LOOK, MR. MEYER-- I DON'T BELIEVE IN GHOSTS--
. . . YOUR EYES CAN PLAY TRICKS ON YOU AT NIGHT; THE WEATHER CAN CAUSE A HOUSE TO MAKE ODD NOISES, AND SO FORTH--
PLUS, IF I WENT TO COURT AND SAID YOUR HOUSE WAS HAUNTED-- WHY, I'D BE RIDICULED FOR THAT KIND OF DEFENSE!
BUT I DO BELIEVE MY NOW EX-BOSS WILL PURSUE HIS PERSONAL INJURY SUIT AGAINST US!
AND THERE IS DEFINITELY SOMETHING WEIRD HAPPENING TO OUR HOUSE EVERY FULL MOON!
TELL YOU WHAT . . .
. . . LET ME SPEND THE NIGHT AT YOUR HOUSE. EH-EH . . . I'LL FIND PLAUSIBLE EXPLANATIONS FOR ALL YOUR SPOOKS . . .
I'M A NATURAL DEBUNKER, I'M AFRAID . . .
AND ON THE NEXT FULL MOON . . .
YAARGH!
MR. MEYER!
GASP! HE WAS SO FRIGHTENED, HIS HAIR TURNED WHITE!
AYYAAAH!
THIS . . . THIS IS TERRIBLE! I SEE ANOTHER LAWSUIT COMING!
TOM-- NOW CAN WE CALL IN SPECIALISTS?
EH
EH
EH
EH . . .

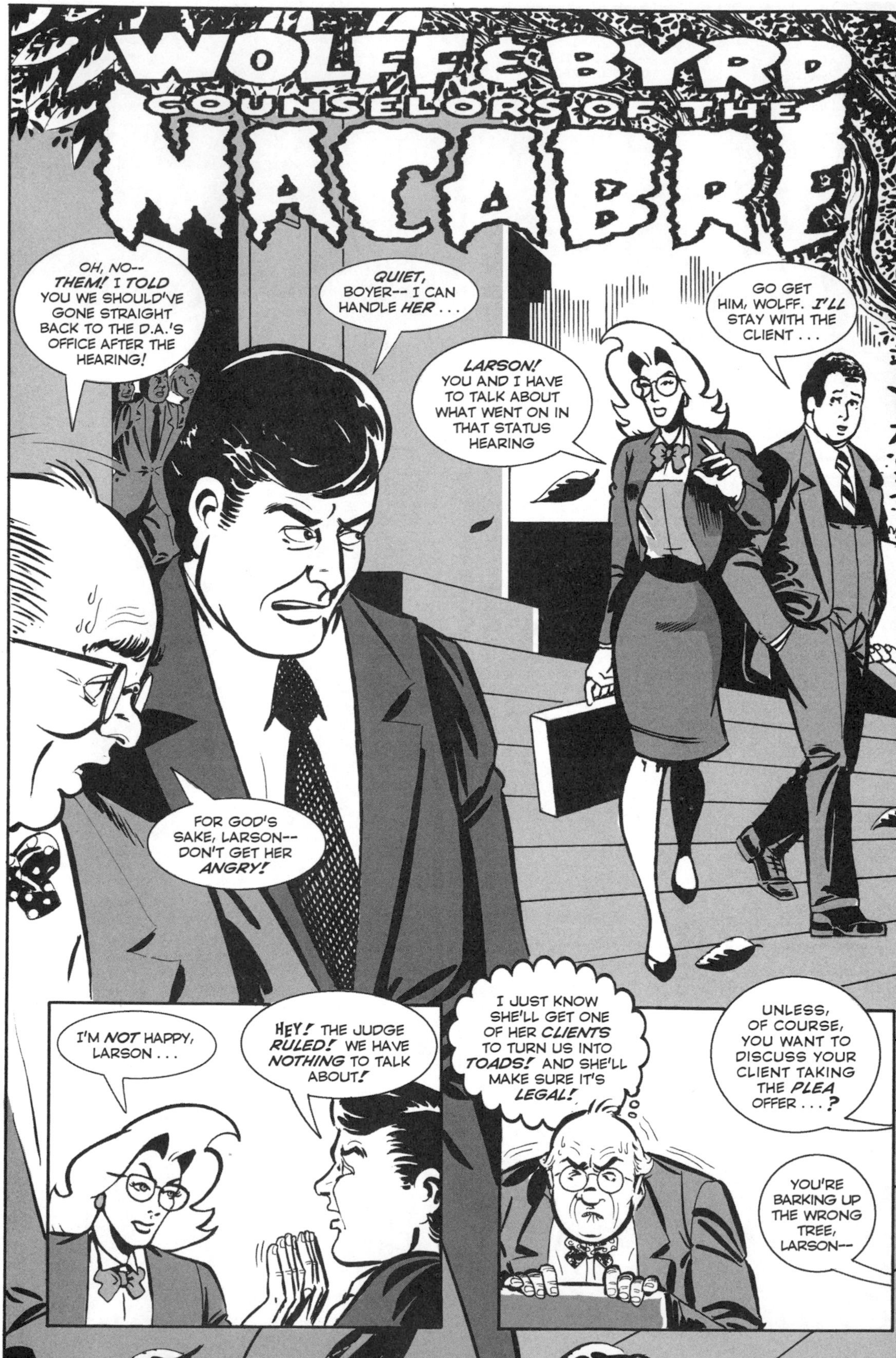
WOLFF & BYRD
COUNSELORS OF THE
MACABRE
OH, NO-- THEM! I TOLD YOU WE SHOULD'VE GONE STRAIGHT BACK TO THE D.A.'S OFFICE AFTER THE HEARING!
QUIET, BOYER-- I CAN HANDLE HER . . .
LARSON! YOU AND I HAVE TO TALK ABOUT WHAT WENT ON IN THAT STATUS HEARING
GO GET HIM, WOLFF. I'LL STAY WITH THE CLIENT . . .
FOR GOD'S SAKE, LARSON-- DON'T GET HER ANGRY!
I'M NOT HAPPY, LARSON . . .
HEY! THE JUDGE RULED! WE HAVE NOTHING TO TALK ABOUT!
I JUST KNOW SHE'LL GET ONE OF HER CLIENTS TO TURN US INTO TOADS! AND SHE'LL MAKE SURE IT'S LEGAL!
UNLESS, OF COURSE, YOU WANT TO DISCUSS YOUR CLIENT TAKING THE PLEA OFFER . . .?
YOU'RE BARKING UP THE WRONG TREE, LARSON--

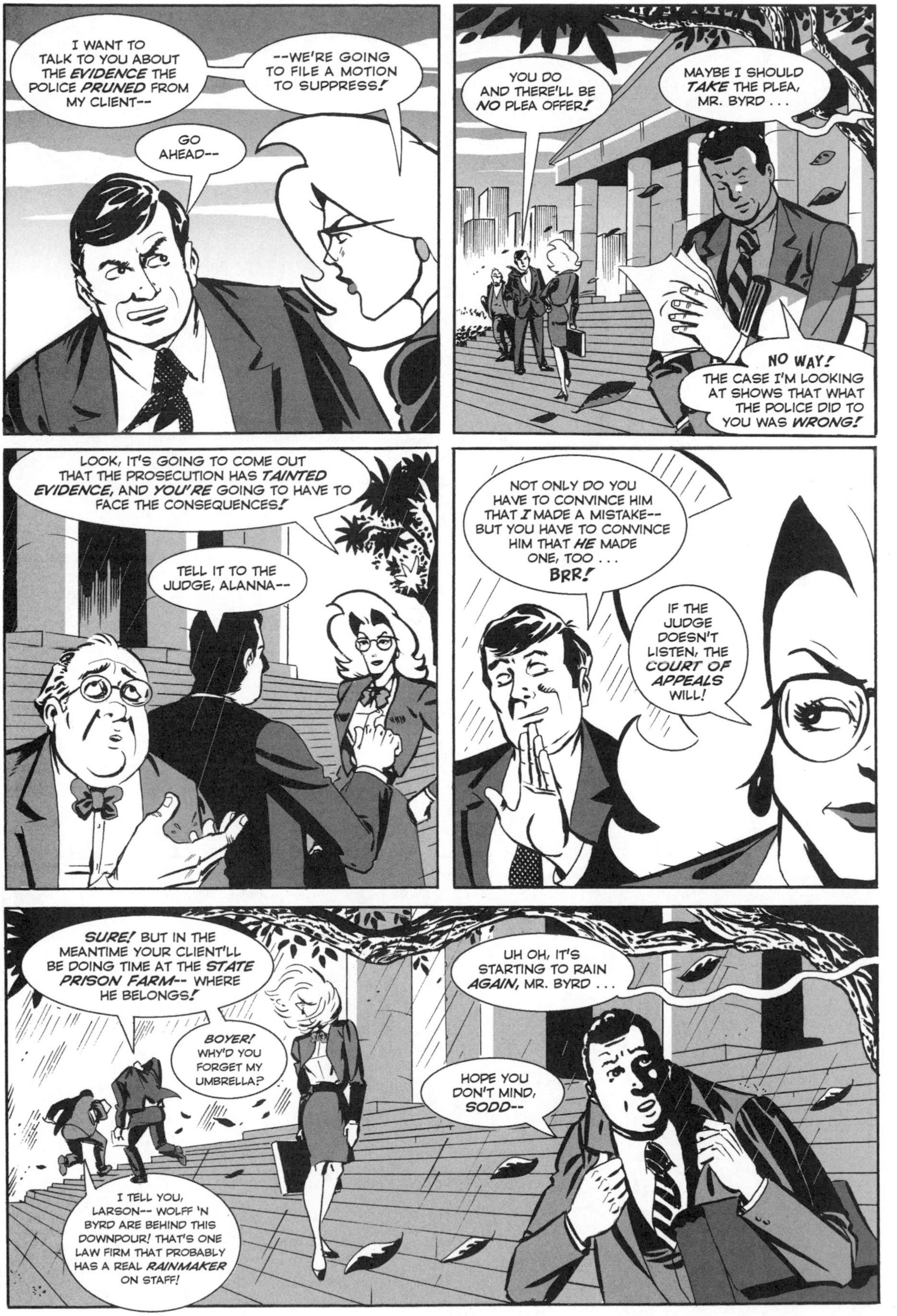
I WANT TO TALK TO YOU ABOUT THE EVIDENCE THE POLICE PRUNED FROM MY CLIENT--
--WE'RE GOING TO FILE A MOTION TO SUPPRESS!
GO AHEAD--
YOU DO AND THERE'LL BE NO PLEA OFFER!
MAYBE I SHOULD TAKE THE PLEA, MR. BYRD . . .
NO WAY! THE CASE I'M LOOKING AT SHOWS THAT WHAT THE POLICE DID TO YOU WAS WRONG!
LOOK, IT'S GOING TO COME OUT THAT THE PROSECUTION HAS TAINTED EVIDENCE, AND YOU'RE GOING TO HAVE TO FACE THE CONSEQUENCES!
TELL IT TO THE JUDGE, ALANNA--
NOT ONLY DO YOU HAVE TO CONVINCE HIM THAT I MADE A MISTAKE-- BUT YOU HAVE TO CONVINCE HIM THAT HE MADE ONE, TOO . . . BRR!
IF THE JUDGE DOESN'T LISTEN, THE COURT OF APPEALS WILL!
SURE! BUT IN THE MEANTIME YOUR CLIENT'LL BE DOING TIME AT THE STATE PRISON FARM-- WHERE HE BELONGS!
BOYER! WHY'D YOU FORGET MY UMBRELLA?
UH OH, IT'S STARTING TO RAIN AGAIN, MR. BYRD . . .
HOPE YOU DON'T MIND, SODD--
I TELL YOU, LARSON-- WOLFF 'N BYRD ARE BEHIND THIS DOWNPOUR! THAT'S ONE LAW FIRM THAT PROBABLY HAS A REAL RAINMAKER ON STAFF!

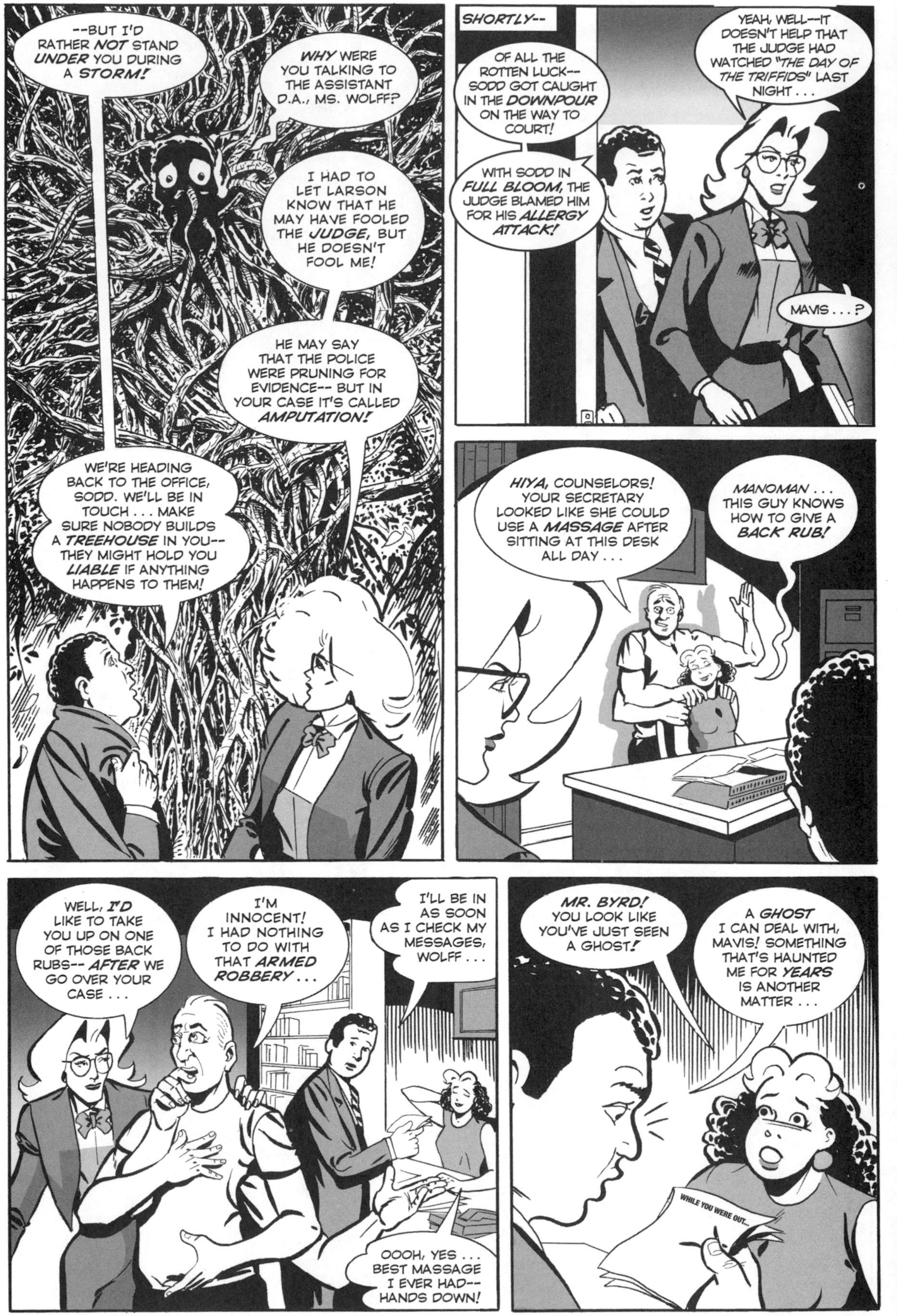
--BUT I'D RATHER NOT STAND UNDER YOU DURING A STORM!
WHY WERE YOU TALKING TO THE ASSISTANT D.A., MS. WOLFF?
I HAD TO LET LARSON KNOW THAT HE MAY HAVE FOOLED THE JUDGE, BUT HE DOESN'T FOOL ME!
HE MAY SAY THAT THE POLICE WERE PRUNING FOR EVIDENCE-- BUT IN YOUR CASE IT'S CALLED AMPUTATION!
WE'RE HEADING BACK TO THE OFFICE, SODD. WE'LL BE IN TOUCH . . . MAKE SURE NOBODY BUILDS A TREEHOUSE IN YOU-- THEY MIGHT HOLD YOU LIABLE IF ANYTHING HAPPENS TO THEM!
SHORTLY--
OF ALL THE ROTTEN LUCK-- SODD GOT CAUGHT IN THE DOWNPOUR ON THE WAY TO COURT!
WITH SODD IN FULL BLOOM, THE JUDGE BLAMED HIM FOR HIS ALLERGY ATTACK!
YEAH, WELL--IT DOESN'T HELP THAT THE JUDGE HAD WATCHED "THE DAY OF THE TRIFFIDS" LAST NIGHT . . .
MAVIS . . .?
HIYA, COUNSELORS! YOUR SECRETARY LOOKED LIKE SHE COULD USE A MASSAGE AFTER SITTING AT THIS DESK ALL DAY . . .
MANOMAN . . . THIS GUY KNOWS HOW TO GIVE A BACK RUB!
WELL, I'D LIKE TO TAKE YOU UP ON ONE OF THOSE BACK RUBS-- AFTER WE GO OVER YOUR CASE . . .
I'M INNOCENT! I HAD NOTHING TO DO WITH THAT ARMED ROBBERY . . .
I'LL BE IN AS SOON AS I CHECK MY MESSAGES, WOLFF . . .
OOOH, YES . . . BEST MASSAGE I EVER HAD-- HANDS DOWN!
MR. BYRD! YOU LOOK LIKE YOU'VE JUST SEEN A GHOST!
A GHOST I CAN DEAL WITH, MAVIS! SOMETHING THAT'S HAUNTED ME FOR YEARS IS ANOTHER MATTER . . .
WHILE YOU WERE OUT...

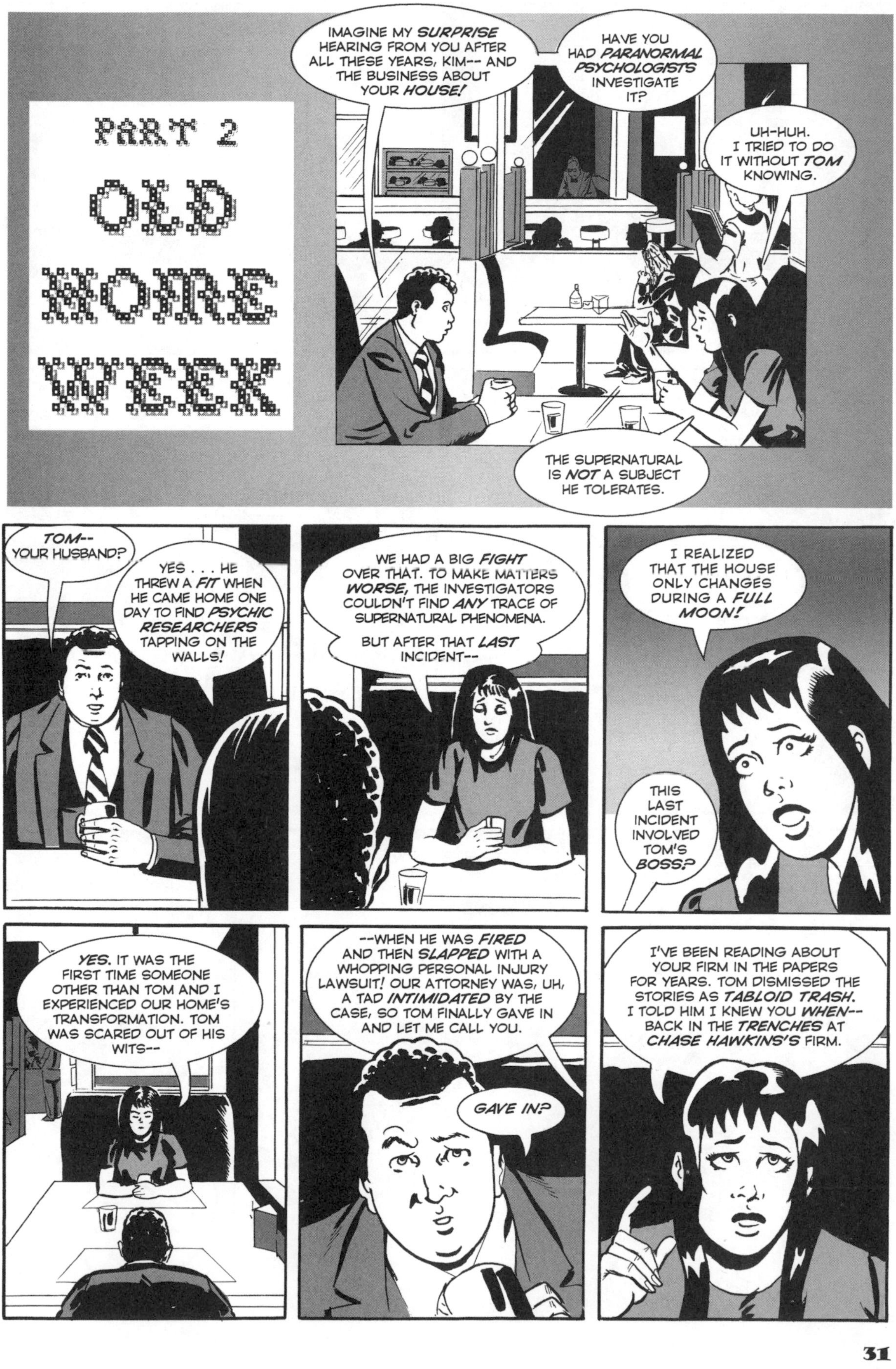
PART 2
OLD NOIRE WEEK
IMAGINE MY SURPRISE HEARING FROM YOU AFTER ALL THESE YEARS, KIM-- AND THE BUSINESS ABOUT YOUR HOUSE!
HAVE YOU HAD PARANORMAL PSYCHOLOGISTS INVESTIGATE IT?
UH-HUH. I TRIED TO DO IT WITHOUT TOM KNOWING.
THE SUPERNATURAL IS NOT A SUBJECT HE TOLERATES.
TOM-- YOUR HUSBAND?
YES . . . HE THREW A FIT WHEN HE CAME HOME ONE DAY TO FIND PSYCHIC RESEARCHERS TAPPING ON THE WALLS!
WE HAD A BIG FIGHT OVER THAT. TO MAKE MATTERS WORSE, THE INVESTIGATORS COULDN'T FIND ANY TRACE OF SUPERNATURAL PHENOMENA.
BUT AFTER THAT LAST INCIDENT--
I REALIZED THAT THE HOUSE ONLY CHANGES DURING A FULL MOON!
THIS LAST INCIDENT INVOLVED TOM'S BOSS?
YES. IT WAS THE FIRST TIME SOMEONE OTHER THAN TOM AND I EXPERIENCED OUR HOME'S TRANSFORMATION. TOM WAS SCARED OUT OF HIS WITS--
--WHEN HE WAS FIRED AND THEN SLAPPED WITH A WHOPPING PERSONAL INJURY LAWSUIT! OUR ATTORNEY WAS, UH, A TAD INTIMIDATED BY THE CASE, SO TOM FINALLY GAVE IN AND LET ME CALL YOU.
GAVE IN?
I'VE BEEN READING ABOUT YOUR FIRM IN THE PAPERS FOR YEARS. TOM DISMISSED THE STORIES AS TABLOID TRASH. I TOLD HIM I KNEW YOU WHEN-- BACK IN THE TRENCHES AT CHASE HAWKINS'S FIRM.

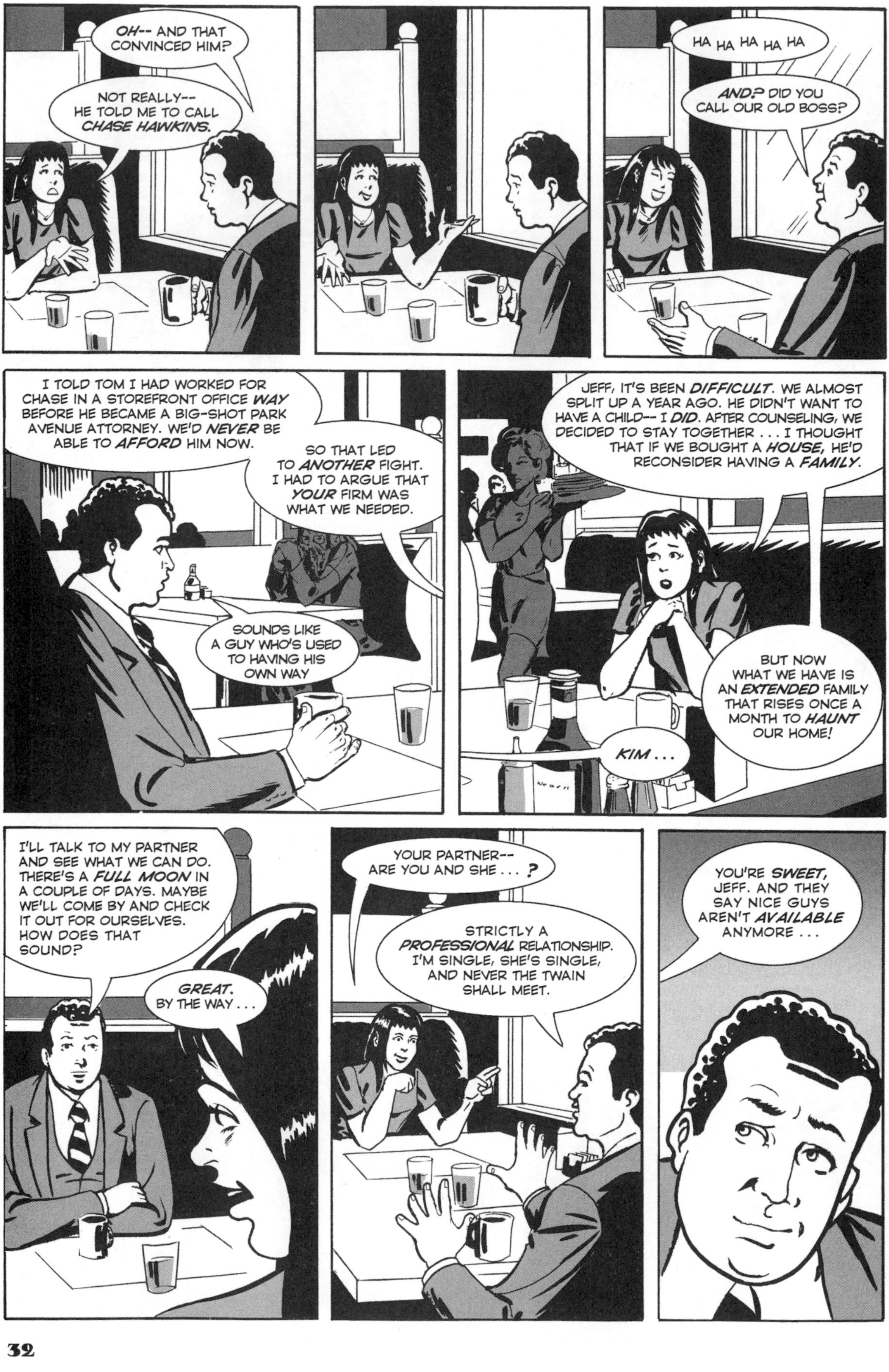
OH-- AND THAT CONVINCED HIM?
NOT REALLY-- HE TOLD ME TO CALL CHASE HAWKINS.
HA HA HA HA HA
AND? DID YOU CALL OUR OLD BOSS?
I TOLD TOM I HAD WORKED FOR CHASE IN A STOREFRONT OFFICE WAY BEFORE HE BECAME A BIG-SHOT PARK AVENUE ATTORNEY. WE'D NEVER BE ABLE TO AFFORD HIM NOW.
SO THAT LED TO ANOTHER FIGHT. I HAD TO ARGUE THAT YOUR FIRM WAS WHAT WE NEEDED.
SOUNDS LIKE A GUY WHO'S USED TO HAVING HIS OWN WAY
JEFF, IT'S BEEN DIFFICULT. WE ALMOST SPLIT UP A YEAR AGO. HE DIDN'T WANT TO HAVE A CHILD-- I DID. AFTER COUNSELING, WE DECIDED TO STAY TOGETHER . . . I THOUGHT THAT IF WE BOUGHT A HOUSE, HE'D RECONSIDER HAVING A FAMILY.
BUT NOW WHAT WE HAVE IS AN EXTENDED FAMILY THAT RISES ONCE A MONTH TO HAUNT OUR HOME!
KIM . . .
I'LL TALK TO MY PARTNER AND SEE WHAT WE CAN DO. THERE'S A FULL MOON IN A COUPLE OF DAYS. MAYBE WE'LL COME BY AND CHECK IT OUT FOR OURSELVES. HOW DOES THAT SOUND?
GREAT. BY THE WAY . . .
YOUR PARTNER-- ARE YOU AND SHE . . . ?
STRICTLY A PROFESSIONAL RELATIONSHIP. I'M SINGLE, SHE'S SINGLE, AND NEVER THE TWAIN SHALL MEET.
YOU'RE SWEET, JEFF. AND THEY SAY NICE GUYS AREN'T AVAILABLE ANYMORE . . .

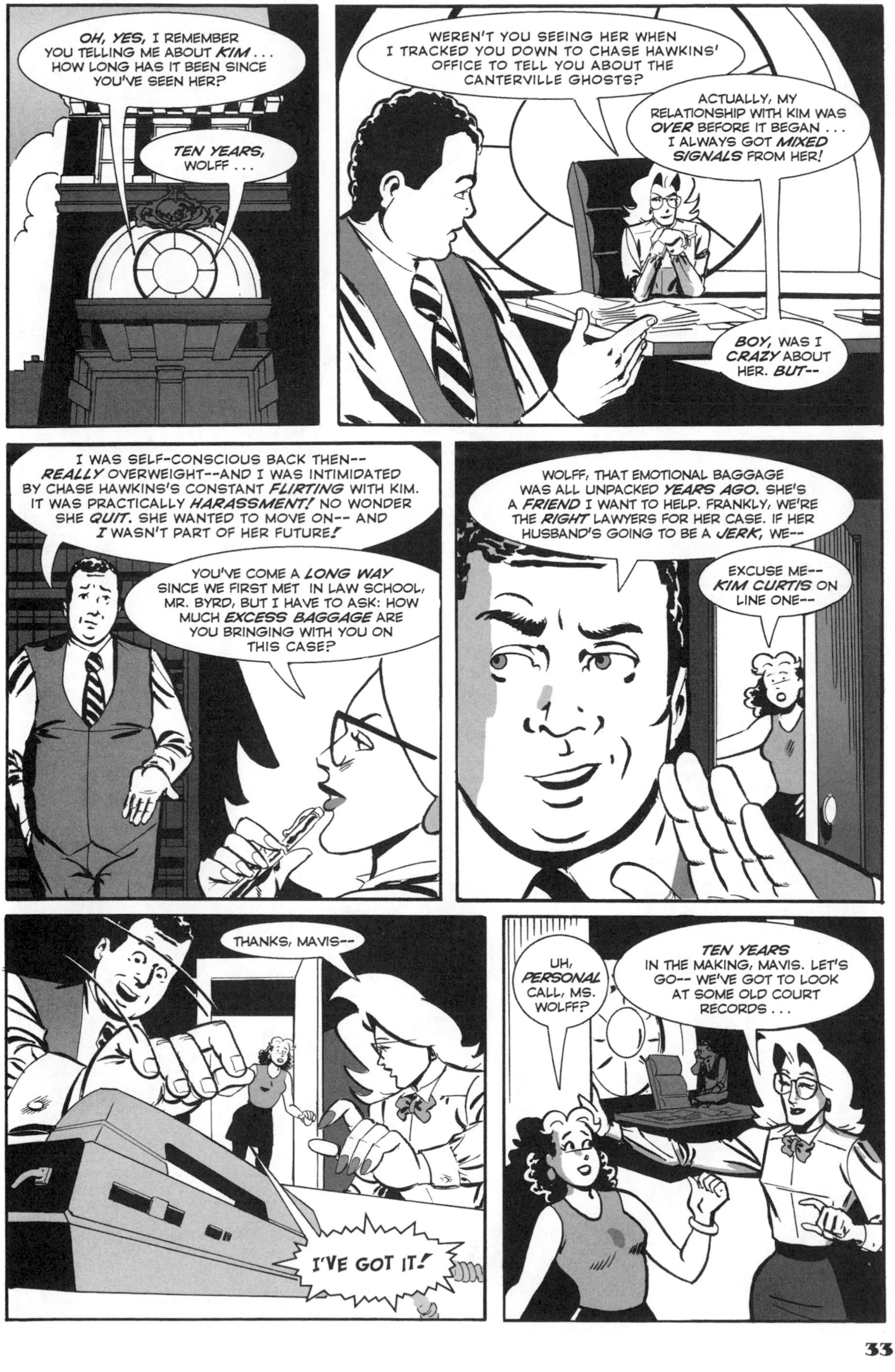
OH, YES, I REMEMBER YOU TELLING ME ABOUT KIM . . . HOW LONG HAS IT BEEN SINCE YOU'VE SEEN HER?
TEN YEARS, WOLFF . . .
WEREN'T YOU SEEING HER WHEN I TRACKED YOU DOWN TO CHASE HAWKINS' OFFICE TO TELL YOU ABOUT THE CANTERVILLE GHOSTS?
ACTUALLY, MY RELATIONSHIP WITH KIM WAS OVER BEFORE IT BEGAN . . . I ALWAYS GOT MIXED SIGNALS FROM HER!
BOY, WAS I CRAZY ABOUT HER. BUT--
I WAS SELF-CONSCIOUS BACK THEN-- REALLY OVERWEIGHT--AND I WAS INTIMIDATED BY CHASE HAWKINS'S CONSTANT FLIRTING WITH KIM. IT WAS PRACTICALLY HARASSMENT! NO WONDER SHE QUIT. SHE WANTED TO MOVE ON-- AND I WASN'T PART OF HER FUTURE!
YOU'VE COME A LONG WAY SINCE WE FIRST MET IN LAW SCHOOL, MR. BYRD, BUT I HAVE TO ASK: HOW MUCH EXCESS BAGGAGE ARE YOU BRINGING WITH YOU ON THIS CASE?
WOLFF, THAT EMOTIONAL BAGGAGE WAS ALL UNPACKED YEARS AGO. SHE'S A FRIEND I WANT TO HELP. FRANKLY, WE'RE THE RIGHT LAWYERS FOR HER CASE. IF HER HUSBAND'S GOING TO BE A JERK, WE--
EXCUSE ME-- KIM CURTIS ON LINE ONE--
THANKS, MAVIS--
I'VE GOT IT!
UH, PERSONAL CALL, MS. WOLFF?
TEN YEARS IN THE MAKING, MAVIS. LET'S GO-- WE'VE GOT TO LOOK AT SOME OLD COURT RECORDS . . .

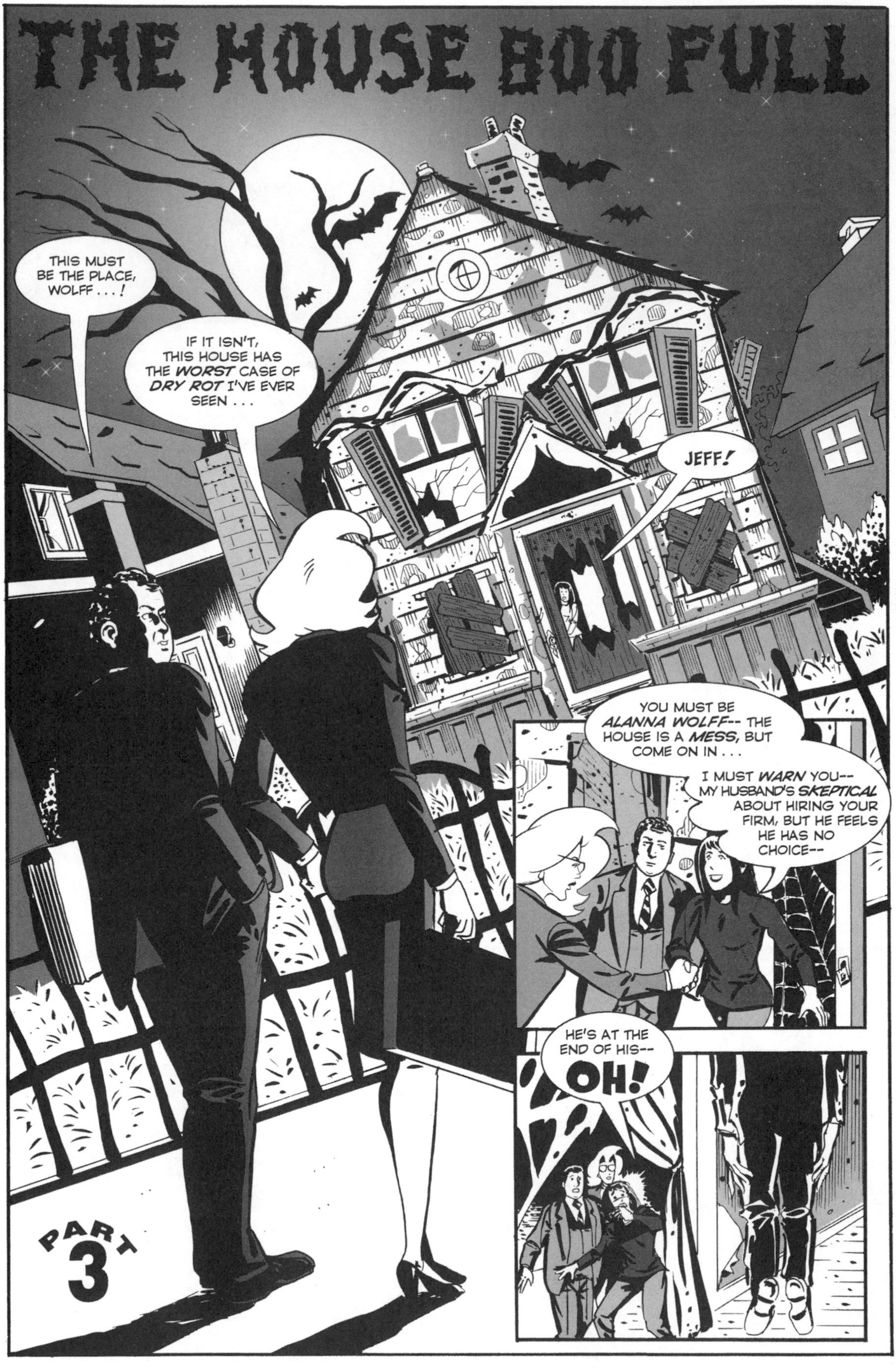
THE HOUSE BOO FULL
THIS MUST BE THE PLACE, WOLFF . . . !
IF IT ISN'T, THIS HOUSE HAS THE WORST CASE OF DRY ROT I'VE EVER SEEN . . .
JEFF!
PART 3
YOU MUST BE ALANNA WOLFF-- THE HOUSE IS A MESS, BUT COME ON IN . . .
I MUST WARN YOU-- MY HUSBAND'S SKEPTICAL ABOUT HIRING YOUR FIRM, BUT HE FEELS HE HAS NO CHOICE--
HE'S AT THE END OF HIS--
OH!

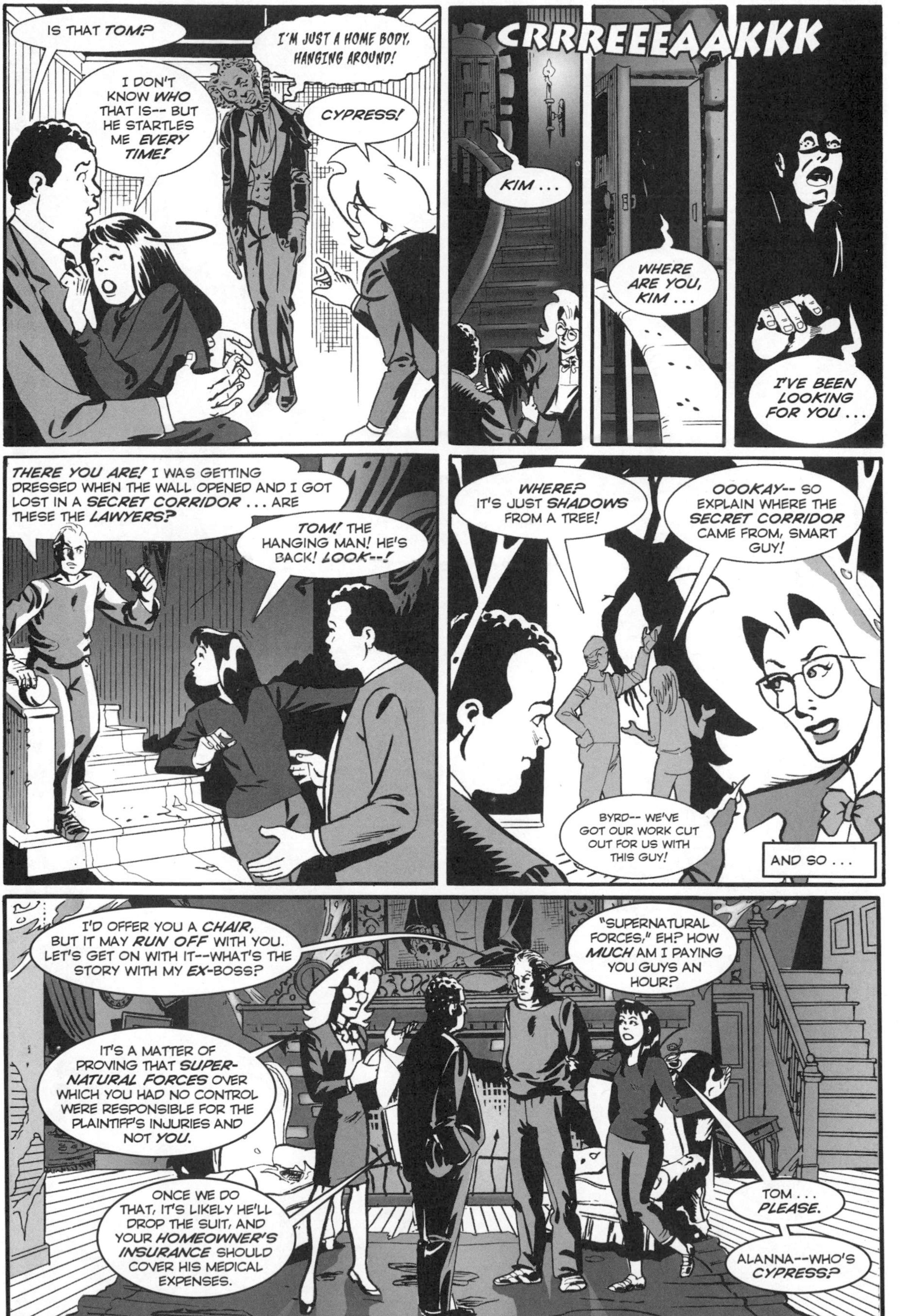

IS THAT TOM?
I DON'T KNOW WHO THAT IS-- BUT HE STARTLES ME EVERY TIME!
I'M JUST A HOME BODY, HANGING AROUND!
CYPRESS!
CRRRREEEAAKKK
KIM ...
WHERE ARE YOU, KIM ...
I'VE BEEN LOOKING FOR YOU ...
THERE YOU ARE! I WAS GETTING DRESSED WHEN THE WALL OPENED AND I GOT LOST IN A SECRET CORRIDOR ... ARE THESE THE LAWYERS?
TOM! THE HANGING MAN! HE'S BACK! LOOK--!
WHERE? IT'S JUST SHADOWS FROM A TREE!
OOOKAY-- SO EXPLAIN WHERE THE SECRET CORRIDOR CAME FROM, SMART GUY!
BYRD-- WE'VE GOT OUR WORK CUT OUT FOR US WITH THIS GUY!
AND SO ...
I'D OFFER YOU A CHAIR, BUT IT MAY RUN OFF WITH YOU. LET'S GET ON WITH IT--WHAT'S THE STORY WITH MY EX-BOSS?
"SUPERNATURAL FORCES," EH? HOW MUCH AM I PAYING YOU GUYS AN HOUR?
IT'S A MATTER OF PROVING THAT SUPER-NATURAL FORCES OVER WHICH YOU HAD NO CONTROL WERE RESPONSIBLE FOR THE PLAINTIFF'S INJURIES AND NOT YOU.
ONCE WE DO THAT, IT'S LIKELY HE'LL DROP THE SUIT, AND YOUR HOMEOWNER'S INSURANCE SHOULD COVER HIS MEDICAL EXPENSES.
TOM ... PLEASE.
ALANNA--WHO'S CYPRESS?

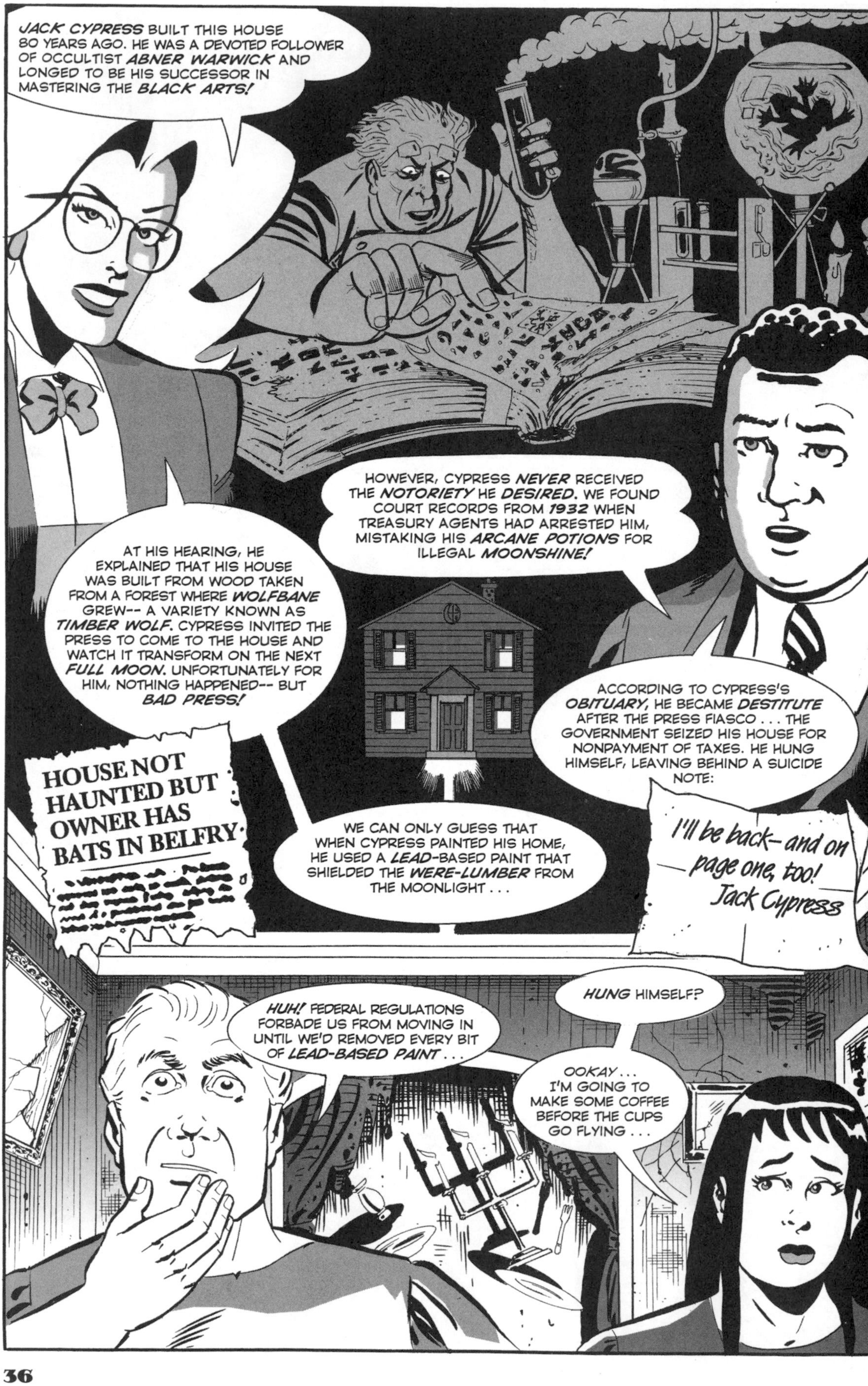
JACK CYPRESS BUILT THIS HOUSE 80 YEARS AGO. HE WAS A DEVOTED FOLLOWER OF OCCULTIST ABNER WARWICK AND LONGED TO BE HIS SUCCESSOR IN MASTERING THE BLACK ARTS!
HOWEVER, CYPRESS NEVER RECEIVED THE NOTORIETY HE DESIRED. WE FOUND COURT RECORDS FROM 1932 WHEN TREASURY AGENTS HAD ARRESTED HIM, MISTAKING HIS ARCANE POTIONS FOR ILLEGAL MOONSHINE!
AT HIS HEARING, HE EXPLAINED THAT HIS HOUSE WAS BUILT FROM WOOD TAKEN FROM A FOREST WHERE WOLFBANE GREW-- A VARIETY KNOWN AS TIMBER WOLF. CYPRESS INVITED THE PRESS TO COME TO THE HOUSE AND WATCH IT TRANSFORM ON THE NEXT FULL MOON. UNFORTUNATELY FOR HIM, NOTHING HAPPENED-- BUT BAD PRESS!
HOUSE NOT HAUNTED BUT OWNER HAS BATS IN BELFRY
WE CAN ONLY GUESS THAT WHEN CYPRESS PAINTED HIS HOME, HE USED A LEAD-BASED PAINT THAT SHIELDED THE WERE-LUMBER FROM THE MOONLIGHT . . .
ACCORDING TO CYPRESS'S OBITUARY, HE BECAME DESTITUTE AFTER THE PRESS FIASCO . . . THE GOVERNMENT SEIZED HIS HOUSE FOR NONPAYMENT OF TAXES. HE HUNG HIMSELF, LEAVING BEHIND A SUICIDE NOTE:
I'll be back—and on page one, too! Jack Cypress
HUH! FEDERAL REGULATIONS FORBADE US FROM MOVING IN UNTIL WE'D REMOVED EVERY BIT OF LEAD-BASED PAINT . . .
HUNG HIMSELF?
OOKAY . . . I'M GOING TO MAKE SOME COFFEE BEFORE THE CUPS GO FLYING . . .

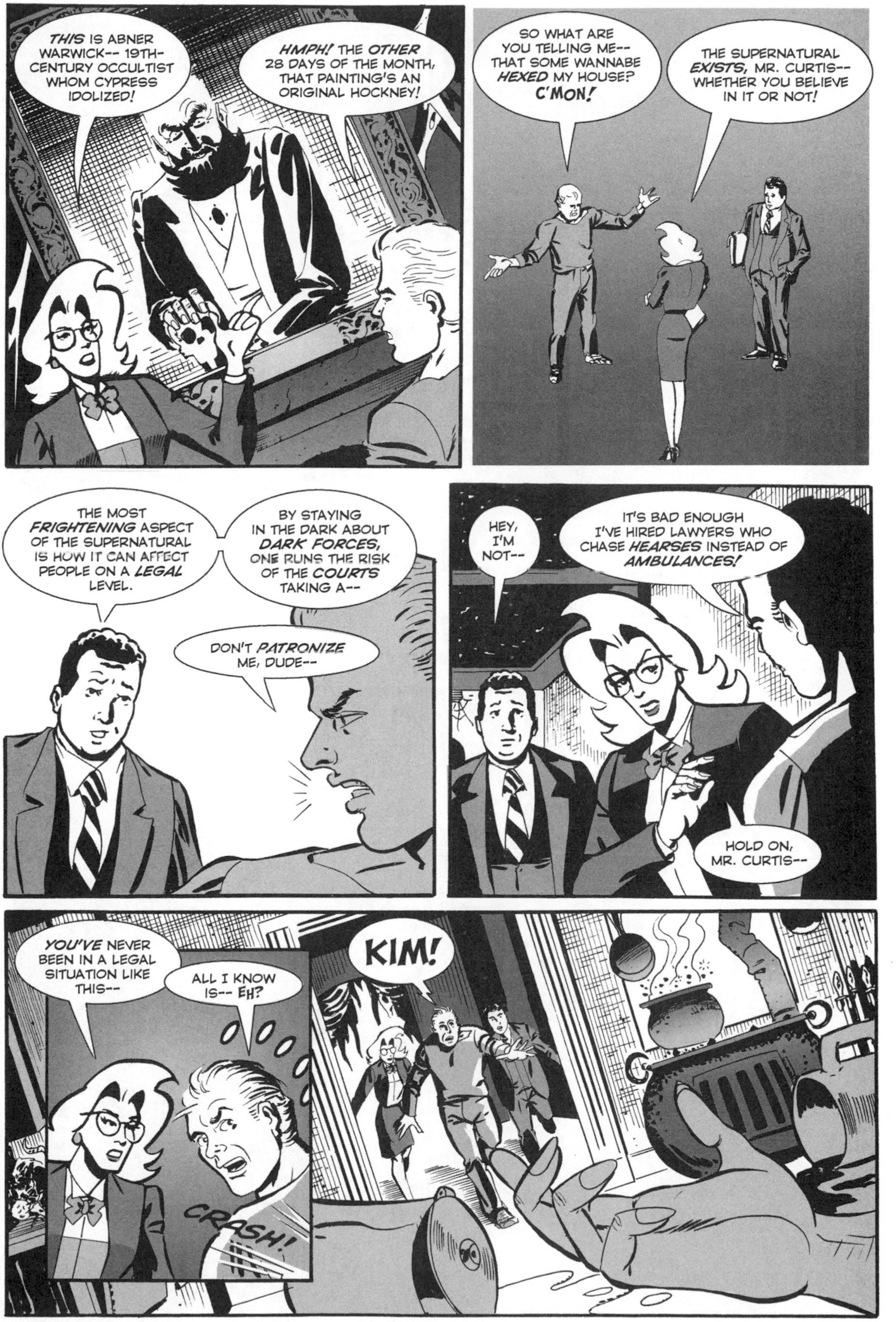
THIS IS ABNER WARWICK-- 19TH-CENTURY OCCULTIST WHOM CYPRESS IDOLIZED!
HMPH! THE OTHER 28 DAYS OF THE MONTH, THAT PAINTING'S AN ORIGINAL HOCKNEY!
SO WHAT ARE YOU TELLING ME-- THAT SOME WANNABE HEXED MY HOUSE? C'MON!
THE SUPERNATURAL EXISTS, MR. CURTIS-- WHETHER YOU BELIEVE IN IT OR NOT!
THE MOST FRIGHTENING ASPECT OF THE SUPERNATURAL IS HOW IT CAN AFFECT PEOPLE ON A LEGAL LEVEL.
BY STAYING IN THE DARK ABOUT DARK FORCES, ONE RUNS THE RISK OF THE COURTS TAKING A--
DON'T PATRONIZE ME, DUDE--
HEY, I'M NOT--
IT'S BAD ENOUGH I'VE HIRED LAWYERS WHO CHASE HEARSES INSTEAD OF AMBULANCES!
HOLD ON, MR. CURTIS--
YOU'VE NEVER BEEN IN A LEGAL SITUATION LIKE THIS--
ALL I KNOW IS-- EH?
CRASH!
KIM!

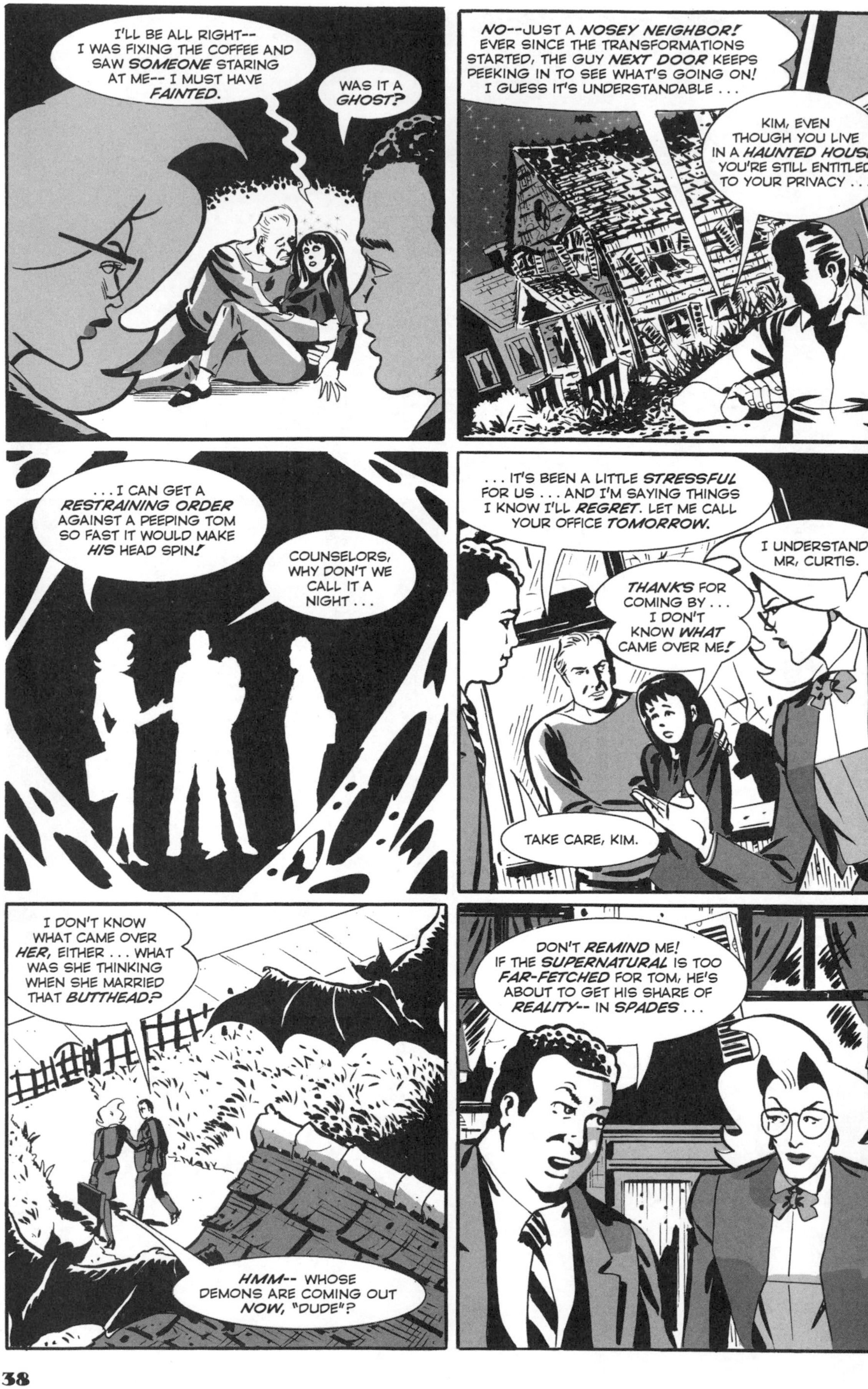
I'LL BE ALL RIGHT-- I WAS FIXING THE COFFEE AND SAW SOMEONE STARING AT ME-- I MUST HAVE FAINTED.
WAS IT A GHOST?
NO--JUST A NOSEY NEIGHBOR! EVER SINCE THE TRANSFORMATIONS STARTED, THE GUY NEXT DOOR KEEPS PEEKING IN TO SEE WHAT'S GOING ON! I GUESS IT'S UNDERSTANDABLE . . .
KIM, EVEN THOUGH YOU LIVE IN A HAUNTED HOUSE, YOU'RE STILL ENTITLED TO YOUR PRIVACY . . .
. . . I CAN GET A RESTRAINING ORDER AGAINST A PEEPING TOM SO FAST IT WOULD MAKE HIS HEAD SPIN!
COUNSELORS, WHY DON'T WE CALL IT A NIGHT . . .
. . . IT'S BEEN A LITTLE STRESSFUL FOR US . . . AND I'M SAYING THINGS I KNOW I'LL REGRET. LET ME CALL YOUR OFFICE TOMORROW.
I UNDERSTAND, MR. CURTIS.
THANKS FOR COMING BY . . . I DON'T KNOW WHAT CAME OVER ME!
TAKE CARE, KIM.
I DON'T KNOW WHAT CAME OVER HER, EITHER . . . WHAT WAS SHE THINKING WHEN SHE MARRIED THAT BUTTHEAD?
HMM-- WHOSE DEMONS ARE COMING OUT NOW, "DUDE"?
DON'T REMIND ME! IF THE SUPERNATURAL IS TOO FAR-FETCHED FOR TOM, HE'S ABOUT TO GET HIS SHARE OF REALITY-- IN SPADES . . .

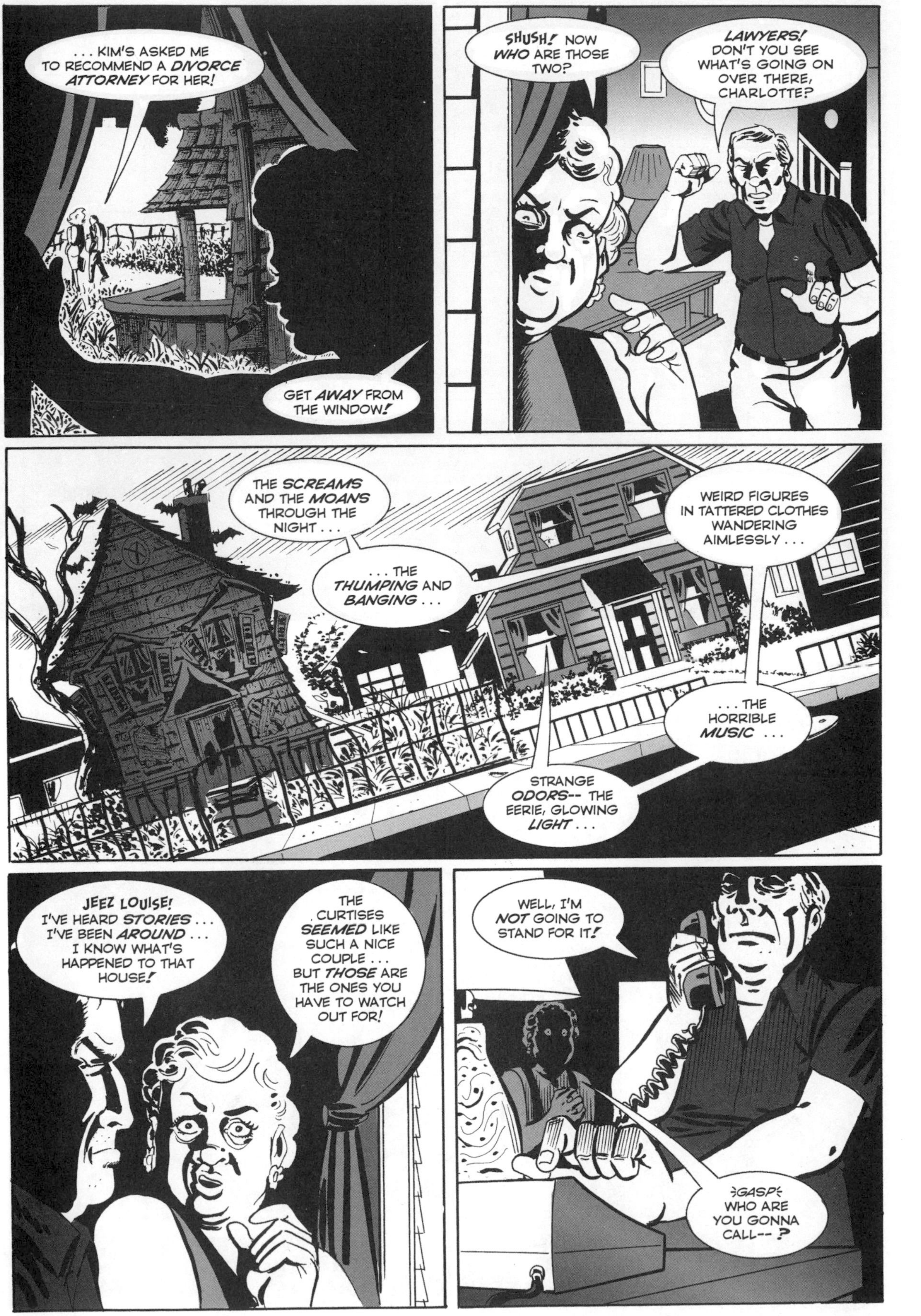

. . . KIM'S ASKED ME TO RECOMMEND A *DIVORCE ATTORNEY* FOR HER!
GET *AWAY* FROM THE WINDOW!
SHUSH! NOW *WHO* ARE THOSE TWO?
LAWYERS! DON'T YOU SEE WHAT'S GOING ON OVER THERE, CHARLOTTE?
THE *SCREAMS* AND THE *MOANS* THROUGH THE NIGHT . . .
. . . THE *THUMPING* AND *BANGING* . . .
WEIRD FIGURES IN TATTERED CLOTHES WANDERING AIMLESSLY . . .
. . . THE HORRIBLE *MUSIC* . . .
STRANGE *ODORS--* THE EERIE, GLOWING *LIGHT* . . .
JEEZ LOUISE! I'VE HEARD *STORIES* . . . I'VE BEEN *AROUND* . . . I KNOW WHAT'S HAPPENED TO THAT HOUSE!
THE CURTISES *SEEMED* LIKE SUCH A NICE COUPLE . . . BUT *THOSE* ARE THE ONES YOU HAVE TO WATCH OUT FOR!
WELL, I'M *NOT* GOING TO STAND FOR IT!
GASP WHO ARE YOU GONNA CALL-- ?

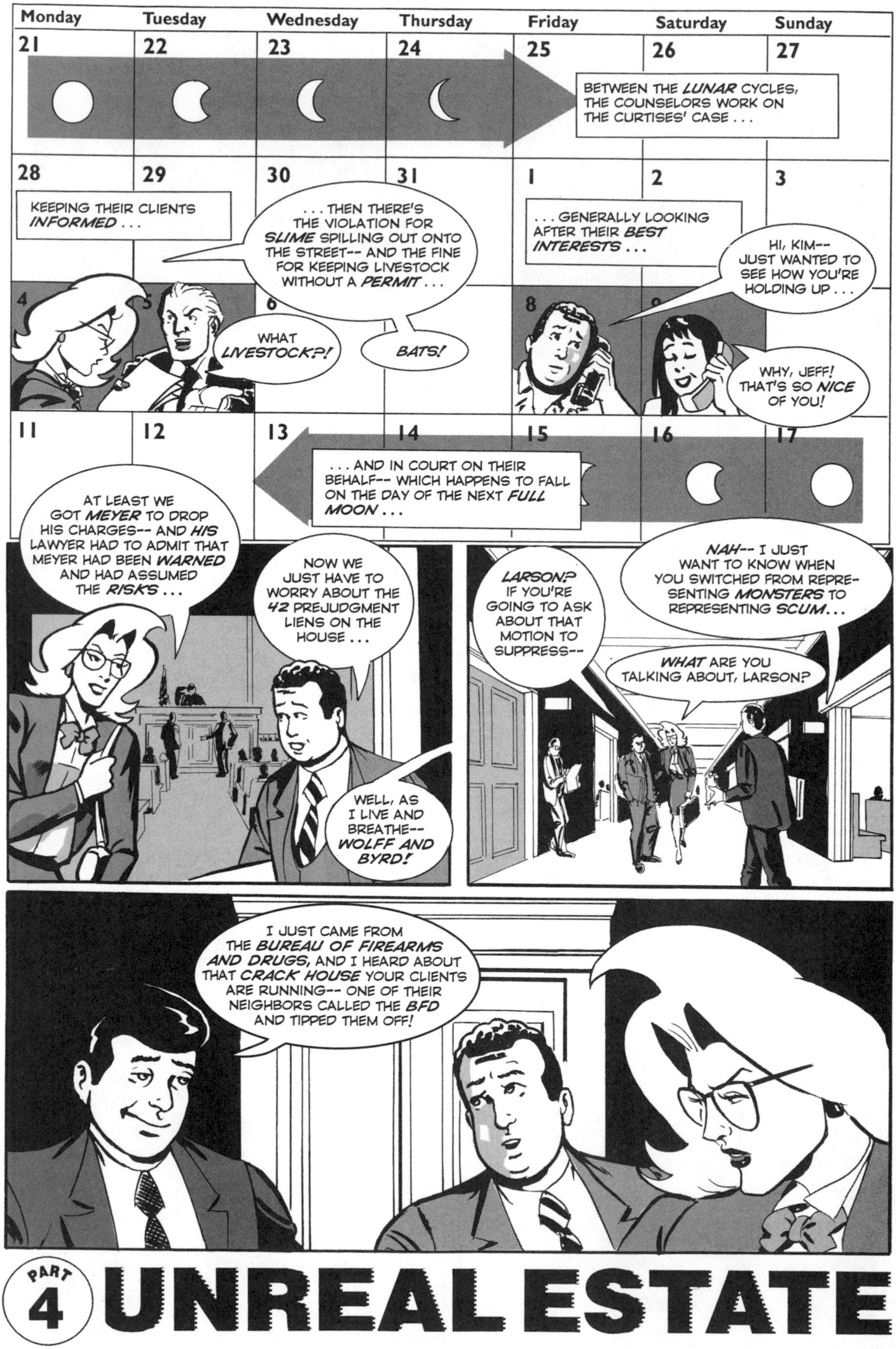
Monday
Tuesday
Wednesday
Thursday
Friday
Saturday
Sunday
BETWEEN THE LUNAR CYCLES, THE COUNSELORS WORK ON THE CURTISES' CASE . . .
KEEPING THEIR CLIENTS INFORMED . . .
. . . THEN THERE'S THE VIOLATION FOR SLIME SPILLING OUT ONTO THE STREET-- AND THE FINE FOR KEEPING LIVESTOCK WITHOUT A PERMIT . . .
WHAT LIVESTOCK?!
BATS!
. . . GENERALLY LOOKING AFTER THEIR BEST INTERESTS . . .
HI, KIM-- JUST WANTED TO SEE HOW YOU'RE HOLDING UP . . .
WHY, JEFF! THAT'S SO NICE OF YOU!
. . . AND IN COURT ON THEIR BEHALF-- WHICH HAPPENS TO FALL ON THE DAY OF THE NEXT FULL MOON . . .
AT LEAST WE GOT MEYER TO DROP HIS CHARGES-- AND HIS LAWYER HAD TO ADMIT THAT MEYER HAD BEEN WARNED AND HAD ASSUMED THE RISKS . . .
NOW WE JUST HAVE TO WORRY ABOUT THE 42 PREJUDGMENT LIENS ON THE HOUSE . . .
WELL, AS I LIVE AND BREATHE-- WOLFF AND BYRD!
LARSON? IF YOU'RE GOING TO ASK ABOUT THAT MOTION TO SUPPRESS--
NAH-- I JUST WANT TO KNOW WHEN YOU SWITCHED FROM REPRESENTING MONSTERS TO REPRESENTING SCUM . . .
WHAT ARE YOU TALKING ABOUT, LARSON?
I JUST CAME FROM THE BUREAU OF FIREARMS AND DRUGS, AND I HEARD ABOUT THAT CRACK HOUSE YOUR CLIENTS ARE RUNNING-- ONE OF THEIR NEIGHBORS CALLED THE BFD AND TIPPED THEM OFF!

PART 4 UNREAL ESTATE

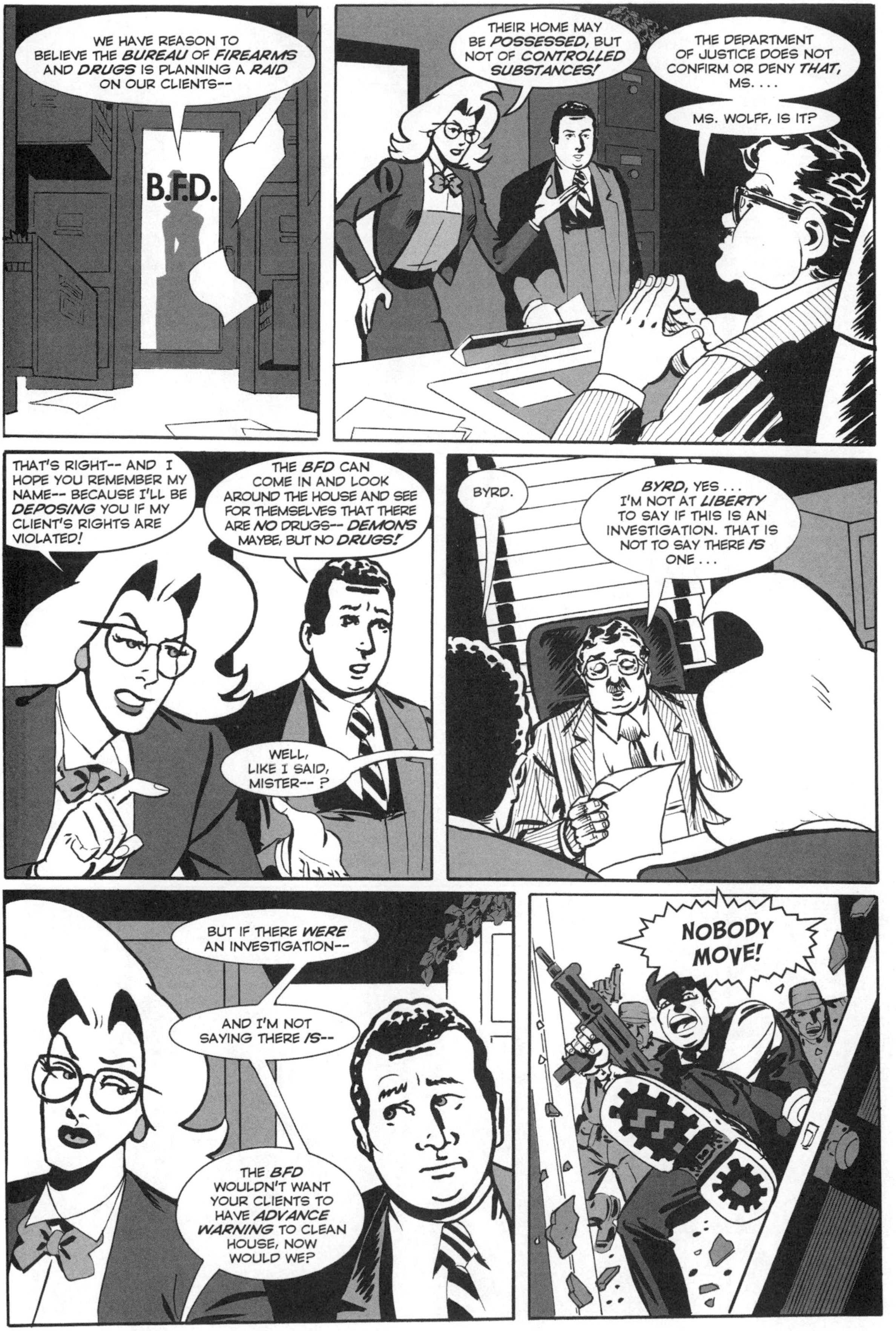
WE HAVE REASON TO BELIEVE THE BUREAU OF FIREARMS AND DRUGS IS PLANNING A RAID ON OUR CLIENTS--
B.F.D.
THEIR HOME MAY BE POSSESSED, BUT NOT OF CONTROLLED SUBSTANCES!
THE DEPARTMENT OF JUSTICE DOES NOT CONFIRM OR DENY THAT, MS. . . .
MS. WOLFF, IS IT?
THAT'S RIGHT-- AND I HOPE YOU REMEMBER MY NAME-- BECAUSE I'LL BE DEPOSING YOU IF MY CLIENT'S RIGHTS ARE VIOLATED!
THE BFD CAN COME IN AND LOOK AROUND THE HOUSE AND SEE FOR THEMSELVES THAT THERE ARE NO DRUGS-- DEMONS MAYBE, BUT NO DRUGS!
WELL, LIKE I SAID, MISTER-- ?
BYRD.
BYRD, YES . . . I'M NOT AT LIBERTY TO SAY IF THIS IS AN INVESTIGATION. THAT IS NOT TO SAY THERE IS ONE . . .
BUT IF THERE WERE AN INVESTIGATION--
AND I'M NOT SAYING THERE IS--
THE BFD WOULDN'T WANT YOUR CLIENTS TO HAVE ADVANCE WARNING TO CLEAN HOUSE, NOW WOULD WE?
NOBODY MOVE!

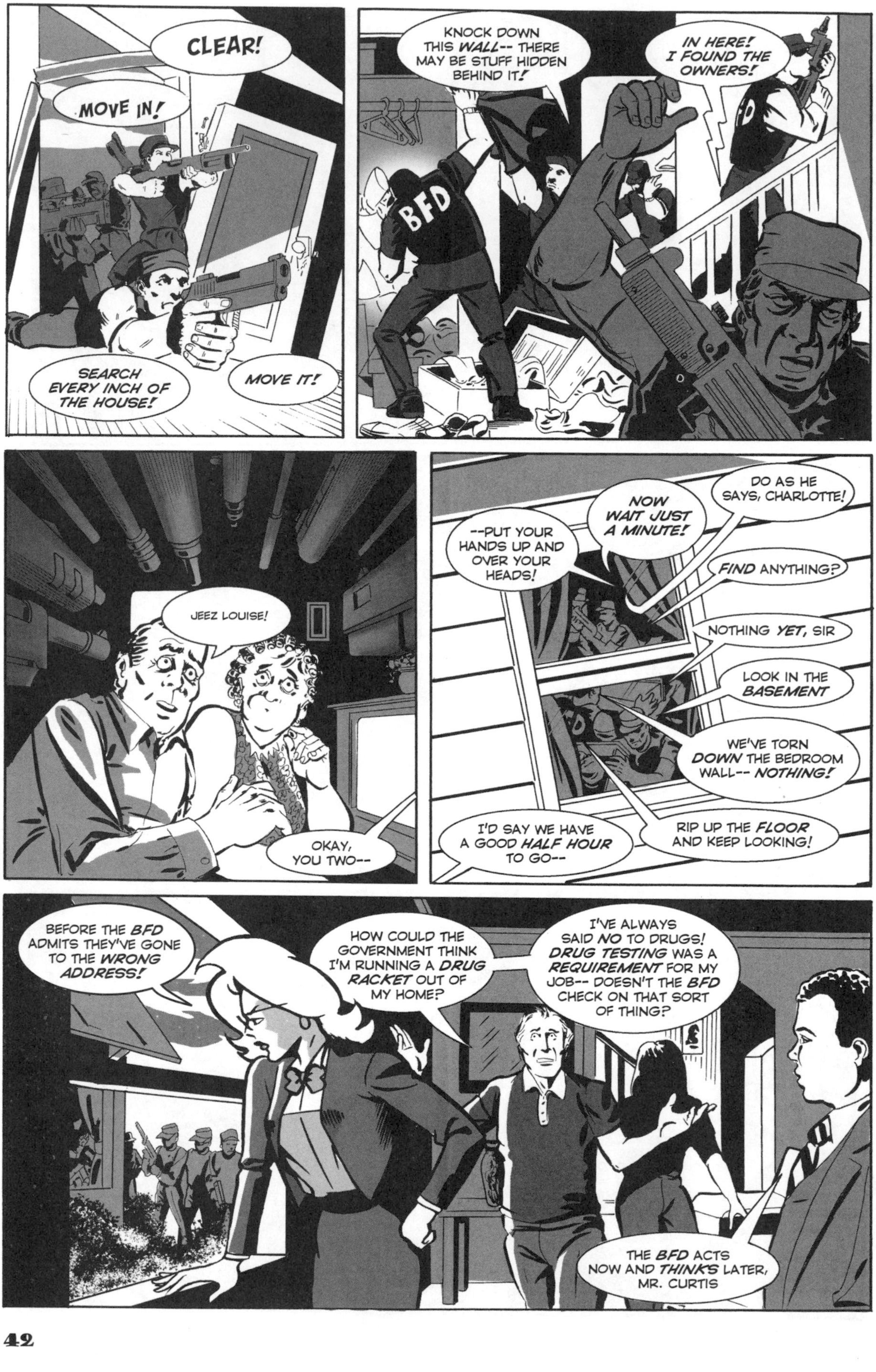
CLEAR!
MOVE IN!
SEARCH EVERY INCH OF THE HOUSE!
MOVE IT!
KNOCK DOWN THIS WALL-- THERE MAY BE STUFF HIDDEN BEHIND IT!
IN HERE! I FOUND THE OWNERS!
BFD
JEEZ LOUISE!
OKAY, YOU TWO--
--PUT YOUR HANDS UP AND OVER YOUR HEADS!
NOW WAIT JUST A MINUTE!
DO AS HE SAYS, CHARLOTTE!
FIND ANYTHING?
NOTHING YET, SIR
LOOK IN THE BASEMENT
WE'VE TORN DOWN THE BEDROOM WALL-- NOTHING!
RIP UP THE FLOOR AND KEEP LOOKING!
I'D SAY WE HAVE A GOOD HALF HOUR TO GO--
BEFORE THE BFD ADMITS THEY'VE GONE TO THE WRONG ADDRESS!
HOW COULD THE GOVERNMENT THINK I'M RUNNING A DRUG RACKET OUT OF MY HOME?
I'VE ALWAYS SAID NO TO DRUGS! DRUG TESTING WAS A REQUIREMENT FOR MY JOB-- DOESN'T THE BFD CHECK ON THAT SORT OF THING?
THE BFD ACTS NOW AND THINKS LATER, MR. CURTIS

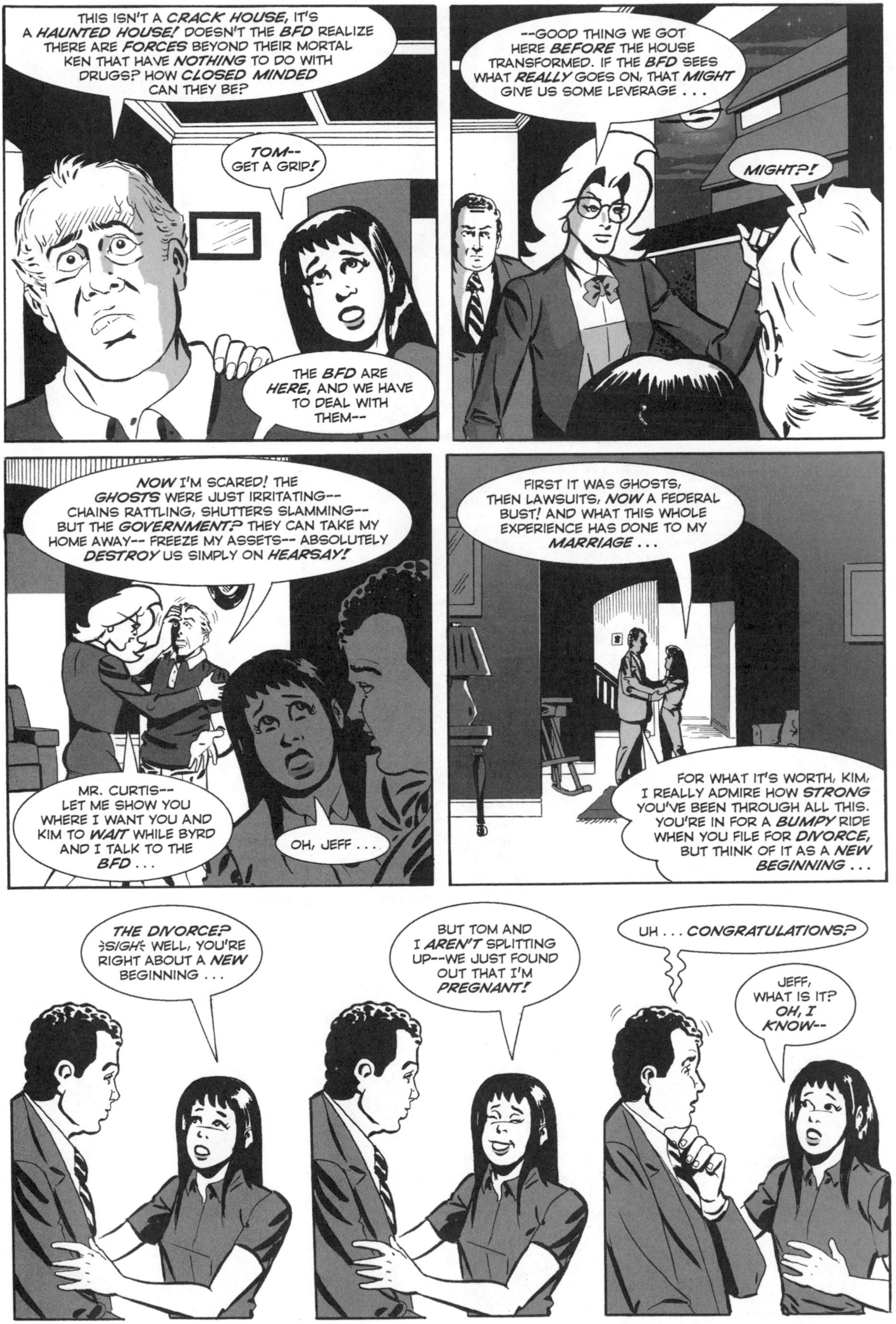
THIS ISN'T A CRACK HOUSE, IT'S A HAUNTED HOUSE! DOESN'T THE BFD REALIZE THERE ARE FORCES BEYOND THEIR MORTAL KEN THAT HAVE NOTHING TO DO WITH DRUGS? HOW CLOSED MINDED CAN THEY BE?
TOM-- GET A GRIP!
THE BFD ARE HERE, AND WE HAVE TO DEAL WITH THEM--
--GOOD THING WE GOT HERE BEFORE THE HOUSE TRANSFORMED. IF THE BFD SEES WHAT REALLY GOES ON, THAT MIGHT GIVE US SOME LEVERAGE . . .
MIGHT?!
NOW I'M SCARED! THE GHOSTS WERE JUST IRRITATING-- CHAINS RATTLING, SHUTTERS SLAMMING-- BUT THE GOVERNMENT? THEY CAN TAKE MY HOME AWAY-- FREEZE MY ASSETS-- ABSOLUTELY DESTROY US SIMPLY ON HEARSAY!
MR. CURTIS-- LET ME SHOW YOU WHERE I WANT YOU AND KIM TO WAIT WHILE BYRD AND I TALK TO THE BFD . . .
OH, JEFF . . .
FIRST IT WAS GHOSTS, THEN LAWSUITS, NOW A FEDERAL BUST! AND WHAT THIS WHOLE EXPERIENCE HAS DONE TO MY MARRIAGE . . .
FOR WHAT IT'S WORTH, KIM, I REALLY ADMIRE HOW STRONG YOU'VE BEEN THROUGH ALL THIS. YOU'RE IN FOR A BUMPY RIDE WHEN YOU FILE FOR DIVORCE, BUT THINK OF IT AS A NEW BEGINNING . . .
THE DIVORCE? SIGH WELL, YOU'RE RIGHT ABOUT A NEW BEGINNING . . .
BUT TOM AND I AREN'T SPLITTING UP--WE JUST FOUND OUT THAT I'M PREGNANT!
UH . . . CONGRATULATIONS?
JEFF, WHAT IS IT? OH, I KNOW--

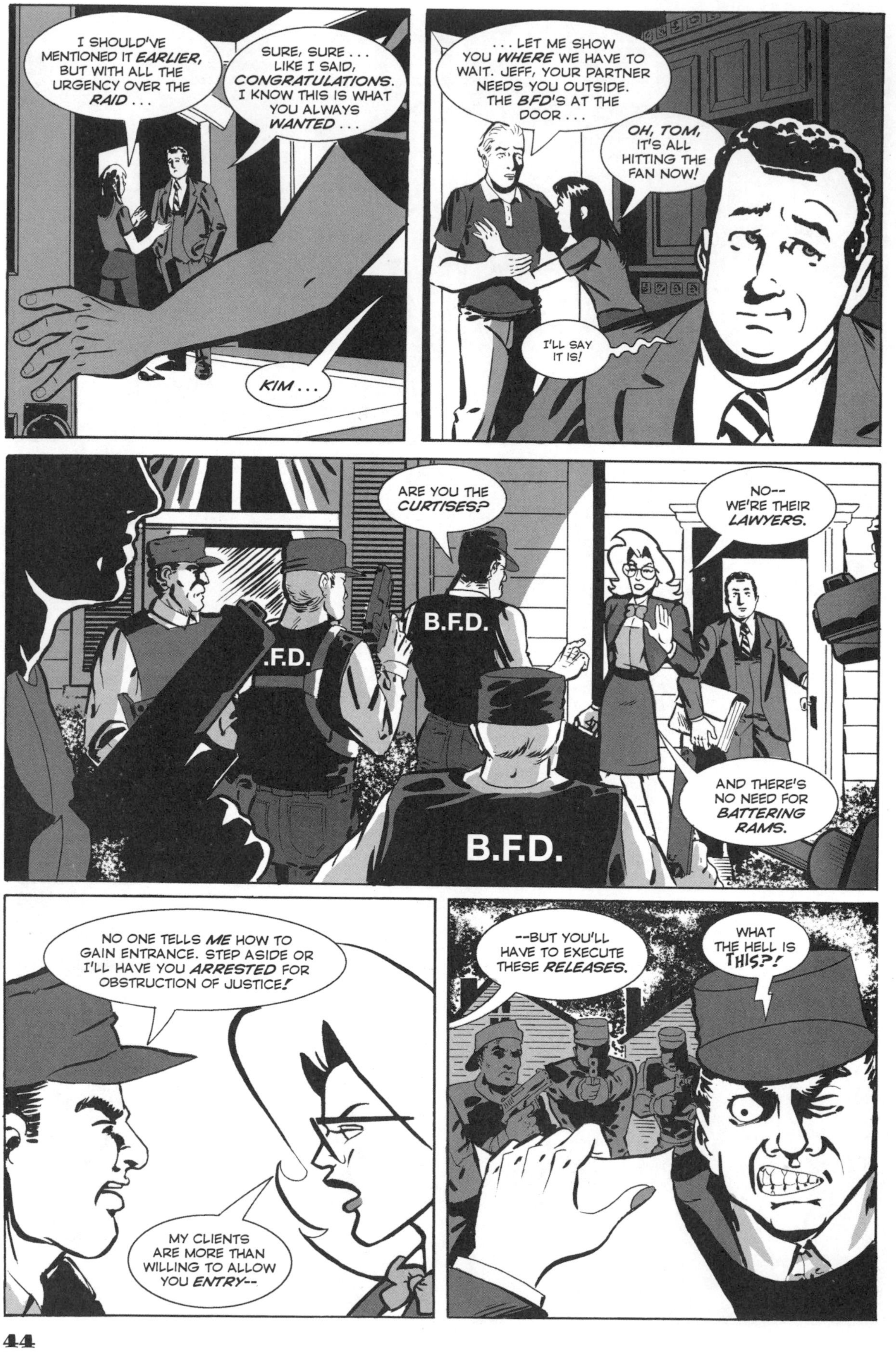
I SHOULD'VE MENTIONED IT EARLIER, BUT WITH ALL THE URGENCY OVER THE RAID . . .
SURE, SURE . . . LIKE I SAID, CONGRATULATIONS. I KNOW THIS IS WHAT YOU ALWAYS WANTED . . .
KIM . . .
. . . LET ME SHOW YOU WHERE WE HAVE TO WAIT. JEFF, YOUR PARTNER NEEDS YOU OUTSIDE. THE BFD'S AT THE DOOR . . .
OH, TOM, IT'S ALL HITTING THE FAN NOW!
I'LL SAY IT IS!
ARE YOU THE CURTISES?
NO-- WE'RE THEIR LAWYERS.
B.F.D.
B.F.D.
AND THERE'S NO NEED FOR BATTERING RAMS.
NO ONE TELLS ME HOW TO GAIN ENTRANCE. STEP ASIDE OR I'LL HAVE YOU ARRESTED FOR OBSTRUCTION OF JUSTICE!
MY CLIENTS ARE MORE THAN WILLING TO ALLOW YOU ENTRY--
--BUT YOU'LL HAVE TO EXECUTE THESE RELEASES.
WHAT THE HELL IS THIS?!

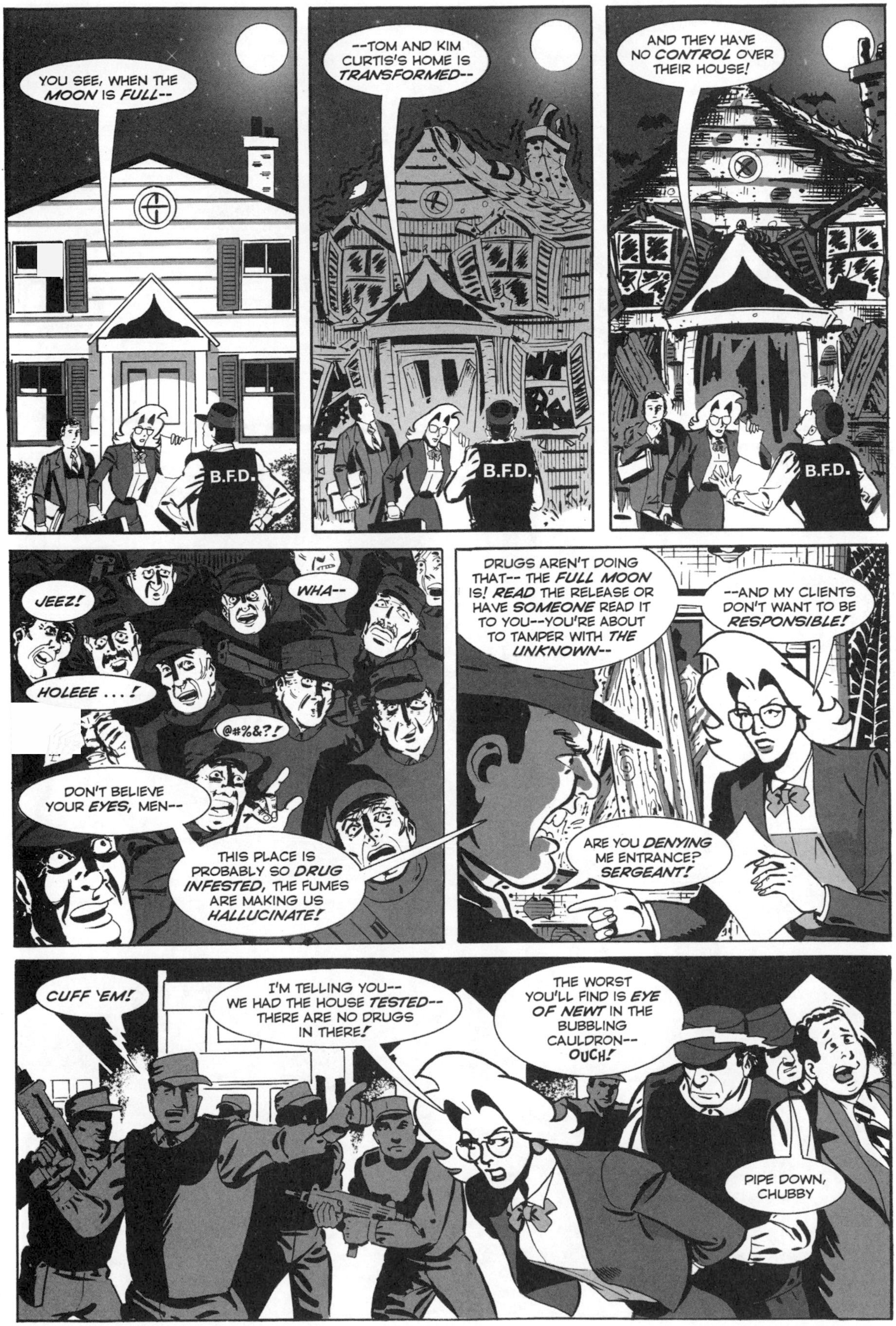
YOU SEE, WHEN THE MOON IS FULL--
--TOM AND KIM CURTIS'S HOME IS TRANSFORMED--
AND THEY HAVE NO CONTROL OVER THEIR HOUSE!
B.F.D.
JEEZ!
WHA--
HOLEEE . . . !
@#%&?!
DON'T BELIEVE YOUR EYES, MEN--
THIS PLACE IS PROBABLY SO DRUG INFESTED, THE FUMES ARE MAKING US HALLUCINATE!
DRUGS AREN'T DOING THAT-- THE FULL MOON IS! READ THE RELEASE OR HAVE SOMEONE READ IT TO YOU--YOU'RE ABOUT TO TAMPER WITH THE UNKNOWN--
--AND MY CLIENTS DON'T WANT TO BE RESPONSIBLE!
ARE YOU DENYING ME ENTRANCE? SERGEANT!
CUFF 'EM!
I'M TELLING YOU-- WE HAD THE HOUSE TESTED-- THERE ARE NO DRUGS IN THERE!
THE WORST YOU'LL FIND IS EYE OF NEWT IN THE BUBBLING CAULDRON-- OUCH!
PIPE DOWN, CHUBBY

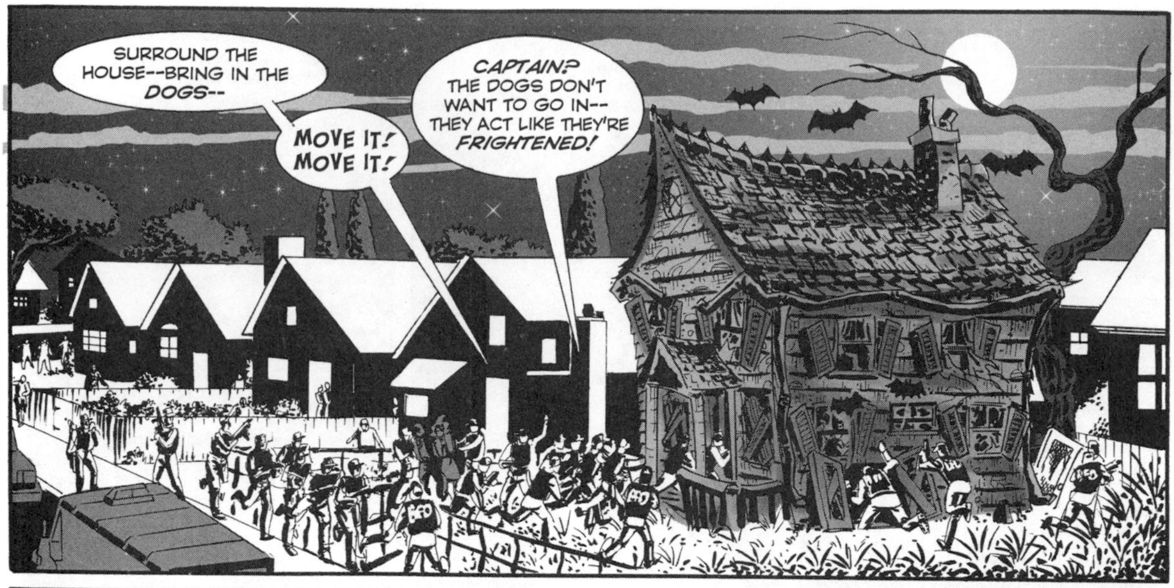
SURROUND THE HOUSE--BRING IN THE DOGS--
MOVE IT! MOVE IT!
CAPTAIN? THE DOGS DON'T WANT TO GO IN-- THEY ACT LIKE THEY'RE FRIGHTENED!

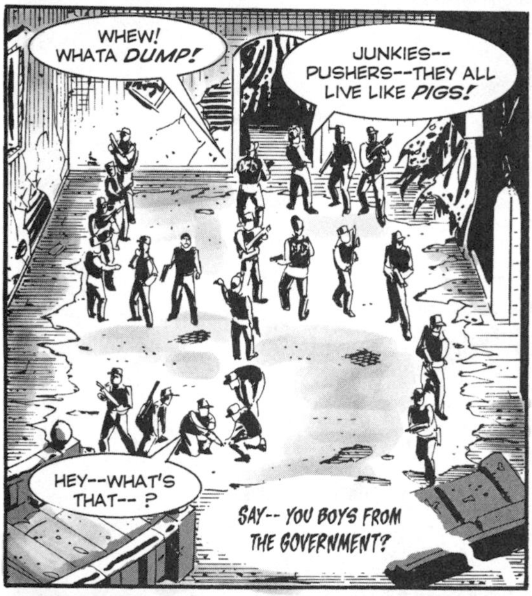
WHEW! WHATA DUMP!
JUNKIES-- PUSHERS--THEY ALL LIVE LIKE PIGS!
HEY--WHAT'S THAT-- ?
SAY-- YOU BOYS FROM THE GOVERNMENT?

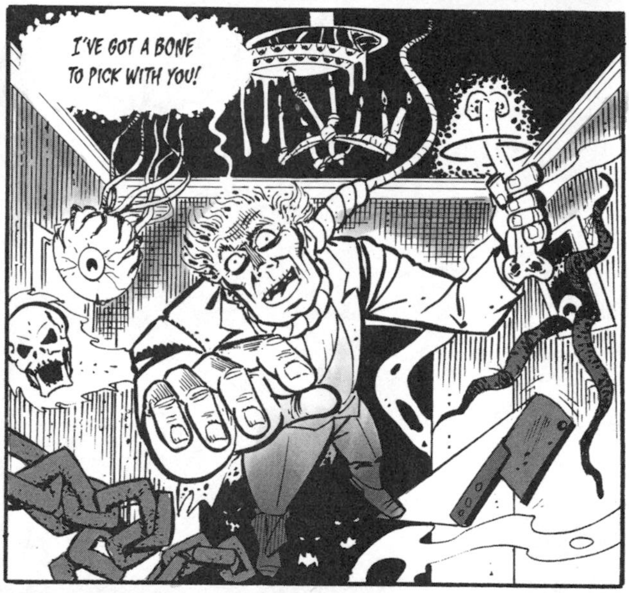
I'VE GOT A BONE TO PICK WITH YOU!

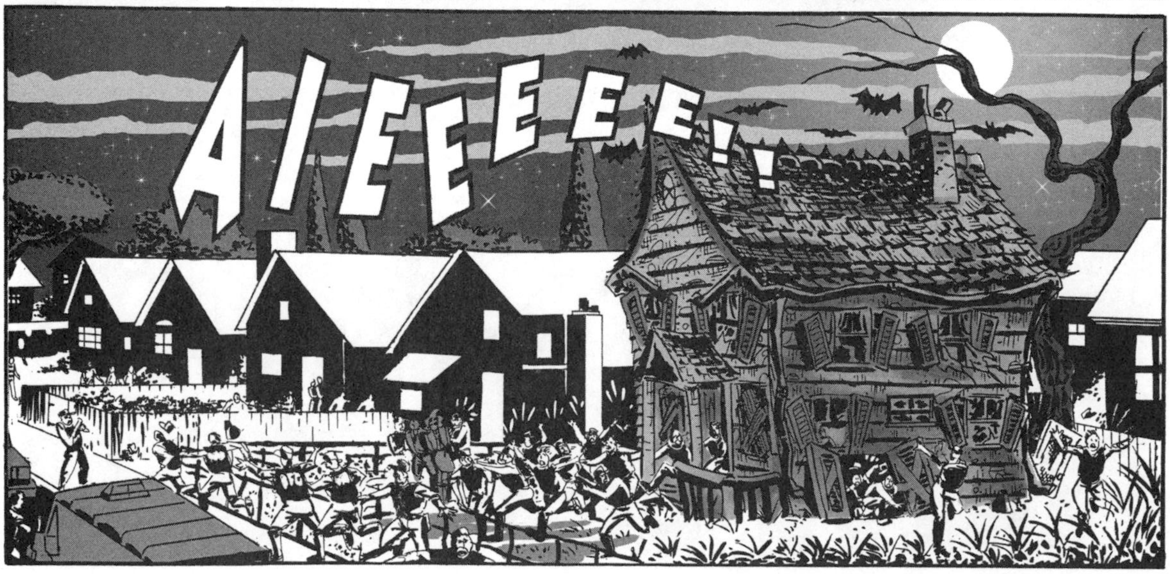
AIEEEEE!!

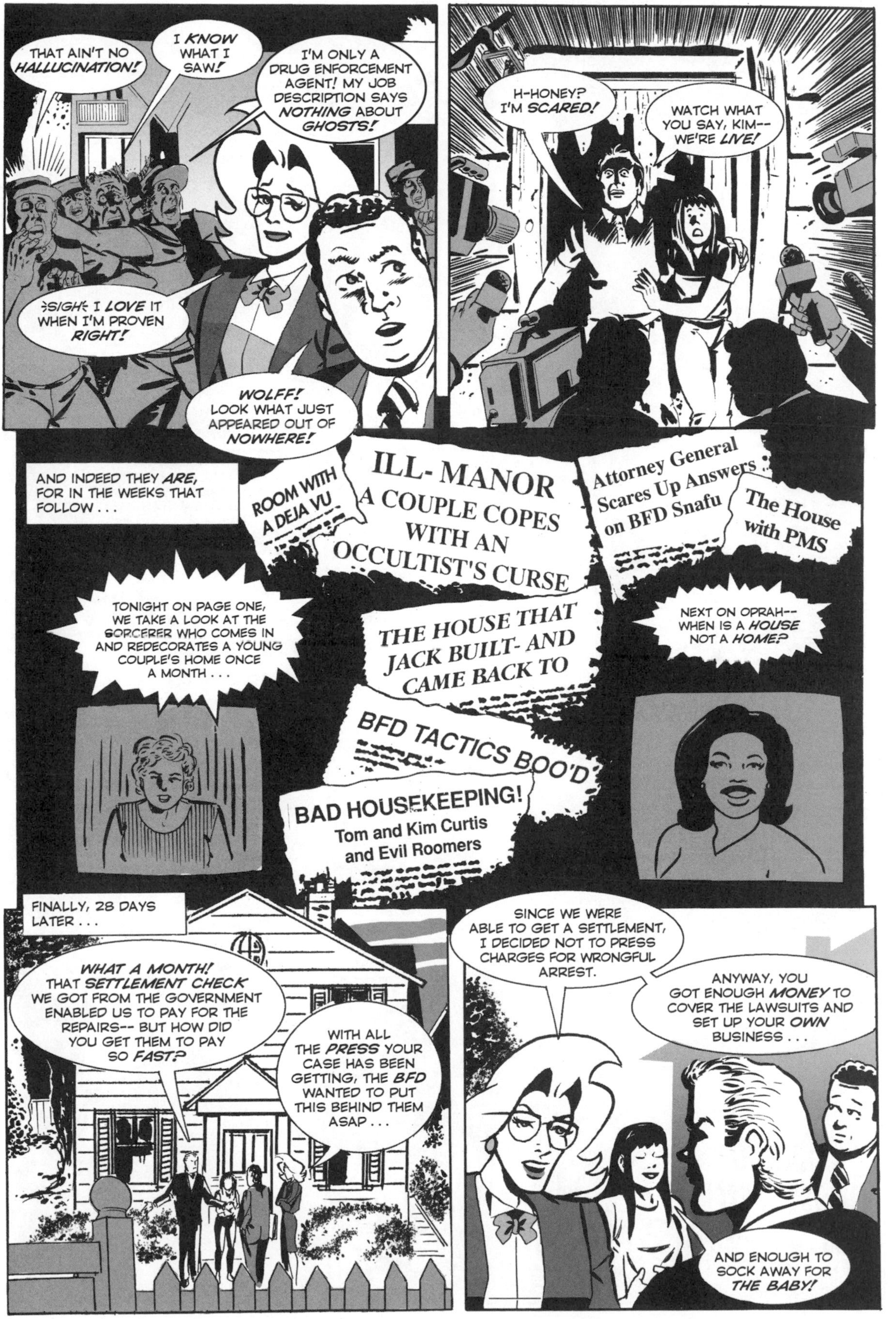
THAT AIN'T NO HALLUCINATION!
I KNOW WHAT I SAW!
I'M ONLY A DRUG ENFORCEMENT AGENT! MY JOB DESCRIPTION SAYS NOTHING ABOUT GHOSTS!
SIGH I LOVE IT WHEN I'M PROVEN RIGHT!
WOLFF! LOOK WHAT JUST APPEARED OUT OF NOWHERE!
H-HONEY? I'M SCARED!
WATCH WHAT YOU SAY, KIM-- WE'RE LIVE!
AND INDEED THEY ARE, FOR IN THE WEEKS THAT FOLLOW . . .
ROOM WITH A DEJA VU
ILL- MANOR
A COUPLE COPES WITH AN OCCULTIST'S CURSE
Attorney General Scares Up Answers on BFD Snafu
The House with PMS
TONIGHT ON PAGE ONE, WE TAKE A LOOK AT THE SORCERER WHO COMES IN AND REDECORATES A YOUNG COUPLE'S HOME ONCE A MONTH . . .
THE HOUSE THAT JACK BUILT- AND CAME BACK TO
NEXT ON OPRAH-- WHEN IS A HOUSE NOT A HOME?
BFD TACTICS BOO'D
BAD HOUSEKEEPING!
Tom and Kim Curtis and Evil Roomers
FINALLY, 28 DAYS LATER . . .
WHAT A MONTH! THAT SETTLEMENT CHECK WE GOT FROM THE GOVERNMENT ENABLED US TO PAY FOR THE REPAIRS-- BUT HOW DID YOU GET THEM TO PAY SO FAST?
WITH ALL THE PRESS YOUR CASE HAS BEEN GETTING, THE BFD WANTED TO PUT THIS BEHIND THEM ASAP . . .
SINCE WE WERE ABLE TO GET A SETTLEMENT, I DECIDED NOT TO PRESS CHARGES FOR WRONGFUL ARREST.
ANYWAY, YOU GOT ENOUGH MONEY TO COVER THE LAWSUITS AND SET UP YOUR OWN BUSINESS . . .
AND ENOUGH TO SOCK AWAY FOR THE BABY!

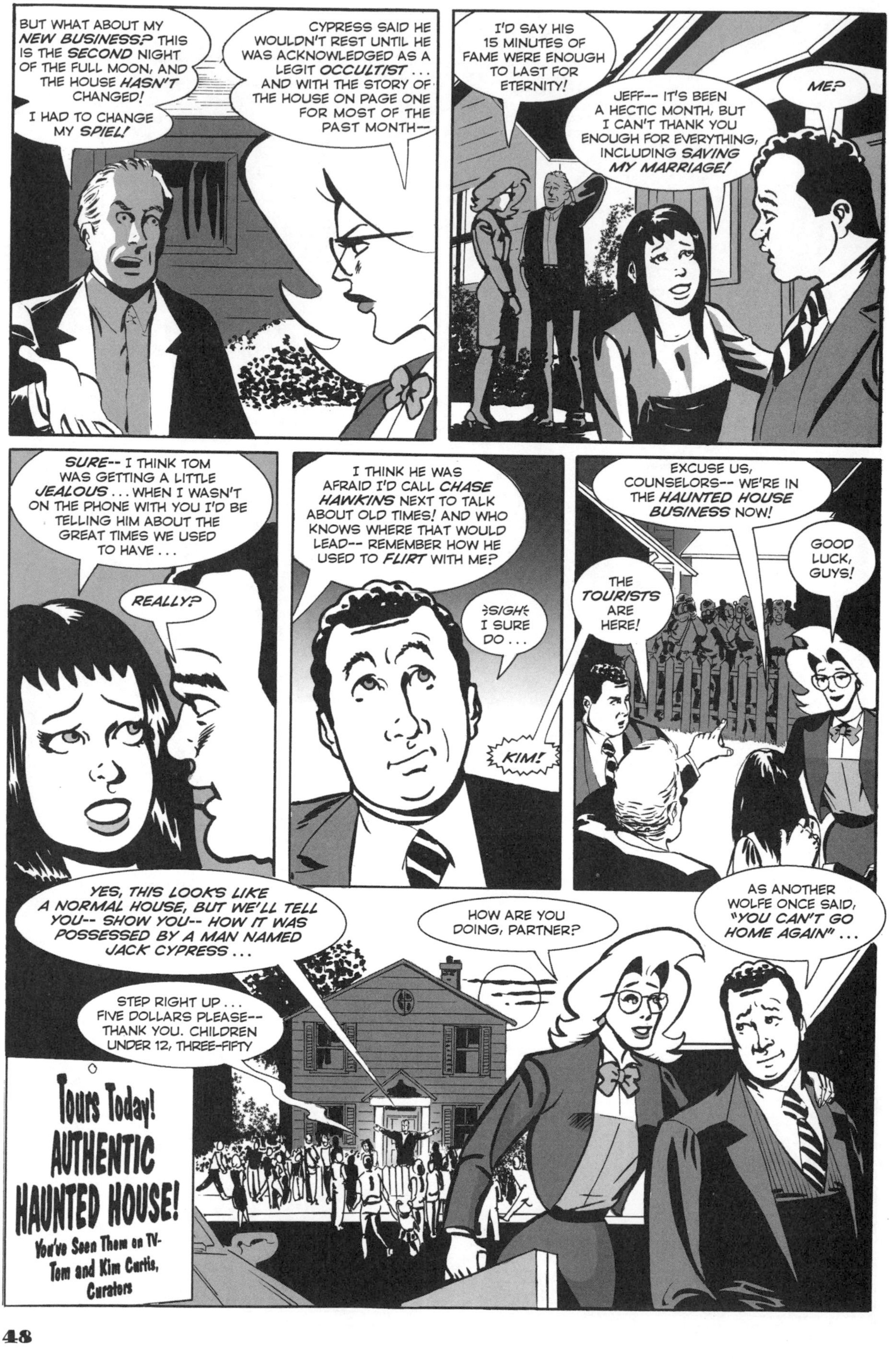
BUT WHAT ABOUT MY NEW BUSINESS? THIS IS THE SECOND NIGHT OF THE FULL MOON, AND THE HOUSE HASN'T CHANGED!
I HAD TO CHANGE MY SPIEL!
CYPRESS SAID HE WOULDN'T REST UNTIL HE WAS ACKNOWLEDGED AS A LEGIT OCCULTIST . . . AND WITH THE STORY OF THE HOUSE ON PAGE ONE FOR MOST OF THE PAST MONTH--
I'D SAY HIS 15 MINUTES OF FAME WERE ENOUGH TO LAST FOR ETERNITY!
JEFF-- IT'S BEEN A HECTIC MONTH, BUT I CAN'T THANK YOU ENOUGH FOR EVERYTHING, INCLUDING SAVING MY MARRIAGE!
ME?
SURE-- I THINK TOM WAS GETTING A LITTLE JEALOUS . . . WHEN I WASN'T ON THE PHONE WITH YOU I'D BE TELLING HIM ABOUT THE GREAT TIMES WE USED TO HAVE . . .
REALLY?
I THINK HE WAS AFRAID I'D CALL CHASE HAWKINS NEXT TO TALK ABOUT OLD TIMES! AND WHO KNOWS WHERE THAT WOULD LEAD-- REMEMBER HOW HE USED TO FLIRT WITH ME?
SIGH I SURE DO . . .
KIM!
EXCUSE US, COUNSELORS-- WE'RE IN THE HAUNTED HOUSE BUSINESS NOW!
THE TOURISTS ARE HERE!
GOOD LUCK, GUYS!
YES, THIS LOOKS LIKE A NORMAL HOUSE, BUT WE'LL TELL YOU-- SHOW YOU-- HOW IT WAS POSSESSED BY A MAN NAMED JACK CYPRESS . . .
STEP RIGHT UP . . . FIVE DOLLARS PLEASE-- THANK YOU. CHILDREN UNDER 12, THREE-FIFTY
HOW ARE YOU DOING, PARTNER?
AS ANOTHER WOLFE ONCE SAID, "YOU CAN'T GO HOME AGAIN" . . .
Tours Today! AUTHENTIC HAUNTED HOUSE!
You've Seen Them on TV- Tom and Kim Curtis, Curators

A Long Night's Journey into Day

Featuring:

The Zombies Strike at Midnight

Court of Public Opinion

Wolff & Byrd's Secretary, Mavis

Things That Go Bump in the Night . . . and Day!

The Man Who Broke the Laws of Gravity
(and Landed in Court)

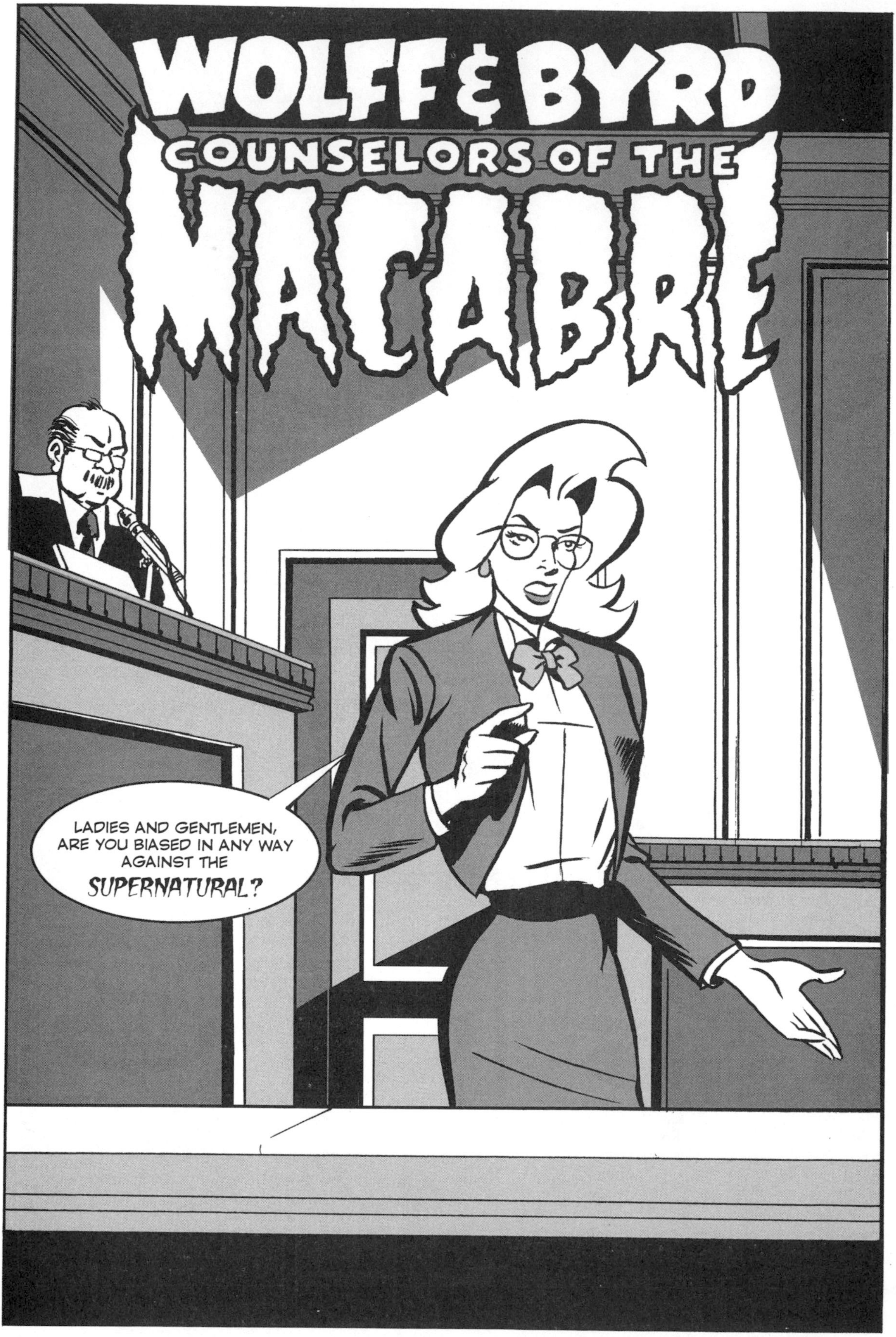
WOLFF & BYRD
COUNSELORS OF THE
MACABRE
LADIES AND GENTLEMEN, ARE YOU BIASED IN ANY WAY AGAINST THE SUPERNATURAL?

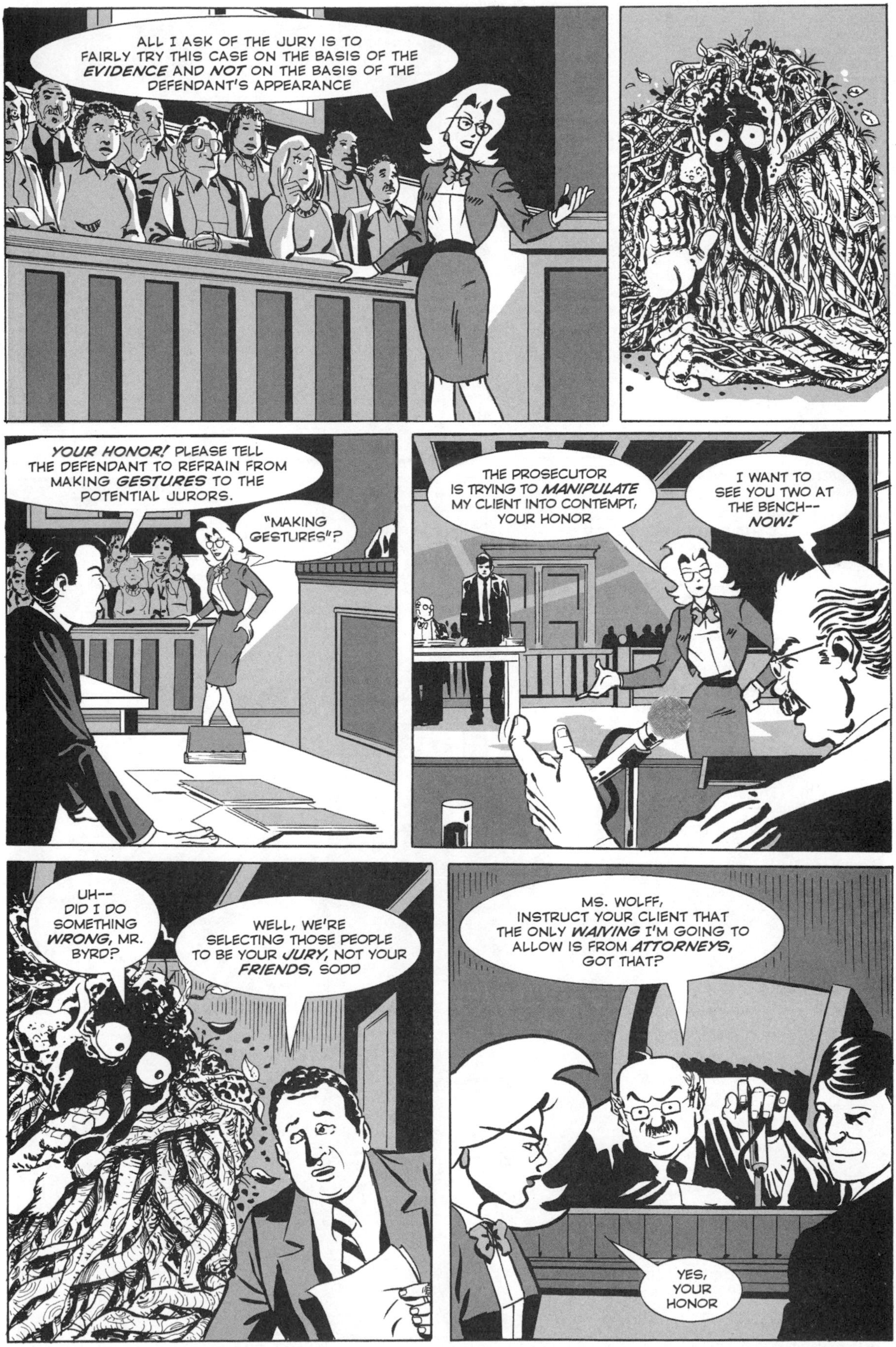
ALL I ASK OF THE JURY IS TO FAIRLY TRY THIS CASE ON THE BASIS OF THE EVIDENCE AND NOT ON THE BASIS OF THE DEFENDANT'S APPEARANCE
YOUR HONOR! PLEASE TELL THE DEFENDANT TO REFRAIN FROM MAKING GESTURES TO THE POTENTIAL JURORS.
"MAKING GESTURES"?
THE PROSECUTOR IS TRYING TO MANIPULATE MY CLIENT INTO CONTEMPT, YOUR HONOR
I WANT TO SEE YOU TWO AT THE BENCH-- NOW!
UH-- DID I DO SOMETHING WRONG, MR. BYRD?
WELL, WE'RE SELECTING THOSE PEOPLE TO BE YOUR JURY, NOT YOUR FRIENDS, SODD
MS. WOLFF, INSTRUCT YOUR CLIENT THAT THE ONLY WAIVING I'M GOING TO ALLOW IS FROM ATTORNEYS, GOT THAT?
YES, YOUR HONOR

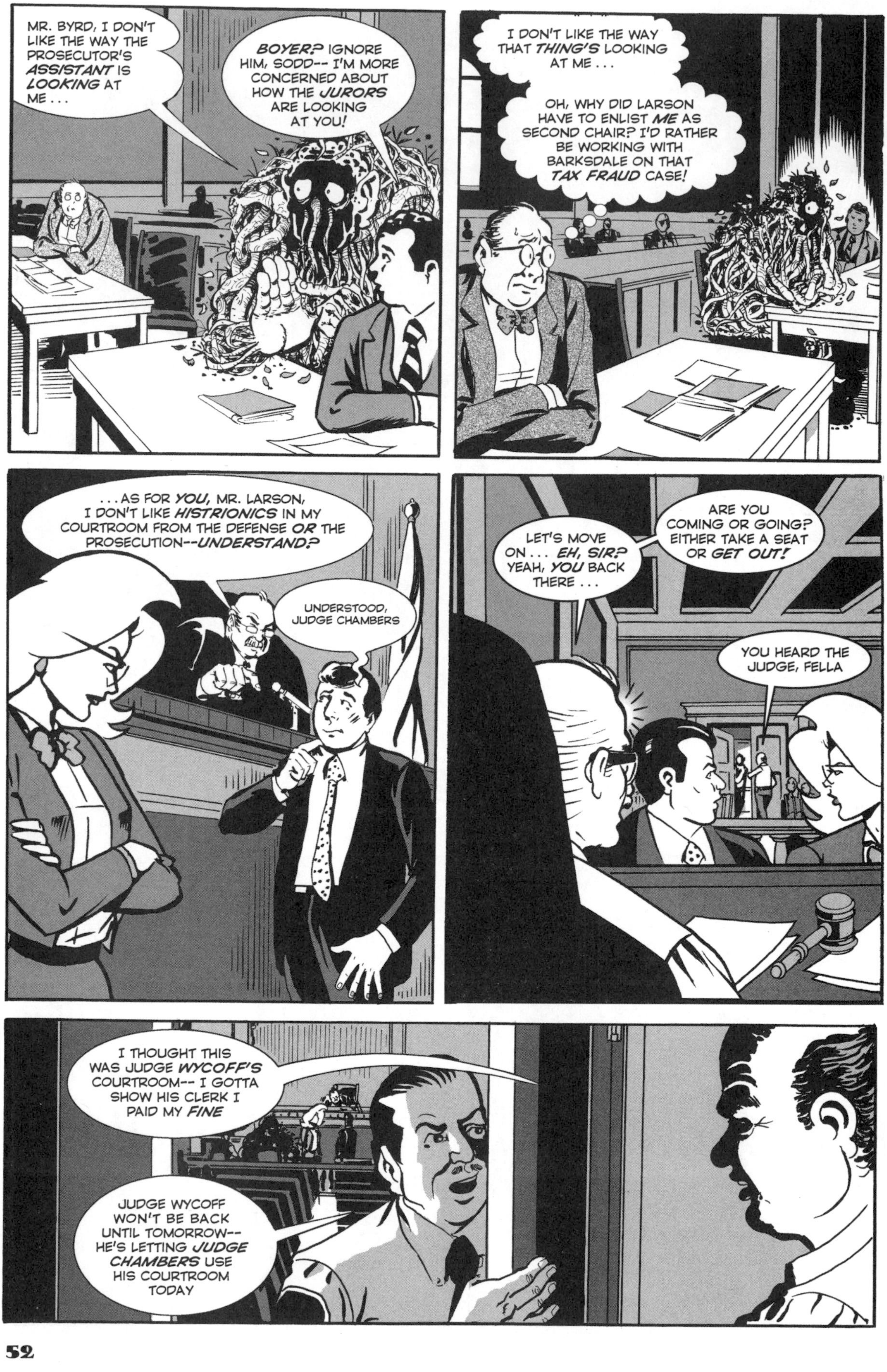
MR. BYRD, I DON'T LIKE THE WAY THE PROSECUTOR'S ASSISTANT IS LOOKING AT ME . . .
BOYER? IGNORE HIM, SODD-- I'M MORE CONCERNED ABOUT HOW THE JURORS ARE LOOKING AT YOU!
I DON'T LIKE THE WAY THAT THING'S LOOKING AT ME . . .
OH, WHY DID LARSON HAVE TO ENLIST ME AS SECOND CHAIR? I'D RATHER BE WORKING WITH BARKSDALE ON THAT TAX FRAUD CASE!
. . . AS FOR YOU, MR. LARSON, I DON'T LIKE HISTRIONICS IN MY COURTROOM FROM THE DEFENSE OR THE PROSECUTION--UNDERSTAND?
UNDERSTOOD, JUDGE CHAMBERS
LET'S MOVE ON . . . EH, SIR? YEAH, YOU BACK THERE . . .
ARE YOU COMING OR GOING? EITHER TAKE A SEAT OR GET OUT!
YOU HEARD THE JUDGE, FELLA
I THOUGHT THIS WAS JUDGE WYCOFF'S COURTROOM-- I GOTTA SHOW HIS CLERK I PAID MY FINE
JUDGE WYCOFF WON'T BE BACK UNTIL TOMORROW-- HE'S LETTING JUDGE CHAMBERS USE HIS COURTROOM TODAY

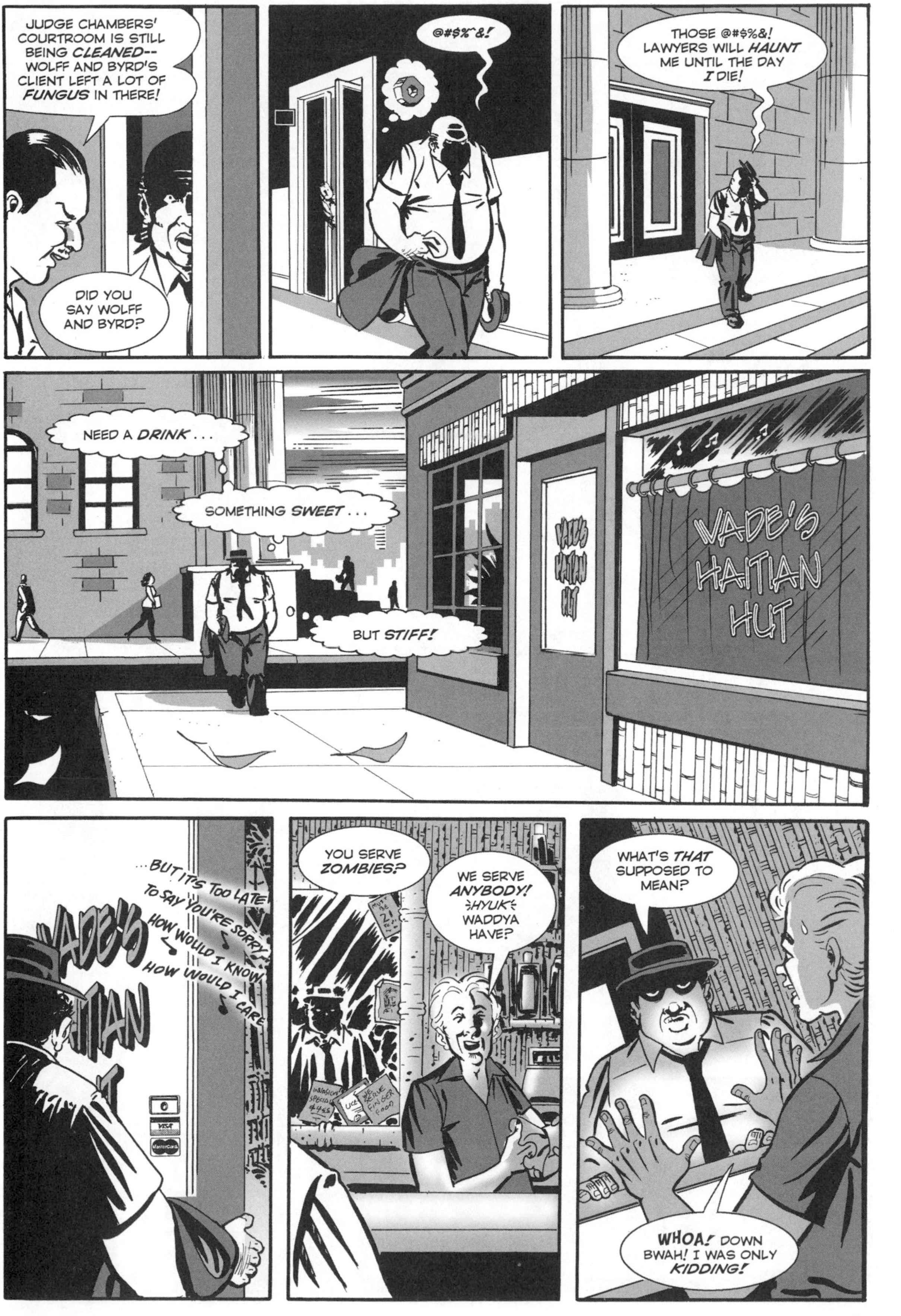
JUDGE CHAMBERS' COURTROOM IS STILL BEING CLEANED-- WOLFF AND BYRD'S CLIENT LEFT A LOT OF FUNGUS IN THERE!
DID YOU SAY WOLFF AND BYRD?
@#$%~&!
THOSE @#$%&! LAWYERS WILL HAUNT ME UNTIL THE DAY I DIE!
NEED A DRINK . . .
SOMETHING SWEET . . .
BUT STIFF!
WADE'S HAITIAN HUT
WADE'S HAITIAN HUT
...BUT IT'S TOO LATE TO SAY YOU'RE SORRY HOW WOULD I KNOW HOW WOULD I CARE
YOU SERVE ZOMBIES?
WE SERVE ANYBODY! HYUK WADDYA HAVE?
WHAT'S THAT SUPPOSED TO MEAN?
WHOA! DOWN BWAH! I WAS ONLY KIDDING!

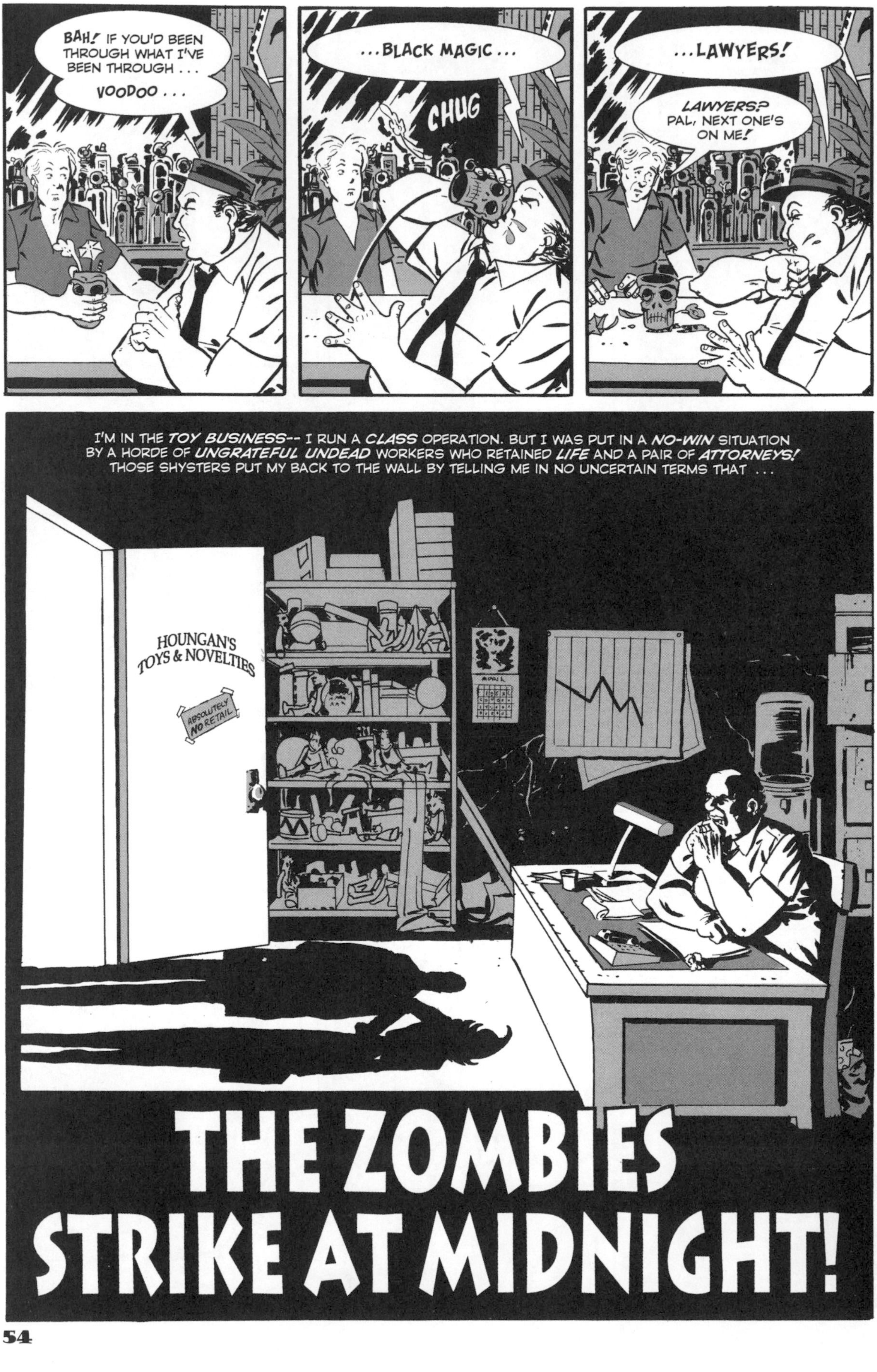
BAH! IF YOU'D BEEN THROUGH WHAT I'VE BEEN THROUGH . . .
VOODOO . . .
. . . BLACK MAGIC . . .
CHUG
. . . LAWYERS!
LAWYERS? PAL, NEXT ONE'S ON ME!
I'M IN THE TOY BUSINESS-- I RUN A CLASS OPERATION. BUT I WAS PUT IN A NO-WIN SITUATION BY A HORDE OF UNGRATEFUL UNDEAD WORKERS WHO RETAINED LIFE AND A PAIR OF ATTORNEYS! THOSE SHYSTERS PUT MY BACK TO THE WALL BY TELLING ME IN NO UNCERTAIN TERMS THAT . . .
HOUNGAN'S TOYS & NOVELTIES
ABSOLUTELY NO RETAIL
THE ZOMBIES STRIKE AT MIDNIGHT!

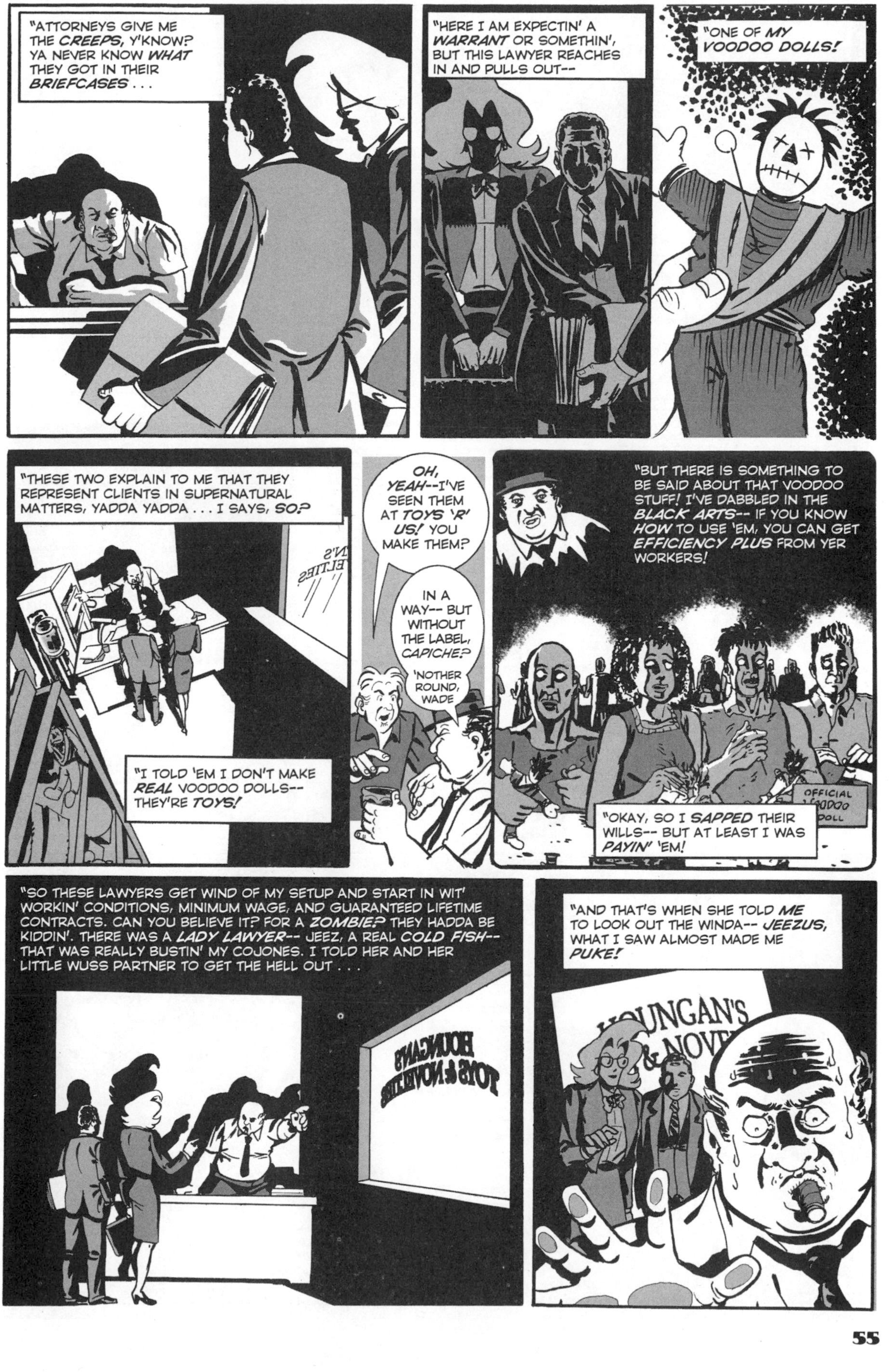
"ATTORNEYS GIVE ME THE CREEPS, Y'KNOW? YA NEVER KNOW WHAT THEY GOT IN THEIR BRIEFCASES . . .
"HERE I AM EXPECTIN' A WARRANT OR SOMETHIN', BUT THIS LAWYER REACHES IN AND PULLS OUT--
"ONE OF MY VOODOO DOLLS!
"THESE TWO EXPLAIN TO ME THAT THEY REPRESENT CLIENTS IN SUPERNATURAL MATTERS, YADDA YADDA . . . I SAYS, SO?
"I TOLD 'EM I DON'T MAKE REAL VOODOO DOLLS-- THEY'RE TOYS!
OH, YEAH--I'VE SEEN THEM AT TOYS 'R' US! YOU MAKE THEM?
IN A WAY-- BUT WITHOUT THE LABEL, CAPICHE?
'NOTHER ROUND, WADE
"BUT THERE IS SOMETHING TO BE SAID ABOUT THAT VOODOO STUFF! I'VE DABBLED IN THE BLACK ARTS-- IF YOU KNOW HOW TO USE 'EM, YOU CAN GET EFFICIENCY PLUS FROM YER WORKERS!
"OKAY, SO I SAPPED THEIR WILLS-- BUT AT LEAST I WAS PAYIN' 'EM!
"SO THESE LAWYERS GET WIND OF MY SETUP AND START IN WIT' WORKIN' CONDITIONS, MINIMUM WAGE, AND GUARANTEED LIFETIME CONTRACTS. CAN YOU BELIEVE IT? FOR A ZOMBIE? THEY HADDA BE KIDDIN'. THERE WAS A LADY LAWYER-- JEEZ, A REAL COLD FISH-- THAT WAS REALLY BUSTIN' MY COJONES. I TOLD HER AND HER LITTLE WUSS PARTNER TO GET THE HELL OUT . . .
HOUNGAN'S TOYS & NOVELTIES
"AND THAT'S WHEN SHE TOLD ME TO LOOK OUT THE WINDA-- JEEZUS, WHAT I SAW ALMOST MADE ME PUKE!
HOUNGAN'S

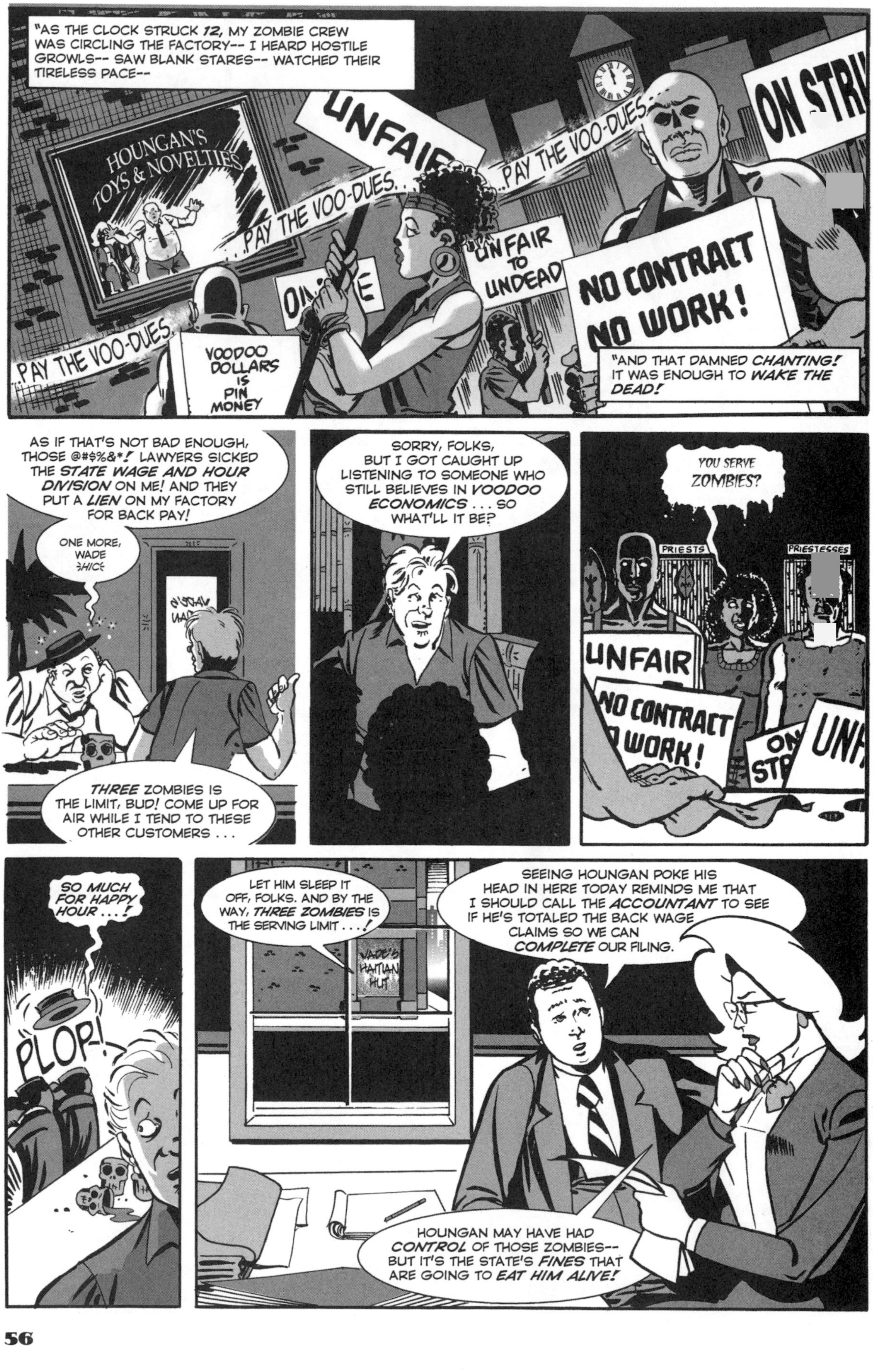

"AS THE CLOCK STRUCK 12, MY ZOMBIE CREW WAS CIRCLING THE FACTORY-- I HEARD HOSTILE GROWLS-- SAW BLANK STARES-- WATCHED THEIR TIRELESS PACE--
HOUNGAN'S TOYS & NOVELTIES
UNFAIR
PAY THE VOO-DUES
ON STRI
PAY THE VOO-DUES
PAY THE VOO-DUES
UNFAIR TO UNDEAD
NO CONTRACT NO WORK!
PAY THE VOO-DUES
VOODOO DOLLARS IS PIN MONEY
"AND THAT DAMNED CHANTING! IT WAS ENOUGH TO WAKE THE DEAD!
AS IF THAT'S NOT BAD ENOUGH, THOSE @#$%&*! LAWYERS SICKED THE STATE WAGE AND HOUR DIVISION ON ME! AND THEY PUT A LIEN ON MY FACTORY FOR BACK PAY!
ONE MORE, WADE *HIC*
THREE ZOMBIES IS THE LIMIT, BUD! COME UP FOR AIR WHILE I TEND TO THESE OTHER CUSTOMERS . . .
SORRY, FOLKS, BUT I GOT CAUGHT UP LISTENING TO SOMEONE WHO STILL BELIEVES IN VOODOO ECONOMICS . . . SO WHAT'LL IT BE?
YOU SERVE ZOMBIES?
PRIESTS
PRIESTESSES
UNFAIR
NO CONTRACT NO WORK!
ON STR
UNF
SO MUCH FOR HAPPY HOUR . . . !
PLOP!
LET HIM SLEEP IT OFF, FOLKS. AND BY THE WAY, THREE ZOMBIES IS THE SERVING LIMIT . . . !
WADE'S HAITIAN HUT
SEEING HOUNGAN POKE HIS HEAD IN HERE TODAY REMINDS ME THAT I SHOULD CALL THE ACCOUNTANT TO SEE IF HE'S TOTALED THE BACK WAGE CLAIMS SO WE CAN COMPLETE OUR FILING.
HOUNGAN MAY HAVE HAD CONTROL OF THOSE ZOMBIES-- BUT IT'S THE STATE'S FINES THAT ARE GOING TO EAT HIM ALIVE!

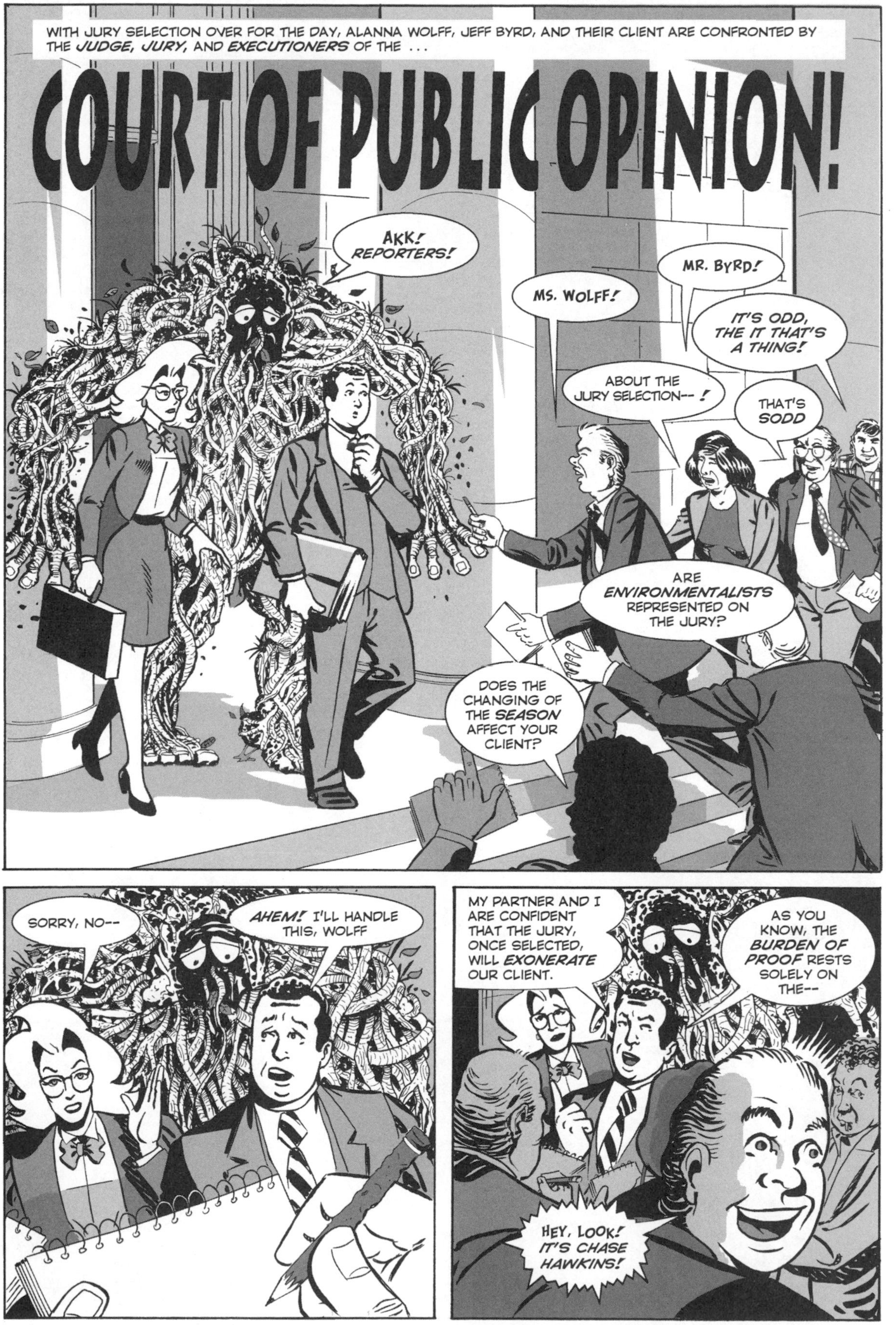
WITH JURY SELECTION OVER FOR THE DAY, ALANNA WOLFF, JEFF BYRD, AND THEIR CLIENT ARE CONFRONTED BY THE JUDGE, JURY, AND EXECUTIONERS OF THE . . .
COURT OF PUBLIC OPINION!
AKK! REPORTERS!
MS. WOLFF!
MR. BYRD!
IT'S ODD, THE IT THAT'S A THING!
ABOUT THE JURY SELECTION-- !
THAT'S SODD
ARE ENVIRONMENTALISTS REPRESENTED ON THE JURY?
DOES THE CHANGING OF THE SEASON AFFECT YOUR CLIENT?
SORRY, NO--
AHEM! I'LL HANDLE THIS, WOLFF
MY PARTNER AND I ARE CONFIDENT THAT THE JURY, ONCE SELECTED, WILL EXONERATE OUR CLIENT.
AS YOU KNOW, THE BURDEN OF PROOF RESTS SOLELY ON THE--
HEY, LOOK! IT'S CHASE HAWKINS!

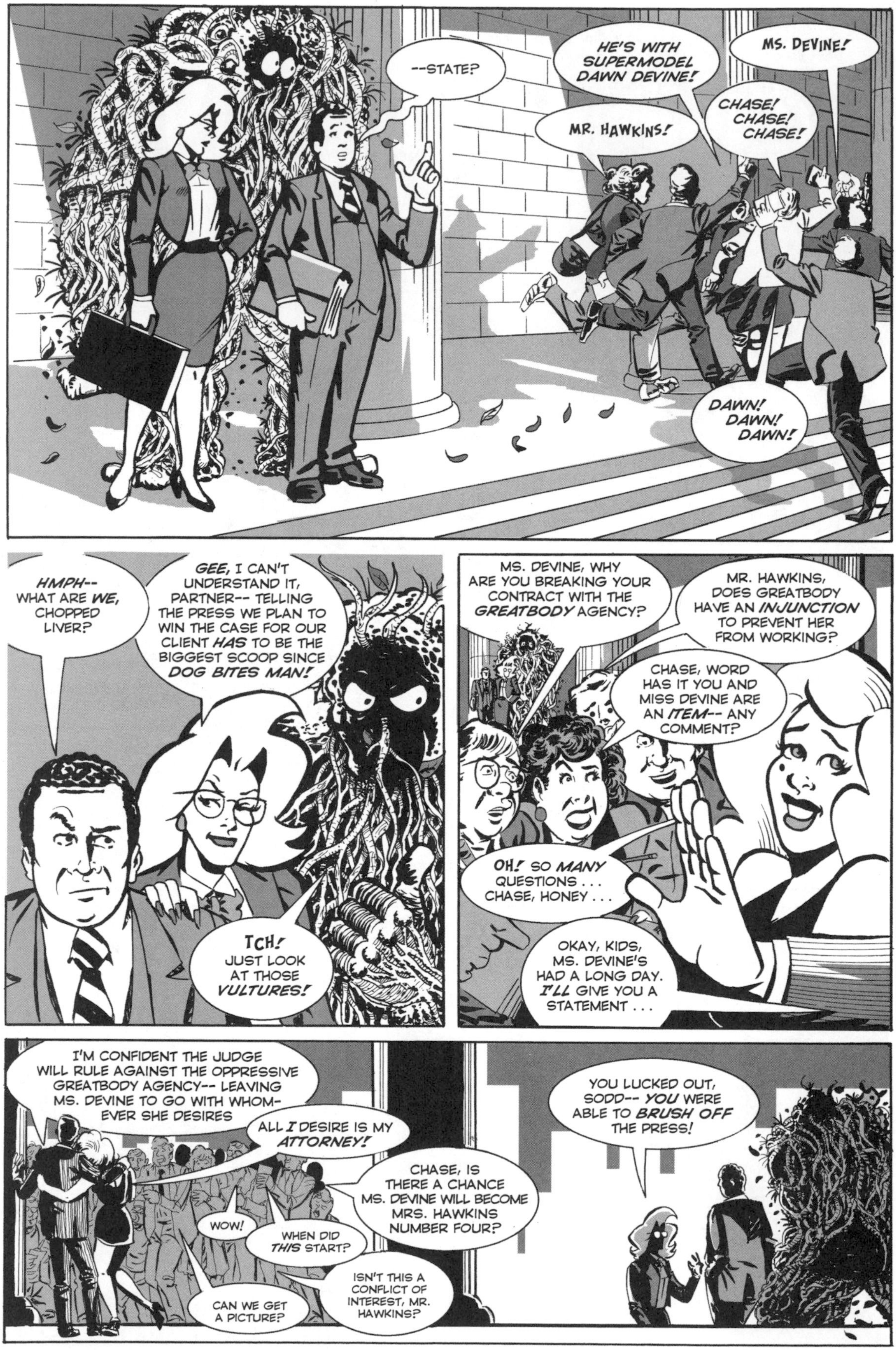

--STATE?
HE'S WITH SUPERMODEL DAWN DEVINE!
MS. DEVINE!
MR. HAWKINS!
CHASE! CHASE! CHASE!
DAWN! DAWN! DAWN!
HMPH-- WHAT ARE WE, CHOPPED LIVER?
GEE, I CAN'T UNDERSTAND IT, PARTNER-- TELLING THE PRESS WE PLAN TO WIN THE CASE FOR OUR CLIENT HAS TO BE THE BIGGEST SCOOP SINCE DOG BITES MAN!
TCH! JUST LOOK AT THOSE VULTURES!
MS. DEVINE, WHY ARE YOU BREAKING YOUR CONTRACT WITH THE GREATBODY AGENCY?
MR. HAWKINS, DOES GREATBODY HAVE AN INJUNCTION TO PREVENT HER FROM WORKING?
CHASE, WORD HAS IT YOU AND MISS DEVINE ARE AN ITEM-- ANY COMMENT?
OH! SO MANY QUESTIONS . . . CHASE, HONEY . . .
OKAY, KIDS, MS. DEVINE'S HAD A LONG DAY. I'LL GIVE YOU A STATEMENT . . .
I'M CONFIDENT THE JUDGE WILL RULE AGAINST THE OPPRESSIVE GREATBODY AGENCY-- LEAVING MS. DEVINE TO GO WITH WHOM-EVER SHE DESIRES
ALL I DESIRE IS MY ATTORNEY!
CHASE, IS THERE A CHANCE MS. DEVINE WILL BECOME MRS. HAWKINS NUMBER FOUR?
WOW!
WHEN DID THIS START?
ISN'T THIS A CONFLICT OF INTEREST, MR. HAWKINS?
CAN WE GET A PICTURE?
YOU LUCKED OUT, SODD-- YOU WERE ABLE TO BRUSH OFF THE PRESS!

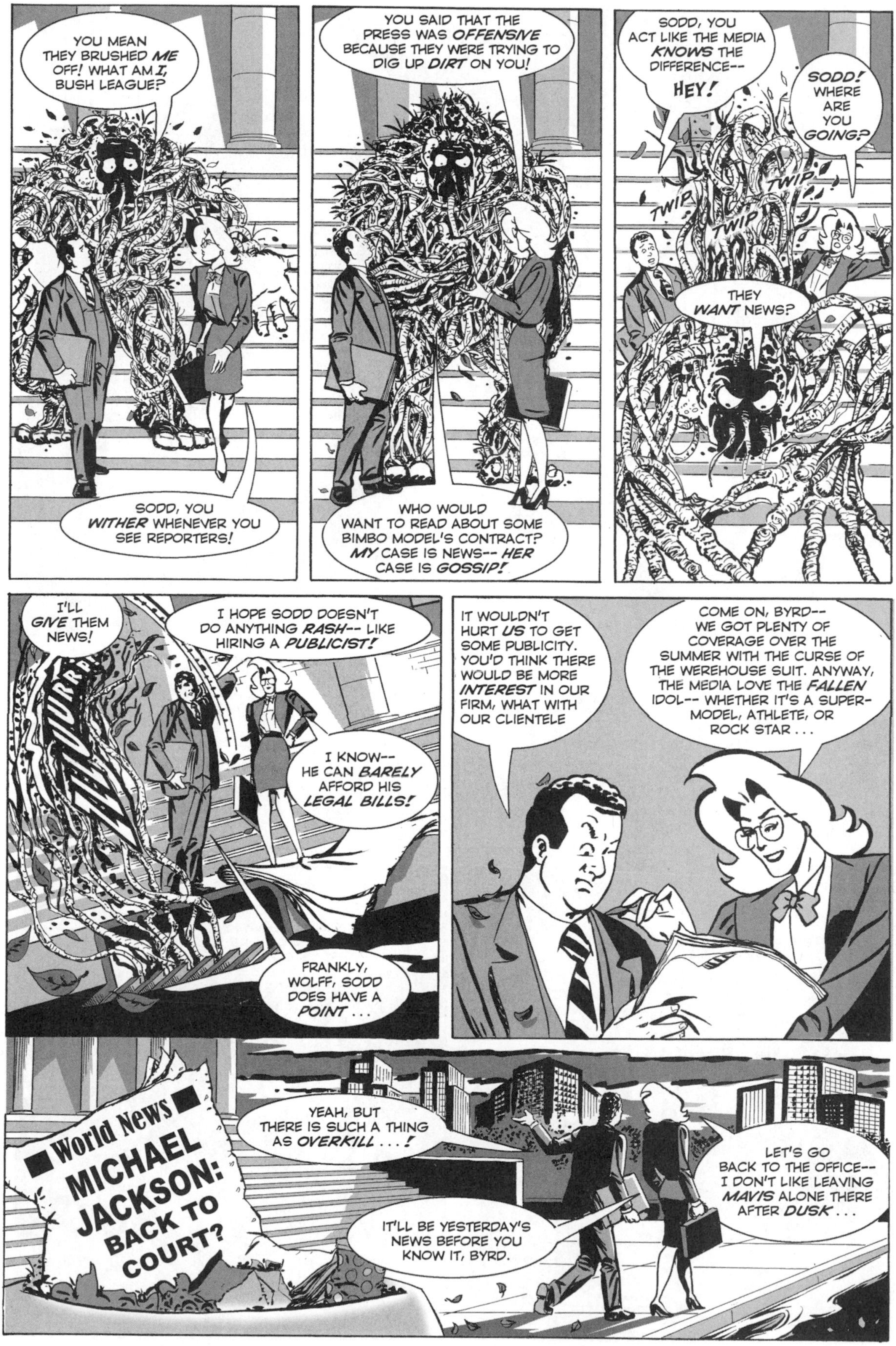
YOU MEAN THEY BRUSHED ME OFF! WHAT AM I, BUSH LEAGUE?
SODD, YOU WITHER WHENEVER YOU SEE REPORTERS!
YOU SAID THAT THE PRESS WAS OFFENSIVE BECAUSE THEY WERE TRYING TO DIG UP DIRT ON YOU!
WHO WOULD WANT TO READ ABOUT SOME BIMBO MODEL'S CONTRACT? MY CASE IS NEWS-- HER CASE IS GOSSIP!
SODD, YOU ACT LIKE THE MEDIA KNOWS THE DIFFERENCE--
HEY!
SODD! WHERE ARE YOU GOING?
TWIP TWIP TWIP
THEY WANT NEWS?
I'LL GIVE THEM NEWS!
I HOPE SODD DOESN'T DO ANYTHING RASH-- LIKE HIRING A PUBLICIST!
I KNOW-- HE CAN BARELY AFFORD HIS LEGAL BILLS!
FRANKLY, WOLFF, SODD DOES HAVE A POINT . . .
IT WOULDN'T HURT US TO GET SOME PUBLICITY. YOU'D THINK THERE WOULD BE MORE INTEREST IN OUR FIRM, WHAT WITH OUR CLIENTELE
COME ON, BYRD-- WE GOT PLENTY OF COVERAGE OVER THE SUMMER WITH THE CURSE OF THE WEREHOUSE SUIT. ANYWAY, THE MEDIA LOVE THE FALLEN IDOL-- WHETHER IT'S A SUPER-MODEL, ATHLETE, OR ROCK STAR . . .
World News
MICHAEL JACKSON: BACK TO COURT?
YEAH, BUT THERE IS SUCH A THING AS OVERKILL . . . !
IT'LL BE YESTERDAY'S NEWS BEFORE YOU KNOW IT, BYRD.
LET'S GO BACK TO THE OFFICE-- I DON'T LIKE LEAVING MAVIS ALONE THERE AFTER DUSK . . .

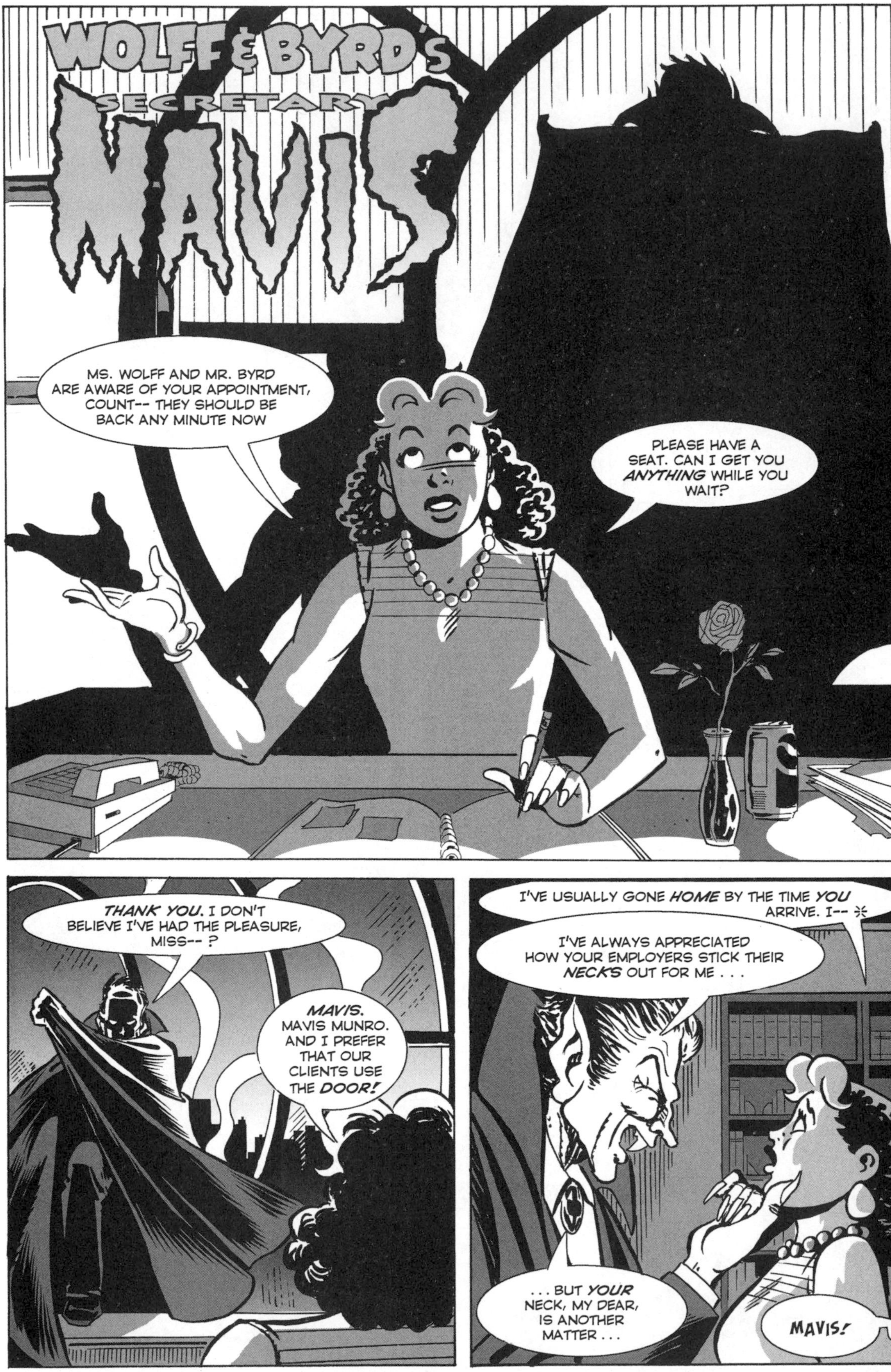
WOLFF & BYRD'S
SECRETARY
MAVIS
MS. WOLFF AND MR. BYRD ARE AWARE OF YOUR APPOINTMENT, COUNT-- THEY SHOULD BE BACK ANY MINUTE NOW
PLEASE HAVE A SEAT. CAN I GET YOU ANYTHING WHILE YOU WAIT?
THANK YOU. I DON'T BELIEVE I'VE HAD THE PLEASURE, MISS-- ?
MAVIS. MAVIS MUNRO. AND I PREFER THAT OUR CLIENTS USE THE DOOR!
I'VE USUALLY GONE HOME BY THE TIME YOU ARRIVE. I--
I'VE ALWAYS APPRECIATED HOW YOUR EMPLOYERS STICK THEIR NECKS OUT FOR ME . . .
. . . BUT YOUR NECK, MY DEAR, IS ANOTHER MATTER . . .
MAVIS!

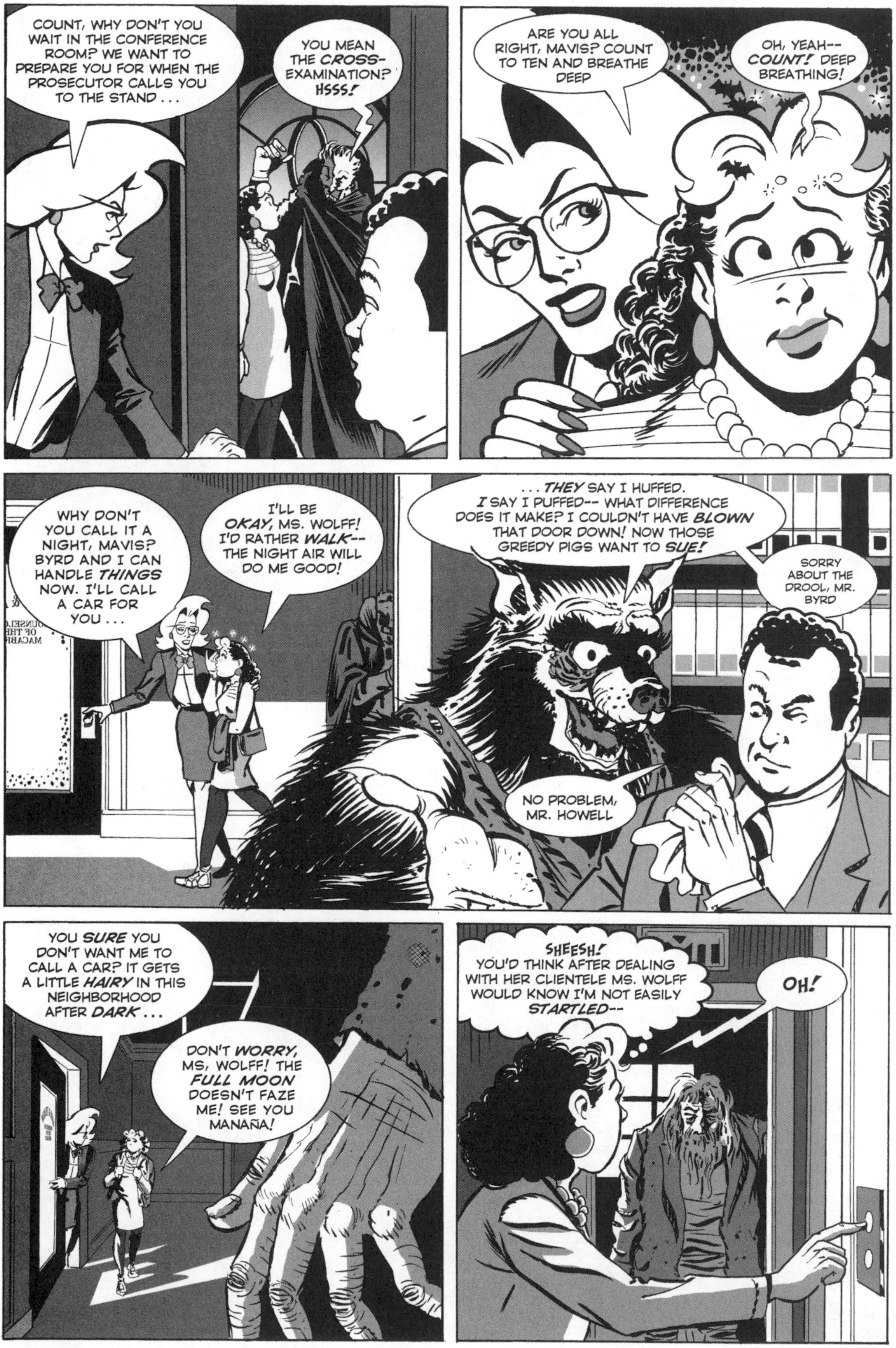
COUNT, WHY DON'T YOU WAIT IN THE CONFERENCE ROOM? WE WANT TO PREPARE YOU FOR WHEN THE PROSECUTOR CALLS YOU TO THE STAND . . .
YOU MEAN THE *CROSS*-EXAMINATION? *HSSS!*
ARE YOU ALL RIGHT, MAVIS? COUNT TO TEN AND BREATHE DEEP
OH, YEAH-- *COUNT!* DEEP BREATHING!
WHY DON'T YOU CALL IT A NIGHT, MAVIS? BYRD AND I CAN HANDLE *THINGS* NOW. I'LL CALL A CAR FOR YOU . . .
I'LL BE *OKAY,* MS. WOLFF! I'D RATHER *WALK*-- THE NIGHT AIR WILL DO ME GOOD!
. . . *THEY* SAY I HUFFED. *I* SAY I PUFFED-- WHAT DIFFERENCE DOES IT MAKE? I COULDN'T HAVE *BLOWN* THAT DOOR DOWN! NOW THOSE GREEDY PIGS WANT TO *SUE!*
SORRY ABOUT THE DROOL, MR. BYRD
NO PROBLEM, MR. HOWELL
YOU *SURE* YOU DON'T WANT ME TO CALL A CAR? IT GETS A LITTLE *HAIRY* IN THIS NEIGHBORHOOD AFTER *DARK* . . .
DON'T *WORRY,* MS, WOLFF! THE *FULL MOON* DOESN'T FAZE ME! SEE YOU MAÑAÑA!
SHEESH! YOU'D THINK AFTER DEALING WITH HER CLIENTELE MS. WOLFF WOULD KNOW I'M NOT EASILY *STARTLED*--
OH!

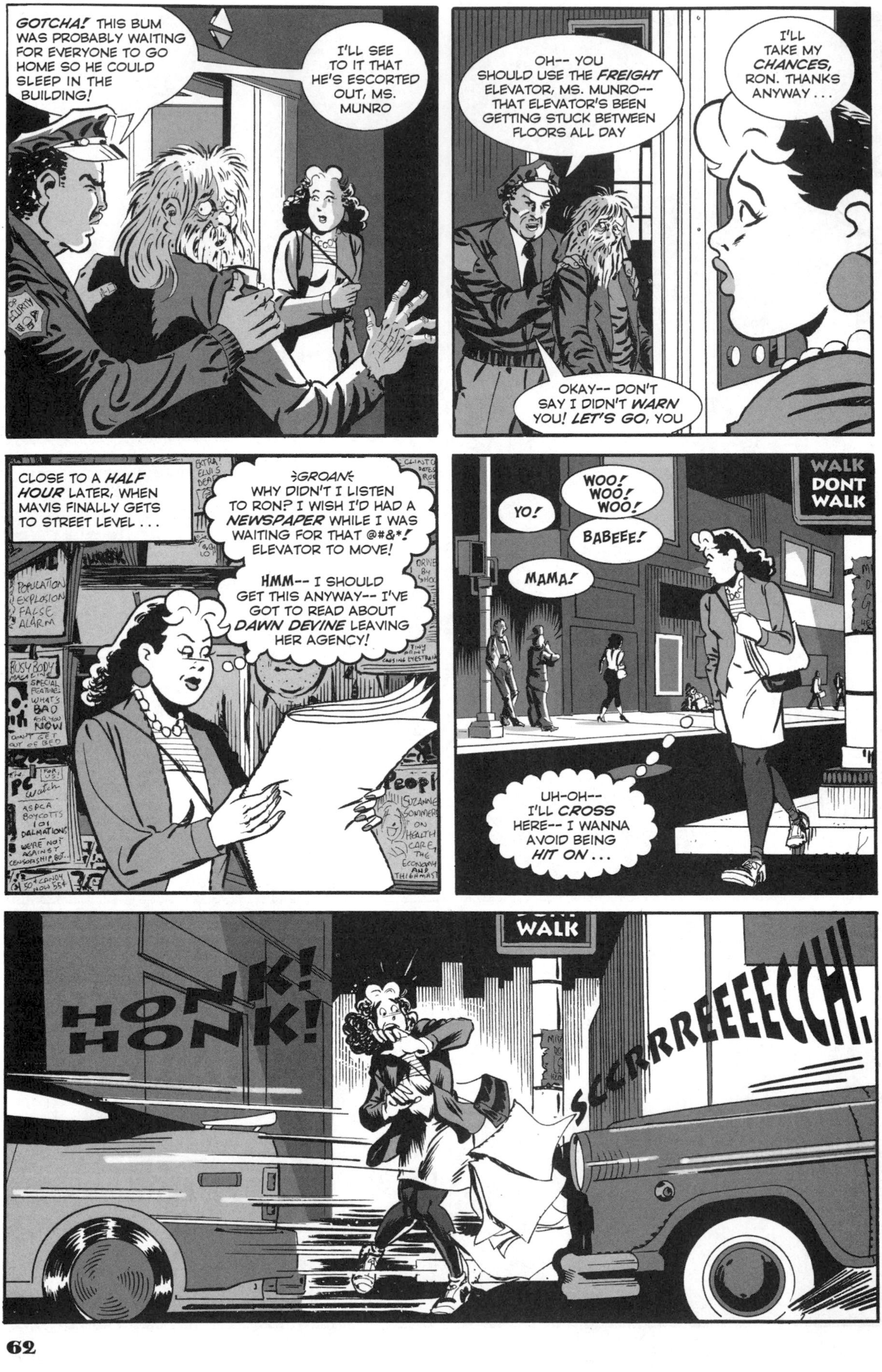
GOTCHA! THIS BUM WAS PROBABLY WAITING FOR EVERYONE TO GO HOME SO HE COULD SLEEP IN THE BUILDING!
I'LL SEE TO IT THAT HE'S ESCORTED OUT, MS. MUNRO
OH-- YOU SHOULD USE THE FREIGHT ELEVATOR, MS. MUNRO-- THAT ELEVATOR'S BEEN GETTING STUCK BETWEEN FLOORS ALL DAY
I'LL TAKE MY CHANCES, RON. THANKS ANYWAY . . .
OKAY-- DON'T SAY I DIDN'T WARN YOU! LET'S GO, YOU
CLOSE TO A HALF HOUR LATER, WHEN MAVIS FINALLY GETS TO STREET LEVEL . . .
GROAN
WHY DIDN'T I LISTEN TO RON? I WISH I'D HAD A NEWSPAPER WHILE I WAS WAITING FOR THAT @#&*! ELEVATOR TO MOVE!
HMM-- I SHOULD GET THIS ANYWAY-- I'VE GOT TO READ ABOUT DAWN DEVINE LEAVING HER AGENCY!
POPULATION EXPLOSION FALSE ALARM
WALK
DONT WALK
YO!
WOO! WOO! WOO!
BABEEE!
MAMA!
UH-OH-- I'LL CROSS HERE-- I WANNA AVOID BEING HIT ON . . .
WALK
HONK! HONK!
SCCRRREEEEECCH!

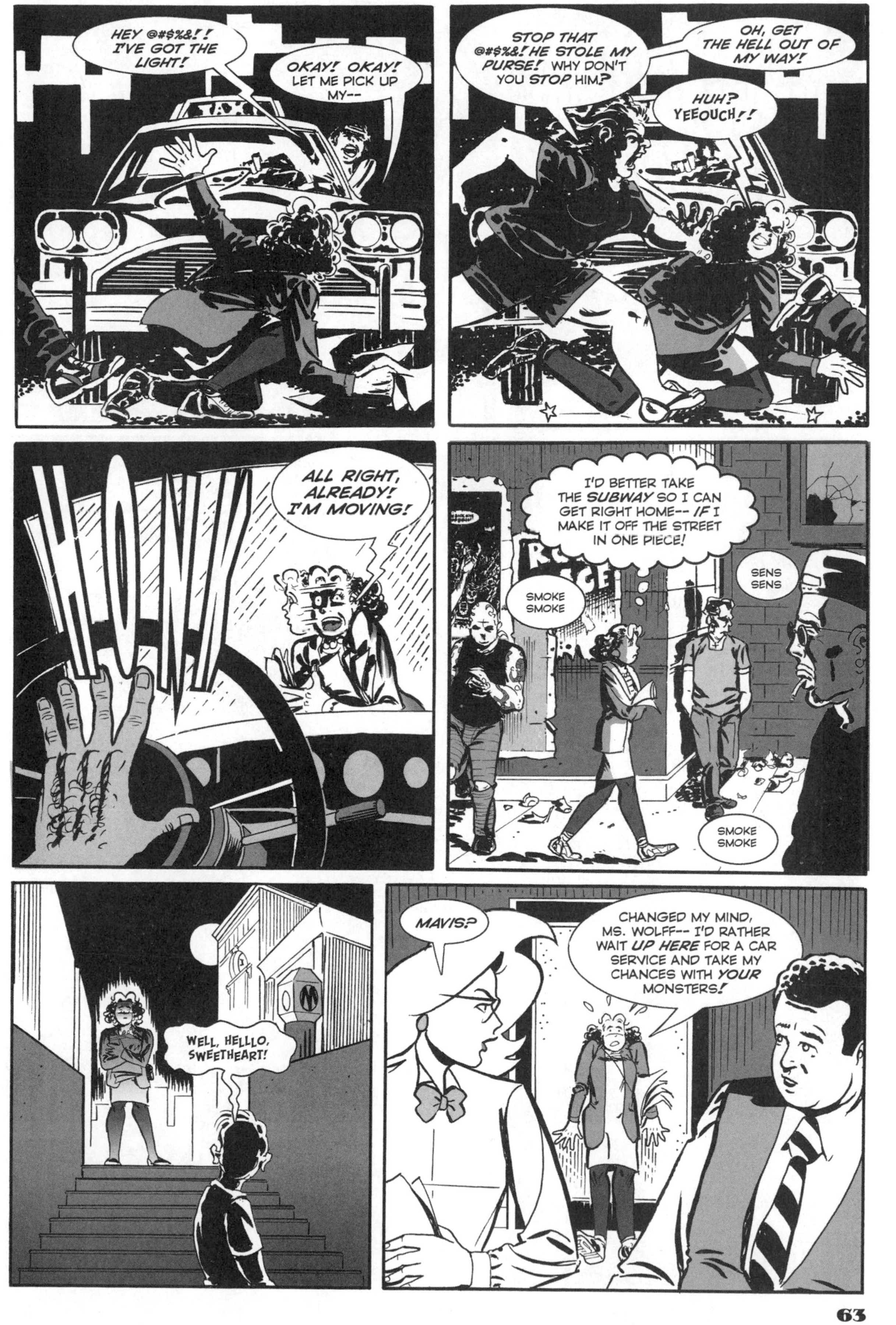
HEY @#$%&!! I'VE GOT THE LIGHT!
OKAY! OKAY! LET ME PICK UP MY--
STOP THAT @#$%&! HE STOLE MY PURSE! WHY DON'T YOU STOP HIM?
OH, GET THE HELL OUT OF MY WAY!
HUH? YEEOUCH!!
HONK
ALL RIGHT, ALREADY! I'M MOVING!
I'D BETTER TAKE THE SUBWAY SO I CAN GET RIGHT HOME-- IF I MAKE IT OFF THE STREET IN ONE PIECE!
SMOKE SMOKE
SENS SENS
SMOKE SMOKE
WELL, HELLLO, SWEETHEART!
MAVIS?
CHANGED MY MIND, MS. WOLFF-- I'D RATHER WAIT UP HERE FOR A CAR SERVICE AND TAKE MY CHANCES WITH YOUR MONSTERS!

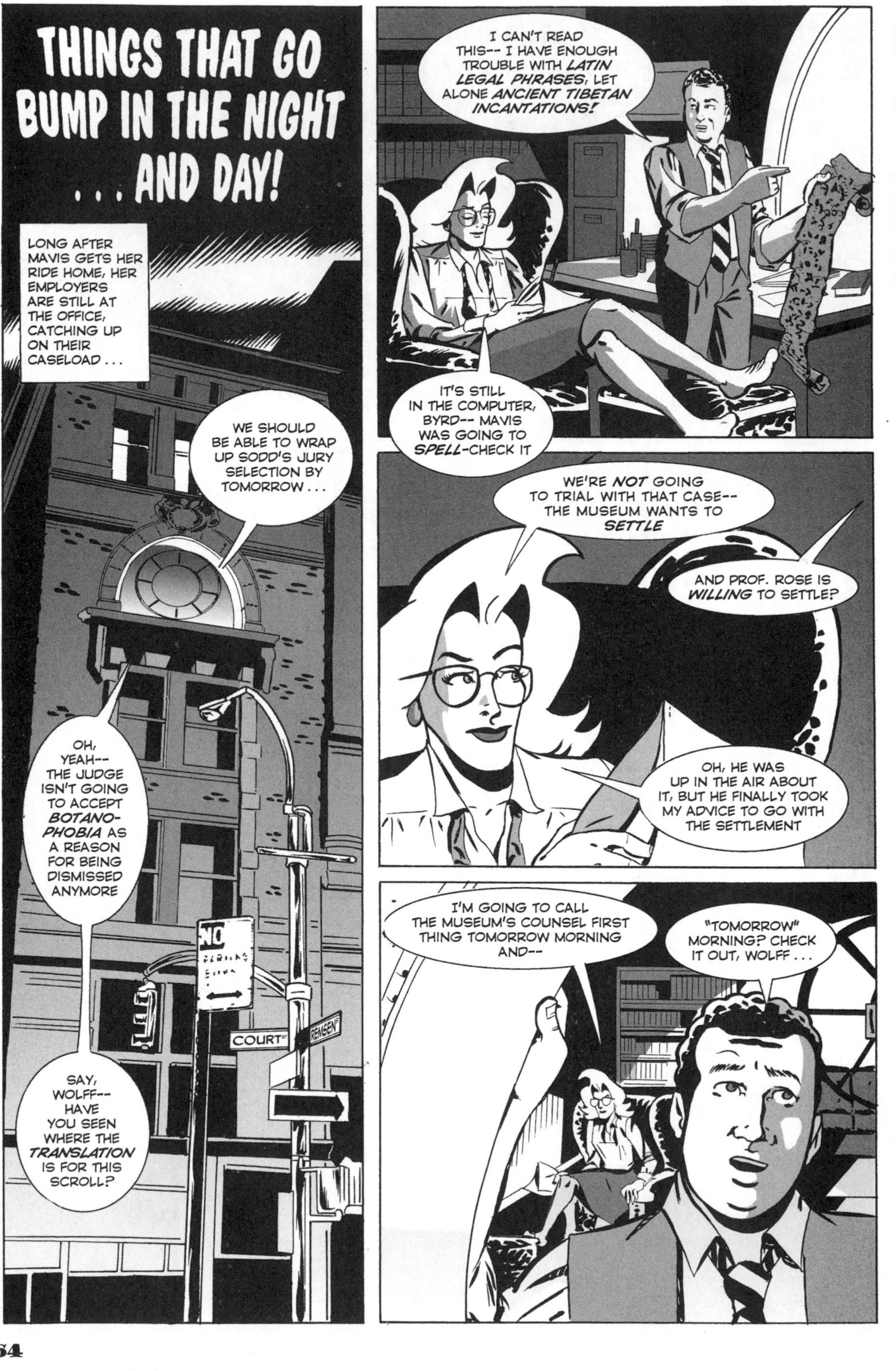
THINGS THAT GO BUMP IN THE NIGHT ...AND DAY!
LONG AFTER MAVIS GETS HER RIDE HOME, HER EMPLOYERS ARE STILL AT THE OFFICE, CATCHING UP ON THEIR CASELOAD . . .
WE SHOULD BE ABLE TO WRAP UP SODD'S JURY SELECTION BY TOMORROW . . .
OH, YEAH-- THE JUDGE ISN'T GOING TO ACCEPT *BOTANO-PHOBIA* AS A REASON FOR BEING DISMISSED ANYMORE
SAY, WOLFF-- HAVE YOU SEEN WHERE THE *TRANSLATION* IS FOR THIS SCROLL?
NO
COURT ST
REMSEN ST
I CAN'T READ THIS-- I HAVE ENOUGH TROUBLE WITH *LATIN LEGAL PHRASES*, LET ALONE *ANCIENT TIBETAN INCANTATIONS!*
IT'S STILL IN THE COMPUTER, BYRD-- MAVIS WAS GOING TO *SPELL*-CHECK IT
WE'RE *NOT* GOING TO TRIAL WITH THAT CASE-- THE MUSEUM WANTS TO *SETTLE*
AND PROF. ROSE IS *WILLING* TO SETTLE?
OH, HE WAS UP IN THE AIR ABOUT IT, BUT HE FINALLY TOOK MY ADVICE TO GO WITH THE SETTLEMENT
I'M GOING TO CALL THE MUSEUM'S COUNSEL FIRST THING TOMORROW MORNING AND--
"TOMORROW" MORNING? CHECK IT OUT, WOLFF . . .

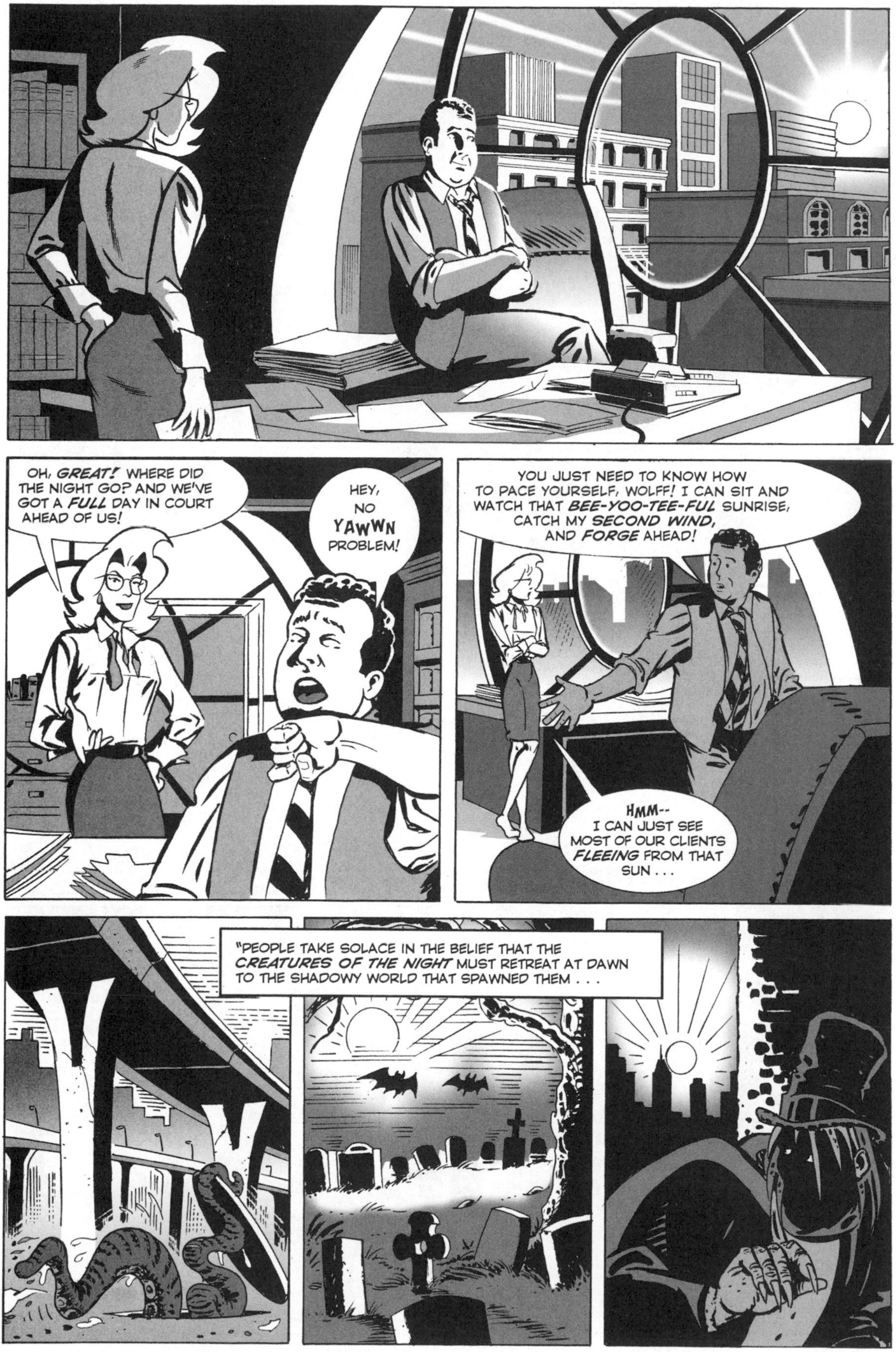

OH, GREAT! WHERE DID THE NIGHT GO? AND WE'VE GOT A FULL DAY IN COURT AHEAD OF US!
HEY, NO YAWWN PROBLEM!
YOU JUST NEED TO KNOW HOW TO PACE YOURSELF, WOLFF! I CAN SIT AND WATCH THAT BEE-YOO-TEE-FUL SUNRISE, CATCH MY SECOND WIND, AND FORGE AHEAD!
HMM-- I CAN JUST SEE MOST OF OUR CLIENTS FLEEING FROM THAT SUN . . .
"PEOPLE TAKE SOLACE IN THE BELIEF THAT THE CREATURES OF THE NIGHT MUST RETREAT AT DAWN TO THE SHADOWY WORLD THAT SPAWNED THEM . . .

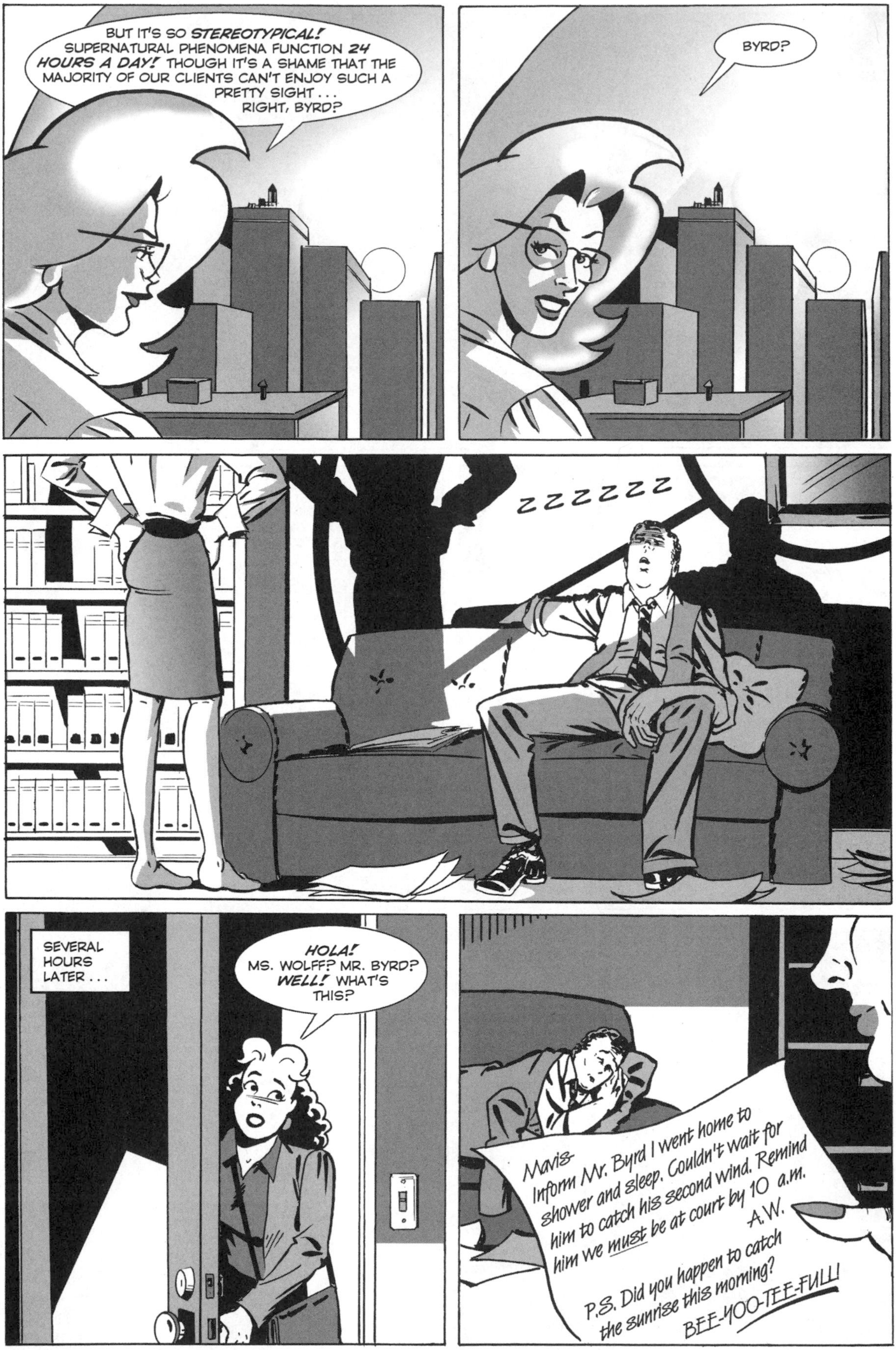
BUT IT'S SO **STEREOTYPICAL!** SUPERNATURAL PHENOMENA FUNCTION **24 HOURS A DAY!** THOUGH IT'S A SHAME THAT THE MAJORITY OF OUR CLIENTS CAN'T ENJOY SUCH A PRETTY SIGHT . . . RIGHT, BYRD?
BYRD?
ZZZZZZ
SEVERAL HOURS LATER . . .
HOLA! MS. WOLFF? MR. BYRD? **WELL!** WHAT'S THIS?
Mavis-
Inform Mr. Byrd I went home to shower and sleep. Couldn't wait for him to catch his second wind. Remind him we must be at court by 10 a.m.
A.W.
P.S. Did you happen to catch the sunrise this morning?
BEE-YOO-TEE-FULL!

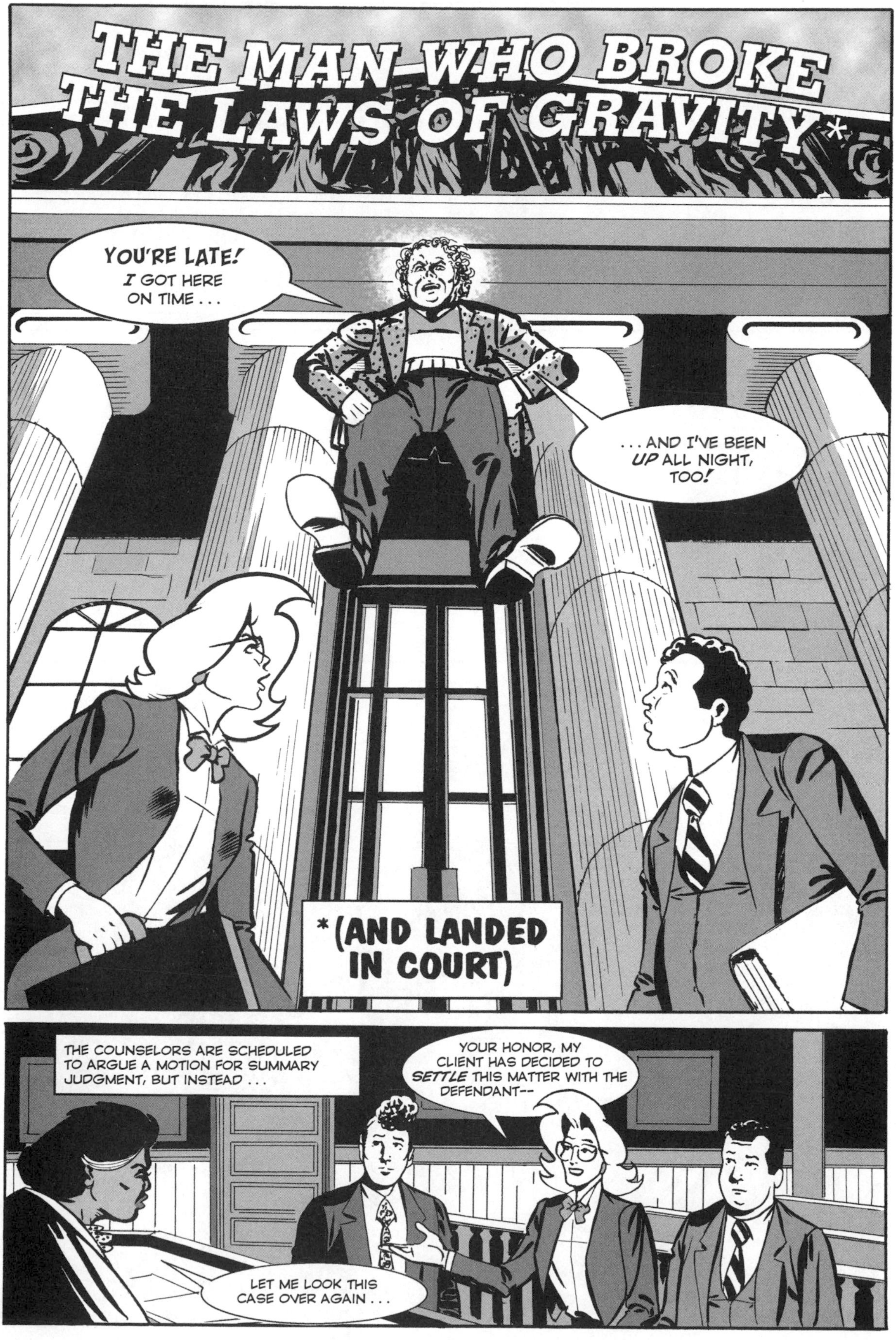
THE MAN WHO BROKE THE LAWS OF GRAVITY*
YOU'RE LATE! I GOT HERE ON TIME . . .
. . . AND I'VE BEEN UP ALL NIGHT, TOO!
*(AND LANDED IN COURT)
THE COUNSELORS ARE SCHEDULED TO ARGUE A MOTION FOR SUMMARY JUDGMENT, BUT INSTEAD . . .
YOUR HONOR, MY CLIENT HAS DECIDED TO SETTLE THIS MATTER WITH THE DEFENDANT--
LET ME LOOK THIS CASE OVER AGAIN . . .

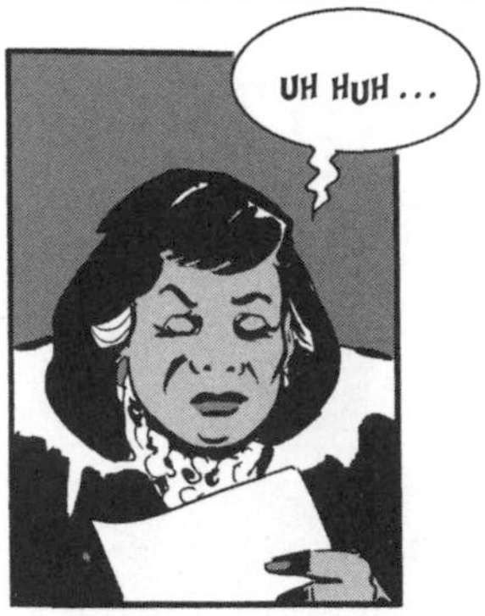
UH HUH . . .

Alanna Wolff, Jeffrey Byrd
Attorneys for the Plaintiff

Professor Lowell M. Rose seeks compensation for personal injuries caused as a result of gross negligence of Blackwood Museum (hereafter, "the Defendant") . . . Rose was hired to catalog artifacts, items, and papers for spring exhibition . . . Rose was told to translate ancient Tibetan scroll containing arcane incantations and spells . . . As Rose orally checked accuracy of ancient writ on levitation, Rose rose, finding himself hovering several feet above his desk. Buoyant at first, he was dismayed to learn he couldn't alight . . . Defendant terminated Rose's employment, citing tampering with museum property and holding up the project . . . Rose requests court to regard his plight, as he now has no visible means of support . . . asks for punitive damages in amount of 20 million dollars, and ownership of Tibetan scrolls, to study for remedy . . .

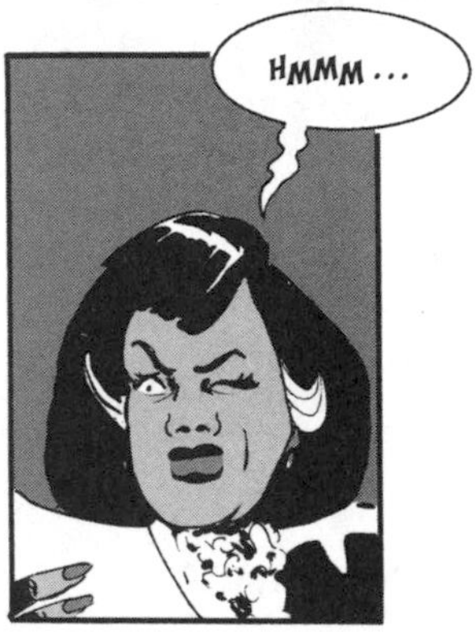
HMMM . . .

Tobias J. Bascoe
Attorney for the Defendant

Plaintiff constantly looked down his nose at Blackwood Museum's owners, curators, and other employees . . . He was upset over not getting a raise, even though Museum was employing him only for duration of exhibit . . . Plaintiff dabbled outside scope of his employment when he practiced spells inscribed on scrolls he was translating, resulting in his present state . . . Learning of Plaintiff's gravity-impaired condition, Museum was willing to work with Plaintiff, to monetary benefit of both. Plaintiff was apparently setting his sights high . . . demanded lofty position on Museum's board and pay scale that would escalate quarterly . . . When Museum would not yield, Plaintiff filed suit . . . Museum fired him, since elevated physical condition put mystic artifacts exhibition behind schedule . . .

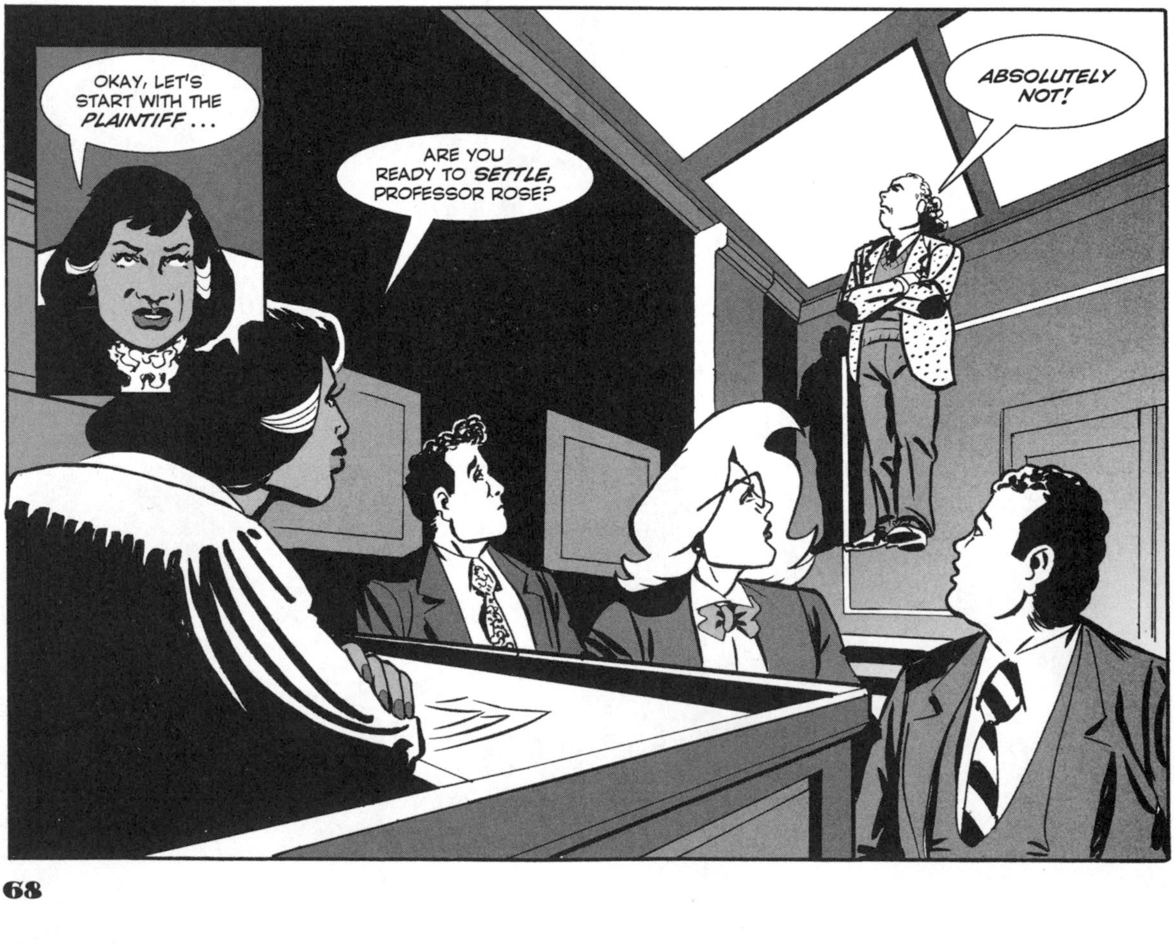
OKAY, LET'S START WITH THE *PLAINTIFF* . . .
ARE YOU READY TO *SETTLE*, PROFESSOR ROSE?
ABSOLUTELY NOT!

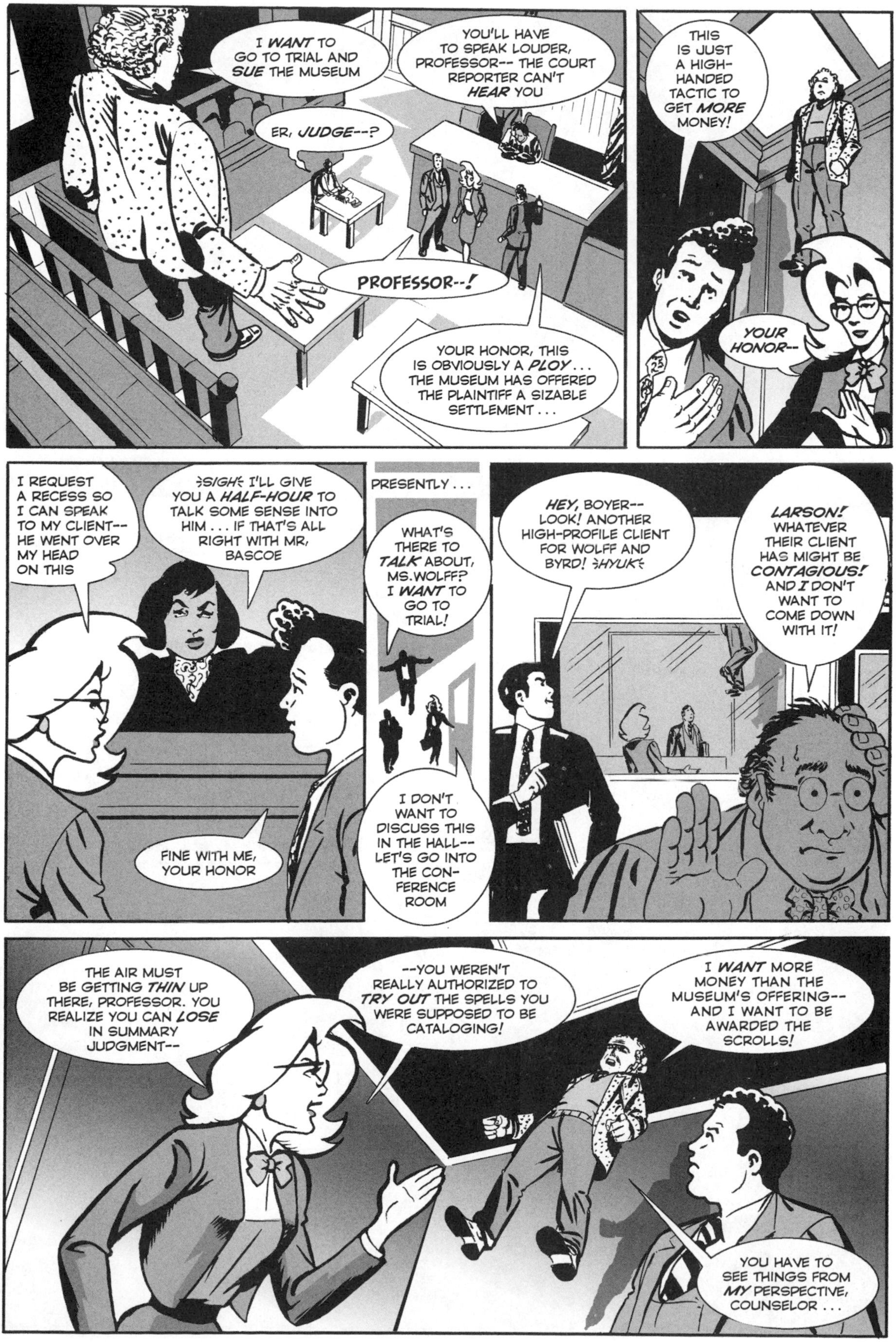
I WANT TO GO TO TRIAL AND SUE THE MUSEUM
YOU'LL HAVE TO SPEAK LOUDER, PROFESSOR-- THE COURT REPORTER CAN'T HEAR YOU
ER, JUDGE--?
PROFESSOR--!
YOUR HONOR, THIS IS OBVIOUSLY A PLOY . . . THE MUSEUM HAS OFFERED THE PLAINTIFF A SIZABLE SETTLEMENT . . .
THIS IS JUST A HIGH-HANDED TACTIC TO GET MORE MONEY!
YOUR HONOR--
I REQUEST A RECESS SO I CAN SPEAK TO MY CLIENT-- HE WENT OVER MY HEAD ON THIS
SIGH I'LL GIVE YOU A HALF-HOUR TO TALK SOME SENSE INTO HIM . . . IF THAT'S ALL RIGHT WITH MR, BASCOE
FINE WITH ME, YOUR HONOR
PRESENTLY . . .
WHAT'S THERE TO TALK ABOUT, MS.WOLFF? I WANT TO GO TO TRIAL!
I DON'T WANT TO DISCUSS THIS IN THE HALL-- LET'S GO INTO THE CONFERENCE ROOM
HEY, BOYER-- LOOK! ANOTHER HIGH-PROFILE CLIENT FOR WOLFF AND BYRD! HYUK
LARSON! WHATEVER THEIR CLIENT HAS MIGHT BE CONTAGIOUS! AND I DON'T WANT TO COME DOWN WITH IT!
THE AIR MUST BE GETTING THIN UP THERE, PROFESSOR. YOU REALIZE YOU CAN LOSE IN SUMMARY JUDGMENT--
--YOU WEREN'T REALLY AUTHORIZED TO TRY OUT THE SPELLS YOU WERE SUPPOSED TO BE CATALOGING!
I WANT MORE MONEY THAN THE MUSEUM'S OFFERING-- AND I WANT TO BE AWARDED THE SCROLLS!
YOU HAVE TO SEE THINGS FROM MY PERSPECTIVE, COUNSELOR . . .

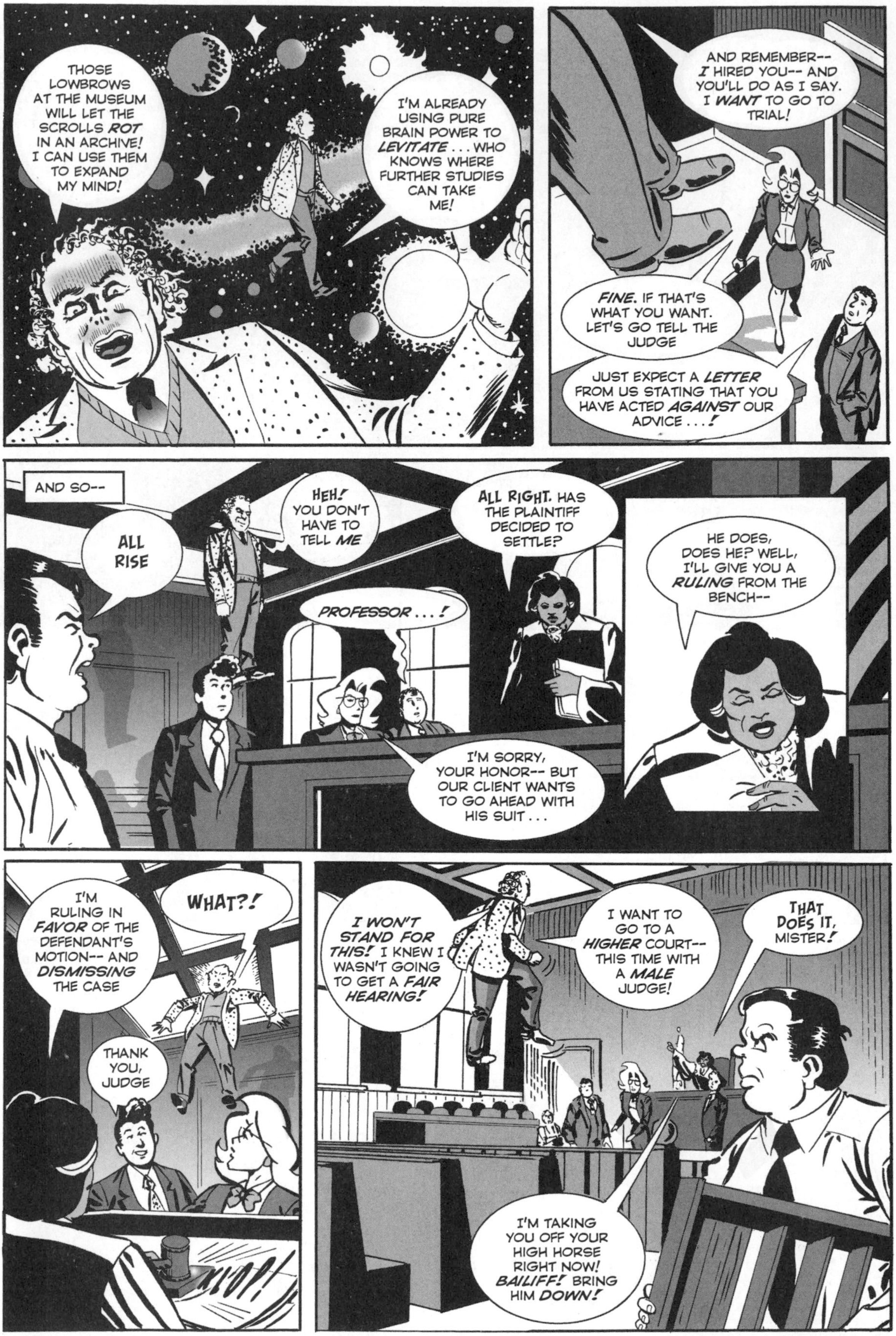
THOSE LOWBROWS AT THE MUSEUM WILL LET THE SCROLLS ROT IN AN ARCHIVE! I CAN USE THEM TO EXPAND MY MIND!
I'M ALREADY USING PURE BRAIN POWER TO LEVITATE . . . WHO KNOWS WHERE FURTHER STUDIES CAN TAKE ME!
AND REMEMBER-- I HIRED YOU-- AND YOU'LL DO AS I SAY. I WANT TO GO TO TRIAL!
FINE. IF THAT'S WHAT YOU WANT. LET'S GO TELL THE JUDGE
JUST EXPECT A LETTER FROM US STATING THAT YOU HAVE ACTED AGAINST OUR ADVICE . . .!
AND SO--
ALL RISE
HEH! YOU DON'T HAVE TO TELL ME
ALL RIGHT. HAS THE PLAINTIFF DECIDED TO SETTLE?
PROFESSOR . . . !
I'M SORRY, YOUR HONOR-- BUT OUR CLIENT WANTS TO GO AHEAD WITH HIS SUIT . . .
HE DOES, DOES HE? WELL, I'LL GIVE YOU A RULING FROM THE BENCH--
I'M RULING IN FAVOR OF THE DEFENDANT'S MOTION-- AND DISMISSING THE CASE
WHAT?!
THANK YOU, JUDGE
I WON'T STAND FOR THIS! I KNEW I WASN'T GOING TO GET A FAIR HEARING!
I WANT TO GO TO A HIGHER COURT-- THIS TIME WITH A MALE JUDGE!
THAT DOES IT, MISTER!
I'M TAKING YOU OFF YOUR HIGH HORSE RIGHT NOW! BAILIFF! BRING HIM DOWN!

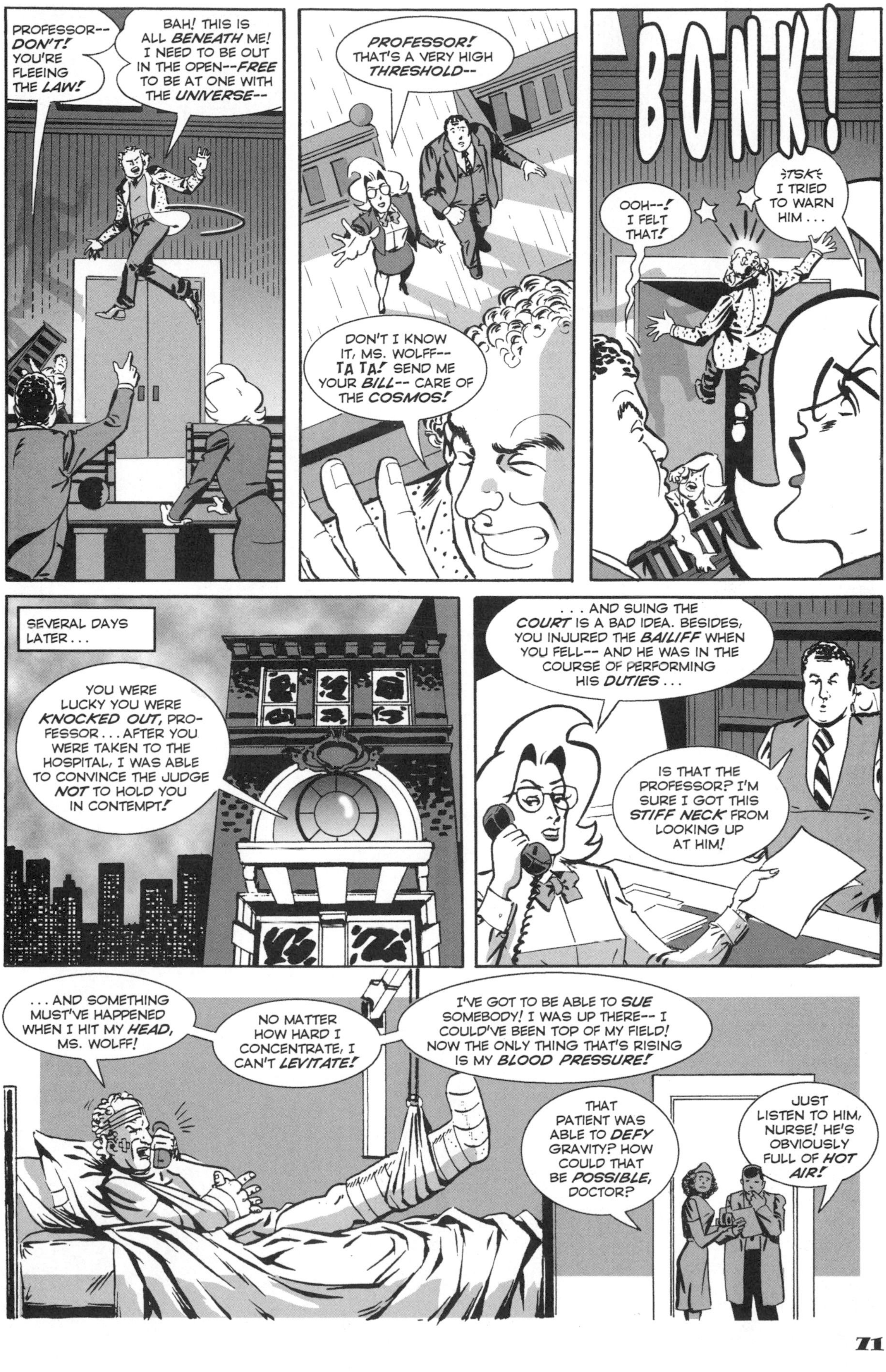
PROFESSOR-- DON'T! YOU'RE FLEEING THE LAW!
BAH! THIS IS ALL BENEATH ME! I NEED TO BE OUT IN THE OPEN--FREE TO BE AT ONE WITH THE UNIVERSE--
PROFESSOR! THAT'S A VERY HIGH THRESHOLD--
DON'T I KNOW IT, MS. WOLFF-- TA TA! SEND ME YOUR BILL-- CARE OF THE COSMOS!
BONK!
OOH--! I FELT THAT!
TSK I TRIED TO WARN HIM . . .
SEVERAL DAYS LATER . . .
YOU WERE LUCKY YOU WERE KNOCKED OUT, PROFESSOR . . . AFTER YOU WERE TAKEN TO THE HOSPITAL, I WAS ABLE TO CONVINCE THE JUDGE NOT TO HOLD YOU IN CONTEMPT!
. . . AND SUING THE COURT IS A BAD IDEA. BESIDES, YOU INJURED THE BAILIFF WHEN YOU FELL-- AND HE WAS IN THE COURSE OF PERFORMING HIS DUTIES . . .
IS THAT THE PROFESSOR? I'M SURE I GOT THIS STIFF NECK FROM LOOKING UP AT HIM!
. . . AND SOMETHING MUST'VE HAPPENED WHEN I HIT MY HEAD, MS. WOLFF!
NO MATTER HOW HARD I CONCENTRATE, I CAN'T LEVITATE!
I'VE GOT TO BE ABLE TO SUE SOMEBODY! I WAS UP THERE-- I COULD'VE BEEN TOP OF MY FIELD! NOW THE ONLY THING THAT'S RISING IS MY BLOOD PRESSURE!
THAT PATIENT WAS ABLE TO DEFY GRAVITY? HOW COULD THAT BE POSSIBLE, DOCTOR?
JUST LISTEN TO HIM, NURSE! HE'S OBVIOUSLY FULL OF HOT AIR!

A Host of Horrors

A HOST OF HORRORS

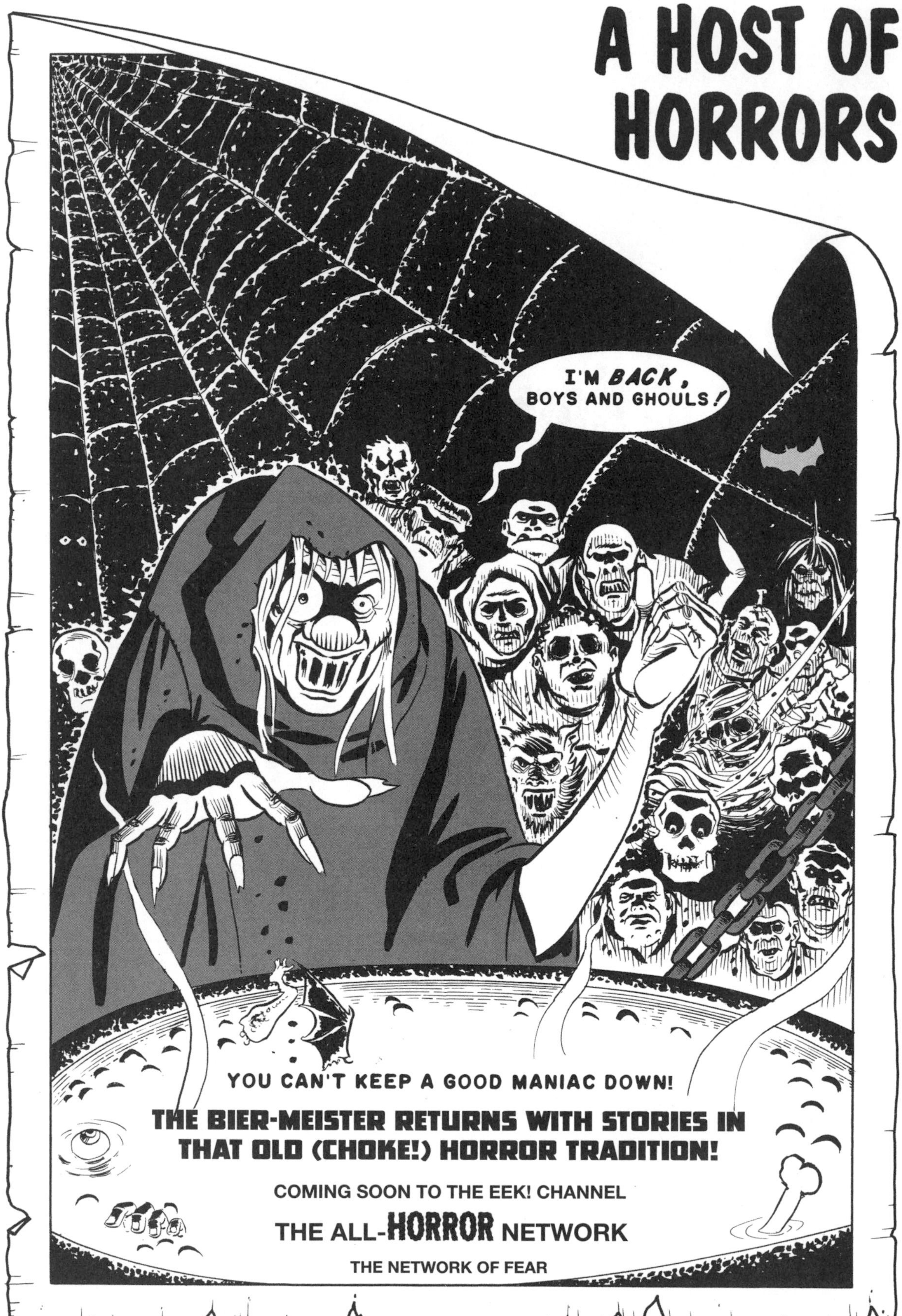

I'M BACK, BOYS AND GHOULS!
YOU CAN'T KEEP A GOOD MANIAC DOWN!
THE BIER-MEISTER RETURNS WITH STORIES IN THAT OLD (CHOKE!) HORROR TRADITION!
COMING SOON TO THE EEK! CHANNEL
THE ALL-HORROR NETWORK
THE NETWORK OF FEAR

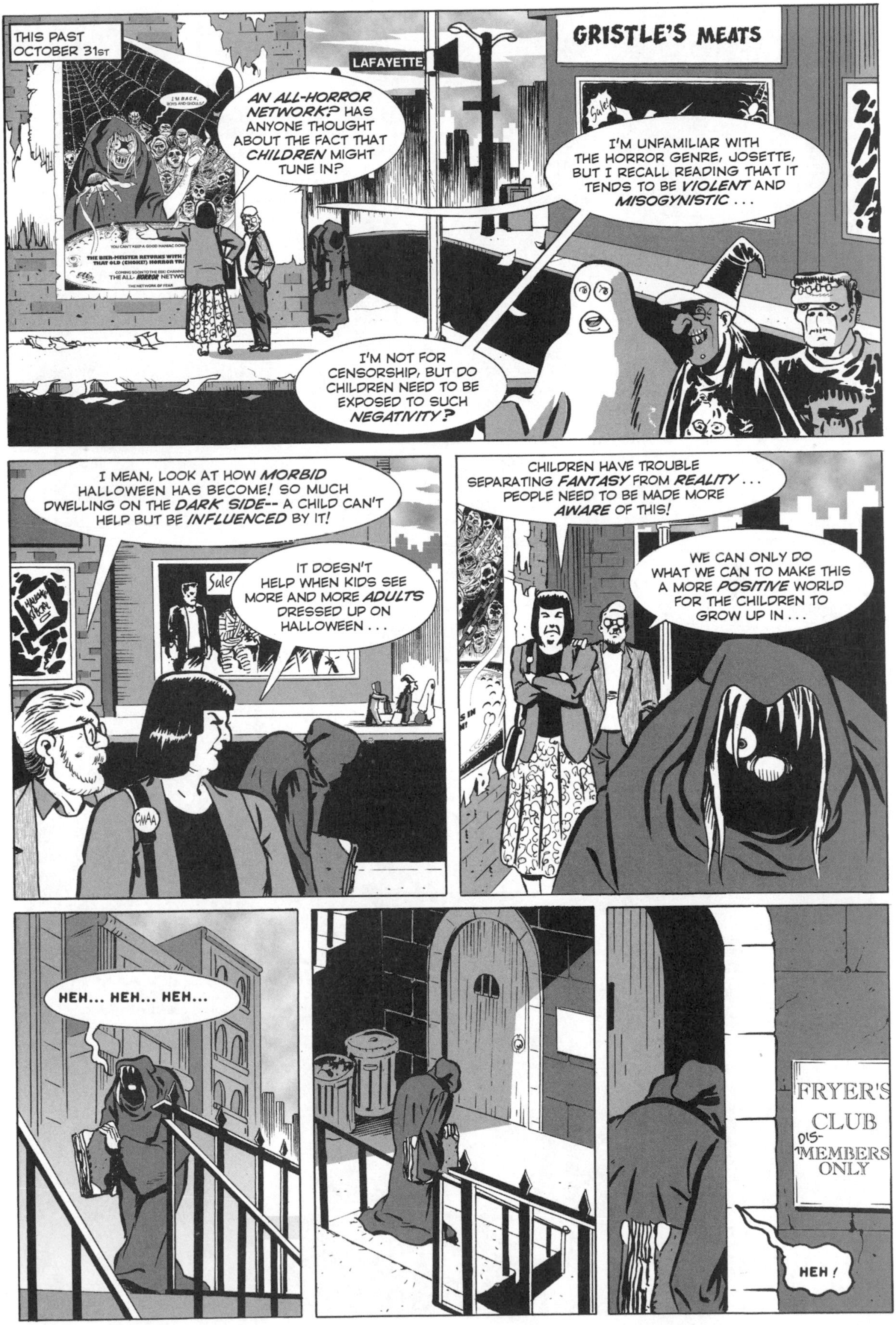
THIS PAST OCTOBER 31ST
LAFAYETTE
GRISTLE'S MEATS
AN ALL-HORROR NETWORK? HAS ANYONE THOUGHT ABOUT THE FACT THAT CHILDREN MIGHT TUNE IN?
I'M UNFAMILIAR WITH THE HORROR GENRE, JOSETTE, BUT I RECALL READING THAT IT TENDS TO BE VIOLENT AND MISOGYNISTIC . . .
I'M NOT FOR CENSORSHIP, BUT DO CHILDREN NEED TO BE EXPOSED TO SUCH NEGATIVITY?
I MEAN, LOOK AT HOW MORBID HALLOWEEN HAS BECOME! SO MUCH DWELLING ON THE DARK SIDE-- A CHILD CAN'T HELP BUT BE INFLUENCED BY IT!
IT DOESN'T HELP WHEN KIDS SEE MORE AND MORE ADULTS DRESSED UP ON HALLOWEEN . . .
CHILDREN HAVE TROUBLE SEPARATING FANTASY FROM REALITY . . . PEOPLE NEED TO BE MADE MORE AWARE OF THIS!
WE CAN ONLY DO WHAT WE CAN TO MAKE THIS A MORE POSITIVE WORLD FOR THE CHILDREN TO GROW UP IN . . .
CMAA
HEH... HEH... HEH...
FRYER'S CLUB DIS-MEMBERS ONLY
HEH!

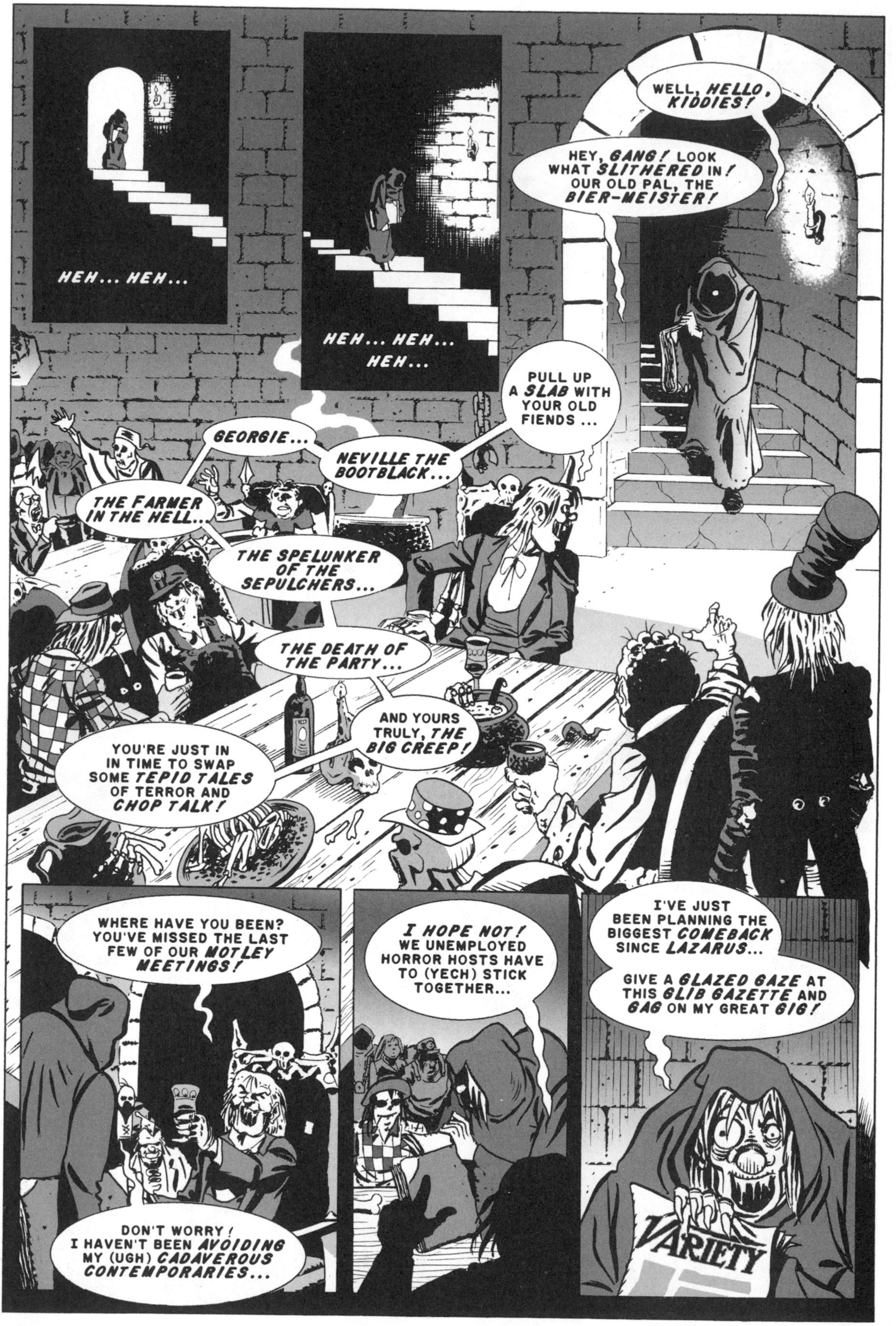
HEH... HEH...
HEH... HEH... HEH...
WELL, HELLO, KIDDIES!
HEY, GANG! LOOK WHAT SLITHERED IN! OUR OLD PAL, THE BIER-MEISTER!
PULL UP A SLAB WITH YOUR OLD FIENDS ...
GEORGIE...
NEVILLE THE BOOTBLACK...
THE FARMER IN THE HELL...
THE SPELUNKER OF THE SEPULCHERS...
THE DEATH OF THE PARTY...
AND YOURS TRULY, THE BIG CREEP!
YOU'RE JUST IN IN TIME TO SWAP SOME TEPID TALES OF TERROR AND CHOP TALK!
WHERE HAVE YOU BEEN? YOU'VE MISSED THE LAST FEW OF OUR MOTLEY MEETINGS!
DON'T WORRY! I HAVEN'T BEEN AVOIDING MY (UGH) CADAVEROUS CONTEMPORARIES...
I HOPE NOT! WE UNEMPLOYED HORROR HOSTS HAVE TO (YECH) STICK TOGETHER...
I'VE JUST BEEN PLANNING THE BIGGEST COMEBACK SINCE LAZARUS...
GIVE A GLAZED GAZE AT THIS GLIB GAZETTE AND GAG ON MY GREAT GIG!
VARIETY

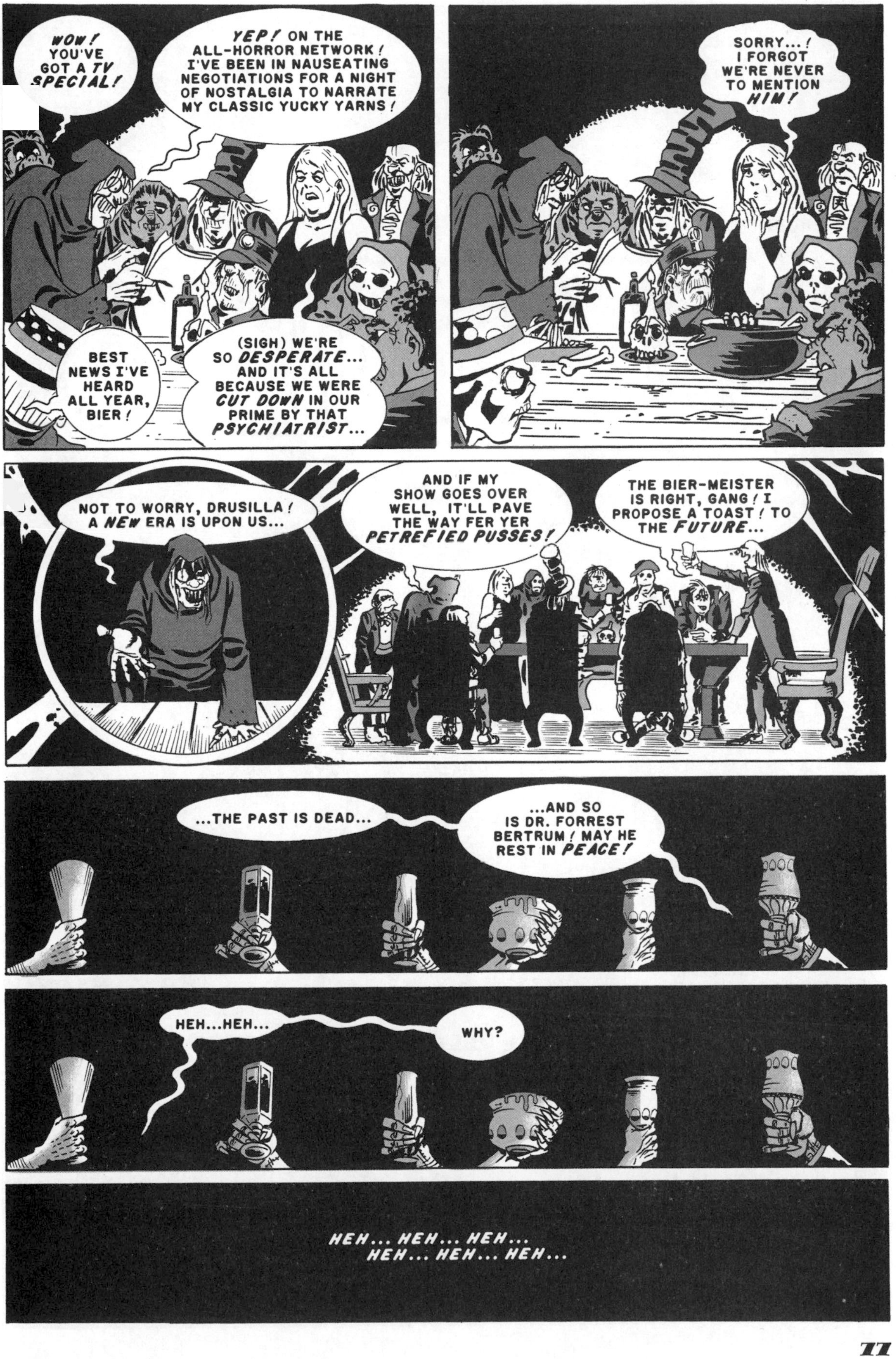
WOW! YOU'VE GOT A TV SPECIAL!
YEP! ON THE ALL-HORROR NETWORK! I'VE BEEN IN NAUSEATING NEGOTIATIONS FOR A NIGHT OF NOSTALGIA TO NARRATE MY CLASSIC YUCKY YARNS!
BEST NEWS I'VE HEARD ALL YEAR, BIER!
(SIGH) WE'RE SO DESPERATE... AND IT'S ALL BECAUSE WE WERE CUT DOWN IN OUR PRIME BY THAT PSYCHIATRIST...
SORRY...! I FORGOT WE'RE NEVER TO MENTION HIM!
NOT TO WORRY, DRUSILLA! A NEW ERA IS UPON US...
AND IF MY SHOW GOES OVER WELL, IT'LL PAVE THE WAY FER YER PETREFIED PUSSES!
THE BIER-MEISTER IS RIGHT, GANG! I PROPOSE A TOAST! TO THE FUTURE...
...THE PAST IS DEAD...
...AND SO IS DR. FORREST BERTRUM! MAY HE REST IN PEACE!
HEH...HEH...
WHY?
HEH... HEH... HEH...
HEH... HEH... HEH...

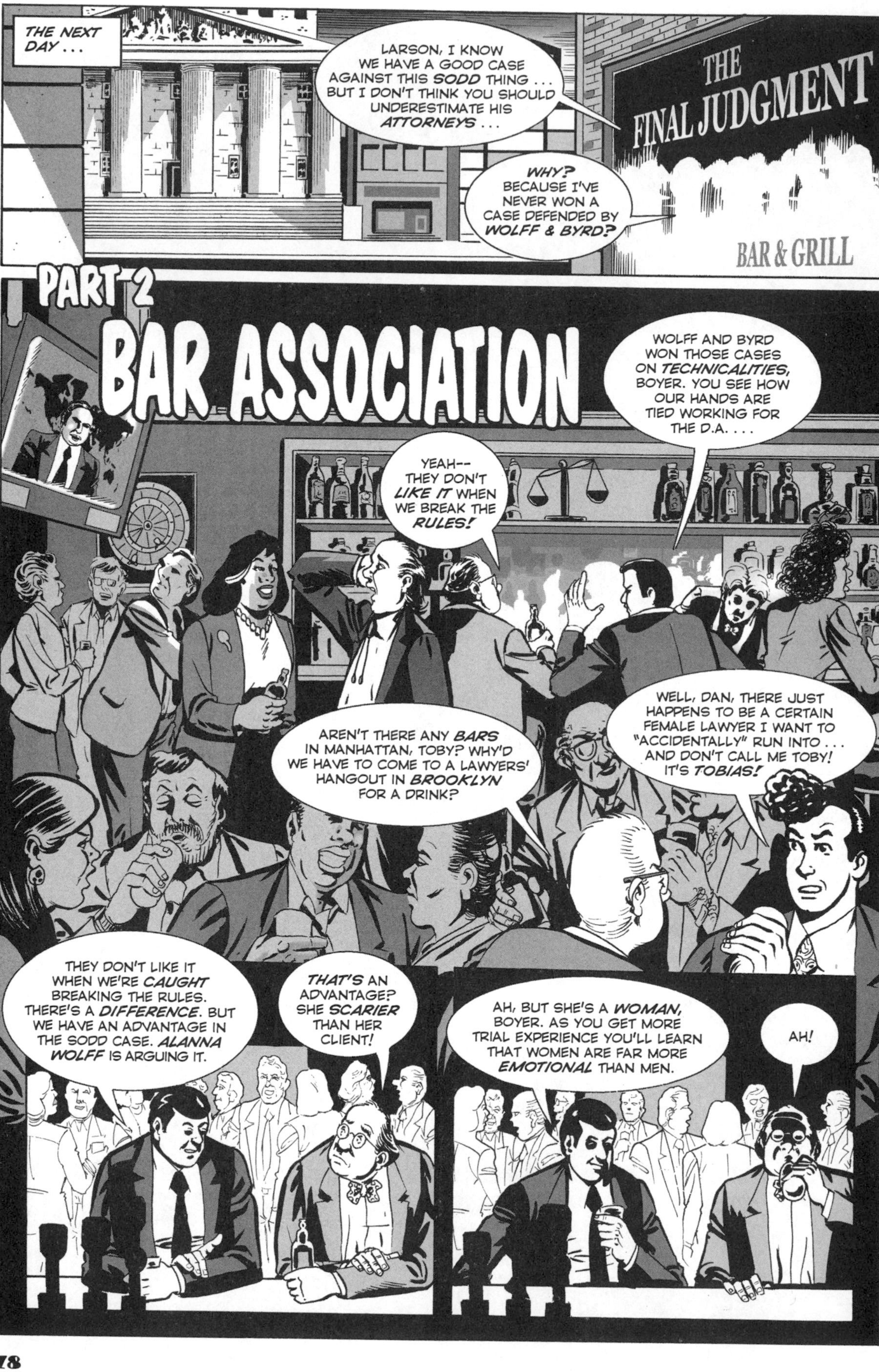
THE NEXT DAY . . .
LARSON, I KNOW WE HAVE A GOOD CASE AGAINST THIS SODD THING . . . BUT I DON'T THINK YOU SHOULD UNDERESTIMATE HIS ATTORNEYS . . .
THE FINAL JUDGMENT
BAR & GRILL
WHY? BECAUSE I'VE NEVER WON A CASE DEFENDED BY WOLFF & BYRD?
PART 2
BAR ASSOCIATION
WOLFF AND BYRD WON THOSE CASES ON TECHNICALITIES, BOYER. YOU SEE HOW OUR HANDS ARE TIED WORKING FOR THE D.A. . . .
YEAH-- THEY DON'T LIKE IT WHEN WE BREAK THE RULES!
AREN'T THERE ANY BARS IN MANHATTAN, TOBY? WHY'D WE HAVE TO COME TO A LAWYERS' HANGOUT IN BROOKLYN FOR A DRINK?
WELL, DAN, THERE JUST HAPPENS TO BE A CERTAIN FEMALE LAWYER I WANT TO "ACCIDENTALLY" RUN INTO . . . AND DON'T CALL ME TOBY! IT'S TOBIAS!
THEY DON'T LIKE IT WHEN WE'RE CAUGHT BREAKING THE RULES. THERE'S A DIFFERENCE. BUT WE HAVE AN ADVANTAGE IN THE SODD CASE. ALANNA WOLFF IS ARGUING IT.
THAT'S AN ADVANTAGE? SHE SCARIER THAN HER CLIENT!
AH, BUT SHE'S A WOMAN, BOYER. AS YOU GET MORE TRIAL EXPERIENCE YOU'LL LEARN THAT WOMEN ARE FAR MORE EMOTIONAL THAN MEN.
AH!

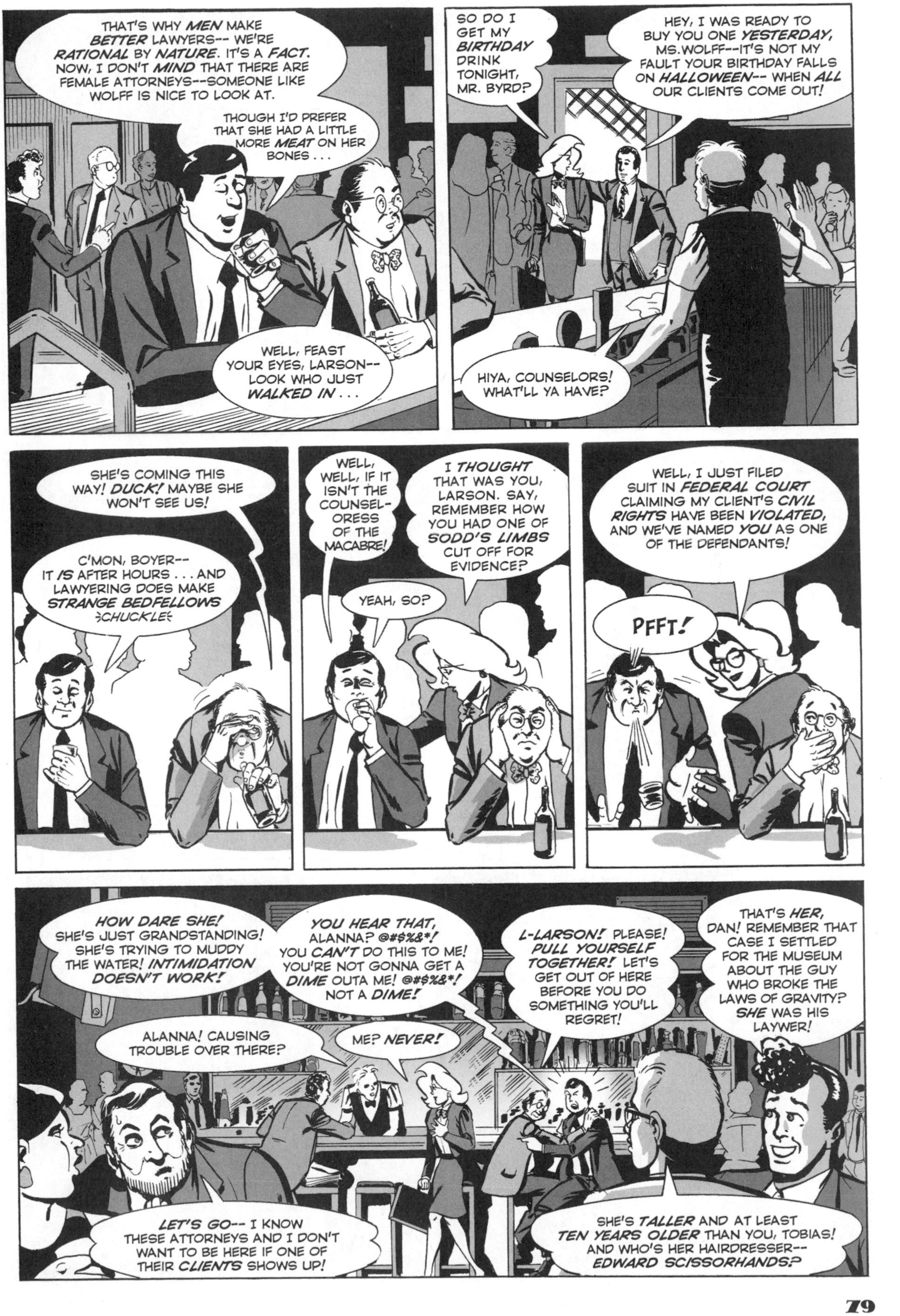

THAT'S WHY MEN MAKE BETTER LAWYERS-- WE'RE RATIONAL BY NATURE. IT'S A FACT. NOW, I DON'T MIND THAT THERE ARE FEMALE ATTORNEYS--SOMEONE LIKE WOLFF IS NICE TO LOOK AT.
THOUGH I'D PREFER THAT SHE HAD A LITTLE MORE MEAT ON HER BONES . . .
WELL, FEAST YOUR EYES, LARSON-- LOOK WHO JUST WALKED IN . . .
SO DO I GET MY BIRTHDAY DRINK TONIGHT, MR. BYRD?
HEY, I WAS READY TO BUY YOU ONE YESTERDAY, MS.WOLFF--IT'S NOT MY FAULT YOUR BIRTHDAY FALLS ON HALLOWEEN-- WHEN ALL OUR CLIENTS COME OUT!
HIYA, COUNSELORS! WHAT'LL YA HAVE?
SHE'S COMING THIS WAY! DUCK! MAYBE SHE WON'T SEE US!
C'MON, BOYER-- IT IS AFTER HOURS . . . AND LAWYERING DOES MAKE STRANGE BEDFELLOWS
CHUCKLE
WELL, WELL, IF IT ISN'T THE COUNSEL-ORESS OF THE MACABRE!
I THOUGHT THAT WAS YOU, LARSON. SAY, REMEMBER HOW YOU HAD ONE OF SODD'S LIMBS CUT OFF FOR EVIDENCE?
YEAH, SO?
WELL, I JUST FILED SUIT IN FEDERAL COURT CLAIMING MY CLIENT'S CIVIL RIGHTS HAVE BEEN VIOLATED, AND WE'VE NAMED YOU AS ONE OF THE DEFENDANTS!
PFFT!
HOW DARE SHE! SHE'S JUST GRANDSTANDING! SHE'S TRYING TO MUDDY THE WATER! INTIMIDATION DOESN'T WORK!
YOU HEAR THAT, ALANNA? @#$%&*! YOU CAN'T DO THIS TO ME! YOU'RE NOT GONNA GET A DIME OUTA ME! @#$%&*! NOT A DIME!
L-LARSON! PLEASE! PULL YOURSELF TOGETHER! LET'S GET OUT OF HERE BEFORE YOU DO SOMETHING YOU'LL REGRET!
THAT'S HER, DAN! REMEMBER THAT CASE I SETTLED FOR THE MUSEUM ABOUT THE GUY WHO BROKE THE LAWS OF GRAVITY? SHE WAS HIS LAYWER!
ALANNA! CAUSING TROUBLE OVER THERE?
ME? NEVER!
LET'S GO-- I KNOW THESE ATTORNEYS AND I DON'T WANT TO BE HERE IF ONE OF THEIR CLIENTS SHOWS UP!
SHE'S TALLER AND AT LEAST TEN YEARS OLDER THAN YOU, TOBIAS! AND WHO'S HER HAIRDRESSER-- EDWARD SCISSORHANDS?

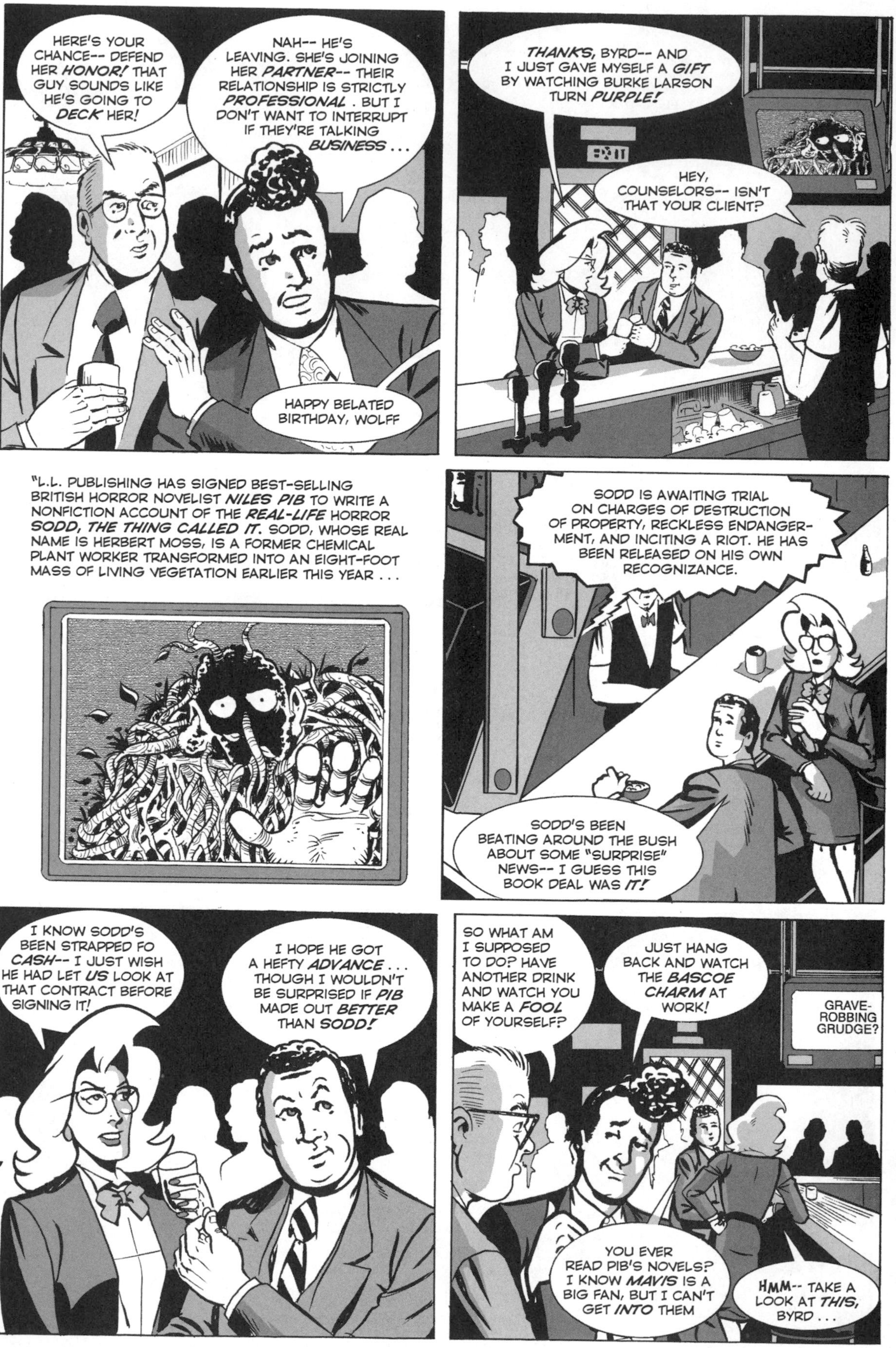
HERE'S YOUR CHANCE-- DEFEND HER HONOR! THAT GUY SOUNDS LIKE HE'S GOING TO DECK HER!
NAH-- HE'S LEAVING. SHE'S JOINING HER PARTNER-- THEIR RELATIONSHIP IS STRICTLY PROFESSIONAL . BUT I DON'T WANT TO INTERRUPT IF THEY'RE TALKING BUSINESS . . .
HAPPY BELATED BIRTHDAY, WOLFF
THANKS, BYRD-- AND I JUST GAVE MYSELF A GIFT BY WATCHING BURKE LARSON TURN PURPLE!
HEY, COUNSELORS-- ISN'T THAT YOUR CLIENT?
"L.L. PUBLISHING HAS SIGNED BEST-SELLING BRITISH HORROR NOVELIST NILES PIB TO WRITE A NONFICTION ACCOUNT OF THE REAL-LIFE HORROR SODD, THE THING CALLED IT. SODD, WHOSE REAL NAME IS HERBERT MOSS, IS A FORMER CHEMICAL PLANT WORKER TRANSFORMED INTO AN EIGHT-FOOT MASS OF LIVING VEGETATION EARLIER THIS YEAR . . .
SODD IS AWAITING TRIAL ON CHARGES OF DESTRUCTION OF PROPERTY, RECKLESS ENDANGERMENT, AND INCITING A RIOT. HE HAS BEEN RELEASED ON HIS OWN RECOGNIZANCE.
SODD'S BEEN BEATING AROUND THE BUSH ABOUT SOME "SURPRISE" NEWS-- I GUESS THIS BOOK DEAL WAS IT!
I KNOW SODD'S BEEN STRAPPED FO CASH-- I JUST WISH HE HAD LET US LOOK AT THAT CONTRACT BEFORE SIGNING IT!
I HOPE HE GOT A HEFTY ADVANCE . . . THOUGH I WOULDN'T BE SURPRISED IF PIB MADE OUT BETTER THAN SODD!
SO WHAT AM I SUPPOSED TO DO? HAVE ANOTHER DRINK AND WATCH YOU MAKE A FOOL OF YOURSELF?
JUST HANG BACK AND WATCH THE BASCOE CHARM AT WORK!
GRAVE-ROBBING GRUDGE?
YOU EVER READ PIB'S NOVELS? I KNOW MAVIS IS A BIG FAN, BUT I CAN'T GET INTO THEM
HMM-- TAKE A LOOK AT THIS, BYRD . . .

"A *GRAVE-ROBBING* INCIDENT OCCURRED EARLY THIS MORNING AT ST. WILLIAMS CEMETERY. AFTER RESPONDING TO CALLS COMPLAINING OF LOUD NOISES COMING FROM THE CEMETERY, THE POLICE CAME UPON A GROUP OF PEOPLE HUDDLED AROUND THE OPEN *GRAVE* OF *DR. FORREST BERTRUM,* A NOTED PSYCHIATRIST WHO DIED LAST YEAR. THE BODY WAS NOWHERE TO BE FOUND.

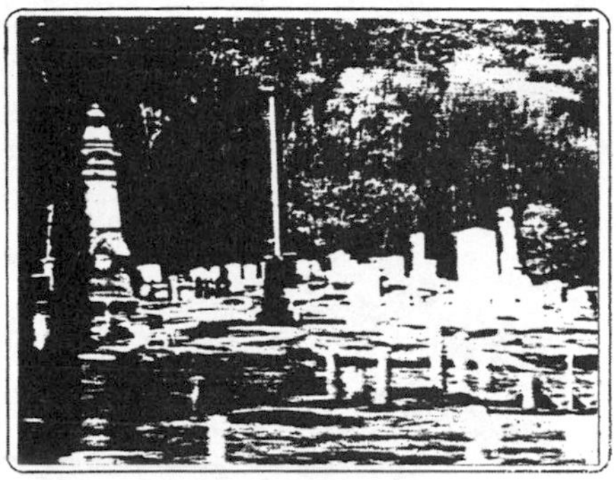

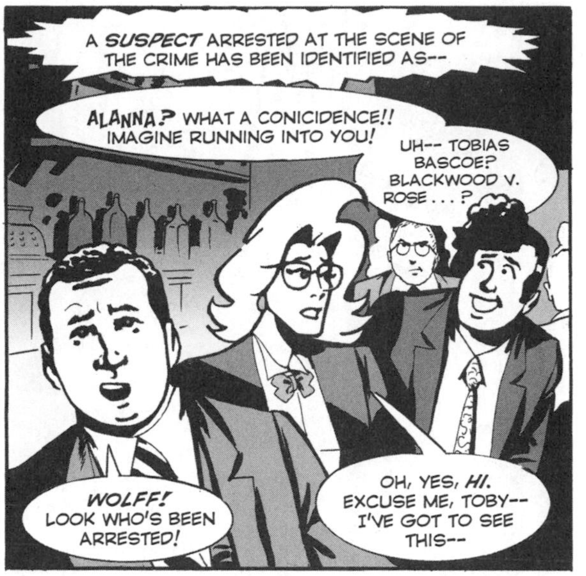
A *SUSPECT* ARRESTED AT THE SCENE OF THE CRIME HAS BEEN IDENTIFIED AS--
ALANNA? WHAT A CONICIDENCE!! IMAGINE RUNNING INTO YOU!
UH-- TOBIAS BASCOE? BLACKWOOD V. ROSE . . . ?
WOLFF! LOOK WHO'S BEEN ARRESTED!
OH, YES, *HI.* EXCUSE ME, TOBY-- I'VE GOT TO SEE THIS--

"THE BIER-MEISTER IS A *GHOUL* WHOSE CELEBRITY CAME 40 YEARS AGO AS A "HORROR HOST" WHO SPUN *VIOLENT* TALES OF THE *SUPERNATURAL* FOR PRIMARILY A *YOUNG* AUDIENCE. A GHOUL IS BELIEVED TO *FEAST* ON THE LIVING OR DEAD *FLESH* OF HUMANS. THE BIER-MEISTER CLAIMS TO BE A STRICT VEGETARIAN . . .

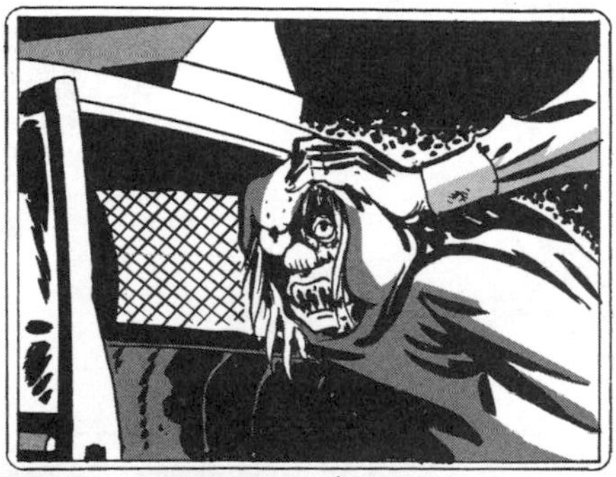

"THE HORROR HOST PROFESSION SUFFERED A *SEVERE BLOW* IN THE *1950S* WHEN DR. BERTRUM RELEASED A STUDY *LINKING* HORROR STORIES TO *JUVENILE DELINQUENCY.* ALTHOUGH BERTRUM'S THEORIES WERE *NEVER* PROVEN, HE INFLUENCED PARENTS' GROUPS TO URGE *CONGRESS* TO PASS A LAW *BANNING* HORROR STORIES FOR ANYONE UNDER THE AGE OF 18. THE HORROR HOSTS CALLED IT QUITS *BEFORE* ANY SUCH LAW COULD BE INTRODUCED . . .

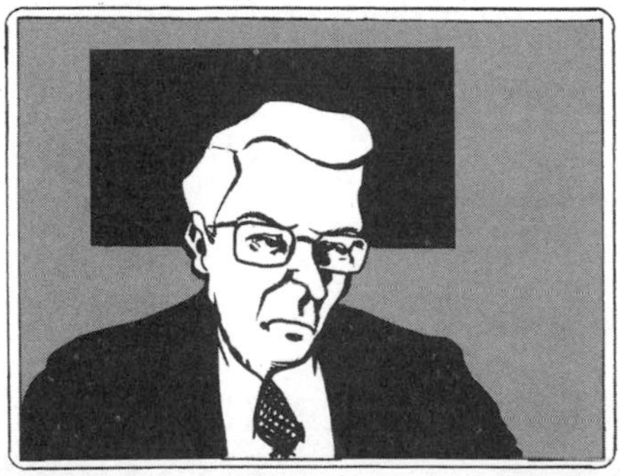

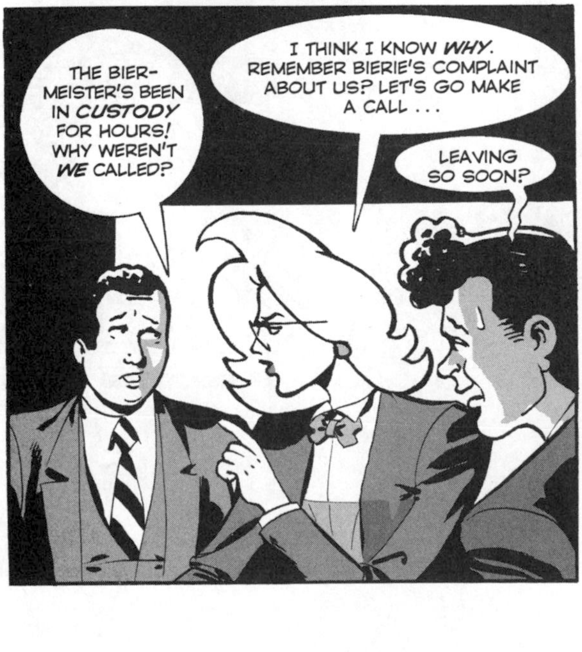
THE BIER-MEISTER'S BEEN IN *CUSTODY* FOR HOURS! WHY WEREN'T *WE* CALLED?
I THINK I KNOW *WHY.* REMEMBER BIERIE'S COMPLAINT ABOUT US? LET'S GO MAKE A CALL . . .
LEAVING SO SOON?

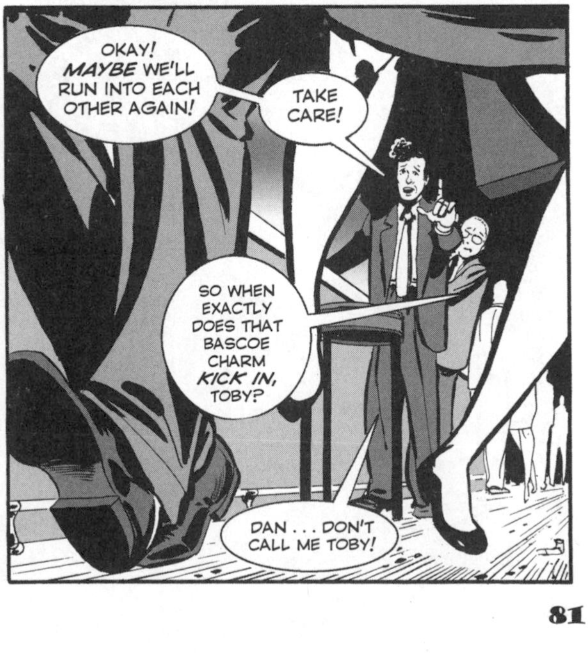
OKAY! *MAYBE* WE'LL RUN INTO EACH OTHER AGAIN!
TAKE CARE!
SO WHEN EXACTLY DOES THAT BASCOE CHARM *KICK IN,* TOBY?
DAN . . . DON'T CALL ME TOBY!

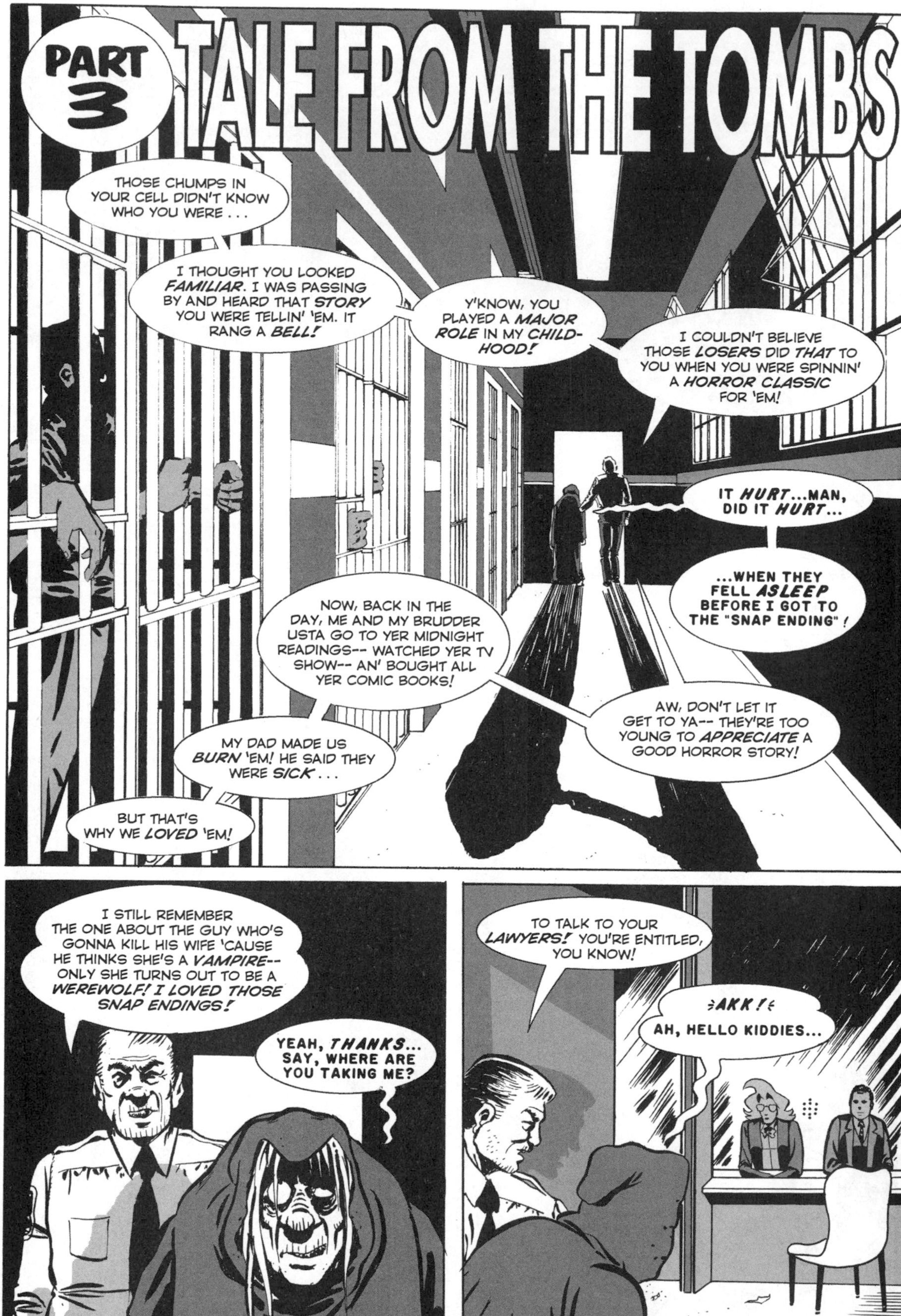
PART 3
TALE FROM THE TOMBS
THOSE CHUMPS IN YOUR CELL DIDN'T KNOW WHO YOU WERE . . .
I THOUGHT YOU LOOKED FAMILIAR. I WAS PASSING BY AND HEARD THAT STORY YOU WERE TELLIN' 'EM. IT RANG A BELL!
Y'KNOW, YOU PLAYED A MAJOR ROLE IN MY CHILD-HOOD!
I COULDN'T BELIEVE THOSE LOSERS DID THAT TO YOU WHEN YOU WERE SPINNIN' A HORROR CLASSIC FOR 'EM!
IT HURT...MAN, DID IT HURT...
...WHEN THEY FELL ASLEEP BEFORE I GOT TO THE "SNAP ENDING"!
NOW, BACK IN THE DAY, ME AND MY BRUDDER USTA GO TO YER MIDNIGHT READINGS-- WATCHED YER TV SHOW-- AN' BOUGHT ALL YER COMIC BOOKS!
AW, DON'T LET IT GET TO YA-- THEY'RE TOO YOUNG TO APPRECIATE A GOOD HORROR STORY!
MY DAD MADE US BURN 'EM! HE SAID THEY WERE SICK . . .
BUT THAT'S WHY WE LOVED 'EM!
I STILL REMEMBER THE ONE ABOUT THE GUY WHO'S GONNA KILL HIS WIFE 'CAUSE HE THINKS SHE'S A VAMPIRE-- ONLY SHE TURNS OUT TO BE A WEREWOLF! I LOVED THOSE SNAP ENDINGS!
YEAH, THANKS... SAY, WHERE ARE YOU TAKING ME?
TO TALK TO YOUR LAWYERS! YOU'RE ENTITLED, YOU KNOW!
AKK!
AH, HELLO KIDDIES...

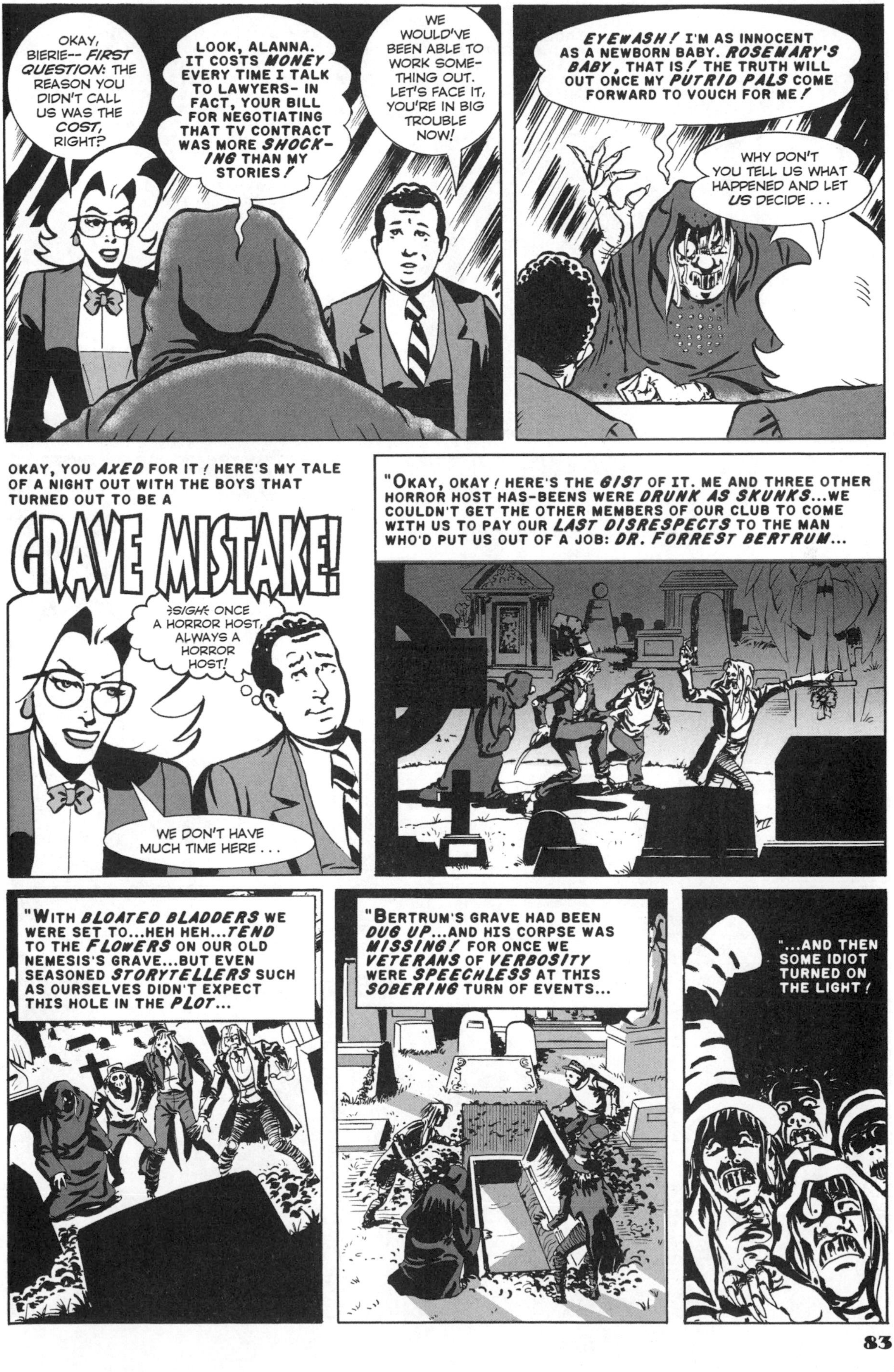

OKAY, BIERIE-- FIRST QUESTION: THE REASON YOU DIDN'T CALL US WAS THE COST, RIGHT?
LOOK, ALANNA. IT COSTS MONEY EVERY TIME I TALK TO LAWYERS- IN FACT, YOUR BILL FOR NEGOTIATING THAT TV CONTRACT WAS MORE SHOCK-ING THAN MY STORIES!
WE WOULD'VE BEEN ABLE TO WORK SOME-THING OUT. LET'S FACE IT, YOU'RE IN BIG TROUBLE NOW!
EYEWASH! I'M AS INNOCENT AS A NEWBORN BABY. ROSEMARY'S BABY, THAT IS! THE TRUTH WILL OUT ONCE MY PUTRID PALS COME FORWARD TO VOUCH FOR ME!
WHY DON'T YOU TELL US WHAT HAPPENED AND LET US DECIDE . . .
OKAY, YOU AXED FOR IT! HERE'S MY TALE OF A NIGHT OUT WITH THE BOYS THAT TURNED OUT TO BE A
GRAVE MISTAKE!
SIGH ONCE A HORROR HOST, ALWAYS A HORROR HOST!
WE DON'T HAVE MUCH TIME HERE . . .
"OKAY, OKAY! HERE'S THE GIST OF IT. ME AND THREE OTHER HORROR HOST HAS-BEENS WERE DRUNK AS SKUNKS...WE COULDN'T GET THE OTHER MEMBERS OF OUR CLUB TO COME WITH US TO PAY OUR LAST DISRESPECTS TO THE MAN WHO'D PUT US OUT OF A JOB: DR. FORREST BERTRUM...
"WITH BLOATED BLADDERS WE WERE SET TO...HEH HEH...TEND TO THE FLOWERS ON OUR OLD NEMESIS'S GRAVE...BUT EVEN SEASONED STORYTELLERS SUCH AS OURSELVES DIDN'T EXPECT THIS HOLE IN THE PLOT...
"BERTRUM'S GRAVE HAD BEEN DUG UP...AND HIS CORPSE WAS MISSING! FOR ONCE WE VETERANS OF VERBOSITY WERE SPEECHLESS AT THIS SOBERING TURN OF EVENTS...
"...AND THEN SOME IDIOT TURNED ON THE LIGHT!

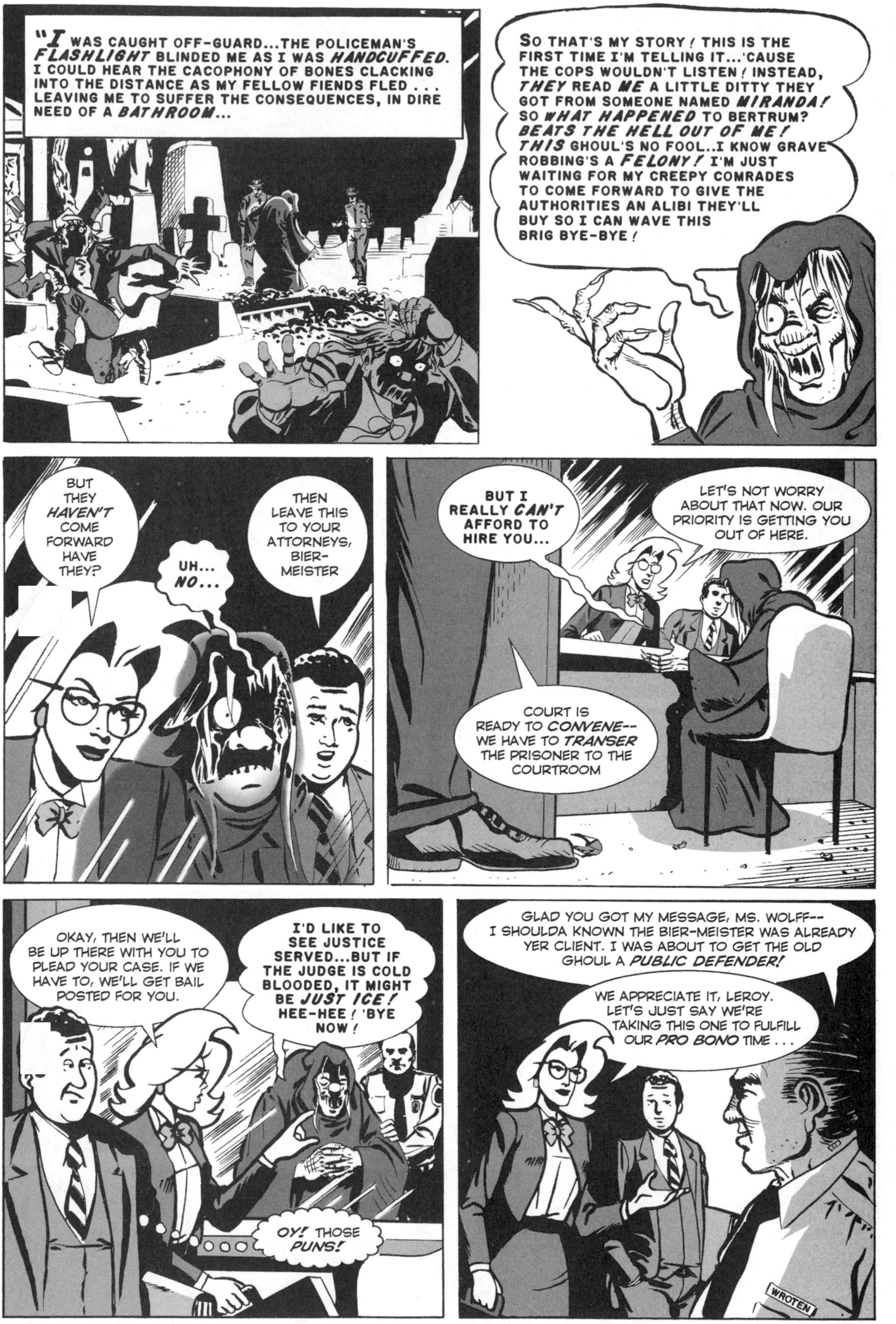

"I WAS CAUGHT OFF-GUARD...THE POLICEMAN'S FLASHLIGHT BLINDED ME AS I WAS HANDCUFFED. I COULD HEAR THE CACOPHONY OF BONES CLACKING INTO THE DISTANCE AS MY FELLOW FIENDS FLED . . . LEAVING ME TO SUFFER THE CONSEQUENCES, IN DIRE NEED OF A BATHROOM...
SO THAT'S MY STORY! THIS IS THE FIRST TIME I'M TELLING IT...'CAUSE THE COPS WOULDN'T LISTEN! INSTEAD, THEY READ ME A LITTLE DITTY THEY GOT FROM SOMEONE NAMED MIRANDA! SO WHAT HAPPENED TO BERTRUM? BEATS THE HELL OUT OF ME! THIS GHOUL'S NO FOOL..I KNOW GRAVE ROBBING'S A FELONY! I'M JUST WAITING FOR MY CREEPY COMRADES TO COME FORWARD TO GIVE THE AUTHORITIES AN ALIBI THEY'LL BUY SO I CAN WAVE THIS BRIG BYE-BYE!
BUT THEY HAVEN'T COME FORWARD HAVE THEY?
UH... NO...
THEN LEAVE THIS TO YOUR ATTORNEYS, BIER-MEISTER
BUT I REALLY CAN'T AFFORD TO HIRE YOU...
LET'S NOT WORRY ABOUT THAT NOW. OUR PRIORITY IS GETTING YOU OUT OF HERE.
COURT IS READY TO CONVENE-- WE HAVE TO TRANSER THE PRISONER TO THE COURTROOM
OKAY, THEN WE'LL BE UP THERE WITH YOU TO PLEAD YOUR CASE. IF WE HAVE TO, WE'LL GET BAIL POSTED FOR YOU.
I'D LIKE TO SEE JUSTICE SERVED...BUT IF THE JUDGE IS COLD BLOODED, IT MIGHT BE JUST ICE! HEE-HEE! 'BYE NOW!
OY! THOSE PUNS!
GLAD YOU GOT MY MESSAGE, MS. WOLFF-- I SHOULDA KNOWN THE BIER-MEISTER WAS ALREADY YER CLIENT. I WAS ABOUT TO GET THE OLD GHOUL A PUBLIC DEFENDER!
WE APPRECIATE IT, LEROY. LET'S JUST SAY WE'RE TAKING THIS ONE TO FULFILL OUR PRO BONO TIME . . .
WROTEN

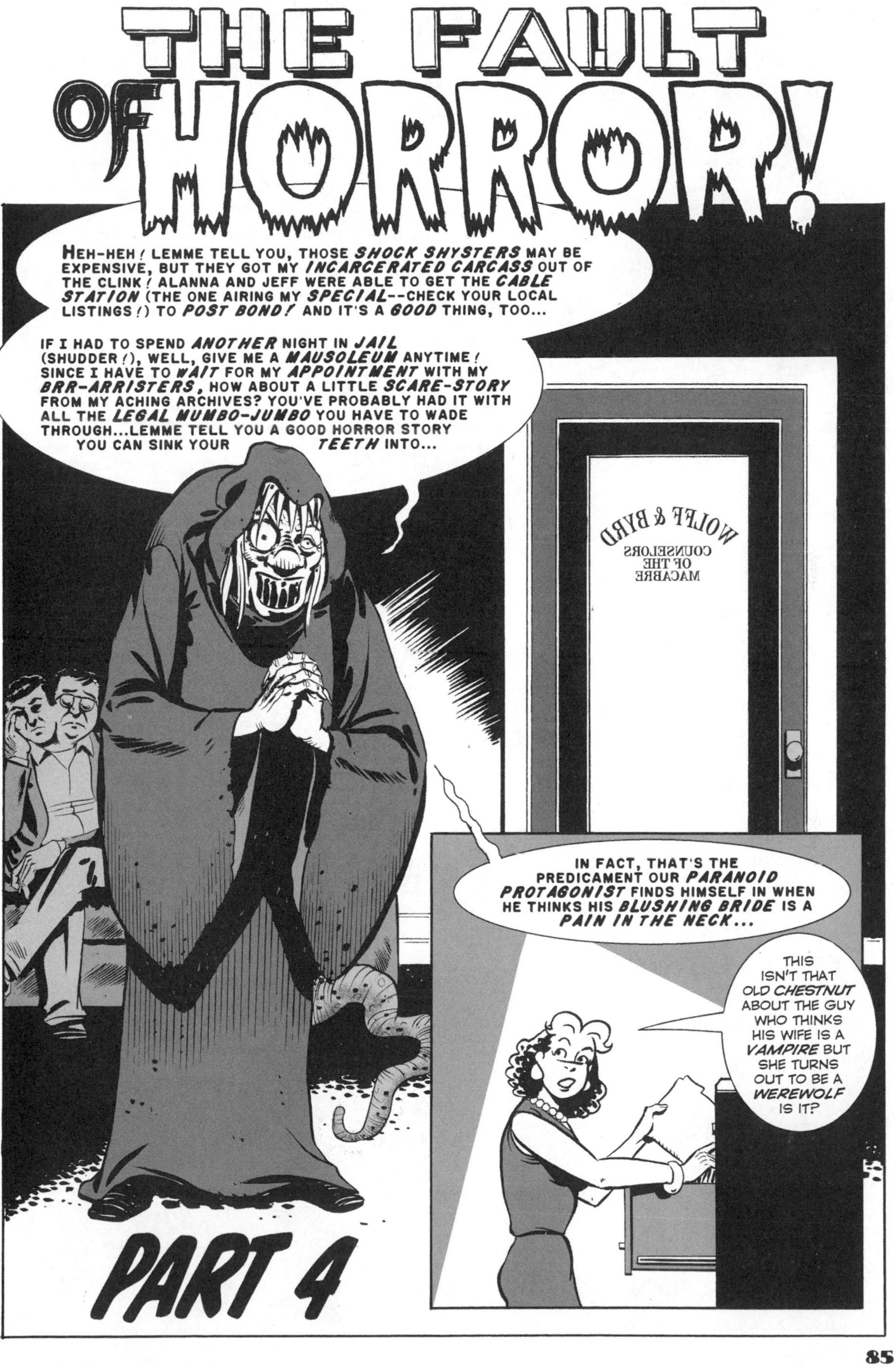
THE FAULT OF HORROR!
HEH-HEH! LEMME TELL YOU, THOSE SHOCK SHYSTERS MAY BE EXPENSIVE, BUT THEY GOT MY INCARCERATED CARCASS OUT OF THE CLINK! ALANNA AND JEFF WERE ABLE TO GET THE CABLE STATION (THE ONE AIRING MY SPECIAL--CHECK YOUR LOCAL LISTINGS!) TO POST BOND! AND IT'S A GOOD THING, TOO...
IF I HAD TO SPEND ANOTHER NIGHT IN JAIL (SHUDDER!), WELL, GIVE ME A MAUSOLEUM ANYTIME! SINCE I HAVE TO WAIT FOR MY APPOINTMENT WITH MY BRR-ARRISTERS, HOW ABOUT A LITTLE SCARE-STORY FROM MY ACHING ARCHIVES? YOU'VE PROBABLY HAD IT WITH ALL THE LEGAL MUMBO-JUMBO YOU HAVE TO WADE THROUGH...LEMME TELL YOU A GOOD HORROR STORY YOU CAN SINK YOUR TEETH INTO...
WOLFF & BYRD COUNSELORS OF THE MACABRE
IN FACT, THAT'S THE PREDICAMENT OUR PARANOID PROTAGONIST FINDS HIMSELF IN WHEN HE THINKS HIS BLUSHING BRIDE IS A PAIN IN THE NECK...
THIS ISN'T THAT OLD CHESTNUT ABOUT THE GUY WHO THINKS HIS WIFE IS A VAMPIRE BUT SHE TURNS OUT TO BE A WEREWOLF IS IT?
PART 4

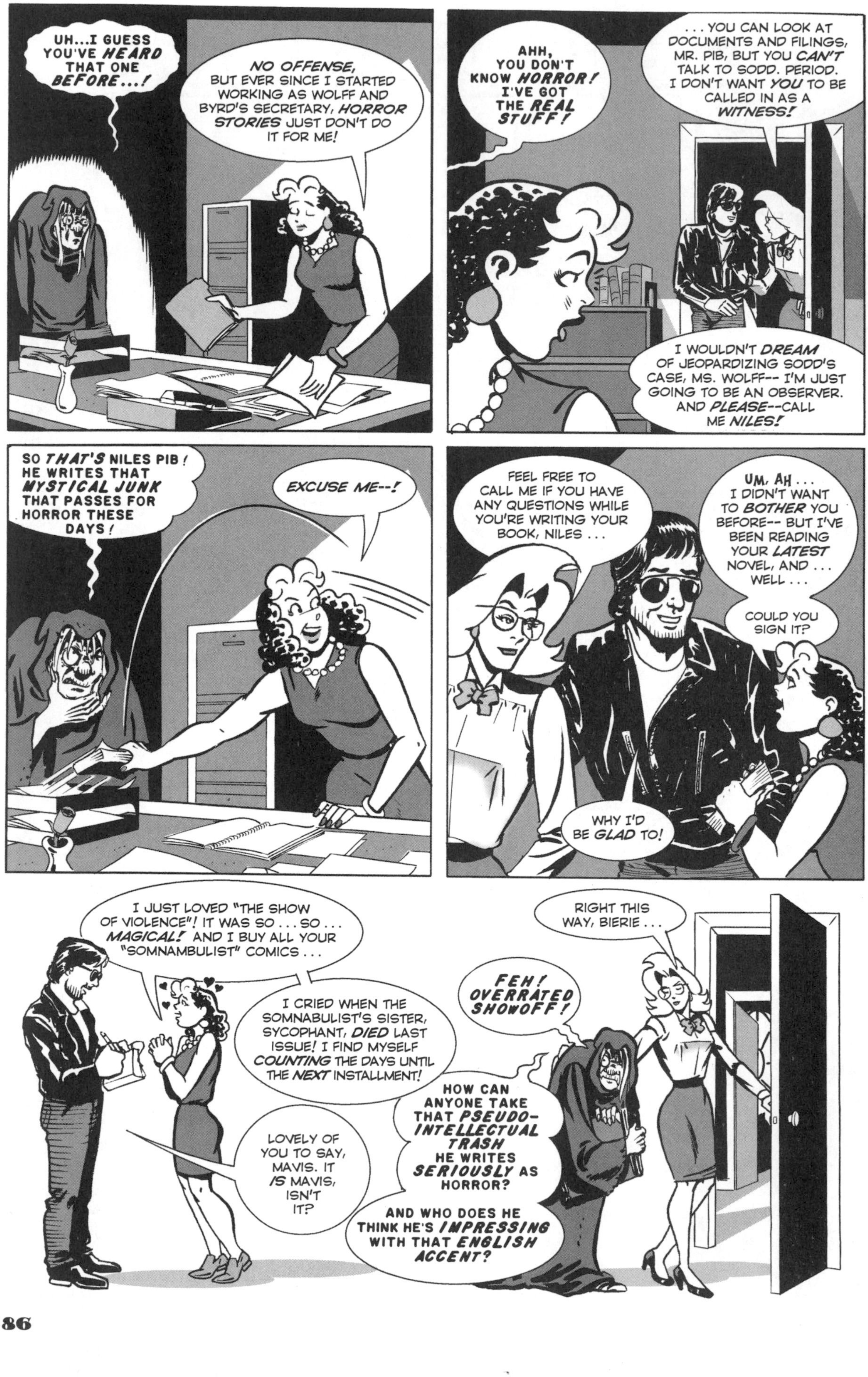

UH...I GUESS YOU'VE HEARD THAT ONE BEFORE...!
NO OFFENSE, BUT EVER SINCE I STARTED WORKING AS WOLFF AND BYRD'S SECRETARY, HORROR STORIES JUST DON'T DO IT FOR ME!
AHH, YOU DON'T KNOW HORROR! I'VE GOT THE REAL STUFF!
. . . YOU CAN LOOK AT DOCUMENTS AND FILINGS, MR. PIB, BUT YOU CAN'T TALK TO SODD. PERIOD. I DON'T WANT YOU TO BE CALLED IN AS A WITNESS!
I WOULDN'T DREAM OF JEOPARDIZING SODD'S CASE, MS. WOLFF-- I'M JUST GOING TO BE AN OBSERVER. AND PLEASE--CALL ME NILES!
SO THAT'S NILES PIB! HE WRITES THAT MYSTICAL JUNK THAT PASSES FOR HORROR THESE DAYS!
EXCUSE ME--!
FEEL FREE TO CALL ME IF YOU HAVE ANY QUESTIONS WHILE YOU'RE WRITING YOUR BOOK, NILES . . .
UM, AH . . . I DIDN'T WANT TO BOTHER YOU BEFORE-- BUT I'VE BEEN READING YOUR LATEST NOVEL, AND . . . WELL . . .
COULD YOU SIGN IT?
WHY I'D BE GLAD TO!
I JUST LOVED "THE SHOW OF VIOLENCE"! IT WAS SO . . . SO . . . MAGICAL! AND I BUY ALL YOUR "SOMNAMBULIST" COMICS . . .
I CRIED WHEN THE SOMNABULIST'S SISTER, SYCOPHANT, DIED LAST ISSUE! I FIND MYSELF COUNTING THE DAYS UNTIL THE NEXT INSTALLMENT!
LOVELY OF YOU TO SAY, MAVIS. IT IS MAVIS, ISN'T IT?
RIGHT THIS WAY, BIERIE . . .
FEH! OVERRATED SHOWOFF!
HOW CAN ANYONE TAKE THAT PSEUDO-INTELLECTUAL TRASH HE WRITES SERIOUSLY AS HORROR?
AND WHO DOES HE THINK HE'S IMPRESSING WITH THAT ENGLISH ACCENT?

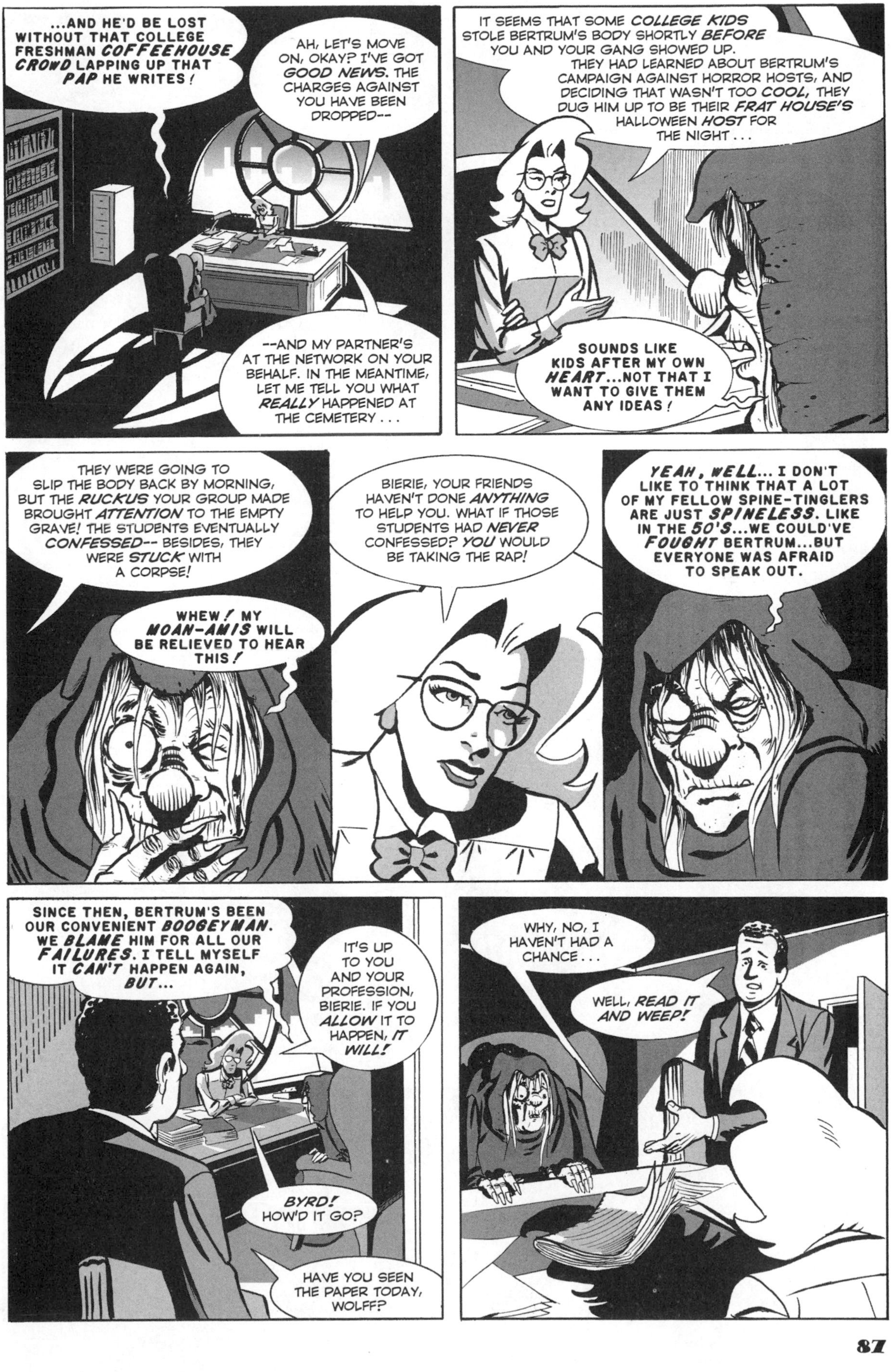
...AND HE'D BE LOST WITHOUT THAT COLLEGE FRESHMAN COFFEEHOUSE CROWD LAPPING UP THAT PAP HE WRITES!
AH, LET'S MOVE ON, OKAY? I'VE GOT GOOD NEWS. THE CHARGES AGAINST YOU HAVE BEEN DROPPED--
--AND MY PARTNER'S AT THE NETWORK ON YOUR BEHALF. IN THE MEANTIME, LET ME TELL YOU WHAT REALLY HAPPENED AT THE CEMETERY...
IT SEEMS THAT SOME COLLEGE KIDS STOLE BERTRUM'S BODY SHORTLY BEFORE YOU AND YOUR GANG SHOWED UP. THEY HAD LEARNED ABOUT BERTRUM'S CAMPAIGN AGAINST HORROR HOSTS, AND DECIDING THAT WASN'T TOO COOL, THEY DUG HIM UP TO BE THEIR FRAT HOUSE'S HALLOWEEN HOST FOR THE NIGHT...
SOUNDS LIKE KIDS AFTER MY OWN HEART...NOT THAT I WANT TO GIVE THEM ANY IDEAS!
THEY WERE GOING TO SLIP THE BODY BACK BY MORNING, BUT THE RUCKUS YOUR GROUP MADE BROUGHT ATTENTION TO THE EMPTY GRAVE! THE STUDENTS EVENTUALLY CONFESSED-- BESIDES, THEY WERE STUCK WITH A CORPSE!
WHEW! MY MOAN-AMIS WILL BE RELIEVED TO HEAR THIS!
BIERIE, YOUR FRIENDS HAVEN'T DONE ANYTHING TO HELP YOU. WHAT IF THOSE STUDENTS HAD NEVER CONFESSED? YOU WOULD BE TAKING THE RAP!
YEAH, WELL... I DON'T LIKE TO THINK THAT A LOT OF MY FELLOW SPINE-TINGLERS ARE JUST SPINELESS. LIKE IN THE 50'S...WE COULD'VE FOUGHT BERTRUM...BUT EVERYONE WAS AFRAID TO SPEAK OUT.
SINCE THEN, BERTRUM'S BEEN OUR CONVENIENT BOOGEYMAN. WE BLAME HIM FOR ALL OUR FAILURES. I TELL MYSELF IT CAN'T HAPPEN AGAIN, BUT...
IT'S UP TO YOU AND YOUR PROFESSION, BIERIE. IF YOU ALLOW IT TO HAPPEN, IT WILL!
BYRD! HOW'D IT GO?
HAVE YOU SEEN THE PAPER TODAY, WOLFF?
WHY, NO, I HAVEN'T HAD A CHANCE...
WELL, READ IT AND WEEP!

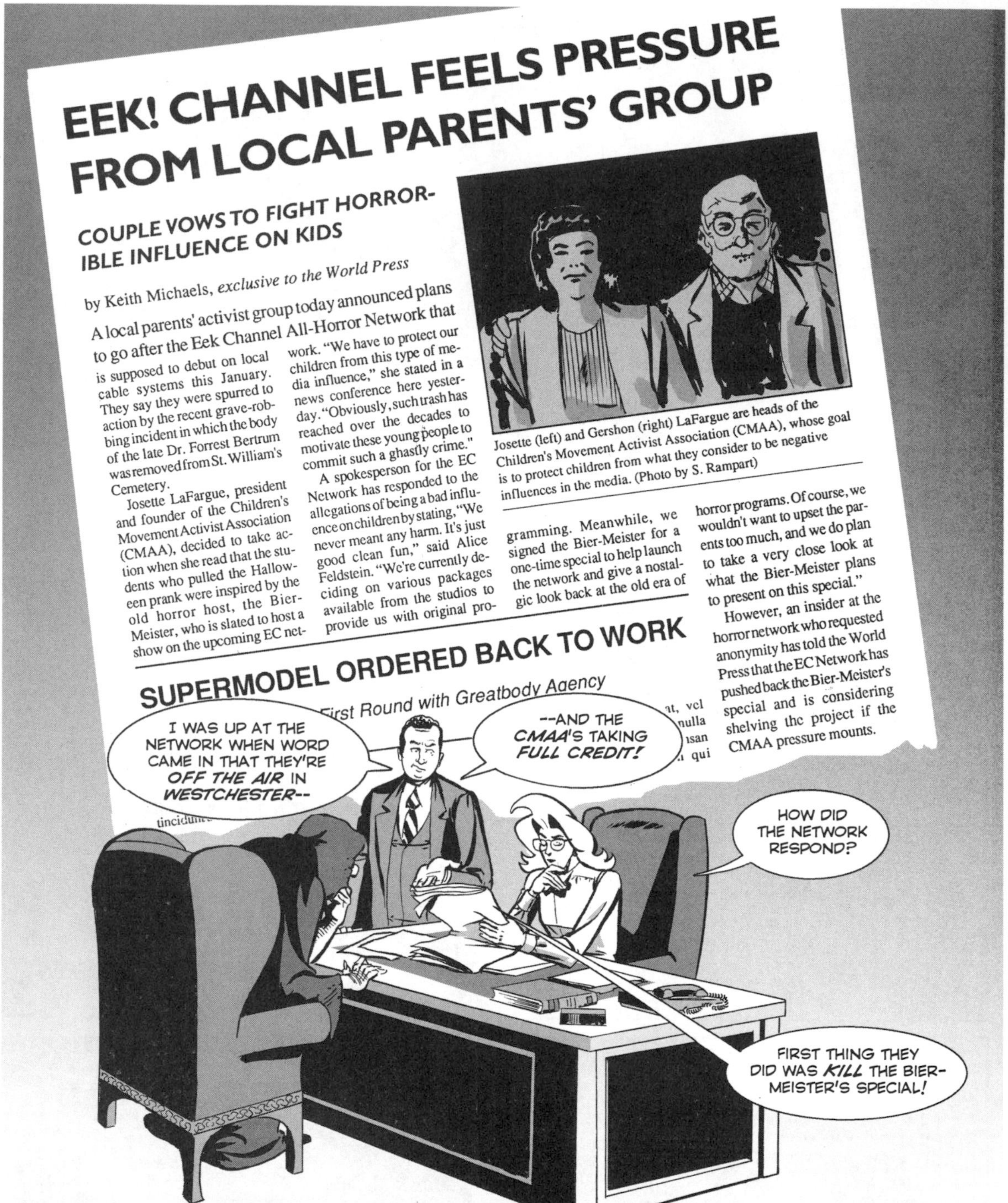

EEK! CHANNEL FEELS PRESSURE FROM LOCAL PARENTS' GROUP
COUPLE VOWS TO FIGHT HORROR-IBLE INFLUENCE ON KIDS
by Keith Michaels, exclusive to the World Press
A local parents' activist group today announced plans to go after the Eek Channel All-Horror Network that is supposed to debut on local cable systems this January. They say they were spurred to action by the recent grave-robbing incident in which the body of the late Dr. Forrest Bertrum was removed from St. William's Cemetery.
Josette LaFargue, president and founder of the Children's Movement Activist Association (CMAA), decided to take action when she read that the students who pulled the Halloween prank were inspired by the old horror host, the Bier-Meister, who is slated to host a show on the upcoming EC network. "We have to protect our children from this type of media influence," she stated in a news conference here yesterday. "Obviously, such trash has reached over the decades to motivate these young people to commit such a ghastly crime."
A spokesperson for the EC Network has responded to the allegations of being a bad influence on children by stating, "We never meant any harm. It's just good clean fun," said Alice Feldstein. "We're currently deciding on various packages available from the studios to provide us with original programming. Meanwhile, we signed the Bier-Meister for a one-time special to help launch the network and give a nostalgic look back at the old era of horror programs. Of course, we wouldn't want to upset the parents too much, and we do plan to take a very close look at what the Bier-Meister plans to present on this special."
However, an insider at the horror network who requested anonymity has told the World Press that the EC Network has pushed back the Bier-Meister's special and is considering shelving the project if the CMAA pressure mounts.
Josette (left) and Gershon (right) LaFargue are heads of the Children's Movement Activist Association (CMAA), whose goal is to protect children from what they consider to be negative influences in the media. (Photo by S. Rampart)
SUPERMODEL ORDERED BACK TO WORK
First Round with Greatbody Agency
I WAS UP AT THE NETWORK WHEN WORD CAME IN THAT THEY'RE *OFF THE AIR* IN *WESTCHESTER*--
--AND THE *CMAA*'S TAKING *FULL CREDIT!*
HOW DID THE NETWORK RESPOND?
FIRST THING THEY DID WAS *KILL* THE BIER-MEISTER'S SPECIAL!

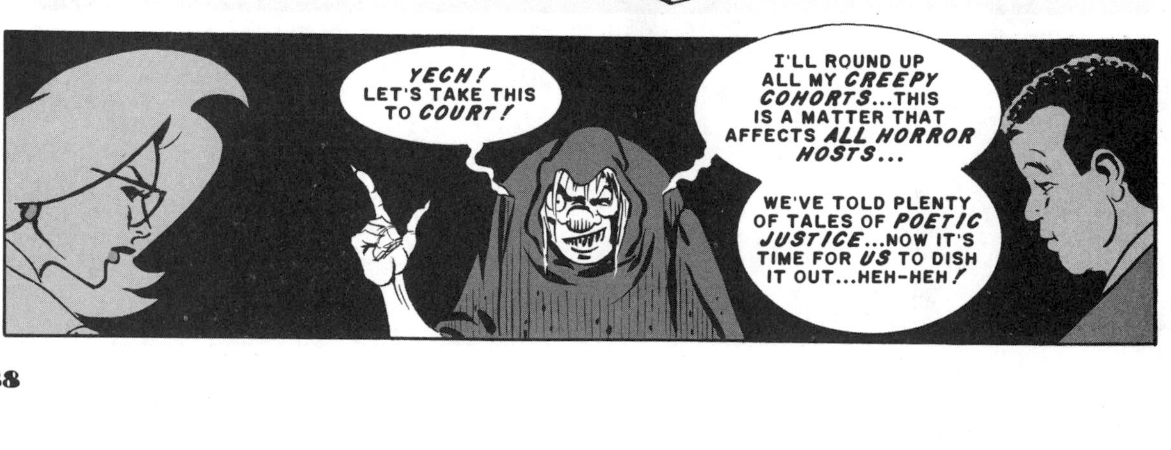

YECH! LET'S TAKE THIS TO *COURT!*
I'LL ROUND UP ALL MY *CREEPY COHORTS*...THIS IS A MATTER THAT AFFECTS *ALL HORROR HOSTS*...
WE'VE TOLD PLENTY OF TALES OF *POETIC JUSTICE*...NOW IT'S TIME FOR *US* TO DISH IT OUT...HEH-HEH*!*

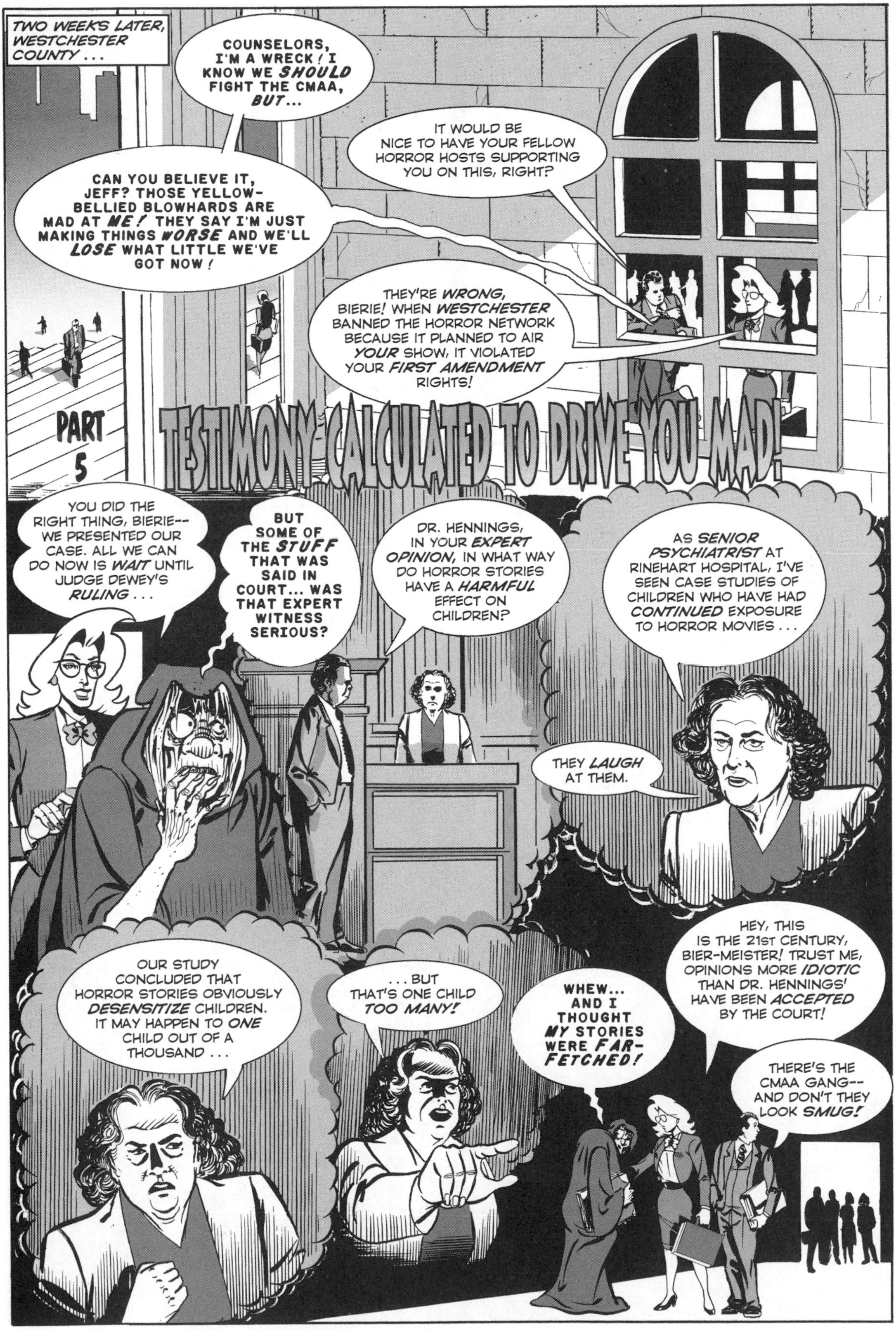
TWO WEEKS LATER, WESTCHESTER COUNTY . . .
COUNSELORS, I'M A WRECK! I KNOW WE SHOULD FIGHT THE CMAA, BUT...
IT WOULD BE NICE TO HAVE YOUR FELLOW HORROR HOSTS SUPPORTING YOU ON THIS, RIGHT?
CAN YOU BELIEVE IT, JEFF? THOSE YELLOW-BELLIED BLOWHARDS ARE MAD AT ME! THEY SAY I'M JUST MAKING THINGS WORSE AND WE'LL LOSE WHAT LITTLE WE'VE GOT NOW!
THEY'RE WRONG, BIERIE! WHEN WESTCHESTER BANNED THE HORROR NETWORK BECAUSE IT PLANNED TO AIR YOUR SHOW, IT VIOLATED YOUR FIRST AMENDMENT RIGHTS!
PART 5
TESTIMONY CALCULATED TO DRIVE YOU MAD!
YOU DID THE RIGHT THING, BIERIE-- WE PRESENTED OUR CASE. ALL WE CAN DO NOW IS WAIT UNTIL JUDGE DEWEY'S RULING . . .
BUT SOME OF THE STUFF THAT WAS SAID IN COURT... WAS THAT EXPERT WITNESS SERIOUS?
DR. HENNINGS, IN YOUR EXPERT OPINION, IN WHAT WAY DO HORROR STORIES HAVE A HARMFUL EFFECT ON CHILDREN?
AS SENIOR PSYCHIATRIST AT RINEHART HOSPITAL, I'VE SEEN CASE STUDIES OF CHILDREN WHO HAVE HAD CONTINUED EXPOSURE TO HORROR MOVIES . . .
THEY LAUGH AT THEM.
OUR STUDY CONCLUDED THAT HORROR STORIES OBVIOUSLY DESENSITIZE CHILDREN. IT MAY HAPPEN TO ONE CHILD OUT OF A THOUSAND . . .
. . . BUT THAT'S ONE CHILD TOO MANY!
WHEW... AND I THOUGHT MY STORIES WERE FAR-FETCHED!
HEY, THIS IS THE 21ST CENTURY, BIER-MEISTER! TRUST ME, OPINIONS MORE IDIOTIC THAN DR. HENNINGS' HAVE BEEN ACCEPTED BY THE COURT!
THERE'S THE CMAA GANG-- AND DON'T THEY LOOK SMUG!

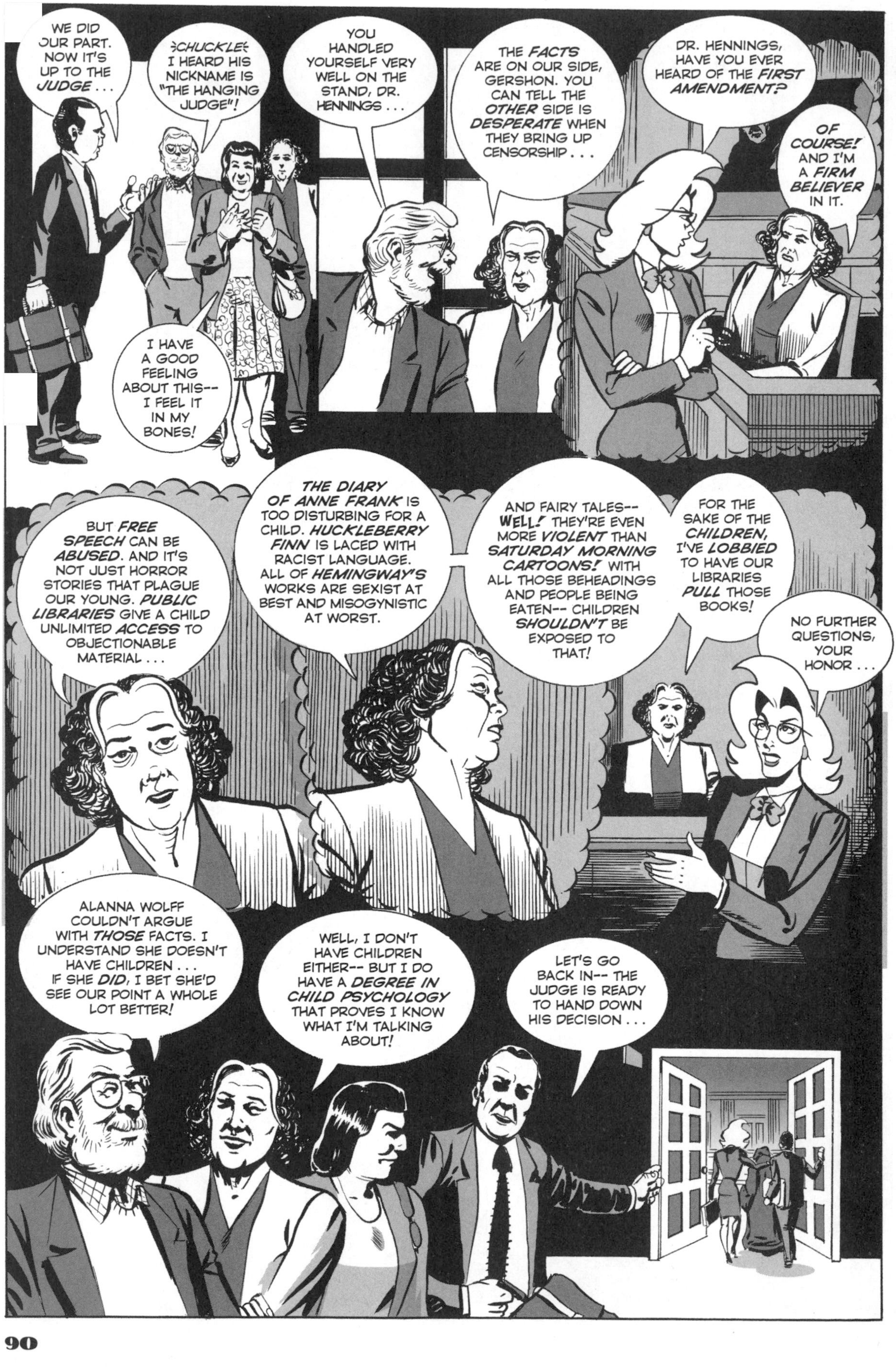
WE DID OUR PART. NOW IT'S UP TO THE JUDGE . . .
CHUCKLE I HEARD HIS NICKNAME IS "THE HANGING JUDGE"!
I HAVE A GOOD FEELING ABOUT THIS-- I FEEL IT IN MY BONES!
YOU HANDLED YOURSELF VERY WELL ON THE STAND, DR. HENNINGS . . .
THE FACTS ARE ON OUR SIDE, GERSHON. YOU CAN TELL THE OTHER SIDE IS DESPERATE WHEN THEY BRING UP CENSORSHIP . . .
DR. HENNINGS, HAVE YOU EVER HEARD OF THE FIRST AMENDMENT?
OF COURSE! AND I'M A FIRM BELIEVER IN IT.
BUT FREE SPEECH CAN BE ABUSED. AND IT'S NOT JUST HORROR STORIES THAT PLAGUE OUR YOUNG. PUBLIC LIBRARIES GIVE A CHILD UNLIMITED ACCESS TO OBJECTIONABLE MATERIAL . . .
THE DIARY OF ANNE FRANK IS TOO DISTURBING FOR A CHILD. HUCKLEBERRY FINN IS LACED WITH RACIST LANGUAGE. ALL OF HEMINGWAY'S WORKS ARE SEXIST AT BEST AND MISOGYNISTIC AT WORST.
AND FAIRY TALES-- WELL! THEY'RE EVEN MORE VIOLENT THAN SATURDAY MORNING CARTOONS! WITH ALL THOSE BEHEADINGS AND PEOPLE BEING EATEN-- CHILDREN SHOULDN'T BE EXPOSED TO THAT!
FOR THE SAKE OF THE CHILDREN, I'VE LOBBIED TO HAVE OUR LIBRARIES PULL THOSE BOOKS!
NO FURTHER QUESTIONS, YOUR HONOR . . .
ALANNA WOLFF COULDN'T ARGUE WITH THOSE FACTS. I UNDERSTAND SHE DOESN'T HAVE CHILDREN . . . IF SHE DID, I BET SHE'D SEE OUR POINT A WHOLE LOT BETTER!
WELL, I DON'T HAVE CHILDREN EITHER-- BUT I DO HAVE A DEGREE IN CHILD PSYCHOLOGY THAT PROVES I KNOW WHAT I'M TALKING ABOUT!
LET'S GO BACK IN-- THE JUDGE IS READY TO HAND DOWN HIS DECISION . . .

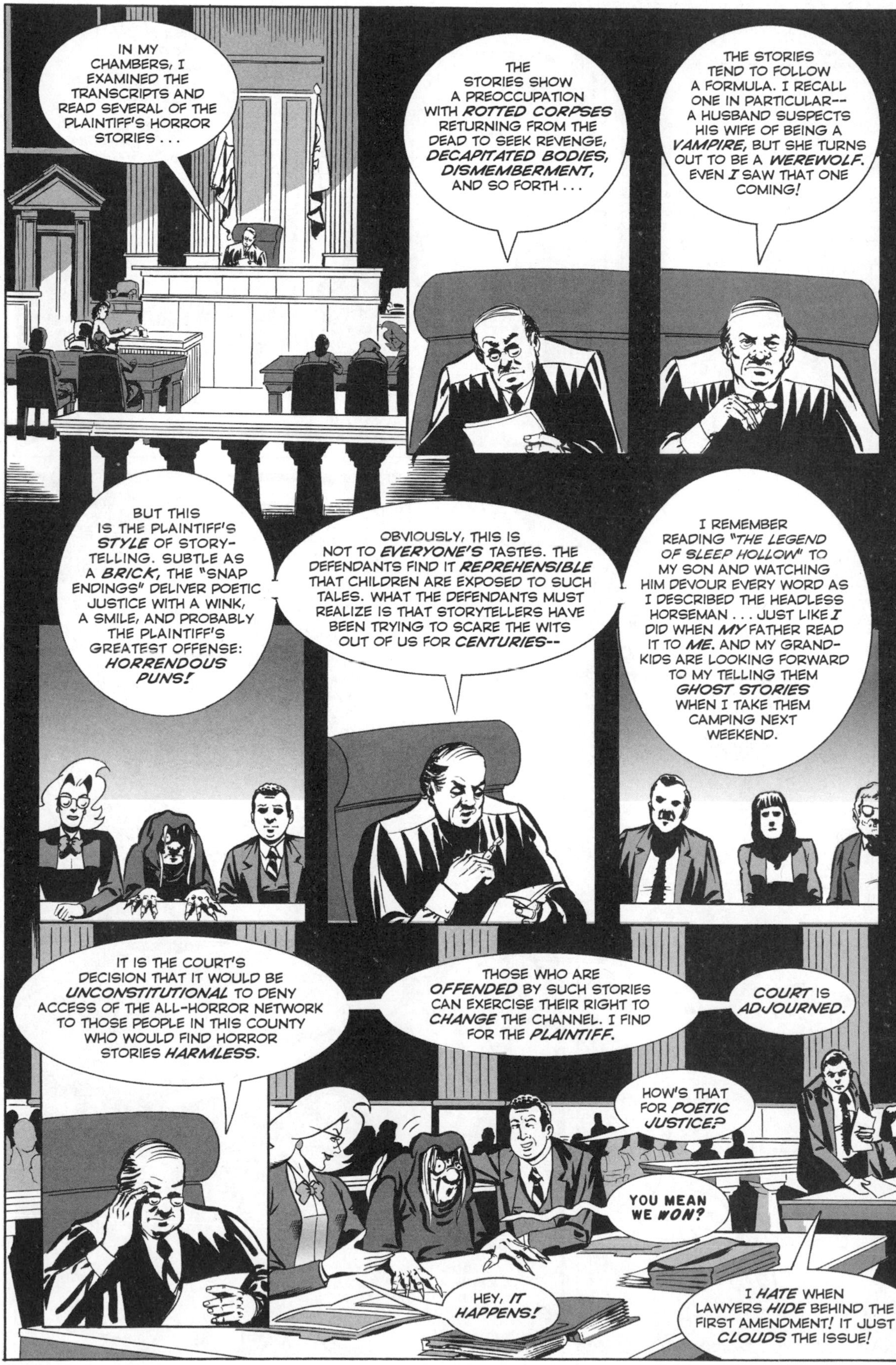
IN MY CHAMBERS, I EXAMINED THE TRANSCRIPTS AND READ SEVERAL OF THE PLAINTIFF'S HORROR STORIES . . .
THE STORIES SHOW A PREOCCUPATION WITH *ROTTED CORPSES* RETURNING FROM THE DEAD TO SEEK REVENGE, *DECAPITATED BODIES, DISMEMBERMENT,* AND SO FORTH . . .
THE STORIES TEND TO FOLLOW A FORMULA. I RECALL ONE IN PARTICULAR-- A HUSBAND SUSPECTS HIS WIFE OF BEING A *VAMPIRE,* BUT SHE TURNS OUT TO BE A *WEREWOLF.* EVEN *I* SAW THAT ONE COMING!
BUT THIS IS THE PLAINTIFF'S *STYLE* OF STORY-TELLING. SUBTLE AS A *BRICK,* THE "SNAP ENDINGS" DELIVER POETIC JUSTICE WITH A WINK, A SMILE, AND PROBABLY THE PLAINTIFF'S GREATEST OFFENSE: *HORRENDOUS PUNS!*
OBVIOUSLY, THIS IS NOT TO *EVERYONE'S* TASTES. THE DEFENDANTS FIND IT *REPREHENSIBLE* THAT CHILDREN ARE EXPOSED TO SUCH TALES. WHAT THE DEFENDANTS MUST REALIZE IS THAT STORYTELLERS HAVE BEEN TRYING TO SCARE THE WITS OUT OF US FOR *CENTURIES*--
I REMEMBER READING *"THE LEGEND OF SLEEP HOLLOW"* TO MY SON AND WATCHING HIM DEVOUR EVERY WORD AS I DESCRIBED THE HEADLESS HORSEMAN . . . JUST LIKE *I* DID WHEN *MY* FATHER READ IT TO *ME.* AND MY GRAND-KIDS ARE LOOKING FORWARD TO MY TELLING THEM *GHOST STORIES* WHEN I TAKE THEM CAMPING NEXT WEEKEND.
IT IS THE COURT'S DECISION THAT IT WOULD BE *UNCONSTITUTIONAL* TO DENY ACCESS OF THE ALL-HORROR NETWORK TO THOSE PEOPLE IN THIS COUNTY WHO WOULD FIND HORROR STORIES *HARMLESS.*
THOSE WHO ARE *OFFENDED* BY SUCH STORIES CAN EXERCISE THEIR RIGHT TO *CHANGE* THE CHANNEL. I FIND FOR THE *PLAINTIFF.*
COURT IS *ADJOURNED.*
HOW'S THAT FOR *POETIC JUSTICE?*
YOU MEAN WE *WON?*
HEY, *IT HAPPENS!*
I *HATE* WHEN LAWYERS *HIDE* BEHIND THE FIRST AMENDMENT! IT JUST *CLOUDS* THE ISSUE!

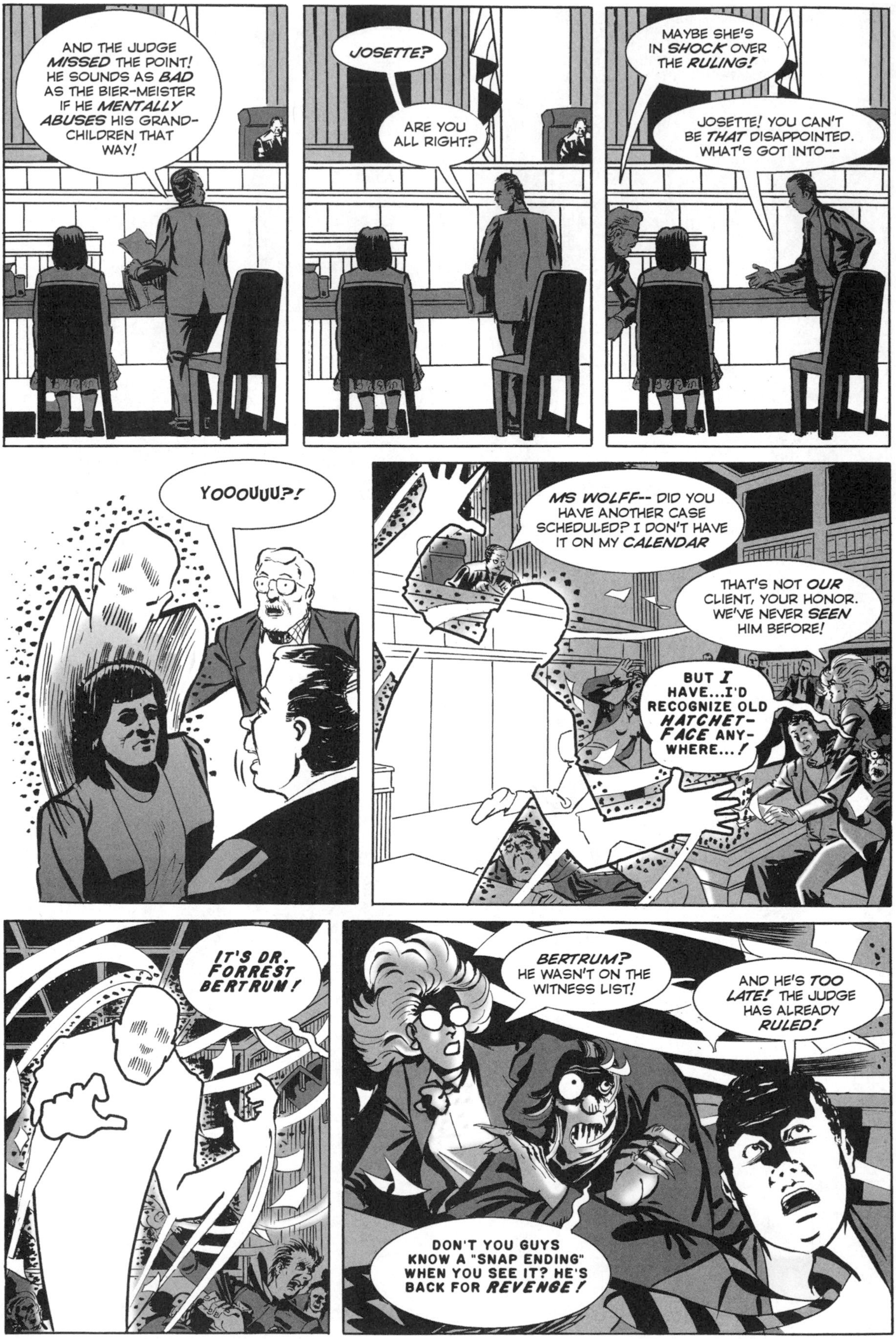
AND THE JUDGE MISSED THE POINT! HE SOUNDS AS BAD AS THE BIER-MEISTER IF HE MENTALLY ABUSES HIS GRAND-CHILDREN THAT WAY!
JOSETTE?
ARE YOU ALL RIGHT?
MAYBE SHE'S IN SHOCK OVER THE RULING!
JOSETTE! YOU CAN'T BE THAT DISAPPOINTED. WHAT'S GOT INTO--
YOOOUUU?!
MS WOLFF-- DID YOU HAVE ANOTHER CASE SCHEDULED? I DON'T HAVE IT ON MY CALENDAR
THAT'S NOT OUR CLIENT, YOUR HONOR. WE'VE NEVER SEEN HIM BEFORE!
BUT I HAVE...I'D RECOGNIZE OLD HATCHET-FACE ANY-WHERE...!
IT'S DR. FORREST BERTRUM!
BERTRUM? HE WASN'T ON THE WITNESS LIST!
AND HE'S TOO LATE! THE JUDGE HAS ALREADY RULED!
DON'T YOU GUYS KNOW A "SNAP ENDING" WHEN YOU SEE IT? HE'S BACK FOR REVENGE!

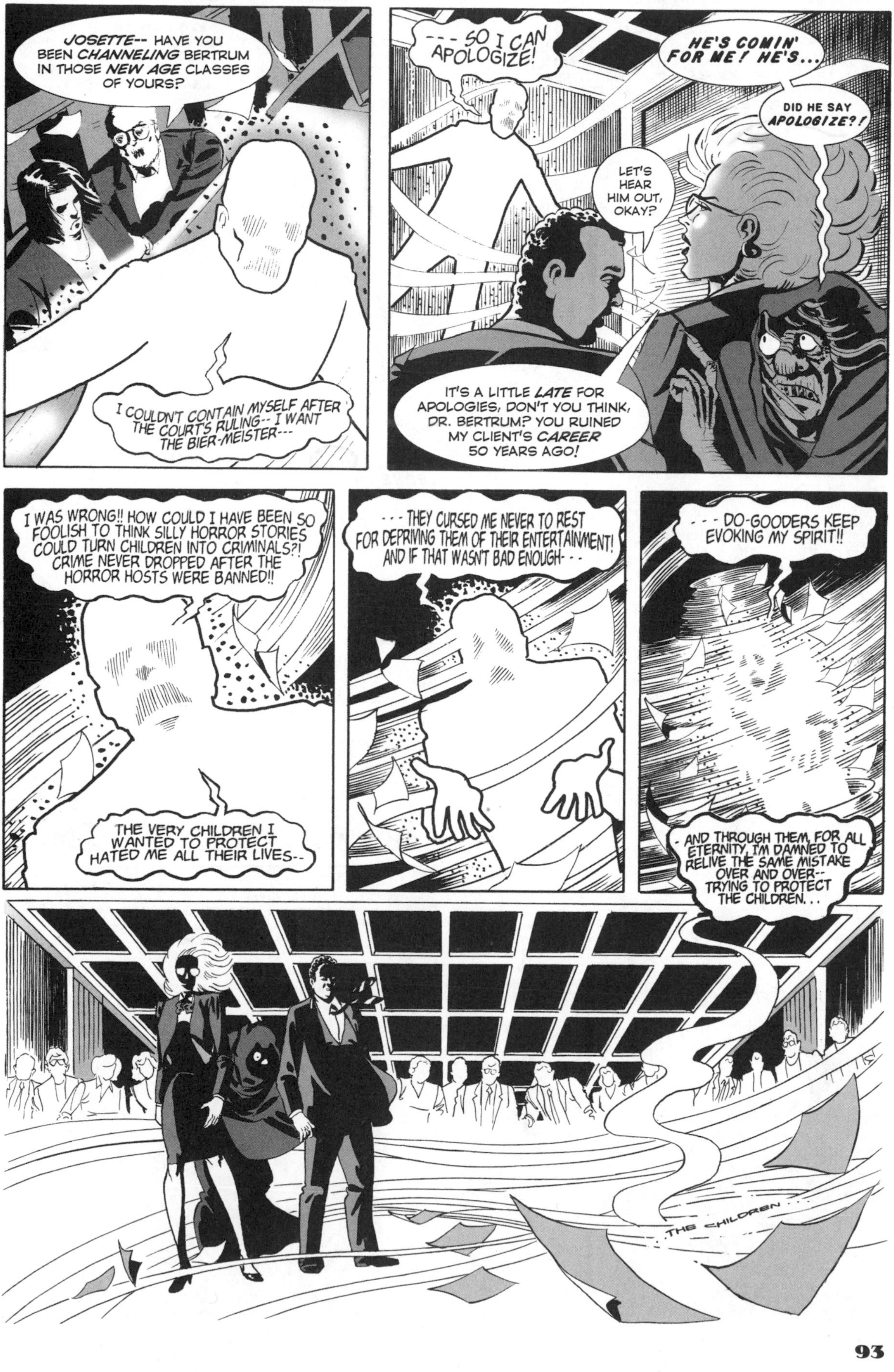
JOSETTE-- HAVE YOU BEEN CHANNELING BERTRUM IN THOSE NEW AGE CLASSES OF YOURS?
I COULDN'T CONTAIN MYSELF AFTER THE COURT'S RULING-- I WANT THE BIER-MEISTER---
---SO I CAN APOLOGIZE!
HE'S COMIN' FOR ME! HE'S...
DID HE SAY APOLOGIZE?!
LET'S HEAR HIM OUT, OKAY?
IT'S A LITTLE LATE FOR APOLOGIES, DON'T YOU THINK, DR. BERTRUM? YOU RUINED MY CLIENT'S CAREER 50 YEARS AGO!
I WAS WRONG!! HOW COULD I HAVE BEEN SO FOOLISH TO THINK SILLY HORROR STORIES COULD TURN CHILDREN INTO CRIMINALS?! CRIME NEVER DROPPED AFTER THE HORROR HOSTS WERE BANNED!!
THE VERY CHILDREN I WANTED TO PROTECT HATED ME ALL THEIR LIVES--
---THEY CURSED ME NEVER TO REST FOR DEPRIVING THEM OF THEIR ENTERTAINMENT! AND IF THAT WASN'T BAD ENOUGH---
---DO-GOODERS KEEP EVOKING MY SPIRIT!!
-AND THROUGH THEM, FOR ALL ETERNITY, I'M DAMNED TO RELIVE THE SAME MISTAKE OVER AND OVER-- TRYING TO PROTECT THE CHILDREN...
...THE CHILDREN...

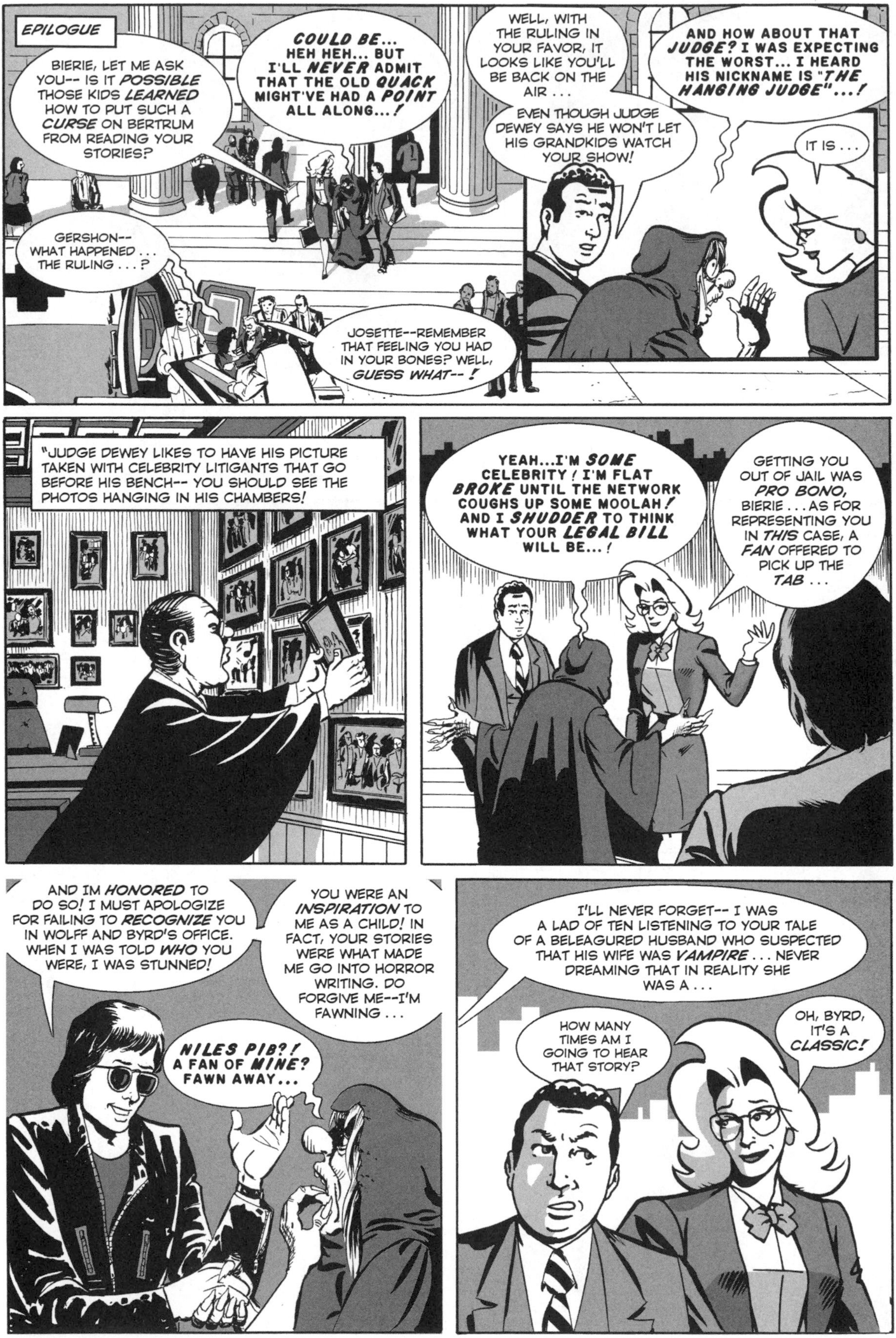
EPILOGUE
BIERIE, LET ME ASK YOU-- IS IT POSSIBLE THOSE KIDS LEARNED HOW TO PUT SUCH A CURSE ON BERTRUM FROM READING YOUR STORIES?
COULD BE... HEH HEH... BUT I'LL NEVER ADMIT THAT THE OLD QUACK MIGHT'VE HAD A POINT ALL ALONG...!
GERSHON-- WHAT HAPPENED . . . THE RULING . . .?
JOSETTE--REMEMBER THAT FEELING YOU HAD IN YOUR BONES? WELL, GUESS WHAT-- !
WELL, WITH THE RULING IN YOUR FAVOR, IT LOOKS LIKE YOU'LL BE BACK ON THE AIR . . .
EVEN THOUGH JUDGE DEWEY SAYS HE WON'T LET HIS GRANDKIDS WATCH YOUR SHOW!
AND HOW ABOUT THAT JUDGE? I WAS EXPECTING THE WORST... I HEARD HIS NICKNAME IS "THE HANGING JUDGE"...!
IT IS . . .
"JUDGE DEWEY LIKES TO HAVE HIS PICTURE TAKEN WITH CELEBRITY LITIGANTS THAT GO BEFORE HIS BENCH-- YOU SHOULD SEE THE PHOTOS HANGING IN HIS CHAMBERS!
YEAH...I'M SOME CELEBRITY! I'M FLAT BROKE UNTIL THE NETWORK COUGHS UP SOME MOOLAH! AND I SHUDDER TO THINK WHAT YOUR LEGAL BILL WILL BE...!
GETTING YOU OUT OF JAIL WAS PRO BONO, BIERIE . . . AS FOR REPRESENTING YOU IN THIS CASE, A FAN OFFERED TO PICK UP THE TAB . . .
AND IM HONORED TO DO SO! I MUST APOLOGIZE FOR FAILING TO RECOGNIZE YOU IN WOLFF AND BYRD'S OFFICE. WHEN I WAS TOLD WHO YOU WERE, I WAS STUNNED!
YOU WERE AN INSPIRATION TO ME AS A CHILD! IN FACT, YOUR STORIES WERE WHAT MADE ME GO INTO HORROR WRITING. DO FORGIVE ME--I'M FAWNING . . .
NILES PIB?! A FAN OF MINE? FAWN AWAY...
I'LL NEVER FORGET-- I WAS A LAD OF TEN LISTENING TO YOUR TALE OF A BELEAGURED HUSBAND WHO SUSPECTED THAT HIS WIFE WAS VAMPIRE . . . NEVER DREAMING THAT IN REALITY SHE WAS A . . .
HOW MANY TIMES AM I GOING TO HEAR THAT STORY?
OH, BYRD, IT'S A CLASSIC!

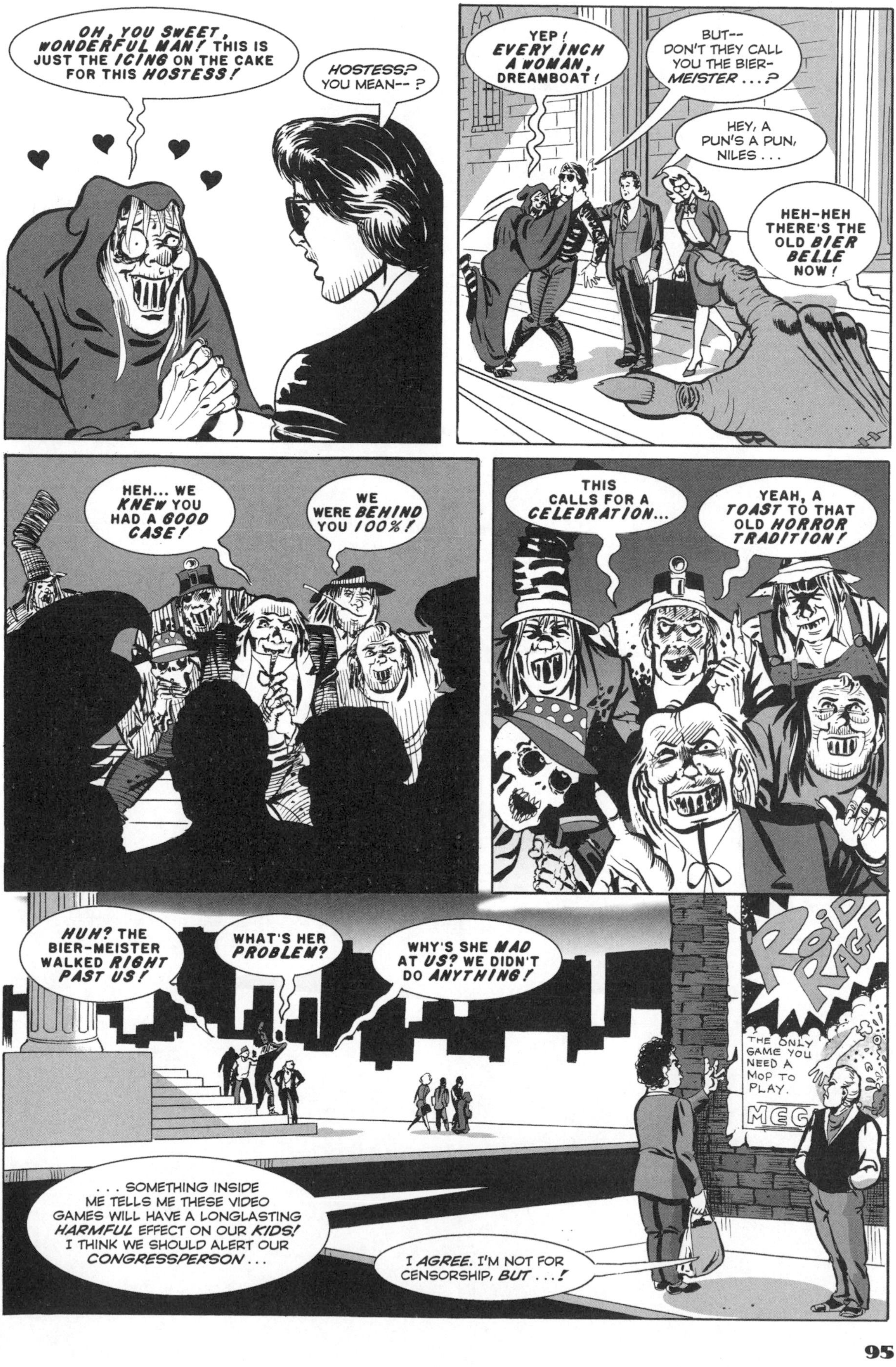
OH, YOU SWEET, WONDERFUL MAN! THIS IS JUST THE ICING ON THE CAKE FOR THIS HOSTESS!
HOSTESS? YOU MEAN-- ?
YEP! EVERY INCH A WOMAN, DREAMBOAT!
BUT-- DON'T THEY CALL YOU THE BIER-MEISTER ...?
HEY, A PUN'S A PUN, NILES ...
HEH-HEH THERE'S THE OLD BIER BELLE NOW!
HEH... WE KNEW YOU HAD A GOOD CASE!
WE WERE BEHIND YOU 100%!
THIS CALLS FOR A CELEBRATION...
YEAH, A TOAST TO THAT OLD HORROR TRADITION!
HUH? THE BIER-MEISTER WALKED RIGHT PAST US!
WHAT'S HER PROBLEM?
WHY'S SHE MAD AT US? WE DIDN'T DO ANYTHING!
ROID RAGE
THE ONLY GAME YOU NEED A MOP TO PLAY.
MEG
... SOMETHING INSIDE ME TELLS ME THESE VIDEO GAMES WILL HAVE A LONGLASTING HARMFUL EFFECT ON OUR KIDS! I THINK WE SHOULD ALERT OUR CONGRESSPERSON ...
I AGREE. I'M NOT FOR CENSORSHIP, BUT ...!

That Model Client

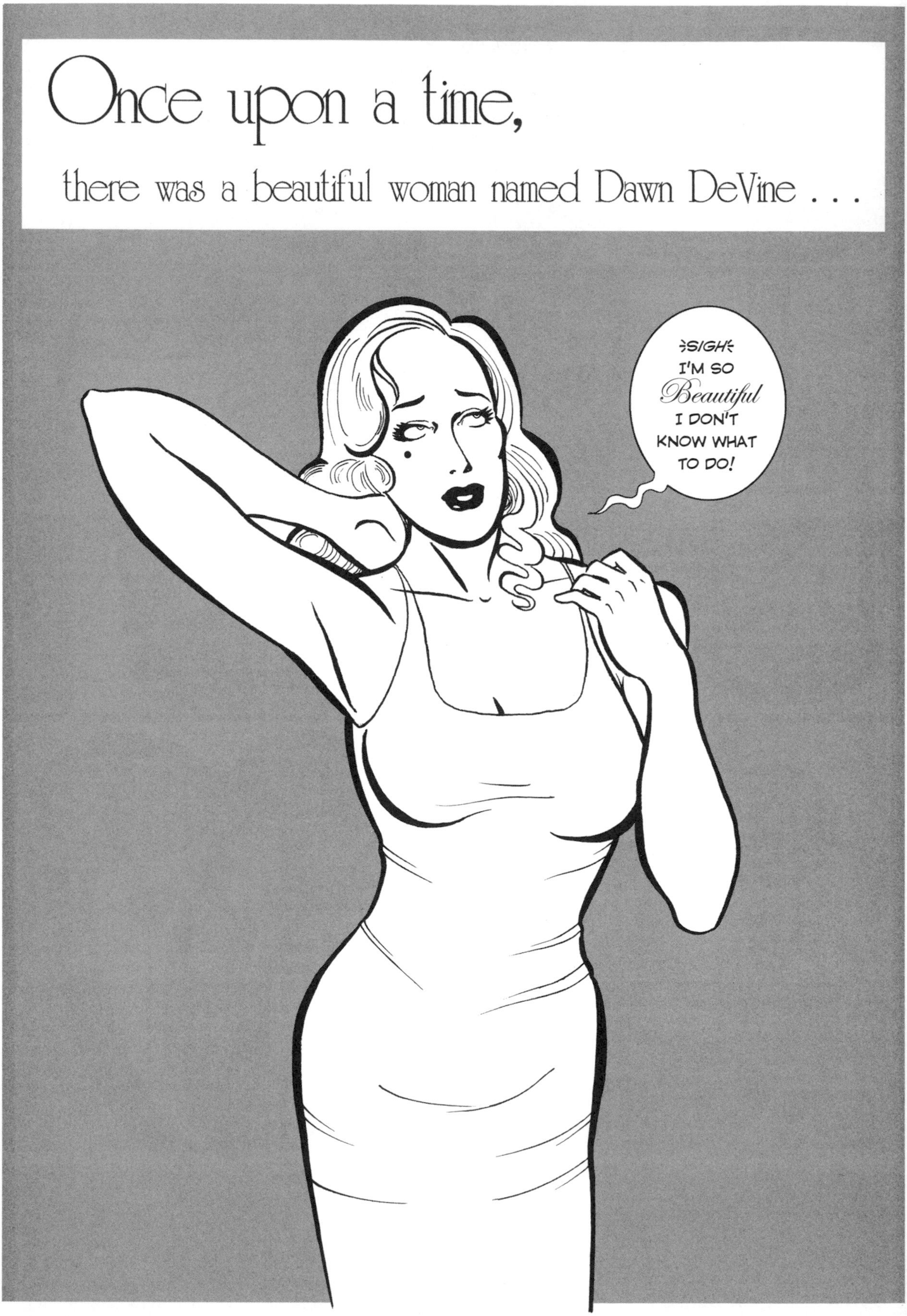
Once upon a time,
there was a beautiful woman named Dawn DeVine . . .
SIGH I'M SO Beautiful I DON'T KNOW WHAT TO DO!

Dawn was a fashion model whose face was known throughout the land (and her form was also well known and adored by those who followed a certain sporting publication with an annual swimsuit issue). As a result, she was treated like royalty . . .

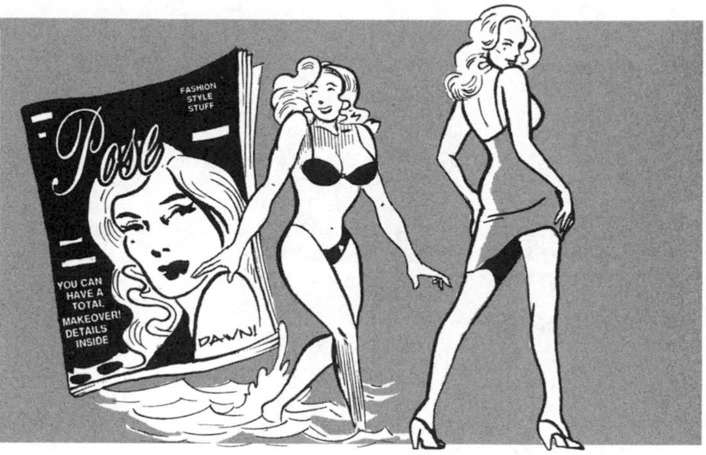

Pose
FASHION STYLE STUFF
YOU CAN HAVE A TOTAL MAKEOVER! DETAILS INSIDE
DAWN!

If one could find fault with Dawn, it might be that she was all too aware of her beauty and of how highly beauty was prized by the people of her land. In short, she was quite *vain!*

As time passed, Dawn became unhappy with her lot. She grieved to see most of her earnings go to her agency, and not to her wardrobe. "I know I could make a lot more money if I went out on my own," she thought. Her entourage was quite concerned . . .

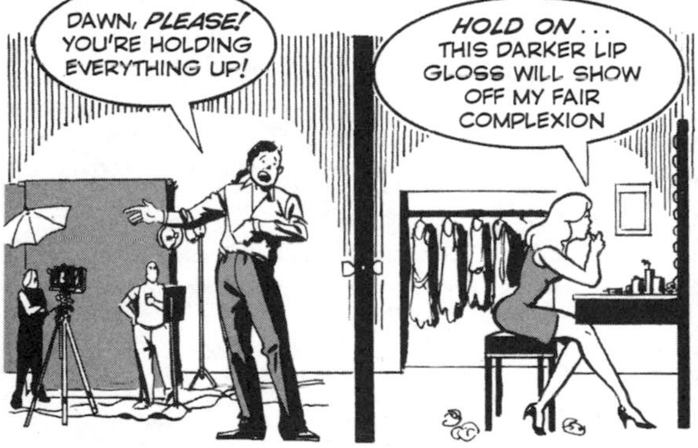

DAWN, *PLEASE!* YOU'RE HOLDING EVERYTHING UP!
HOLD ON . . . THIS DARKER LIP GLOSS WILL SHOW OFF MY FAIR COMPLEXION

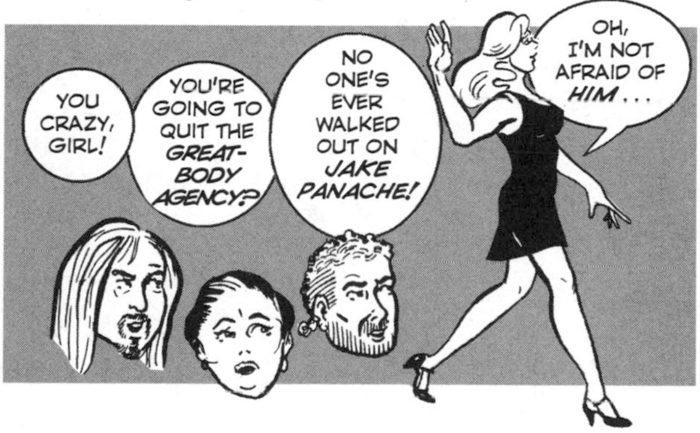

YOU CRAZY, GIRL!
YOU'RE GOING TO QUIT THE *GREAT-BODY AGENCY?*
NO ONE'S EVER WALKED OUT ON *JAKE PANACHE!*
OH, I'M NOT AFRAID OF *HIM* . . .

And concerned they should be, for this most supreme of models was the source of their livelihoods. For all her fame and sucess, Dawn was still under the thrall of Jake Panache, who ruled the Greatbody Agency with an iron hand. Jake did not take kindly to Dawn's wanting to find her own way in the world. He realized that Dawn sometimes had her head in the clouds and that life to her was a storybook fantasy.

Occasionally, this would get on his nerves (as you might well agree at this point), and he found it necessary to bring her back down to earth . . .

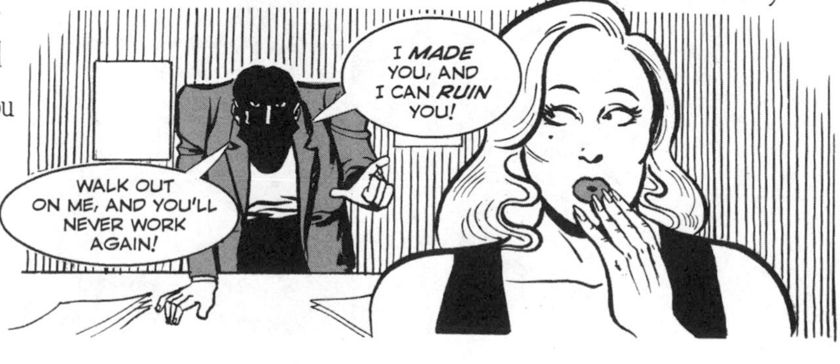

I *MADE* YOU, AND I CAN *RUIN* YOU!
WALK OUT ON ME, AND YOU'LL NEVER WORK AGAIN!

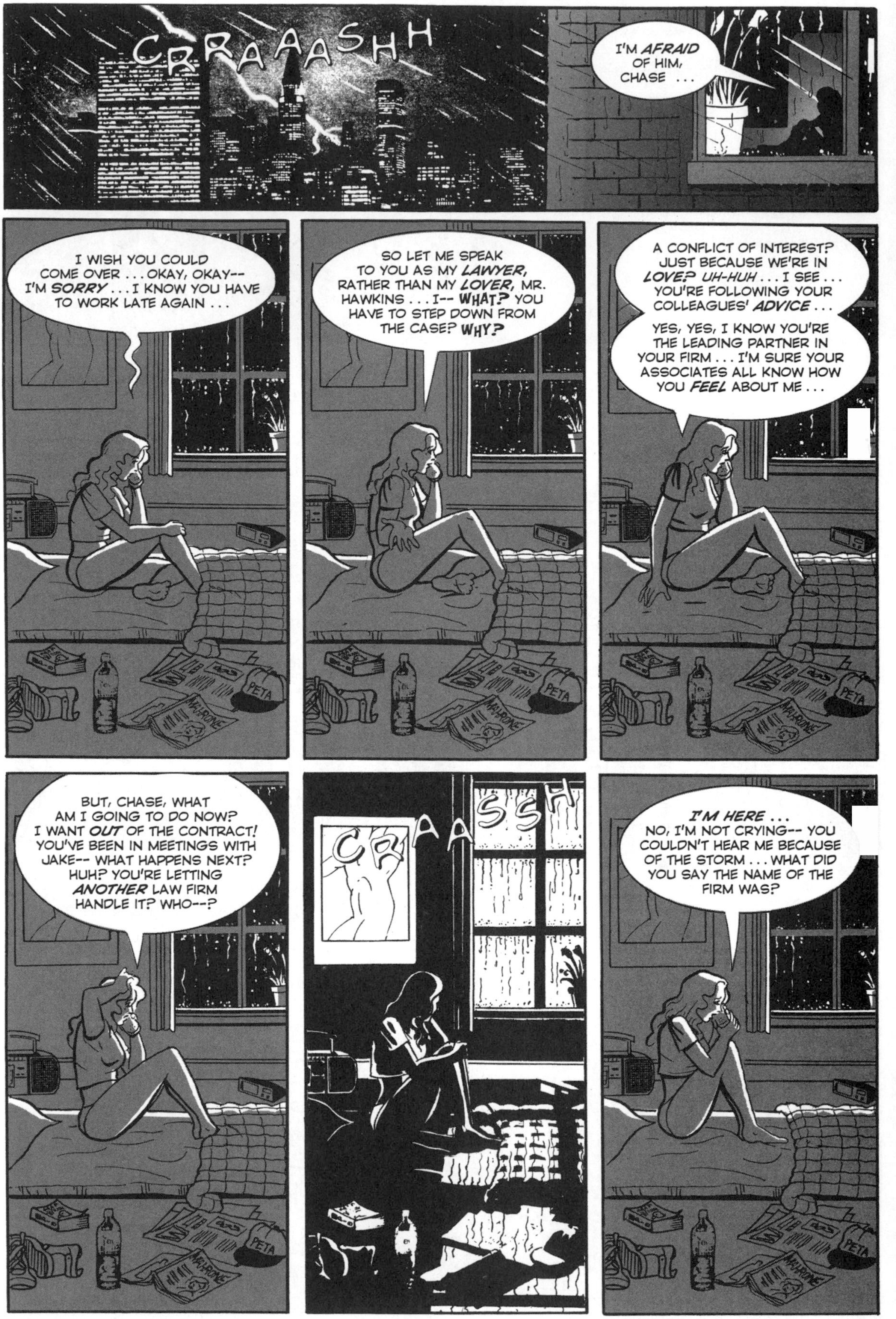

CRRAAASHH
I'M AFRAID OF HIM, CHASE . . .
I WISH YOU COULD COME OVER . . . OKAY, OKAY-- I'M SORRY . . . I KNOW YOU HAVE TO WORK LATE AGAIN . . .
SO LET ME SPEAK TO YOU AS MY LAWYER, RATHER THAN MY LOVER, MR. HAWKINS . . . I-- WHAT? YOU HAVE TO STEP DOWN FROM THE CASE? WHY?
A CONFLICT OF INTEREST? JUST BECAUSE WE'RE IN LOVE? UH-HUH . . . I SEE . . . YOU'RE FOLLOWING YOUR COLLEAGUES' ADVICE . . .
YES, YES, I KNOW YOU'RE THE LEADING PARTNER IN YOUR FIRM . . . I'M SURE YOUR ASSOCIATES ALL KNOW HOW YOU FEEL ABOUT ME . . .
BUT, CHASE, WHAT AM I GOING TO DO NOW? I WANT OUT OF THE CONTRACT! YOU'VE BEEN IN MEETINGS WITH JAKE-- WHAT HAPPENS NEXT? HUH? YOU'RE LETTING ANOTHER LAW FIRM HANDLE IT? WHO--?
CRAASSH
I'M HERE . . . NO, I'M NOT CRYING-- YOU COULDN'T HEAR ME BECAUSE OF THE STORM . . . WHAT DID YOU SAY THE NAME OF THE FIRM WAS?

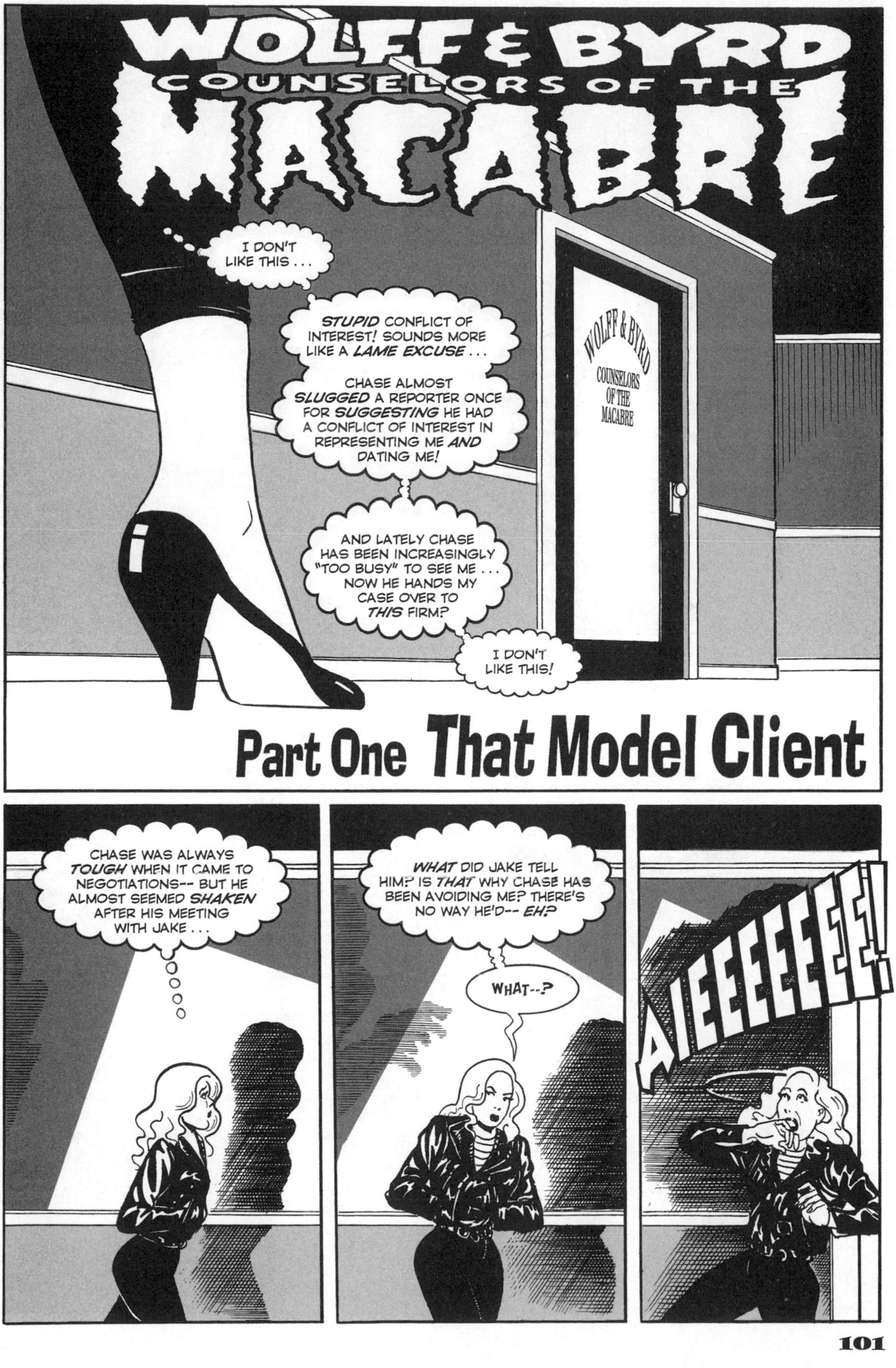
WOLFF & BYRD
COUNSELORS OF THE
MACABRE
I DON'T LIKE THIS . . .
STUPID CONFLICT OF INTEREST! SOUNDS MORE LIKE A LAME EXCUSE . . .
CHASE ALMOST SLUGGED A REPORTER ONCE FOR SUGGESTING HE HAD A CONFLICT OF INTEREST IN REPRESENTING ME AND DATING ME!
AND LATELY CHASE HAS BEEN INCREASINGLY "TOO BUSY" TO SEE ME . . . NOW HE HANDS MY CASE OVER TO THIS FIRM?
I DON'T LIKE THIS!
WOLFF & BYRD
COUNSELORS OF THE MACABRE
Part One That Model Client
CHASE WAS ALWAYS TOUGH WHEN IT CAME TO NEGOTIATIONS-- BUT HE ALMOST SEEMED SHAKEN AFTER HIS MEETING WITH JAKE . . .
WHAT DID JAKE TELL HIM? IS THAT WHY CHASE HAS BEEN AVOIDING ME? THERE'S NO WAY HE'D-- EH?
WHAT--?
AIEEEEEEE!

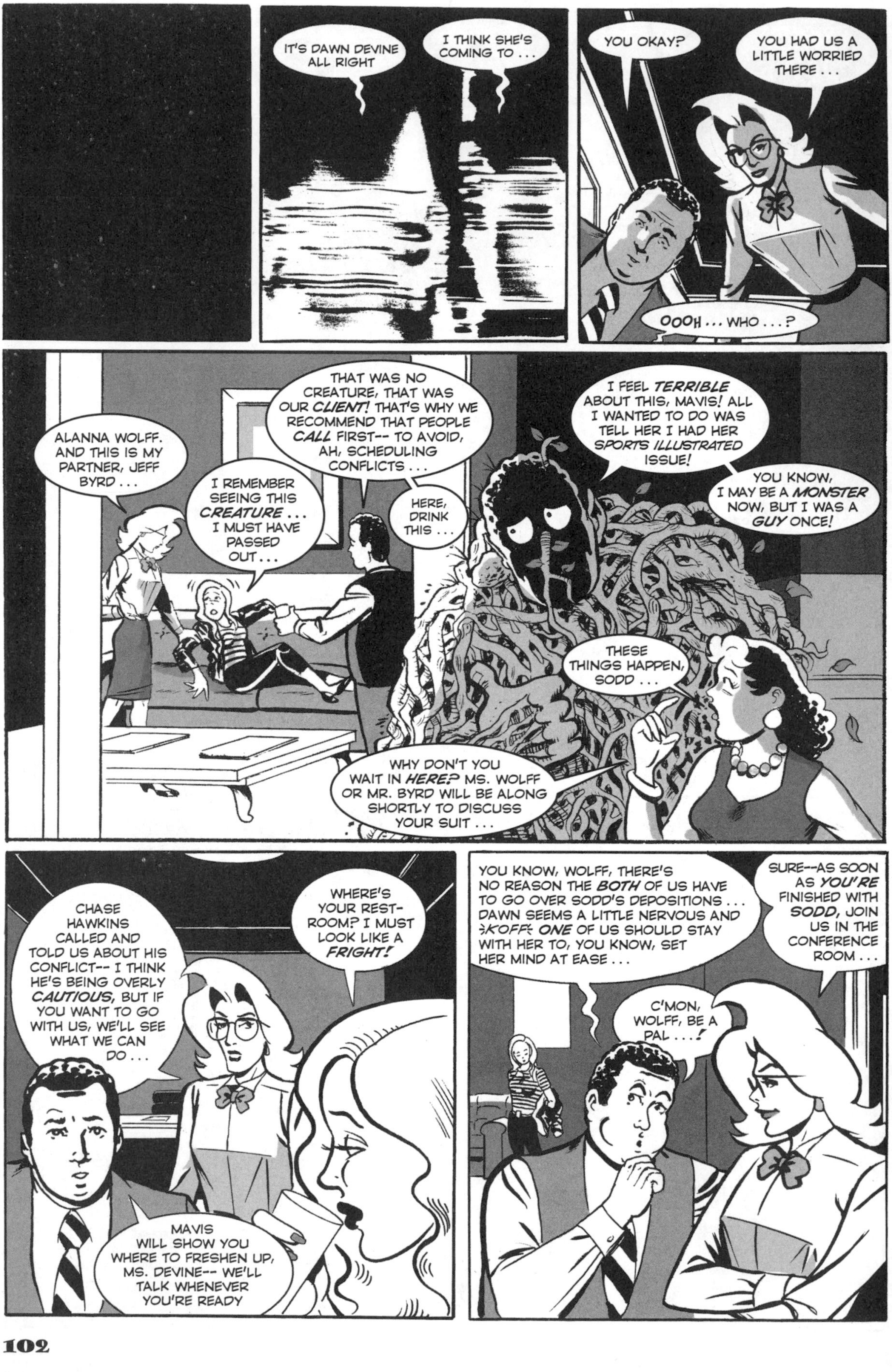

IT'S DAWN DEVINE ALL RIGHT
I THINK SHE'S COMING TO . . .
YOU OKAY?
YOU HAD US A LITTLE WORRIED THERE . . .
OOOH . . . WHO . . . ?
ALANNA WOLFF. AND THIS IS MY PARTNER, JEFF BYRD . . .
I REMEMBER SEEING THIS CREATURE . . . I MUST HAVE PASSED OUT . . .
THAT WAS NO CREATURE, THAT WAS OUR CLIENT! THAT'S WHY WE RECOMMEND THAT PEOPLE CALL FIRST-- TO AVOID, AH, SCHEDULING CONFLICTS . . .
HERE, DRINK THIS . . .
I FEEL TERRIBLE ABOUT THIS, MAVIS! ALL I WANTED TO DO WAS TELL HER I HAD HER SPORTS ILLUSTRATED ISSUE!
YOU KNOW, I MAY BE A MONSTER NOW, BUT I WAS A GUY ONCE!
THESE THINGS HAPPEN, SODD . . .
WHY DON'T YOU WAIT IN HERE? MS. WOLFF OR MR. BYRD WILL BE ALONG SHORTLY TO DISCUSS YOUR SUIT . . .
CHASE HAWKINS CALLED AND TOLD US ABOUT HIS CONFLICT-- I THINK HE'S BEING OVERLY CAUTIOUS, BUT IF YOU WANT TO GO WITH US, WE'LL SEE WHAT WE CAN DO . . .
WHERE'S YOUR REST-ROOM? I MUST LOOK LIKE A FRIGHT!
MAVIS WILL SHOW YOU WHERE TO FRESHEN UP, MS. DEVINE-- WE'LL TALK WHENEVER YOU'RE READY
YOU KNOW, WOLFF, THERE'S NO REASON THE BOTH OF US HAVE TO GO OVER SODD'S DEPOSITIONS . . . DAWN SEEMS A LITTLE NERVOUS AND *KOFF* ONE OF US SHOULD STAY WITH HER TO, YOU KNOW, SET HER MIND AT EASE . . .
SURE--AS SOON AS YOU'RE FINISHED WITH SODD, JOIN US IN THE CONFERENCE ROOM . . .
C'MON, WOLFF, BE A PAL . . . !

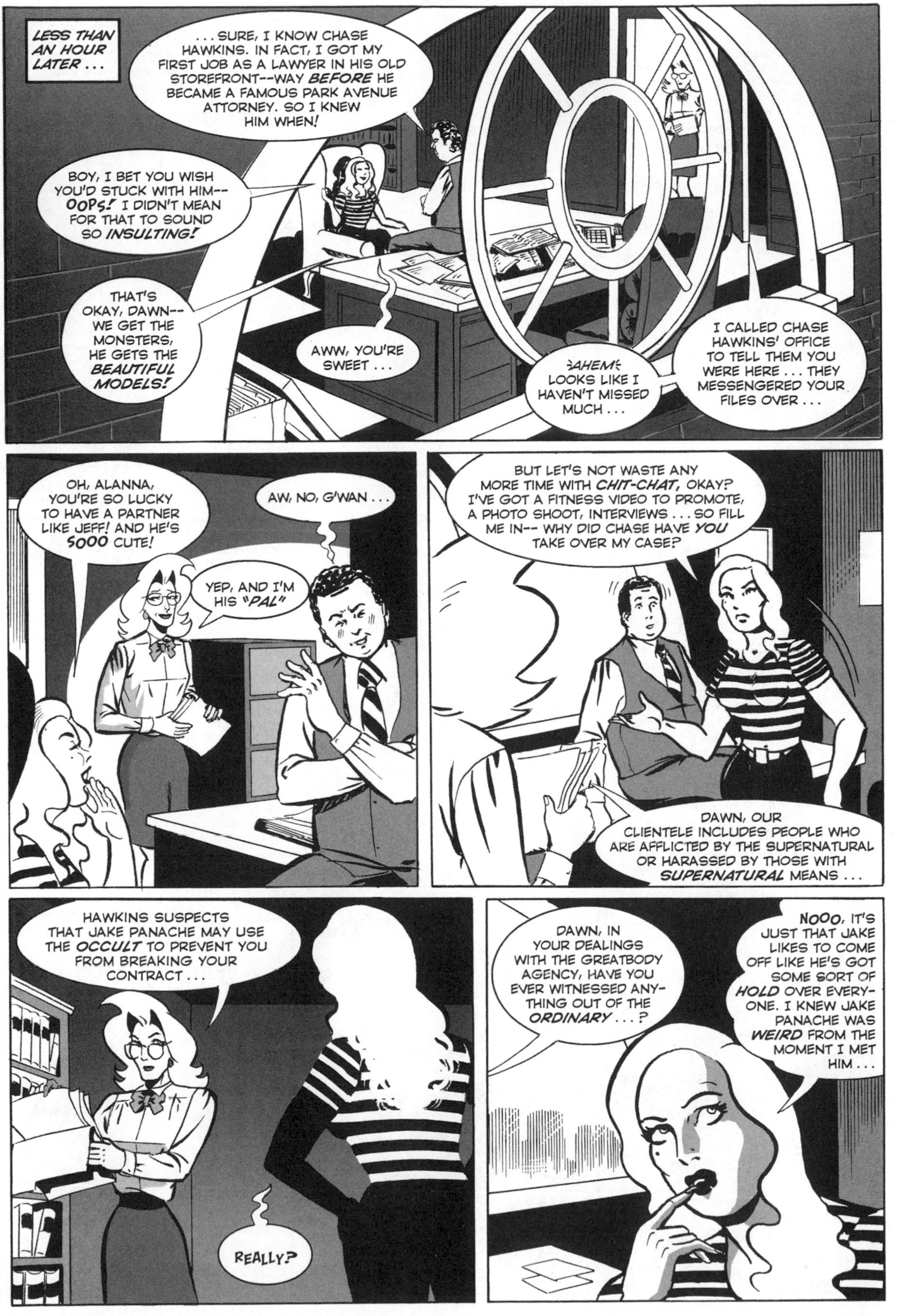

LESS THAN AN HOUR LATER . . .
. . . SURE, I KNOW CHASE HAWKINS. IN FACT, I GOT MY FIRST JOB AS A LAWYER IN HIS OLD STOREFRONT--WAY BEFORE HE BECAME A FAMOUS PARK AVENUE ATTORNEY. SO I KNEW HIM WHEN!
BOY, I BET YOU WISH YOU'D STUCK WITH HIM-- OOPS! I DIDN'T MEAN FOR THAT TO SOUND SO INSULTING!
THAT'S OKAY, DAWN-- WE GET THE MONSTERS, HE GETS THE BEAUTIFUL MODELS!
AWW, YOU'RE SWEET . . .
AHEM LOOKS LIKE I HAVEN'T MISSED MUCH . . .
I CALLED CHASE HAWKINS' OFFICE TO TELL THEM YOU WERE HERE . . . THEY MESSENGERED YOUR FILES OVER . . .
OH, ALANNA, YOU'RE SO LUCKY TO HAVE A PARTNER LIKE JEFF! AND HE'S SOOO CUTE!
AW, NO, G'WAN . . .
YEP, AND I'M HIS "PAL"
BUT LET'S NOT WASTE ANY MORE TIME WITH CHIT-CHAT, OKAY? I'VE GOT A FITNESS VIDEO TO PROMOTE, A PHOTO SHOOT, INTERVIEWS . . . SO FILL ME IN-- WHY DID CHASE HAVE YOU TAKE OVER MY CASE?
DAWN, OUR CLIENTELE INCLUDES PEOPLE WHO ARE AFFLICTED BY THE SUPERNATURAL OR HARASSED BY THOSE WITH SUPERNATURAL MEANS . . .
HAWKINS SUSPECTS THAT JAKE PANACHE MAY USE THE OCCULT TO PREVENT YOU FROM BREAKING YOUR CONTRACT . . .
REALLY?
DAWN, IN YOUR DEALINGS WITH THE GREATBODY AGENCY, HAVE YOU EVER WITNESSED ANYTHING OUT OF THE ORDINARY . . . ?
NOOO, IT'S JUST THAT JAKE LIKES TO COME OFF LIKE HE'S GOT SOME SORT OF HOLD OVER EVERYONE. I KNEW JAKE PANACHE WAS WEIRD FROM THE MOMENT I MET HIM . . .

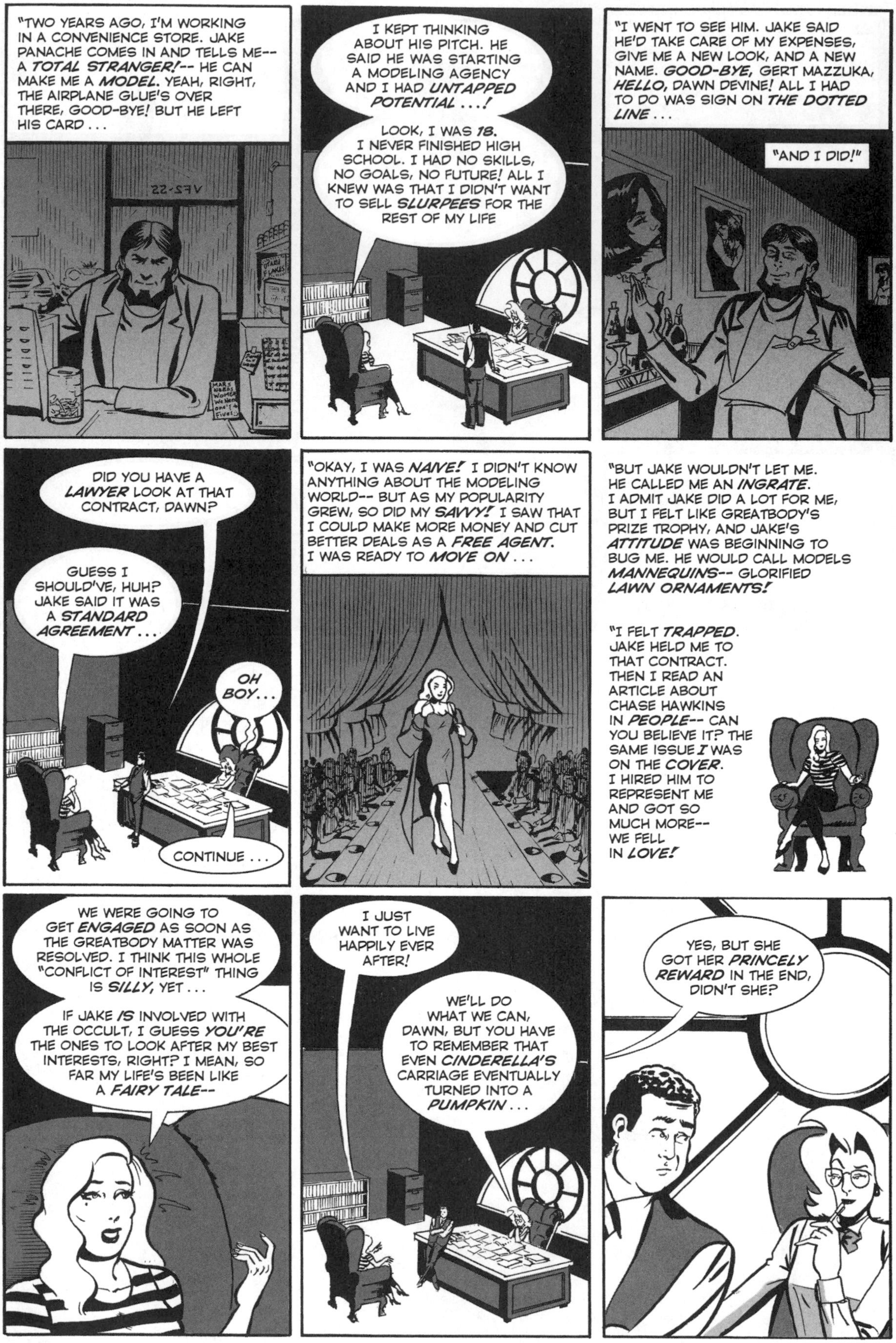
"TWO YEARS AGO, I'M WORKING IN A CONVENIENCE STORE. JAKE PANACHE COMES IN AND TELLS ME-- A TOTAL STRANGER!-- HE CAN MAKE ME A MODEL. YEAH, RIGHT, THE AIRPLANE GLUE'S OVER THERE, GOOD-BYE! BUT HE LEFT HIS CARD . . .
I KEPT THINKING ABOUT HIS PITCH. HE SAID HE WAS STARTING A MODELING AGENCY AND I HAD UNTAPPED POTENTIAL . . .!
LOOK, I WAS 18. I NEVER FINISHED HIGH SCHOOL. I HAD NO SKILLS, NO GOALS, NO FUTURE! ALL I KNEW WAS THAT I DIDN'T WANT TO SELL SLURPEES FOR THE REST OF MY LIFE
"I WENT TO SEE HIM. JAKE SAID HE'D TAKE CARE OF MY EXPENSES, GIVE ME A NEW LOOK, AND A NEW NAME. GOOD-BYE, GERT MAZZUKA, HELLO, DAWN DEVINE! ALL I HAD TO DO WAS SIGN ON THE DOTTED LINE . . .
"AND I DID!"
DID YOU HAVE A LAWYER LOOK AT THAT CONTRACT, DAWN?
GUESS I SHOULD'VE, HUH? JAKE SAID IT WAS A STANDARD AGREEMENT . . .
OH BOY . . .
CONTINUE . . .
"OKAY, I WAS NAIVE! I DIDN'T KNOW ANYTHING ABOUT THE MODELING WORLD-- BUT AS MY POPULARITY GREW, SO DID MY SAVVY! I SAW THAT I COULD MAKE MORE MONEY AND CUT BETTER DEALS AS A FREE AGENT. I WAS READY TO MOVE ON . . .
"BUT JAKE WOULDN'T LET ME. HE CALLED ME AN INGRATE. I ADMIT JAKE DID A LOT FOR ME, BUT I FELT LIKE GREATBODY'S PRIZE TROPHY, AND JAKE'S ATTITUDE WAS BEGINNING TO BUG ME. HE WOULD CALL MODELS MANNEQUINS-- GLORIFIED LAWN ORNAMENTS!
"I FELT TRAPPED. JAKE HELD ME TO THAT CONTRACT. THEN I READ AN ARTICLE ABOUT CHASE HAWKINS IN PEOPLE-- CAN YOU BELIEVE IT? THE SAME ISSUE I WAS ON THE COVER. I HIRED HIM TO REPRESENT ME AND GOT SO MUCH MORE-- WE FELL IN LOVE!
WE WERE GOING TO GET ENGAGED AS SOON AS THE GREATBODY MATTER WAS RESOLVED. I THINK THIS WHOLE "CONFLICT OF INTEREST" THING IS SILLY, YET . . .
IF JAKE IS INVOLVED WITH THE OCCULT, I GUESS YOU'RE THE ONES TO LOOK AFTER MY BEST INTERESTS, RIGHT? I MEAN, SO FAR MY LIFE'S BEEN LIKE A FAIRY TALE--
I JUST WANT TO LIVE HAPPILY EVER AFTER!
WE'LL DO WHAT WE CAN, DAWN, BUT YOU HAVE TO REMEMBER THAT EVEN CINDERELLA'S CARRIAGE EVENTUALLY TURNED INTO A PUMPKIN . . .
YES, BUT SHE GOT HER PRINCELY REWARD IN THE END, DIDN'T SHE?

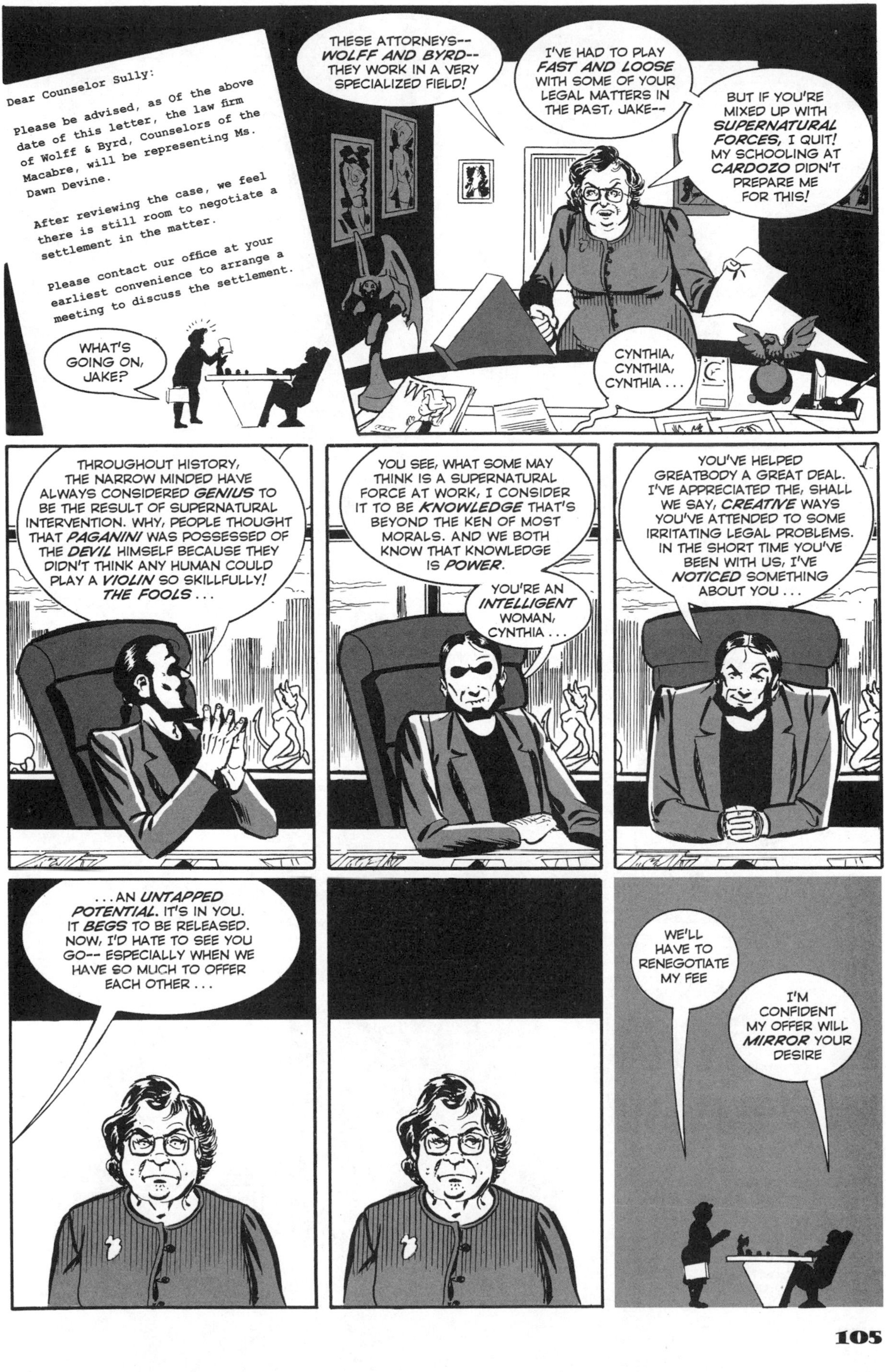
Dear Counselor Sully:
Please be advised, as Of the above date of this letter, the law firm of Wolff & Byrd, Counselors of the Macabre, will be representing Ms. Dawn Devine.
After reviewing the case, we feel there is still room to negotiate a settlement in the matter.
Please contact our office at your earliest convenience to arrange a meeting to discuss the settlement.
WHAT'S GOING ON, JAKE?
THESE ATTORNEYS-- WOLFF AND BYRD-- THEY WORK IN A VERY SPECIALIZED FIELD!
I'VE HAD TO PLAY FAST AND LOOSE WITH SOME OF YOUR LEGAL MATTERS IN THE PAST, JAKE--
BUT IF YOU'RE MIXED UP WITH SUPERNATURAL FORCES, I QUIT! MY SCHOOLING AT CARDOZO DIDN'T PREPARE ME FOR THIS!
CYNTHIA, CYNTHIA, CYNTHIA . . .
THROUGHOUT HISTORY, THE NARROW MINDED HAVE ALWAYS CONSIDERED GENIUS TO BE THE RESULT OF SUPERNATURAL INTERVENTION. WHY, PEOPLE THOUGHT THAT PAGANINI WAS POSSESSED OF THE DEVIL HIMSELF BECAUSE THEY DIDN'T THINK ANY HUMAN COULD PLAY A VIOLIN SO SKILLFULLY! THE FOOLS . . .
YOU SEE, WHAT SOME MAY THINK IS A SUPERNATURAL FORCE AT WORK, I CONSIDER IT TO BE KNOWLEDGE THAT'S BEYOND THE KEN OF MOST MORALS. AND WE BOTH KNOW THAT KNOWLEDGE IS POWER.
YOU'RE AN INTELLIGENT WOMAN, CYNTHIA . . .
YOU'VE HELPED GREATBODY A GREAT DEAL. I'VE APPRECIATED THE, SHALL WE SAY, CREATIVE WAYS YOU'VE ATTENDED TO SOME IRRITATING LEGAL PROBLEMS. IN THE SHORT TIME YOU'VE BEEN WITH US, I'VE NOTICED SOMETHING ABOUT YOU . . .
. . . AN UNTAPPED POTENTIAL. IT'S IN YOU. IT BEGS TO BE RELEASED. NOW, I'D HATE TO SEE YOU GO-- ESPECIALLY WHEN WE HAVE SO MUCH TO OFFER EACH OTHER . . .
WE'LL HAVE TO RENEGOTIATE MY FEE
I'M CONFIDENT MY OFFER WILL MIRROR YOUR DESIRE

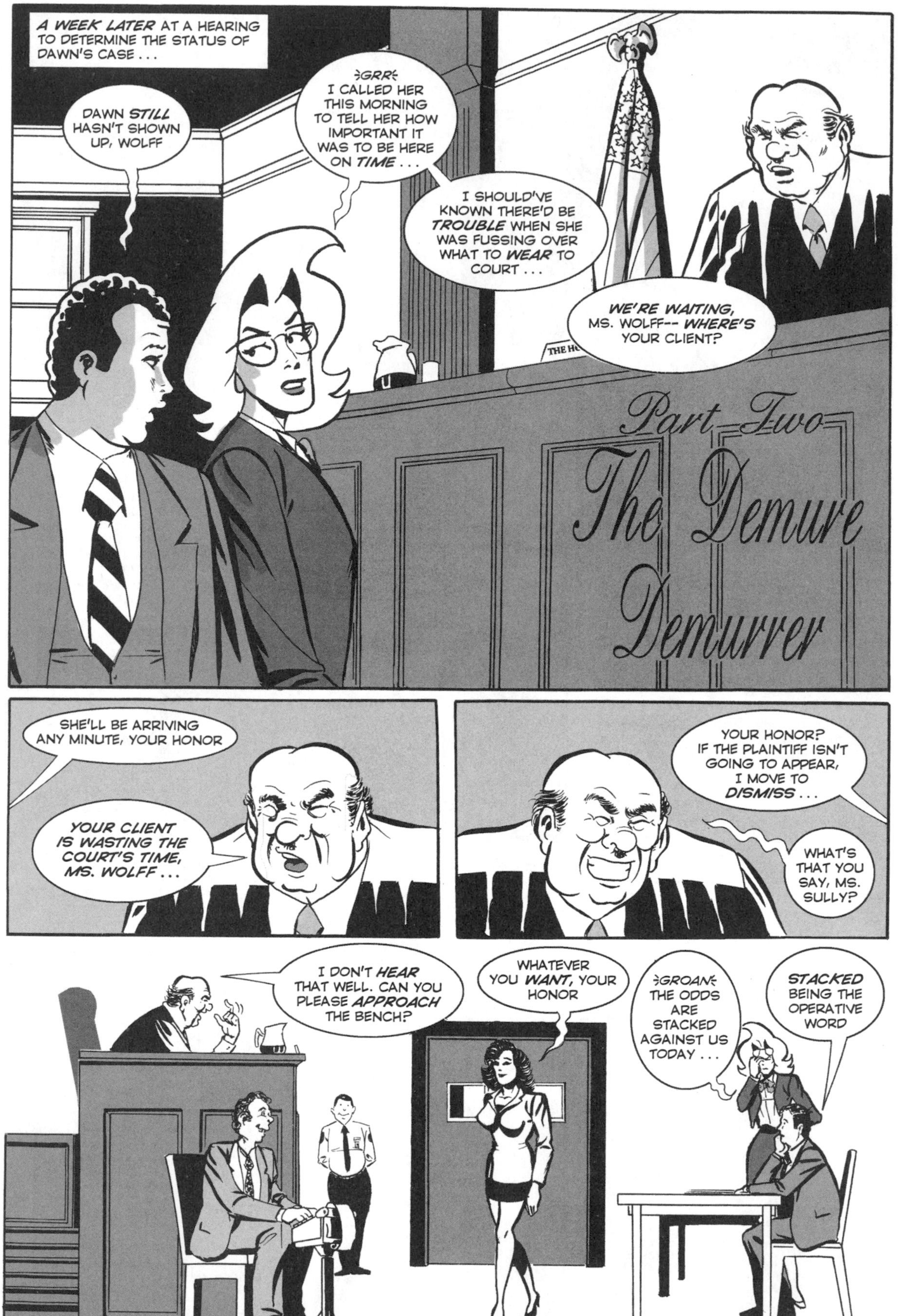
A WEEK LATER AT A HEARING TO DETERMINE THE STATUS OF DAWN'S CASE . . .
DAWN STILL HASN'T SHOWN UP, WOLFF
GRR I CALLED HER THIS MORNING TO TELL HER HOW IMPORTANT IT WAS TO BE HERE ON TIME . . .
I SHOULD'VE KNOWN THERE'D BE TROUBLE WHEN SHE WAS FUSSING OVER WHAT TO WEAR TO COURT . . .
WE'RE WAITING, MS. WOLFF-- WHERE'S YOUR CLIENT?
Part Two
The Demure Demurrer
SHE'LL BE ARRIVING ANY MINUTE, YOUR HONOR
YOUR CLIENT IS WASTING THE COURT'S TIME, MS. WOLFF . . .
YOUR HONOR? IF THE PLAINTIFF ISN'T GOING TO APPEAR, I MOVE TO DISMISS . . .
WHAT'S THAT YOU SAY, MS. SULLY?
I DON'T HEAR THAT WELL. CAN YOU PLEASE APPROACH THE BENCH?
WHATEVER YOU WANT, YOUR HONOR
GROAN THE ODDS ARE STACKED AGAINST US TODAY . . .
STACKED BEING THE OPERATIVE WORD

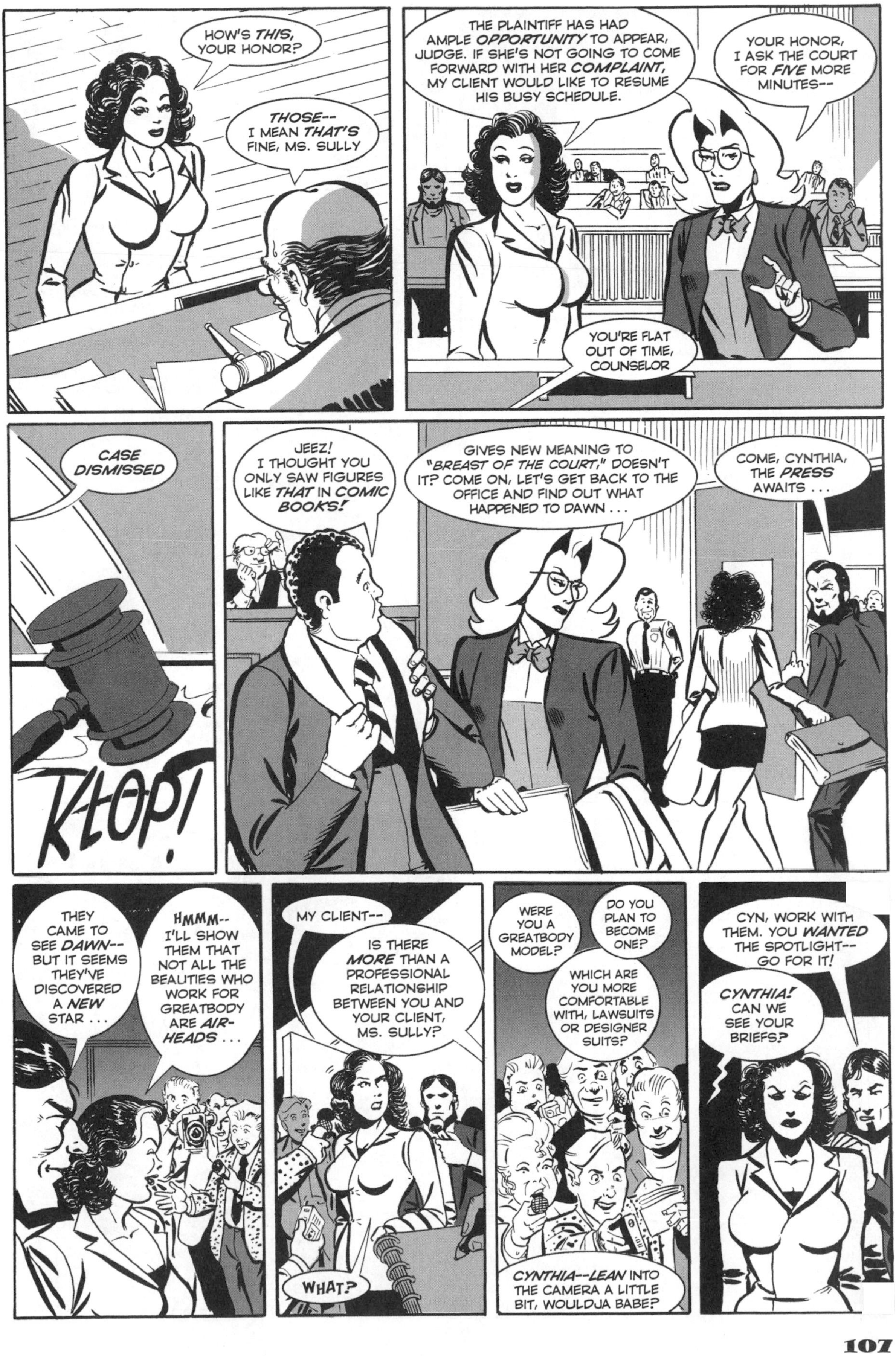
HOW'S THIS, YOUR HONOR?
THOSE-- I MEAN THAT'S FINE, MS. SULLY
THE PLAINTIFF HAS HAD AMPLE OPPORTUNITY TO APPEAR, JUDGE. IF SHE'S NOT GOING TO COME FORWARD WITH HER COMPLAINT, MY CLIENT WOULD LIKE TO RESUME HIS BUSY SCHEDULE.
YOUR HONOR, I ASK THE COURT FOR FIVE MORE MINUTES--
YOU'RE FLAT OUT OF TIME, COUNSELOR
CASE DISMISSED
KLOP!
JEEZ! I THOUGHT YOU ONLY SAW FIGURES LIKE THAT IN COMIC BOOKS!
GIVES NEW MEANING TO "BREAST OF THE COURT," DOESN'T IT? COME ON, LET'S GET BACK TO THE OFFICE AND FIND OUT WHAT HAPPENED TO DAWN . . .
COME, CYNTHIA, THE PRESS AWAITS . . .
THEY CAME TO SEE DAWN-- BUT IT SEEMS THEY'VE DISCOVERED A NEW STAR . . .
HMMM-- I'LL SHOW THEM THAT NOT ALL THE BEAUTIES WHO WORK FOR GREATBODY ARE AIR-HEADS . . .
MY CLIENT--
IS THERE MORE THAN A PROFESSIONAL RELATIONSHIP BETWEEN YOU AND YOUR CLIENT, MS. SULLY?
WHAT?
WERE YOU A GREATBODY MODEL?
DO YOU PLAN TO BECOME ONE?
WHICH ARE YOU MORE COMFORTABLE WITH, LAWSUITS OR DESIGNER SUITS?
CYNTHIA--LEAN INTO THE CAMERA A LITTLE BIT, WOULDJA BABE?
CYN, WORK WITH THEM. YOU WANTED THE SPOTLIGHT-- GO FOR IT!
CYNTHIA! CAN WE SEE YOUR BRIEFS?

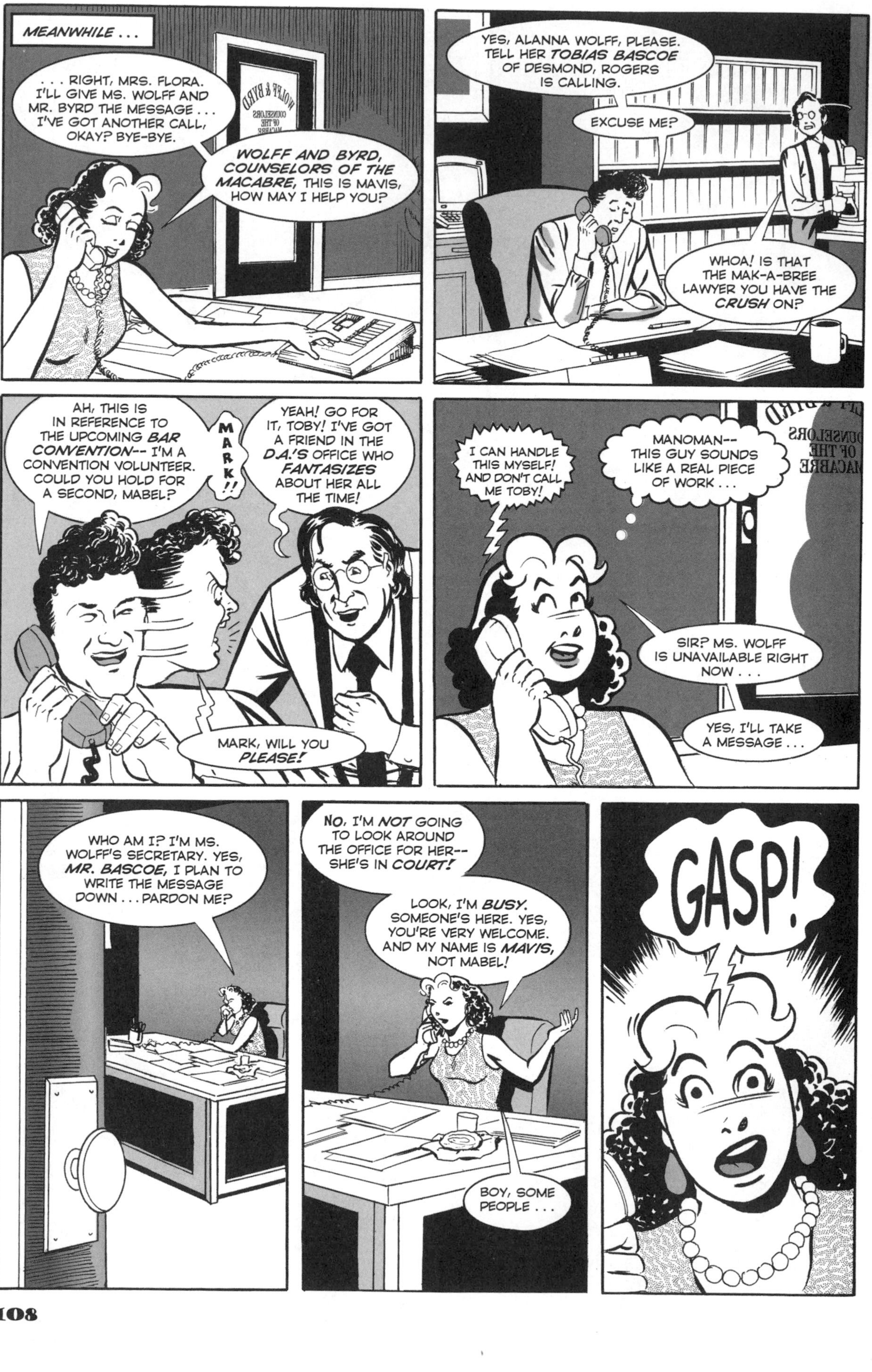

MEANWHILE . . .
. . . RIGHT, MRS. FLORA. I'LL GIVE MS. WOLFF AND MR. BYRD THE MESSAGE . . . I'VE GOT ANOTHER CALL, OKAY? BYE-BYE.
WOLFF AND BYRD, COUNSELORS OF THE MACABRE, THIS IS MAVIS, HOW MAY I HELP YOU?
YES, ALANNA WOLFF, PLEASE. TELL HER TOBIAS BASCOE OF DESMOND, ROGERS IS CALLING.
EXCUSE ME?
WHOA! IS THAT THE MAK-A-BREE LAWYER YOU HAVE THE CRUSH ON?
AH, THIS IS IN REFERENCE TO THE UPCOMING BAR CONVENTION-- I'M A CONVENTION VOLUNTEER. COULD YOU HOLD FOR A SECOND, MABEL?
MARK!!
YEAH! GO FOR IT, TOBY! I'VE GOT A FRIEND IN THE D.A.'S OFFICE WHO FANTASIZES ABOUT HER ALL THE TIME!
MARK, WILL YOU PLEASE!
I CAN HANDLE THIS MYSELF! AND DON'T CALL ME TOBY!
MANOMAN-- THIS GUY SOUNDS LIKE A REAL PIECE OF WORK . . .
SIR? MS. WOLFF IS UNAVAILABLE RIGHT NOW . . .
YES, I'LL TAKE A MESSAGE . . .
WHO AM I? I'M MS. WOLFF'S SECRETARY. YES, MR. BASCOE, I PLAN TO WRITE THE MESSAGE DOWN . . . PARDON ME?
NO, I'M NOT GOING TO LOOK AROUND THE OFFICE FOR HER-- SHE'S IN COURT!
LOOK, I'M BUSY. SOMEONE'S HERE. YES, YOU'RE VERY WELCOME. AND MY NAME IS MAVIS, NOT MABEL!
BOY, SOME PEOPLE . . .
GASP!

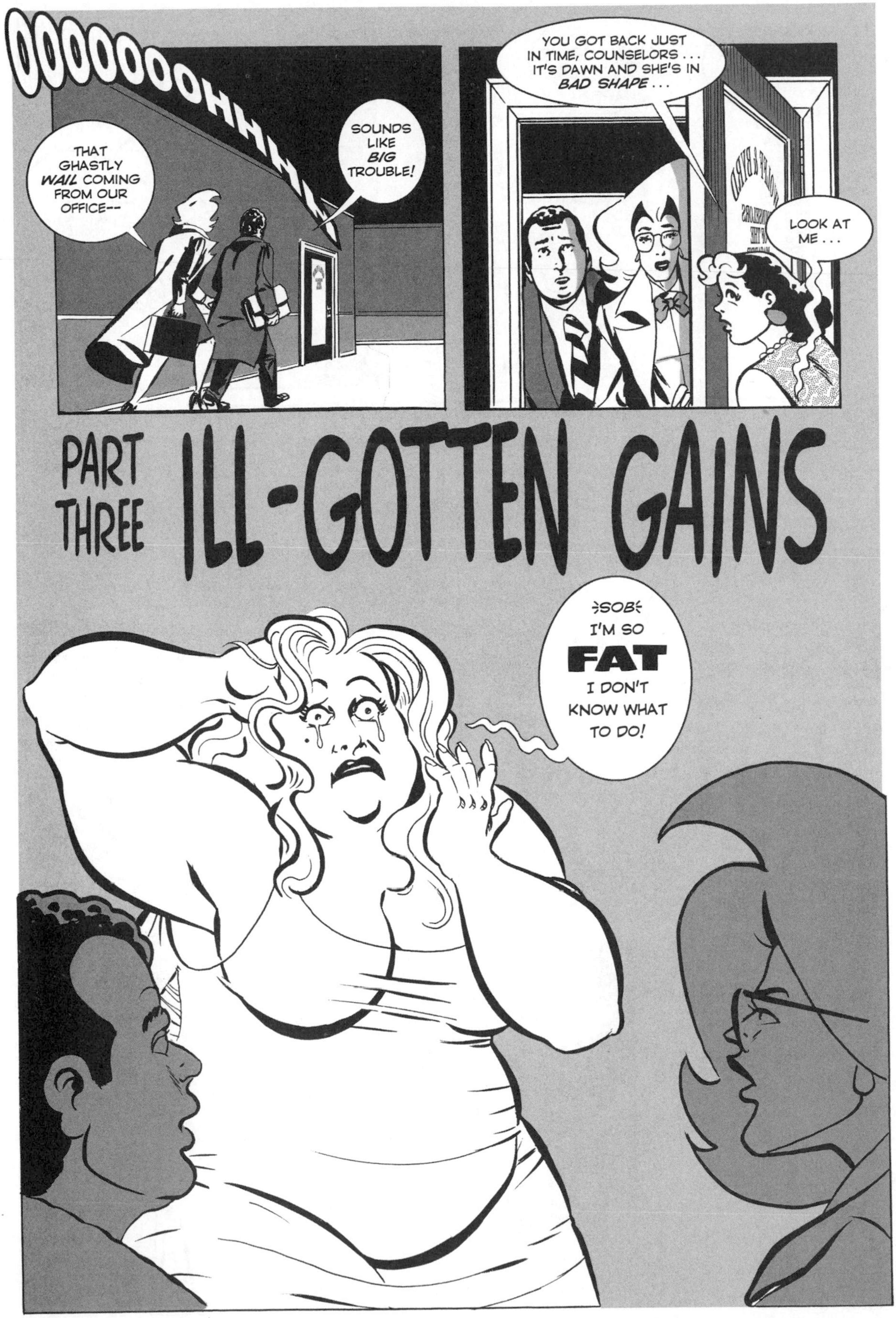
OOOOOOOHHHHH
THAT GHASTLY WAIL COMING FROM OUR OFFICE--
SOUNDS LIKE BIG TROUBLE!
YOU GOT BACK JUST IN TIME, COUNSELORS . . . IT'S DAWN AND SHE'S IN BAD SHAPE . . .
LOOK AT ME . . .
PART THREE ILL-GOTTEN GAINS
SOB I'M SO FAT I DON'T KNOW WHAT TO DO!

PANACHE KNEW YOU'D BE TOO *HUMILIATED* TO APPEAR IN PUBLIC IN THIS CONDITION!

WE'LL GET A *COURT ORDER* FOR HIM TO *REMOVE* THIS SPELL

I- I STARTED *EXPANDING* ON THE WAY TO COURT-- I- I NEVER THOUGHT IT WOULD COME TO THIS . . . ЗCHOKEЄ

BUT JAKE *DIDN'T* PUT A SPELL ON ME--

HE TOOK IT OFF! ЗSOBЄ THIS IS WHAT I LOOKED LIKE WHEN JAKE MET ME!!

I KNOW WHAT YOU MUST BE GOING THROUGH, BUT I WISH YOU'D *LEVELED* WITH US FROM THE BEGINNING--

YOU HAVE NO IDEA WHAT I'M GOING THROUGH, ALANNA! I'LL BET YOU'VE NEVER HAD A *WEIGHT PROBLEM* IN YOUR LIFE!

AND *YOU*, JEFF-- YOU'RE NOT FLIRTING WITH ME *NOW*, ARE YOU? I'M *STILL* THE *SAME* PERSON, BUT IT'S *DIFFERENT* NOW, ISN'T IT?

UHH-- DIDN'T YOU THINK PANACHE WOULD *REVERSE* THE SPELL IF YOU CAUSED HIM *TROUBLE*?

ЗSOBЄ HE TOLD ME MY NEW FORM WAS *PERMANENT!* I NEVER WANTED TO *REMEMBER* HOW I WAS-- THAT'S WHY I DIDN'T TELL YOU ЗCHOKEЄ I DIDN'T THINK I'D *EVER* CHANGE!

PLEASE . . . I NEED TO TALK TO CHASE . . .

SURE-- WE'LL BE OUT HERE IF YOU NEED US . . .

WELL, HER FAIRY TALE JUST GOT *GRIM* . . .

AND I WOULDN'T COUNT ON PRINCE CHARMING TO SAVE THE DAY . . .

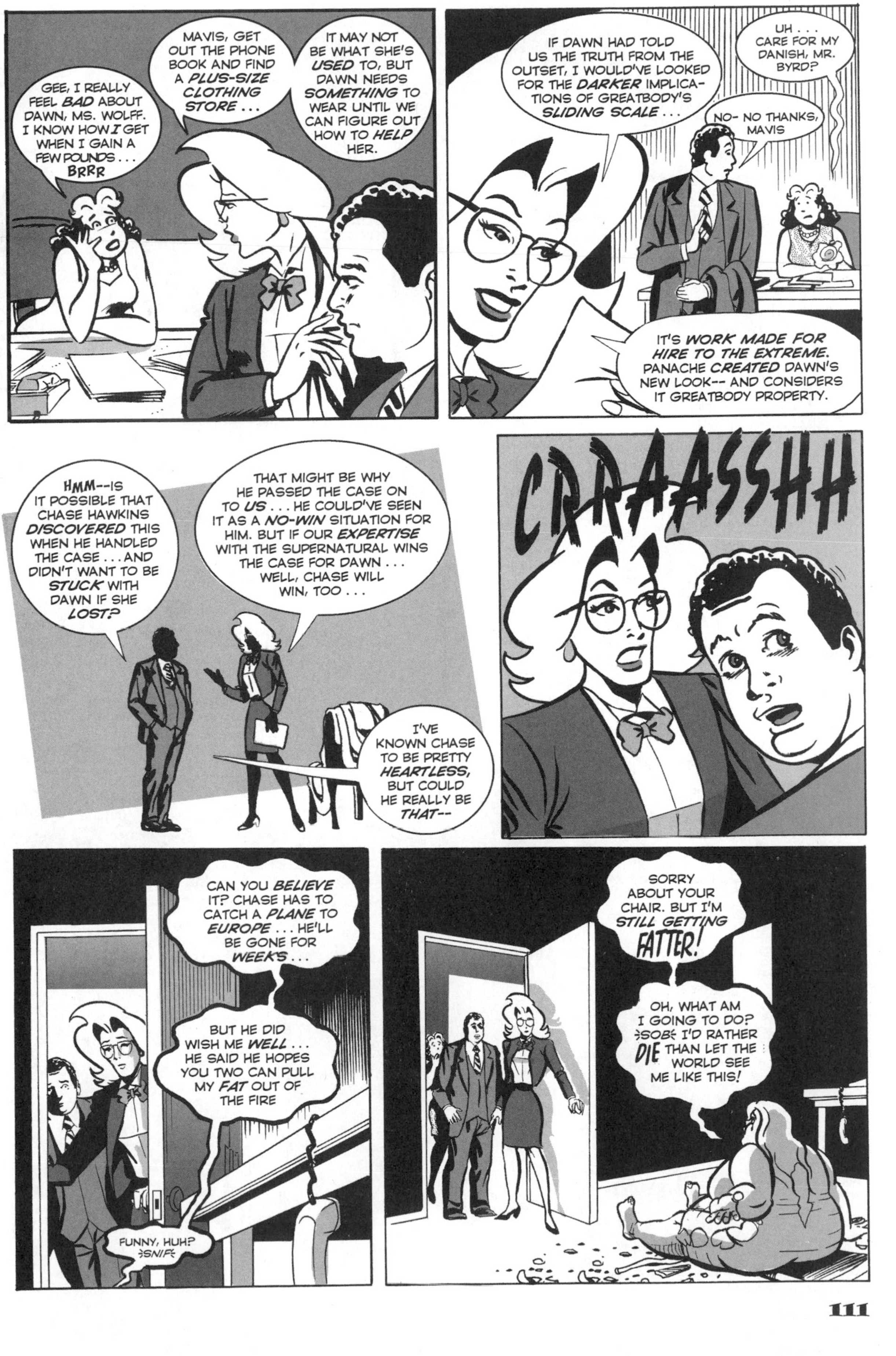
GEE, I REALLY FEEL BAD ABOUT DAWN, MS. WOLFF. I KNOW HOW I GET WHEN I GAIN A FEW POUNDS . . . BRRR
MAVIS, GET OUT THE PHONE BOOK AND FIND A PLUS-SIZE CLOTHING STORE . . .
IT MAY NOT BE WHAT SHE'S USED TO, BUT DAWN NEEDS SOMETHING TO WEAR UNTIL WE CAN FIGURE OUT HOW TO HELP HER.
IF DAWN HAD TOLD US THE TRUTH FROM THE OUTSET, I WOULD'VE LOOKED FOR THE DARKER IMPLICATIONS OF GREATBODY'S SLIDING SCALE . . .
UH . . . CARE FOR MY DANISH, MR. BYRD?
NO- NO THANKS, MAVIS
IT'S WORK MADE FOR HIRE TO THE EXTREME. PANACHE CREATED DAWN'S NEW LOOK-- AND CONSIDERS IT GREATBODY PROPERTY.
HMM--IS IT POSSIBLE THAT CHASE HAWKINS DISCOVERED THIS WHEN HE HANDLED THE CASE . . . AND DIDN'T WANT TO BE STUCK WITH DAWN IF SHE LOST?
THAT MIGHT BE WHY HE PASSED THE CASE ON TO US . . . HE COULD'VE SEEN IT AS A NO-WIN SITUATION FOR HIM. BUT IF OUR EXPERTISE WITH THE SUPERNATURAL WINS THE CASE FOR DAWN . . . WELL, CHASE WILL WIN, TOO . . .
I'VE KNOWN CHASE TO BE PRETTY HEARTLESS, BUT COULD HE REALLY BE THAT--
CRRAASSHH
CAN YOU BELIEVE IT? CHASE HAS TO CATCH A PLANE TO EUROPE . . . HE'LL BE GONE FOR WEEKS . . .
BUT HE DID WISH ME WELL . . . HE SAID HE HOPES YOU TWO CAN PULL MY FAT OUT OF THE FIRE
FUNNY, HUH? ⟩SNIF⟨
SORRY ABOUT YOUR CHAIR. BUT I'M STILL GETTING FATTER!
OH, WHAT AM I GOING TO DO? ⟩SOB⟨ I'D RATHER DIE THAN LET THE WORLD SEE ME LIKE THIS!

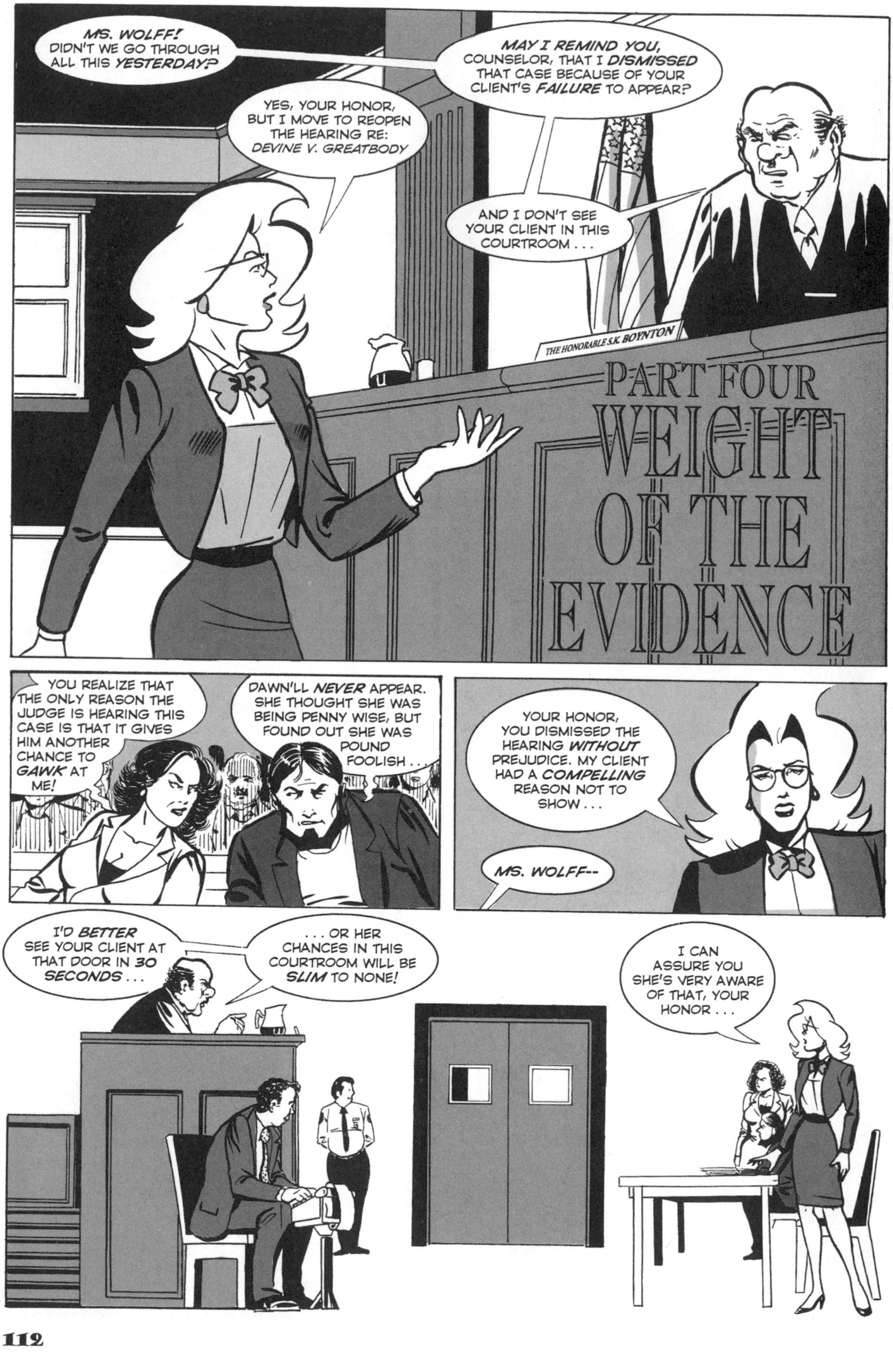
MS. WOLFF! DIDN'T WE GO THROUGH ALL THIS YESTERDAY?
YES, YOUR HONOR, BUT I MOVE TO REOPEN THE HEARING RE: DEVINE V. GREATBODY
MAY I REMIND YOU, COUNSELOR, THAT I DISMISSED THAT CASE BECAUSE OF YOUR CLIENT'S FAILURE TO APPEAR?
AND I DON'T SEE YOUR CLIENT IN THIS COURTROOM . . .
THE HONORABLE S.K. BOYNTON
PART FOUR
WEIGHT OF THE EVIDENCE
YOU REALIZE THAT THE ONLY REASON THE JUDGE IS HEARING THIS CASE IS THAT IT GIVES HIM ANOTHER CHANCE TO GAWK AT ME!
DAWN'LL NEVER APPEAR. SHE THOUGHT SHE WAS BEING PENNY WISE, BUT FOUND OUT SHE WAS POUND FOOLISH . . .
YOUR HONOR, YOU DISMISSED THE HEARING WITHOUT PREJUDICE. MY CLIENT HAD A COMPELLING REASON NOT TO SHOW . . .
MS. WOLFF--
I'D BETTER SEE YOUR CLIENT AT THAT DOOR IN 30 SECONDS . . .
. . . OR HER CHANCES IN THIS COURTROOM WILL BE SLIM TO NONE!
I CAN ASSURE YOU SHE'S VERY AWARE OF THAT, YOUR HONOR . . .

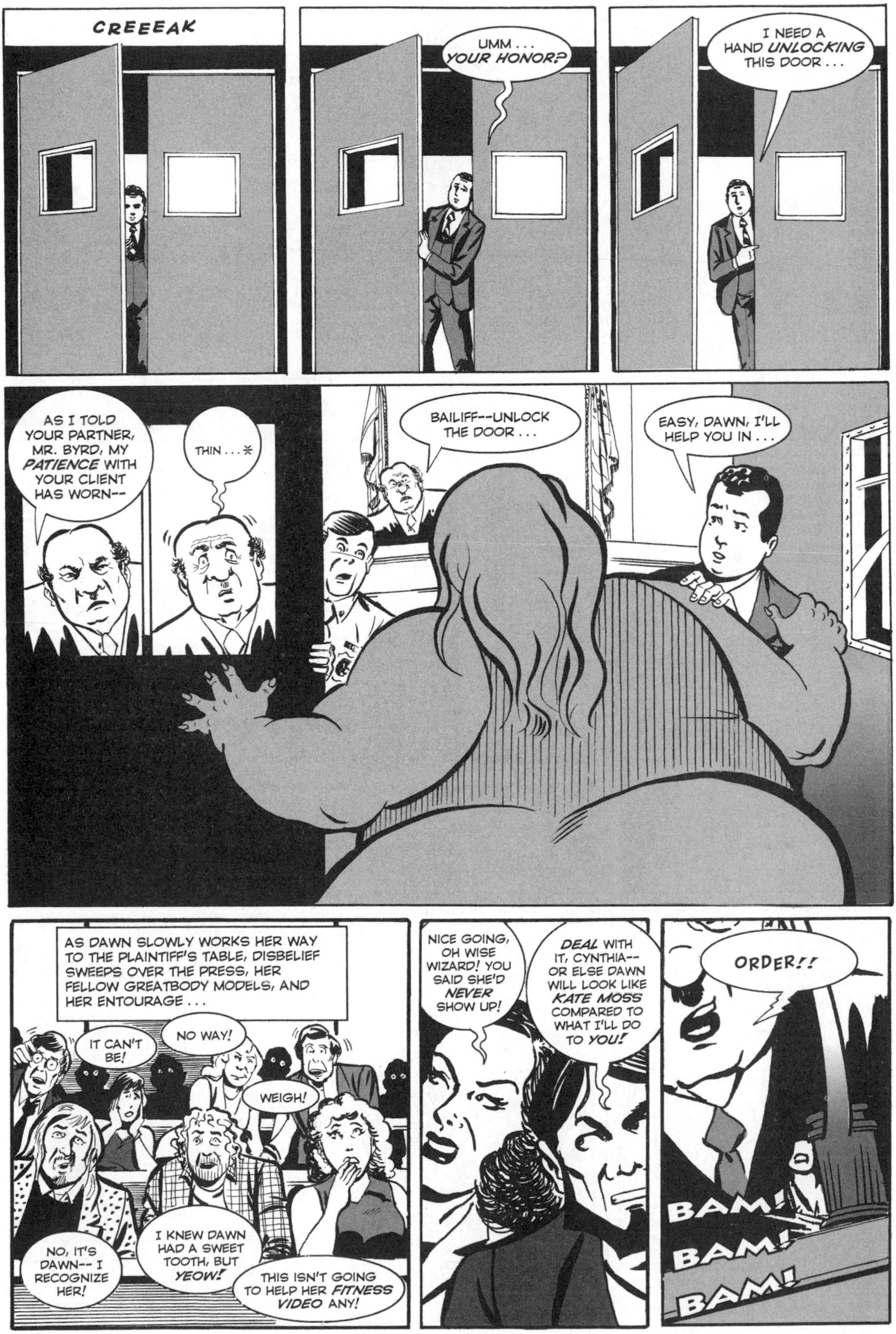
CREEEAK
UMM . . . YOUR HONOR?
I NEED A HAND UNLOCKING THIS DOOR . . .
AS I TOLD YOUR PARTNER, MR. BYRD, MY PATIENCE WITH YOUR CLIENT HAS WORN--
THIN . . .
BAILIFF--UNLOCK THE DOOR . . .
EASY, DAWN, I'LL HELP YOU IN . . .
AS DAWN SLOWLY WORKS HER WAY TO THE PLAINTIFF'S TABLE, DISBELIEF SWEEPS OVER THE PRESS, HER FELLOW GREATBODY MODELS, AND HER ENTOURAGE . . .
IT CAN'T BE!
NO WAY!
WEIGH!
NO, IT'S DAWN-- I RECOGNIZE HER!
I KNEW DAWN HAD A SWEET TOOTH, BUT YEOW!
THIS ISN'T GOING TO HELP HER FITNESS VIDEO ANY!
NICE GOING, OH WISE WIZARD! YOU SAID SHE'D NEVER SHOW UP!
DEAL WITH IT, CYNTHIA-- OR ELSE DAWN WILL LOOK LIKE KATE MOSS COMPARED TO WHAT I'LL DO TO YOU!
ORDER!!
BAM!
BAM!
BAM!

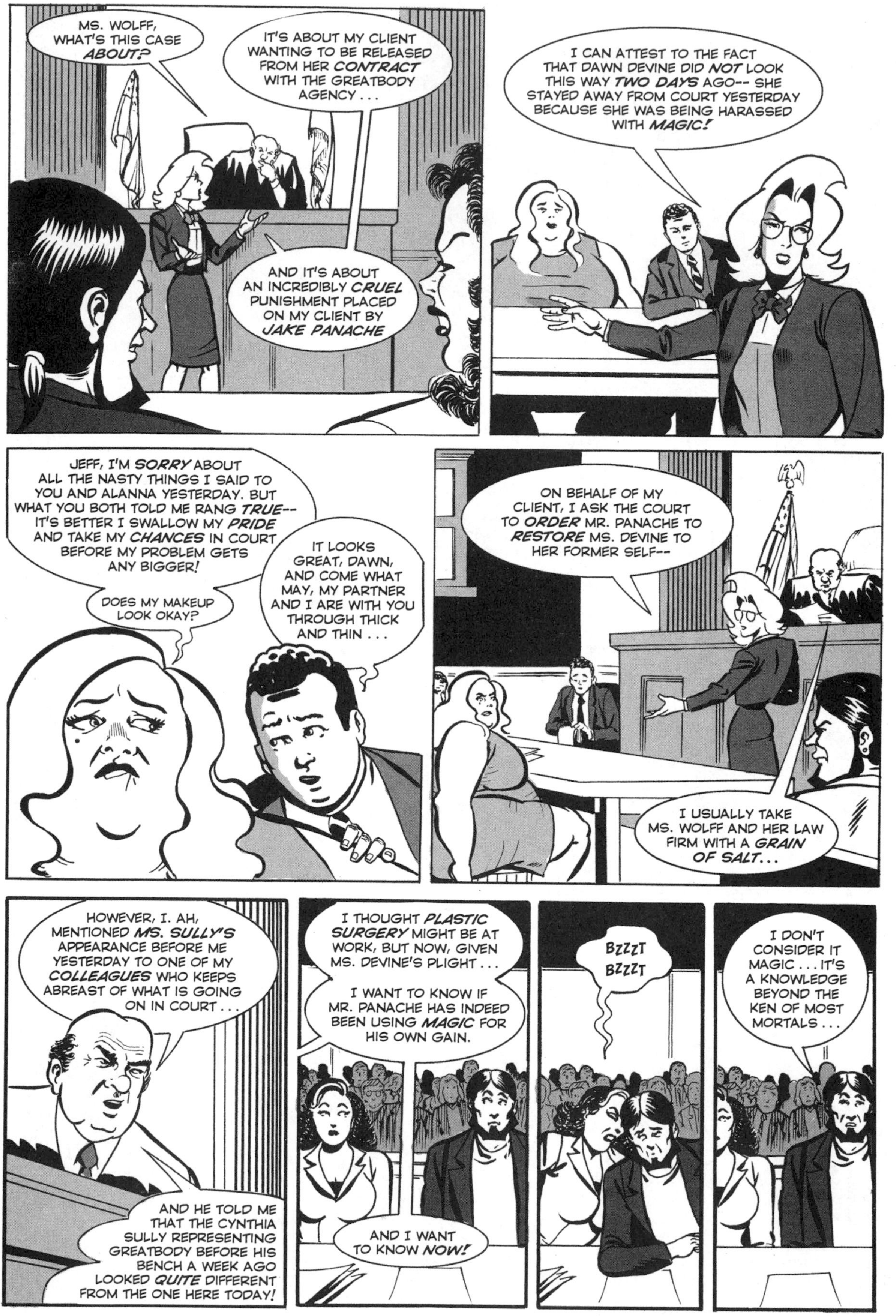
MS. WOLFF, WHAT'S THIS CASE ABOUT?
IT'S ABOUT MY CLIENT WANTING TO BE RELEASED FROM HER CONTRACT WITH THE GREATBODY AGENCY . . .
AND IT'S ABOUT AN INCREDIBLY CRUEL PUNISHMENT PLACED ON MY CLIENT BY JAKE PANACHE
I CAN ATTEST TO THE FACT THAT DAWN DEVINE DID NOT LOOK THIS WAY TWO DAYS AGO-- SHE STAYED AWAY FROM COURT YESTERDAY BECAUSE SHE WAS BEING HARASSED WITH MAGIC!
JEFF, I'M SORRY ABOUT ALL THE NASTY THINGS I SAID TO YOU AND ALANNA YESTERDAY. BUT WHAT YOU BOTH TOLD ME RANG TRUE-- IT'S BETTER I SWALLOW MY PRIDE AND TAKE MY CHANCES IN COURT BEFORE MY PROBLEM GETS ANY BIGGER!
DOES MY MAKEUP LOOK OKAY?
IT LOOKS GREAT, DAWN, AND COME WHAT MAY, MY PARTNER AND I ARE WITH YOU THROUGH THICK AND THIN . . .
ON BEHALF OF MY CLIENT, I ASK THE COURT TO ORDER MR. PANACHE TO RESTORE MS. DEVINE TO HER FORMER SELF--
I USUALLY TAKE MS. WOLFF AND HER LAW FIRM WITH A GRAIN OF SALT . . .
HOWEVER, I. AH, MENTIONED MS. SULLY'S APPEARANCE BEFORE ME YESTERDAY TO ONE OF MY COLLEAGUES WHO KEEPS ABREAST OF WHAT IS GOING ON IN COURT . . .
AND HE TOLD ME THAT THE CYNTHIA SULLY REPRESENTING GREATBODY BEFORE HIS BENCH A WEEK AGO LOOKED QUITE DIFFERENT FROM THE ONE HERE TODAY!
I THOUGHT PLASTIC SURGERY MIGHT BE AT WORK, BUT NOW, GIVEN MS. DEVINE'S PLIGHT . . .
I WANT TO KNOW IF MR. PANACHE HAS INDEED BEEN USING MAGIC FOR HIS OWN GAIN.
AND I WANT TO KNOW NOW!
BZZZT BZZZT
I DON'T CONSIDER IT MAGIC . . . IT'S A KNOWLEDGE BEYOND THE KEN OF MOST MORTALS . . .

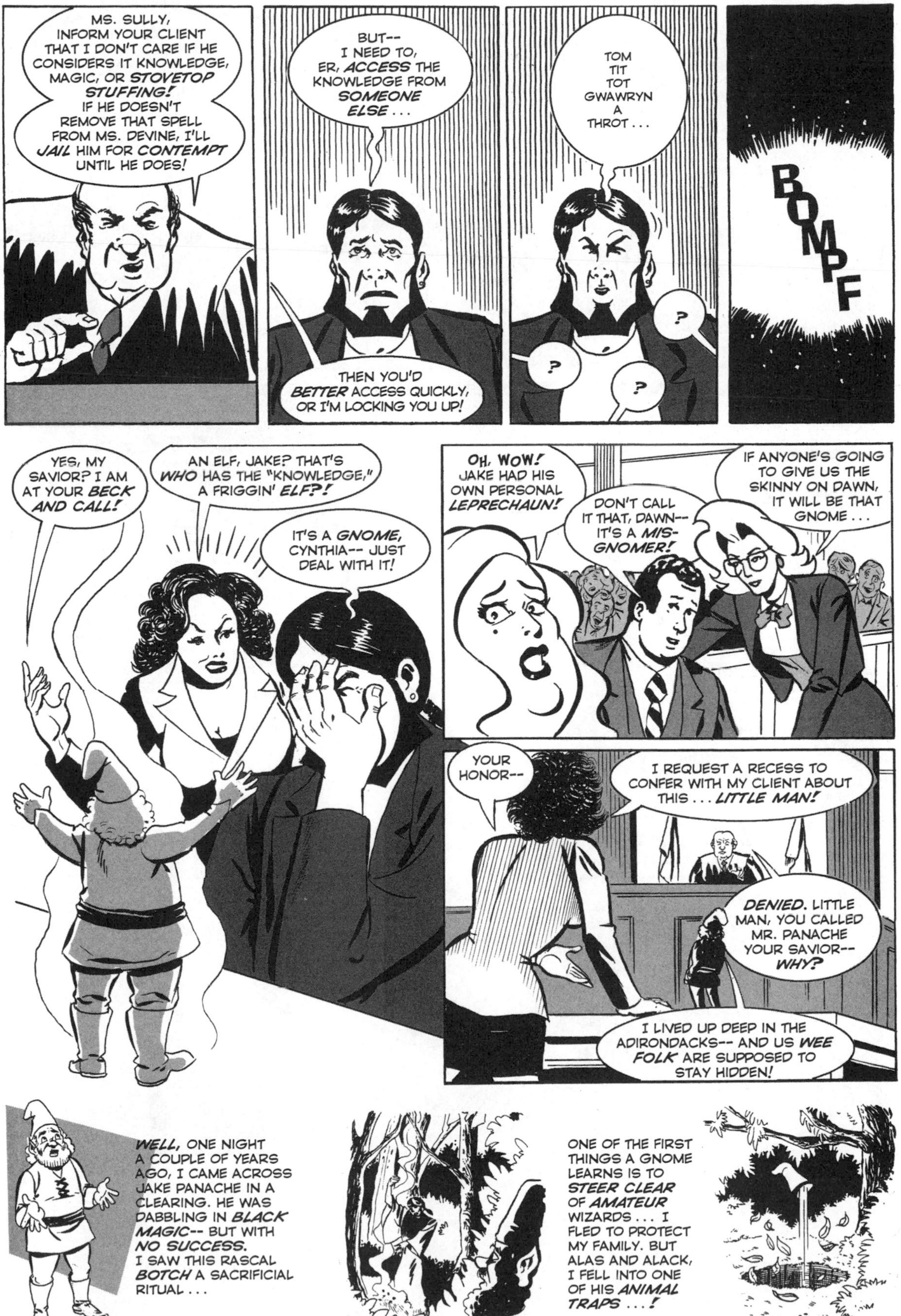

MS. SULLY, INFORM YOUR CLIENT THAT I DON'T CARE IF HE CONSIDERS IT KNOWLEDGE, MAGIC, OR STOVETOP STUFFING! IF HE DOESN'T REMOVE THAT SPELL FROM MS. DEVINE, I'LL JAIL HIM FOR CONTEMPT UNTIL HE DOES!
BUT-- I NEED TO, ER, ACCESS THE KNOWLEDGE FROM SOMEONE ELSE . . .
THEN YOU'D BETTER ACCESS QUICKLY, OR I'M LOCKING YOU UP!
TOM TIT TOT GWAWRYN A THROT . . .
?
?
?
BOMPF
YES, MY SAVIOR? I AM AT YOUR BECK AND CALL!
AN ELF, JAKE? THAT'S WHO HAS THE "KNOWLEDGE," A FRIGGIN' ELF?!
IT'S A GNOME, CYNTHIA-- JUST DEAL WITH IT!
OH, WOW! JAKE HAD HIS OWN PERSONAL LEPRECHAUN!
DON'T CALL IT THAT, DAWN-- IT'S A MIS-GNOMER!
IF ANYONE'S GOING TO GIVE US THE SKINNY ON DAWN, IT WILL BE THAT GNOME . . .
YOUR HONOR--
I REQUEST A RECESS TO CONFER WITH MY CLIENT ABOUT THIS . . . LITTLE MAN!
DENIED. LITTLE MAN, YOU CALLED MR. PANACHE YOUR SAVIOR-- WHY?
I LIVED UP DEEP IN THE ADIRONDACKS-- AND US WEE FOLK ARE SUPPOSED TO STAY HIDDEN!
WELL, ONE NIGHT A COUPLE OF YEARS AGO, I CAME ACROSS JAKE PANACHE IN A CLEARING. HE WAS DABBLING IN BLACK MAGIC-- BUT WITH NO SUCCESS. I SAW THIS RASCAL BOTCH A SACRIFICIAL RITUAL . . .
ONE OF THE FIRST THINGS A GNOME LEARNS IS TO STEER CLEAR OF AMATEUR WIZARDS . . . I FLED TO PROTECT MY FAMILY. BUT ALAS AND ALACK, I FELL INTO ONE OF HIS ANIMAL TRAPS . . . !

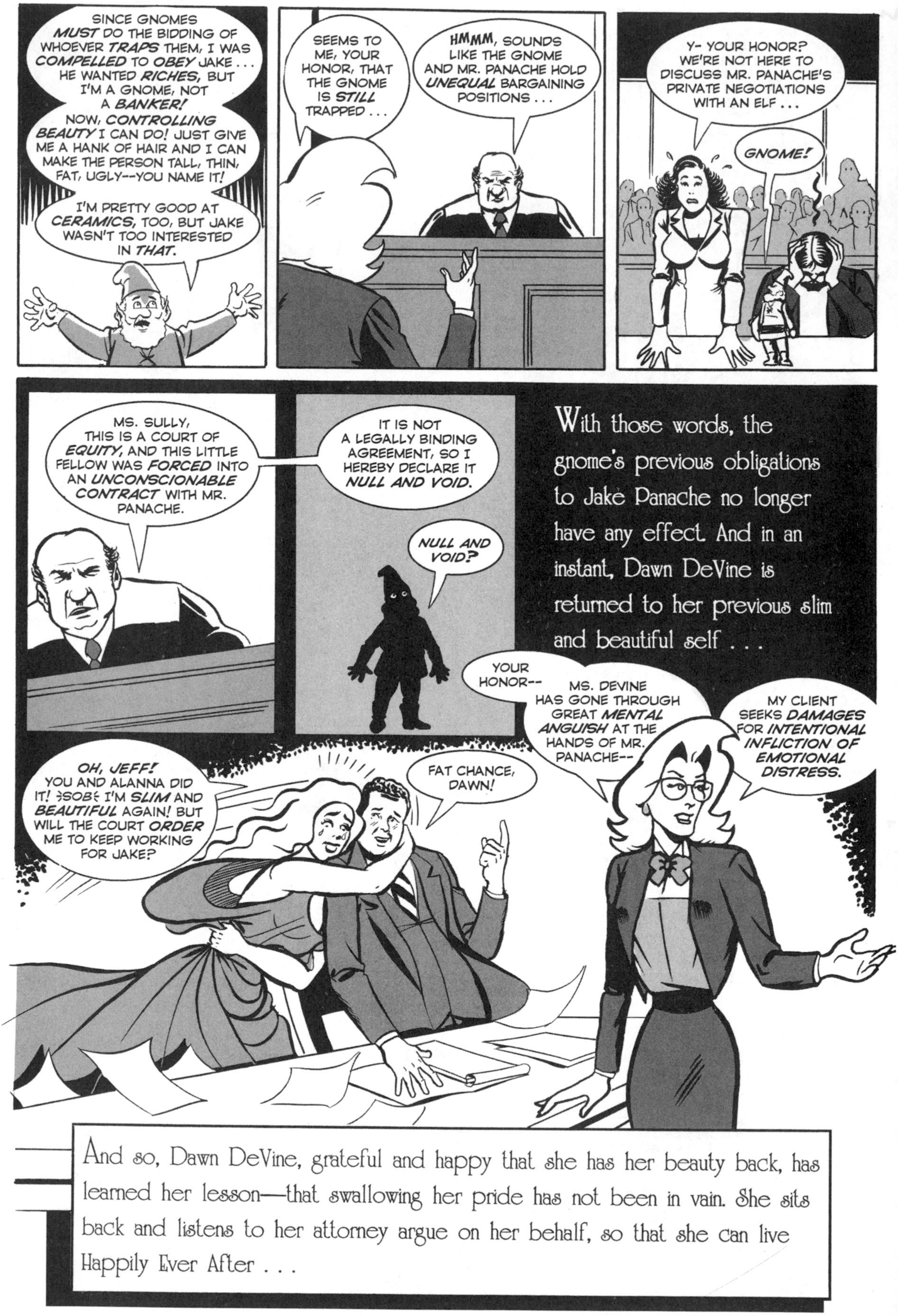
SINCE GNOMES MUST DO THE BIDDING OF WHOEVER TRAPS THEM, I WAS COMPELLED TO OBEY JAKE . . . HE WANTED RICHES, BUT I'M A GNOME, NOT A BANKER!
NOW, CONTROLLING BEAUTY I CAN DO! JUST GIVE ME A HANK OF HAIR AND I CAN MAKE THE PERSON TALL, THIN, FAT, UGLY--YOU NAME IT!
I'M PRETTY GOOD AT CERAMICS, TOO, BUT JAKE WASN'T TOO INTERESTED IN THAT.
SEEMS TO ME, YOUR HONOR, THAT THE GNOME IS STILL TRAPPED . . .
HMMM, SOUNDS LIKE THE GNOME AND MR. PANACHE HOLD UNEQUAL BARGAINING POSITIONS . . .
Y- YOUR HONOR? WE'RE NOT HERE TO DISCUSS MR. PANACHE'S PRIVATE NEGOTIATIONS WITH AN ELF . . .
GNOME!
MS. SULLY, THIS IS A COURT OF EQUITY, AND THIS LITTLE FELLOW WAS FORCED INTO AN UNCONSCIONABLE CONTRACT WITH MR. PANACHE.
IT IS NOT A LEGALLY BINDING AGREEMENT, SO I HEREBY DECLARE IT NULL AND VOID.
NULL AND VOID?
With those words, the gnome's previous obligations to Jake Panache no longer have any effect. And in an instant, Dawn DeVine is returned to her previous slim and beautiful self . . .
OH, JEFF! YOU AND ALANNA DID IT! *SOB* I'M SLIM AND BEAUTIFUL AGAIN! BUT WILL THE COURT ORDER ME TO KEEP WORKING FOR JAKE?
FAT CHANCE, DAWN!
YOUR HONOR--
MS. DEVINE HAS GONE THROUGH GREAT MENTAL ANGUISH AT THE HANDS OF MR. PANACHE--
MY CLIENT SEEKS DAMAGES FOR INTENTIONAL INFLICTION OF EMOTIONAL DISTRESS.
And so, Dawn DeVine, grateful and happy that she has her beauty back, has learned her lesson—that swallowing her pride has not been in vain. She sits back and listens to her attorney argue on her behalf, so that she can live Happily Ever After . . .

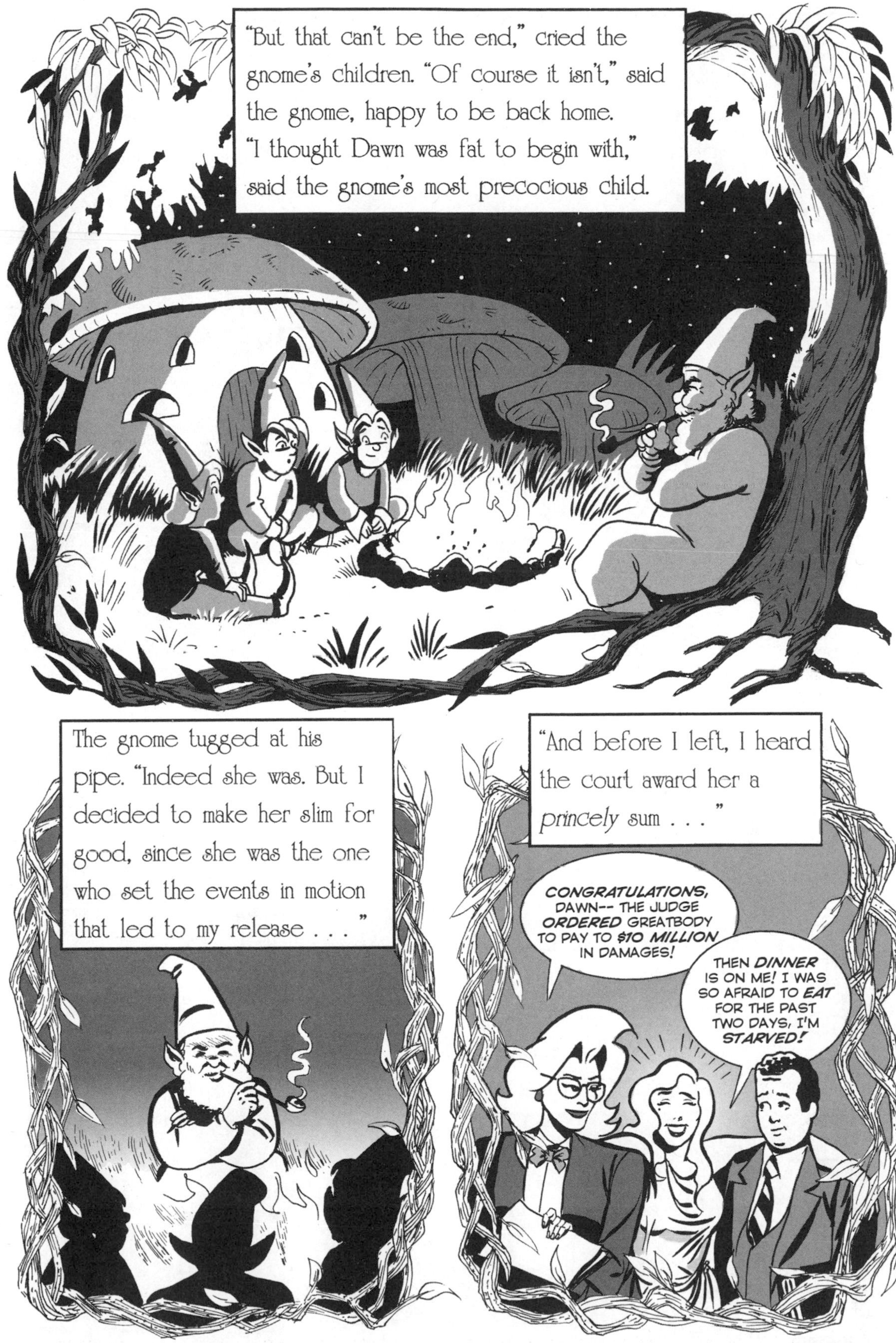
"But that can't be the end," cried the gnome's children. "Of course it isn't," said the gnome, happy to be back home. "I thought Dawn was fat to begin with," said the gnome's most precocious child.
The gnome tugged at his pipe. "Indeed she was. But I decided to make her slim for good, since she was the one who set the events in motion that led to my release . . . "
"And before I left, I heard the court award her a *princely* sum . . . "
CONGRATULATIONS, DAWN-- THE JUDGE ORDERED GREATBODY TO PAY TO $10 MILLION IN DAMAGES!
THEN DINNER IS ON ME! I WAS SO AFRAID TO EAT FOR THE PAST TWO DAYS, I'M STARVED!

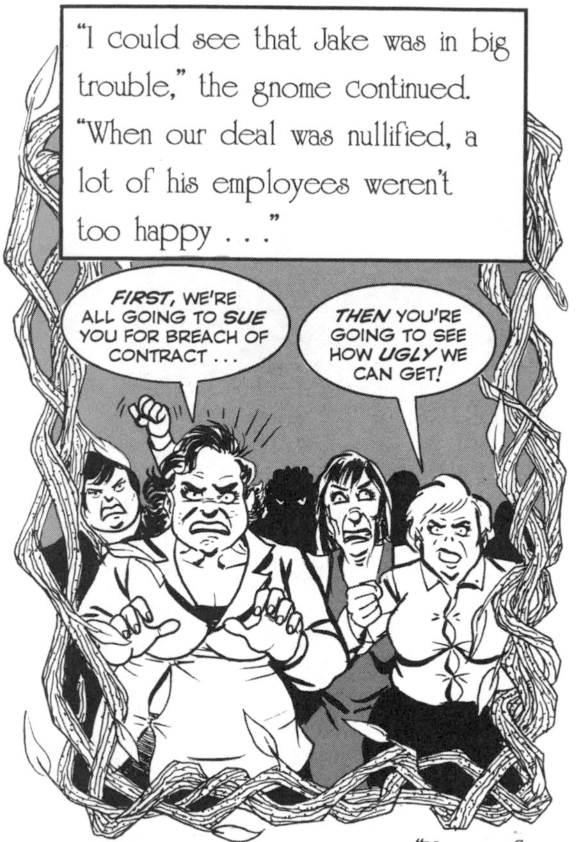
"I could see that Jake was in big trouble," the gnome continued. "When our deal was nullified, a lot of his employees weren't too happy . . ."
FIRST, WE'RE ALL GOING TO *SUE* YOU FOR BREACH OF CONTRACT . . .
THEN YOU'RE GOING TO SEE HOW *UGLY* WE CAN GET!

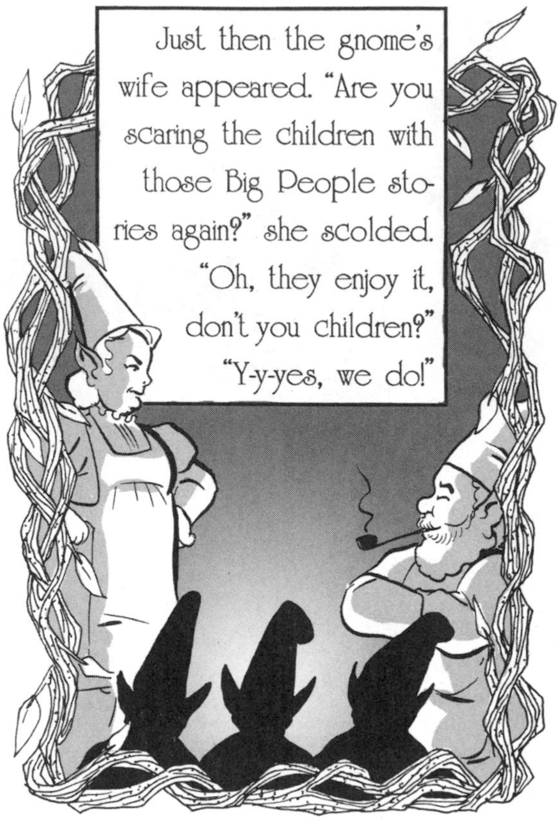
Just then the gnome's wife appeared. "Are you scaring the children with those Big People stories again?" she scolded. "Oh, they enjoy it, don't you children?" "Y-y-yes, we do!"

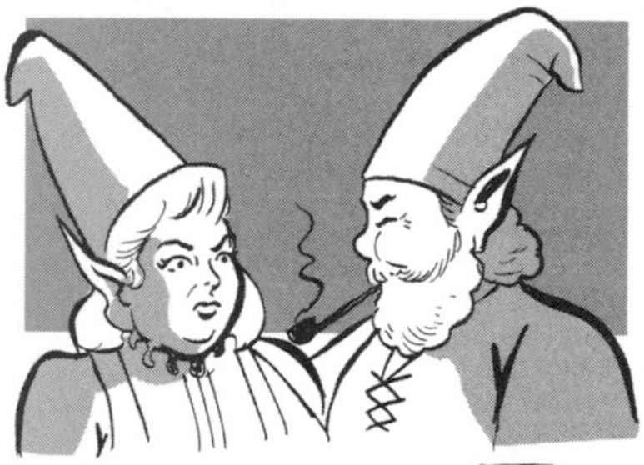

"Now, of course I'm happy to see you back safe and sound," said his wife. "But did you have to bring . . . that *thing* home with you? It's so tacky." The gnome smiled. He knew she would never believe that sometimes justice is not served in the outside world. He did not want to risk that his captor would go *unpunished* . . .

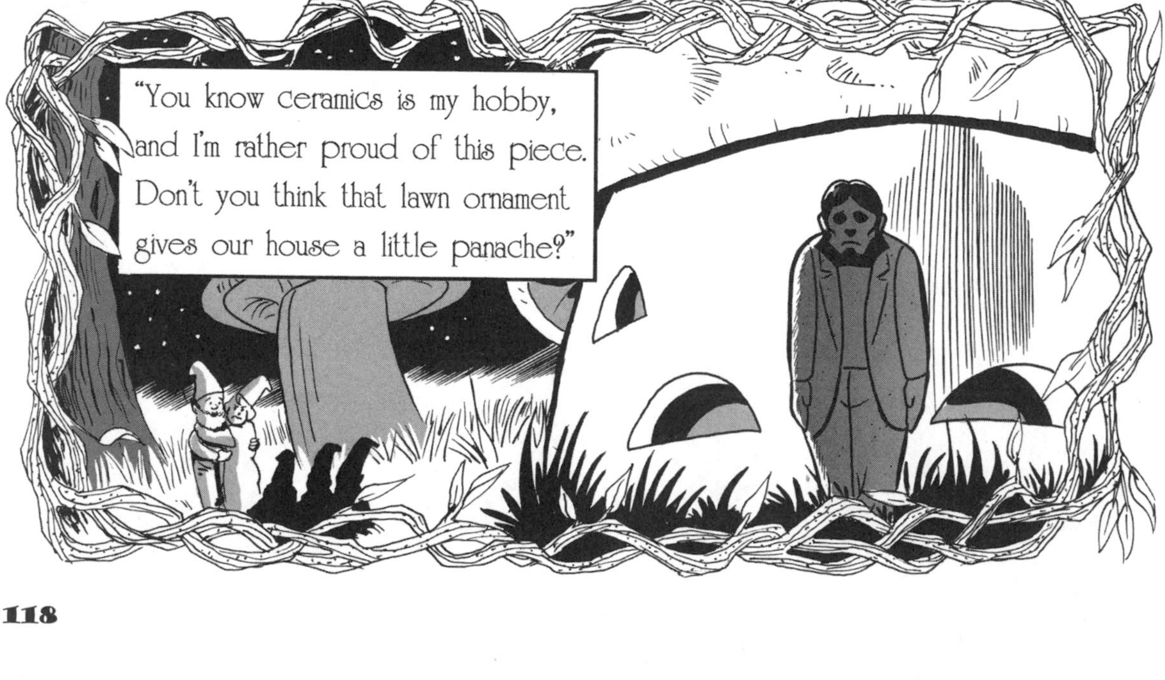
"You know ceramics is my hobby, and I'm rather proud of this piece. Don't you think that lawn ornament gives our house a little panache?"

It Stalks the Public Domain

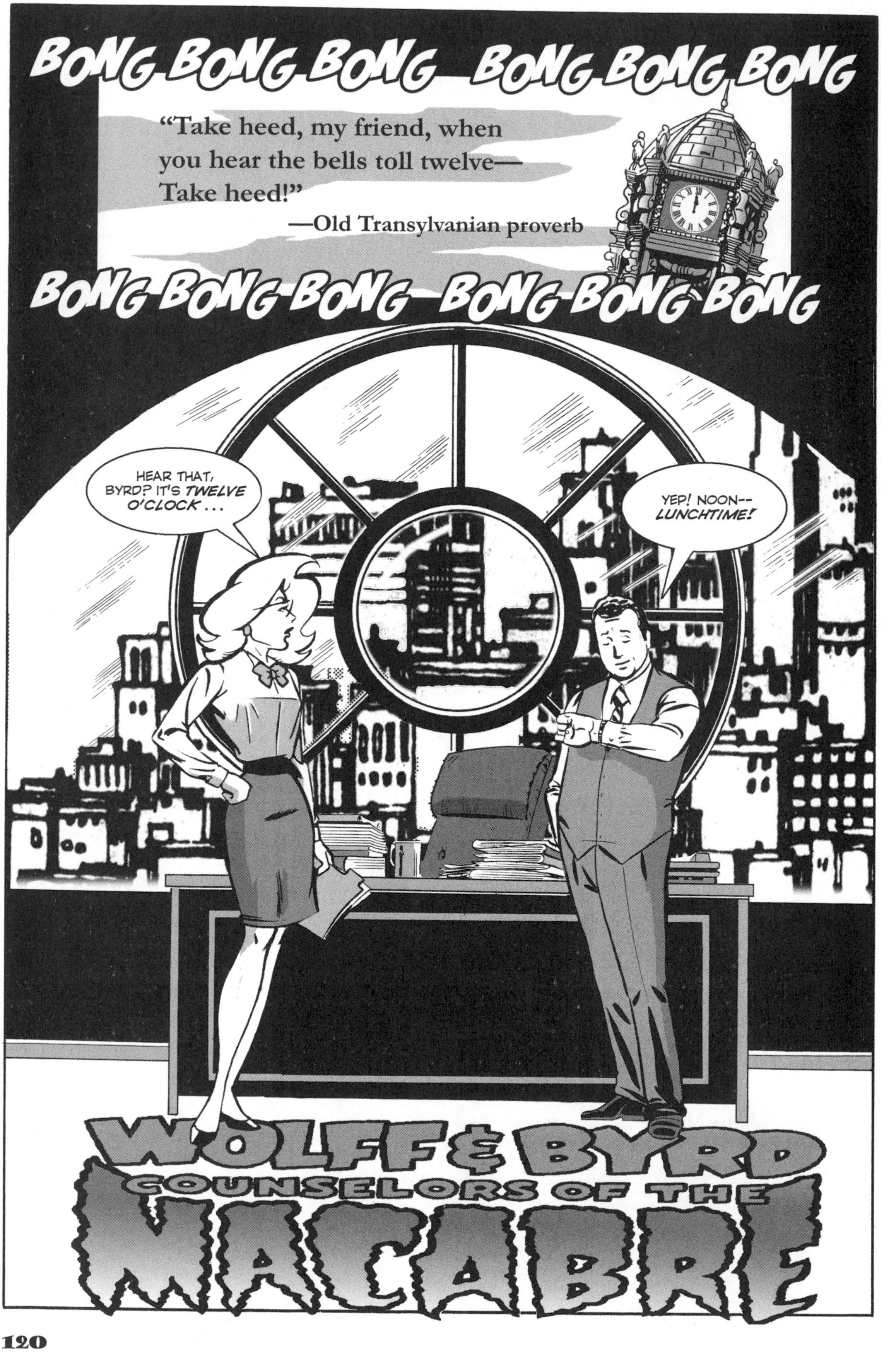
BONG BONG BONG BONG BONG BONG
"Take heed, my friend, when you hear the bells toll twelve— Take heed!"
—Old Transylvanian proverb
BONG BONG BONG BONG BONG BONG
HEAR THAT, BYRD? IT'S *TWELVE O'CLOCK* . . .
YEP! NOON-- *LUNCHTIME!*
WOLFF & BYRD
COUNSELORS OF THE
MACABRE

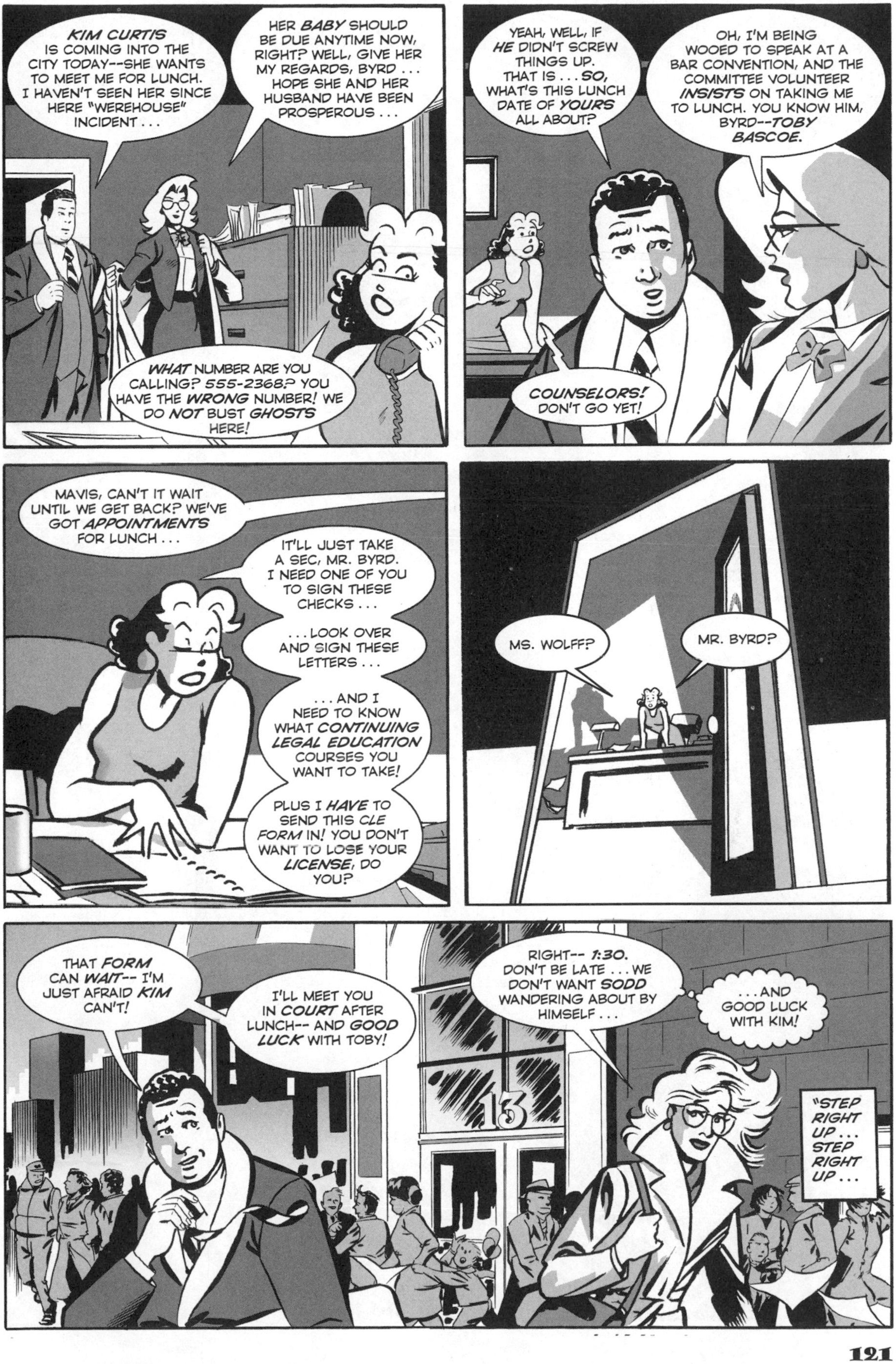
KIM CURTIS IS COMING INTO THE CITY TODAY--SHE WANTS TO MEET ME FOR LUNCH. I HAVEN'T SEEN HER SINCE HERE "WEREHOUSE" INCIDENT . . .
HER BABY SHOULD BE DUE ANYTIME NOW, RIGHT? WELL, GIVE HER MY REGARDS, BYRD . . . HOPE SHE AND HER HUSBAND HAVE BEEN PROSPEROUS . . .
WHAT NUMBER ARE YOU CALLING? 555-2368? YOU HAVE THE WRONG NUMBER! WE DO NOT BUST GHOSTS HERE!
YEAH, WELL, IF HE DIDN'T SCREW THINGS UP. THAT IS . . . SO, WHAT'S THIS LUNCH DATE OF YOURS ALL ABOUT?
OH, I'M BEING WOOED TO SPEAK AT A BAR CONVENTION, AND THE COMMITTEE VOLUNTEER INSISTS ON TAKING ME TO LUNCH. YOU KNOW HIM, BYRD--TOBY BASCOE.
COUNSELORS! DON'T GO YET!
MAVIS, CAN'T IT WAIT UNTIL WE GET BACK? WE'VE GOT APPOINTMENTS FOR LUNCH . . .
IT'LL JUST TAKE A SEC, MR. BYRD. I NEED ONE OF YOU TO SIGN THESE CHECKS . . .
. . . LOOK OVER AND SIGN THESE LETTERS . . .
. . . AND I NEED TO KNOW WHAT CONTINUING LEGAL EDUCATION COURSES YOU WANT TO TAKE!
PLUS I HAVE TO SEND THIS CLE FORM IN! YOU DON'T WANT TO LOSE YOUR LICENSE, DO YOU?
MS. WOLFF?
MR. BYRD?
THAT FORM CAN WAIT-- I'M JUST AFRAID KIM CAN'T!
I'LL MEET YOU IN COURT AFTER LUNCH-- AND GOOD LUCK WITH TOBY!
RIGHT-- 1:30. DON'T BE LATE . . . WE DON'T WANT SODD WANDERING ABOUT BY HIMSELF . . .
. . . AND GOOD LUCK WITH KIM!
13
"STEP RIGHT UP . . . STEP RIGHT UP . . .

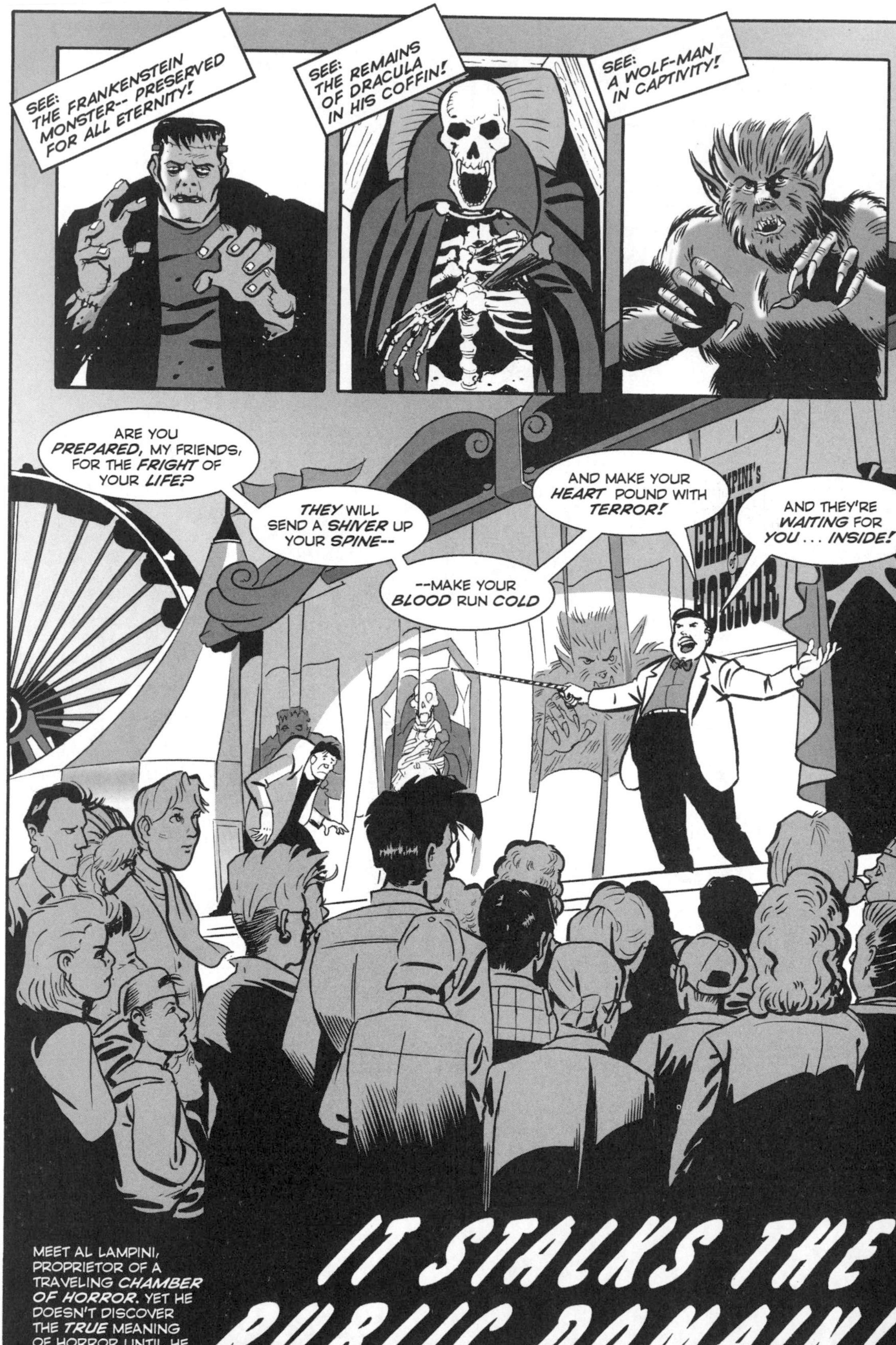
SEE: THE FRANKENSTEIN MONSTER-- PRESERVED FOR ALL ETERNITY!
SEE: THE REMAINS OF DRACULA IN HIS COFFIN!
SEE: A WOLF-MAN IN CAPTIVITY!
ARE YOU PREPARED, MY FRIENDS, FOR THE FRIGHT OF YOUR LIFE?
THEY WILL SEND A SHIVER UP YOUR SPINE--
--MAKE YOUR BLOOD RUN COLD
AND MAKE YOUR HEART POUND WITH TERROR!
AND THEY'RE WAITING FOR YOU . . . INSIDE!
HORROR
MEET AL LAMPINI, PROPRIETOR OF A TRAVELING CHAMBER OF HORROR. YET HE DOESN'T DISCOVER THE TRUE MEANING OF HORROR UNTIL HE LEARNS THAT . . .
IT STALKS THE PUBLIC DOMAIN!

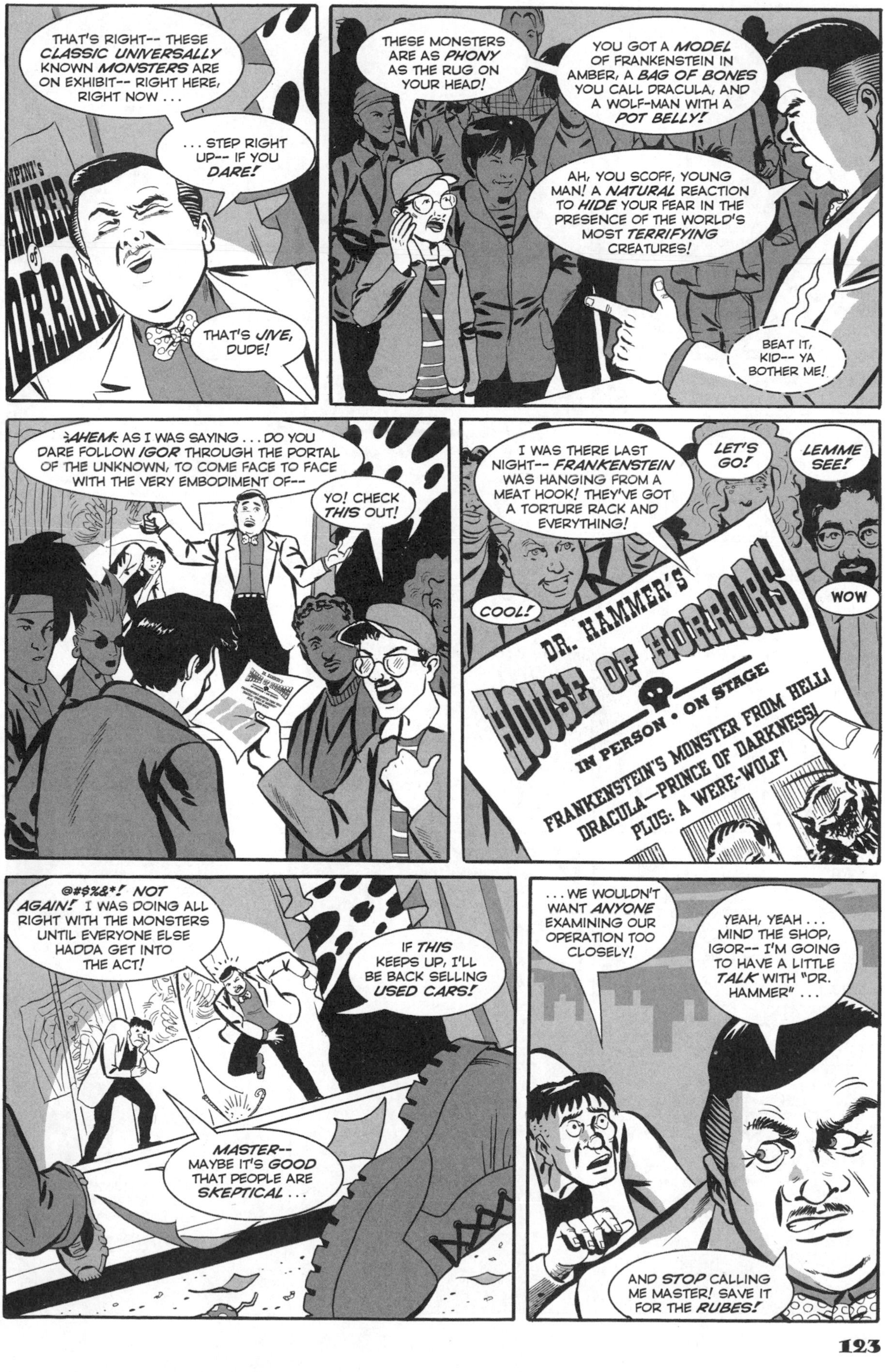
THAT'S RIGHT-- THESE CLASSIC UNIVERSALLY KNOWN MONSTERS ARE ON EXHIBIT-- RIGHT HERE, RIGHT NOW . . .
. . . STEP RIGHT UP-- IF YOU DARE!
THAT'S JIVE, DUDE!
THESE MONSTERS ARE AS PHONY AS THE RUG ON YOUR HEAD!
YOU GOT A MODEL OF FRANKENSTEIN IN AMBER, A BAG OF BONES YOU CALL DRACULA, AND A WOLF-MAN WITH A POT BELLY!
AH, YOU SCOFF, YOUNG MAN! A NATURAL REACTION TO HIDE YOUR FEAR IN THE PRESENCE OF THE WORLD'S MOST TERRIFYING CREATURES!
BEAT IT, KID-- YA BOTHER ME!
-AHEM- AS I WAS SAYING . . . DO YOU DARE FOLLOW IGOR THROUGH THE PORTAL OF THE UNKNOWN, TO COME FACE TO FACE WITH THE VERY EMBODIMENT OF--
YO! CHECK THIS OUT!
I WAS THERE LAST NIGHT-- FRANKENSTEIN WAS HANGING FROM A MEAT HOOK! THEY'VE GOT A TORTURE RACK AND EVERYTHING!
LET'S GO!
LEMME SEE!
COOL!
WOW
DR. HAMMER'S
HOUSE OF HORRORS
IN PERSON • ON STAGE
FRANKENSTEIN'S MONSTER FROM HELL!
DRACULA—PRINCE OF DARKNESS!
PLUS: A WERE-WOLF!
@#$%&*! NOT AGAIN! I WAS DOING ALL RIGHT WITH THE MONSTERS UNTIL EVERYONE ELSE HADDA GET INTO THE ACT!
IF THIS KEEPS UP, I'LL BE BACK SELLING USED CARS!
MASTER-- MAYBE IT'S GOOD THAT PEOPLE ARE SKEPTICAL . . .
. . . WE WOULDN'T WANT ANYONE EXAMINING OUR OPERATION TOO CLOSELY!
YEAH, YEAH . . . MIND THE SHOP, IGOR-- I'M GOING TO HAVE A LITTLE TALK WITH "DR. HAMMER" . . .
AND STOP CALLING ME MASTER! SAVE IT FOR THE RUBES!

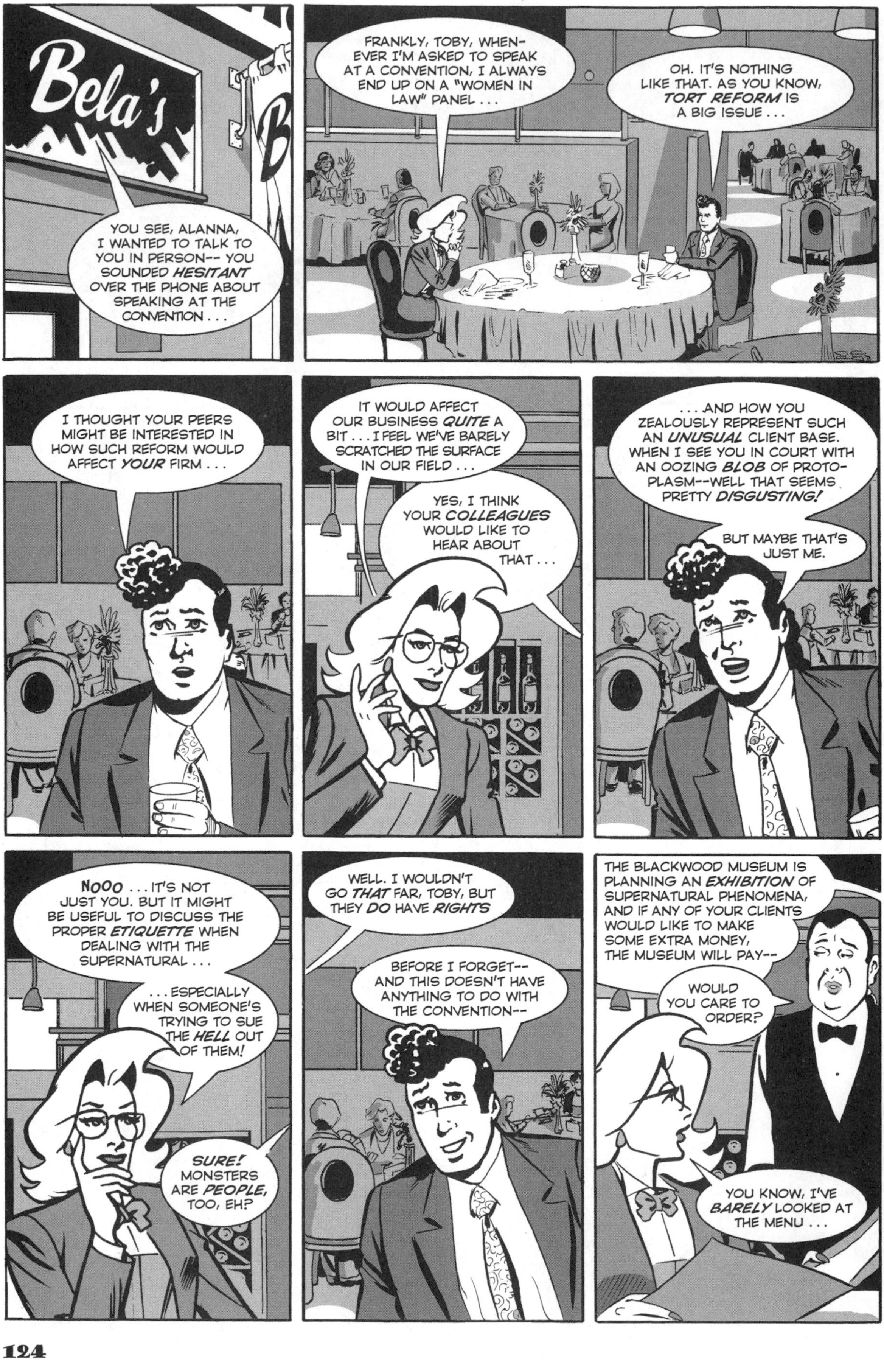
Bela's
YOU SEE, ALANNA, I WANTED TO TALK TO YOU IN PERSON-- YOU SOUNDED HESITANT OVER THE PHONE ABOUT SPEAKING AT THE CONVENTION . . .
FRANKLY, TOBY, WHENEVER I'M ASKED TO SPEAK AT A CONVENTION, I ALWAYS END UP ON A "WOMEN IN LAW" PANEL . . .
OH. IT'S NOTHING LIKE THAT. AS YOU KNOW, TORT REFORM IS A BIG ISSUE . . .
I THOUGHT YOUR PEERS MIGHT BE INTERESTED IN HOW SUCH REFORM WOULD AFFECT YOUR FIRM . . .
IT WOULD AFFECT OUR BUSINESS QUITE A BIT . . . I FEEL WE'VE BARELY SCRATCHED THE SURFACE IN OUR FIELD . . .
YES, I THINK YOUR COLLEAGUES WOULD LIKE TO HEAR ABOUT THAT . . .
. . . AND HOW YOU ZEALOUSLY REPRESENT SUCH AN UNUSUAL CLIENT BASE. WHEN I SEE YOU IN COURT WITH AN OOZING BLOB OF PROTOPLASM--WELL THAT SEEMS PRETTY DISGUSTING!
BUT MAYBE THAT'S JUST ME.
NOOO . . . IT'S NOT JUST YOU. BUT IT MIGHT BE USEFUL TO DISCUSS THE PROPER ETIQUETTE WHEN DEALING WITH THE SUPERNATURAL . . .
. . . ESPECIALLY WHEN SOMEONE'S TRYING TO SUE THE HELL OUT OF THEM!
SURE! MONSTERS ARE PEOPLE, TOO, EH?
WELL. I WOULDN'T GO THAT FAR, TOBY, BUT THEY DO HAVE RIGHTS
BEFORE I FORGET-- AND THIS DOESN'T HAVE ANYTHING TO DO WITH THE CONVENTION--
THE BLACKWOOD MUSEUM IS PLANNING AN EXHIBITION OF SUPERNATURAL PHENOMENA, AND IF ANY OF YOUR CLIENTS WOULD LIKE TO MAKE SOME EXTRA MONEY, THE MUSEUM WILL PAY--
WOULD YOU CARE TO ORDER?
YOU KNOW, I'VE BARELY LOOKED AT THE MENU . . .

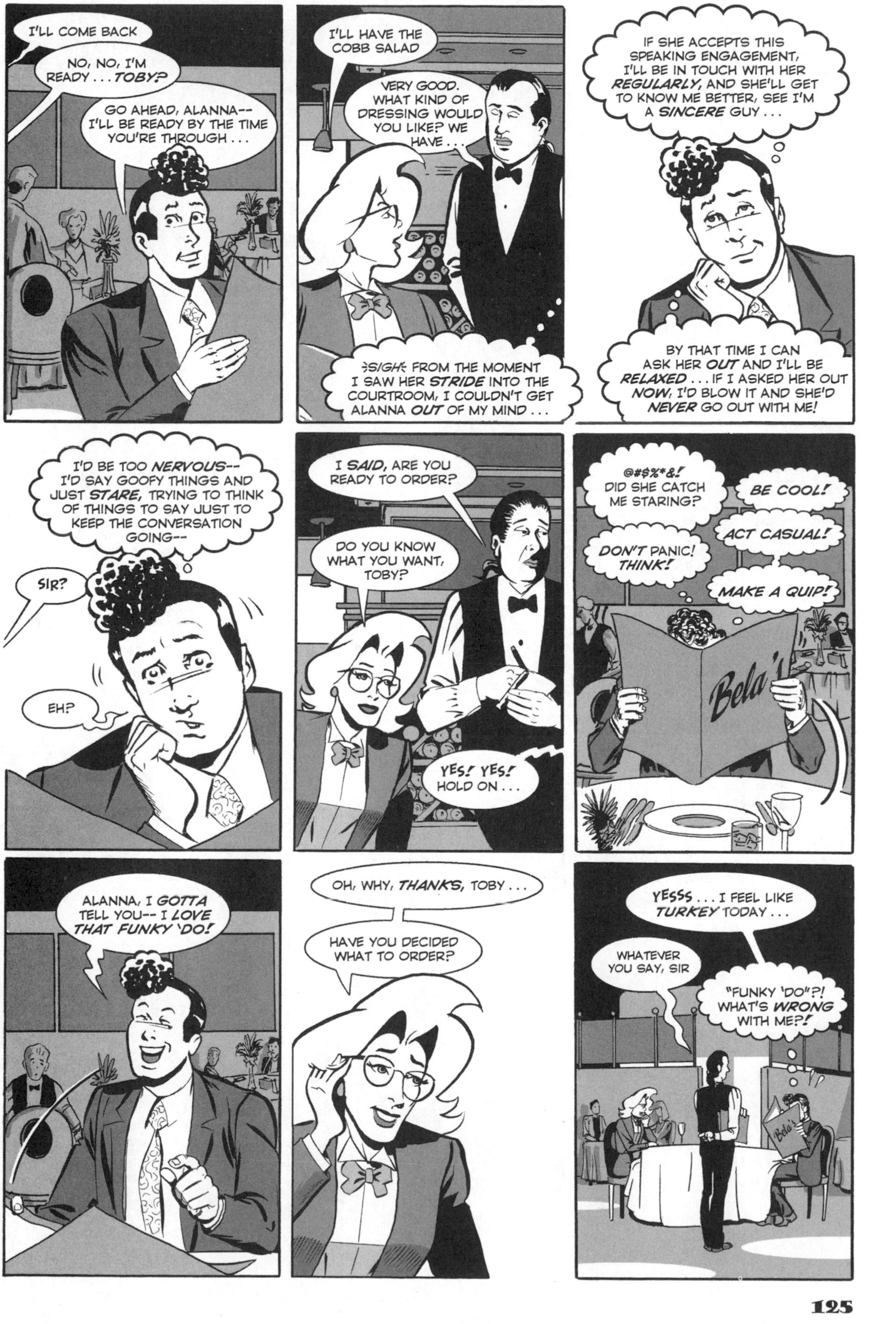
I'LL COME BACK
NO, NO, I'M READY . . . TOBY?
GO AHEAD, ALANNA-- I'LL BE READY BY THE TIME YOU'RE THROUGH . . .
I'LL HAVE THE COBB SALAD
VERY GOOD. WHAT KIND OF DRESSING WOULD YOU LIKE? WE HAVE . . .
SIGH FROM THE MOMENT I SAW HER STRIDE INTO THE COURTROOM, I COULDN'T GET ALANNA OUT OF MY MIND . . .
IF SHE ACCEPTS THIS SPEAKING ENGAGEMENT, I'LL BE IN TOUCH WITH HER REGULARLY, AND SHE'LL GET TO KNOW ME BETTER, SEE I'M A SINCERE GUY . . .
BY THAT TIME I CAN ASK HER OUT AND I'LL BE RELAXED . . . IF I ASKED HER OUT NOW, I'D BLOW IT AND SHE'D NEVER GO OUT WITH ME!
I'D BE TOO NERVOUS-- I'D SAY GOOFY THINGS AND JUST STARE, TRYING TO THINK OF THINGS TO SAY JUST TO KEEP THE CONVERSATION GOING--
SIR?
EH?
I SAID, ARE YOU READY TO ORDER?
DO YOU KNOW WHAT YOU WANT, TOBY?
YES! YES! HOLD ON . . .
@#$%*&! DID SHE CATCH ME STARING?
BE COOL!
ACT CASUAL!
DON'T PANIC! THINK!
MAKE A QUIP!
Bela's
ALANNA, I GOTTA TELL YOU-- I LOVE THAT FUNKY 'DO!
OH, WHY, THANKS, TOBY . . .
HAVE YOU DECIDED WHAT TO ORDER?
YESSS . . . I FEEL LIKE TURKEY TODAY . . .
WHATEVER YOU SAY, SIR
"FUNKY 'DO"?! WHAT'S WRONG WITH ME?!
Bela's

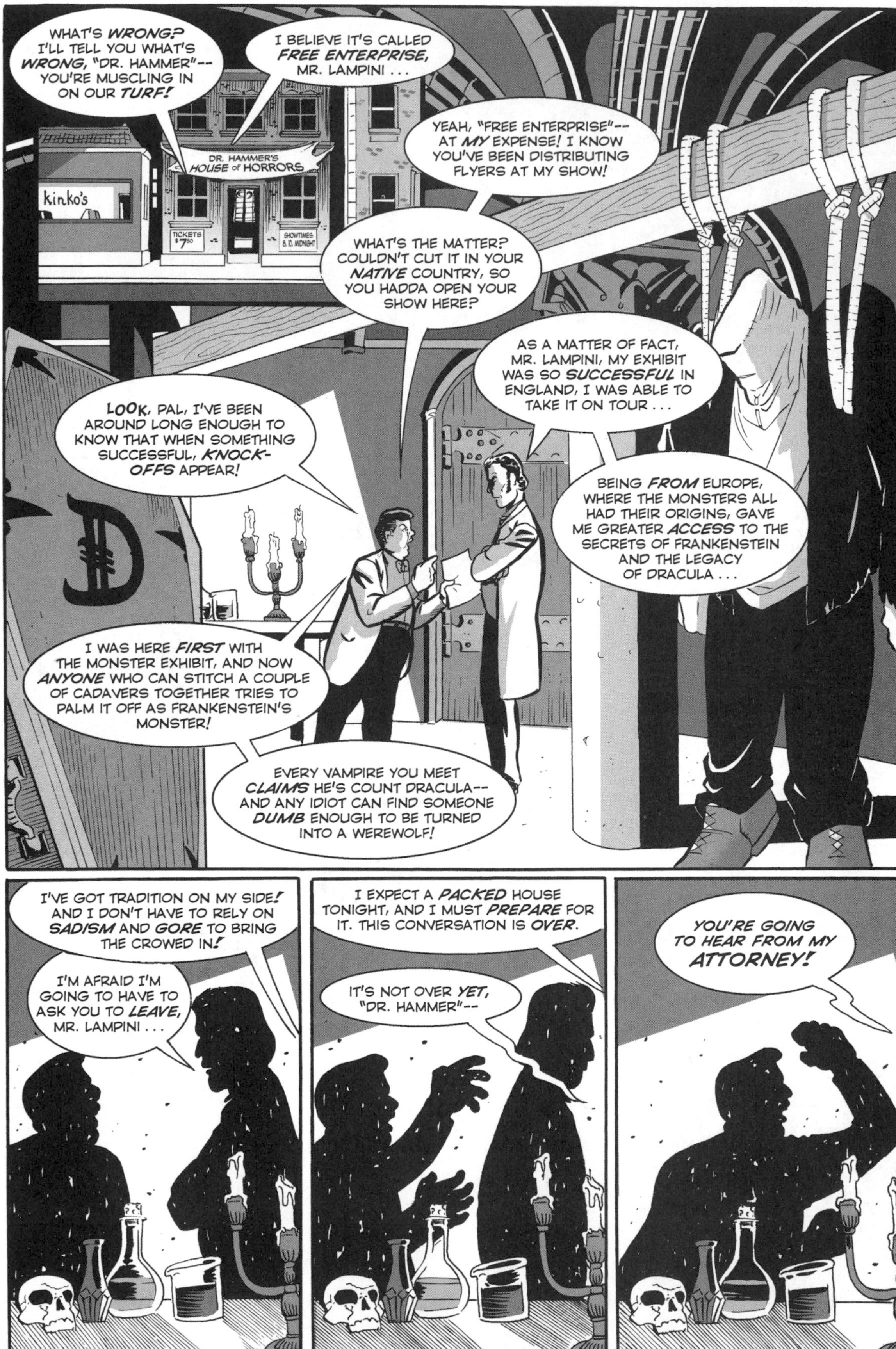
WHAT'S WRONG? I'LL TELL YOU WHAT'S WRONG, "DR. HAMMER"-- YOU'RE MUSCLING IN ON OUR TURF!
I BELIEVE IT'S CALLED FREE ENTERPRISE, MR. LAMPINI . . .
DR. HAMMER'S HOUSE of HORRORS
kinko's
TICKETS $7.50
SHOWTIMES: 8, 10, MIDNIGHT
YEAH, "FREE ENTERPRISE"-- AT MY EXPENSE! I KNOW YOU'VE BEEN DISTRIBUTING FLYERS AT MY SHOW!
WHAT'S THE MATTER? COULDN'T CUT IT IN YOUR NATIVE COUNTRY, SO YOU HADDA OPEN YOUR SHOW HERE?
AS A MATTER OF FACT, MR. LAMPINI, MY EXHIBIT WAS SO SUCCESSFUL IN ENGLAND, I WAS ABLE TO TAKE IT ON TOUR . . .
LOOK, PAL, I'VE BEEN AROUND LONG ENOUGH TO KNOW THAT WHEN SOMETHING SUCCESSFUL, KNOCK-OFFS APPEAR!
BEING FROM EUROPE, WHERE THE MONSTERS ALL HAD THEIR ORIGINS, GAVE ME GREATER ACCESS TO THE SECRETS OF FRANKENSTEIN AND THE LEGACY OF DRACULA . . .
I WAS HERE FIRST WITH THE MONSTER EXHIBIT, AND NOW ANYONE WHO CAN STITCH A COUPLE OF CADAVERS TOGETHER TRIES TO PALM IT OFF AS FRANKENSTEIN'S MONSTER!
EVERY VAMPIRE YOU MEET CLAIMS HE'S COUNT DRACULA-- AND ANY IDIOT CAN FIND SOMEONE DUMB ENOUGH TO BE TURNED INTO A WEREWOLF!
I'VE GOT TRADITION ON MY SIDE! AND I DON'T HAVE TO RELY ON SADISM AND GORE TO BRING THE CROWED IN!
I'M AFRAID I'M GOING TO HAVE TO ASK YOU TO LEAVE, MR. LAMPINI . . .
I EXPECT A PACKED HOUSE TONIGHT, AND I MUST PREPARE FOR IT. THIS CONVERSATION IS OVER.
IT'S NOT OVER YET, "DR. HAMMER"--
YOU'RE GOING TO HEAR FROM MY ATTORNEY!

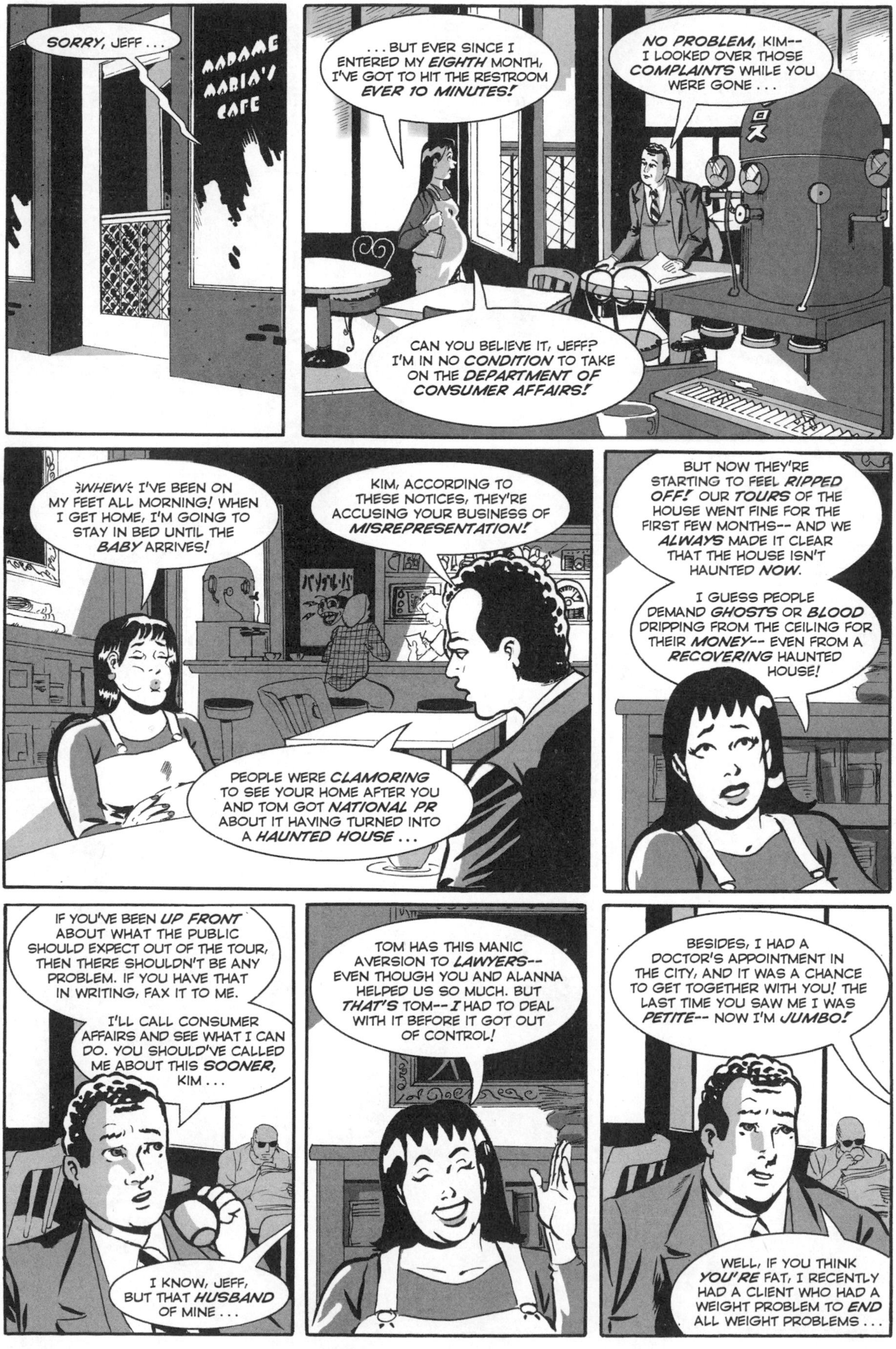
SORRY, JEFF . . .
MADAME MARIA'S CAFE
. . . BUT EVER SINCE I ENTERED MY EIGHTH MONTH, I'VE GOT TO HIT THE RESTROOM EVER 10 MINUTES!
NO PROBLEM, KIM-- I LOOKED OVER THOSE COMPLAINTS WHILE YOU WERE GONE . . .
CAN YOU BELIEVE IT, JEFF? I'M IN NO CONDITION TO TAKE ON THE DEPARTMENT OF CONSUMER AFFAIRS!
WHEW I'VE BEEN ON MY FEET ALL MORNING! WHEN I GET HOME, I'M GOING TO STAY IN BED UNTIL THE BABY ARRIVES!
KIM, ACCORDING TO THESE NOTICES, THEY'RE ACCUSING YOUR BUSINESS OF MISREPRESENTATION!
PEOPLE WERE CLAMORING TO SEE YOUR HOME AFTER YOU AND TOM GOT NATIONAL PR ABOUT IT HAVING TURNED INTO A HAUNTED HOUSE . . .
BUT NOW THEY'RE STARTING TO FEEL RIPPED OFF! OUR TOURS OF THE HOUSE WENT FINE FOR THE FIRST FEW MONTHS-- AND WE ALWAYS MADE IT CLEAR THAT THE HOUSE ISN'T HAUNTED NOW.
I GUESS PEOPLE DEMAND GHOSTS OR BLOOD DRIPPING FROM THE CEILING FOR THEIR MONEY-- EVEN FROM A RECOVERING HAUNTED HOUSE!
IF YOU'VE BEEN UP FRONT ABOUT WHAT THE PUBLIC SHOULD EXPECT OUT OF THE TOUR, THEN THERE SHOULDN'T BE ANY PROBLEM. IF YOU HAVE THAT IN WRITING, FAX IT TO ME.
I'LL CALL CONSUMER AFFAIRS AND SEE WHAT I CAN DO. YOU SHOULD'VE CALLED ME ABOUT THIS SOONER, KIM . . .
I KNOW, JEFF, BUT THAT HUSBAND OF MINE . . .
TOM HAS THIS MANIC AVERSION TO LAWYERS-- EVEN THOUGH YOU AND ALANNA HELPED US SO MUCH. BUT THAT'S TOM-- I HAD TO DEAL WITH IT BEFORE IT GOT OUT OF CONTROL!
BESIDES, I HAD A DOCTOR'S APPOINTMENT IN THE CITY, AND IT WAS A CHANCE TO GET TOGETHER WITH YOU! THE LAST TIME YOU SAW ME I WAS PETITE-- NOW I'M JUMBO!
WELL, IF YOU THINK YOU'RE FAT, I RECENTLY HAD A CLIENT WHO HAD A WEIGHT PROBLEM TO END ALL WEIGHT PROBLEMS . . .

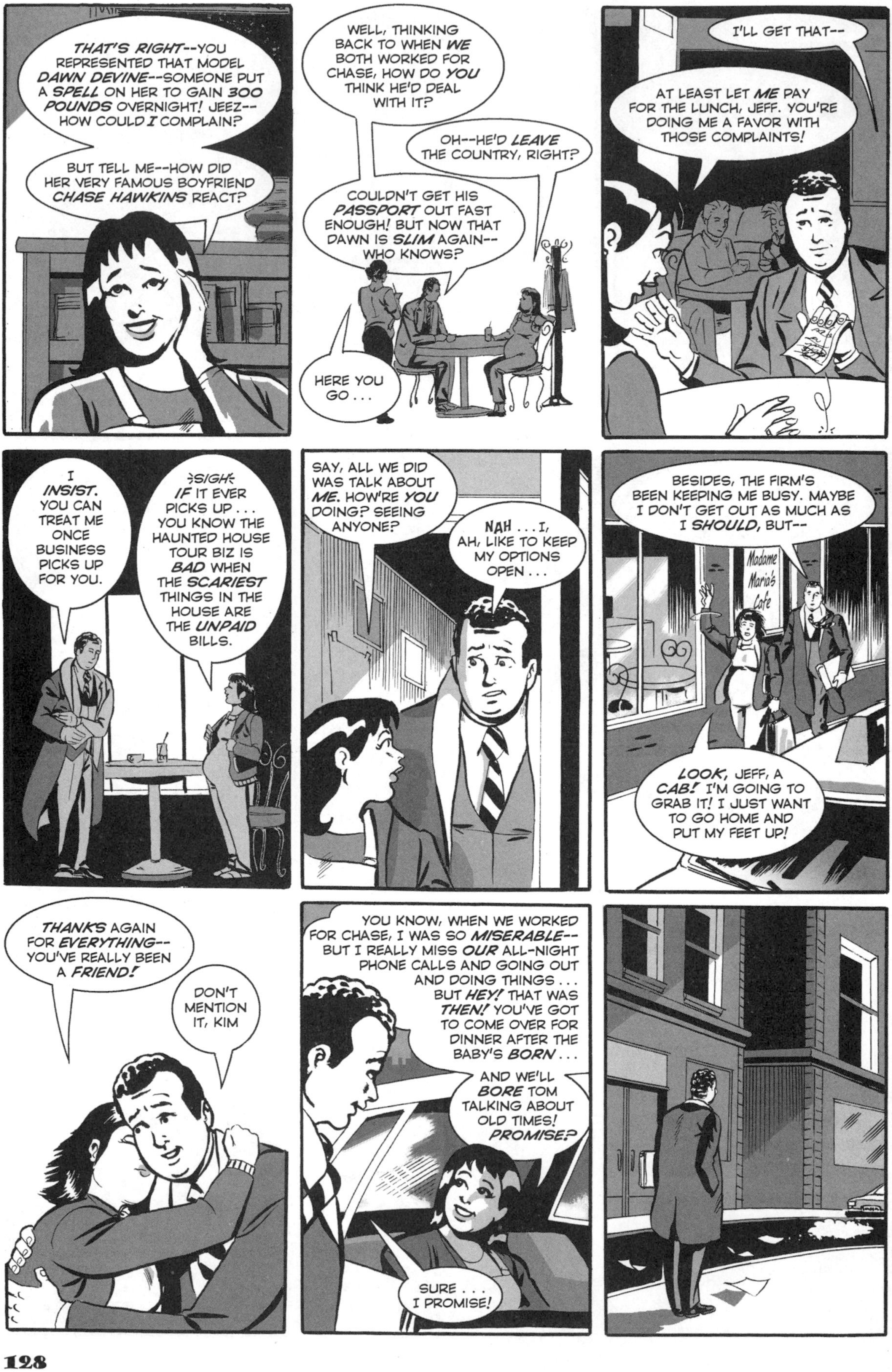

THAT'S RIGHT--YOU REPRESENTED THAT MODEL DAWN DEVINE--SOMEONE PUT A SPELL ON HER TO GAIN 300 POUNDS OVERNIGHT! JEEZ--HOW COULD I COMPLAIN?
BUT TELL ME--HOW DID HER VERY FAMOUS BOYFRIEND CHASE HAWKINS REACT?
WELL, THINKING BACK TO WHEN WE BOTH WORKED FOR CHASE, HOW DO YOU THINK HE'D DEAL WITH IT?
OH--HE'D LEAVE THE COUNTRY, RIGHT?
COULDN'T GET HIS PASSPORT OUT FAST ENOUGH! BUT NOW THAT DAWN IS SLIM AGAIN--WHO KNOWS?
HERE YOU GO . . .
I'LL GET THAT--
AT LEAST LET ME PAY FOR THE LUNCH, JEFF. YOU'RE DOING ME A FAVOR WITH THOSE COMPLAINTS!
I INSIST. YOU CAN TREAT ME ONCE BUSINESS PICKS UP FOR YOU.
SIGH IF IT EVER PICKS UP . . . YOU KNOW THE HAUNTED HOUSE TOUR BIZ IS BAD WHEN THE SCARIEST THINGS IN THE HOUSE ARE THE UNPAID BILLS.
SAY, ALL WE DID WAS TALK ABOUT ME. HOW'RE YOU DOING? SEEING ANYONE?
NAH . . . I, AH, LIKE TO KEEP MY OPTIONS OPEN . . .
BESIDES, THE FIRM'S BEEN KEEPING ME BUSY. MAYBE I DON'T GET OUT AS MUCH AS I SHOULD, BUT--
Madame Maria's Cafe
LOOK, JEFF, A CAB! I'M GOING TO GRAB IT! I JUST WANT TO GO HOME AND PUT MY FEET UP!
THANKS AGAIN FOR EVERYTHING--YOU'VE REALLY BEEN A FRIEND!
DON'T MENTION IT, KIM
YOU KNOW, WHEN WE WORKED FOR CHASE, I WAS SO MISERABLE--BUT I REALLY MISS OUR ALL-NIGHT PHONE CALLS AND GOING OUT AND DOING THINGS . . . BUT HEY! THAT WAS THEN! YOU'VE GOT TO COME OVER FOR DINNER AFTER THE BABY'S BORN . . .
AND WE'LL BORE TOM TALKING ABOUT OLD TIMES! PROMISE?
SURE . . . I PROMISE!

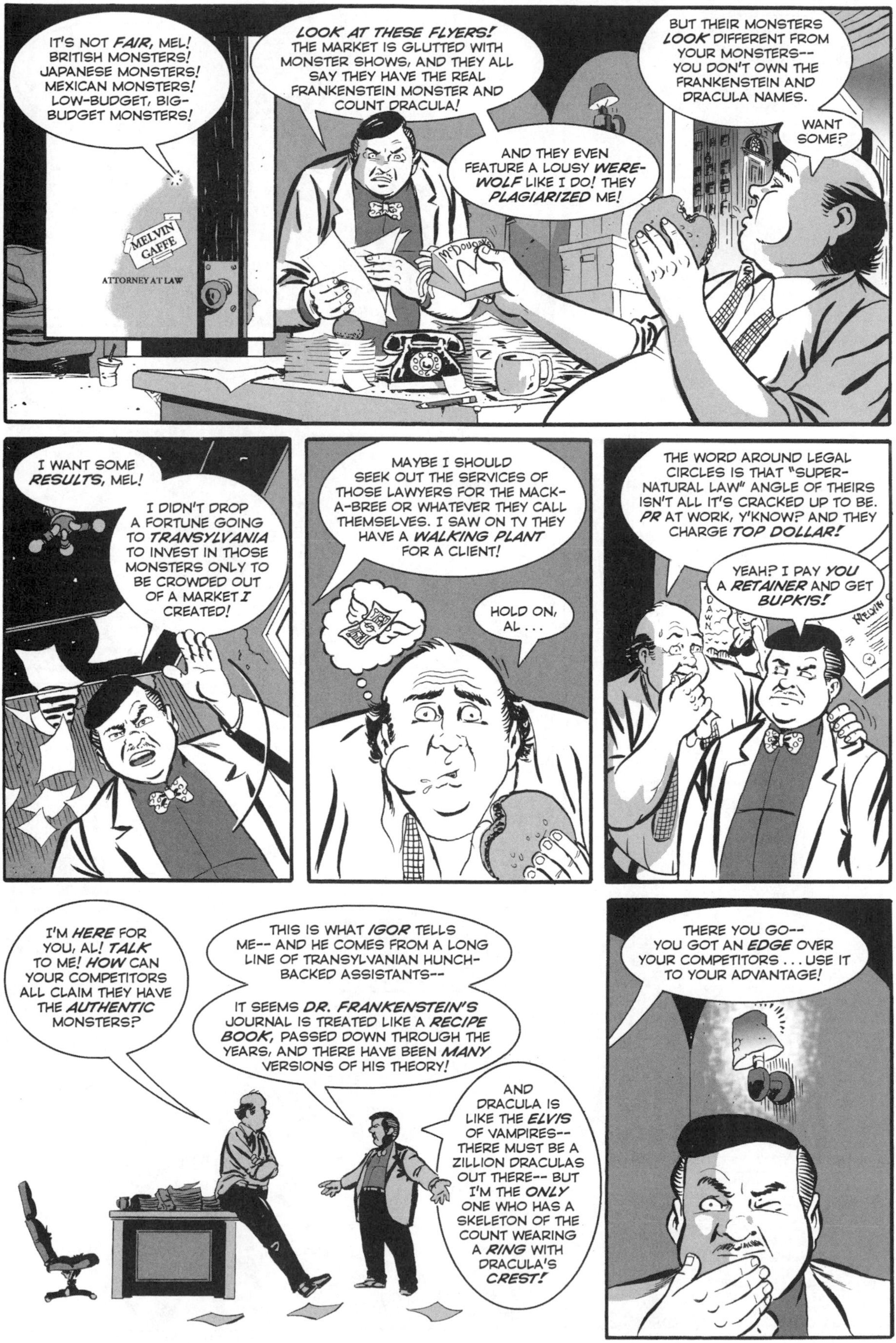
IT'S NOT FAIR, MEL! BRITISH MONSTERS! JAPANESE MONSTERS! MEXICAN MONSTERS! LOW-BUDGET, BIG-BUDGET MONSTERS!
LOOK AT THESE FLYERS! THE MARKET IS GLUTTED WITH MONSTER SHOWS, AND THEY ALL SAY THEY HAVE THE REAL FRANKENSTEIN MONSTER AND COUNT DRACULA!
AND THEY EVEN FEATURE A LOUSY WERE-WOLF LIKE I DO! THEY PLAGIARIZED ME!
BUT THEIR MONSTERS LOOK DIFFERENT FROM YOUR MONSTERS-- YOU DON'T OWN THE FRANKENSTEIN AND DRACULA NAMES.
WANT SOME?
MELVIN GAFFE
ATTORNEY AT LAW
McDOUGAL'S
I WANT SOME RESULTS, MEL!
I DIDN'T DROP A FORTUNE GOING TO TRANSYLVANIA TO INVEST IN THOSE MONSTERS ONLY TO BE CROWDED OUT OF A MARKET I CREATED!
MAYBE I SHOULD SEEK OUT THE SERVICES OF THOSE LAWYERS FOR THE MACK-A-BREE OR WHATEVER THEY CALL THEMSELVES. I SAW ON TV THEY HAVE A WALKING PLANT FOR A CLIENT!
HOLD ON, AL . . .
THE WORD AROUND LEGAL CIRCLES IS THAT "SUPER-NATURAL LAW" ANGLE OF THEIRS ISN'T ALL IT'S CRACKED UP TO BE. PR AT WORK, Y'KNOW? AND THEY CHARGE TOP DOLLAR!
YEAH? I PAY YOU A RETAINER AND GET BUPKIS!
I'M HERE FOR YOU, AL! TALK TO ME! HOW CAN YOUR COMPETITORS ALL CLAIM THEY HAVE THE AUTHENTIC MONSTERS?
THIS IS WHAT IGOR TELLS ME-- AND HE COMES FROM A LONG LINE OF TRANSYLVANIAN HUNCH-BACKED ASSISTANTS--
IT SEEMS DR. FRANKENSTEIN'S JOURNAL IS TREATED LIKE A RECIPE BOOK, PASSED DOWN THROUGH THE YEARS, AND THERE HAVE BEEN MANY VERSIONS OF HIS THEORY!
AND DRACULA IS LIKE THE ELVIS OF VAMPIRES-- THERE MUST BE A ZILLION DRACULAS OUT THERE-- BUT I'M THE ONLY ONE WHO HAS A SKELETON OF THE COUNT WEARING A RING WITH DRACULA'S CREST!
THERE YOU GO-- YOU GOT AN EDGE OVER YOUR COMPETITORS . . . USE IT TO YOUR ADVANTAGE!

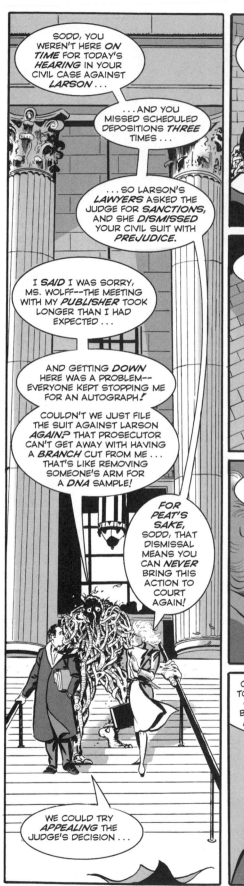

SODD, YOU WEREN'T HERE ON TIME FOR TODAY'S HEARING IN YOUR CIVIL CASE AGAINST LARSON...

...AND YOU MISSED SCHEDULED DEPOSITIONS THREE TIMES...

...SO LARSON'S LAWYERS ASKED THE JUDGE FOR SANCTIONS, AND SHE DISMISSED YOUR CIVIL SUIT WITH PREJUDICE.

I SAID I WAS SORRY, MS. WOLFF--THE MEETING WITH MY PUBLISHER TOOK LONGER THAN I HAD EXPECTED...

AND GETTING DOWN HERE WAS A PROBLEM-- EVERYONE KEPT STOPPING ME FOR AN AUTOGRAPH!

COULDN'T WE JUST FILE THE SUIT AGAINST LARSON AGAIN? THAT PROSECUTOR CAN'T GET AWAY WITH HAVING A BRANCH CUT FROM ME... THAT'S LIKE REMOVING SOMEONE'S ARM FOR A DNA SAMPLE!

FOR PEAT'S SAKE, SODD, THAT DISMISSAL MEANS YOU CAN NEVER BRING THIS ACTION TO COURT AGAIN!

WE COULD TRY APPEALING THE JUDGE'S DECISION...

...BUT IT DOESN'T HELP THAT YOU'VE BEEN SELLING LEAVES OFF YOUR BODY ON EBAY!

I WAS ONLY DOING THAT TO DEFRAY THE LEGAL COSTS!

LOOK, SODD, WE'RE NOT OUT OF THE WOODS YET WITH YOUR CRIMINAL CHARGES!

WHILE YOUR BOOK DEAL'S IMPORTANT, YOUR CASE COMES FIRST! I HOPE ALL THIS NOTORIETY HASN'T GONE TO YOUR HEAD...

OF COURSE IT HASN'T. OOPS... GOTTA RUN--

THE STUDIO'S PICKING ME UP TO DISCUSS A MOVIE-OF-THE WEEK!

OH-- AND I WANT TO TALK TO YOU ABOUT TRADEMARKING MY NAME! I DON'T WANT ANYONE USING "SODD" WITHOUT MY PERMISSION... LIKE THEY DO WITH THOSE OTHER MONSTERS! CIAO!

CIAO? YEOW! WHAT HAPPENED TO OUR NERVOUS, SELF-EFFACING CLIENT WHO WAS ASHAMED OF BEING TURNED INTO A MONSTER AND ONLY WANTED TO RETURN TO NORMAL?

WHAT USUALLY HAPPENS, BYRD-- ALL THE MEDIA ATTENTION HAS CREATED A FRANKEN-STEIN!

130

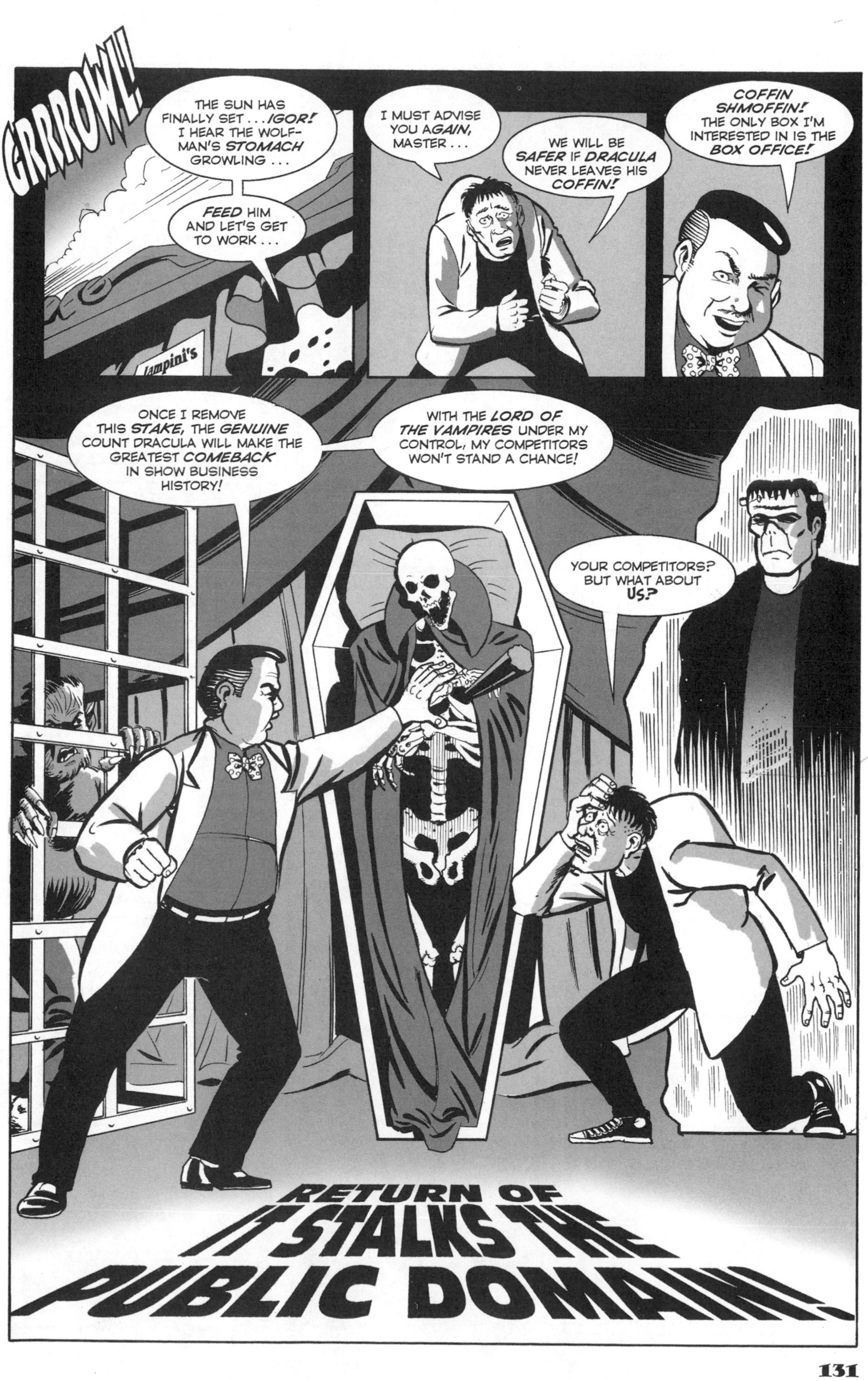
GRRROWL!
THE SUN HAS FINALLY SET . . . IGOR! I HEAR THE WOLF-MAN'S STOMACH GROWLING . . .
FEED HIM AND LET'S GET TO WORK . . .
Zampini's
I MUST ADVISE YOU AGAIN, MASTER . . .
WE WILL BE SAFER IF DRACULA NEVER LEAVES HIS COFFIN!
COFFIN SHMOFFIN! THE ONLY BOX I'M INTERESTED IN IS THE BOX OFFICE!
ONCE I REMOVE THIS STAKE, THE GENUINE COUNT DRACULA WILL MAKE THE GREATEST COMEBACK IN SHOW BUSINESS HISTORY!
WITH THE LORD OF THE VAMPIRES UNDER MY CONTROL, MY COMPETITORS WON'T STAND A CHANCE!
YOUR COMPETITORS? BUT WHAT ABOUT US?
RETURN OF IT STALKS THE PUBLIC DOMAIN!

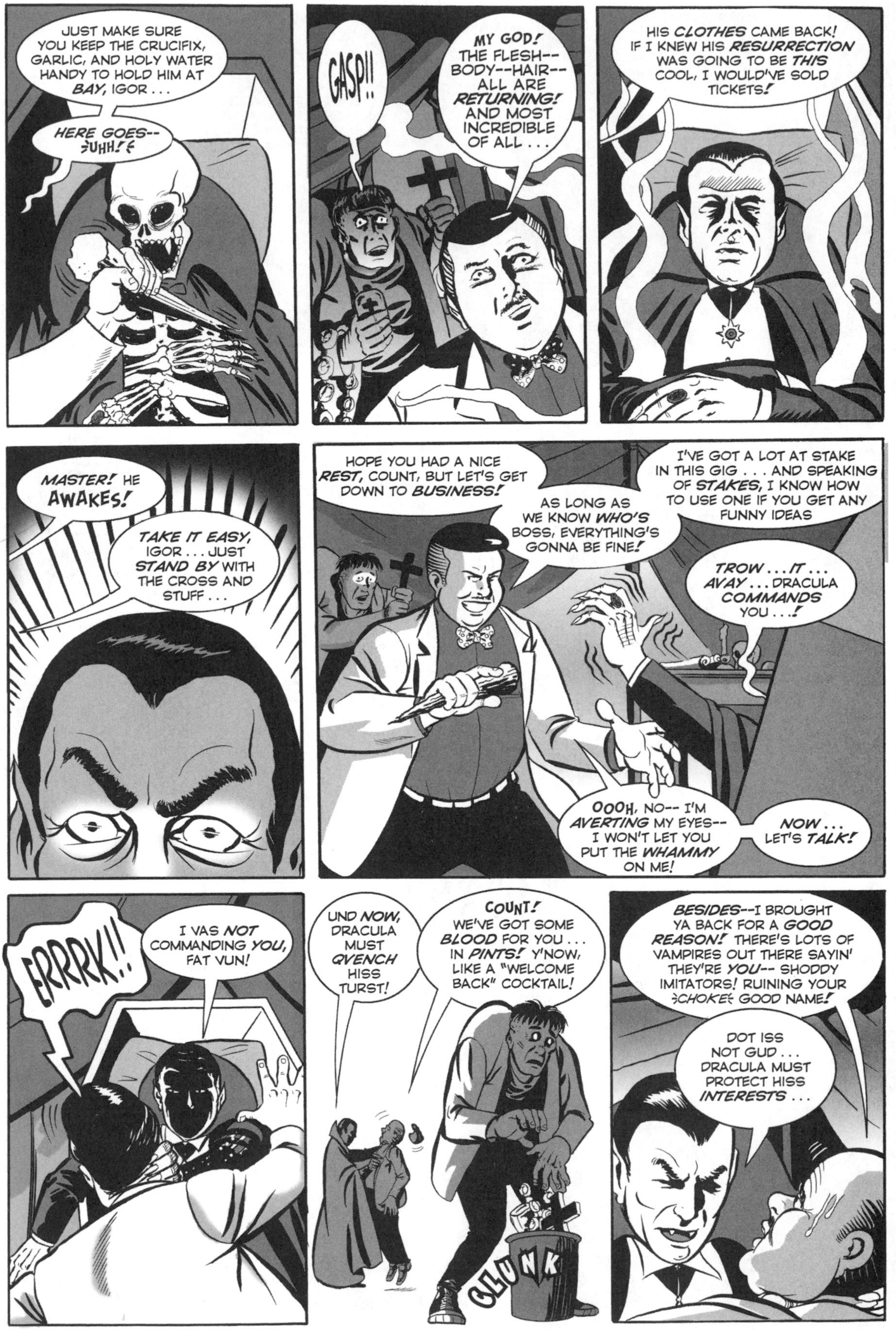

JUST MAKE SURE YOU KEEP THE CRUCIFIX, GARLIC, AND HOLY WATER HANDY TO HOLD HIM AT BAY, IGOR . . .
HERE GOES-- UHH!
GASP!!
MY GOD! THE FLESH-- BODY--HAIR-- ALL ARE RETURNING! AND MOST INCREDIBLE OF ALL . . .
HIS CLOTHES CAME BACK! IF I KNEW HIS RESURRECTION WAS GOING TO BE THIS COOL, I WOULD'VE SOLD TICKETS!
MASTER! HE AWAKES!
TAKE IT EASY, IGOR . . . JUST STAND BY WITH THE CROSS AND STUFF . . .
HOPE YOU HAD A NICE REST, COUNT, BUT LET'S GET DOWN TO BUSINESS!
AS LONG AS WE KNOW WHO'S BOSS, EVERYTHING'S GONNA BE FINE!
I'VE GOT A LOT AT STAKE IN THIS GIG . . . AND SPEAKING OF STAKES, I KNOW HOW TO USE ONE IF YOU GET ANY FUNNY IDEAS
TROW . . . IT . . . AVAY . . . DRACULA COMMANDS YOU . . .!
OOOH, NO-- I'M AVERTING MY EYES-- I WON'T LET YOU PUT THE WHAMMY ON ME!
NOW . . . LET'S TALK!
ERRRK!!
I VAS NOT COMMANDING YOU, FAT VUN!
UND NOW, DRACULA MUST QVENCH HISS TURST!
COUNT! WE'VE GOT SOME BLOOD FOR YOU . . . IN PINTS! Y'NOW, LIKE A "WELCOME BACK" COCKTAIL!
CLUNK
BESIDES--I BROUGHT YA BACK FOR A GOOD REASON! THERE'S LOTS OF VAMPIRES OUT THERE SAYIN' THEY'RE YOU-- SHODDY IMITATORS! RUINING YOUR CHOKE GOOD NAME!
DOT ISS NOT GUD . . . DRACULA MUST PROTECT HISS INTERESTS . . .

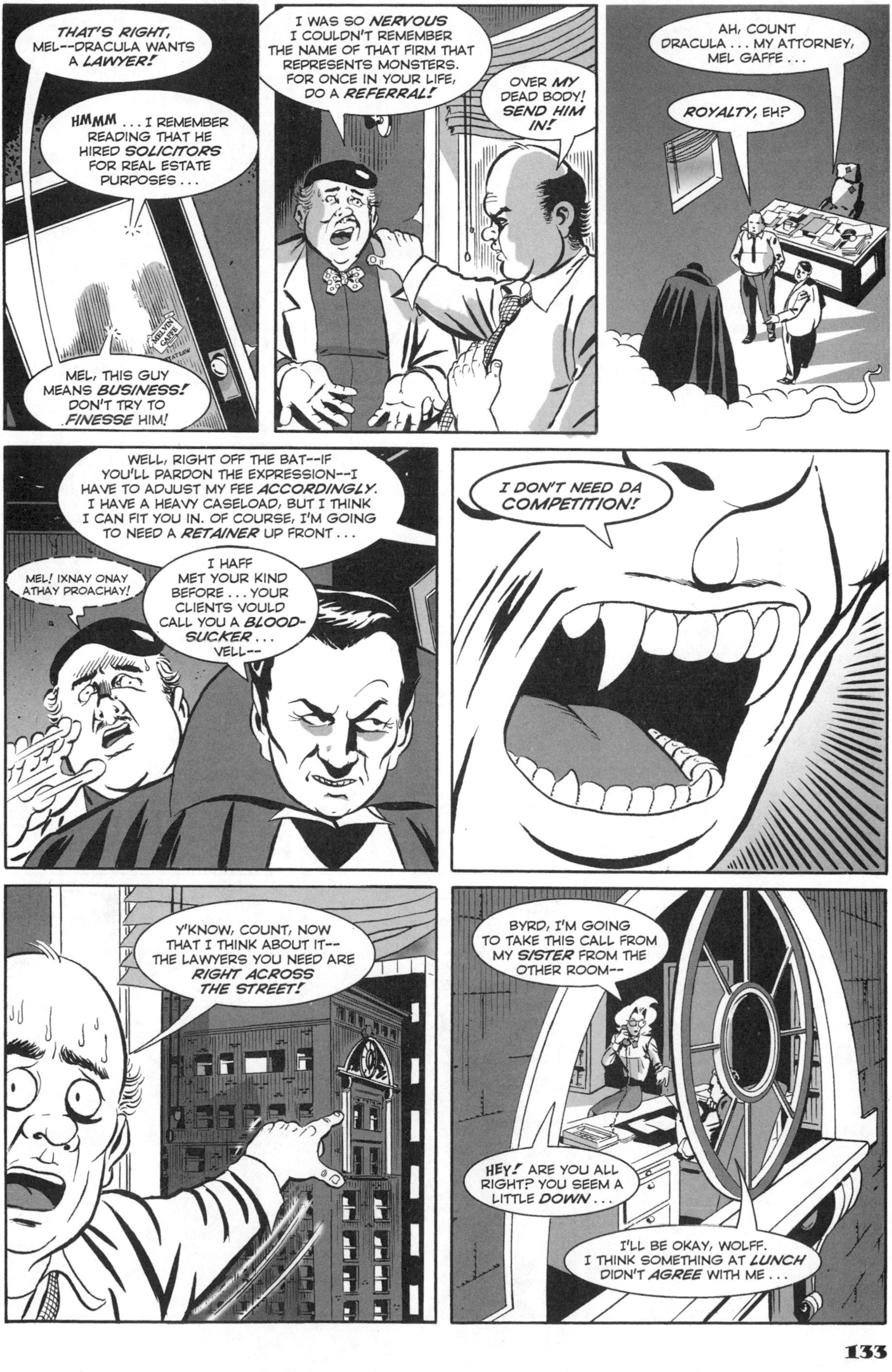
THAT'S RIGHT, MEL--DRACULA WANTS A LAWYER!
HMMM . . . I REMEMBER READING THAT HE HIRED SOLICITORS FOR REAL ESTATE PURPOSES . . .
MEL, THIS GUY MEANS BUSINESS! DON'T TRY TO FINESSE HIM!
I WAS SO NERVOUS I COULDN'T REMEMBER THE NAME OF THAT FIRM THAT REPRESENTS MONSTERS. FOR ONCE IN YOUR LIFE, DO A REFERRAL!
OVER MY DEAD BODY! SEND HIM IN!
AH, COUNT DRACULA . . . MY ATTORNEY, MEL GAFFE . . .
ROYALTY, EH?
WELL, RIGHT OFF THE BAT--IF YOU'LL PARDON THE EXPRESSION--I HAVE TO ADJUST MY FEE ACCORDINGLY. I HAVE A HEAVY CASELOAD, BUT I THINK I CAN FIT YOU IN. OF COURSE, I'M GOING TO NEED A RETAINER UP FRONT . . .
MEL! IXNAY ONAY ATHAY PROACHAY!
I HAFF MET YOUR KIND BEFORE . . . YOUR CLIENTS VOULD CALL YOU A BLOOD-SUCKER . . . VELL--
I DON'T NEED DA COMPETITION!
Y'KNOW, COUNT, NOW THAT I THINK ABOUT IT-- THE LAWYERS YOU NEED ARE RIGHT ACROSS THE STREET!
BYRD, I'M GOING TO TAKE THIS CALL FROM MY SISTER FROM THE OTHER ROOM--
HEY! ARE YOU ALL RIGHT? YOU SEEM A LITTLE DOWN . . .
I'LL BE OKAY, WOLFF. I THINK SOMETHING AT LUNCH DIDN'T AGREE WITH ME . . .

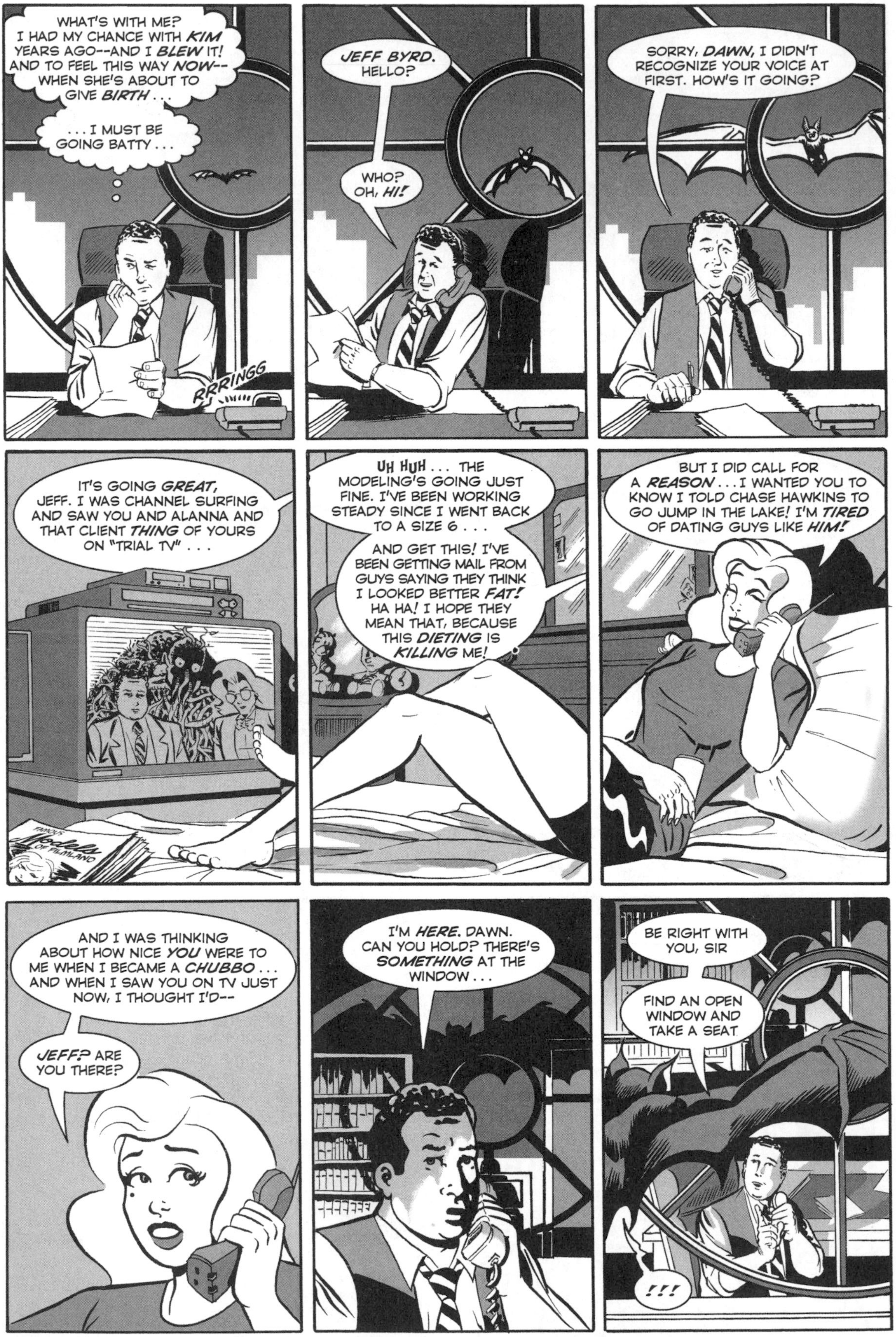
WHAT'S WITH ME? I HAD MY CHANCE WITH KIM YEARS AGO--AND I BLEW IT! AND TO FEEL THIS WAY NOW-- WHEN SHE'S ABOUT TO GIVE BIRTH . . .
. . . I MUST BE GOING BATTY . . .
RRRINGG
JEFF BYRD. HELLO?
WHO? OH, HI!
SORRY, DAWN, I DIDN'T RECOGNIZE YOUR VOICE AT FIRST. HOW'S IT GOING?
IT'S GOING GREAT, JEFF. I WAS CHANNEL SURFING AND SAW YOU AND ALANNA AND THAT CLIENT THING OF YOURS ON "TRIAL TV" . . .
UH HUH . . . THE MODELING'S GOING JUST FINE. I'VE BEEN WORKING STEADY SINCE I WENT BACK TO A SIZE 6 . . .
AND GET THIS! I'VE BEEN GETTING MAIL FROM GUYS SAYING THEY THINK I LOOKED BETTER FAT! HA HA! I HOPE THEY MEAN THAT, BECAUSE THIS DIETING IS KILLING ME!
BUT I DID CALL FOR A REASON . . . I WANTED YOU TO KNOW I TOLD CHASE HAWKINS TO GO JUMP IN THE LAKE! I'M TIRED OF DATING GUYS LIKE HIM!
AND I WAS THINKING ABOUT HOW NICE YOU WERE TO ME WHEN I BECAME A CHUBBO . . . AND WHEN I SAW YOU ON TV JUST NOW, I THOUGHT I'D--
JEFF? ARE YOU THERE?
I'M HERE. DAWN. CAN YOU HOLD? THERE'S SOMETHING AT THE WINDOW . . .
BE RIGHT WITH YOU, SIR
FIND AN OPEN WINDOW AND TAKE A SEAT
!!!

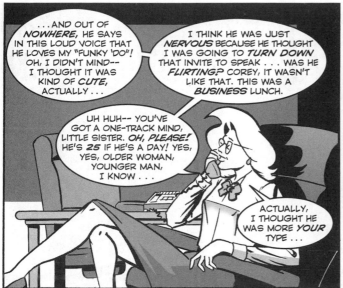

...AND OUT OF *NOWHERE,* HE SAYS IN THIS LOUD VOICE THAT HE LOVES MY "FUNKY 'DO"! OH, I DIDN'T MIND-- I THOUGHT IT WAS KIND OF *CUTE,* ACTUALLY...

I THINK HE WAS JUST *NERVOUS* BECAUSE HE THOUGHT I WAS GOING TO *TURN DOWN* THAT INVITE TO SPEAK... WAS HE *FLIRTING?* COREY, IT WASN'T LIKE THAT. THIS WAS A *BUSINESS* LUNCH.

UH HUH-- YOU'VE GOT A ONE-TRACK MIND, LITTLE SISTER. OH, PLEASE! HE'S *25* IF HE'S A DAY! YES, OLDER WOMAN, YOUNGER MAN, I KNOW...

ACTUALLY, I THOUGHT HE WAS MORE *YOUR* TYPE...

AH-HAH! *NOW* YOU WANT TO KNOW MORE, EH? WELL, I'VE GOT TO *GO*--THE OTHER LINE IS RINGING AND BYRD'S NOT PICKING UP

YES, I'LL COME UP TO VISIT SOON. EH? *WHAT* DID YOU SAY ABOUT TOBY? YOU'RE *INCORRIGIBLE,* COREY. GIVE MY LOVE TO DAD.

ALANNA WOLFF... *TOBY?* I WAS JUST-- *EXCUSE ME?* NO, I HAVEN'T... OKAY, I'LL TURN IT ON RIGHT NOW...

IT'S A REGULAR *MONSTERSCENE* HERE ON THE GREAT WHITE WAY-- AND NO ONE KNOWS *WHY!*

CLICK

WHOA! YOU'RE RIGHT, TOBY--THIS *IS* SOMETHING I'D BE INTERESTED IN...

"SO FAR, IT'S BEEN A *PEACEFUL* PROCESSION, AND THE ONLY THING *CERTAIN* IS THAT THESE *FAMOUS MONSTERS* ARE HEADING *DOWNTOWN!* THERE SEEM TO BE SEVERAL VERSIONS OF FRANKENSTEIN'S MONSTER, A BEVY OF BATS, AND A PACK OF WEREWOLVES. IT'S BELIEVED THAT THEY'RE FROM THE VARIOUS MONSTER SHOWS THAT HAVE FLOODED THE MARKET LATELY..."

LIVE

I HAVE *NO* IDEA WHAT THIS IS ALL ABOUT, TOBY... HOWEVER, THERE *IS* A *FULL MOON* TONIGHT, SO I'M NOT TOO SURPRISED.

ANYWAY, LET ME TELL MY PARTNER ABOUT THIS... IT MIGHT REQUIRE OUR SERVICES... *EH?*

OH, I HAD A NICE TIME AT LUNCH, TOO. UH HUH. BYE.

COUNT... DRACULA... IS... WAITING... TO... SEE... YOU...

THE COUNT DRACULA? THAT MAY EXPLAIN...

BYRD! WHAT IS IT?

YOUR *EYES*-- GLAZED OVER... LIKE YOUR IN A TRANCE!

HUH? OH, SORRY, WOLFF-- BUT THE DAMNDEST THING HAPPENED JUST BEFORE THE COUNT FLEW IN... *DAWN DEVINE* ASKED ME OUT ON A *DATE!*

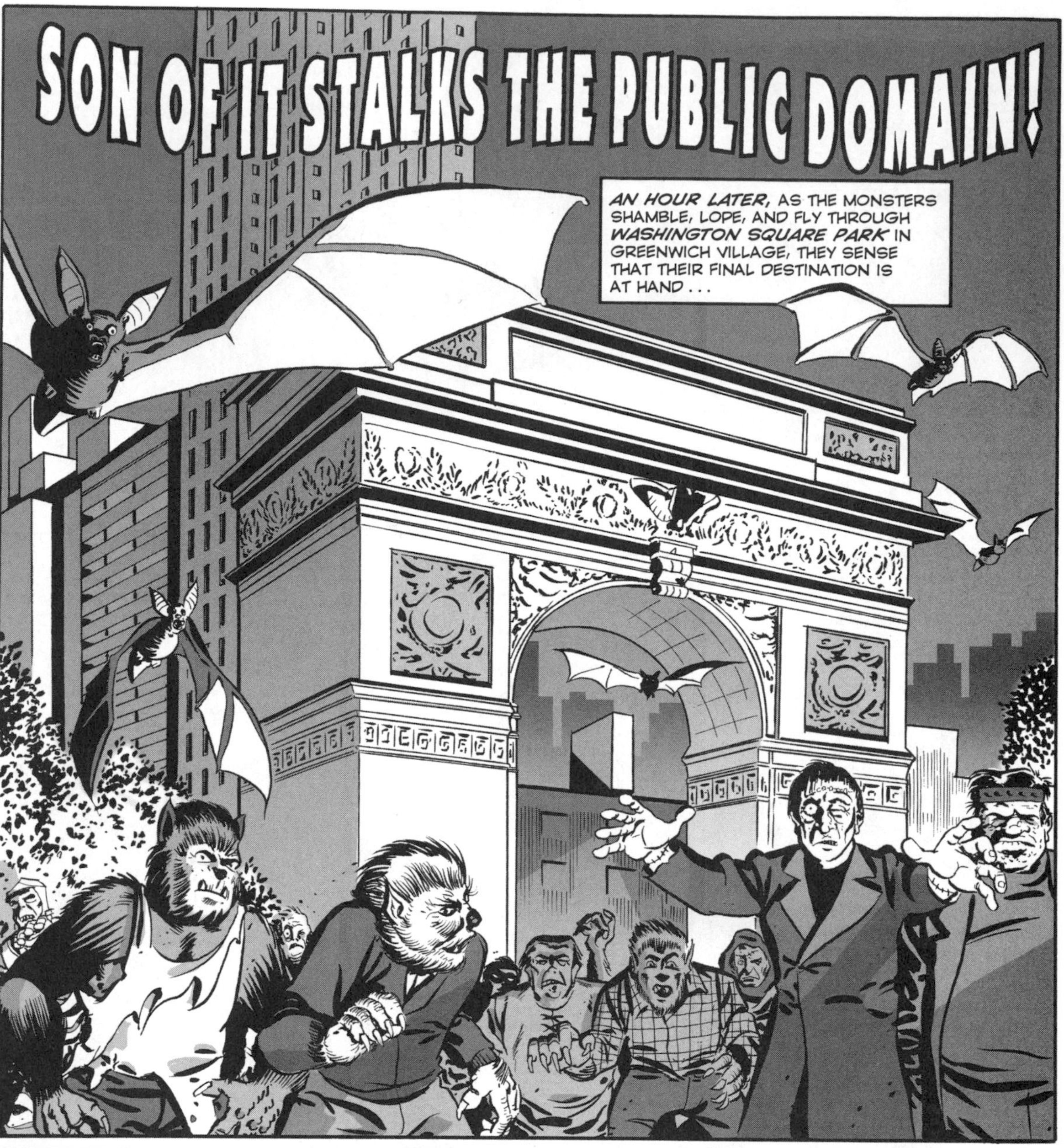
SON OF IT STALKS THE PUBLIC DOMAIN!
AN HOUR LATER, AS THE MONSTERS SHAMBLE, LOPE, AND FLY THROUGH WASHINGTON SQUARE PARK IN GREENWICH VILLAGE, THEY SENSE THAT THEIR FINAL DESTINATION IS AT HAND . . .

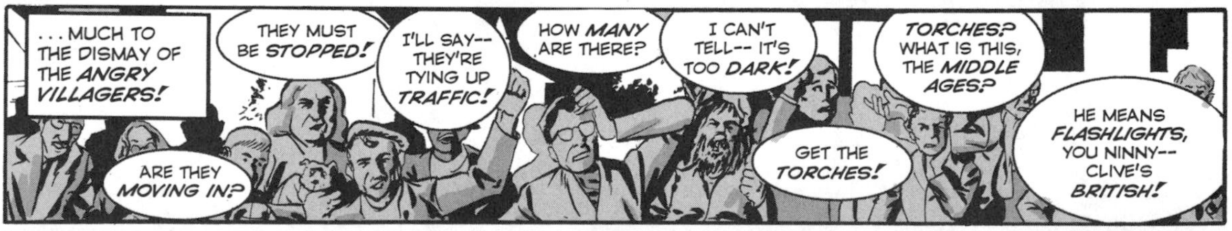
. . . MUCH TO THE DISMAY OF THE ANGRY VILLAGERS!
THEY MUST BE STOPPED!
ARE THEY MOVING IN?
I'LL SAY-- THEY'RE TYING UP TRAFFIC!
HOW MANY ARE THERE?
I CAN'T TELL-- IT'S TOO DARK!
GET THE TORCHES!
TORCHES? WHAT IS THIS, THE MIDDLE AGES?
HE MEANS FLASHLIGHTS, YOU NINNY-- CLIVE'S BRITISH!

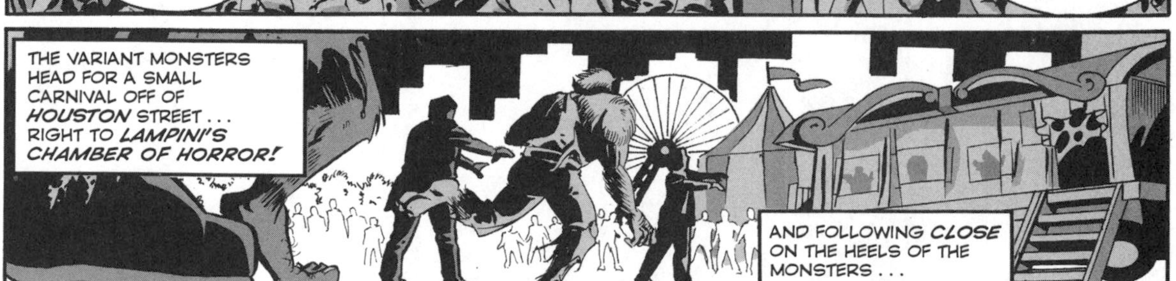
THE VARIANT MONSTERS HEAD FOR A SMALL CARNIVAL OFF OF HOUSTON STREET . . . RIGHT TO LAMPINI'S CHAMBER OF HORROR!
AND FOLLOWING CLOSE ON THE HEELS OF THE MONSTERS . . .

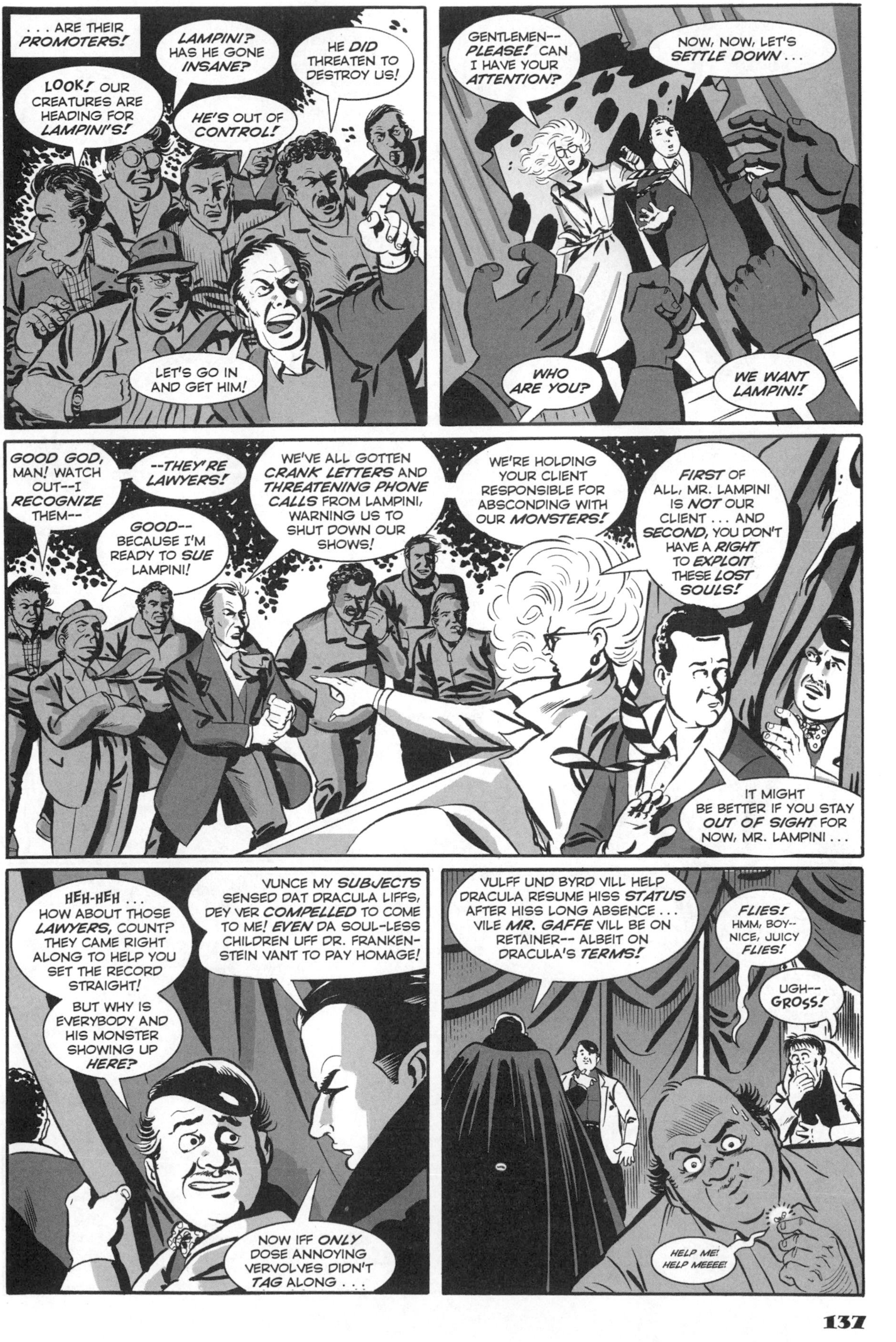
. . . ARE THEIR PROMOTERS!
LOOK! OUR CREATURES ARE HEADING FOR LAMPINI'S!
LAMPINI? HAS HE GONE INSANE?
HE'S OUT OF CONTROL!
HE DID THREATEN TO DESTROY US!
LET'S GO IN AND GET HIM!
GENTLEMEN-- PLEASE! CAN I HAVE YOUR ATTENTION?
NOW, NOW, LET'S SETTLE DOWN . . .
WHO ARE YOU?
WE WANT LAMPINI!
GOOD GOD, MAN! WATCH OUT--I RECOGNIZE THEM--
--THEY'RE LAWYERS!
GOOD-- BECAUSE I'M READY TO SUE LAMPINI!
WE'VE ALL GOTTEN CRANK LETTERS AND THREATENING PHONE CALLS FROM LAMPINI, WARNING US TO SHUT DOWN OUR SHOWS!
WE'RE HOLDING YOUR CLIENT RESPONSIBLE FOR ABSCONDING WITH OUR MONSTERS!
FIRST OF ALL, MR. LAMPINI IS NOT OUR CLIENT . . . AND SECOND, YOU DON'T HAVE A RIGHT TO EXPLOIT THESE LOST SOULS!
IT MIGHT BE BETTER IF YOU STAY OUT OF SIGHT FOR NOW, MR. LAMPINI . . .
HEH-HEH . . . HOW ABOUT THOSE LAWYERS, COUNT? THEY CAME RIGHT ALONG TO HELP YOU SET THE RECORD STRAIGHT!
BUT WHY IS EVERYBODY AND HIS MONSTER SHOWING UP HERE?
VUNCE MY SUBJECTS SENSED DAT DRACULA LIFFS, DEY VER COMPELLED TO COME TO ME! EVEN DA SOUL-LESS CHILDREN UFF DR. FRANKENSTEIN VANT TO PAY HOMAGE!
NOW IFF ONLY DOSE ANNOYING VERVOLVES DIDN'T TAG ALONG . . .
VULFF UND BYRD VILL HELP DRACULA RESUME HISS STATUS AFTER HISS LONG ABSENCE . . . VILE MR. GAFFE VILL BE ON RETAINER-- ALBEIT ON DRACULA'S TERMS!
FLIES! HMM, BOY-- NICE, JUICY FLIES!
UGH-- GROSS!
HELP ME! HELP MEEEE!

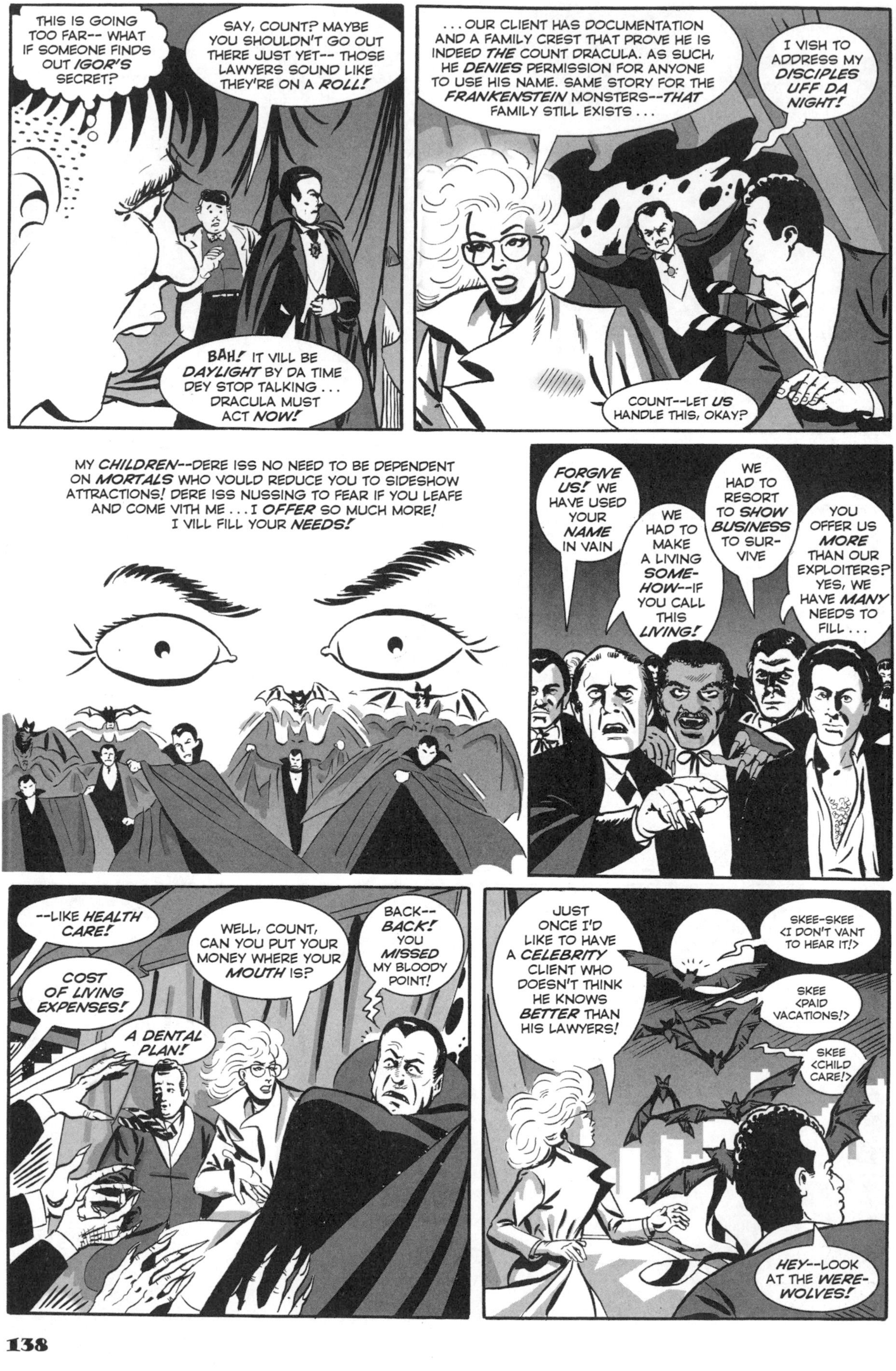
THIS IS GOING TOO FAR-- WHAT IF SOMEONE FINDS OUT IGOR'S SECRET?
SAY, COUNT? MAYBE YOU SHOULDN'T GO OUT THERE JUST YET-- THOSE LAWYERS SOUND LIKE THEY'RE ON A ROLL!
BAH! IT VILL BE DAYLIGHT BY DA TIME DEY STOP TALKING . . . DRACULA MUST ACT NOW!
. . . OUR CLIENT HAS DOCUMENTATION AND A FAMILY CREST THAT PROVE HE IS INDEED THE COUNT DRACULA. AS SUCH, HE DENIES PERMISSION FOR ANYONE TO USE HIS NAME. SAME STORY FOR THE FRANKENSTEIN MONSTERS--THAT FAMILY STILL EXISTS . . .
I VISH TO ADDRESS MY DISCIPLES UFF DA NIGHT!
COUNT--LET US HANDLE THIS, OKAY?
MY CHILDREN--DERE ISS NO NEED TO BE DEPENDENT ON MORTALS WHO VOULD REDUCE YOU TO SIDESHOW ATTRACTIONS! DERE ISS NUSSING TO FEAR IF YOU LEAFE AND COME VITH ME . . . I OFFER SO MUCH MORE! I VILL FILL YOUR NEEDS!
FORGIVE US! WE HAVE USED YOUR NAME IN VAIN
WE HAD TO MAKE A LIVING SOME-HOW--IF YOU CALL THIS LIVING!
WE HAD TO RESORT TO SHOW BUSINESS TO SUR-VIVE
YOU OFFER US MORE THAN OUR EXPLOITERS? YES, WE HAVE MANY NEEDS TO FILL . . .
--LIKE HEALTH CARE!
COST OF LIVING EXPENSES!
A DENTAL PLAN!
WELL, COUNT, CAN YOU PUT YOUR MONEY WHERE YOUR MOUTH IS?
BACK--BACK! YOU MISSED MY BLOODY POINT!
JUST ONCE I'D LIKE TO HAVE A CELEBRITY CLIENT WHO DOESN'T THINK HE KNOWS BETTER THAN HIS LAWYERS!
SKEE-SKEE <I DON'T VANT TO HEAR IT!>
SKEE <PAID VACATIONS!>
SKEE <CHILD CARE!>
HEY--LOOK AT THE WERE-WOLVES!

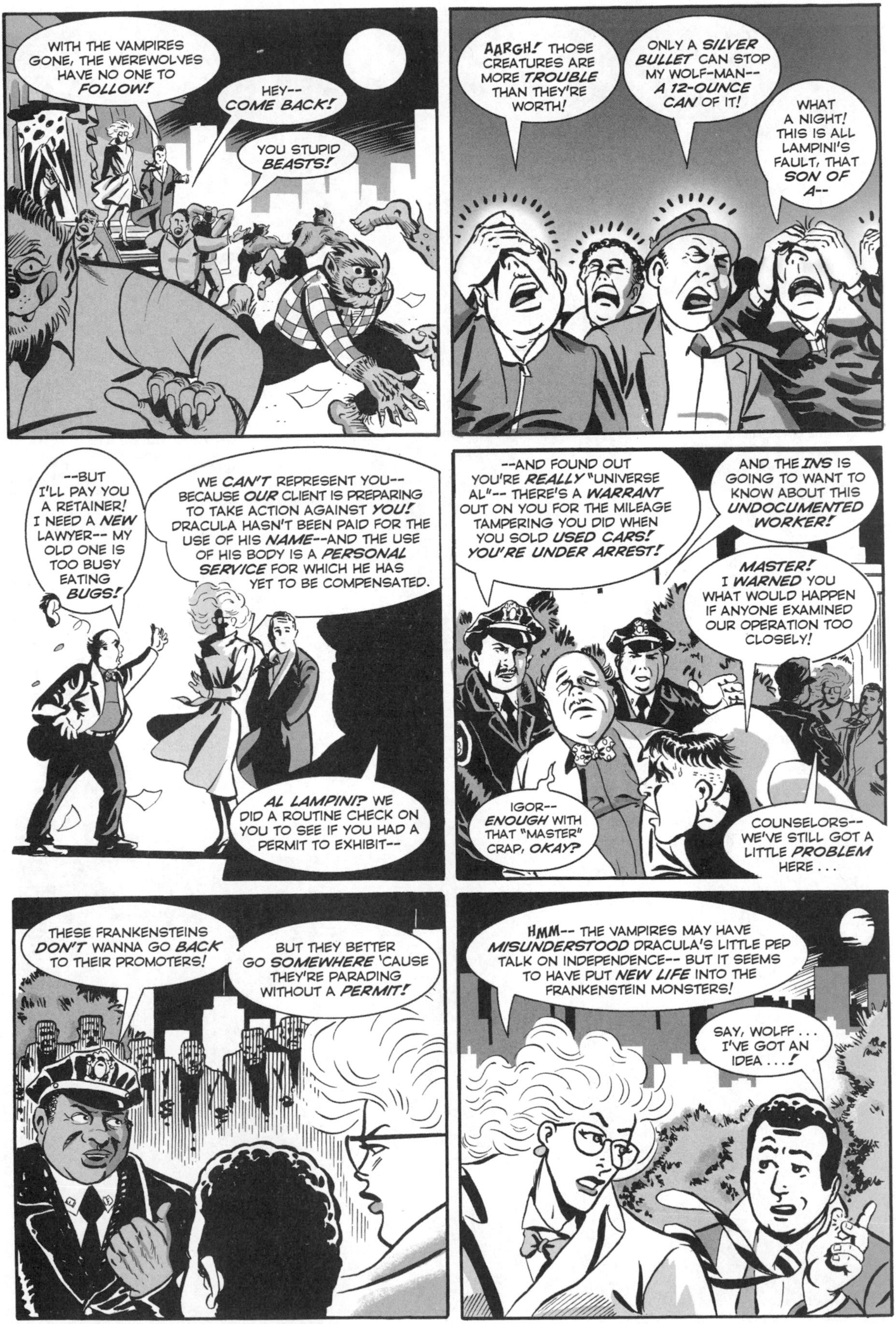
WITH THE VAMPIRES GONE, THE WEREWOLVES HAVE NO ONE TO FOLLOW!
HEY-- COME BACK!
YOU STUPID BEASTS!
AARGH! THOSE CREATURES ARE MORE TROUBLE THAN THEY'RE WORTH!
ONLY A SILVER BULLET CAN STOP MY WOLF-MAN-- A 12-OUNCE CAN OF IT!
WHAT A NIGHT! THIS IS ALL LAMPINI'S FAULT, THAT SON OF A--
--BUT I'LL PAY YOU A RETAINER! I NEED A NEW LAWYER-- MY OLD ONE IS TOO BUSY EATING BUGS!
WE CAN'T REPRESENT YOU-- BECAUSE OUR CLIENT IS PREPARING TO TAKE ACTION AGAINST YOU! DRACULA HASN'T BEEN PAID FOR THE USE OF HIS NAME--AND THE USE OF HIS BODY IS A PERSONAL SERVICE FOR WHICH HE HAS YET TO BE COMPENSATED.
AL LAMPINI? WE DID A ROUTINE CHECK ON YOU TO SEE IF YOU HAD A PERMIT TO EXHIBIT--
--AND FOUND OUT YOU'RE REALLY "UNIVERSE AL"-- THERE'S A WARRANT OUT ON YOU FOR THE MILEAGE TAMPERING YOU DID WHEN YOU SOLD USED CARS! YOU'RE UNDER ARREST!
AND THE INS IS GOING TO WANT TO KNOW ABOUT THIS UNDOCUMENTED WORKER!
MASTER! I WARNED YOU WHAT WOULD HAPPEN IF ANYONE EXAMINED OUR OPERATION TOO CLOSELY!
IGOR-- ENOUGH WITH THAT "MASTER" CRAP, OKAY?
COUNSELORS-- WE'VE STILL GOT A LITTLE PROBLEM HERE . . .
THESE FRANKENSTEINS DON'T WANNA GO BACK TO THEIR PROMOTERS!
BUT THEY BETTER GO SOMEWHERE 'CAUSE THEY'RE PARADING WITHOUT A PERMIT!
HMM-- THE VAMPIRES MAY HAVE MISUNDERSTOOD DRACULA'S LITTLE PEP TALK ON INDEPENDENCE-- BUT IT SEEMS TO HAVE PUT NEW LIFE INTO THE FRANKENSTEIN MONSTERS!
SAY, WOLFF . . . I'VE GOT AN IDEA . . . !

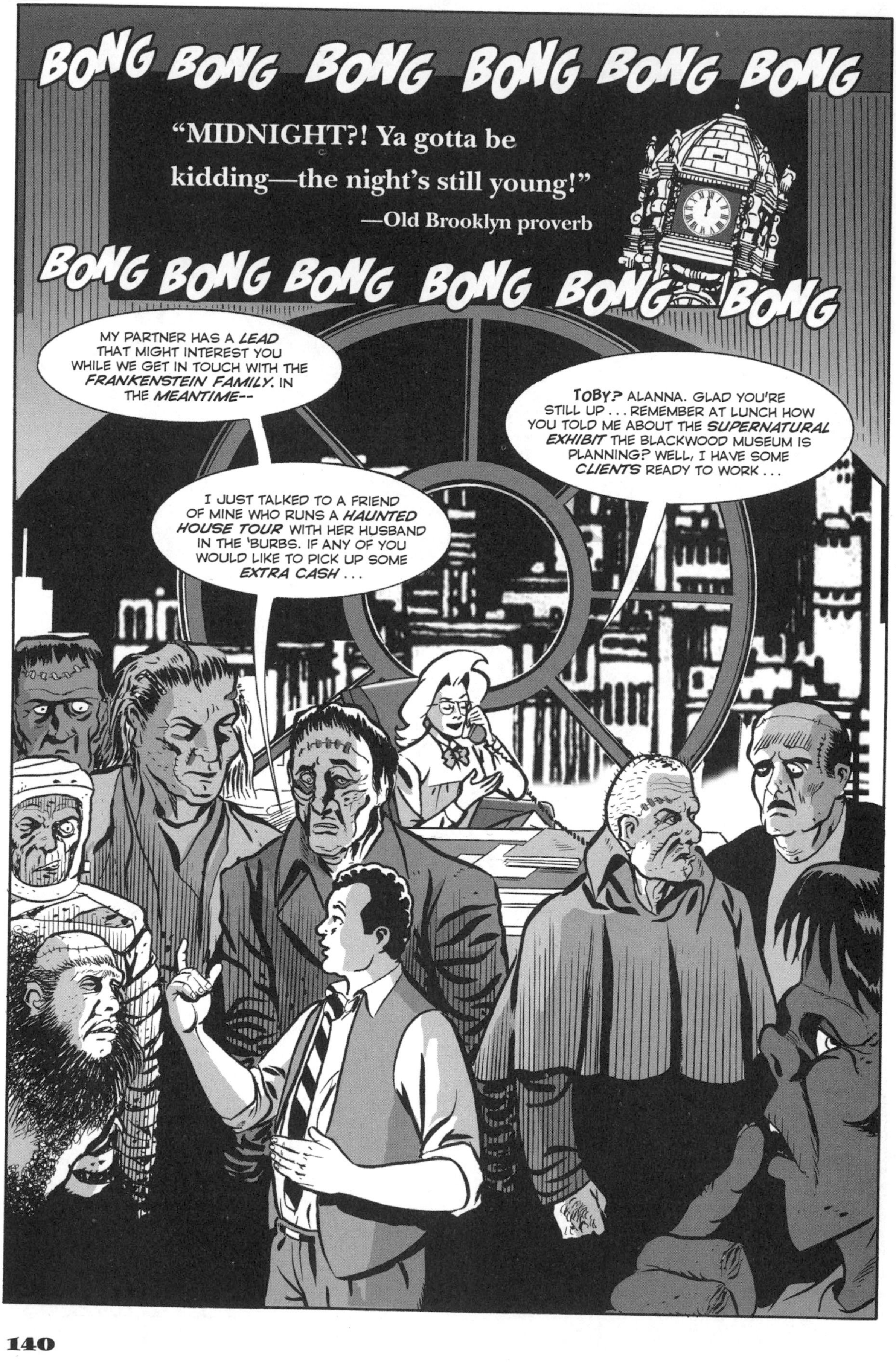
BONG BONG BONG BONG BONG BONG
"MIDNIGHT?! Ya gotta be kidding—the night's still young!"
—Old Brooklyn proverb
BONG BONG BONG BONG BONG BONG
MY PARTNER HAS A LEAD THAT MIGHT INTEREST YOU WHILE WE GET IN TOUCH WITH THE FRANKENSTEIN FAMILY. IN THE MEANTIME--
I JUST TALKED TO A FRIEND OF MINE WHO RUNS A HAUNTED HOUSE TOUR WITH HER HUSBAND IN THE 'BURBS. IF ANY OF YOU WOULD LIKE TO PICK UP SOME EXTRA CASH . . .
TOBY? ALANNA. GLAD YOU'RE STILL UP . . . REMEMBER AT LUNCH HOW YOU TOLD ME ABOUT THE SUPERNATURAL EXHIBIT THE BLACKWOOD MUSEUM IS PLANNING? WELL, I HAVE SOME CLIENTS READY TO WORK . . .

Fungi and Dolls

Featuring:

I, Sodd

The Bequeathing of Hodge the Flunky

I Turned a Dream Date into a Nightmare

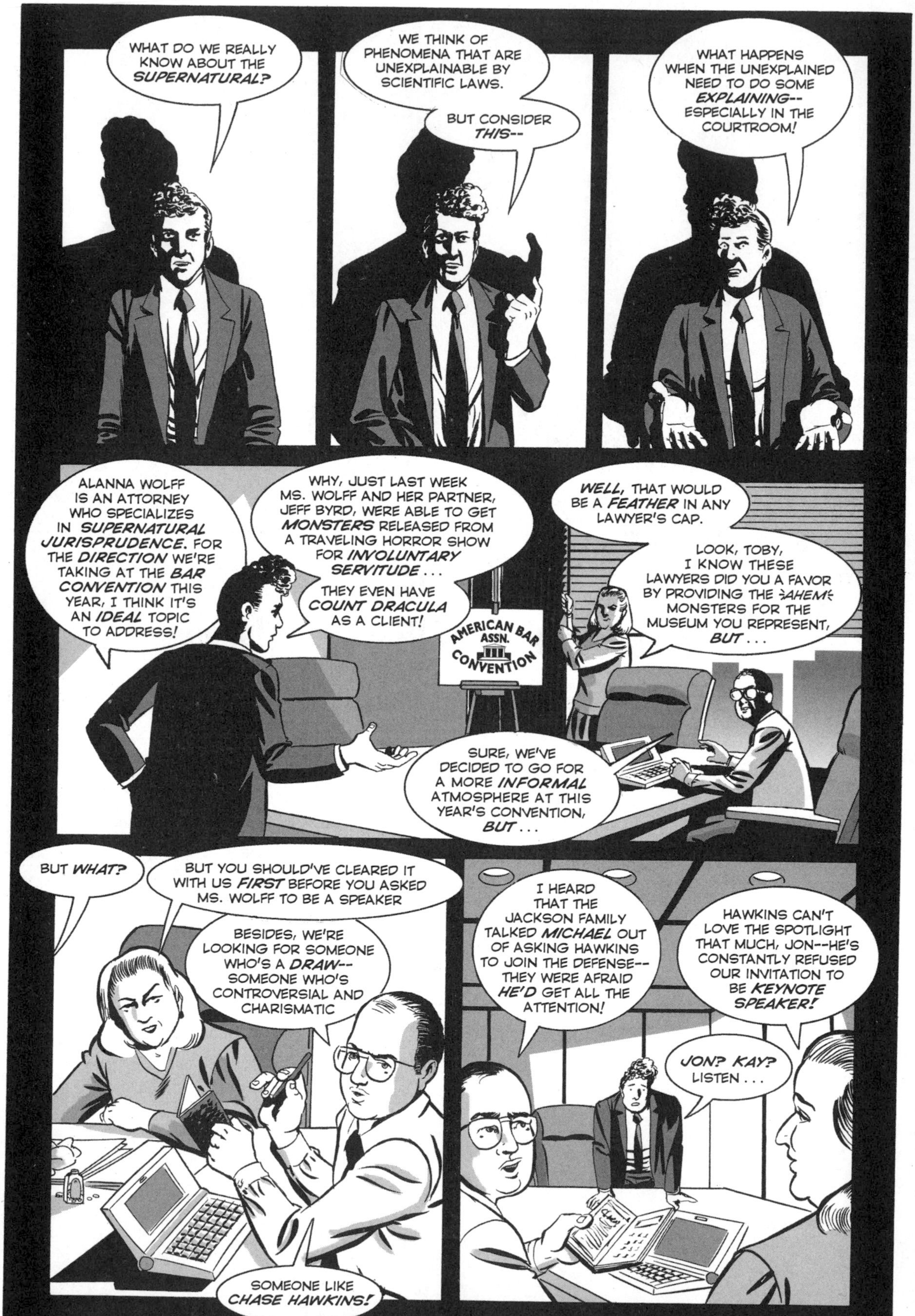
WHAT DO WE REALLY KNOW ABOUT THE SUPERNATURAL?
WE THINK OF PHENOMENA THAT ARE UNEXPLAINABLE BY SCIENTIFIC LAWS.
BUT CONSIDER THIS--
WHAT HAPPENS WHEN THE UNEXPLAINED NEED TO DO SOME EXPLAINING-- ESPECIALLY IN THE COURTROOM!
ALANNA WOLFF IS AN ATTORNEY WHO SPECIALIZES IN SUPERNATURAL JURISPRUDENCE. FOR THE DIRECTION WE'RE TAKING AT THE BAR CONVENTION THIS YEAR, I THINK IT'S AN IDEAL TOPIC TO ADDRESS!
WHY, JUST LAST WEEK MS. WOLFF AND HER PARTNER, JEFF BYRD, WERE ABLE TO GET MONSTERS RELEASED FROM A TRAVELING HORROR SHOW FOR INVOLUNTARY SERVITUDE . . .
THEY EVEN HAVE COUNT DRACULA AS A CLIENT!
AMERICAN BAR ASSN. CONVENTION
WELL, THAT WOULD BE A FEATHER IN ANY LAWYER'S CAP.
LOOK, TOBY, I KNOW THESE LAWYERS DID YOU A FAVOR BY PROVIDING THE *AHEM* MONSTERS FOR THE MUSEUM YOU REPRESENT, BUT . . .
SURE, WE'VE DECIDED TO GO FOR A MORE INFORMAL ATMOSPHERE AT THIS YEAR'S CONVENTION, BUT . . .
BUT WHAT?
BUT YOU SHOULD'VE CLEARED IT WITH US FIRST BEFORE YOU ASKED MS. WOLFF TO BE A SPEAKER
BESIDES, WE'RE LOOKING FOR SOMEONE WHO'S A DRAW-- SOMEONE WHO'S CONTROVERSIAL AND CHARISMATIC
SOMEONE LIKE CHASE HAWKINS!
I HEARD THAT THE JACKSON FAMILY TALKED MICHAEL OUT OF ASKING HAWKINS TO JOIN THE DEFENSE-- THEY WERE AFRAID HE'D GET ALL THE ATTENTION!
HAWKINS CAN'T LOVE THE SPOTLIGHT THAT MUCH, JON--HE'S CONSTANTLY REFUSED OUR INVITATION TO BE KEYNOTE SPEAKER!
JON? KAY? LISTEN . . .

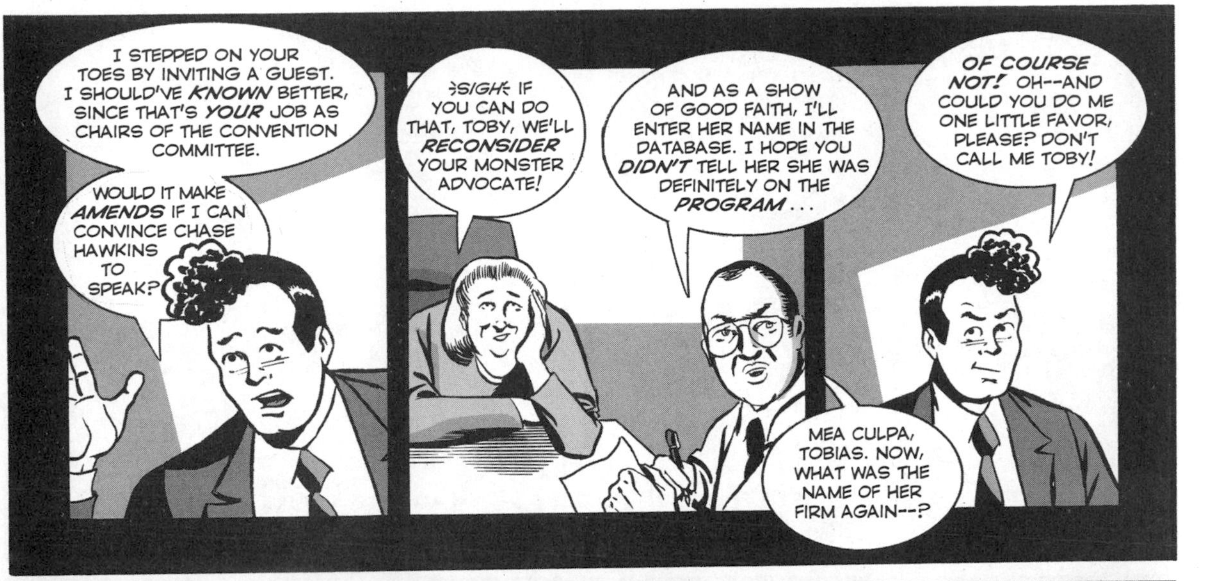
I STEPPED ON YOUR TOES BY INVITING A GUEST. I SHOULD'VE KNOWN BETTER, SINCE THAT'S YOUR JOB AS CHAIRS OF THE CONVENTION COMMITTEE.
WOULD IT MAKE AMENDS IF I CAN CONVINCE CHASE HAWKINS TO SPEAK?
>SIGH< IF YOU CAN DO THAT, TOBY, WE'LL RECONSIDER YOUR MONSTER ADVOCATE!
AND AS A SHOW OF GOOD FAITH, I'LL ENTER HER NAME IN THE DATABASE. I HOPE YOU DIDN'T TELL HER SHE WAS DEFINITELY ON THE PROGRAM...
OF COURSE NOT! OH--AND COULD YOU DO ME ONE LITTLE FAVOR, PLEASE? DON'T CALL ME TOBY!
MEA CULPA, TOBIAS. NOW, WHAT WAS THE NAME OF HER FIRM AGAIN--?

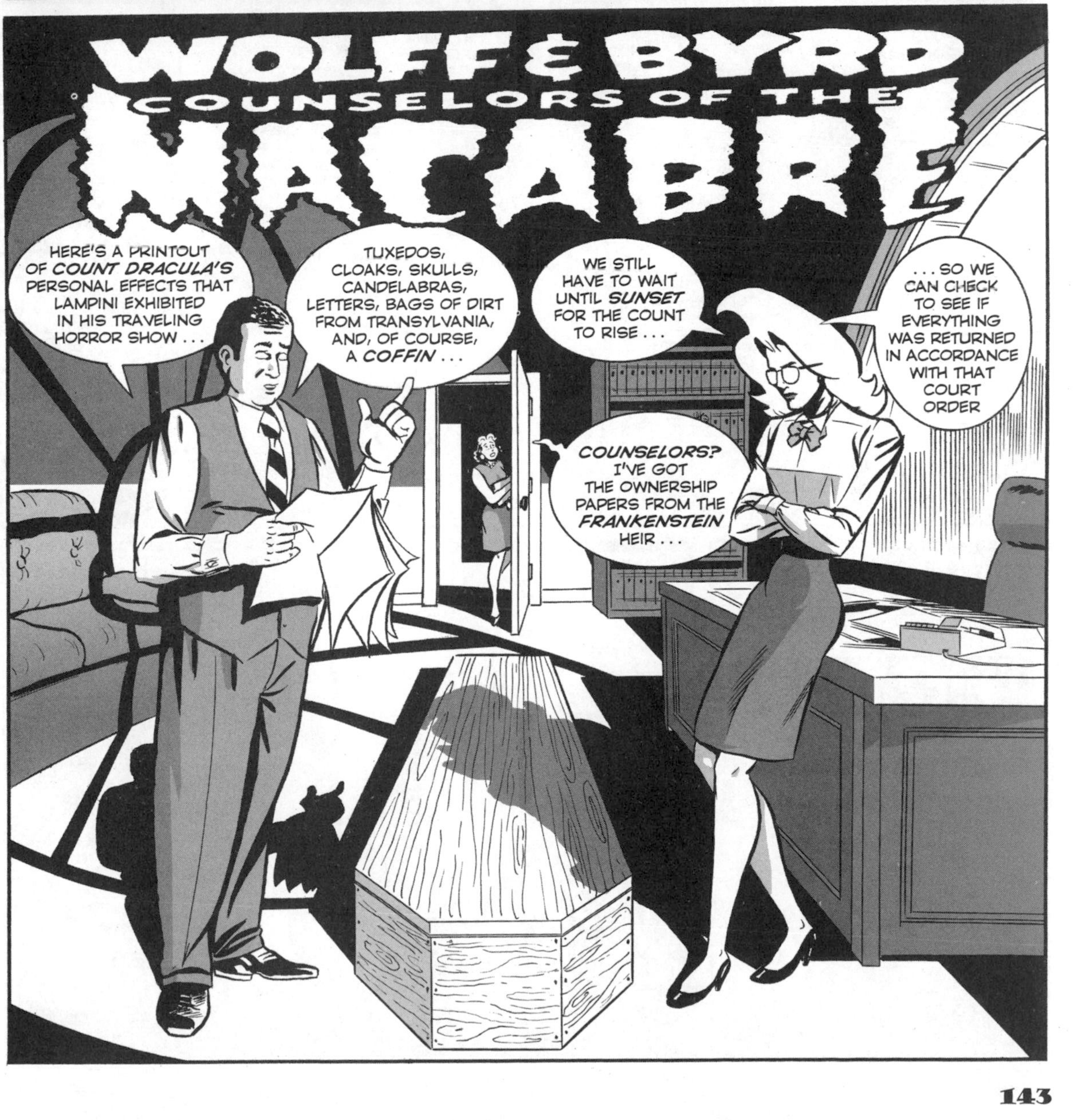
WOLFF & BYRD
COUNSELORS OF THE
MACABRE
HERE'S A PRINTOUT OF COUNT DRACULA'S PERSONAL EFFECTS THAT LAMPINI EXHIBITED IN HIS TRAVELING HORROR SHOW...
TUXEDOS, CLOAKS, SKULLS, CANDELABRAS, LETTERS, BAGS OF DIRT FROM TRANSYLVANIA, AND, OF COURSE, A COFFIN...
WE STILL HAVE TO WAIT UNTIL SUNSET FOR THE COUNT TO RISE...
...SO WE CAN CHECK TO SEE IF EVERYTHING WAS RETURNED IN ACCORDANCE WITH THAT COURT ORDER
COUNSELORS? I'VE GOT THE OWNERSHIP PAPERS FROM THE FRANKENSTEIN HEIR...

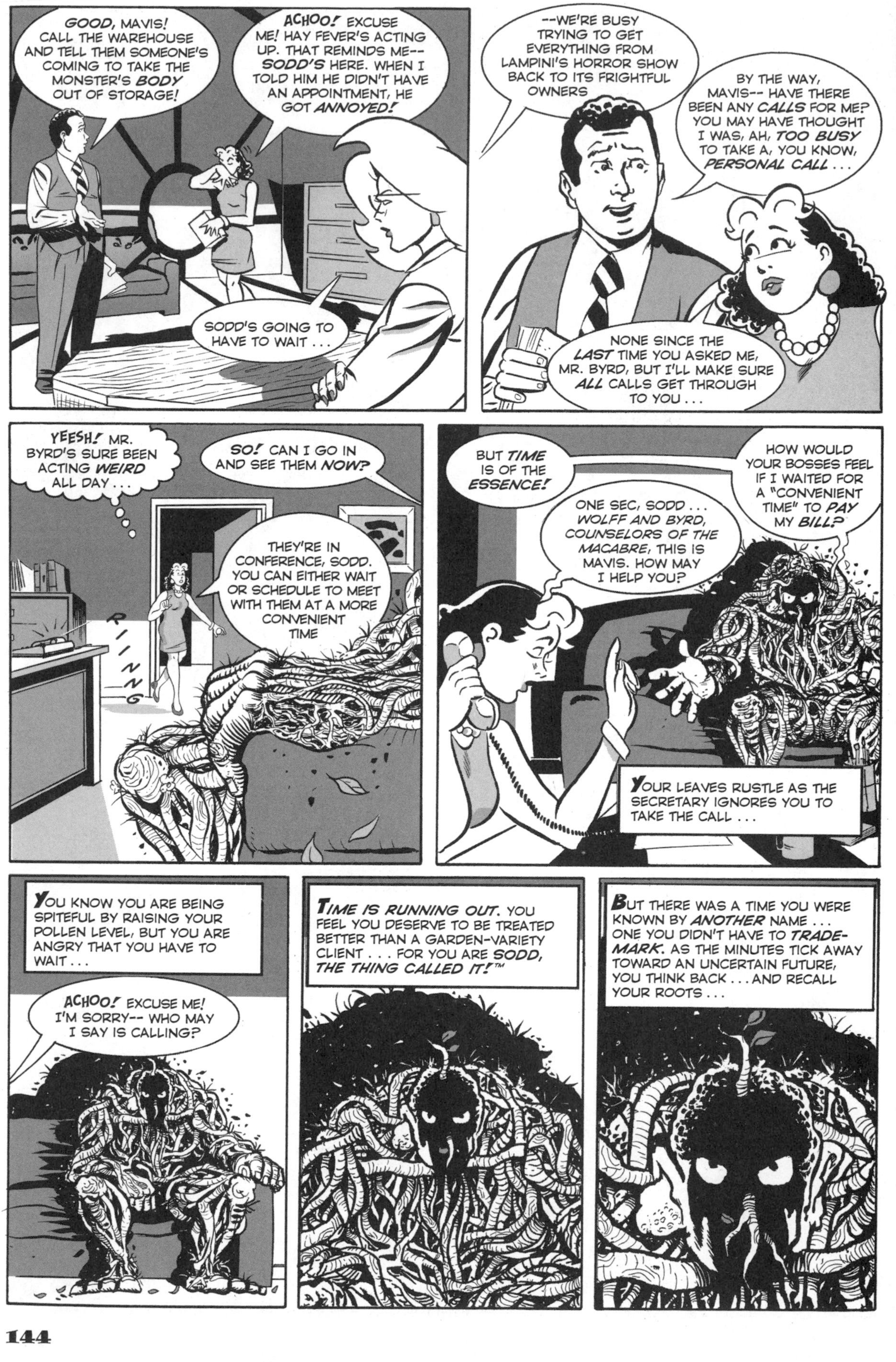
GOOD, MAVIS! CALL THE WAREHOUSE AND TELL THEM SOMEONE'S COMING TO TAKE THE MONSTER'S BODY OUT OF STORAGE!
ACHOO! EXCUSE ME! HAY FEVER'S ACTING UP. THAT REMINDS ME-- SODD'S HERE. WHEN I TOLD HIM HE DIDN'T HAVE AN APPOINTMENT, HE GOT ANNOYED!
SODD'S GOING TO HAVE TO WAIT . . .
--WE'RE BUSY TRYING TO GET EVERYTHING FROM LAMPINI'S HORROR SHOW BACK TO ITS FRIGHTFUL OWNERS
BY THE WAY, MAVIS-- HAVE THERE BEEN ANY CALLS FOR ME? YOU MAY HAVE THOUGHT I WAS, AH, TOO BUSY TO TAKE A, YOU KNOW, PERSONAL CALL . . .
NONE SINCE THE LAST TIME YOU ASKED ME, MR. BYRD, BUT I'LL MAKE SURE ALL CALLS GET THROUGH TO YOU . . .
YEESH! MR. BYRD'S SURE BEEN ACTING WEIRD ALL DAY . . .
SO! CAN I GO IN AND SEE THEM NOW?
THEY'RE IN CONFERENCE, SODD. YOU CAN EITHER WAIT OR SCHEDULE TO MEET WITH THEM AT A MORE CONVENIENT TIME
RIIING
BUT TIME IS OF THE ESSENCE!
HOW WOULD YOUR BOSSES FEEL IF I WAITED FOR A "CONVENIENT TIME" TO PAY MY BILL?
ONE SEC, SODD . . . WOLFF AND BYRD, COUNSELORS OF THE MACABRE, THIS IS MAVIS. HOW MAY I HELP YOU?
YOUR LEAVES RUSTLE AS THE SECRETARY IGNORES YOU TO TAKE THE CALL . . .
YOU KNOW YOU ARE BEING SPITEFUL BY RAISING YOUR POLLEN LEVEL, BUT YOU ARE ANGRY THAT YOU HAVE TO WAIT . . .
ACHOO! EXCUSE ME! I'M SORRY-- WHO MAY I SAY IS CALLING?
TIME IS RUNNING OUT. YOU FEEL YOU DESERVE TO BE TREATED BETTER THAN A GARDEN-VARIETY CLIENT . . . FOR YOU ARE SODD, THE THING CALLED IT!™
BUT THERE WAS A TIME YOU WERE KNOWN BY ANOTHER NAME . . . ONE YOU DIDN'T HAVE TO TRADE-MARK. AS THE MINUTES TICK AWAY TOWARD AN UNCERTAIN FUTURE, YOU THINK BACK . . . AND RECALL YOUR ROOTS . . .

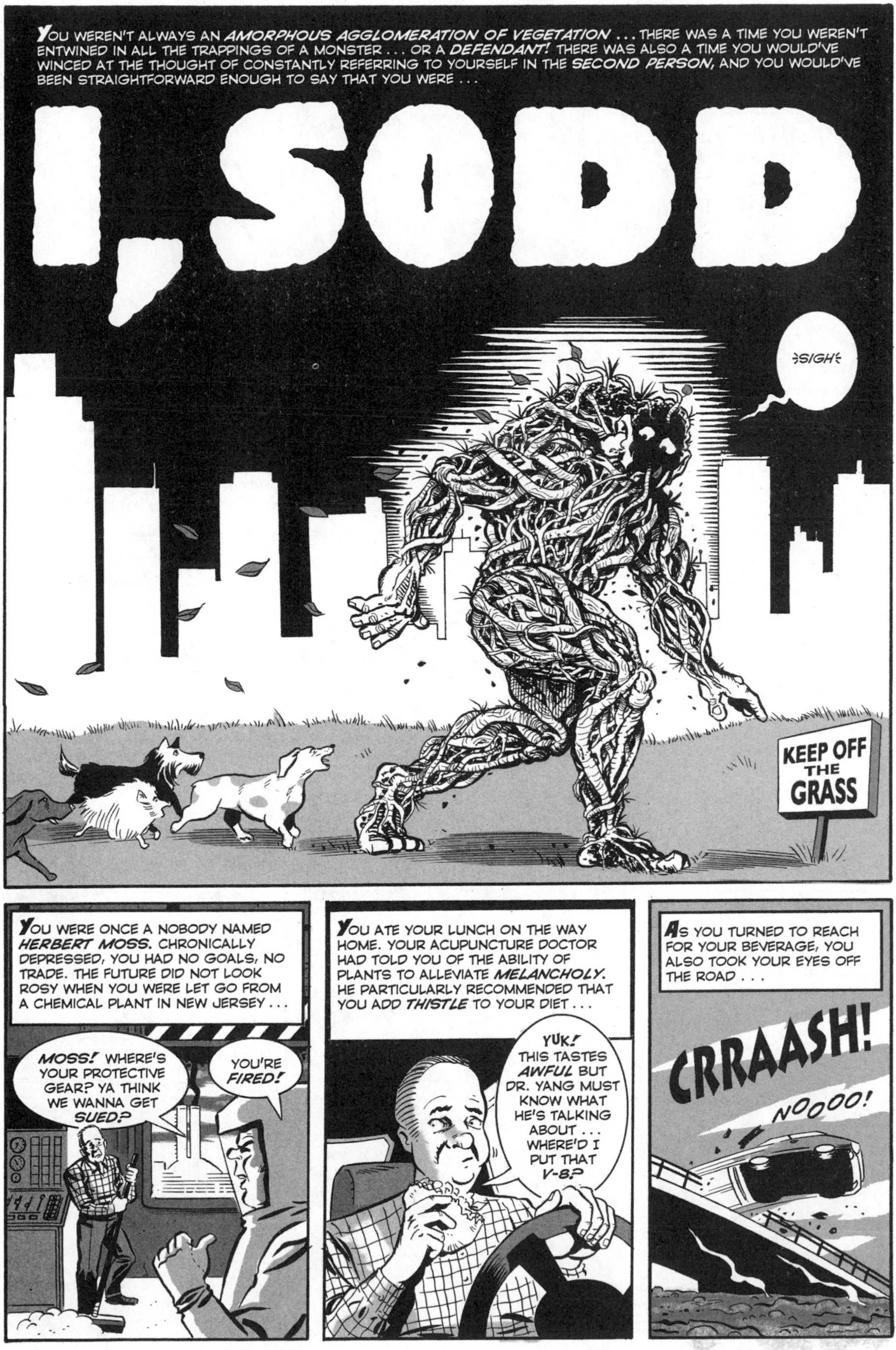
YOU WEREN'T ALWAYS AN AMORPHOUS AGGLOMERATION OF VEGETATION . . . THERE WAS A TIME YOU WEREN'T ENTWINED IN ALL THE TRAPPINGS OF A MONSTER . . . OR A DEFENDANT! THERE WAS ALSO A TIME YOU WOULD'VE WINCED AT THE THOUGHT OF CONSTANTLY REFERRING TO YOURSELF IN THE SECOND PERSON, AND YOU WOULD'VE BEEN STRAIGHTFORWARD ENOUGH TO SAY THAT YOU WERE . . .
I, SODD
SIGH
KEEP OFF THE GRASS
YOU WERE ONCE A NOBODY NAMED HERBERT MOSS. CHRONICALLY DEPRESSED, YOU HAD NO GOALS, NO TRADE. THE FUTURE DID NOT LOOK ROSY WHEN YOU WERE LET GO FROM A CHEMICAL PLANT IN NEW JERSEY . . .
MOSS! WHERE'S YOUR PROTECTIVE GEAR? YA THINK WE WANNA GET SUED?
YOU'RE FIRED!
YOU ATE YOUR LUNCH ON THE WAY HOME. YOUR ACUPUNCTURE DOCTOR HAD TOLD YOU OF THE ABILITY OF PLANTS TO ALLEVIATE MELANCHOLY. HE PARTICULARLY RECOMMENDED THAT YOU ADD THISTLE TO YOUR DIET . . .
YUK! THIS TASTES AWFUL BUT DR. YANG MUST KNOW WHAT HE'S TALKING ABOUT . . . WHERE'D I PUT THAT V-8?
AS YOU TURNED TO REACH FOR YOUR BEVERAGE, YOU ALSO TOOK YOUR EYES OFF THE ROAD . . .
CRRAASH!
NOOOO!

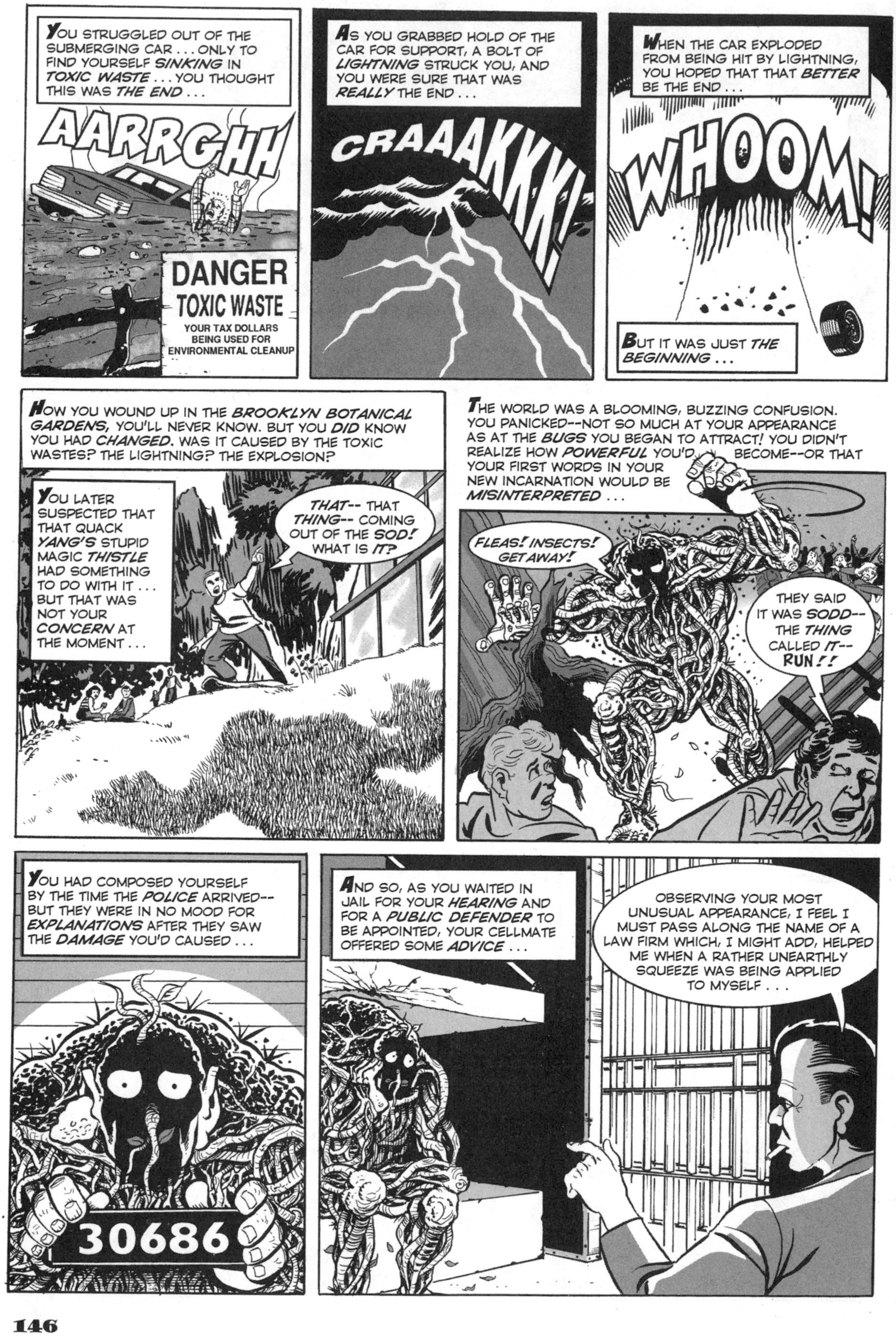
YOU STRUGGLED OUT OF THE SUBMERGING CAR . . . ONLY TO FIND YOURSELF SINKING IN TOXIC WASTE . . . YOU THOUGHT THIS WAS THE END . . .
AARRGHH
DANGER
TOXIC WASTE
YOUR TAX DOLLARS BEING USED FOR ENVIRONMENTAL CLEANUP
AS YOU GRABBED HOLD OF THE CAR FOR SUPPORT, A BOLT OF LIGHTNING STRUCK YOU, AND YOU WERE SURE THAT WAS REALLY THE END . . .
CRAAAKKK!
WHEN THE CAR EXPLODED FROM BEING HIT BY LIGHTNING, YOU HOPED THAT THAT BETTER BE THE END . . .
WHOOM!
BUT IT WAS JUST THE BEGINNING . . .
HOW YOU WOUND UP IN THE BROOKLYN BOTANICAL GARDENS, YOU'LL NEVER KNOW. BUT YOU DID KNOW YOU HAD CHANGED. WAS IT CAUSED BY THE TOXIC WASTES? THE LIGHTNING? THE EXPLOSION?
YOU LATER SUSPECTED THAT THAT QUACK YANG'S STUPID MAGIC THISTLE HAD SOMETHING TO DO WITH IT . . . BUT THAT WAS NOT YOUR CONCERN AT THE MOMENT . . .
THAT-- THAT THING-- COMING OUT OF THE SOD! WHAT IS IT?
THE WORLD WAS A BLOOMING, BUZZING CONFUSION. YOU PANICKED--NOT SO MUCH AT YOUR APPEARANCE AS AT THE BUGS YOU BEGAN TO ATTRACT! YOU DIDN'T REALIZE HOW POWERFUL YOU'D BECOME--OR THAT YOUR FIRST WORDS IN YOUR NEW INCARNATION WOULD BE MISINTERPRETED . . .
FLEAS! INSECTS! GET AWAY!
THEY SAID IT WAS SODD-- THE THING CALLED IT-- RUN!!
YOU HAD COMPOSED YOURSELF BY THE TIME THE POLICE ARRIVED-- BUT THEY WERE IN NO MOOD FOR EXPLANATIONS AFTER THEY SAW THE DAMAGE YOU'D CAUSED . . .
30686
AND SO, AS YOU WAITED IN JAIL FOR YOUR HEARING AND FOR A PUBLIC DEFENDER TO BE APPOINTED, YOUR CELLMATE OFFERED SOME ADVICE . . .
OBSERVING YOUR MOST UNUSUAL APPEARANCE, I FEEL I MUST PASS ALONG THE NAME OF A LAW FIRM WHICH, I MIGHT ADD, HELPED ME WHEN A RATHER UNEARTHLY SQUEEZE WAS BEING APPLIED TO MYSELF . . .

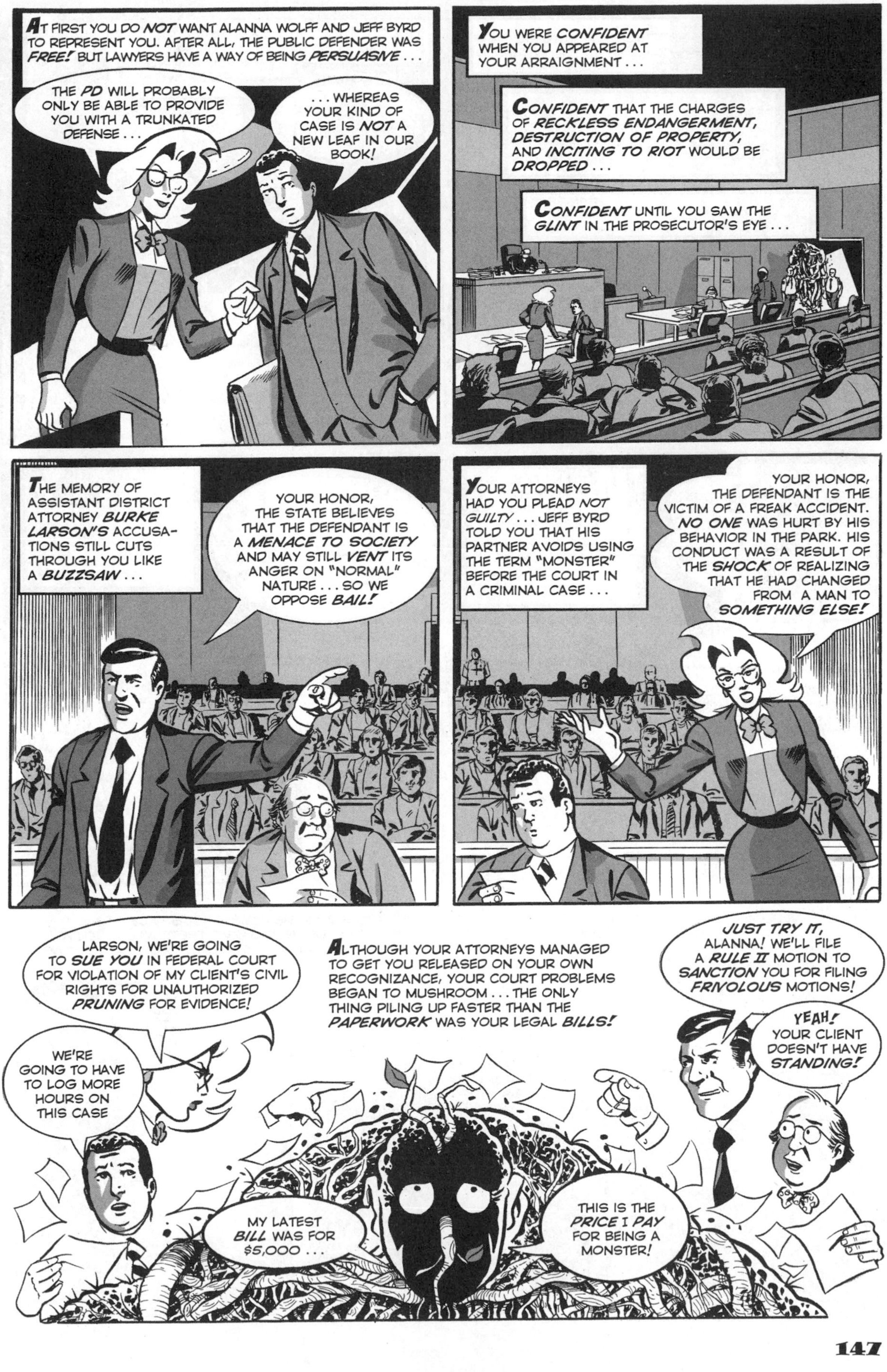
AT FIRST YOU DO NOT WANT ALANNA WOLFF AND JEFF BYRD TO REPRESENT YOU. AFTER ALL, THE PUBLIC DEFENDER WAS FREE! BUT LAWYERS HAVE A WAY OF BEING PERSUASIVE . . .
THE PD WILL PROBABLY ONLY BE ABLE TO PROVIDE YOU WITH A TRUNKATED DEFENSE . . .
. . . WHEREAS YOUR KIND OF CASE IS NOT A NEW LEAF IN OUR BOOK!
YOU WERE CONFIDENT WHEN YOU APPEARED AT YOUR ARRAIGNMENT . . .
CONFIDENT THAT THE CHARGES OF RECKLESS ENDANGERMENT, DESTRUCTION OF PROPERTY, AND INCITING TO RIOT WOULD BE DROPPED . . .
CONFIDENT UNTIL YOU SAW THE GLINT IN THE PROSECUTOR'S EYE . . .
THE MEMORY OF ASSISTANT DISTRICT ATTORNEY BURKE LARSON'S ACCUSATIONS STILL CUTS THROUGH YOU LIKE A BUZZSAW . . .
YOUR HONOR, THE STATE BELIEVES THAT THE DEFENDANT IS A MENACE TO SOCIETY AND MAY STILL VENT ITS ANGER ON "NORMAL" NATURE . . . SO WE OPPOSE BAIL!
YOUR ATTORNEYS HAD YOU PLEAD NOT GUILTY . . . JEFF BYRD TOLD YOU THAT HIS PARTNER AVOIDS USING THE TERM "MONSTER" BEFORE THE COURT IN A CRIMINAL CASE . . .
YOUR HONOR, THE DEFENDANT IS THE VICTIM OF A FREAK ACCIDENT. NO ONE WAS HURT BY HIS BEHAVIOR IN THE PARK. HIS CONDUCT WAS A RESULT OF THE SHOCK OF REALIZING THAT HE HAD CHANGED FROM A MAN TO SOMETHING ELSE!
LARSON, WE'RE GOING TO SUE YOU IN FEDERAL COURT FOR VIOLATION OF MY CLIENT'S CIVIL RIGHTS FOR UNAUTHORIZED PRUNING FOR EVIDENCE!
ALTHOUGH YOUR ATTORNEYS MANAGED TO GET YOU RELEASED ON YOUR OWN RECOGNIZANCE, YOUR COURT PROBLEMS BEGAN TO MUSHROOM . . . THE ONLY THING PILING UP FASTER THAN THE PAPERWORK WAS YOUR LEGAL BILLS!
JUST TRY IT, ALANNA! WE'LL FILE A RULE II MOTION TO SANCTION YOU FOR FILING FRIVOLOUS MOTIONS!
YEAH! YOUR CLIENT DOESN'T HAVE STANDING!
WE'RE GOING TO HAVE TO LOG MORE HOURS ON THIS CASE
MY LATEST BILL WAS FOR $5,000 . . .
THIS IS THE PRICE I PAY FOR BEING A MONSTER!

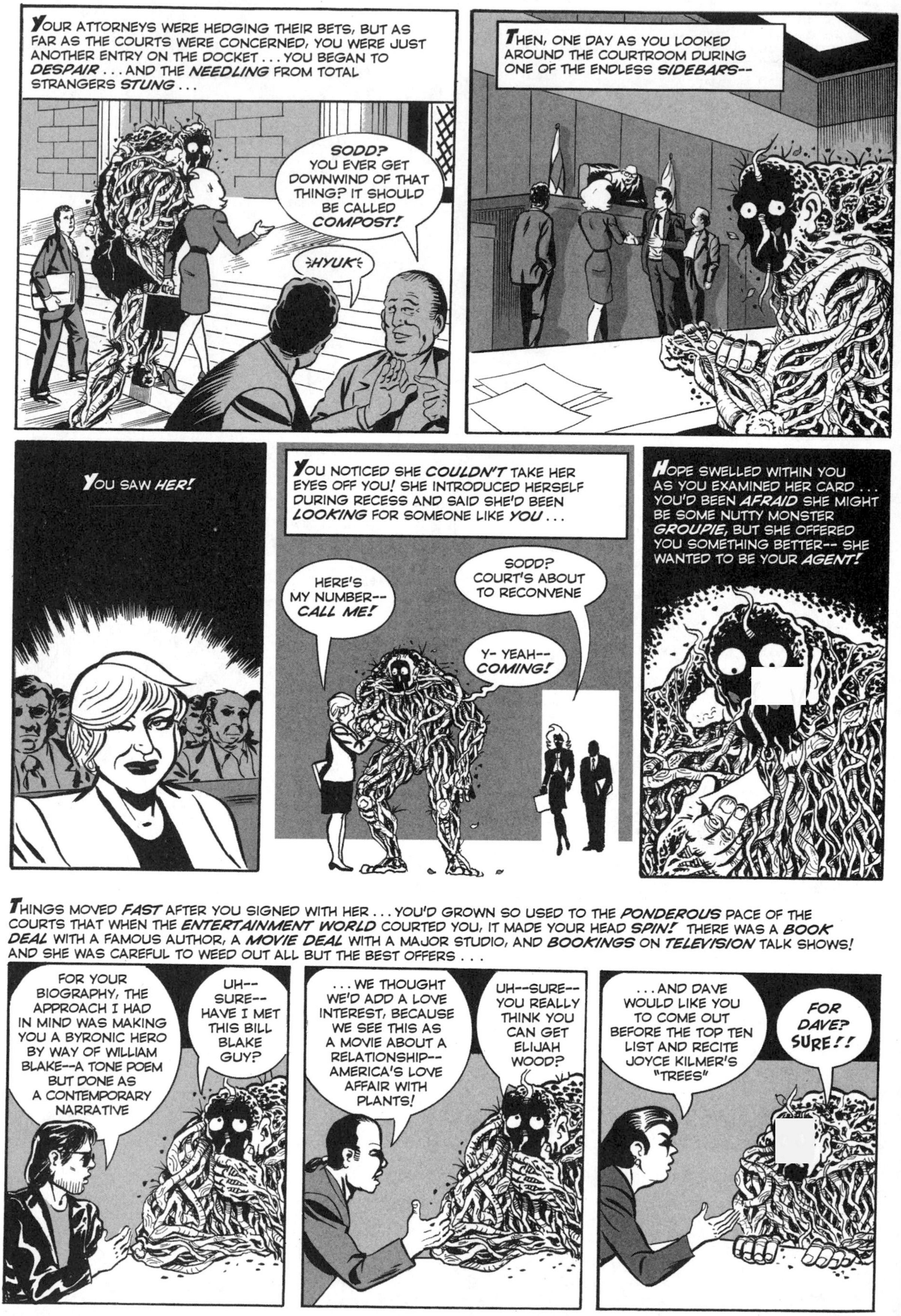
YOUR ATTORNEYS WERE HEDGING THEIR BETS, BUT AS FAR AS THE COURTS WERE CONCERNED, YOU WERE JUST ANOTHER ENTRY ON THE DOCKET . . . YOU BEGAN TO DESPAIR . . . AND THE NEEDLING FROM TOTAL STRANGERS STUNG . . .
SODD? YOU EVER GET DOWNWIND OF THAT THING? IT SHOULD BE CALLED COMPOST!
HYUK
THEN, ONE DAY AS YOU LOOKED AROUND THE COURTROOM DURING ONE OF THE ENDLESS SIDEBARS--
YOU SAW HER!
YOU NOTICED SHE COULDN'T TAKE HER EYES OFF YOU! SHE INTRODUCED HERSELF DURING RECESS AND SAID SHE'D BEEN LOOKING FOR SOMEONE LIKE YOU . . .
HERE'S MY NUMBER-- CALL ME!
SODD? COURT'S ABOUT TO RECONVENE
Y- YEAH-- COMING!
HOPE SWELLED WITHIN YOU AS YOU EXAMINED HER CARD . . . YOU'D BEEN AFRAID SHE MIGHT BE SOME NUTTY MONSTER GROUPIE, BUT SHE OFFERED YOU SOMETHING BETTER-- SHE WANTED TO BE YOUR AGENT!
THINGS MOVED FAST AFTER YOU SIGNED WITH HER . . . YOU'D GROWN SO USED TO THE PONDEROUS PACE OF THE COURTS THAT WHEN THE ENTERTAINMENT WORLD COURTED YOU, IT MADE YOUR HEAD SPIN! THERE WAS A BOOK DEAL WITH A FAMOUS AUTHOR, A MOVIE DEAL WITH A MAJOR STUDIO, AND BOOKINGS ON TELEVISION TALK SHOWS! AND SHE WAS CAREFUL TO WEED OUT ALL BUT THE BEST OFFERS . . .
FOR YOUR BIOGRAPHY, THE APPROACH I HAD IN MIND WAS MAKING YOU A BYRONIC HERO BY WAY OF WILLIAM BLAKE--A TONE POEM BUT DONE AS A CONTEMPORARY NARRATIVE
UH-- SURE-- HAVE I MET THIS BILL BLAKE GUY?
. . . WE THOUGHT WE'D ADD A LOVE INTEREST, BECAUSE WE SEE THIS AS A MOVIE ABOUT A RELATIONSHIP-- AMERICA'S LOVE AFFAIR WITH PLANTS!
UH--SURE-- YOU REALLY THINK YOU CAN GET ELIJAH WOOD?
. . . AND DAVE WOULD LIKE YOU TO COME OUT BEFORE THE TOP TEN LIST AND RECITE JOYCE KILMER'S "TREES"
FOR DAVE? SURE!!

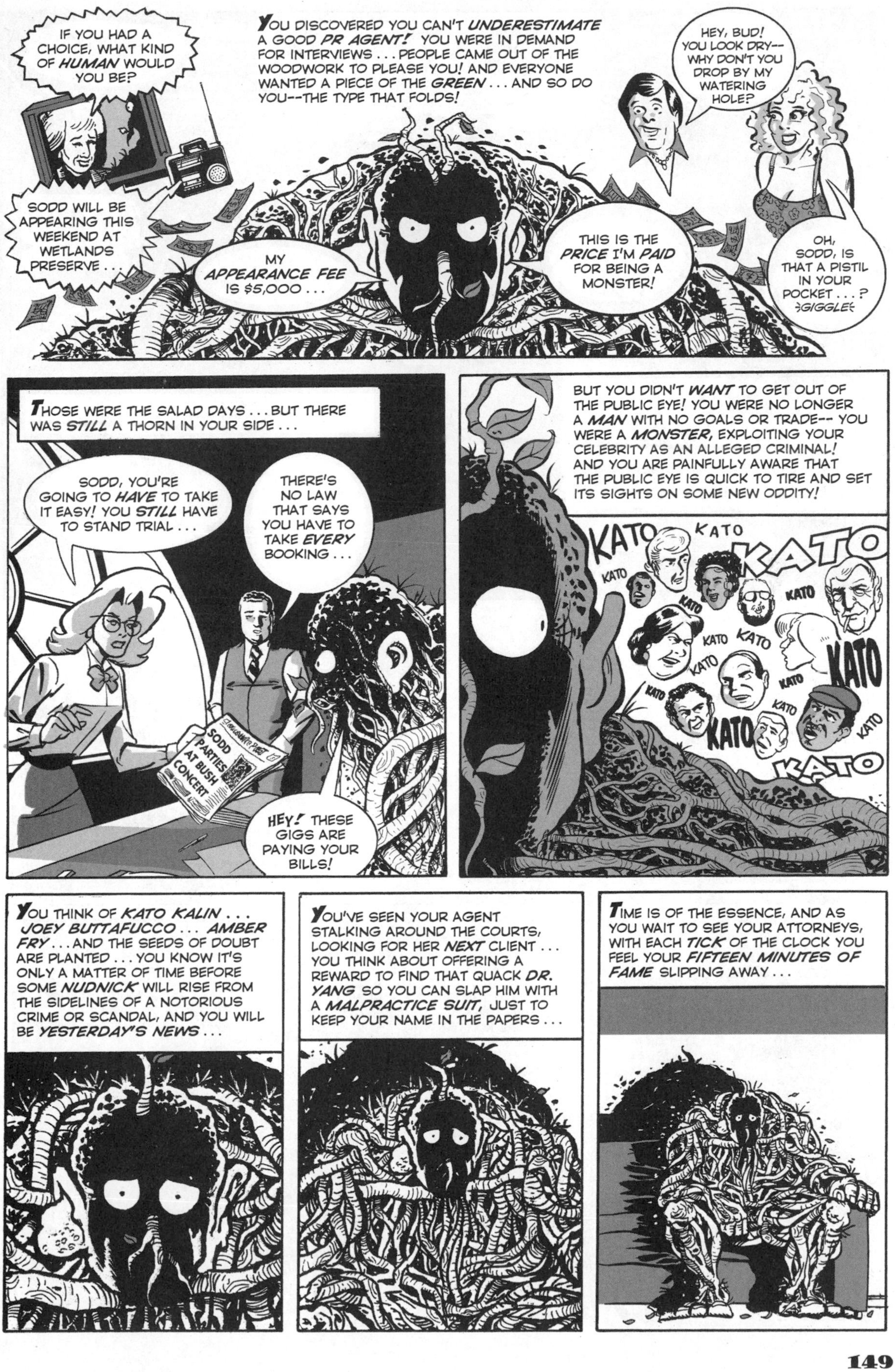
IF YOU HAD A CHOICE, WHAT KIND OF *HUMAN* WOULD YOU BE?
SODD WILL BE APPEARING THIS WEEKEND AT WETLANDS PRESERVE . . .
YOU DISCOVERED YOU CAN'T *UNDERESTIMATE* A GOOD *PR AGENT!* YOU WERE IN DEMAND FOR INTERVIEWS . . . PEOPLE CAME OUT OF THE WOODWORK TO PLEASE YOU! AND EVERYONE WANTED A PIECE OF THE *GREEN* . . . AND SO DO YOU--THE TYPE THAT FOLDS!
MY *APPEARANCE FEE* IS $5,000 . . .
THIS IS THE *PRICE* I'M *PAID* FOR BEING A MONSTER!
HEY, BUD! YOU LOOK DRY-- WHY DON'T YOU DROP BY MY WATERING HOLE?
OH, SODD, IS THAT A PISTIL IN YOUR POCKET . . . ? *GIGGLE*
THOSE WERE THE SALAD DAYS . . . BUT THERE WAS *STILL* A THORN IN YOUR SIDE . . .
SODD, YOU'RE GOING TO *HAVE* TO TAKE IT EASY! YOU *STILL* HAVE TO STAND TRIAL . . .
THERE'S NO LAW THAT SAYS YOU HAVE TO TAKE *EVERY* BOOKING . . .
SODD PARTIES AT BUSH CONCERT
HEY! THESE GIGS ARE PAYING YOUR BILLS!
BUT YOU DIDN'T *WANT* TO GET OUT OF THE PUBLIC EYE! YOU WERE NO LONGER A *MAN* WITH NO GOALS OR TRADE-- YOU WERE A *MONSTER*, EXPLOITING YOUR CELEBRITY AS AN ALLEGED CRIMINAL! AND YOU ARE PAINFULLY AWARE THAT THE PUBLIC EYE IS QUICK TO TIRE AND SET ITS SIGHTS ON SOME NEW ODDITY!
KATO KATO KATO KATO KATO KATO KATO KATO KATO KATO KATO KATO KATO KATO KATO KATO
YOU THINK OF *KATO KALIN* . . . *JOEY BUTTAFUCCO* . . . *AMBER FRY* . . . AND THE SEEDS OF DOUBT ARE PLANTED . . . YOU KNOW IT'S ONLY A MATTER OF TIME BEFORE SOME *NUDNICK* WILL RISE FROM THE SIDELINES OF A NOTORIOUS CRIME OR SCANDAL, AND YOU WILL BE *YESTERDAY'S NEWS* . . .
YOU'VE SEEN YOUR AGENT STALKING AROUND THE COURTS, LOOKING FOR HER *NEXT* CLIENT . . . YOU THINK ABOUT OFFERING A REWARD TO FIND THAT QUACK *DR. YANG* SO YOU CAN SLAP HIM WITH A *MALPRACTICE SUIT,* JUST TO KEEP YOUR NAME IN THE PAPERS . . .
TIME IS OF THE ESSENCE, AND AS YOU WAIT TO SEE YOUR ATTORNEYS, WITH EACH *TICK* OF THE CLOCK YOU FEEL YOUR *FIFTEEN MINUTES OF FAME* SLIPPING AWAY . . .

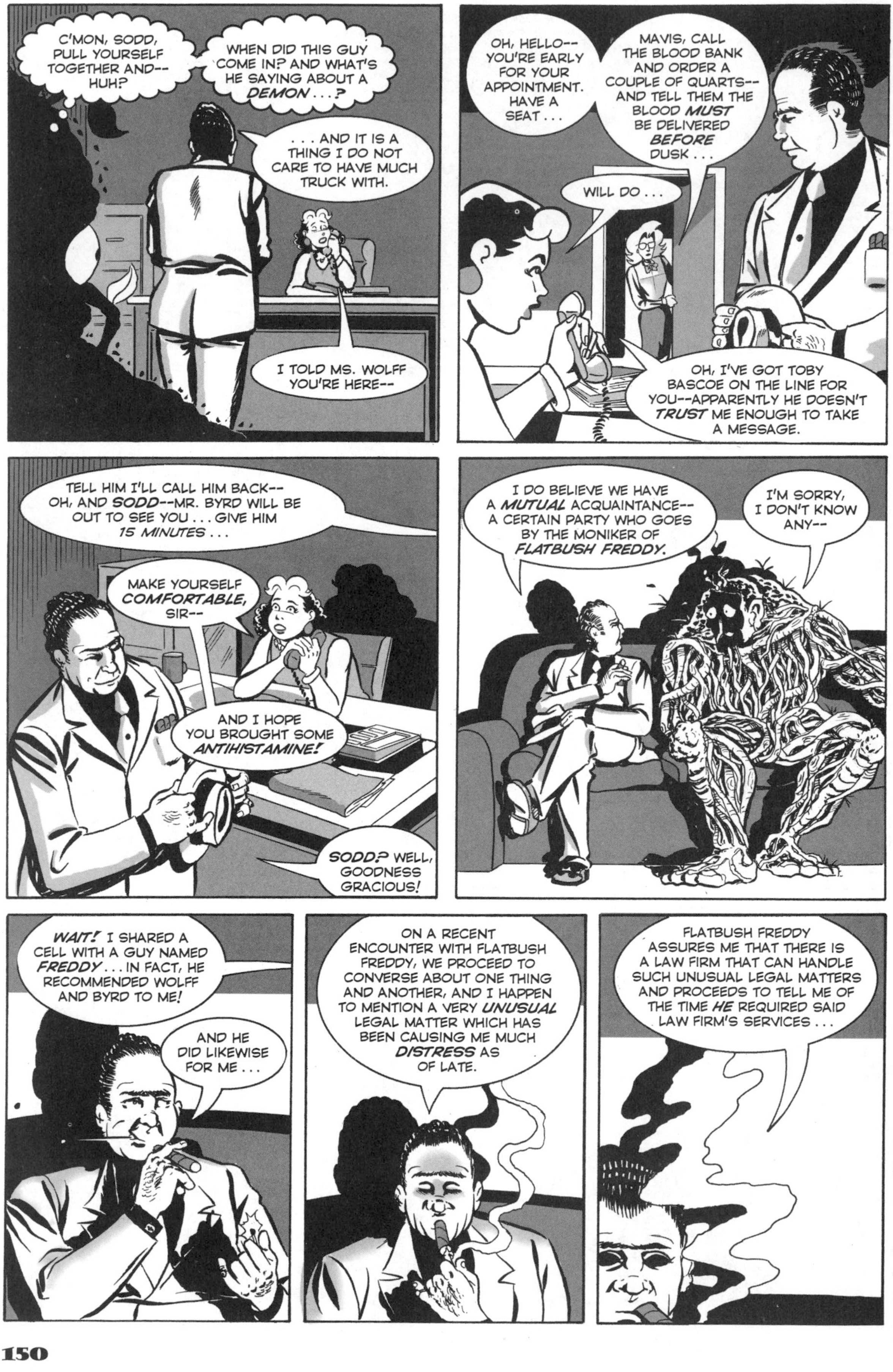
C'MON, SODD, PULL YOURSELF TOGETHER AND-- HUH?
WHEN DID THIS GUY COME IN? AND WHAT'S HE SAYING ABOUT A DEMON . . .?
. . . AND IT IS A THING I DO NOT CARE TO HAVE MUCH TRUCK WITH.
I TOLD MS. WOLFF YOU'RE HERE--
OH, HELLO-- YOU'RE EARLY FOR YOUR APPOINTMENT. HAVE A SEAT . . .
MAVIS, CALL THE BLOOD BANK AND ORDER A COUPLE OF QUARTS-- AND TELL THEM THE BLOOD MUST BE DELIVERED BEFORE DUSK . . .
WILL DO . . .
OH, I'VE GOT TOBY BASCOE ON THE LINE FOR YOU--APPARENTLY HE DOESN'T TRUST ME ENOUGH TO TAKE A MESSAGE.
TELL HIM I'LL CALL HIM BACK-- OH, AND SODD--MR. BYRD WILL BE OUT TO SEE YOU . . . GIVE HIM 15 MINUTES . . .
MAKE YOURSELF COMFORTABLE, SIR--
AND I HOPE YOU BROUGHT SOME ANTIHISTAMINE!
SODD? WELL, GOODNESS GRACIOUS!
I DO BELIEVE WE HAVE A MUTUAL ACQUAINTANCE-- A CERTAIN PARTY WHO GOES BY THE MONIKER OF FLATBUSH FREDDY.
I'M SORRY, I DON'T KNOW ANY--
WAIT! I SHARED A CELL WITH A GUY NAMED FREDDY . . . IN FACT, HE RECOMMENDED WOLFF AND BYRD TO ME!
AND HE DID LIKEWISE FOR ME . . .
ON A RECENT ENCOUNTER WITH FLATBUSH FREDDY, WE PROCEED TO CONVERSE ABOUT ONE THING AND ANOTHER, AND I HAPPEN TO MENTION A VERY UNUSUAL LEGAL MATTER WHICH HAS BEEN CAUSING ME MUCH DISTRESS AS OF LATE.
FLATBUSH FREDDY ASSURES ME THAT THERE IS A LAW FIRM THAT CAN HANDLE SUCH UNUSUAL LEGAL MATTERS AND PROCEEDS TO TELL ME OF THE TIME HE REQUIRED SAID LAW FIRM'S SERVICES . . .

THE BEQUEATHING OF HODGE THE FLUNKY

We are enjoying a fine repast in a restaurant where Mindy's used to be, and Flatbush Freddy tells me how he came to engage the services of Miss Alanna Wolff and Mister Jeffrey Byrd, Esq.

Flatbush Freddy sets up an appointment with said attorneys when Flatbush Freddy becomes a beneficiary in Big Al's last will and testament. Now, Flatbush Freddy and Big Al were competitors, each working different ends of Brooklyn, so let us just say there was no love lost between them. In fact, upon hearing of Big Al's passing, Flatbush Freddy does not even dress in any more black than he usually does.

Be that as it may, Flatbush Freddy is quite surprised upon being notified that he is one of the beneficiaries named in Big Al's will. Flatbush Freddy had heard that several dolls picked up a few bob from the will, and Big Al's associate Two-Ton Tony was the recipient of the opulent digs Big Al had called his own. So Flatbush Freddy gets to thinking that perhaps Big Al is having some post-mortem fun when he is left the services of Big Al's A-number-one valet, one Hodge the Flunky.

Now, everyone knows that Hodge the Flunky is currently playing a harp, having stepped in to stop a slug intended for his boss. No one could take away that Hodge the Flunky had been the most loyal of flunkies, although he was none too bright and had a proclivity to irritate citizens in his eagerness to please.

Flatbush Freddy thinks Big Al's bequeathing is very frivolous indeed, but when Flatbush Freddy takes out a cigarette, he sees a match floating in front of him and hears a voice come out of thin air: "Let me light that for you, sir." Flatbush Freddy reaches for his John Roscoe, as this voice comes as quite a surprise to him. Flatbush Freddy always gives his premises the once-over before he settles in, to see if anyone has dropped by in his absence. "You look a little tired, sir, let me help you get a load off your feet," says the voice. Flatbush Freddy is plopped into a nearby easychair and feels his legs propped up onto the ottoman. "What is this," says Flatbush Freddy, "some kind of gag? Come out where I can see you!" This is when Hodge the Flunky commences to appear before Flatbush Freddy. "You sound a little parched, sir. Let me fetch you

a cold beverage," says Hodge the Flunky. Flatbush Freddy then lets John Roscoe do the talking for him, but this does not deter Hodge the Flunky from going about his duties, and Flatbush Freddy realizes that he has indeed inherited the services of Big Al's A-number-one valet.

Now, Flatbush Freddy knows next to nothing about the supernatural and does not want to unintentionally open a can of worms in trying to exterminate a ghost who is waiting on him hand and foot. Being the savvy guy that he is, Flatbush Freddy figures that if a ghost is bequeathed to him in a will, this may be a matter with which a lawyer might help him.

Flatbush Freddy gets on the horn to his usual mouthpiece, who is very busy upstate and will not be available for several years but knows a law firm that 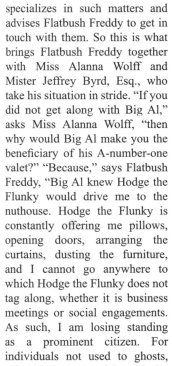 specializes in such matters and advises Flatbush Freddy to get in touch with them. So this is what brings Flatbush Freddy together with Miss Alanna Wolff and Mister Jeffrey Byrd, Esq., who take his situation in stride. "If you did not get along with Big Al," asks Miss Alanna Wolff, "then why would Big Al make you the beneficiary of his A-number-one valet?" "Because," says Flatbush Freddy, "Big Al knew Hodge the Flunky would drive me to the nuthouse. Hodge the Flunky is constantly offering me pillows, opening doors, arranging the curtains, dusting the furniture, and I cannot go anywhere to which Hodge the Flunky does not tag along, whether it is business meetings or social engagements. As such, I am losing standing as a prominent citizen. For individuals not used to ghosts, these apparitions can be quite distracting. And the majority want no truck with them—especially dolls who are of the opinion that three's a crowd, ghost or no ghost."

Mister Jeffrey Byrd asks, "So where is this ghost now?" "Fetching coffee. In fact," says Flatbush Freddy, "here he is now. Could you open the window? A cup of coffee cannot pass through solid objects as easily as he can." Miss Alanna Wolff lets Hodge the Flunky in, who commences to bring the java right over to Flatbush Freddy. "They didn't have cream, boss. Is half and half all right? I can go find some cream if you really want it," says Hodge the Flunky. Flatbush Freddy introduces Hodge the Flunky to Miss Alanna Wolff and Mister Jeffrey Byrd, Esq. "Are they giving you a hard time, boss? You want I should lean on them?" Flatbush Freddy says that it is not necessary and tells Hodge the Flunky to cool his heels.

Miss Alanna Wolff then proceeds to ask Hodge the Flunky some questions, while Mister Jeffrey Byrd takes notes. "The ghost of an individual usually remains on Earth because of some unfinished business," says Miss Alanna Wolff. "Was Big Al aware of your present condition?" "Big Al most certainly knew of my present condition," says Hodge the Flunky, "for I had owed Big Al big time and left him a marker that I would serve him as long as he lived. Since I do not welch on a marker, I found it my duty to come back from the grave to make good my promise. In fact, the only time I let Big Al out of my sight is when he gives me strict orders to mind the house—and that is the night he takes his most unfortunate car ride and—" Miss Alanna Wolff hands Hodge the Flunky a tissue. Once he honks his beezer, he continues, "And now that Big Al is gone, I am bound to carry out his final wish, which is to serve my new boss forever . . . Let me stir that for you, boss."

"I can stir my own coffee, thank you," says Flatbush Freddy, who then says to the lawyers, "This is my situation. The biggest break Big Al ever got was that car wreck, for I do not know how he could take Hodge the Flunky nonstop." At that point Hodge the Flunky leans over and picks a piece of lint off Flatbush Freddy's lapel, saying, "You want I should get this suit cleaned, boss?" Being somewhat in tears, Flatbush Freddy turns to the attorneys and says, "I would not wish Hodge the Flunky on my worst enemy, but it seems Big Al would. Please tell me there is some loophole that can get me out of being a beneficiary, or else I will never have a private moment to myself again."

Being lawyers and all, Miss Alanna Wolff and Mister Jeffrey Byrd, Esq. turn on the meter and get to work to see what they can do about Flatbush Freddy's situation. First they get ahold of Big Al's will and see what was doled out and to whom. They see that Two-Ton Tony has been bequeathed Big Al's palatial home, which has gotten Two-Ton Tony in dutch with the local gendarmes, because it is suspected that Two-Ton Tony arranged a quick demise for his long-time associate in order to move into such swell digs. But Two-Ton Tony has an ironclad alibi and the coppers can't get anything to stick to Two-Ton

Tony, who not only resides in Big Al's home but is now CEO of Big Al's distribution operations.

Miss Alanna Wolff is able to procure a copy of Big Al's death certificate, which leads to a discussion with the coroner, who, it turns out, had very little to do with the matter of Big Al's remains, as the car wreck that did him in was so bad, there was nothing left to piece together. Meanwhile, Mister Jeffrey Byrd finds out from the D.A.'s office that the local prosecutors are in mourning over Big Al, for they were ready to bring Big Al up on charges and Big Al's explosive car ride has rendered the paperwork moot. But one assistant D.A. confides to Mister Jeffrey Byrd that Big Al knew the heat was on, and the sudden lack of Big Al in the world was very suspicious indeed.

Anyway, Miss Alanna Wolff and Mister Jeffrey Byrd, Esq. arrange with Big Al's estate attorney to set up a meeting with Two-Ton Tony in Big Al's home, suggesting that Two-Ton Tony still has something coming to him from Big Al. Miss Alanna Wolff wastes no time to tell Two-Ton Tony and the estate attorney that she and her partner are representing Flatbush Freddy. Two-Ton Tony begins to go pale, but the estate attorney picks up the slack and asks her what of it. Miss Alanna Wolff says, "In accordance with your late client's last will and testament, my client is the beneficiary of Big Al's A-number-one valet, Hodge the Flunky. However, there is a slight problem, and I hope we can settle this amicably. Big Al made a final request of his A-number-one valet that was not stipulated in his will, and the recipient does not feel quite right about it. I am sure it was just an oversight and can be resolves with all speed."

Now Two-Ton Tony is beginning to swat above his lip, for since he was a close associate of Big Al's he is well aware of Hodge the Flunky. The estate attorney, conversely, does not know of Hodge the Flunky, for Big Al is not someone who would admit he has a ghost hanging around. And even though Two-Ton Tony has observed Hodge the Flunky going about his business, let us say he was not envious of the attention the spirit lavished upon Big Al.

So the estate attorney asks Miss Alanna Wolff to specify exactly to what it is she is referring. Miss Alanna Wolff nods to Mister Jeffrey Byrd, who goes over to the door and lets in Flatbush Freddy. When Flatbush Freddy approaches the table, a chair pulls out by itself for Flatbush Freddy to sit down. Now the estate attorney is quite puzzled, but Two-Ton Tony is bug-eyed at this point. Two-Ton Tony reaches for his cigar and falls backward in his chair when a Zippo floats toward him. The estate attorney demands to know what is going on. Miss Alanna Wolff says, "My client wishes to contest being the beneficiary of Big Al's A-number-one valet, for he does not feel he deserves such a bequest." Flatbush Freddy says amen to that, and Miss Alanna Wolff continues, "Since Big Al's valet is a ghost, Big Al told him to stay here while Big Al took care of business, which we all know resulted in a tragic trip into town. This is where things get sticky, for this was Big Al's last request which he made to a ghost who was his servant in residence, and the usual standard and practice of a ghost is to stay put and attend to unfinished business, especially in the house said ghost resided in as a mortal."

Now at this point Two-Ton Tony gets up from the floor but not of his own power. A small brush whisks around Two-Ton Tony's suit, and he feels the sleeves of his jacket being tugged and straightened. "Hodge?" says Two-Ton Tony. It is then that Hodge the Flunky materializes, whisk broom in hand. "I am certainly in a very peculiar situation," says Hodge the Flunky.

"Although I feel obligated to follow Big Al's wishes as stated in his will and serve Flatbush Freddy for all eternity, Miss Alanna Wolff and Mister Jeffrey Byrd, Esq. have pointed out that Big Al himself made one last request of me, and I feel I will be delinquent in my duties if I do not follow it. Furthermore, I can see that the premises need me, for the carpet is filthy and the windows need to be washed. Let me clean out that ashtray for you, Mr. Two-Ton Tony. Can I offer anyone a refreshment?"

Well, with that, Hodge the Flunky passes through the wall into the kitchen and Two-Ton Tony pulls his chair over to Miss Alanna Wolff. "I did not want to have any truck with Hodge the Flunky while he was alive because his is so attentive you are ready to blow your brains out. And since he is a ghost now, he is on the watch day and night, and Big Al has said there is nowhere in the house where he will not follow you to see to your needs—and I mean anywhere!"

"You said it," says Flatbush Freddy.

At that point Hodge the Flunky's head pokes through the wall and says, "The kitchen is a mess, but I will have it spic and span in a jiffy. And if I may make a suggestion, perhaps Mr. Freddy can move in with Mr. Two-Ton so Big Al's final request can be carried out."

With that, Hodge the Flunky's head sinks back into the wall and the sounds of dishes being washed and Hodge the Flunky singing "Luck Be a Lady Tonight" waft from the kitchen. Two-Ton Tony decides to put his foot down. "No dice! This was not part of the deal!" Miss Alanna Wolff and Mister Jeffrey Byrd, Esq. look at each other and then back at Two-Ton Tony, when the estate attorney stands up and says, "Deal? What deal?"

Two-Ton Tony dummies up and proceeds to throw everyone out of the house, when Hodge the Flunky floats in with an armful of dirty laundry to get the door. This proves too much for Two-Ton Tony, who breaks down and comes clean. Big Al (says Two-Ton Tony), under pressure of John Law and fully fed up with his A-number-one valet, has faked his death and has skipped town. Well, the estate attorney feels it is his duty to report an inconsistency such as this, and Miss Alanna Wolff and Mister Jeffrey Byrd, Esq. rush over to the courthouse, where they inform a judge of this misdeed and ask that Big Al's will be declared null and void, since Big Al is really alive and well and, according to Two-Ton Tony, living the high life somewhere out of the country by now.

With Big Al's will nullified, Flatbush Freddy is no longer the recipient of Hodge the Flunky and is left to fend for himself. Flatbush Freddy tries taking over Big Al's side of town, now that Two-Ton Tony is due to move into a 10 by 6 room upstate. This proves to be Flatbush Freddy's undoing, for it is too much for him to handle alone. As a result of running a sloppy operation, Flatbush Freddy tells me that things do not look good for him, for he is sure a judge is about to approve an all-expenses-paid vacation for him upstate, and with his luck he will be sharing that 10 by 6 room with Two-Ton Tony. But Flatbush Freddy thinks that with good behavior he will be back in Brooklyn by the time he turns fifty, which he thinks is preferable to faking your own death and suffering the consequences. For, from what Flatbush Freddy hears, Big Al made a quick exit via the 48th floor of a high-class hostelry on the Mexican Riviera not too long ago.

Flatbush Freddy assumes that Big Al's A-number-one valet finally tracked him down, because the doll who was in the hotel room at the time heard Big Al yell, "Hodge, no, I don't need your help!" So it is safe to say that Big Al made no provisions for Hodge the Flunky if he did indeed make a new will. And since Big Al's swan dive cleared Hodge the Flunky's debt to Big Al, it is likely they have gone their separate ways, presumably in very opposite directions of each other.

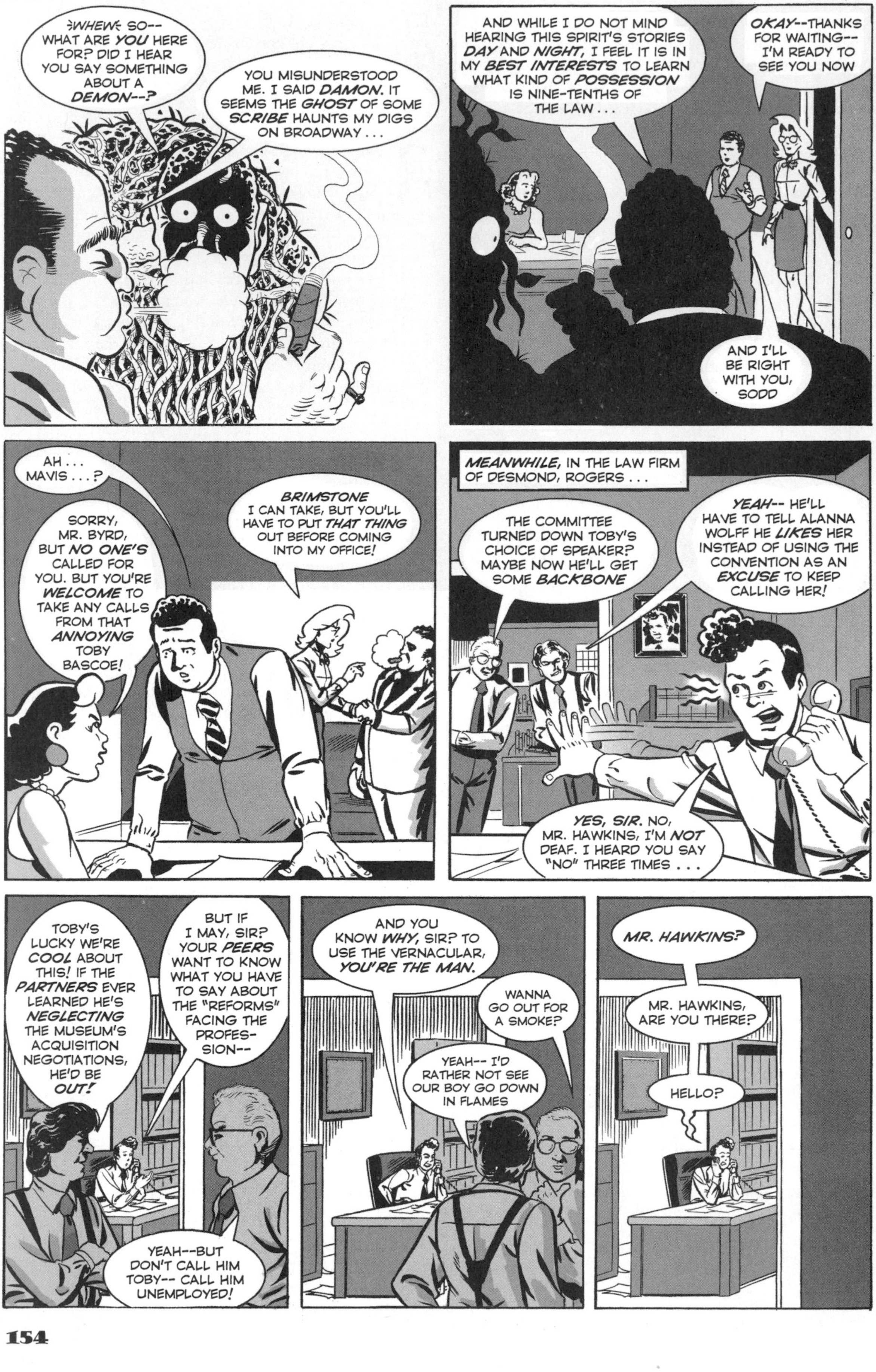
WHEW SO-- WHAT ARE *YOU* HERE FOR? DID I HEAR YOU SAY SOMETHING ABOUT A *DEMON--?*
YOU MISUNDERSTOOD ME. I SAID *DAMON.* IT SEEMS THE *GHOST* OF SOME *SCRIBE* HAUNTS MY DIGS ON BROADWAY . . .
AND WHILE I DO NOT MIND HEARING THIS SPIRIT'S STORIES *DAY* AND *NIGHT,* I FEEL IT IS IN MY *BEST INTERESTS* TO LEARN WHAT KIND OF *POSSESSION* IS NINE-TENTHS OF THE LAW . . .
OKAY--THANKS FOR WAITING-- I'M READY TO SEE YOU NOW
AND I'LL BE RIGHT WITH YOU, SODD
AH . . . MAVIS . . .?
SORRY, MR. BYRD, BUT *NO ONE'S* CALLED FOR YOU. BUT YOU'RE *WELCOME* TO TAKE ANY CALLS FROM THAT *ANNOYING* TOBY BASCOE!
BRIMSTONE I CAN TAKE, BUT YOU'LL HAVE TO PUT *THAT THING* OUT BEFORE COMING INTO MY OFFICE!
MEANWHILE, IN THE LAW FIRM OF DESMOND, ROGERS . . .
THE COMMITTEE TURNED DOWN TOBY'S CHOICE OF SPEAKER? MAYBE NOW HE'LL GET SOME *BACKBONE*
YEAH-- HE'LL HAVE TO TELL ALANNA WOLFF HE *LIKES* HER INSTEAD OF USING THE CONVENTION AS AN *EXCUSE* TO KEEP CALLING HER!
YES, SIR. NO, MR. HAWKINS, I'M *NOT* DEAF. I HEARD YOU SAY "NO" THREE TIMES . . .
TOBY'S LUCKY WE'RE *COOL* ABOUT THIS! IF THE *PARTNERS* EVER LEARNED HE'S *NEGLECTING* THE MUSEUM'S ACQUISITION NEGOTIATIONS, HE'D BE *OUT!*
BUT IF I MAY, SIR? YOUR *PEERS* WANT TO KNOW WHAT YOU HAVE TO SAY ABOUT THE "REFORMS" FACING THE PROFES-SION--
YEAH--BUT DON'T CALL HIM TOBY-- CALL HIM UNEMPLOYED!
AND YOU KNOW *WHY,* SIR? TO USE THE VERNACULAR, *YOU'RE THE MAN.*
WANNA GO OUT FOR A SMOKE?
YEAH-- I'D RATHER NOT SEE OUR BOY GO DOWN IN FLAMES
MR. HAWKINS?
MR. HAWKINS, ARE YOU THERE?
HELLO?

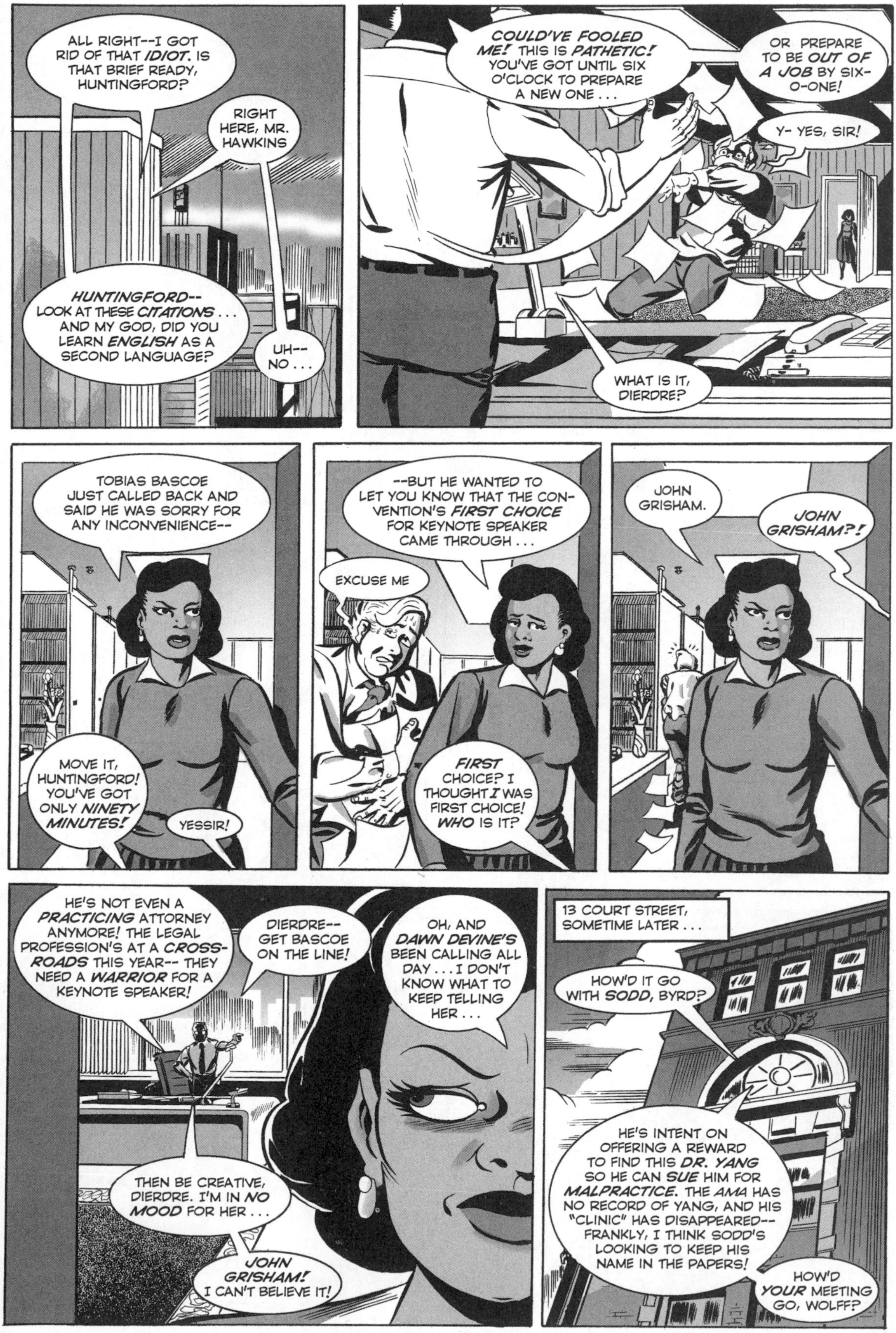
ALL RIGHT--I GOT RID OF THAT IDIOT. IS THAT BRIEF READY, HUNTINGFORD?
RIGHT HERE, MR. HAWKINS
HUNTINGFORD-- LOOK AT THESE CITATIONS . . . AND MY GOD, DID YOU LEARN ENGLISH AS A SECOND LANGUAGE?
UH-- NO . . .
COULD'VE FOOLED ME! THIS IS PATHETIC! YOU'VE GOT UNTIL SIX O'CLOCK TO PREPARE A NEW ONE . . .
OR PREPARE TO BE OUT OF A JOB BY SIX-O-ONE!
Y- YES, SIR!
WHAT IS IT, DIERDRE?
TOBIAS BASCOE JUST CALLED BACK AND SAID HE WAS SORRY FOR ANY INCONVENIENCE--
MOVE IT, HUNTINGFORD! YOU'VE GOT ONLY NINETY MINUTES!
YESSIR!
--BUT HE WANTED TO LET YOU KNOW THAT THE CONVENTION'S FIRST CHOICE FOR KEYNOTE SPEAKER CAME THROUGH . . .
EXCUSE ME
FIRST CHOICE? I THOUGHT I WAS FIRST CHOICE! WHO IS IT?
JOHN GRISHAM.
JOHN GRISHAM?!
HE'S NOT EVEN A PRACTICING ATTORNEY ANYMORE! THE LEGAL PROFESSION'S AT A CROSS-ROADS THIS YEAR-- THEY NEED A WARRIOR FOR A KEYNOTE SPEAKER!
DIERDRE-- GET BASCOE ON THE LINE!
OH, AND DAWN DEVINE'S BEEN CALLING ALL DAY . . . I DON'T KNOW WHAT TO KEEP TELLING HER . . .
THEN BE CREATIVE, DIERDRE. I'M IN NO MOOD FOR HER . . .
JOHN GRISHAM! I CAN'T BELIEVE IT!
13 COURT STREET, SOMETIME LATER . . .
HOW'D IT GO WITH SODD, BYRD?
HE'S INTENT ON OFFERING A REWARD TO FIND THIS DR. YANG SO HE CAN SUE HIM FOR MALPRACTICE. THE AMA HAS NO RECORD OF YANG, AND HIS "CLINIC" HAS DISAPPEARED-- FRANKLY, I THINK SODD'S LOOKING TO KEEP HIS NAME IN THE PAPERS!
HOW'D YOUR MEETING GO, WOLFF?

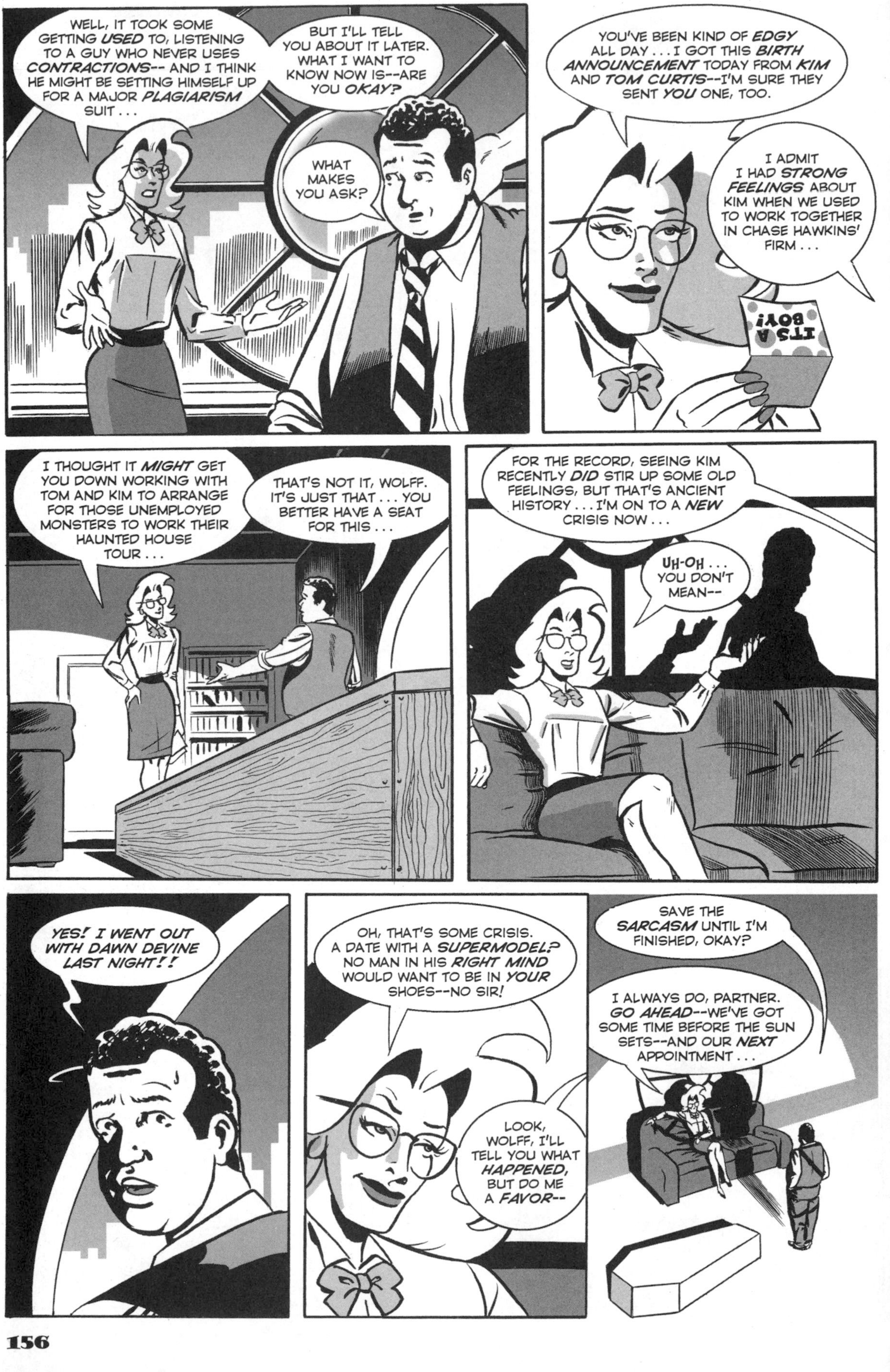
WELL, IT TOOK SOME GETTING USED TO, LISTENING TO A GUY WHO NEVER USES CONTRACTIONS-- AND I THINK HE MIGHT BE SETTING HIMSELF UP FOR A MAJOR PLAGIARISM SUIT . . .
BUT I'LL TELL YOU ABOUT IT LATER. WHAT I WANT TO KNOW NOW IS--ARE YOU OKAY?
WHAT MAKES YOU ASK?
YOU'VE BEEN KIND OF EDGY ALL DAY . . . I GOT THIS BIRTH ANNOUNCEMENT TODAY FROM KIM AND TOM CURTIS--I'M SURE THEY SENT YOU ONE, TOO.
I ADMIT I HAD STRONG FEELINGS ABOUT KIM WHEN WE USED TO WORK TOGETHER IN CHASE HAWKINS' FIRM . . .
IT'S A BOY!
I THOUGHT IT MIGHT GET YOU DOWN WORKING WITH TOM AND KIM TO ARRANGE FOR THOSE UNEMPLOYED MONSTERS TO WORK THEIR HAUNTED HOUSE TOUR . . .
THAT'S NOT IT, WOLFF. IT'S JUST THAT . . . YOU BETTER HAVE A SEAT FOR THIS . . .
FOR THE RECORD, SEEING KIM RECENTLY DID STIR UP SOME OLD FEELINGS, BUT THAT'S ANCIENT HISTORY . . . I'M ON TO A NEW CRISIS NOW . . .
UH-OH . . . YOU DON'T MEAN--
YES! I WENT OUT WITH DAWN DEVINE LAST NIGHT!!
OH, THAT'S SOME CRISIS. A DATE WITH A SUPERMODEL? NO MAN IN HIS RIGHT MIND WOULD WANT TO BE IN YOUR SHOES--NO SIR!
LOOK, WOLFF, I'LL TELL YOU WHAT HAPPENED, BUT DO ME A FAVOR--
SAVE THE SARCASM UNTIL I'M FINISHED, OKAY?
I ALWAYS DO, PARTNER. GO AHEAD--WE'VE GOT SOME TIME BEFORE THE SUN SETS--AND OUR NEXT APPOINTMENT . . .

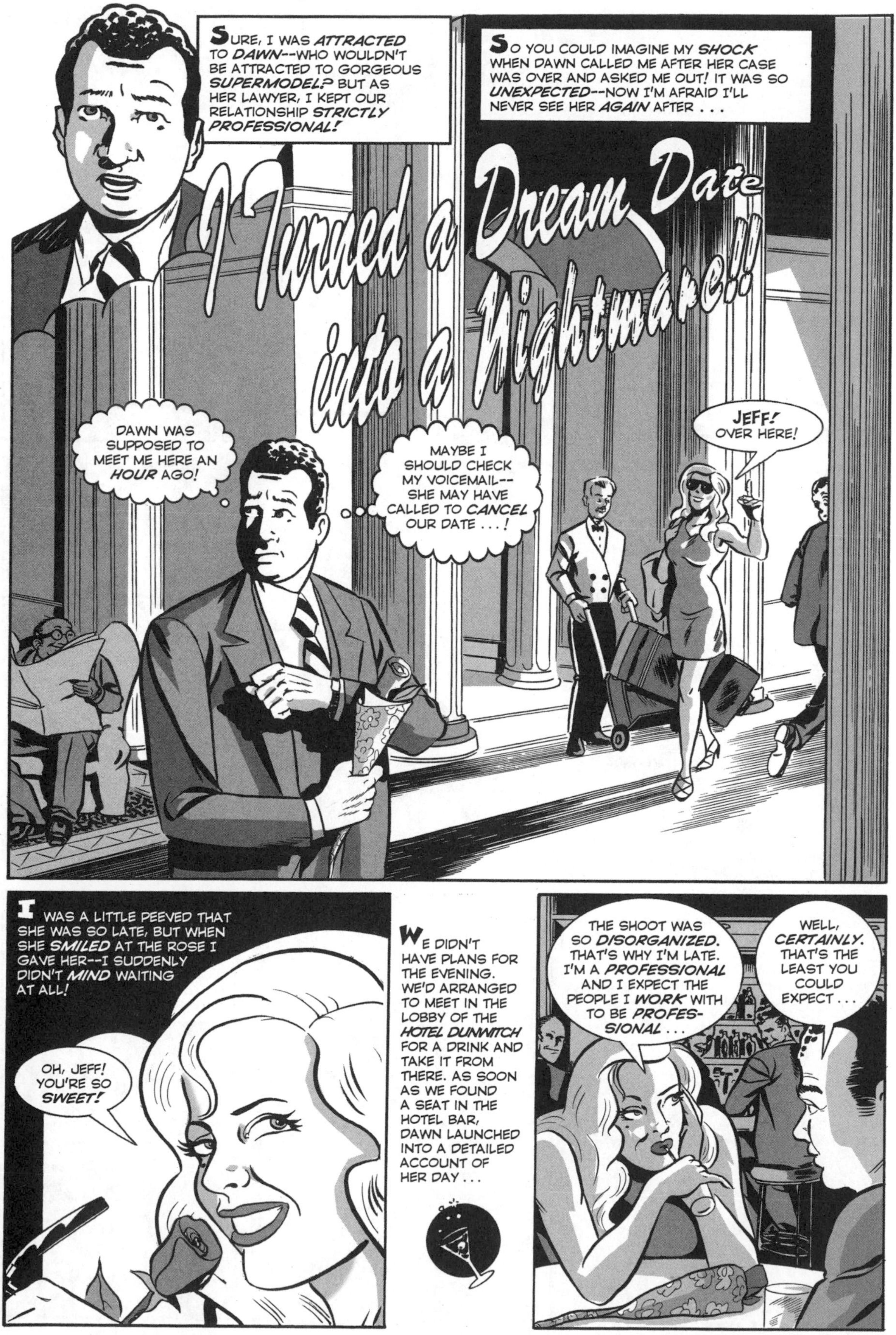
SURE, I WAS ATTRACTED TO DAWN--WHO WOULDN'T BE ATTRACTED TO GORGEOUS SUPERMODEL? BUT AS HER LAWYER, I KEPT OUR RELATIONSHIP STRICTLY PROFESSIONAL!
SO YOU COULD IMAGINE MY SHOCK WHEN DAWN CALLED ME AFTER HER CASE WAS OVER AND ASKED ME OUT! IT WAS SO UNEXPECTED--NOW I'M AFRAID I'LL NEVER SEE HER AGAIN AFTER . . .
I Turned a Dream Date into a Nightmare!!
DAWN WAS SUPPOSED TO MEET ME HERE AN HOUR AGO!
MAYBE I SHOULD CHECK MY VOICEMAIL-- SHE MAY HAVE CALLED TO CANCEL OUR DATE . . . !
JEFF! OVER HERE!
I WAS A LITTLE PEEVED THAT SHE WAS SO LATE, BUT WHEN SHE SMILED AT THE ROSE I GAVE HER--I SUDDENLY DIDN'T MIND WAITING AT ALL!
OH, JEFF! YOU'RE SO SWEET!
WE DIDN'T HAVE PLANS FOR THE EVENING. WE'D ARRANGED TO MEET IN THE LOBBY OF THE HOTEL DUNWICH FOR A DRINK AND TAKE IT FROM THERE. AS SOON AS WE FOUND A SEAT IN THE HOTEL BAR, DAWN LAUNCHED INTO A DETAILED ACCOUNT OF HER DAY . . .
THE SHOOT WAS SO DISORGANIZED. THAT'S WHY I'M LATE. I'M A PROFESSIONAL AND I EXPECT THE PEOPLE I WORK WITH TO BE PROFES-SIONAL . . .
WELL, CERTAINLY. THAT'S THE LEAST YOU COULD EXPECT . . .

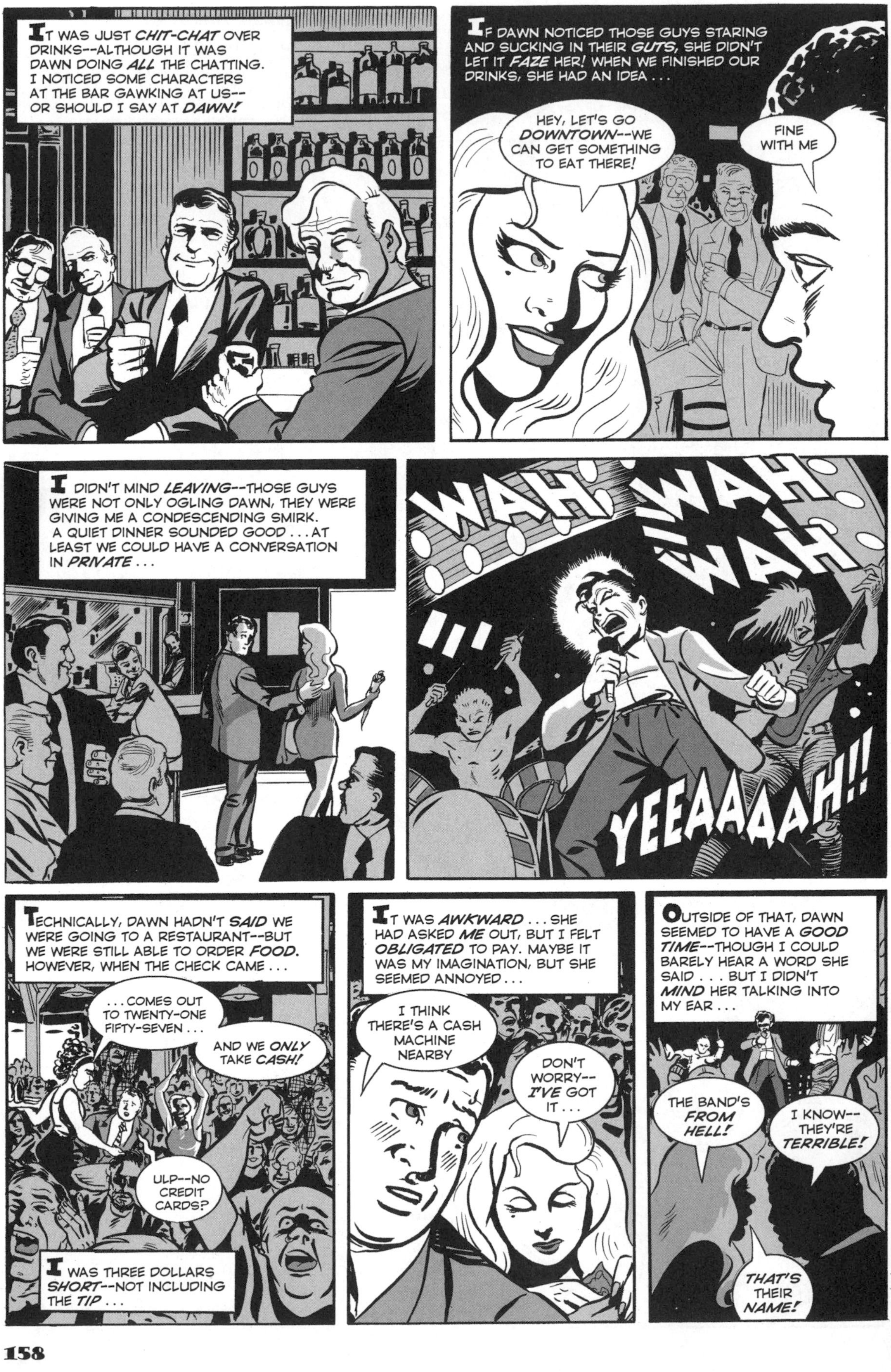
IT WAS JUST CHIT-CHAT OVER DRINKS--ALTHOUGH IT WAS DAWN DOING ALL THE CHATTING. I NOTICED SOME CHARACTERS AT THE BAR GAWKING AT US--OR SHOULD I SAY AT DAWN!
IF DAWN NOTICED THOSE GUYS STARING AND SUCKING IN THEIR GUTS, SHE DIDN'T LET IT FAZE HER! WHEN WE FINISHED OUR DRINKS, SHE HAD AN IDEA . . .
HEY, LET'S GO DOWNTOWN--WE CAN GET SOMETHING TO EAT THERE!
FINE WITH ME
I DIDN'T MIND LEAVING--THOSE GUYS WERE NOT ONLY OGLING DAWN, THEY WERE GIVING ME A CONDESCENDING SMIRK. A QUIET DINNER SOUNDED GOOD . . . AT LEAST WE COULD HAVE A CONVERSATION IN PRIVATE . . .
WAH! WAH! WAH!
!!!
YEEAAAAH!!
TECHNICALLY, DAWN HADN'T SAID WE WERE GOING TO A RESTAURANT--BUT WE WERE STILL ABLE TO ORDER FOOD. HOWEVER, WHEN THE CHECK CAME . . .
. . . COMES OUT TO TWENTY-ONE FIFTY-SEVEN . . .
AND WE ONLY TAKE CASH!
ULP--NO CREDIT CARDS?
I WAS THREE DOLLARS SHORT--NOT INCLUDING THE TIP . . .
IT WAS AWKWARD . . . SHE HAD ASKED ME OUT, BUT I FELT OBLIGATED TO PAY. MAYBE IT WAS MY IMAGINATION, BUT SHE SEEMED ANNOYED . . .
I THINK THERE'S A CASH MACHINE NEARBY
DON'T WORRY--I'VE GOT IT . . .
OUTSIDE OF THAT, DAWN SEEMED TO HAVE A GOOD TIME--THOUGH I COULD BARELY HEAR A WORD SHE SAID . . . BUT I DIDN'T MIND HER TALKING INTO MY EAR . . .
THE BAND'S FROM HELL!
I KNOW--THEY'RE TERRIBLE!
THAT'S THEIR NAME!

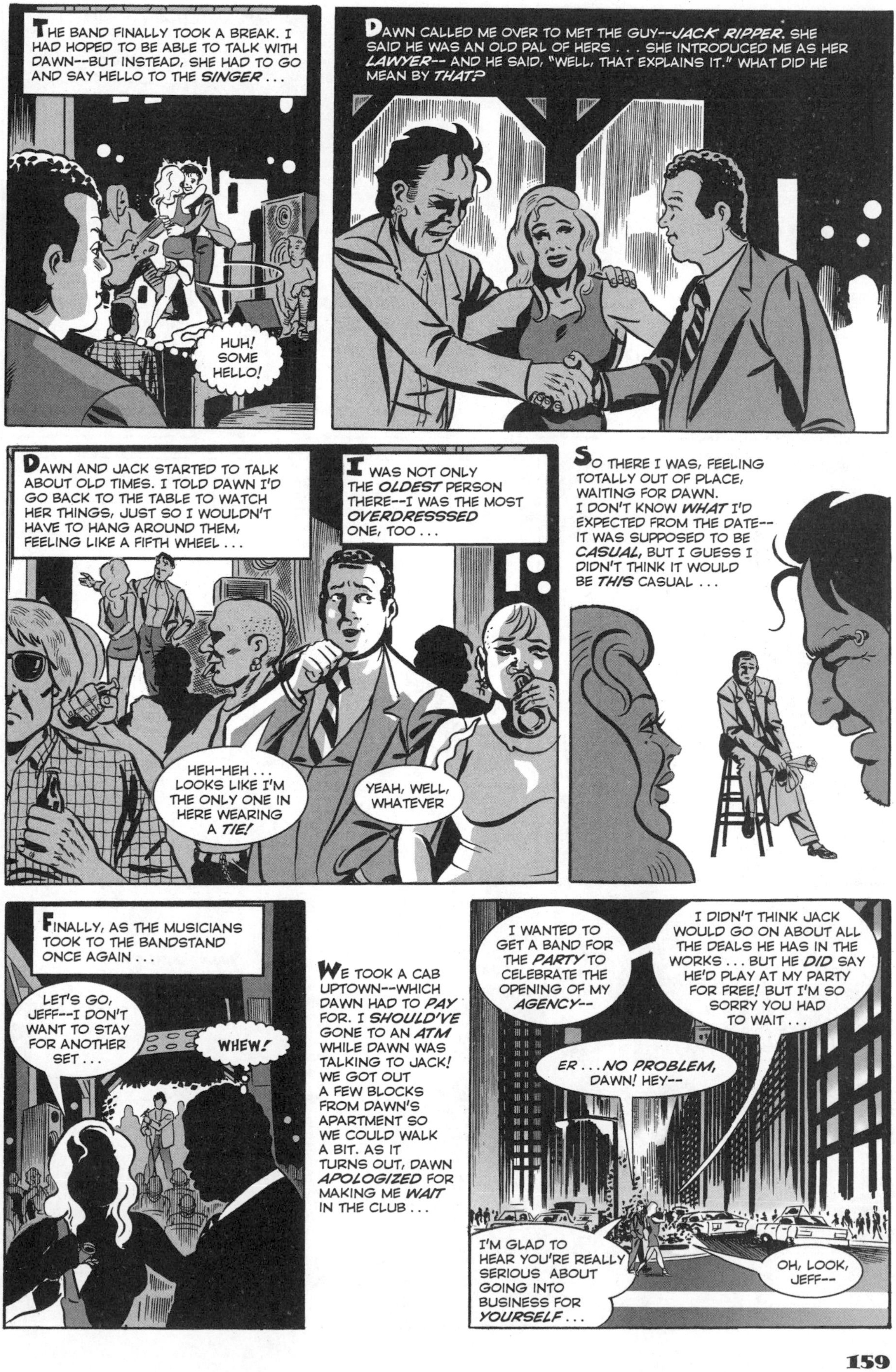
THE BAND FINALLY TOOK A BREAK. I HAD HOPED TO BE ABLE TO TALK WITH DAWN--BUT INSTEAD, SHE HAD TO GO AND SAY HELLO TO THE SINGER . . .
HUH! SOME HELLO!
DAWN CALLED ME OVER TO MET THE GUY--JACK RIPPER. SHE SAID HE WAS AN OLD PAL OF HERS . . . SHE INTRODUCED ME AS HER LAWYER-- AND HE SAID, "WELL, THAT EXPLAINS IT." WHAT DID HE MEAN BY THAT?
DAWN AND JACK STARTED TO TALK ABOUT OLD TIMES. I TOLD DAWN I'D GO BACK TO THE TABLE TO WATCH HER THINGS, JUST SO I WOULDN'T HAVE TO HANG AROUND THEM, FEELING LIKE A FIFTH WHEEL . . .
I WAS NOT ONLY THE OLDEST PERSON THERE--I WAS THE MOST OVERDRESSSED ONE, TOO . . .
HEH-HEH . . . LOOKS LIKE I'M THE ONLY ONE IN HERE WEARING A TIE!
YEAH, WELL, WHATEVER
SO THERE I WAS, FEELING TOTALLY OUT OF PLACE, WAITING FOR DAWN. I DON'T KNOW WHAT I'D EXPECTED FROM THE DATE-- IT WAS SUPPOSED TO BE CASUAL, BUT I GUESS I DIDN'T THINK IT WOULD BE THIS CASUAL . . .
FINALLY, AS THE MUSICIANS TOOK TO THE BANDSTAND ONCE AGAIN . . .
LET'S GO, JEFF--I DON'T WANT TO STAY FOR ANOTHER SET . . .
WHEW!
WE TOOK A CAB UPTOWN--WHICH DAWN HAD TO PAY FOR. I SHOULD'VE GONE TO AN ATM WHILE DAWN WAS TALKING TO JACK! WE GOT OUT A FEW BLOCKS FROM DAWN'S APARTMENT SO WE COULD WALK A BIT. AS IT TURNS OUT, DAWN APOLOGIZED FOR MAKING ME WAIT IN THE CLUB . . .
I WANTED TO GET A BAND FOR THE PARTY TO CELEBRATE THE OPENING OF MY AGENCY--
I DIDN'T THINK JACK WOULD GO ON ABOUT ALL THE DEALS HE HAS IN THE WORKS . . . BUT HE DID SAY HE'D PLAY AT MY PARTY FOR FREE! BUT I'M SO SORRY YOU HAD TO WAIT . . .
ER . . . NO PROBLEM, DAWN! HEY--
I'M GLAD TO HEAR YOU'RE REALLY SERIOUS ABOUT GOING INTO BUSINESS FOR YOURSELF . . .
OH, LOOK, JEFF--

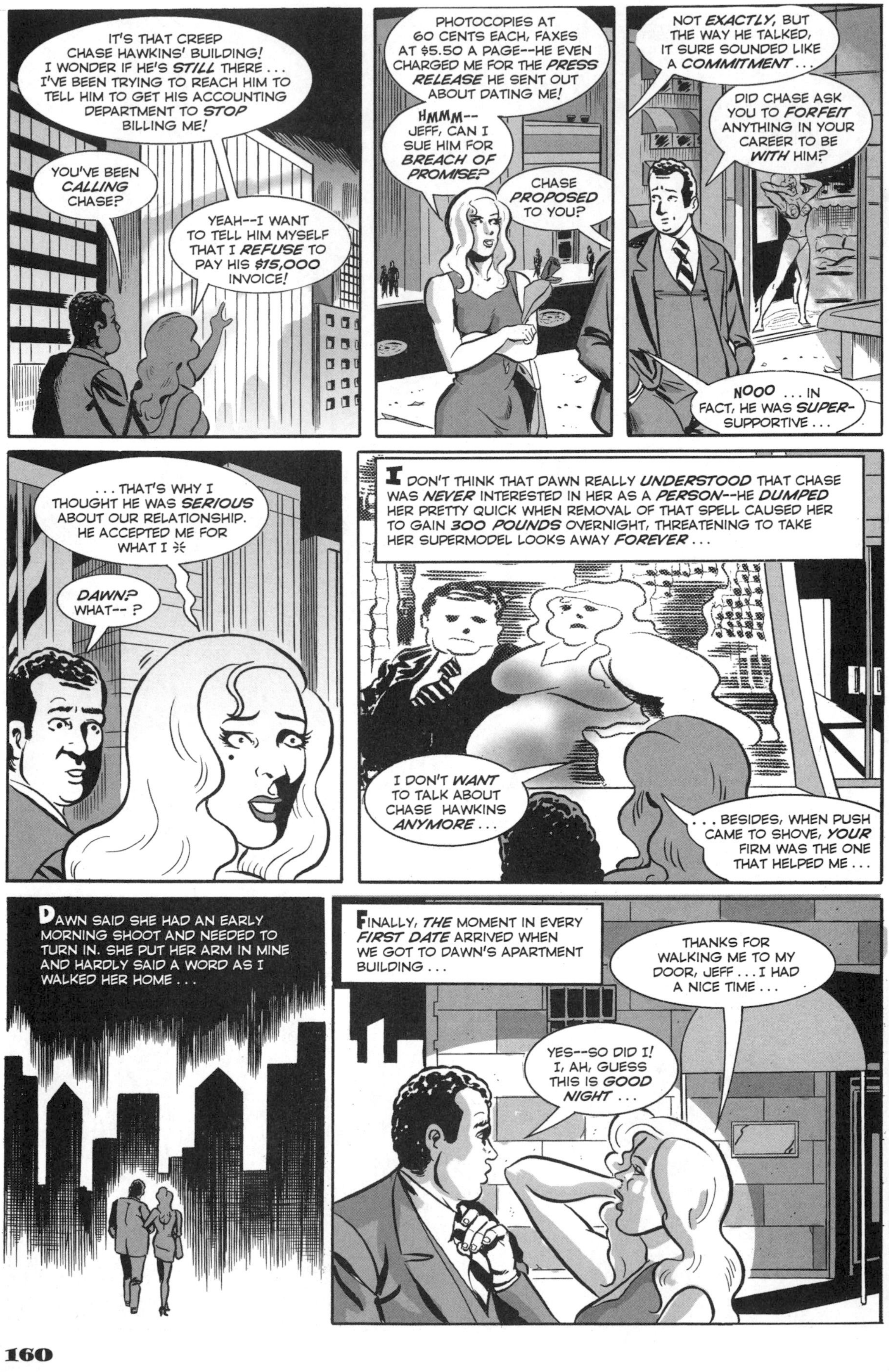
IT'S THAT CREEP CHASE HAWKINS' BUILDING! I WONDER IF HE'S STILL THERE . . . I'VE BEEN TRYING TO REACH HIM TO TELL HIM TO GET HIS ACCOUNTING DEPARTMENT TO STOP BILLING ME!
YOU'VE BEEN CALLING CHASE?
YEAH--I WANT TO TELL HIM MYSELF THAT I REFUSE TO PAY HIS $15,000 INVOICE!
PHOTOCOPIES AT 60 CENTS EACH, FAXES AT $5.50 A PAGE--HE EVEN CHARGED ME FOR THE PRESS RELEASE HE SENT OUT ABOUT DATING ME!
HMMM-- JEFF, CAN I SUE HIM FOR BREACH OF PROMISE?
CHASE PROPOSED TO YOU?
NOT EXACTLY, BUT THE WAY HE TALKED, IT SURE SOUNDED LIKE A COMMITMENT . . .
DID CHASE ASK YOU TO FORFEIT ANYTHING IN YOUR CAREER TO BE WITH HIM?
NOOO . . . IN FACT, HE WAS SUPER-SUPPORTIVE . . .
. . . THAT'S WHY I THOUGHT HE WAS SERIOUS ABOUT OUR RELATIONSHIP. HE ACCEPTED ME FOR WHAT I ✳
DAWN? WHAT-- ?
I DON'T THINK THAT DAWN REALLY UNDERSTOOD THAT CHASE WAS NEVER INTERESTED IN HER AS A PERSON--HE DUMPED HER PRETTY QUICK WHEN REMOVAL OF THAT SPELL CAUSED HER TO GAIN 300 POUNDS OVERNIGHT, THREATENING TO TAKE HER SUPERMODEL LOOKS AWAY FOREVER . . .
I DON'T WANT TO TALK ABOUT CHASE HAWKINS ANYMORE . . .
. . . BESIDES, WHEN PUSH CAME TO SHOVE, YOUR FIRM WAS THE ONE THAT HELPED ME . . .
DAWN SAID SHE HAD AN EARLY MORNING SHOOT AND NEEDED TO TURN IN. SHE PUT HER ARM IN MINE AND HARDLY SAID A WORD AS I WALKED HER HOME . . .
FINALLY, THE MOMENT IN EVERY FIRST DATE ARRIVED WHEN WE GOT TO DAWN'S APARTMENT BUILDING . . .
THANKS FOR WALKING ME TO MY DOOR, JEFF . . . I HAD A NICE TIME . . .
YES--SO DID I! I, AH, GUESS THIS IS GOOD NIGHT . . .

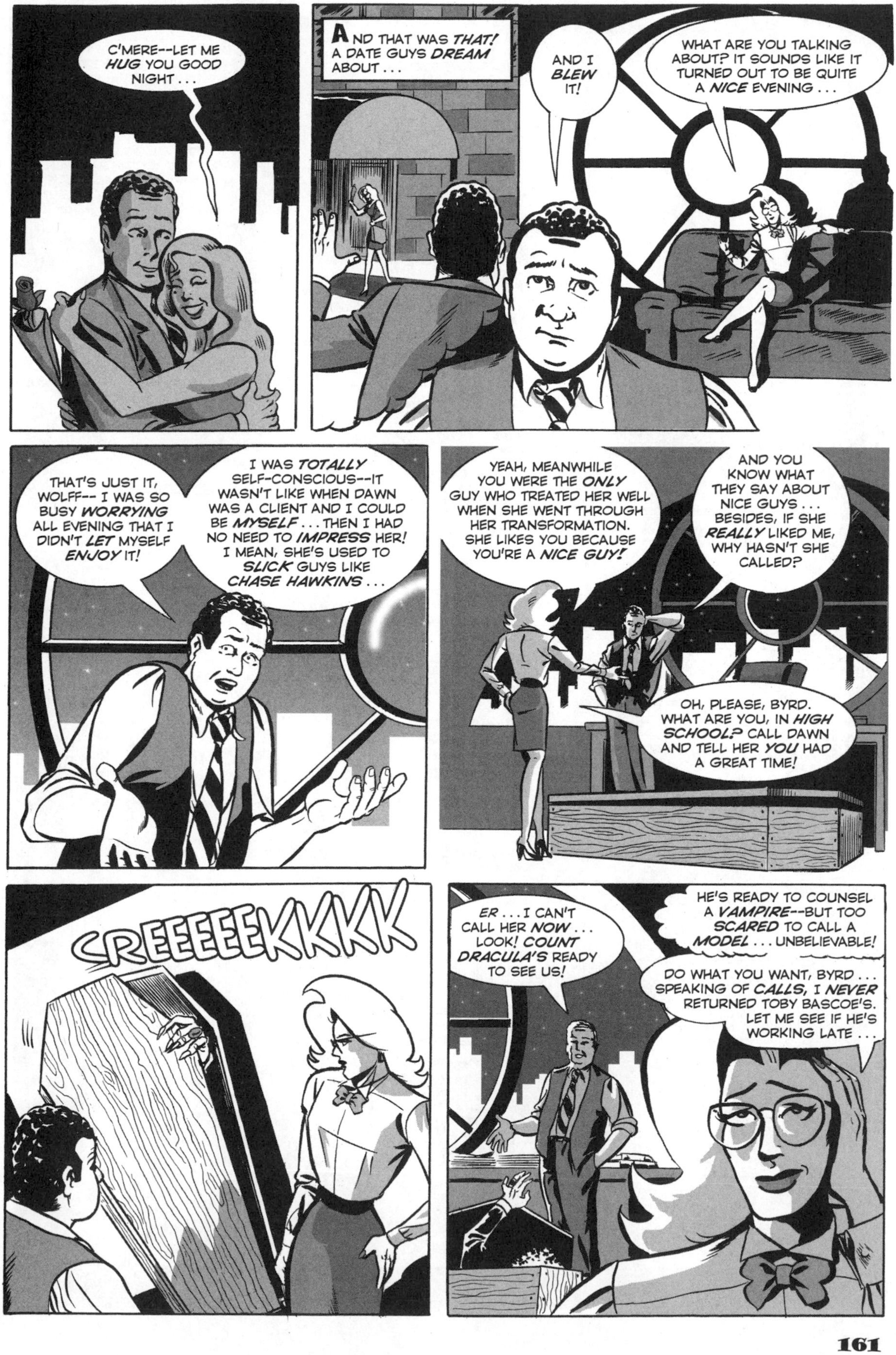
C'MERE--LET ME HUG YOU GOOD NIGHT . . .
AND THAT WAS THAT! A DATE GUYS DREAM ABOUT . . .
AND I BLEW IT!
WHAT ARE YOU TALKING ABOUT? IT SOUNDS LIKE IT TURNED OUT TO BE QUITE A NICE EVENING . . .
THAT'S JUST IT, WOLFF-- I WAS SO BUSY WORRYING ALL EVENING THAT I DIDN'T LET MYSELF ENJOY IT!
I WAS TOTALLY SELF-CONSCIOUS--IT WASN'T LIKE WHEN DAWN WAS A CLIENT AND I COULD BE MYSELF . . . THEN I HAD NO NEED TO IMPRESS HER! I MEAN, SHE'S USED TO SLICK GUYS LIKE CHASE HAWKINS . . .
YEAH, MEANWHILE YOU WERE THE ONLY GUY WHO TREATED HER WELL WHEN SHE WENT THROUGH HER TRANSFORMATION. SHE LIKES YOU BECAUSE YOU'RE A NICE GUY!
AND YOU KNOW WHAT THEY SAY ABOUT NICE GUYS . . . BESIDES, IF SHE REALLY LIKED ME, WHY HASN'T SHE CALLED?
OH, PLEASE, BYRD. WHAT ARE YOU, IN HIGH SCHOOL? CALL DAWN AND TELL HER YOU HAD A GREAT TIME!
CREEEEEEKKKK
ER . . . I CAN'T CALL HER NOW . . . LOOK! COUNT DRACULA'S READY TO SEE US!
HE'S READY TO COUNSEL A VAMPIRE--BUT TOO SCARED TO CALL A MODEL . . . UNBELIEVABLE!
DO WHAT YOU WANT, BYRD . . . SPEAKING OF CALLS, I NEVER RETURNED TOBY BASCOE'S. LET ME SEE IF HE'S WORKING LATE . . .

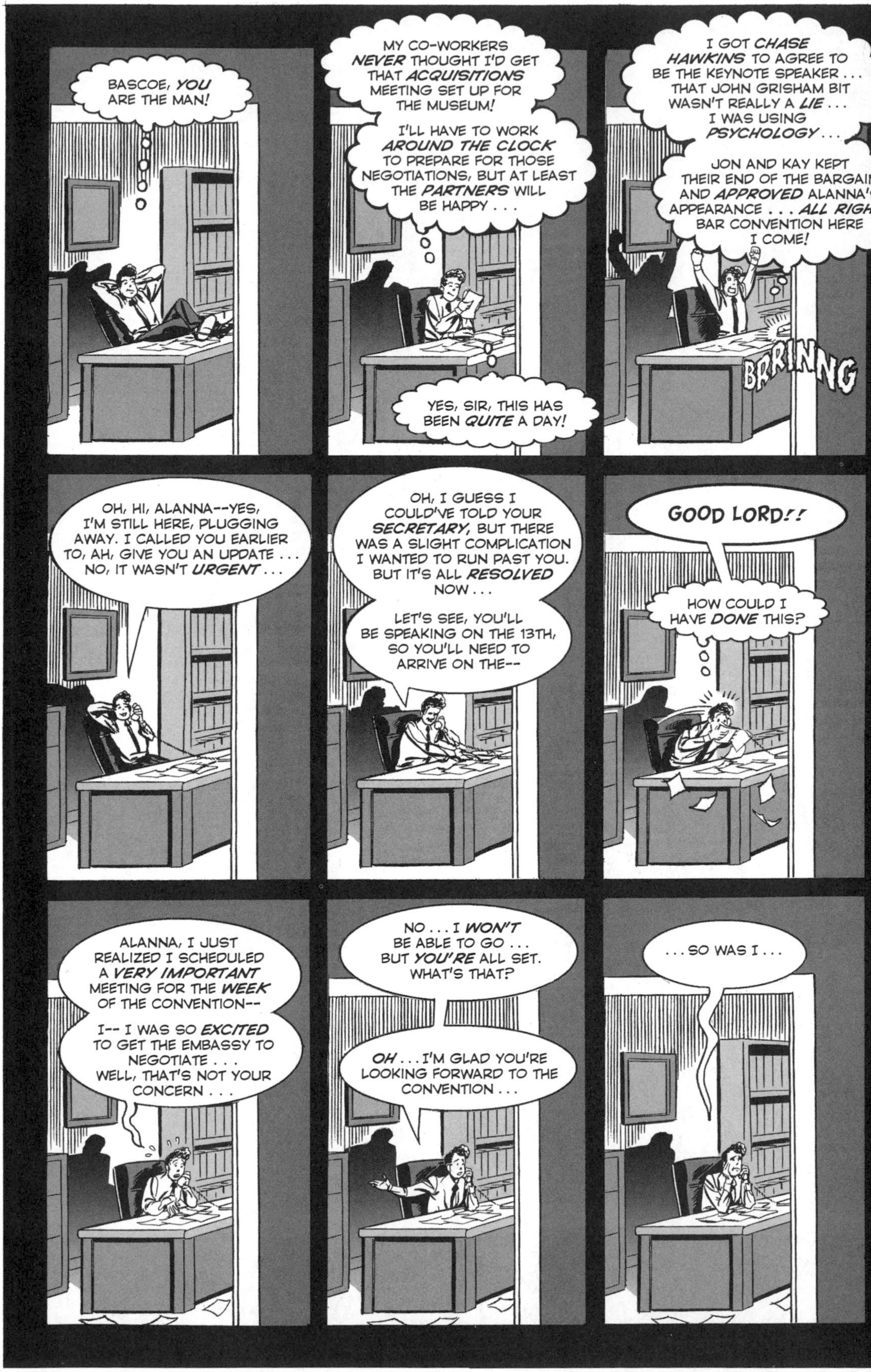
BASCOE, YOU ARE THE MAN!
MY CO-WORKERS NEVER THOUGHT I'D GET THAT ACQUISITIONS MEETING SET UP FOR THE MUSEUM!
I'LL HAVE TO WORK AROUND THE CLOCK TO PREPARE FOR THOSE NEGOTIATIONS, BUT AT LEAST THE PARTNERS WILL BE HAPPY . . .
YES, SIR, THIS HAS BEEN QUITE A DAY!
I GOT CHASE HAWKINS TO AGREE TO BE THE KEYNOTE SPEAKER . . . THAT JOHN GRISHAM BIT WASN'T REALLY A LIE . . . I WAS USING PSYCHOLOGY . . .
JON AND KAY KEPT THEIR END OF THE BARGAIN AND APPROVED ALANNA'S APPEARANCE . . . ALL RIGHT! BAR CONVENTION HERE I COME!
BRRINNG
OH, HI, ALANNA--YES, I'M STILL HERE, PLUGGING AWAY. I CALLED YOU EARLIER TO, AH, GIVE YOU AN UPDATE . . . NO, IT WASN'T URGENT . . .
OH, I GUESS I COULD'VE TOLD YOUR SECRETARY, BUT THERE WAS A SLIGHT COMPLICATION I WANTED TO RUN PAST YOU. BUT IT'S ALL RESOLVED NOW . . .
LET'S SEE, YOU'LL BE SPEAKING ON THE 13TH, SO YOU'LL NEED TO ARRIVE ON THE--
GOOD LORD!!
HOW COULD I HAVE DONE THIS?
ALANNA, I JUST REALIZED I SCHEDULED A VERY IMPORTANT MEETING FOR THE WEEK OF THE CONVENTION--
I-- I WAS SO EXCITED TO GET THE EMBASSY TO NEGOTIATE . . . WELL, THAT'S NOT YOUR CONCERN . . .
NO . . . I WON'T BE ABLE TO GO . . . BUT YOU'RE ALL SET. WHAT'S THAT?
OH . . . I'M GLAD YOU'RE LOOKING FORWARD TO THE CONVENTION . . .
. . . SO WAS I . . .

Bar • Con

INTEROFFICE MEMO

TO: Mavis

FROM: Alanna Wolff

Attached are my airline, hotel, and seminar attendance literature. I'll be checking in for my messages on a daily basis. If you need to reach me otherwise, I'll be at the San Diego Ryatt Hotel (619-555- 8000).

Mrs. Donovan should be by to pick up her husband at the office tomorrow.

Good luck holding down the fort!

A.W.

From the Desk of:

Jeffrey Byrd, Esq.

Mavis:

I cleared my calendar to attend the bar convention. The only client who may need help while I'm away is Sodd. Don't let him take up too much of your time. We've told him that we can't do anything about his case until we get back from San Diego. If by any chance Dawn DeVine calls, make sure she has my cell phone number.

I'll try to bring back some of that California sunshine for you!

J.B.

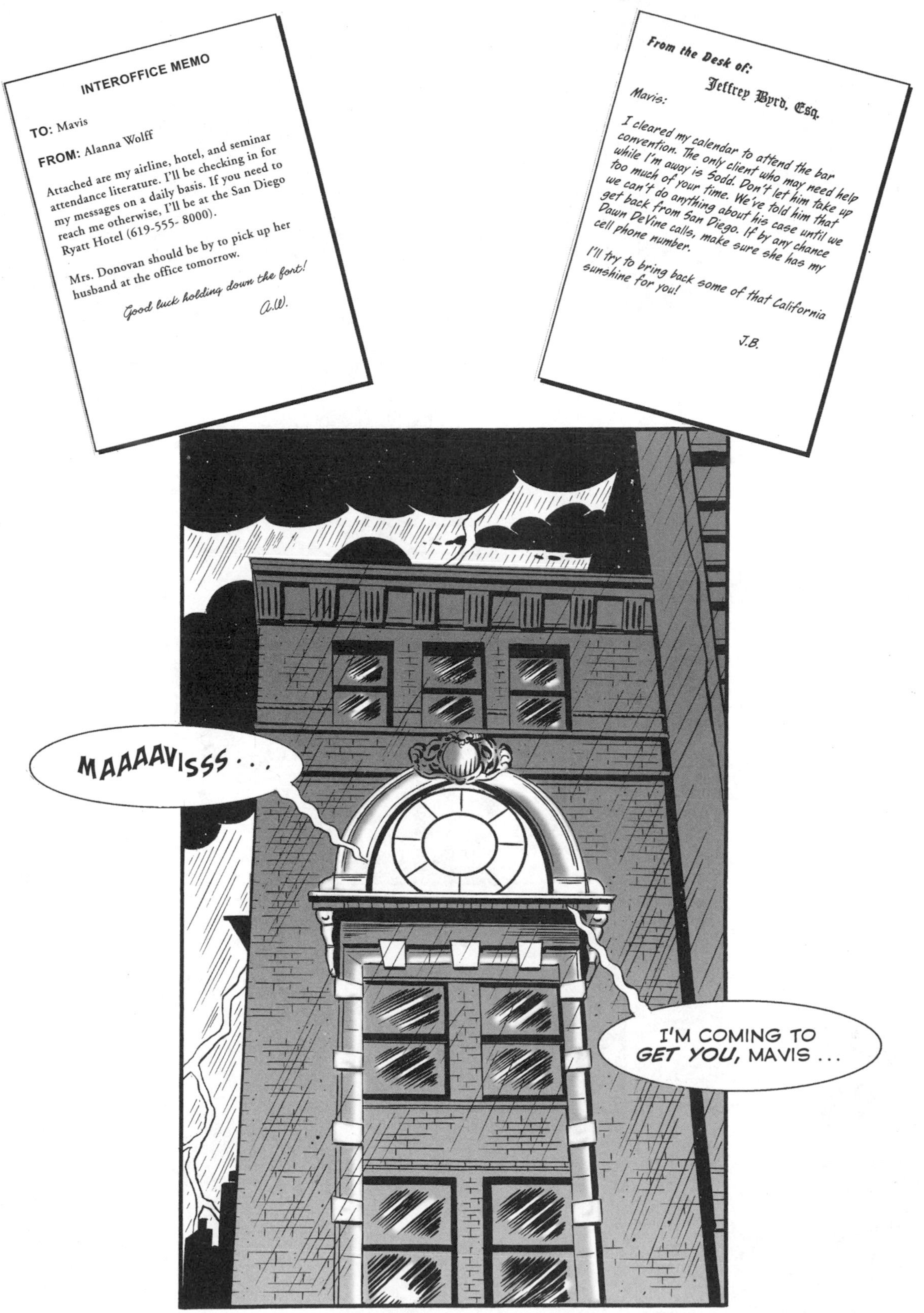
MAAAAVISSS . . .
I'M COMING TO GET YOU, MAVIS . . .

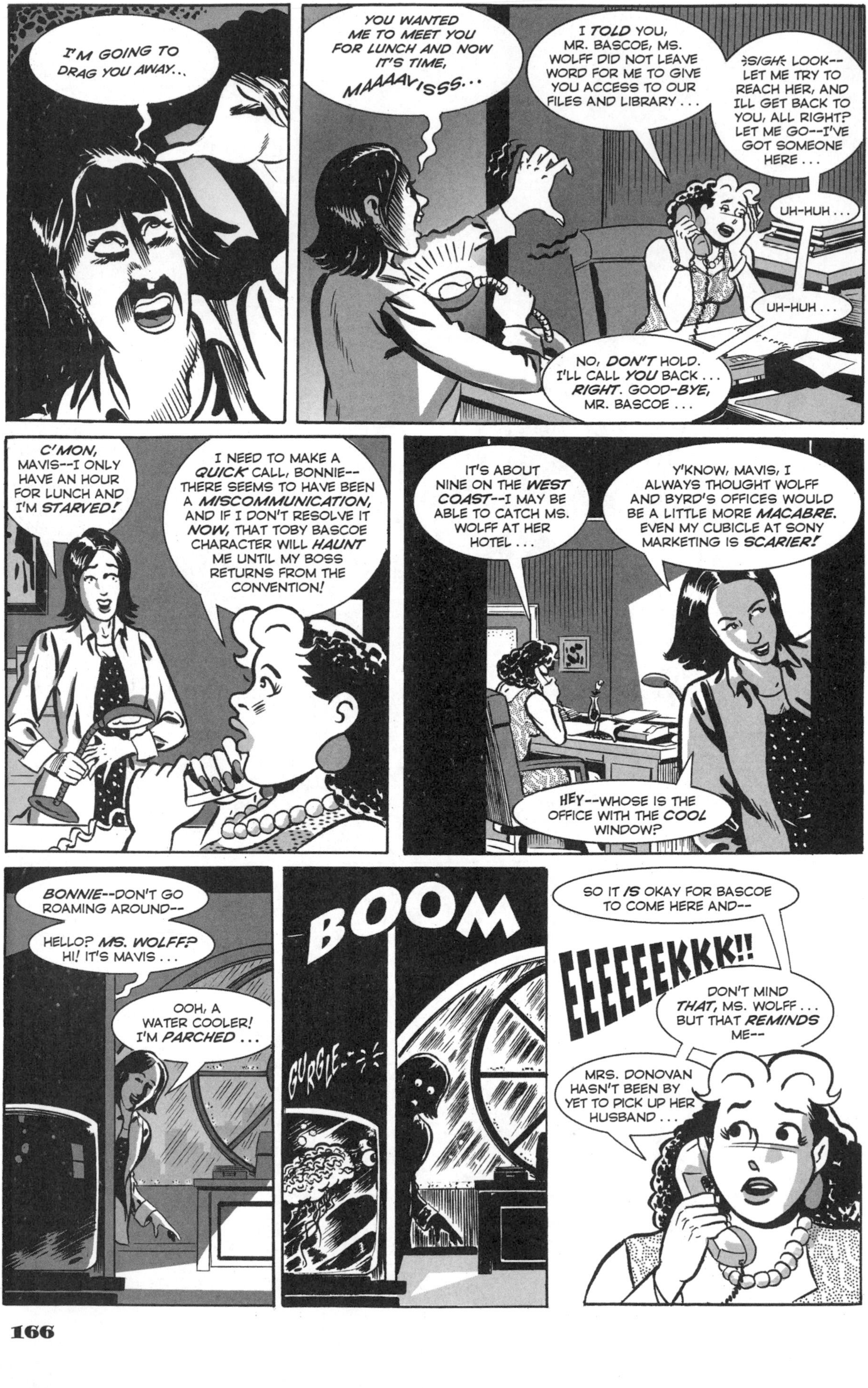
I'M GOING TO DRAG YOU AWAY...
YOU WANTED ME TO MEET YOU FOR LUNCH AND NOW IT'S TIME, MAAAAVISSS...
I TOLD YOU, MR. BASCOE, MS. WOLFF DID NOT LEAVE WORD FOR ME TO GIVE YOU ACCESS TO OUR FILES AND LIBRARY . . .
SIGH LOOK-- LET ME TRY TO REACH HER, AND ILL GET BACK TO YOU, ALL RIGHT? LET ME GO--I'VE GOT SOMEONE HERE . . .
UH-HUH . . .
UH-HUH . . .
NO, DON'T HOLD. I'LL CALL YOU BACK . . . RIGHT. GOOD-BYE, MR. BASCOE . . .
C'MON, MAVIS--I ONLY HAVE AN HOUR FOR LUNCH AND I'M STARVED!
I NEED TO MAKE A QUICK CALL, BONNIE--THERE SEEMS TO HAVE BEEN A MISCOMMUNICATION, AND IF I DON'T RESOLVE IT NOW, THAT TOBY BASCOE CHARACTER WILL HAUNT ME UNTIL MY BOSS RETURNS FROM THE CONVENTION!
IT'S ABOUT NINE ON THE WEST COAST--I MAY BE ABLE TO CATCH MS. WOLFF AT HER HOTEL . . .
Y'KNOW, MAVIS, I ALWAYS THOUGHT WOLFF AND BYRD'S OFFICES WOULD BE A LITTLE MORE MACABRE. EVEN MY CUBICLE AT SONY MARKETING IS SCARIER!
HEY--WHOSE IS THE OFFICE WITH THE COOL WINDOW?
BONNIE--DON'T GO ROAMING AROUND--
HELLO? MS. WOLFF? HI! IT'S MAVIS . . .
OOH, A WATER COOLER! I'M PARCHED . . .
BOOM
GURGLE
SO IT IS OKAY FOR BASCOE TO COME HERE AND--
EEEEEEKKK!!
DON'T MIND THAT, MS. WOLFF . . . BUT THAT REMINDS ME--
MRS. DONOVAN HASN'T BEEN BY YET TO PICK UP HER HUSBAND . . .

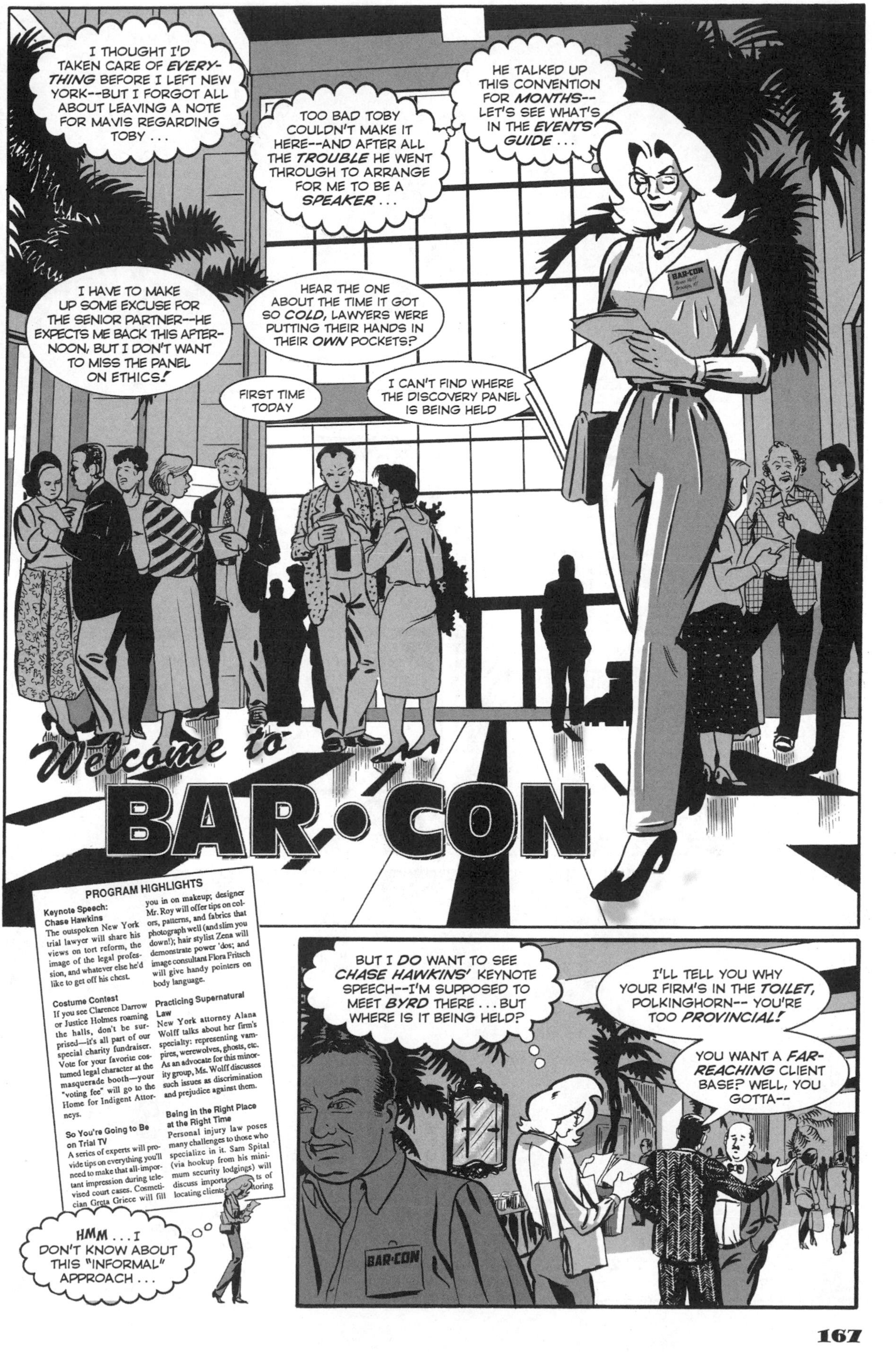
I THOUGHT I'D TAKEN CARE OF EVERYTHING BEFORE I LEFT NEW YORK--BUT I FORGOT ALL ABOUT LEAVING A NOTE FOR MAVIS REGARDING TOBY . . .
TOO BAD TOBY COULDN'T MAKE IT HERE--AND AFTER ALL THE TROUBLE HE WENT THROUGH TO ARRANGE FOR ME TO BE A SPEAKER . . .
HE TALKED UP THIS CONVENTION FOR MONTHS--LET'S SEE WHAT'S IN THE EVENTS GUIDE . . .
I HAVE TO MAKE UP SOME EXCUSE FOR THE SENIOR PARTNER--HE EXPECTS ME BACK THIS AFTERNOON, BUT I DON'T WANT TO MISS THE PANEL ON ETHICS!
HEAR THE ONE ABOUT THE TIME IT GOT SO COLD, LAWYERS WERE PUTTING THEIR HANDS IN THEIR OWN POCKETS?
FIRST TIME TODAY
I CAN'T FIND WHERE THE DISCOVERY PANEL IS BEING HELD
BAR-CON
Welcome to
BAR•CON
PROGRAM HIGHLIGHTS
Keynote Speech: Chase Hawkins
The outspoken New York trial lawyer will share his views on tort reform, the image of the legal profession, and whatever else he'd like to get off his chest.
Costume Contest
If you see Clarence Darrow or Justice Holmes roaming the halls, don't be surprised—it's all part of our special charity fundraiser. Vote for your favorite costumed legal character at the masquerade booth—your "voting fee" will go to the Home for Indigent Attorneys.
So You're Going to Be on Trial TV
A series of experts will provide tips on everything you'll need to make that all-important impression during televised court cases. Cosmetician Greta Griece will fill you in on makeup; designer Mr. Roy will offer tips on colors, patterns, and fabrics that photograph well (and slim you down!); hair stylist Zena will demonstrate power 'dos; and image consultant Flora Fritsch will give handy pointers on body language.
Practicing Supernatural Law
New York attorney Alana Wolff talks about her firm's specialty: representing vampires, werewolves, ghosts, etc. As an advocate for this minority group, Ms. Wolff discusses such issues as discrimination and prejudice against them.
Being in the Right Place at the Right Time
Personal injury law poses many challenges to those who specialize in it. Sam Spital (via hookup from his minimum security lodgings) will discuss importa ts of locating clients, toring
HMM . . . I DON'T KNOW ABOUT THIS "INFORMAL" APPROACH . . .
BUT I DO WANT TO SEE CHASE HAWKINS' KEYNOTE SPEECH--I'M SUPPOSED TO MEET BYRD THERE . . . BUT WHERE IS IT BEING HELD?
I'LL TELL YOU WHY YOUR FIRM'S IN THE TOILET, POLKINGHORN-- YOU'RE TOO PROVINCIAL!
YOU WANT A FAR-REACHING CLIENT BASE? WELL, YOU GOTTA--
BAR-CON

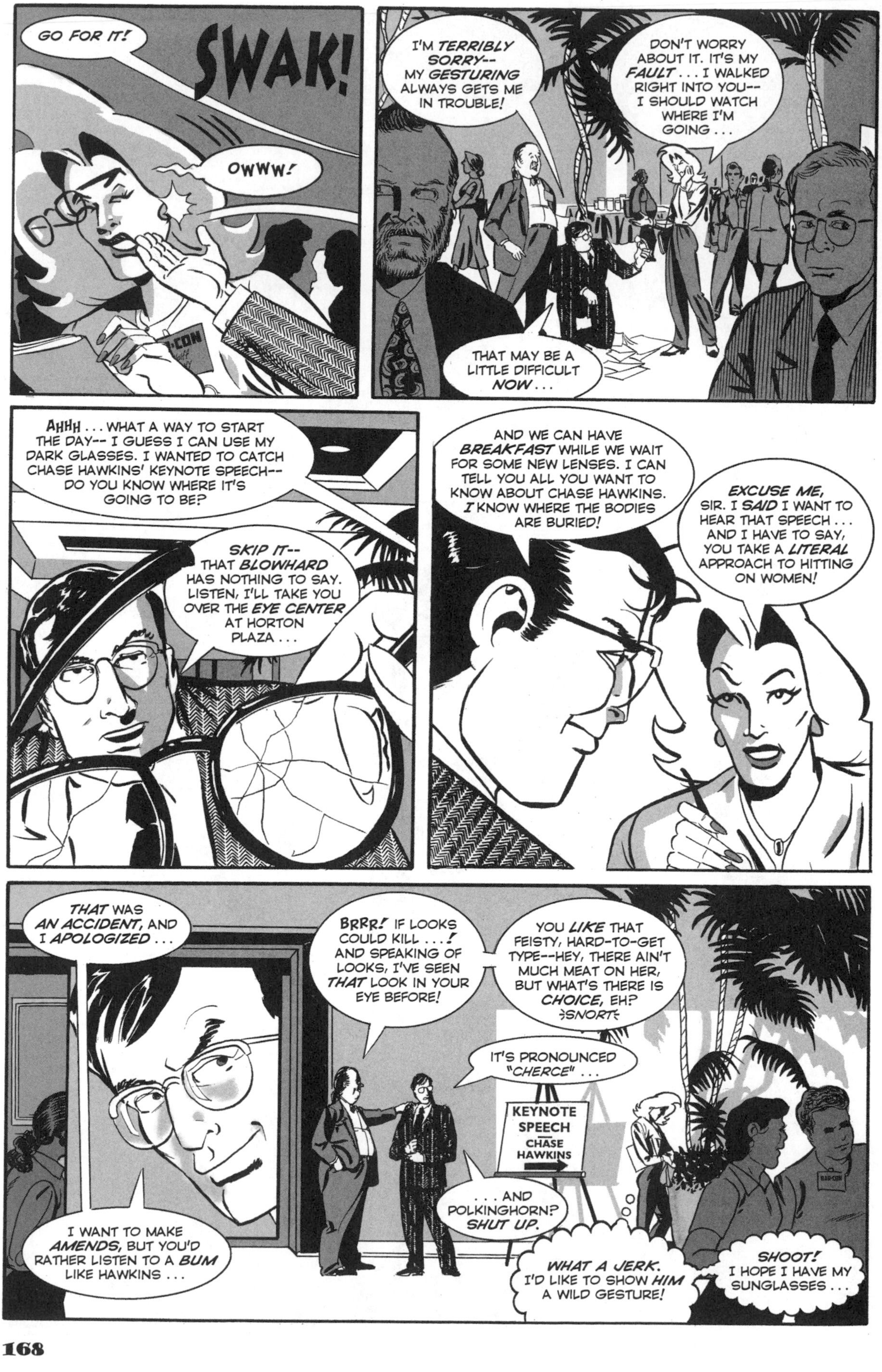
GO FOR IT!
SWAK!
OWWW!
I'M TERRIBLY SORRY-- MY GESTURING ALWAYS GETS ME IN TROUBLE!
DON'T WORRY ABOUT IT. IT'S MY FAULT . . . I WALKED RIGHT INTO YOU-- I SHOULD WATCH WHERE I'M GOING . . .
THAT MAY BE A LITTLE DIFFICULT NOW . . .
AHHH . . . WHAT A WAY TO START THE DAY-- I GUESS I CAN USE MY DARK GLASSES. I WANTED TO CATCH CHASE HAWKINS' KEYNOTE SPEECH-- DO YOU KNOW WHERE IT'S GOING TO BE?
SKIP IT-- THAT BLOWHARD HAS NOTHING TO SAY. LISTEN, I'LL TAKE YOU OVER THE EYE CENTER AT HORTON PLAZA . . .
AND WE CAN HAVE BREAKFAST WHILE WE WAIT FOR SOME NEW LENSES. I CAN TELL YOU ALL YOU WANT TO KNOW ABOUT CHASE HAWKINS. I KNOW WHERE THE BODIES ARE BURIED!
EXCUSE ME, SIR. I SAID I WANT TO HEAR THAT SPEECH . . . AND I HAVE TO SAY, YOU TAKE A LITERAL APPROACH TO HITTING ON WOMEN!
THAT WAS AN ACCIDENT, AND I APOLOGIZED . . .
I WANT TO MAKE AMENDS, BUT YOU'D RATHER LISTEN TO A BUM LIKE HAWKINS . . .
BRRR! IF LOOKS COULD KILL . . .! AND SPEAKING OF LOOKS, I'VE SEEN THAT LOOK IN YOUR EYE BEFORE!
YOU LIKE THAT FEISTY, HARD-TO-GET TYPE--HEY, THERE AIN'T MUCH MEAT ON HER, BUT WHAT'S THERE IS CHOICE, EH? SNORT
IT'S PRONOUNCED "CHERCE" . . .
KEYNOTE SPEECH CHASE HAWKINS
. . . AND POLKINGHORN? SHUT UP.
WHAT A JERK. I'D LIKE TO SHOW HIM A WILD GESTURE!
SHOOT! I HOPE I HAVE MY SUNGLASSES . . .

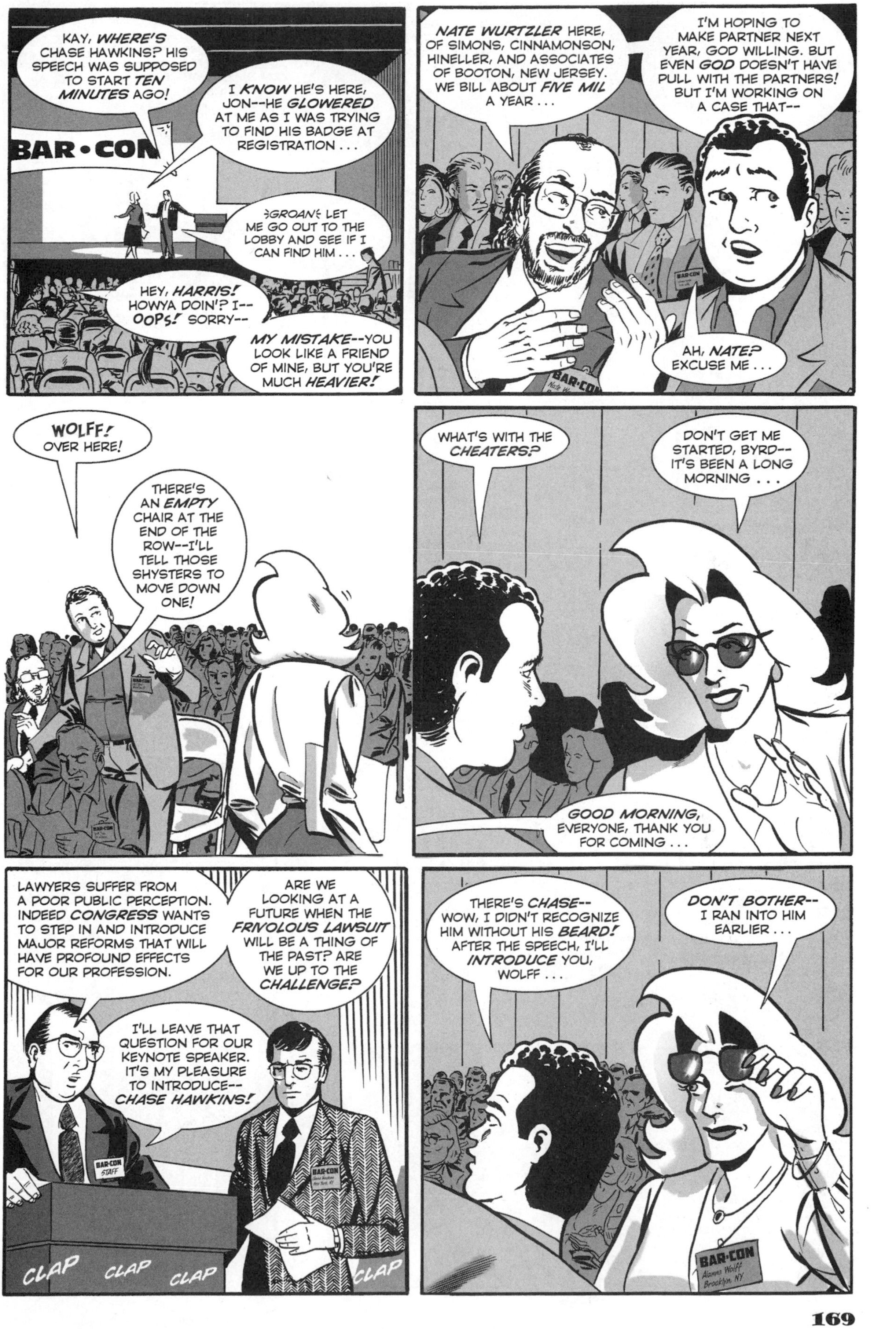
KAY, WHERE'S CHASE HAWKINS? HIS SPEECH WAS SUPPOSED TO START TEN MINUTES AGO!
I KNOW HE'S HERE, JON--HE GLOWERED AT ME AS I WAS TRYING TO FIND HIS BADGE AT REGISTRATION . . .
BAR • CON
GROAN LET ME GO OUT TO THE LOBBY AND SEE IF I CAN FIND HIM . . .
HEY, HARRIS! HOWYA DOIN'? I-- OOPS! SORRY--
MY MISTAKE--YOU LOOK LIKE A FRIEND OF MINE, BUT YOU'RE MUCH HEAVIER!
NATE WURTZLER HERE, OF SIMONS, CINNAMONSON, HINELLER, AND ASSOCIATES OF BOOTON, NEW JERSEY. WE BILL ABOUT FIVE MIL A YEAR . . .
I'M HOPING TO MAKE PARTNER NEXT YEAR, GOD WILLING. BUT EVEN GOD DOESN'T HAVE PULL WITH THE PARTNERS! BUT I'M WORKING ON A CASE THAT--
AH, NATE? EXCUSE ME . . .
WOLFF! OVER HERE!
THERE'S AN EMPTY CHAIR AT THE END OF THE ROW--I'LL TELL THOSE SHYSTERS TO MOVE DOWN ONE!
WHAT'S WITH THE CHEATERS?
DON'T GET ME STARTED, BYRD-- IT'S BEEN A LONG MORNING . . .
GOOD MORNING, EVERYONE, THANK YOU FOR COMING . . .
LAWYERS SUFFER FROM A POOR PUBLIC PERCEPTION. INDEED CONGRESS WANTS TO STEP IN AND INTRODUCE MAJOR REFORMS THAT WILL HAVE PROFOUND EFFECTS FOR OUR PROFESSION.
ARE WE LOOKING AT A FUTURE WHEN THE FRIVOLOUS LAWSUIT WILL BE A THING OF THE PAST? ARE WE UP TO THE CHALLENGE?
I'LL LEAVE THAT QUESTION FOR OUR KEYNOTE SPEAKER. IT'S MY PLEASURE TO INTRODUCE-- CHASE HAWKINS!
BAR•CON STAFF
CLAP CLAP CLAP CLAP
THERE'S CHASE-- WOW, I DIDN'T RECOGNIZE HIM WITHOUT HIS BEARD! AFTER THE SPEECH, I'LL INTRODUCE YOU, WOLFF . . .
DON'T BOTHER-- I RAN INTO HIM EARLIER . . .
BAR•CON Alanna Wolff Brooklyn, NY

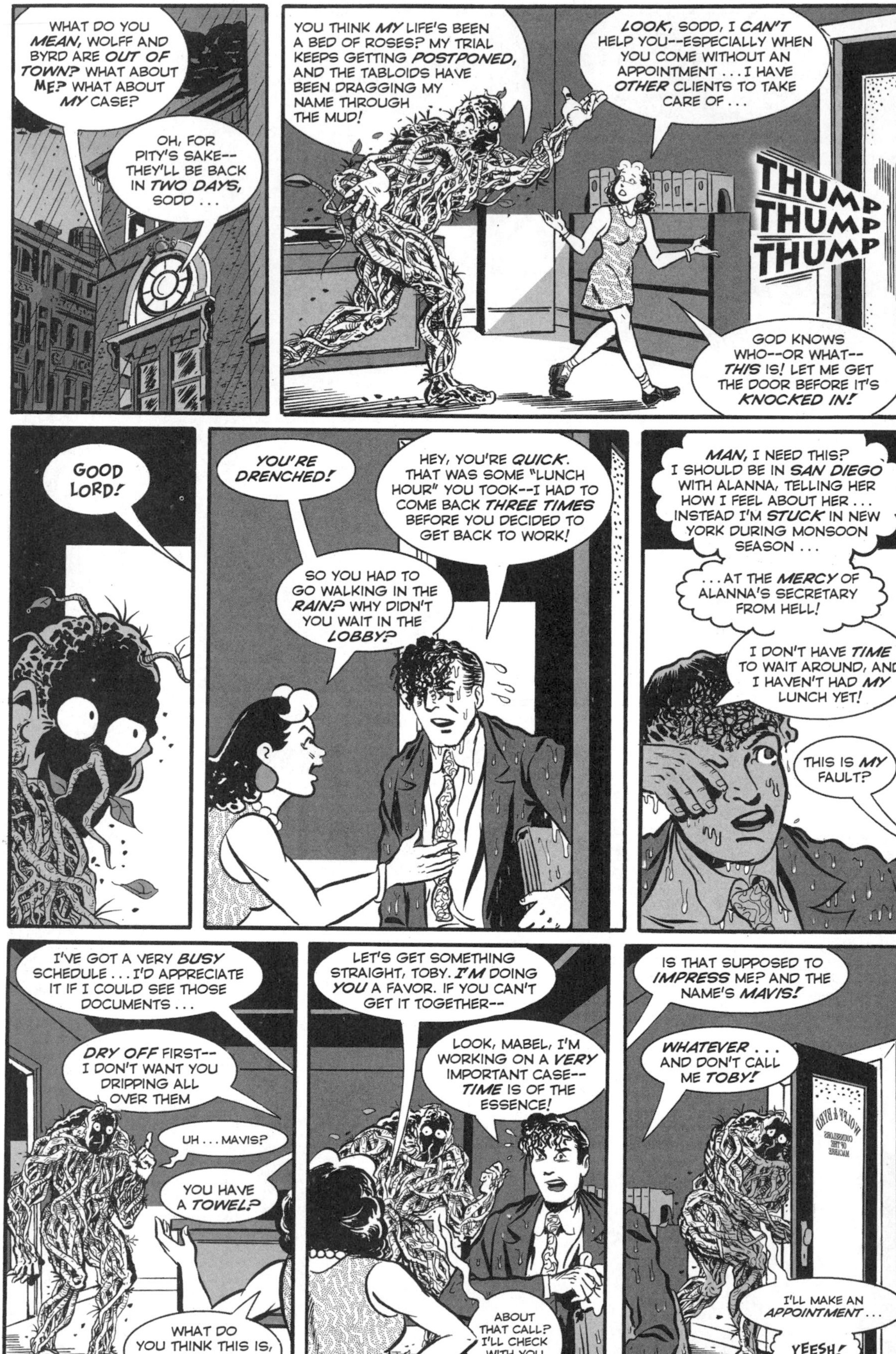
WHAT DO YOU MEAN, WOLFF AND BYRD ARE OUT OF TOWN? WHAT ABOUT ME? WHAT ABOUT MY CASE?
OH, FOR PITY'S SAKE-- THEY'LL BE BACK IN TWO DAYS, SODD . . .
YOU THINK MY LIFE'S BEEN A BED OF ROSES? MY TRIAL KEEPS GETTING POSTPONED, AND THE TABLOIDS HAVE BEEN DRAGGING MY NAME THROUGH THE MUD!
LOOK, SODD, I CAN'T HELP YOU--ESPECIALLY WHEN YOU COME WITHOUT AN APPOINTMENT . . . I HAVE OTHER CLIENTS TO TAKE CARE OF . . .
THUMP THUMP THUMP
GOD KNOWS WHO--OR WHAT-- THIS IS! LET ME GET THE DOOR BEFORE IT'S KNOCKED IN!
GOOD LORD!
YOU'RE DRENCHED!
HEY, YOU'RE QUICK. THAT WAS SOME "LUNCH HOUR" YOU TOOK--I HAD TO COME BACK THREE TIMES BEFORE YOU DECIDED TO GET BACK TO WORK!
SO YOU HAD TO GO WALKING IN THE RAIN? WHY DIDN'T YOU WAIT IN THE LOBBY?
MAN, I NEED THIS? I SHOULD BE IN SAN DIEGO WITH ALANNA, TELLING HER HOW I FEEL ABOUT HER . . . INSTEAD I'M STUCK IN NEW YORK DURING MONSOON SEASON . . .
. . . AT THE MERCY OF ALANNA'S SECRETARY FROM HELL!
I DON'T HAVE TIME TO WAIT AROUND, AND I HAVEN'T HAD MY LUNCH YET!
THIS IS MY FAULT?
I'VE GOT A VERY BUSY SCHEDULE . . . I'D APPRECIATE IT IF I COULD SEE THOSE DOCUMENTS . . .
DRY OFF FIRST-- I DON'T WANT YOU DRIPPING ALL OVER THEM
UH . . . MAVIS?
YOU HAVE A TOWEL?
WHAT DO YOU THINK THIS IS, THE Y?
LET'S GET SOMETHING STRAIGHT, TOBY. I'M DOING YOU A FAVOR. IF YOU CAN'T GET IT TOGETHER--
LOOK, MABEL, I'M WORKING ON A VERY IMPORTANT CASE-- TIME IS OF THE ESSENCE!
ABOUT THAT CALL? I'LL CHECK WITH YOU LATER . . .
IS THAT SUPPOSED TO IMPRESS ME? AND THE NAME'S MAVIS!
WHATEVER . . . AND DON'T CALL ME TOBY!
I'LL MAKE AN APPOINTMENT . . .
YEESH!

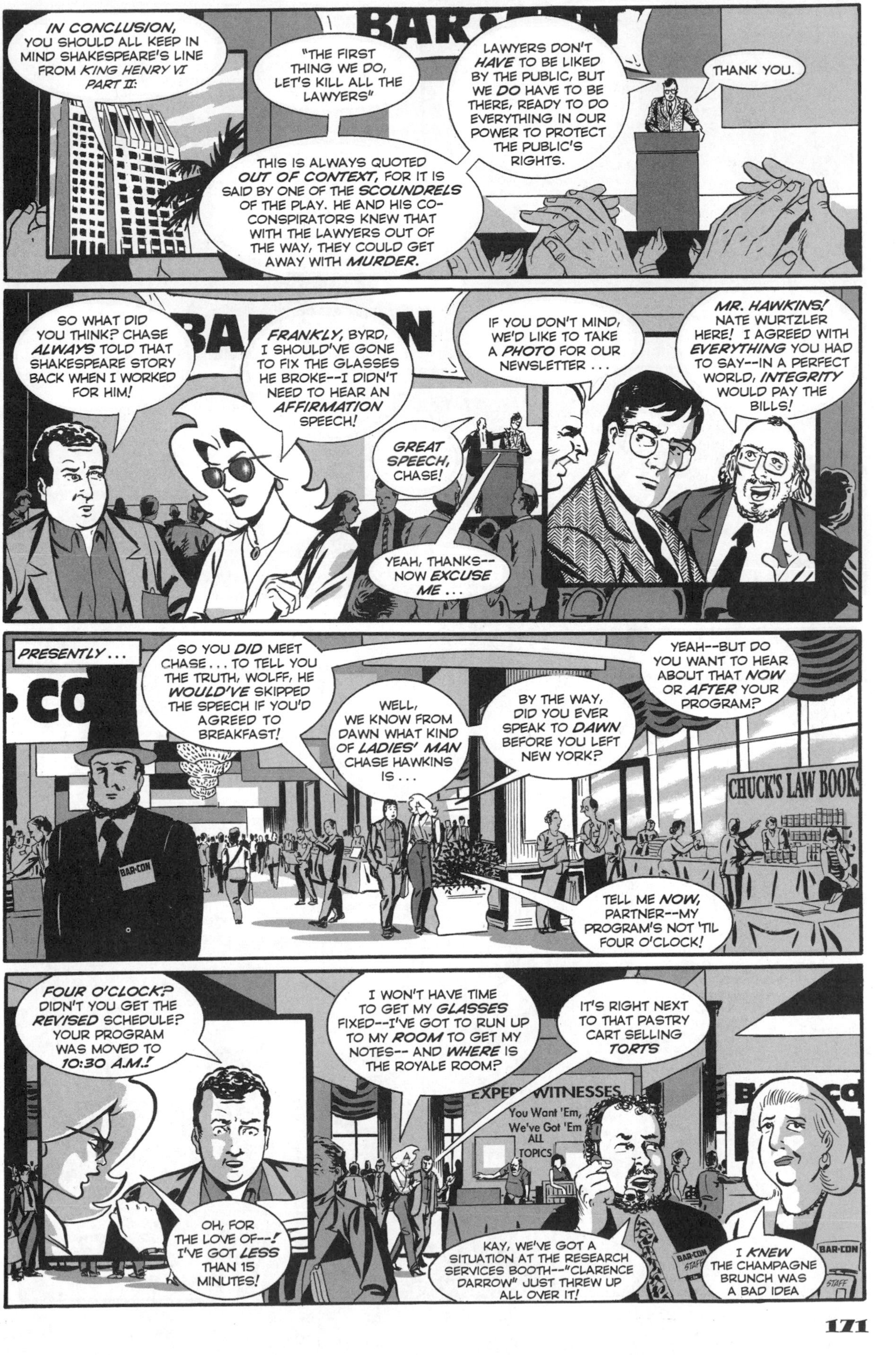

IN CONCLUSION, YOU SHOULD ALL KEEP IN MIND SHAKESPEARE'S LINE FROM KING HENRY VI PART II:
"THE FIRST THING WE DO, LET'S KILL ALL THE LAWYERS"
THIS IS ALWAYS QUOTED OUT OF CONTEXT, FOR IT IS SAID BY ONE OF THE SCOUNDRELS OF THE PLAY. HE AND HIS CO-CONSPIRATORS KNEW THAT WITH THE LAWYERS OUT OF THE WAY, THEY COULD GET AWAY WITH MURDER.
LAWYERS DON'T HAVE TO BE LIKED BY THE PUBLIC, BUT WE DO HAVE TO BE THERE, READY TO DO EVERYTHING IN OUR POWER TO PROTECT THE PUBLIC'S RIGHTS.
THANK YOU.
SO WHAT DID YOU THINK? CHASE ALWAYS TOLD THAT SHAKESPEARE STORY BACK WHEN I WORKED FOR HIM!
FRANKLY, BYRD, I SHOULD'VE GONE TO FIX THE GLASSES HE BROKE--I DIDN'T NEED TO HEAR AN AFFIRMATION SPEECH!
GREAT SPEECH, CHASE!
YEAH, THANKS--NOW EXCUSE ME . . .
IF YOU DON'T MIND, WE'D LIKE TO TAKE A PHOTO FOR OUR NEWSLETTER . . .
MR. HAWKINS! NATE WURTZLER HERE! I AGREED WITH EVERYTHING YOU HAD TO SAY--IN A PERFECT WORLD, INTEGRITY WOULD PAY THE BILLS!
PRESENTLY . . .
SO YOU DID MEET CHASE . . . TO TELL YOU THE TRUTH, WOLFF, HE WOULD'VE SKIPPED THE SPEECH IF YOU'D AGREED TO BREAKFAST!
WELL, WE KNOW FROM DAWN WHAT KIND OF LADIES' MAN CHASE HAWKINS IS . . .
BY THE WAY, DID YOU EVER SPEAK TO DAWN BEFORE YOU LEFT NEW YORK?
YEAH--BUT DO YOU WANT TO HEAR ABOUT THAT NOW OR AFTER YOUR PROGRAM?
TELL ME NOW, PARTNER--MY PROGRAM'S NOT 'TIL FOUR O'CLOCK!
CHUCK'S LAW BOOKS
BAR-CON
FOUR O'CLOCK? DIDN'T YOU GET THE REVISED SCHEDULE? YOUR PROGRAM WAS MOVED TO 10:30 A.M.!
OH, FOR THE LOVE OF--! I'VE GOT LESS THAN 15 MINUTES!
I WON'T HAVE TIME TO GET MY GLASSES FIXED--I'VE GOT TO RUN UP TO MY ROOM TO GET MY NOTES-- AND WHERE IS THE ROYALE ROOM?
IT'S RIGHT NEXT TO THAT PASTRY CART SELLING TORTS
You Want 'Em, We've Got 'Em ALL TOPICS
KAY, WE'VE GOT A SITUATION AT THE RESEARCH SERVICES BOOTH--"CLARENCE DARROW" JUST THREW UP ALL OVER IT!
I KNEW THE CHAMPAGNE BRUNCH WAS A BAD IDEA
BAR-CON STAFF

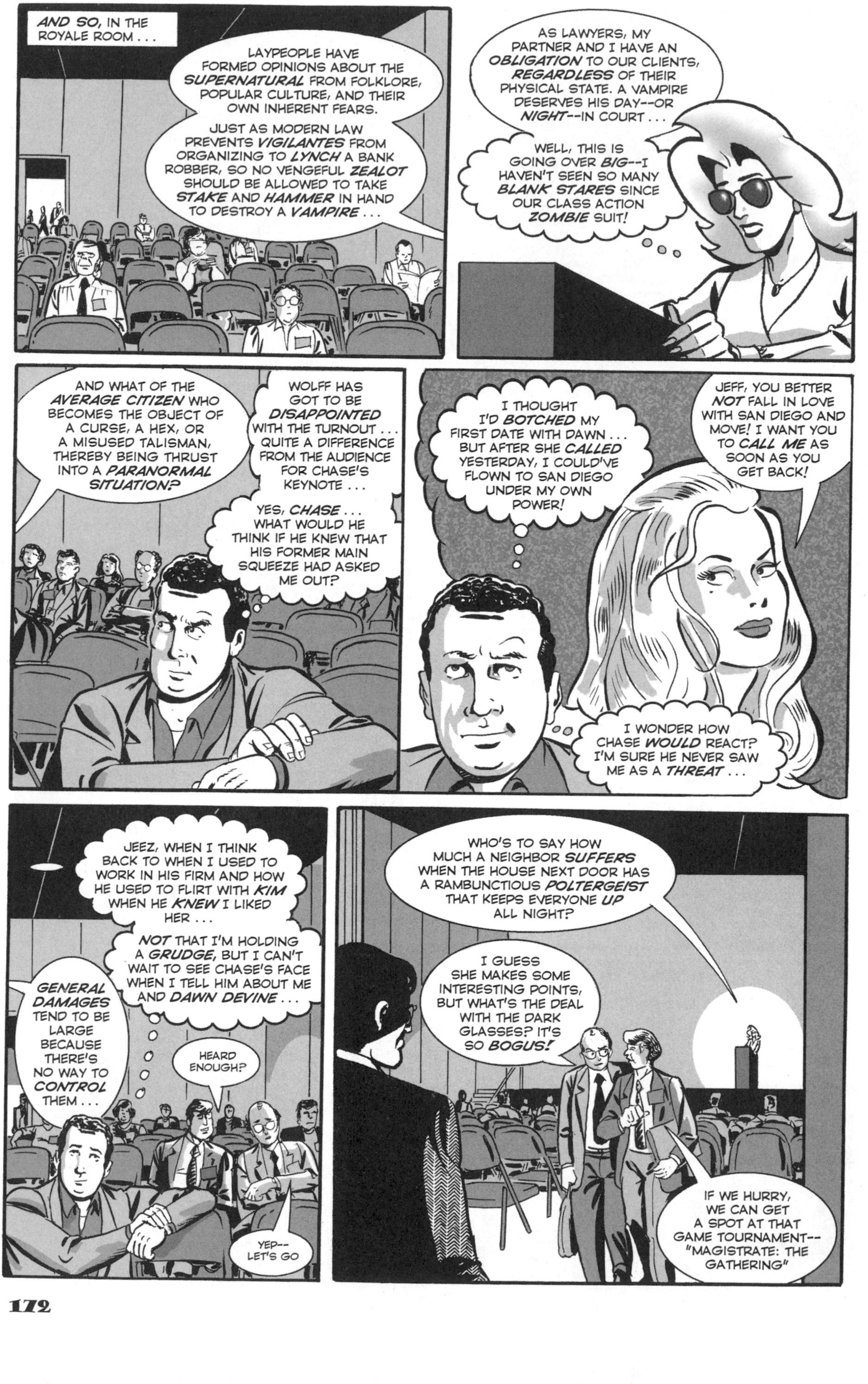

AND SO, IN THE ROYALE ROOM . . .
LAYPEOPLE HAVE FORMED OPINIONS ABOUT THE SUPERNATURAL FROM FOLKLORE, POPULAR CULTURE, AND THEIR OWN INHERENT FEARS.
JUST AS MODERN LAW PREVENTS VIGILANTES FROM ORGANIZING TO LYNCH A BANK ROBBER, SO NO VENGEFUL ZEALOT SHOULD BE ALLOWED TO TAKE STAKE AND HAMMER IN HAND TO DESTROY A VAMPIRE . . .
AS LAWYERS, MY PARTNER AND I HAVE AN OBLIGATION TO OUR CLIENTS, REGARDLESS OF THEIR PHYSICAL STATE. A VAMPIRE DESERVES HIS DAY--OR NIGHT--IN COURT . . .
WELL, THIS IS GOING OVER BIG--I HAVEN'T SEEN SO MANY BLANK STARES SINCE OUR CLASS ACTION ZOMBIE SUIT!
AND WHAT OF THE AVERAGE CITIZEN WHO BECOMES THE OBJECT OF A CURSE, A HEX, OR A MISUSED TALISMAN, THEREBY BEING THRUST INTO A PARANORMAL SITUATION?
WOLFF HAS GOT TO BE DISAPPOINTED WITH THE TURNOUT . . . QUITE A DIFFERENCE FROM THE AUDIENCE FOR CHASE'S KEYNOTE . . .
YES, CHASE . . . WHAT WOULD HE THINK IF HE KNEW THAT HIS FORMER MAIN SQUEEZE HAD ASKED ME OUT?
I THOUGHT I'D BOTCHED MY FIRST DATE WITH DAWN . . . BUT AFTER SHE CALLED YESTERDAY, I COULD'VE FLOWN TO SAN DIEGO UNDER MY OWN POWER!
JEFF, YOU BETTER NOT FALL IN LOVE WITH SAN DIEGO AND MOVE! I WANT YOU TO CALL ME AS SOON AS YOU GET BACK!
I WONDER HOW CHASE WOULD REACT? I'M SURE HE NEVER SAW ME AS A THREAT . . .
JEEZ, WHEN I THINK BACK TO WHEN I USED TO WORK IN HIS FIRM AND HOW HE USED TO FLIRT WITH KIM WHEN HE KNEW I LIKED HER . . .
NOT THAT I'M HOLDING A GRUDGE, BUT I CAN'T WAIT TO SEE CHASE'S FACE WHEN I TELL HIM ABOUT ME AND DAWN DEVINE . . .
GENERAL DAMAGES TEND TO BE LARGE BECAUSE THERE'S NO WAY TO CONTROL THEM . . .
HEARD ENOUGH?
YEP-- LET'S GO
WHO'S TO SAY HOW MUCH A NEIGHBOR SUFFERS WHEN THE HOUSE NEXT DOOR HAS A RAMBUNCTIOUS POLTERGEIST THAT KEEPS EVERYONE UP ALL NIGHT?
I GUESS SHE MAKES SOME INTERESTING POINTS, BUT WHAT'S THE DEAL WITH THE DARK GLASSES? IT'S SO BOGUS!
IF WE HURRY, WE CAN GET A SPOT AT THAT GAME TOURNAMENT-- "MAGISTRATE: THE GATHERING"

YES? YOU HAD A QUESTION--?

KENDALL PETTY, CLERK FOR JUSTICE ENOCH GABLER, NEW YORK STATE COURT OF APPEALS.

UH, MS. WOLFF, I RECALL RESEARCHING A CASE OF YOURS, *IRS V. ROZZOLI*, REGARDING THE AFOREMENTIONED TAX AGENCY'S ABILITY TO PURSUE AN ACTION AGAINST A DECEASED TAXPAYER . . .

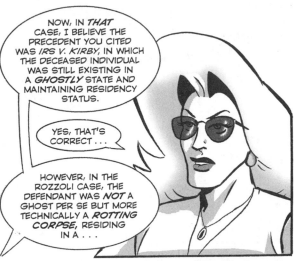

NOW, IN *THAT* CASE, I BELIEVE THE PRECEDENT YOU CITED WAS *IRS V. KIRBY*, IN WHICH THE DECEASED INDIVIDUAL WAS STILL EXISTING IN A *GHOSTLY* STATE AND MAINTAINING RESIDENCY STATUS.

YES, THAT'S CORRECT . . .

HOWEVER, IN THE ROZZOLI CASE, THE DEFENDANT WAS *NOT* A GHOST PER SE BUT MORE TECHNICALLY A *ROTTING CORPSE*, RESIDING IN A . . .

LET'S GO--KENDALL WILL BE CITING CASES ALL AFTERNOON TO SHOW EVERYONE HOW MUCH HE KNOWS

I HEAR SCOTT McZOT IS AUTOGRAPHING "UNDERSTANDING LAW" ON THE MEZZANINE

HOW'S IT GOING, BYRD? IT'S BEEN A *LONG* TIME

CHASE? HI!

BAR-CON

BY THE WAY, *CONGRATULATIONS* ON WINNING *DAWN DEVINE'S* CASE. YOUR FIRM WAS MUCH MORE SUITED TO HANDLING IT THAN MINE . . .

MY ASSOCIATES TELL ME THAT YOU AND YOUR PARTNER WERE SUPERB!

WHY-- WHY, *THANKS*, CHASE

BY ANY CHANCE, ARE YOU STILL IN TOUCH WITH DAWN?

}AHEM{ YOU COULD SAY THAT . . .

DO ME A FAVOR? TELL DAWN TO *STOP* CALLING ME. I *REFUSE* TO TAKE HER CALLS. MY BUSINESS WITH HER IS *OVER*-- PROFESSIONALLY AND PERSONALLY. SINCE YOU'RE HER COUNSEL NOW, ADVISE HER THAT I WON'T HESITATE TO FILE A COMPLAINT IF SHE DOESN'T STOP.

IS-- HAS SHE BEEN CALLING ABOUT HER *BILL?*

I WISH-- BUT I CAN'T SAY ANY MORE. AND ON A *LIGHTER* NOTE . . .

I WANT TO TALK TO YOUR *PARTNER*-- BUT I'LL WAIT OUTSIDE-- I *CAN'T BEAR* TO SIT THROUGH THESE *IMBECILIC* QUESTIONS!

. . . SO MY QUESTION IS, HOW COULD YOU HAVE PROPERLY CITED *IRS V. KIRBY* IN THIS MATTER?

WHAT CAN I SAY? WE JUST WORKED ON THE BASIC ASSUMPTION THAT NOTHING'S CERTAIN BUT *DEATH* AND *TAXES!*

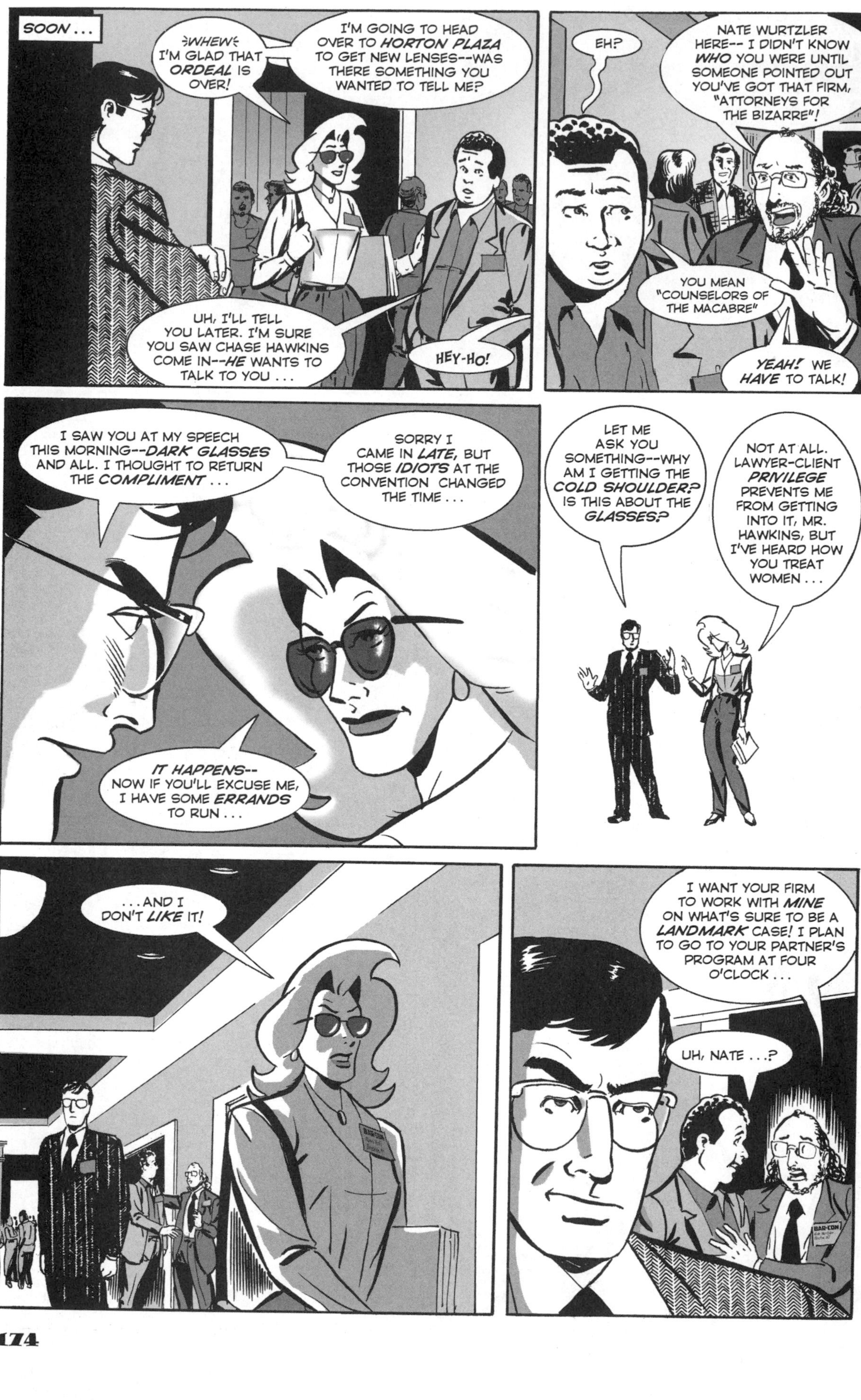
SOON . . .
WHEW! I'M GLAD THAT ORDEAL IS OVER!
I'M GOING TO HEAD OVER TO HORTON PLAZA TO GET NEW LENSES--WAS THERE SOMETHING YOU WANTED TO TELL ME?
UH, I'LL TELL YOU LATER. I'M SURE YOU SAW CHASE HAWKINS COME IN--HE WANTS TO TALK TO YOU . . .
HEY-HO!
EH?
NATE WURTZLER HERE-- I DIDN'T KNOW WHO YOU WERE UNTIL SOMEONE POINTED OUT YOU'VE GOT THAT FIRM, "ATTORNEYS FOR THE BIZARRE"!
YOU MEAN "COUNSELORS OF THE MACABRE"
YEAH! WE HAVE TO TALK!
I SAW YOU AT MY SPEECH THIS MORNING--DARK GLASSES AND ALL. I THOUGHT TO RETURN THE COMPLIMENT . . .
SORRY I CAME IN LATE, BUT THOSE IDIOTS AT THE CONVENTION CHANGED THE TIME . . .
IT HAPPENS-- NOW IF YOU'LL EXCUSE ME, I HAVE SOME ERRANDS TO RUN . . .
LET ME ASK YOU SOMETHING--WHY AM I GETTING THE COLD SHOULDER? IS THIS ABOUT THE GLASSES?
NOT AT ALL. LAWYER-CLIENT PRIVILEGE PREVENTS ME FROM GETTING INTO IT, MR. HAWKINS, BUT I'VE HEARD HOW YOU TREAT WOMEN . . .
. . . AND I DON'T LIKE IT!
I WANT YOUR FIRM TO WORK WITH MINE ON WHAT'S SURE TO BE A LANDMARK CASE! I PLAN TO GO TO YOUR PARTNER'S PROGRAM AT FOUR O'CLOCK . . .
UH, NATE . . .?
BAD-CON

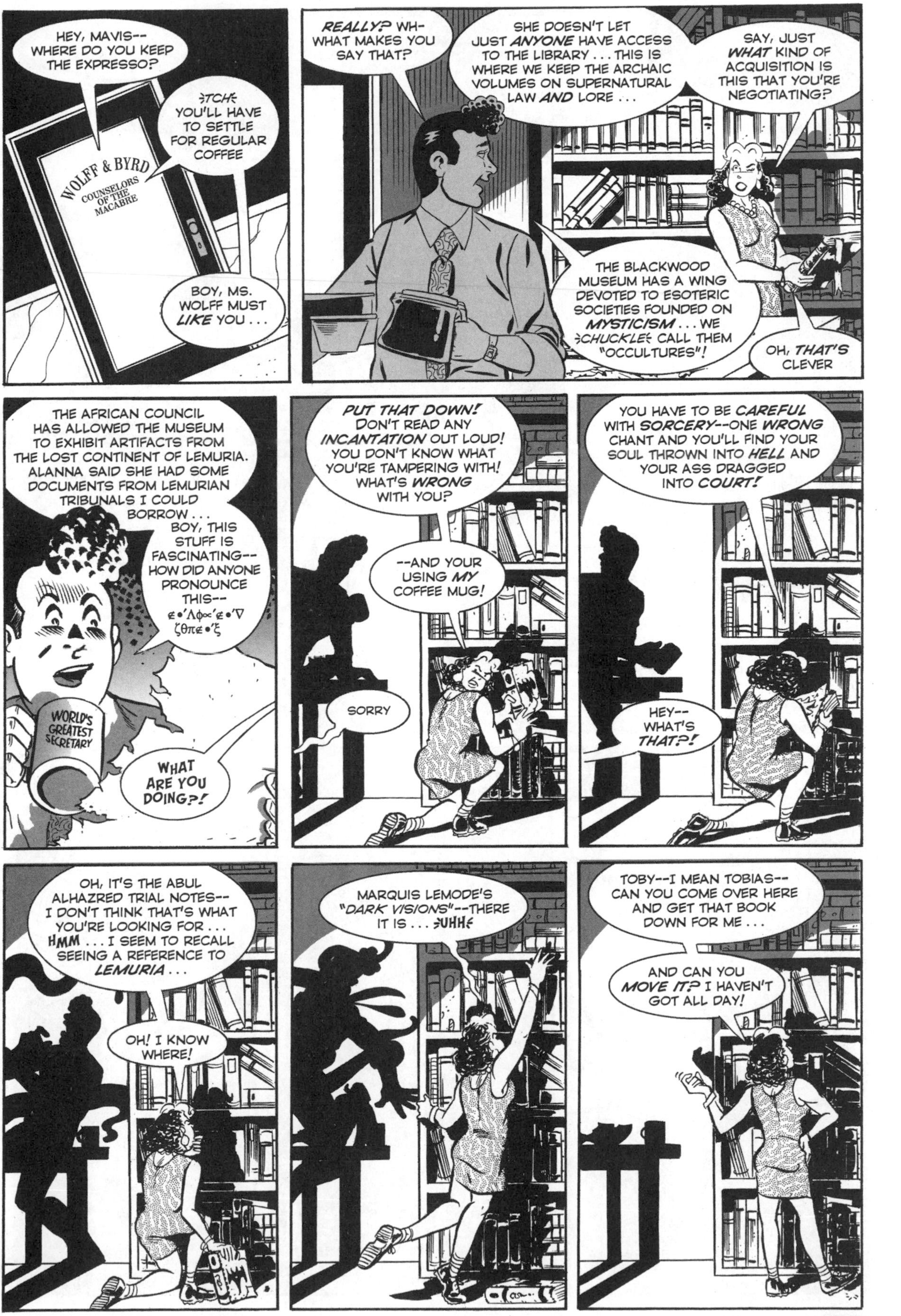

HEY, MAVIS-- WHERE DO YOU KEEP THE EXPRESSO?
WOLFF & BYRD COUNSELORS OF THE MACABRE
≷TCH≶ YOU'LL HAVE TO SETTLE FOR REGULAR COFFEE
BOY, MS. WOLFF MUST *LIKE* YOU . . .
REALLY? WH- WHAT MAKES YOU SAY THAT?
SHE DOESN'T LET JUST *ANYONE* HAVE ACCESS TO THE LIBRARY . . . THIS IS WHERE WE KEEP THE ARCHAIC VOLUMES ON SUPERNATURAL LAW *AND* LORE . . .
SAY, JUST *WHAT* KIND OF ACQUISITION IS THIS THAT YOU'RE NEGOTIATING?
THE BLACKWOOD MUSEUM HAS A WING DEVOTED TO ESOTERIC SOCIETIES FOUNDED ON *MYSTICISM* . . . WE ≷CHUCKLE≶ CALL THEM "OCCULTURES"!
OH, *THAT'S* CLEVER
THE AFRICAN COUNCIL HAS ALLOWED THE MUSEUM TO EXHIBIT ARTIFACTS FROM THE LOST CONTINENT OF LEMURIA. ALANNA SAID SHE HAD SOME DOCUMENTS FROM LEMURIAN TRIBUNALS I COULD BORROW . . .
BOY, THIS STUFF IS FASCINATING-- HOW DID ANYONE PRONOUNCE THIS--
WORLD'S GREATEST SECRETARY
WHAT ARE YOU DOING?!
PUT THAT DOWN! DON'T READ ANY *INCANTATION* OUT LOUD! YOU DON'T KNOW WHAT YOU'RE TAMPERING WITH! WHAT'S *WRONG* WITH YOU?
--AND YOUR USING *MY* COFFEE MUG!
SORRY
YOU HAVE TO BE *CAREFUL* WITH *SORCERY*--ONE *WRONG* CHANT AND YOU'LL FIND YOUR SOUL THROWN INTO *HELL* AND YOUR ASS DRAGGED INTO *COURT!*
HEY-- WHAT'S *THAT?!*
OH, IT'S THE ABUL ALHAZRED TRIAL NOTES-- I DON'T THINK THAT'S WHAT YOU'RE LOOKING FOR . . . HMM . . . I SEEM TO RECALL SEEING A REFERENCE TO *LEMURIA* . . .
OH! I KNOW WHERE!
MARQUIS LEMODE'S "*DARK VISIONS*"--THERE IT IS . . . ≷UHH≶
TOBY--I MEAN TOBIAS-- CAN YOU COME OVER HERE AND GET THAT BOOK DOWN FOR ME . . .
AND CAN YOU *MOVE IT?* I HAVEN'T GOT ALL DAY!

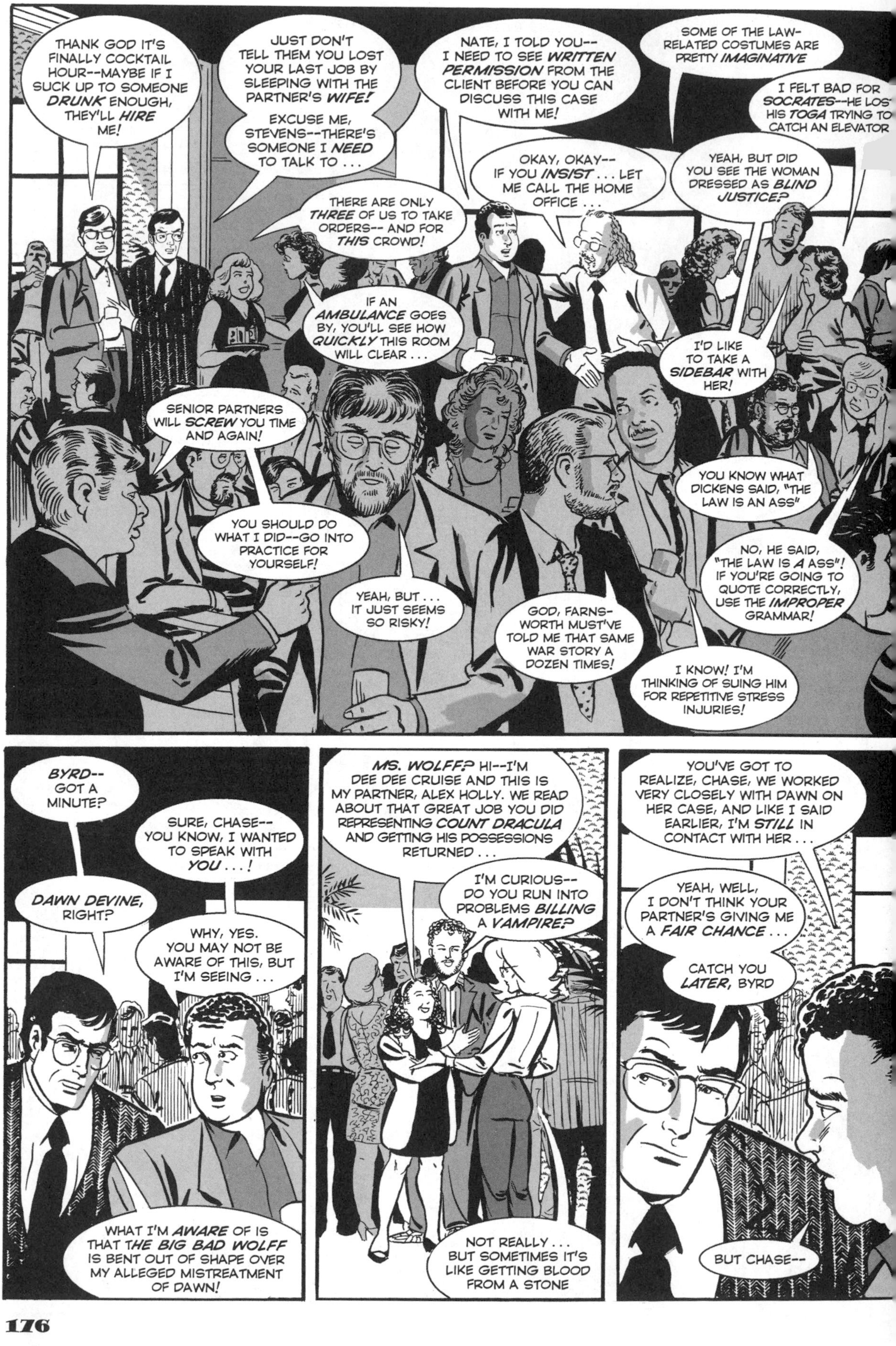

THANK GOD IT'S FINALLY COCKTAIL HOUR--MAYBE IF I SUCK UP TO SOMEONE DRUNK ENOUGH, THEY'LL HIRE ME!
JUST DON'T TELL THEM YOU LOST YOUR LAST JOB BY SLEEPING WITH THE PARTNER'S WIFE!
EXCUSE ME, STEVENS--THERE'S SOMEONE I NEED TO TALK TO . . .
THERE ARE ONLY THREE OF US TO TAKE ORDERS-- AND FOR THIS CROWD!
NATE, I TOLD YOU-- I NEED TO SEE WRITTEN PERMISSION FROM THE CLIENT BEFORE YOU CAN DISCUSS THIS CASE WITH ME!
OKAY, OKAY-- IF YOU INSIST . . . LET ME CALL THE HOME OFFICE . . .
SOME OF THE LAW-RELATED COSTUMES ARE PRETTY IMAGINATIVE
I FELT BAD FOR SOCRATES--HE LOST HIS TOGA TRYING TO CATCH AN ELEVATOR
YEAH, BUT DID YOU SEE THE WOMAN DRESSED AS BLIND JUSTICE?
I'D LIKE TO TAKE A SIDEBAR WITH HER!
IF AN AMBULANCE GOES BY, YOU'LL SEE HOW QUICKLY THIS ROOM WILL CLEAR . . .
SENIOR PARTNERS WILL SCREW YOU TIME AND AGAIN!
YOU SHOULD DO WHAT I DID--GO INTO PRACTICE FOR YOURSELF!
YEAH, BUT . . . IT JUST SEEMS SO RISKY!
GOD, FARNSWORTH MUST'VE TOLD ME THAT SAME WAR STORY A DOZEN TIMES!
I KNOW! I'M THINKING OF SUING HIM FOR REPETITIVE STRESS INJURIES!
YOU KNOW WHAT DICKENS SAID, "THE LAW IS AN ASS"
NO, HE SAID, "THE LAW IS A ASS"! IF YOU'RE GOING TO QUOTE CORRECTLY, USE THE IMPROPER GRAMMAR!
BYRD-- GOT A MINUTE?
SURE, CHASE-- YOU KNOW, I WANTED TO SPEAK WITH YOU . . . !
DAWN DEVINE, RIGHT?
WHY, YES. YOU MAY NOT BE AWARE OF THIS, BUT I'M SEEING . . .
WHAT I'M AWARE OF IS THAT THE BIG BAD WOLFF IS BENT OUT OF SHAPE OVER MY ALLEGED MISTREATMENT OF DAWN!
MS. WOLFF? HI--I'M DEE DEE CRUISE AND THIS IS MY PARTNER, ALEX HOLLY. WE READ ABOUT THAT GREAT JOB YOU DID REPRESENTING COUNT DRACULA AND GETTING HIS POSSESSIONS RETURNED . . .
I'M CURIOUS-- DO YOU RUN INTO PROBLEMS BILLING A VAMPIRE?
NOT REALLY . . . BUT SOMETIMES IT'S LIKE GETTING BLOOD FROM A STONE
YOU'VE GOT TO REALIZE, CHASE, WE WORKED VERY CLOSELY WITH DAWN ON HER CASE, AND LIKE I SAID EARLIER, I'M STILL IN CONTACT WITH HER . . .
YEAH, WELL, I DON'T THINK YOUR PARTNER'S GIVING ME A FAIR CHANCE . . .
CATCH YOU LATER, BYRD
BUT CHASE--

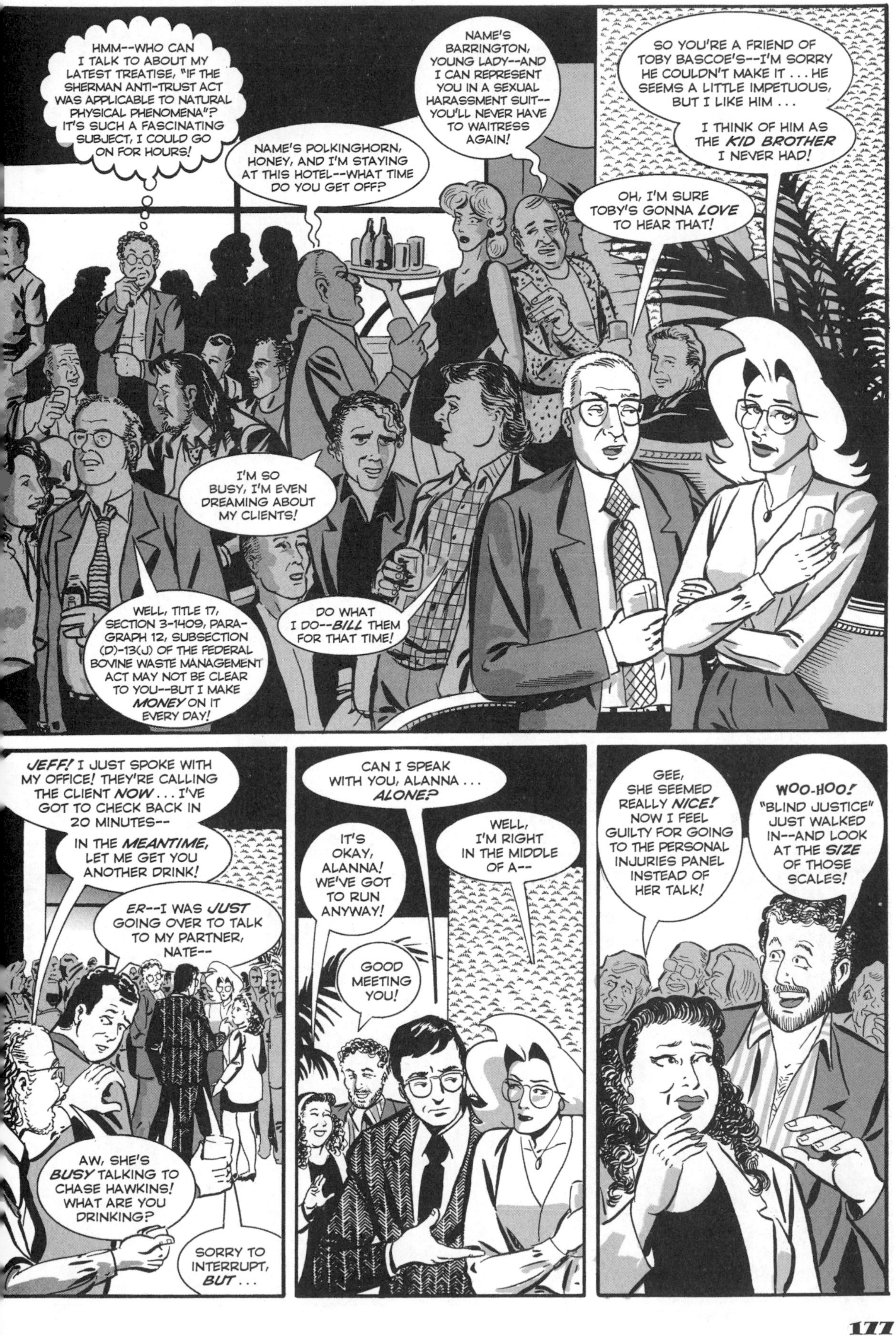
HMM--WHO CAN I TALK TO ABOUT MY LATEST TREATISE, "IF THE SHERMAN ANTI-TRUST ACT WAS APPLICABLE TO NATURAL PHYSICAL PHENOMENA"? IT'S SUCH A FASCINATING SUBJECT, I COULD GO ON FOR HOURS!
NAME'S POLKINGHORN, HONEY, AND I'M STAYING AT THIS HOTEL--WHAT TIME DO YOU GET OFF?
NAME'S BARRINGTON, YOUNG LADY--AND I CAN REPRESENT YOU IN A SEXUAL HARASSMENT SUIT--YOU'LL NEVER HAVE TO WAITRESS AGAIN!
SO YOU'RE A FRIEND OF TOBY BASCOE'S--I'M SORRY HE COULDN'T MAKE IT . . . HE SEEMS A LITTLE IMPETUOUS, BUT I LIKE HIM . . .
I THINK OF HIM AS THE KID BROTHER I NEVER HAD!
OH, I'M SURE TOBY'S GONNA LOVE TO HEAR THAT!
I'M SO BUSY, I'M EVEN DREAMING ABOUT MY CLIENTS!
WELL, TITLE 17, SECTION 3-1409, PARAGRAPH 12, SUBSECTION (D)-13(J) OF THE FEDERAL BOVINE WASTE MANAGEMENT ACT MAY NOT BE CLEAR TO YOU--BUT I MAKE MONEY ON IT EVERY DAY!
DO WHAT I DO--BILL THEM FOR THAT TIME!
JEFF! I JUST SPOKE WITH MY OFFICE! THEY'RE CALLING THE CLIENT NOW . . . I'VE GOT TO CHECK BACK IN 20 MINUTES--
IN THE MEANTIME, LET ME GET YOU ANOTHER DRINK!
ER--I WAS JUST GOING OVER TO TALK TO MY PARTNER, NATE--
AW, SHE'S BUSY TALKING TO CHASE HAWKINS! WHAT ARE YOU DRINKING?
SORRY TO INTERRUPT, BUT . . .
CAN I SPEAK WITH YOU, ALANNA . . . ALONE?
WELL, I'M RIGHT IN THE MIDDLE OF A--
IT'S OKAY, ALANNA! WE'VE GOT TO RUN ANYWAY!
GOOD MEETING YOU!
GEE, SHE SEEMED REALLY NICE! NOW I FEEL GUILTY FOR GOING TO THE PERSONAL INJURIES PANEL INSTEAD OF HER TALK!
WOO-HOO! "BLIND JUSTICE" JUST WALKED IN--AND LOOK AT THE SIZE OF THOSE SCALES!

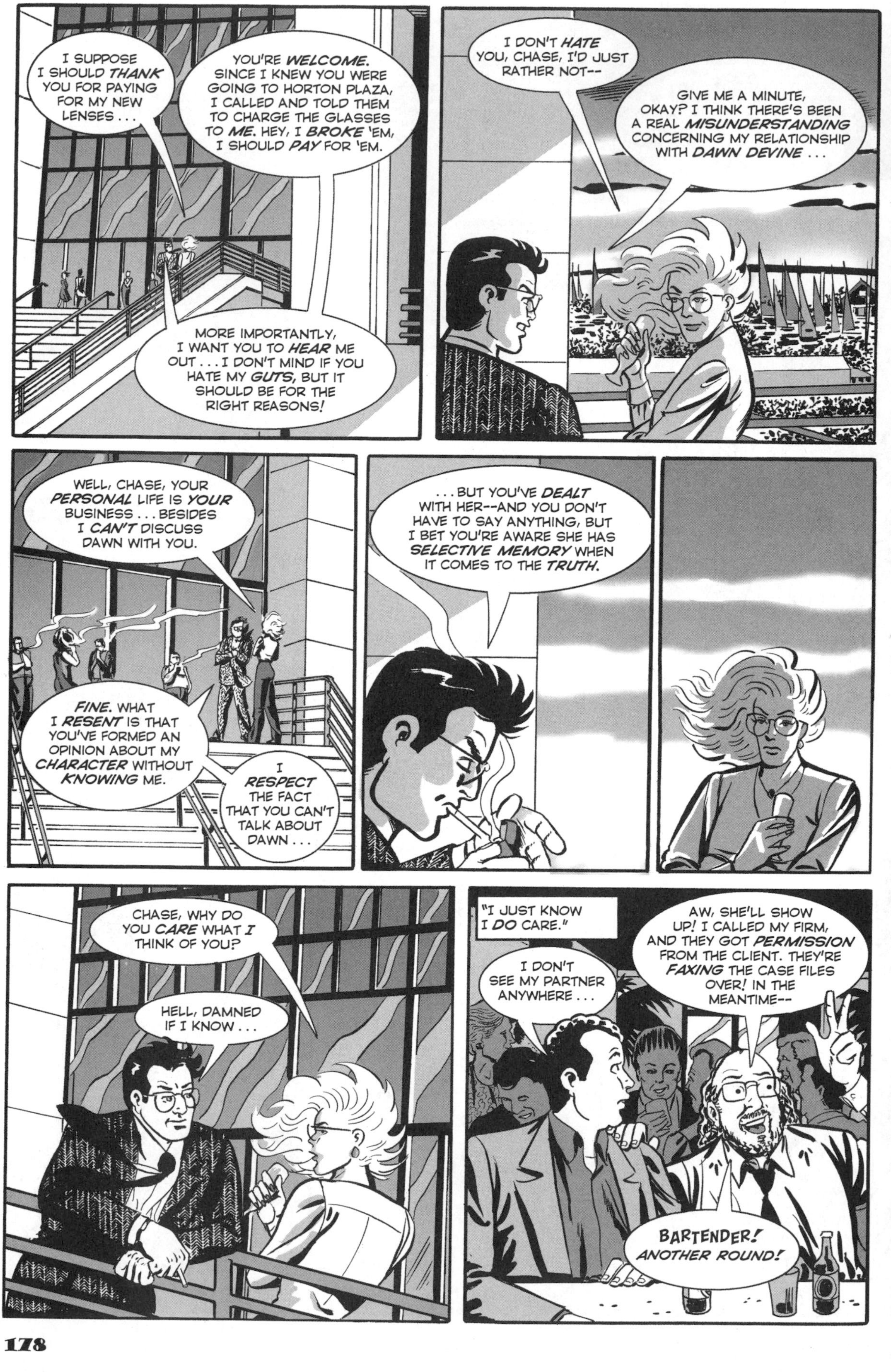
I SUPPOSE I SHOULD THANK YOU FOR PAYING FOR MY NEW LENSES . . .
YOU'RE WELCOME. SINCE I KNEW YOU WERE GOING TO HORTON PLAZA, I CALLED AND TOLD THEM TO CHARGE THE GLASSES TO ME. HEY, I BROKE 'EM, I SHOULD PAY FOR 'EM.
MORE IMPORTANTLY, I WANT YOU TO HEAR ME OUT . . . I DON'T MIND IF YOU HATE MY GUTS, BUT IT SHOULD BE FOR THE RIGHT REASONS!
I DON'T HATE YOU, CHASE, I'D JUST RATHER NOT--
GIVE ME A MINUTE, OKAY? I THINK THERE'S BEEN A REAL MISUNDERSTANDING CONCERNING MY RELATIONSHIP WITH DAWN DEVINE . . .
WELL, CHASE, YOUR PERSONAL LIFE IS YOUR BUSINESS . . . BESIDES I CAN'T DISCUSS DAWN WITH YOU.
FINE. WHAT I RESENT IS THAT YOU'VE FORMED AN OPINION ABOUT MY CHARACTER WITHOUT KNOWING ME.
I RESPECT THE FACT THAT YOU CAN'T TALK ABOUT DAWN . . .
. . . BUT YOU'VE DEALT WITH HER--AND YOU DON'T HAVE TO SAY ANYTHING, BUT I BET YOU'RE AWARE SHE HAS SELECTIVE MEMORY WHEN IT COMES TO THE TRUTH.
CHASE, WHY DO YOU CARE WHAT I THINK OF YOU?
HELL, DAMNED IF I KNOW . . .
"I JUST KNOW I DO CARE."
I DON'T SEE MY PARTNER ANYWHERE . . .
AW, SHE'LL SHOW UP! I CALLED MY FIRM, AND THEY GOT PERMISSION FROM THE CLIENT. THEY'RE FAXING THE CASE FILES OVER! IN THE MEANTIME--
BARTENDER! ANOTHER ROUND!

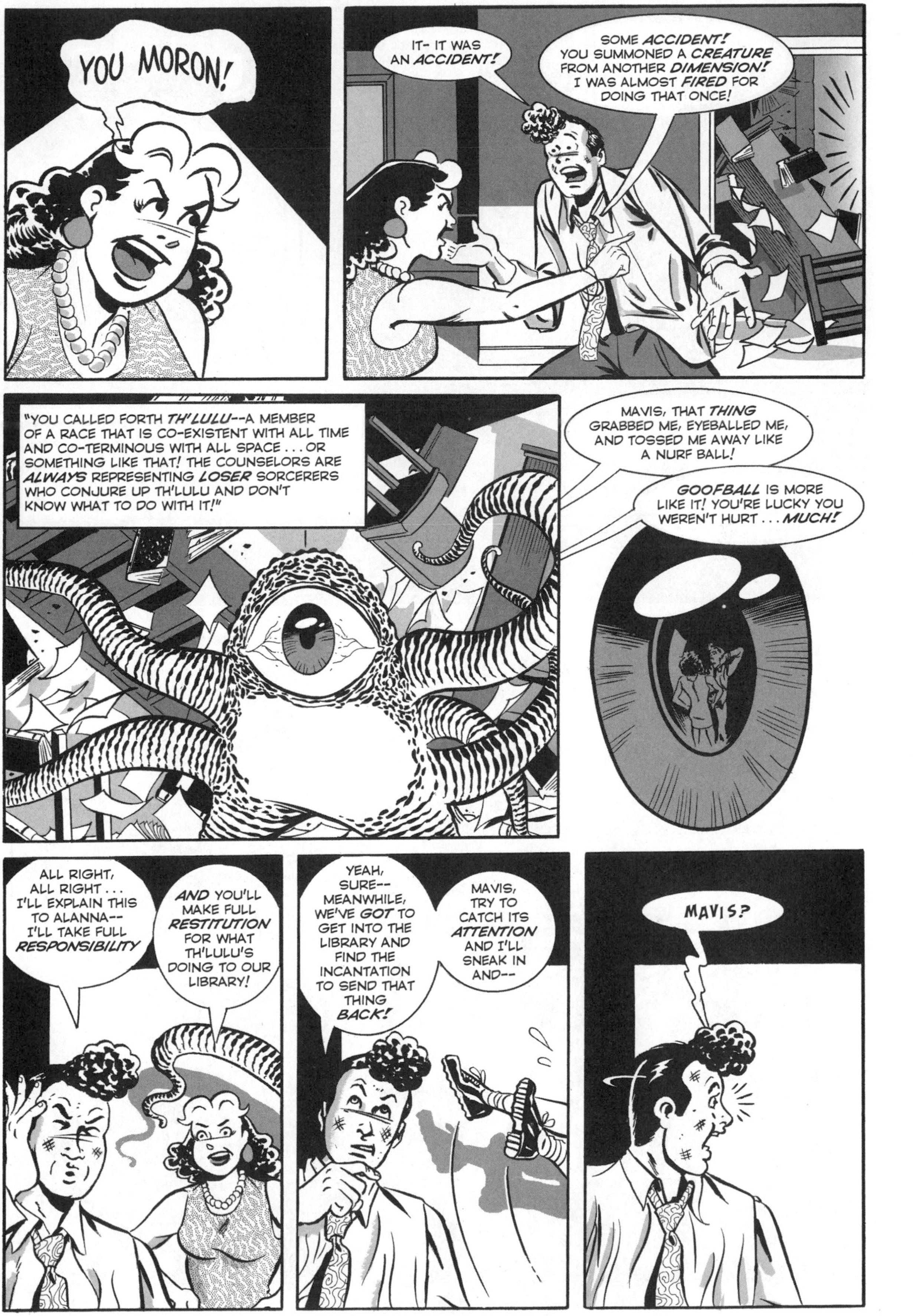

YOU MORON!
IT- IT WAS AN ACCIDENT!
SOME ACCIDENT! YOU SUMMONED A CREATURE FROM ANOTHER DIMENSION! I WAS ALMOST FIRED FOR DOING THAT ONCE!
"YOU CALLED FORTH TH'LULU--A MEMBER OF A RACE THAT IS CO-EXISTENT WITH ALL TIME AND CO-TERMINOUS WITH ALL SPACE . . . OR SOMETHING LIKE THAT! THE COUNSELORS ARE ALWAYS REPRESENTING LOSER SORCERERS WHO CONJURE UP TH'LULU AND DON'T KNOW WHAT TO DO WITH IT!"
MAVIS, THAT THING GRABBED ME, EYEBALLED ME, AND TOSSED ME AWAY LIKE A NURF BALL!
GOOFBALL IS MORE LIKE IT! YOU'RE LUCKY YOU WEREN'T HURT . . . MUCH!
ALL RIGHT, ALL RIGHT . . . I'LL EXPLAIN THIS TO ALANNA-- I'LL TAKE FULL RESPONSIBILITY
AND YOU'LL MAKE FULL RESTITUTION FOR WHAT TH'LULU'S DOING TO OUR LIBRARY!
YEAH, SURE-- MEANWHILE, WE'VE GOT TO GET INTO THE LIBRARY AND FIND THE INCANTATION TO SEND THAT THING BACK!
MAVIS, TRY TO CATCH ITS ATTENTION AND I'LL SNEAK IN AND--
MAVIS?

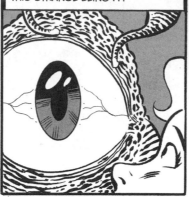

LEGEND HAD DESCRIBED TH'LULU AS INDESCRIBABLE. THE BEST THAT PEOPLE COULD COME UP WITH WAS "THE HAUNTER FROM THE STARS," "SHAMBLER OF THE DARK," OR "THE GREAT OOGLY MOOGLY" . . . IT WAS MERELY *TH'LULU*, AND IT WALKS THE EARTH AGAIN . . .

TH'LULU EXAMINES THE CREATURE BEFORE IT . . . ITS SWEET SCENT IS NOT *UNPLEASANT*, AND ITS SHAPE IS EASY ON THE EYE . . . TH'LULU DOES NOT *UNDERSTAND* THIS STRANGE BEING . . .

. . . BUT TH'LULU *KNOWS* WHAT IT *LIKES!*

≶S'GH≷

RUN, MAVIS! I'LL STOP THIS THING--

BY THE TIME I'M THROUGH WITH IT, ALL THE *VISINE* IN THE WORLD WON'T BE ABLE TO HELP IT!

TOBY! NO! IT DOESN'T MEAN ANY--

#UGH! YGNAIIH?!

CRACK

THUD

WHAM!

BAM

WHACK

CRUNCH

#

BLAM

STOMP

SMASH

CRASH

UF DAH!

ALL RIGHT... HAD ENOUGH ...?

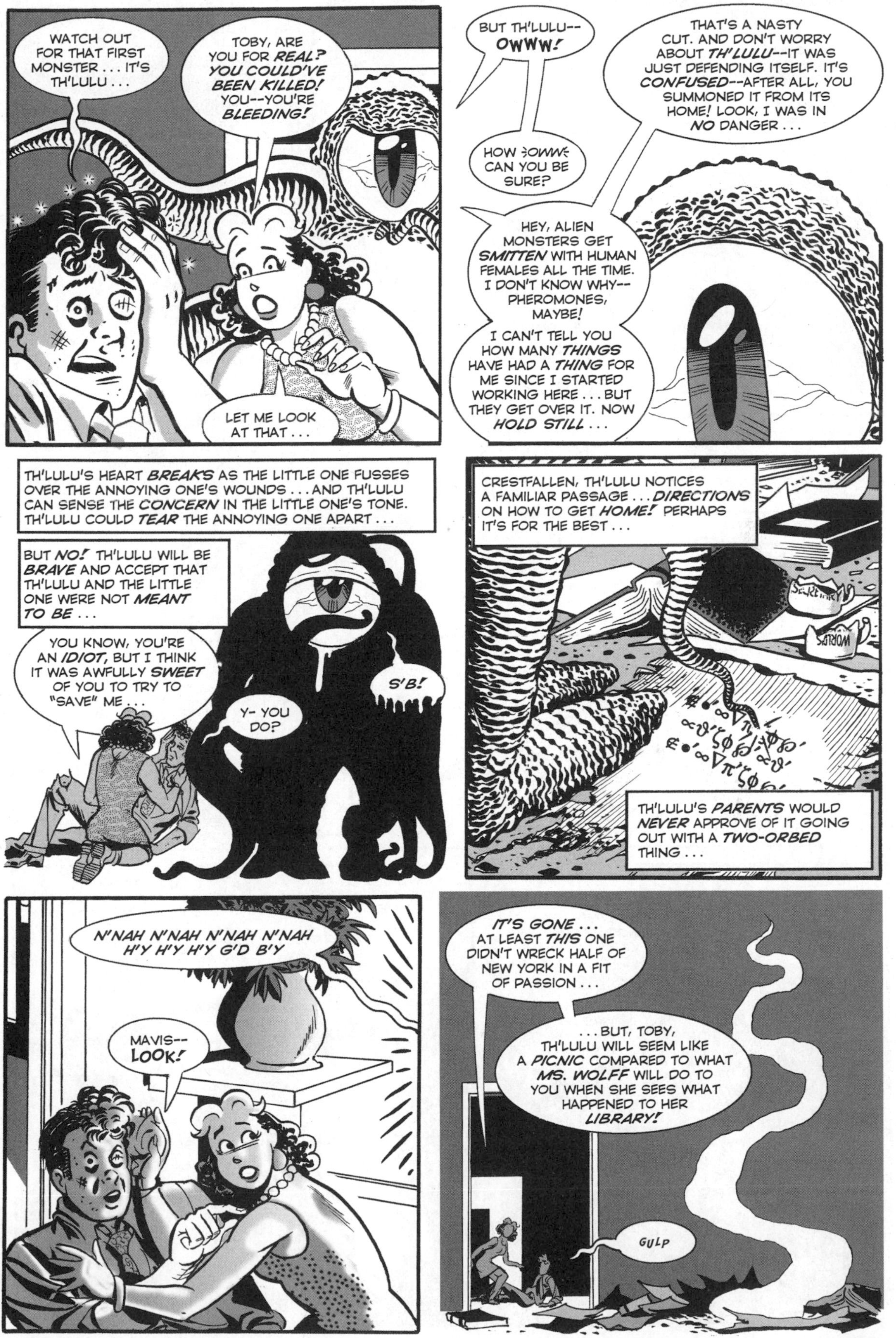
WATCH OUT FOR THAT FIRST MONSTER . . . IT'S TH'LULU . . .
TOBY, ARE YOU FOR *REAL?* *YOU COULD'VE BEEN KILLED!* YOU--YOU'RE *BLEEDING!*
LET ME LOOK AT THAT . . .
BUT TH'LULU-- **OWWW!**
HOW ≶OWW≷ CAN YOU BE SURE?
THAT'S A NASTY CUT. AND DON'T WORRY ABOUT *TH'LULU*--IT WAS JUST DEFENDING ITSELF. IT'S *CONFUSED*--AFTER ALL, YOU SUMMONED IT FROM ITS HOME! LOOK, I WAS IN *NO* DANGER . . .
HEY, ALIEN MONSTERS GET *SMITTEN* WITH HUMAN FEMALES ALL THE TIME. I DON'T KNOW WHY-- PHEROMONES, MAYBE!
I CAN'T TELL YOU HOW MANY *THINGS* HAVE HAD A *THING* FOR ME SINCE I STARTED WORKING HERE . . . BUT THEY GET OVER IT. NOW *HOLD STILL* . . .
TH'LULU'S HEART *BREAKS* AS THE LITTLE ONE FUSSES OVER THE ANNOYING ONE'S WOUNDS . . . AND TH'LULU CAN SENSE THE *CONCERN* IN THE LITTLE ONE'S TONE. TH'LULU COULD *TEAR* THE ANNOYING ONE APART . . .
BUT *NO!* TH'LULU WILL BE *BRAVE* AND ACCEPT THAT TH'LULU AND THE LITTLE ONE WERE NOT *MEANT TO BE* . . .
YOU KNOW, YOU'RE AN *IDIOT*, BUT I THINK IT WAS AWFULLY *SWEET* OF YOU TO TRY TO "SAVE" ME . . .
Y- YOU DO?
S'B!
CRESTFALLEN, TH'LULU NOTICES A FAMILIAR PASSAGE . . . *DIRECTIONS* ON HOW TO GET *HOME!* PERHAPS IT'S FOR THE BEST . . .
TH'LULU'S *PARENTS* WOULD *NEVER* APPROVE OF IT GOING OUT WITH A *TWO-ORBED* THING . . .
N'NAH N'NAH N'NAH N'NAH H'Y H'Y H'Y G'D B'Y
MAVIS-- **LOOK!**
IT'S GONE . . . AT LEAST *THIS* ONE DIDN'T WRECK HALF OF NEW YORK IN A FIT OF PASSION . . .
. . . BUT, TOBY, TH'LULU WILL SEEM LIKE A *PICNIC* COMPARED TO WHAT *MS. WOLFF* WILL DO TO YOU WHEN SHE SEES WHAT HAPPENED TO HER *LIBRARY!*
GULP

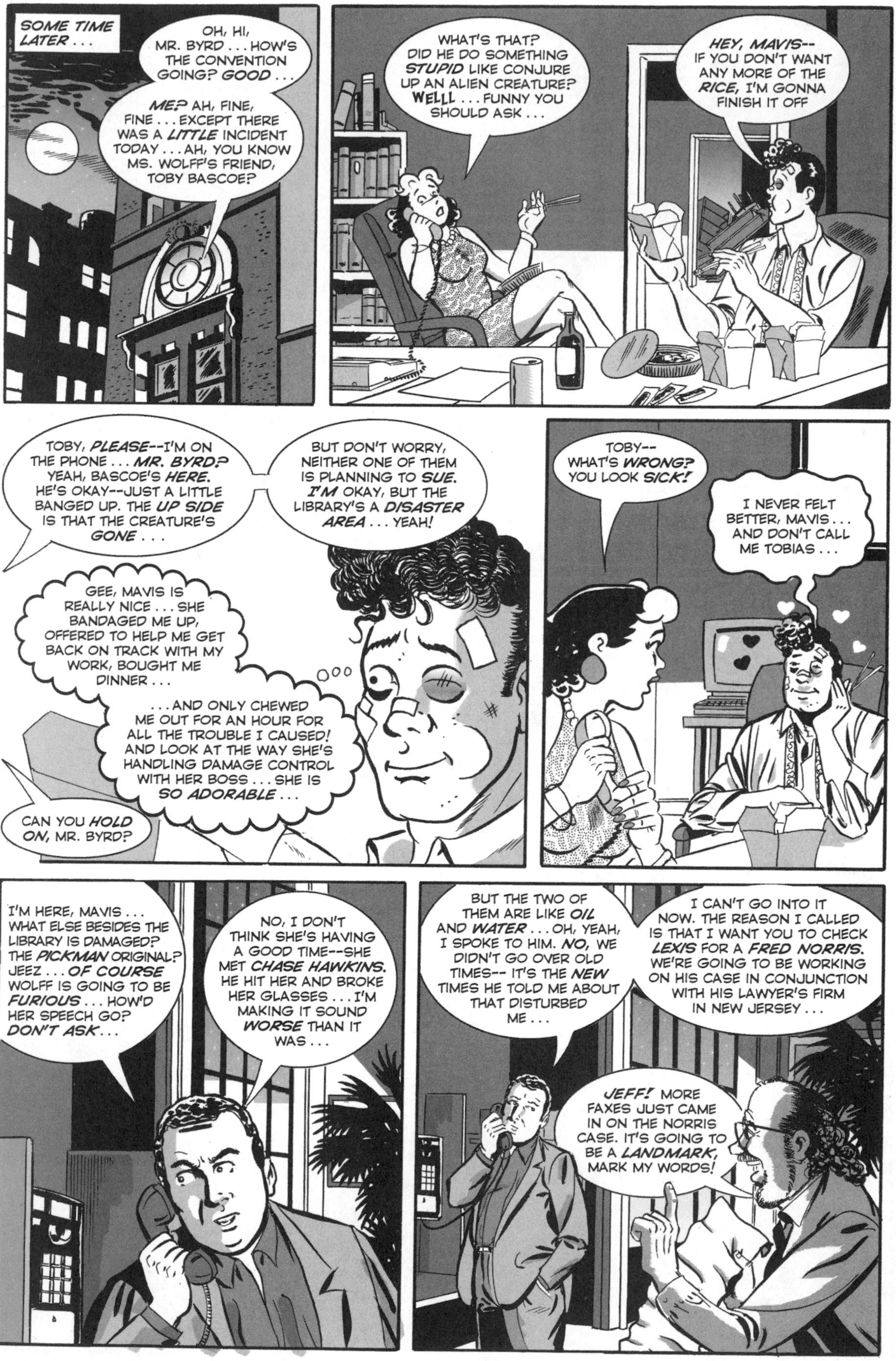
SOME TIME LATER . . .
OH, HI, MR. BYRD . . . HOW'S THE CONVENTION GOING? GOOD . . .
ME? AH, FINE, FINE . . . EXCEPT THERE WAS A LITTLE INCIDENT TODAY . . . AH, YOU KNOW MS. WOLFF'S FRIEND, TOBY BASCOE?
WHAT'S THAT? DID HE DO SOMETHING STUPID LIKE CONJURE UP AN ALIEN CREATURE? WELLL . . . FUNNY YOU SHOULD ASK . . .
HEY, MAVIS-- IF YOU DON'T WANT ANY MORE OF THE RICE, I'M GONNA FINISH IT OFF
TOBY, PLEASE--I'M ON THE PHONE . . . MR. BYRD? YEAH, BASCOE'S HERE. HE'S OKAY--JUST A LITTLE BANGED UP. THE UP SIDE IS THAT THE CREATURE'S GONE . . .
BUT DON'T WORRY, NEITHER ONE OF THEM IS PLANNING TO SUE. I'M OKAY, BUT THE LIBRARY'S A DISASTER AREA . . . YEAH!
GEE, MAVIS IS REALLY NICE . . . SHE BANDAGED ME UP, OFFERED TO HELP ME GET BACK ON TRACK WITH MY WORK, BOUGHT ME DINNER . . .
. . . AND ONLY CHEWED ME OUT FOR AN HOUR FOR ALL THE TROUBLE I CAUSED! AND LOOK AT THE WAY SHE'S HANDLING DAMAGE CONTROL WITH HER BOSS . . . SHE IS SO ADORABLE . . .
CAN YOU HOLD ON, MR. BYRD?
TOBY-- WHAT'S WRONG? YOU LOOK SICK!
I NEVER FELT BETTER, MAVIS . . . AND DON'T CALL ME TOBIAS . . .
I'M HERE, MAVIS . . . WHAT ELSE BESIDES THE LIBRARY IS DAMAGED? THE PICKMAN ORIGINAL? JEEZ . . . OF COURSE WOLFF IS GOING TO BE FURIOUS . . . HOW'D HER SPEECH GO? DON'T ASK . . .
NO, I DON'T THINK SHE'S HAVING A GOOD TIME--SHE MET CHASE HAWKINS. HE HIT HER AND BROKE HER GLASSES . . . I'M MAKING IT SOUND WORSE THAN IT WAS . . .
BUT THE TWO OF THEM ARE LIKE OIL AND WATER . . . OH, YEAH, I SPOKE TO HIM. NO, WE DIDN'T GO OVER OLD TIMES-- IT'S THE NEW TIMES HE TOLD ME ABOUT THAT DISTURBED ME . . .
I CAN'T GO INTO IT NOW. THE REASON I CALLED IS THAT I WANT YOU TO CHECK LEXIS FOR A FRED NORRIS. WE'RE GOING TO BE WORKING ON HIS CASE IN CONJUNCTION WITH HIS LAWYER'S FIRM IN NEW JERSEY . . .
JEFF! MORE FAXES JUST CAME IN ON THE NORRIS CASE. IT'S GOING TO BE A LANDMARK, MARK MY WORDS!

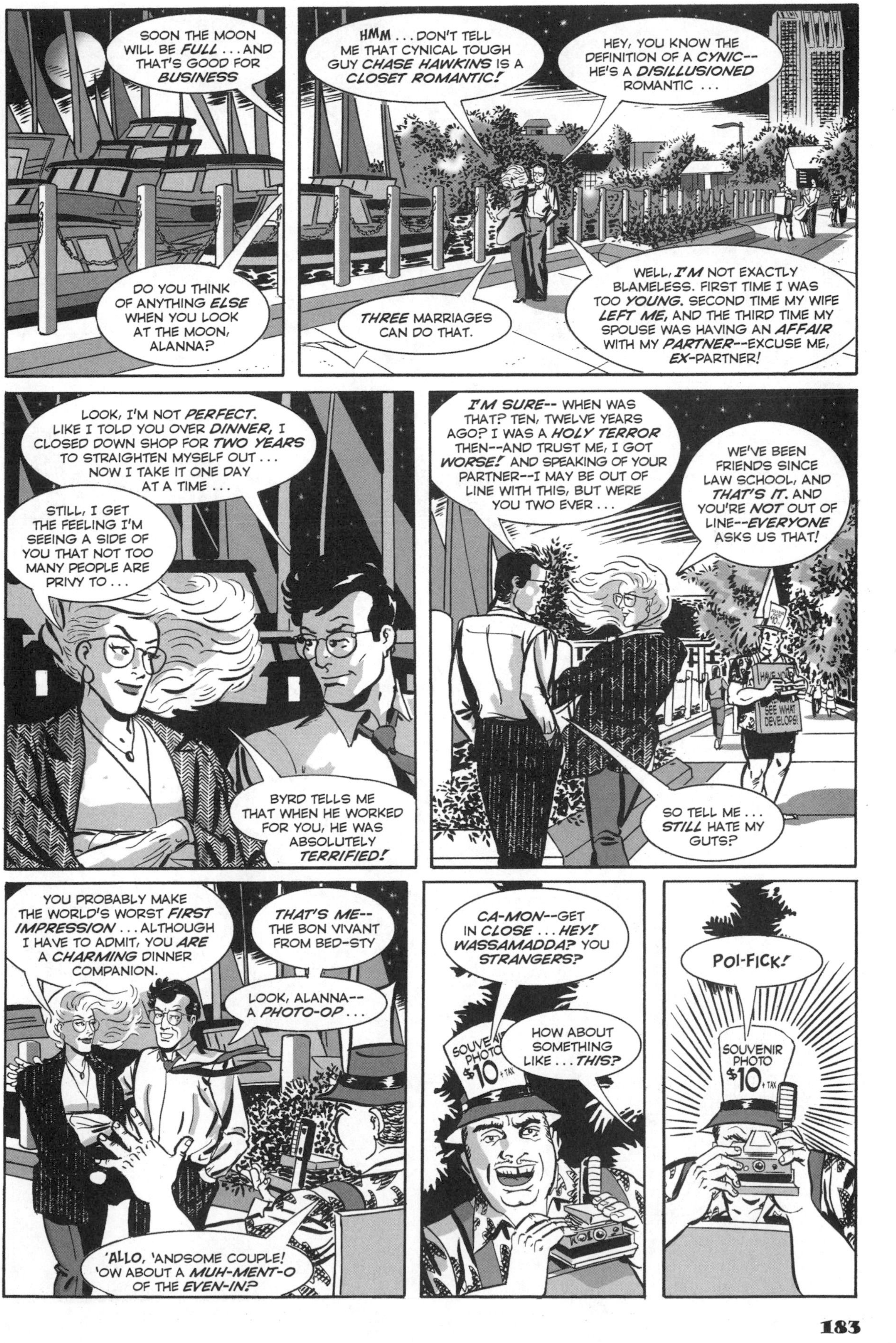
SOON THE MOON WILL BE FULL . . . AND THAT'S GOOD FOR BUSINESS
DO YOU THINK OF ANYTHING ELSE WHEN YOU LOOK AT THE MOON, ALANNA?
HMM . . . DON'T TELL ME THAT CYNICAL TOUGH GUY CHASE HAWKINS IS A CLOSET ROMANTIC!
HEY, YOU KNOW THE DEFINITION OF A CYNIC-- HE'S A DISILLUSIONED ROMANTIC . . .
THREE MARRIAGES CAN DO THAT.
WELL, I'M NOT EXACTLY BLAMELESS. FIRST TIME I WAS TOO YOUNG. SECOND TIME MY WIFE LEFT ME, AND THE THIRD TIME MY SPOUSE WAS HAVING AN AFFAIR WITH MY PARTNER--EXCUSE ME, EX-PARTNER!
LOOK, I'M NOT PERFECT. LIKE I TOLD YOU OVER DINNER, I CLOSED DOWN SHOP FOR TWO YEARS TO STRAIGHTEN MYSELF OUT . . . NOW I TAKE IT ONE DAY AT A TIME . . .
STILL, I GET THE FEELING I'M SEEING A SIDE OF YOU THAT NOT TOO MANY PEOPLE ARE PRIVY TO . . .
BYRD TELLS ME THAT WHEN HE WORKED FOR YOU, HE WAS ABSOLUTELY TERRIFIED!
I'M SURE-- WHEN WAS THAT? TEN, TWELVE YEARS AGO? I WAS A HOLY TERROR THEN--AND TRUST ME, I GOT WORSE! AND SPEAKING OF YOUR PARTNER--I MAY BE OUT OF LINE WITH THIS, BUT WERE YOU TWO EVER . . .
WE'VE BEEN FRIENDS SINCE LAW SCHOOL, AND THAT'S IT. AND YOU'RE NOT OUT OF LINE--EVERYONE ASKS US THAT!
SEE WHAT DEVELOPS!
SO TELL ME . . . STILL HATE MY GUTS?
YOU PROBABLY MAKE THE WORLD'S WORST FIRST IMPRESSION . . . ALTHOUGH I HAVE TO ADMIT, YOU ARE A CHARMING DINNER COMPANION.
THAT'S ME-- THE BON VIVANT FROM BED-STY
LOOK, ALANNA-- A PHOTO-OP . . .
'ALLO, 'ANDSOME COUPLE! 'OW ABOUT A MUH-MENT-O OF THE EVEN-IN?
CA-MON--GET IN CLOSE . . . HEY! WASSAMADDA? YOU STRANGERS?
HOW ABOUT SOMETHING LIKE . . . THIS?
POI-FICK!
SOUVENIR PHOTO $10 + TAX

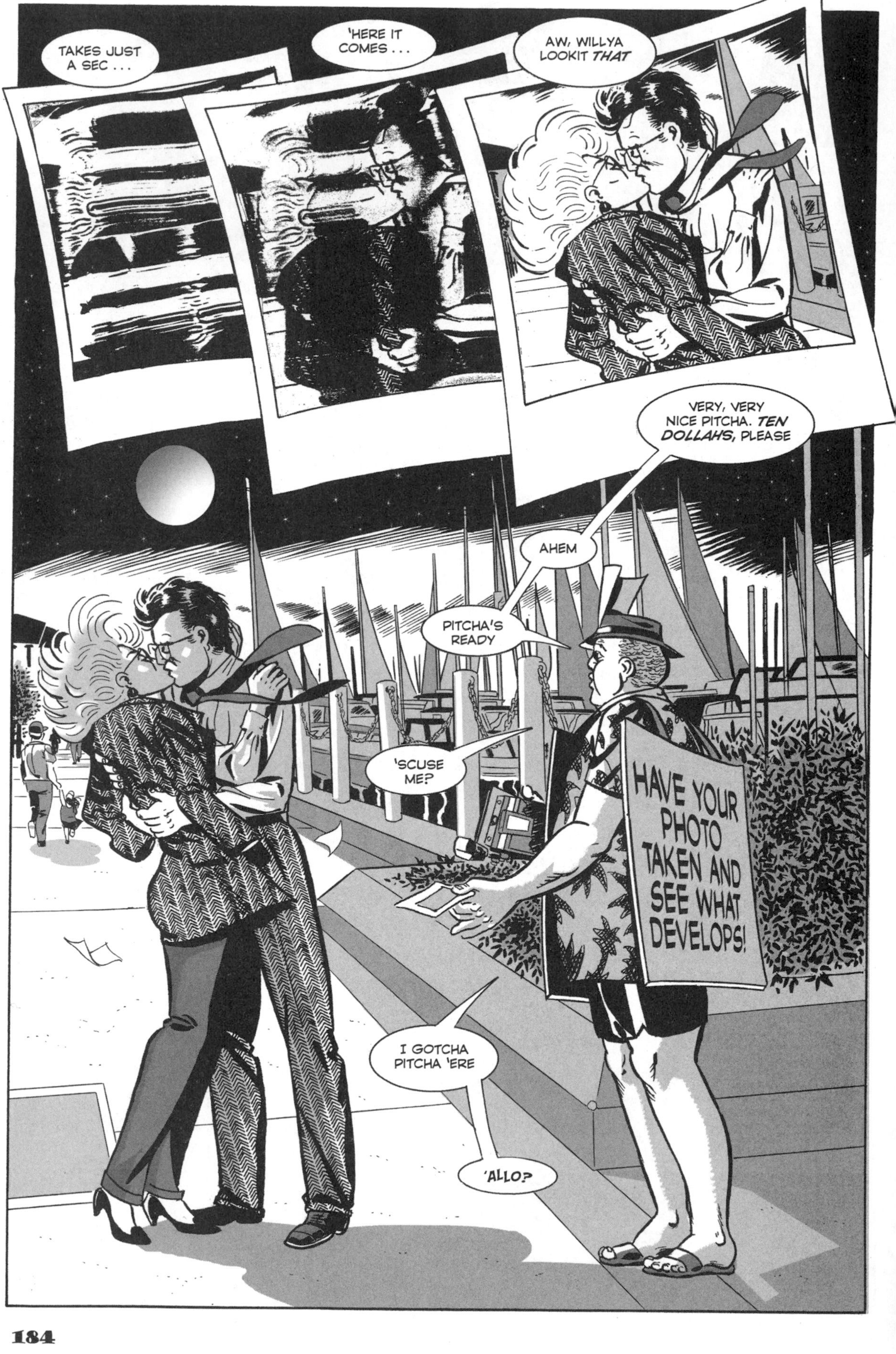
TAKES JUST A SEC . . .
'HERE IT COMES . . .
AW, WILLYA LOOKIT *THAT*
VERY, VERY NICE PITCHA. *TEN DOLLAHS,* PLEASE
AHEM
PITCHA'S READY
'SCUSE ME?
HAVE YOUR PHOTO TAKEN AND SEE WHAT DEVELOPS!
I GOTCHA PITCHA 'ERE
'ALLO?

About the Author

Cartoonist **Batton Lash,** the creator of the humor/horror series *Supernatural Law* (aka *Wolff & Byrd, Counselors of the Macabre*), studied cartooning and graphic arts at the School of Visual Arts in New York, where his instructors included Will Eisner and Harvey Kurtzman.

After graduating he took on various art-related jobs, including copywriting and art for an ad agency and drawings for a variety of magazines, books, and other clients.

In 1979 one of those clients, Brooklyn Paper Publications, asked Lash to create a comic strip, and he came up with "Wolff & Byrd, Counselors of the Macabre," which ran weekly in *The Brooklyn Paper* until 1996 and in *The National Law Journal* from 1983 to 1997.

Since May 1994, Wolff & Byrd have held court in their own comic book series from Exhibit A Press, which Lash established with his wife, Jackie Estrada. Exhibit A has published several trade paperback collections of the comic book issues (see the next page) and two collections of the weekly comic strips, as well as four specials featuring Mavis, W&B's intrepid secretary.

Lash's non-W&B work has included writing *Archie Meets The Punisher,* the 1994 crossover between Archie Comics and Marvel Comics, and the *Radioactive Man* series for Bongo Comics. In 2002 the latter series won the Will Eisner Comic Industry Award for Best Humor Publication. Batton and *Supernatural Law* have been nominated for eight Harvey Awards: two in 2003, three in 2004, and three in 2005. Comic-Con International: San Diego, the premiere event of the comics industry, presented Batton with its Inkpot Award in 2004 for his contributions to comic arts.

Batton is aided and abetted by his wife and Exhibit A co-publisher, **Jackie Estrada.** A professional book editor for over 35 years, Jackie has been involved in the comics industry in various capacities since the 1970s, including having edited the Souvenir Book and onsite Events Guide for Comic-Con International numerous times. Since 1990 she has served as administrator of the Will Eisner Comic Industry Awards (the "Oscars" of the industry). She was one of the founders of Friends of Lulu, a nonprofit organization devoted to getting more women and girls involved in comics, and served as the organization's president for five years. She is particularly proud of having edited Mike Richardson and Steve Duin's *Comics: Between the Panels,* a 500-page four-color hardbound coffeetable book published by Dark Horse Books. In addition to editing all of Exhibit A's publications, Jackie handles the lettering chores.

Even *More* Tales of Supernatural Law:

You can follow the cases of Wolff & Byrd and their secretary Mavis in these trade paperbacks, available at fine comics emporiums and bookstores:

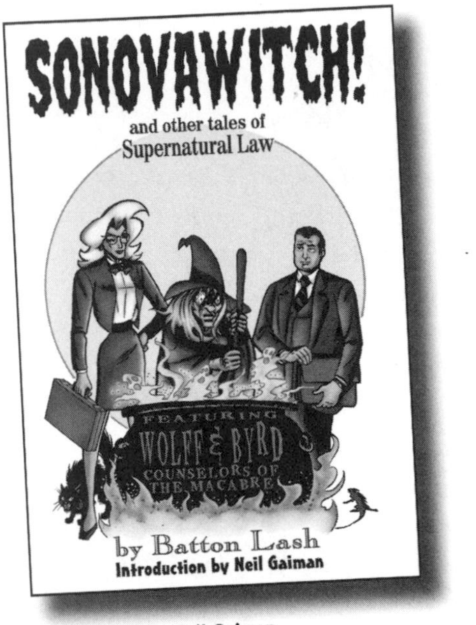
SONOVAWITCH!
and other tales of
Supernatural Law
FEATURING
WOLFF & BYRD
COUNSELORS OF THE MACABRE
by Batton Lash
Introduction by Neil Gaiman

Introduction by Neil Gaiman
ISBN: 0-9633954-6-7 $14.95, 176 pages

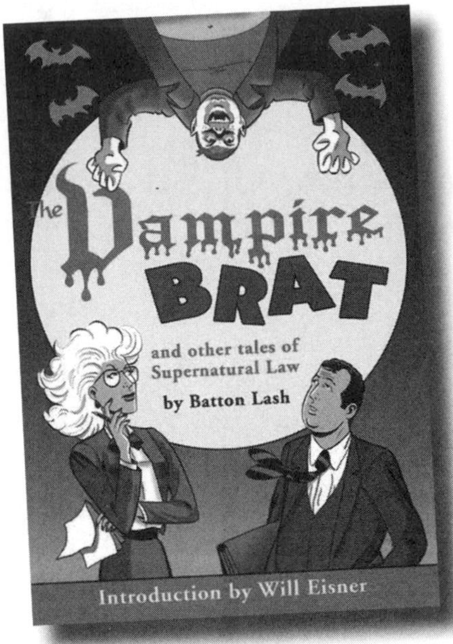
The Vampire BRAT
and other tales of
Supernatural Law
by Batton Lash
Introduction by Will Eisner

Introduction by Will Eisner
ISBN: 0-9633954-7-5 $14.95, 176 pages

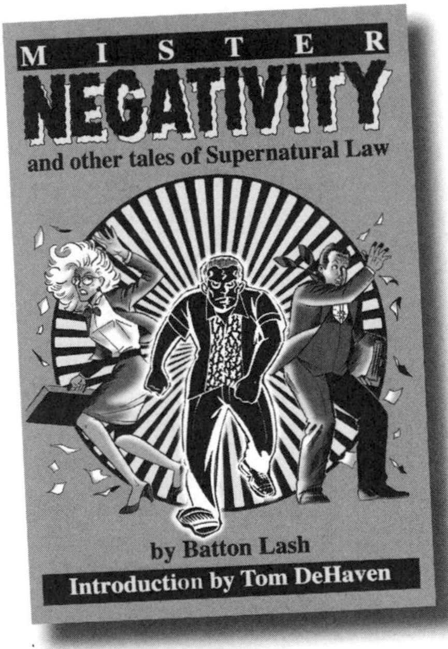
MISTER
NEGATIVITY
and other tales of Supernatural Law
by Batton Lash
Introduction by Tom DeHaven

Introduction byTom DeHaven
ISBN: 0-9633954-8-3 $15.95, 176 pages

Sonovawitch! contains:

- Issues 17–22 of the comic book series
- *Mavis* #1
- The title story's case of "hexual harassment," plus a twist on demonic possession, a giant Japanese monster, vampires in organized crime, and more!

The Vampire Brat contains:

- Issues 23–29 of the comic book series
- *Mavis* #2
- The title story's case of a slacker teenage vampire wanting protection from "Myrtle, the Vampire Hater," plus mad scientists, lost souls, a rampaging purple monster with mother issues, and more!

Mister Negativity contains:

- Issues 31-36 of the comic book series
- *Mavis* #3
- A client who has such a bad attitude, he literally turns negative! Plus: a demon who has been born again, a horror author in a coma, and a talking purple gorilla mob boss!

Visit the Exhibit A website for a full catalogue of *Wolff & Byrd/ Supernatural Law* products, plus news about Batton Lash, a celebrity photo gallery, and other cool stuff!!

Exhibit A Press
4657 Cajon Way
San Diego, Ca 92115

www.exhibitapress.com

mail@exhibitapress.com
Phone: 619-286-6350